THE BORZOI ANTHOLOGY
OF LATIN AMERICAN LITERATURE

Volume I

THE BORZOI ANTHOLOGY OF LATIN AMERICAN LITERATURE

Volume I
From the Time of Columbus
to the Twentieth Century

Edited by
EMIR RODRÍGUEZ MONEGAL

With the assistance of
THOMAS COLCHIE

Alfred A. Knopf   New York   1977

THIS IS A BORZOI BOOK
PUBLISHED BY ALFRED A. KNOPF, INC.

Copyright © 1977 by Alfred A. Knopf, Inc.

*Owing to space limitations, all acknowledgments for permission to reprint
material will be found beginning overleaf of the facing page.*

Library of Congress Cataloging in Publication Data

Main entry under title:

The Borzoi anthology of Latin American literature.

  CONTENTS: v. 1. From the time of Columbus to the twentieth
century.—v. 2. Twentieth century.
    1. Latin American literature—Translations into
English.   2. English literature—Translations from
Spanish.   3. English literature—Translations from
Portuguese.   I. Rodríguez Monegal, Emir.
II. Colchie, Thomas.
PQ7087.E5B6   860'.8   76–19126
ISBN 0–394–73301–0 pbk. (v. 1)
ISBN 0–394–73366–5 pbk. (v. 2)

FIRST EDITION

Assistance in the preparation and translation
of this volume was given by the
Center for Inter-American Relations.

The following selections are reprinted in this volume by the kind permission of the publishers, authors, and individuals hereinafter acknowledged:

"The Green and Beautiful Land." From *Journals and Other Documents on the Life and Voyages of Christopher Columbus.* Published by The Limited Editions Club and The Heritage Club; Copyright © 1963 by Samuel Eliot Morison; used by arrangement with The Heritage Press, Avon, Conn., and by permission of Admiral Morison as translator and editor.

"The Unique Monkey" by Gonzalo Fernández de Oviedo. From *The Golden Land,* edited and translated by Harriet de Onís. Copyright 1948 by Harriet de Onís. Reprinted by permission of Alfred A. Knopf, Inc.

"The Entry of Cortes into Mexico" by Bernal Díaz del Castillo. From *The Conquest of New Spain,* translated by J. M. Cohen, pages 216–41. Copyright © 1963 by J. M. Cohen. Reprinted by permission of Penguin Books, Ltd.

"Encounter with the Amazons" by Gaspar de Carvajal. From *The Golden Land,* edited and translated by Harriet de Onís. Copyright 1948 by Harriet de Onís. Reprinted by permission of Alfred A. Knopf, Inc.

"An Election in Old Araucana" by Alonso de Ercilla y Zuñiga. From *The Historie of Araucana,* edited by Frank Pierce and translated by George Carew (1964). Reprinted by permission of Manchester University Press.

"The Royal Commentaries of the Inca" by Inca Garcilaso de la Vega. From *The Royal Commentaries,* Book 1, Chapter 19; Book 4, Chapters 16 and 20–24; Book 1, Chapter 8; translated by Harold V. Livermore (1966). Reprinted by permission of University of Texas Press.

"Immortal Springtime and Its Tokens" by Bernardo de Balbuena, "Feast by the Manzanares" by Juan Ruiz de Alarcón, "Three Sonnets" by Miguel de Guevara, "Three Sonnets" by Luis Sandoval y Zapata, "Verses Expressing the Feelings of a Lover," "Describes Rationally the Irrational Effects of Love," "Tarry, shadow of my scornful treasure . . .," "Diuturnal infirmity of hope . . .," "This colored counterfeit that thou beholdest . . .," "Divine rose, that in a pleasant garden . . .," "Crimson lute that comest in the dawn, . . ." "Green enravishment of human life . . .," "Amorous of Laura's loveliness, . . ." by Sor Juana Inés de la Cruz. From *Anthology of Mexican Poetry,* compiled and edited by Octavio Paz, translated by Samuel Beckett. Copyright © 1958 by Indiana University Press. Reprinted by permission of the publisher.

"In Acknowledgment of the Praises of European Writers" by Sor Juana Inés de la Cruz. From *An Anthology of Spanish Poetry from Garcilaso to García Lorca,* edited by Angel Flores (Doubleday, 1961). Reprinted by permission of Angel Flores.

"El Dorado" by Juan Rodríguez Freile. From *The Golden Land,* edited and translated by Harriet de Onís. Copyright 1948 by Harriet de Onís. Reprinted by permission of Alfred A. Knopf, Inc. "A Tale of Witchcraft" by Juan Rodríguez Freile. From *The Conquest of the New Granada,* translated by William C. Atkinson (1961). Reprinted by permission of The Folio Society.

"Saint Rose of Lima" by Juan de Meléndez. From *The Green Continent,* edited by Germán Arciniegas, translated by Harriet de Onís. Copyright 1944 and renewed 1972 by Alfred A. Knopf, Inc. Reprinted by permission of the publisher.

"The Happy Captivity" by Francisco Núñez de Pineda y Bascuñán. From *Spanish American Literature in Translation,* Vol. I, edited by Willis Knapp Jones. Copyright © 1966 by Frederick Ungar Publishing Co., Inc. Reprinted by permission of the publisher.

"Atrocities of the Bandeirantes" by Justo Mansilla and Simón Maceta. From

The Bandeirantes: The Historical Role of the Brazilian Pathfinders, edited and translated by Richard M. Morse. Copyright © 1965 by Richard M. Morse. Reprinted by permission of Alfred A. Knopf, Inc.

"How the Indians Make Curare" by José Gumilla. From *The Golden Land*, edited and translated by Harriet de Onís. Copyright 1948 by Harriet de Onís. Reprinted by permission of Alfred A. Knopf, Inc.

"The Wicked Hermit" by Bartolomé Arzáns de Orzúa y Vela. From *Tales of Potosí*, edited by R. C. Padden, translated from the Spanish by Frances M. López-Morillas. Copyright © 1975 by Brown University Press. Reprinted by permission of the publisher.

"Rebellion and Death of Túpac Amaru." From *The Green Continent*, edited by Germán Arciniegas, translated by Harriet de Onís. Copyright 1944 and renewed 1972 by Alfred A. Knopf, Inc. Reprinted by permission of the publisher.

"The Itching Parrot" by José Joaquín Fernández de Lizardi. Chapter 17 from *The Itching Parrot*, translated by Katherine Anne Porter. Copyright 1942 by Doubleday & Company, Inc. Reprinted by permission of the publisher.

"The Slaughterhouse" by Esteban Echeverría. From *The Slaughterhouse*, translated by Angel Flores. Published by Las Americas Publishing Co., 1959. Reprinted by permission of Angel Flores.

"Doctor Faust in the Pampas" by Estanislao del Campo. From *The Golden Land*, translated by Walter Owen, edited by Harriet de Onís. Copyright 1948 by Harriet de Onís. Reprinted by permission of Alfred A. Knopf, Inc.

"The Gaucho Martín Fierro" by José Hernández. From pages 61–8 of *The Gaucho Martín Fierro*, translated by Frank G. Carrino, Alberto J. Carlos, and Norman Mangouni. Copyright © 1974 by State University of New York. Reprinted by permission of the State University of New York Press.

"Enriquillo, the Indian Rebel" by Manuel de Jesús Galván. From *The Cross and the Sword*, translated by Robert Graves. Copyright 1954 by Indiana University Press. Reprinted by permission of the publisher.

"The Goblins of Cuzco" and "Fray Gómez's Scorpion," Parts I and II, by Ricardo Palma. From *The Knights of the Cape*, translated by Harriet de Onís. Copyright 1945 by Alfred A. Knopf, Inc. Reprinted by permission of the publisher.

"Simon Magus" by Tomás Carrasquilla. From *The Golden Land*, edited and translated by Harriet de Onís. Copyright 1948 by Harriet de Onís. Reprinted by permission of Alfred A. Knopf, Inc.

"Dom Casmurro" by Joaquim María Machado de Assis. From *Dom Casmurro*, translated by Helen Caldwell. Translation Copyright 1953 by Helen Caldwell. Reprinted by permission of Farrar, Straus & Giroux, Inc.

"Antonio Conselheiro, the 'Counselor' " by Euclides da Cunha. From *Rebellion in the Backlands*, translated by Samuel Putnam. Copyright 1944 by University of Chicago Press. Reprinted by permission of the publisher.

"The Corpse" and "The Example" by Salvador Díaz Mirón. From *Anthology of Mexican Poetry*, compiled and edited by Octavio Paz, translated by Samuel Beckett. Copyright © 1958 by Indiana University Press. Reprinted by permission of the publisher.

"Symphony in Gray Major," "Far Away and Long Ago," "Doom," and "Eheu!" by Rubén Darío. From *An Anthology of Spanish Poetry from Garcilaso to García Lorca*, edited by Angel Flores (Doubleday, 1961). Reprinted by permission of Angel Flores. "To Roosevelt," "Philosophy," "Leda," and "Pity for Him Who One Day . . ." by Rubén Darío. From *Selected Poems of Rubén Darío*, translated by Lysander Kemp (1965). Reprinted by permission of University of Texas Press.

"The Granite Plain" by José Enrique Rodó. From *The Motives of Proteus*, translated by Angel Flores (George Allen & Unwin Ltd., 1929). Reprinted by permission of Angel Flores.

"Gurí" by Javier de Viana. From *The Golden Land*, edited and translated by Harriet de Onís. Copyright 1948 by Harriet de Onís. Reprinted by permission of Alfred A. Knopf, Inc.

"The Underdogs" by Mariano Azuela. From pages 14 to 38 of *The Underdogs*, translated by E. Munguía, Jr. (1962). Reprinted courtesy of The New American Library, Inc.

"Doña Bárbara" by Rómulo Gallegos. From *Doña Bárbara*, translated by Robert Malloy (Peter Smith Publishers, Inc., 1948). Reprinted by permission of the publisher.

"The Vortex" by José Eustasio Rivera, translated by Earle James. From *The Green Continent*, edited by Germán Arciniegas, translated by Harriet de Onís. Copyright 1944 and renewed 1972 by Alfred A. Knopf, Inc. Reprinted by permission of the publisher.

"Don Segundo Sombra" by Ricardo Güiraldes. From *Don Segundo Sombra*, translated by Harriet de Onís. Copyright 1935, © 1963 by Holt, Rinehart & Winston, Inc. Copyright © 1966 by Harriet de Onís. Reprinted by permission of Holt, Rinehart & Winston, Inc.

"The Eagle and the Serpent" by Martín Luis Guzmán. From *The Eagle and the Serpent*, translated by Harriet de Onís. Copyright 1930 and renewed 1958 by Alfred A. Knopf, Inc. Reprinted by permission of the publisher.

"The Sad End of Policarpo Quaresma" by Lima Barreto. From *O triste fim de Policarpo Quaresma*, published in 1911 by Editora Brasiliense. Translated by Gregory Rabassa. Reprinted by permission of the publisher and the translator.

"The Dog" by Graciliano Ramos. From *Barren Lives*, translated by Ralph Edward Dimmick (1965). Reprinted by permission of University of Texas Press.

"Dead Fires" by José Lins do Rêgo. From *Fogo Morto*, published by José Olympio Editora. Translated by Susan Hertelendy. Reprinted by permission of the publisher and the translator.

"*Haiku* of the Day," "*Haiku* of the Flowerpot," "The Idol in the Porch," and "The Parrot" by José Juan Tablada. From *Anthology of Mexican Poetry*, compiled and edited by Octavio Paz, translated by Samuel Beckett. Copyright © 1958 by Indiana University Press. Reprinted by permission of the publisher. "Flying Fish" by José Juan Tablada, translated by W. S. Merwin; "Alternating Nocturne" by José Juan Tablada, translated by Eliot Weinberger; and "Southern Cross" by José Juan Tablada, translated by Hardie St. Martin. From *New Poetry of Mexico*, edited by Mark Strand. Copyright by Siglo XXI Editores, S.A. English translation Copyright © 1970 by E. P. Dutton & Co., Inc. Reprinted by permission of the publishers.

"Wet Earth" and "The Malefic Return" by Ramón López Velarde. From *Anthology of Mexican Poetry*, compiled and edited by Octavio Paz, translated by Samuel Beckett. Copyright © 1958 by Indiana University Press. Reprinted by permission of the publisher. "The Dream of the Black Gloves" by Ramón López Velarde, translated by Donald Justice, and "The Chandelier" by Ramón López Velarde, translated by Douglas Eichhorn. From *New Poetry of Mexico*, edited by Mark Strand. Copyright by Siglo XXI Editores, S.A. English translation Copyright © 1970 by E. P. Dutton & Co., Inc. Reprinted by permission of the publishers.

"The Prayer" by Gabriela Mistral, translated by Donald D. Walsh. From *An Anthology of Latin American Poetry*, edited by Dudley Fitts. Copyright 1942 by New Directions Publishing Corporation. Reprinted by permission of the publisher. "Ballad" and "Absence" by Gabriela Mistral. From *An Anthology of Spanish Poetry from Garcilaso to García Lorca*, edited by Angel Flores (Doubleday, 1961). Reprinted by permission of Angel Flores. "The Liana" by Gabriela Mistral, translated by Doris Dana. Originally published in *Selected Poems of Gabriela Mistral*, edited and translated by Doris Dana (Johns Hopkins Press, 1971). Reprinted by permission of Doris Dana.

"Tarahumara Herbs," "Scarcely . . .," and "Monterrey Sun" by Alfonso Reyes. From *Anthology of Mexican Poetry,* compiled and edited by Octavio Paz, translated by Samuel Beckett. Copyright © 1958 by Indiana University Press. Reprinted by permission of the publisher.

CONTENTS

GENERAL INTRODUCTION

It cannot yet be said that there is a cohesive Latin American literature, at least in the continental sense. There is, rather, a continental literature in process, an ongoing development, the first manifesto of which was perhaps the "Ode" published in London in 1823 by the Venezuelan Andrés Bello. Latin American literature is more an intention than a fact simply because Latin America itself has never achieved cultural integration. A literature is more than a collection of writers and their works; it is, as Octavio Paz has pointed out, a coherent system of literary communications, a critical space in which works mirror each other and participate in a dialogue with their readers. This space (which exists in Europe and the United States) is still in the process of being created in Latin America. Even the name used to identify this part of the world refers to a geopolitical entity that is actually separated into two main linguistic and cultural groups: Spanish and Portuguese. Despite their common peninsular origin, Spanish America and Brazil have always been separate and apart, since the first days of the discovery and conquest of the New World. The line that divides the Spanish from the Portuguese side of South America may not be as straight today as it was when Pope Alexander VI traced it so imaginatively in 1493, but it is thicker, and hardened by history. Political independence from the respective mother countries brought an even more drastic separation of the new republican regimes of Spanish America from the empire of Brazil.

Cultural contacts between the two blocs remained minimal until quite recently. It is true that the Mexican Sor Juana Inés de la Cruz used to read and comment on the sermons of Father Antônio Vieira, and that the baroque Brazilian satirist Gregorio de Matos knew Góngora's poetry very well. In general, however, Spanish American and Brazilian literature progressed in parallel but separate lines of development until the present century. Even their terminologies differ. What is called modernism in Spanish America corresponds roughly to Brazilian Parnassianism, while the Brazilian modernism of the 1920s is the equivalent of the avant-garde movements in Spanish American letters. In more recent times, there has been more communication between the two literatures. Neruda's poetry and Borges's fiction have been widely read in Brazil, while the Mexican Octavio Paz has been in continuous contact with the Brazilian concrete poets. The new novelists in Spanish America and Brazil have been familiar with one another's works in spite of linguistic and publishing barriers. But complete cultural integration is still a project of the future, and a truly Latin American literature only a blueprint.

There is not even a Spanish American literature before the nineteenth

century, when independence spurred everywhere the creation of a culture different from the peninsular and based on more modern (i.e., French) models. Political independence did not contribute to integration. Bolívar and San Martín
dreamed of unity while the new nations quickly separated under local, and weak,
governments, each keen on fostering its own national culture. Some of the best
writers did have a truly continental perspective and fought hard for the integration of Spanish American literature. But despite their efforts, it took the best part
of fifty years to produce a movement, modernism, that was authentically Spanish
American and that aspired to integrate what had been written in all parts of the
Hispanic world into a new poetic unity (see Part Three, Introduction).

The paradox is that the integration now being sought did exist during
Colonial times: Spanish American and Brazilian writers were part of the respective unities called Spanish and Portuguese literature, and saw themselves essentially as peninsular writers who happened to be on this side of the Atlantic. In
a sense they were right, although we, looking backward, from our very different
perspective, do not see them as such. In approaching the baroque poets, for
instance (see Introduction to Part One), we recognize in them not successful
disciples of Góngora or Quevedo, but the first Latin American poets to attempt
a new departure in their work. For us, therefore, they become the founding
fathers of Latin American literature. This perspective is, of course, anachronistic,
but deliberately so. For the normal diachronic perspective used in literary history
I have substituted a synchronic model in which texts produced in different times
and circumstances are brought together to form a coherent and unified whole.

In the selection of works produced before 1850, I have leaned heavily
on texts that are more significant perhaps to us than they were to their contemporary audience. Many prominent figures have been omitted, either because their
importance is purely historical or simply because they do not travel well in
translation. In the selections of texts that belong to the second half of the
nineteenth or to the twentieth century, I have been generous. More than half
of this anthology is devoted to them because it is in them that the project of a
Latin American literature begins to be fulfilled. I have also deliberately excluded
the Indian literatures, which have contributed so much to Latin American culture. It was a hard decision to make, especially because many of the native myths
and metaphors have strongly influenced writers as diverse and as important as the
Inca Garcilaso, the Argentine José Hernández, the Dominican Manuel de Jesús
Galván, the Guatemalan Miguel Angel Asturias, the Brazilian Mário de Andrade,
the Chilean Pablo Neruda, and the Mexicans Octavio Paz and Juan Rulfo. But
to show how Indian literature can be integrated into Latin American letters
would require a larger and different anthology.

This book is generally confined to texts of either fiction or poetry. No
playwrights or essayists are included—the first, because their works are very
difficult if not impossible to excerpt; the second, because a serious attempt to
illustrate their variety and significance to Latin American letters would require
another volume as large as this one. Only with regard to the Colonial period (Part
One) has a slightly different approach been followed. The best literary prose of

the time is generally not fictional, because the Colonial authorities did not allow novels to circulate in the New World. (Many were smuggled in, but that is another story.) Colonial writers, therefore, knowing they had no chance of having a novel published, abstained from fiction. Nonetheless, fiction thinly disguised as fact, or fact generously contaminated by fiction, was the stuff of some of the most exciting chronicles, memoirs, and documents produced in Colonial times. In truth they do belong to the domain of fiction, and have been treated as such in this anthology.

A new perspective on Latin American letters has been attempted in this book: a perspective which presents New World writing as a permanent quest for a literature of the future, a literary utopia in which an integrated image of a whole continent will be at long last possible.

Part One

THE FABULOUS SOURCES

Although a few of the works written in Latin America under Colonial rule were among the best produced in Spanish and Portuguese in those days, the bulk of Colonial literature is not primarily literary. It consists chiefly of historical chronicles, personal memoirs, confidential reports, letters, and erudite treatises on the New World. But even if the purpose of these documents was to present reality as it then was, they were permeated by the sense of wonder felt by the Europeans as they faced for the first time a reality totally unlike anything they had experienced before. A new image of man and nature was formed in the early days of the discovery and conquest. This image was the product not only of an observation of reality but also of the dreams and fantasies, of the sense of the "marvelous," that the Europeans brought to the New World.

The Middle Ages were still very much alive in Spain and Portugal at the time of the conquest. It is this imaginary reality of the romances of chivalry and the lyrical ballads that the first Europeans projected onto the strange land they had discovered. If Columbus saw mermaids in the Caribbean Sea (selection 1), Fernández de Oviedo (selection 5) would later describe very carefully a monkey with feathers, while Bernal Díaz (7) would compare the Aztec empire with the fabulous kingdoms of chivalry and Ercilla (9) would present the fierce Araucans as proud knights, as attached to a code of honor as were their Spanish counterparts. The Renaissance appetite for discovery and wonder permeated such accounts, changing fact into fiction. Even in more sober times, when Rodríguez Freile (12) was compiling in the early seventeenth century the life and times of his native city, witchcraft and superstition dominated his gossipy chronicle, and in retelling the story of Saint Rose of Lima, Juan de Meléndez (13) dutifully followed the conventions of the Golden Legend. Everything was magic then.

The view we now have of Colonial literature is completely different from the one prevailing at the time. In the first place, readers then saw the work produced on this side of the Atlantic as part of the metropolitan literature—quite properly, of course, not only because the first authors were all Europeans but especially because even those born in America wrote as Europeans, for a European as well as an American audience, and some even went to the peninsula to live there permanently. (The Inca Garcilaso and the Mexican playwright Juan

Ruiz de Alarcón are the best-known examples.) Not until the beginning of the nineteenth century would Latin American writers distinguish themselves from the peninsulars. But the view we now have is different for another very important reason: many works of Colonial times that we now consider essential were, because of their controversial nature, never actually published during that period. They failed to get by the censors, or at least did not circulate freely in the New World. For instance, Vaz de Caminha's letter on the discovery of Brazil (selection 2), written in 1500, was first published in 1817; Las Casas' polemical *History of the Indies* (4), completed in 1566, was censored then, and did not see publication until 1875; Pineda y Bascuñán's *The Happy Captivity* (14), written in 1629, was printed in 1831; Rodríguez Freile's *El Carnero* came out only in 1859, although it had been completed around 1636; Gregorio de Matos's satirical and pornographic poems (17) circulated in his lifetime in manuscript copies, and were not collected and printed until 1831; Bartolomé Arzáns de Orzúa y Vela's chronicle of Potosí (20), written around 1705, was published in 1872. Even the Inca Garcilaso's *Royal Commentaries,* published in Spain in his lifetime, were not allowed to circulate freely in the New World during the seventeenth and eighteenth centuries because of their utopian presentation of the Inca empire as a free and happy society; they were, of course, immediately reprinted by the new independent states. Thus, books written in Colonial times really became nineteenth-century books. Only after independence did a true picture of the state of letters during the Colonial period begin to emerge, and this picture is even today constantly being revised by the discovery of long-forgotten or unknown works. In reading these texts now we see them as they were never seen before: as the fabulous sources of a literature to be. They are closer to us than they were to their nominal contemporaries.

To insist on a new reading of Colonial literature does not preclude the placing of the texts produced during that time in the general context of the peninsular literatures—quite the contrary. It is impossible, for instance, to study the Renaissance epic without including Ercilla's beautiful *Araucana;* in the same way, we cannot consider the historiography of the period without studying very carefully Garcilaso's masterpiece, *The Royal Commentaries of the Inca.* Ruiz de Alarcón's elegant comedies belong to the history of the Spanish theater of the Golden Age as much as Father Vieira's baroque sermons belong to the Portuguese religious prose of the seventeenth century. The entire tradition of Spanish baroque poetry got a renewed lease on life in the New World. The shadow of Luis de Góngora's poetry and poetics loomed large over Spanish American poets, especially the Mexicans. Writers born (like Sor Juana Inés de la Cruz) more than a quarter of a century after his death were still under his spell. His influence was also felt in Brazilian Colonial literature, as the work of Gregorio de Matos attests. Góngora's conception of a poem as a pure object, made exclusively of shining surfaces, informed by a rigorous humanistic code, full of classical allusions and half-disguised "quotations" of Greco-Latin poetry, the product of a learned and witty mind, continued to influence Mexican poetry long after it had ceased to have any impact in Spain. Like a dead star, Góngora was still visible on the

other side of the Atlantic at the end of the seventeenth century. Literary historians of the nineteenth century, such as Menéndez Pelayo, lacked a proper understanding of baroque poetry and mistook Góngora's influence on Spanish America
as a sign of the stagnation of Colonial culture. Today, a reevaluation of the
concept of the baroque and the application to Góngora's texts of a structuralist
method of reading have proved the importance of a poetics that emphasizes the
value of the signifier and opens up the infinite quest for the signified. In his texts
every word, every image, alluded to another word or image, which in turn alluded
to a third, and so on. A superficial poetry, of course, but everything is finally
surface in a poetic text.

It is true that the Spanish and the Spanish American versions of
baroque poetry are different, and many attempts have been made to define this
difference. Theories on the influence of the New World landscape, or the contri-
bution of the native culture to a new vision of reality, have been produced; a
search for some specific "American" ingredient of the baroque texts written in
this part of the world is still going strong. Still one of the most cogent theories
is that of Pedro Henríquez Ureña, who has underlined the existence of a distinctively new baroque style in Spanish American poets. The Mexican Balbuena
(selection 11, 1) was recognized by him as the first to attempt in his descriptive
poetry a synthesis of the elements that appear separated in poets such as Góngora,
Lope, or Quevedo. Following his lead, the most brilliant baroque poet Latin
America ever produced, the Mexican Sor Juana Inés de la Cruz, managed to
blend Góngora's culteranism with Quevedo's conceptism to create a poetry at
once sensual and intellectual. Even baroque prose found in the New World an
elegance and subtlety that were not common in the peninsula, as witness the work
of Father Vieira in Brazil and Sigüenza y Góngora in Peru. In this new reading
of the Latin American baroque, instead of lamenting the imitation in the New
World of a style already defunct in Europe, it is possible to celebrate it as the
first successful attempt to produce a truly new poetry. Following the European
models but with a greater freedom of style, and incorporating elements that were
indigenous to Latin America's nature and societies, the baroque poets (as Octavio
Paz has pointed out) succeeded in creating a distinctively different poetry by
universalizing what was more parochial in the style and themes of the peninsular
baroque. Thus, they anticipated a movement of renewal and expansion which
would be repeated in the modernist and avant-garde quests. The baroque writers
were the first Latin Americans to contribute a really new voice to Hispanic letters.

CHRISTOPHER COLUMBUS

Columbus not only discovered America for the King and Queen of Spain in 1492. He was also the first both to explore the New World and to register his astonishment. His exploit was based on a simple misunderstanding: he seriously miscalculated the nautical distance between Europe and Asia and hoped to reach Cathay (China) and Xipango (Japan) in a few weeks of sailing. He had no idea that the distance was so great and that a vast continent was in his way. Columbus (born in Genoa in 1451) was so determined to discover the new Atlantic route to the Indies that when he finally got to the New World he refused to admit what he beheld. He had read Marco Polo's account of his travels in Asia; he knew, or thought he knew, what to look for. The lands he discovered on his first trip (to the Bahamas, Santo Domingo, and Cuba) were beautiful and exotic; they were peopled by docile naked men who had a few pieces of gold but not a single recognizable spice. The translators he had brought with him were useless: the natives spoke no North African or Eastern language. He felt cheated.

But in this letter about the discovery he tried to disguise his failure. In describing the new land to his patrons, he resorted to literary models. He looked for and saw prodigies Pliny had described in his wildly imaginative *Natural History;* he also remembered Marco Polo's wonders; he exhausted the rhetoric of the "marvelous" he knew from romances of chivalry and Renaissance epic poems. His senses had been trained by European poets: he heard nightingales in Cuba, breathed May air in the tropical November of the Caribbean, and vouched for the existence of Amazons and mermaids, of men with tails. A whole stereotype of the fabulous New World was being created.

Because he met first the mild-mannered, innocent, and handsome Tainos, he believed the conquest was going to be easy and profitable. By calling "Indians" those whom he, as a sincere Christian, intended to convert, Columbus compounded his geographical error. He heard of fiercer tribes in the area, men who ate their captives: the Caribs. (From that word, through "cannibals," Shakespeare would coin the name "Caliban" in *The Tempest.*) Because they were savages, he decided that they were fit to be made slaves, according to the Aristotelian doctrine so popular then. In a single letter, Columbus had planned the future of the New World: discovery, conversion, and conquest were all one for him. In the following century, Las Casas (selection 4) would challenge this blueprint.

Columbus's idyllic description of the new societies he discovered helped to create the myth of the noble savage and to reignite the argument about the exact location of the Garden of Eden. On his fourth trip, he believed, he had found proofs that it was located in South America. Columbus's first letter is the inspiration of future utopias, from More's (1516) to the subtle one suggested by

Montaigne in his essay "On Cannibals" (around 1580) and the satirical version Voltaire presented in his *Candide* (1759).

As a sailor, and first Admiral of the Ocean Sea, Columbus knew he could be proud of his Atlantic crossing; but as the Spanish Crown's representative in the quest for a new sea route to the Far East, he finally realized he was a failure. Still, if his expedition brought back to Spain only a few pieces of gold, some exotic birds and feathers, and seven natives, his account of the expedition was a complete literary success: eight editions in the original Spanish; a Latin version, which was read all over Europe; and a paraphrase in Italian verse. America as a literary and poetic subject was invented by this hyperbolic Genoese.

The Green and Beautiful Land

From Journals and Other Documents on the Life and Voyages of Christopher Columbus, *published by the Limited Editions Club and The Heritage Club; copyright © 1963 by Samuel Eliot Morison. Used by arrangement with The Heritage Press, Avon, Conn., and by permission of Admiral Morison as translator and editor.*

The following translation was made originally for my Christopher Columbus, Mariner *(1955). It was reprinted by Carlos Sanz of Madrid as* A New and Fresh English Translation of the Letter of Columbus Announcing the Discovery of America *(Madrid, 1959). It is also printed as an appendix to his* El gran secreto. *Both editions include a facsimile of the unique copy of the first edition.—S. E. MORISON*

Sir, forasmuch as I know that you will take pleasure in the great triumph with which Our Lord has crowned my voyage, I write this to you, from which you will learn how, in twenty[1] days I reached the Indies with the fleet which the most illustrious King and Queen, our lords, gave to me. And there I found very many islands filled with people without number, and of them all have I taken possession for Their Highnesses, by proclamation and with the royal standard displayed, and nobody objected. To the first island which I found I gave the name *Sant Salvador,* in recognition of His Heavenly Majesty, who marvelously hath given all this; the Indians call it *Guanahani.* To the second I gave the name *Isla de Santa María de Concepción;* to the third, *Ferrandina;* to the fourth, *La Isla Bella;*[2] to the fifth, *La Isla Juana;* and so to each one I gave a new name.

When I reached Juana, I followed its coast to the westward, and I found it to be so long that I thought it must be the mainland, the province of

---

1. *Veinte.* Probably a misprint for *treinta,* or xxxiii. The actual time, as the postcript states, was thirty-three days.

2. Misprint for Isabela, the name he gave to Crooked Island.

Catayo.[3] And since I found neither towns nor cities along the coast, but only small villages, with the people of which I could not have speech because they all fled forthwith, I went forward on the same course, thinking that I should not fail to find great cities and towns. And, at the end of many leagues, seeing that there was no change and that the coast was bearing me northward, which was contrary to my desire since winter was already beginning and I proposed to go thence to the south, and as moreover the wind was favorable, I determined not to wait for a change of weather and backtracked to a certain harbor already noted,[4] and thence I sent two men upcountry to learn if there were a king or great cities. They traveled for three days and found an infinite number of small villages and people without number, but nothing of importance; hence they returned.

I understood sufficiently from other Indians, whom I had already taken, that continually[5] this land was an island, and so I followed its coast eastward 107 leagues up to where it ended. And from that cape I saw toward the east another island, distant 18 leagues from the former, to which I at once gave the name *La Spañola*. And I went there and followed its northern part, as I had in the case of Juana, to the eastward for 178 great leagues in a straight line. As Juana, so all the others are very fertile[6] to an excessive degree, and this one especially. In it there are many harbors on the sea coast, beyond comparison with others which I know in Christendom, and numerous rivers, good and large, which is marvelous. Its lands are lofty and in it there are many sierras and very high mountains, to which the island *Centrefrei*[7] is not comparable. All are most beautiful, of a thousand shapes, and all accessible, and filled with trees of a thousand kinds and tall, and they seem to touch the sky; and I am told that they never lose their foliage, which I can believe, for I saw them as green and beautiful as they are in Spain in May, and some of them were flowering, some with fruit, and some in another condition, according to their quality. And there were singing the nightingale and other little birds of a thousand kinds in the month of November, there where I went. There are palm trees of six or eight kinds, which are a wonder to behold because of their beautiful variety, and so are the other trees and fruits and plants; therein are marvelous pine groves, and extensive meadow country; and there is honey, and there are many kinds of birds and a great variety of fruits. Upcountry there are many mines of metals, and the population is innumerable. *La Spañola* is marvelous, the sierras and the mountains and the plains and the meadows and the lands are so beautiful and rich for planting and sowing, and for livestock of every sort, and for building towns and villages. The harbors of the sea here are such as you could not believe it without seeing them; and so the rivers, many and great, and good streams, the most of which bear gold. And the

3. I.e., a province of China.
4. Puerto Gibara.
5. *continuamente.* Not clear whether he meant that the Indians told him continually that Cuba was an island, or that it was one continual island.
6. *fortissimas.* Probably a printer's error for *fertilissimas*, and 178 is a misprint for 188 leagues, as stated later in the Letter.
7. Misprint for Tenerife.

trees and fruits and plants have great differences from those of La Juana; in this [island] there are many spices and great mines of gold and of other metals.

The people of this island and of all the other islands which I have found and seen, or have not seen, all go naked, men and women, as their mothers bore them, except that some women cover one place only with the leaf of a plant or with a net of cotton which they make for that purpose. They have no iron or steel or weapons, nor are they capable of using them, although they are well-built people of handsome stature, because they are wondrous timid. They have no other arms than arms of canes, [cut] when they are in seed time, to the ends of which they fix a sharp little stick; and they dare not make use of these, for oftentimes it has happened that I have sent ashore two or three men to some town to have speech, and people without number have come out to them, and as soon as they saw them coming, they fled; even a father would not stay for his son; and this not because wrong has been done to anyone; on the contrary, at every point where I have been and have been able to have speech, I have given them of all that I had, such as cloth and many other things, without receiving anything for it; but they are like that, timid beyond cure. It is true that after they have been reassured and have lost this fear, they are so artless and so free with all they possess, that no one would believe it without having seen it. Of anything they have, if you ask them for it, they never say no; rather they invite the person to share it, and show as much love as if they were giving their hearts; and whether the thing be of value or of small price, at once they are content with whatever little thing of whatever kind may be given to them. I forbade that they should be given things so worthless as pieces of broken crockery and broken glass, and lace points, although when they were able to get them, they thought they had the best jewel in the world; thus it was learned that a sailor for a lace point received gold to the weight of two and a half castellanos, and others much more for other things which were worth much less; yea, for new blancas,[8] for them they would give all that they had, although it might be two or three castellanos' weight of gold or an arroba or two of spun cotton; they even took pieces of the broken hoops of the wine casks and, like animals, gave what they had, so that it seemed to me to be wrong and I forbade it, and I gave them a thousand good, pleasing things which I had brought, in order that they might be fond of us, and further-more might become Christians and be inclined to the love and service of Their Highnesses and of the whole Castilian nation, and try to help us and to give us of the things which they have in abundance and which are necessary to us. And they know neither sect nor idolatry, with the exception that all believe that the source of all power and goodness is in the sky, and they believe very firmly that I, with these ships and people, came from the sky, and in this belief they everywhere received me, after they had overcome their fear. And this does not result from their being ignorant (for they are of a very keen intelligence and men who navigate all those seas, so that it is wondrous the good account they give of everything), but because they have never seen people clothed or ships like ours.

8. A copper coin worth half a maravedi, about a third of a cent.

And as soon as I arrived in the Indies, in the first island which I found, I took by force some of them in order that they might learn [Castilian] and give me information of what they had in those parts; it so worked out that they soon understood us, and we them, either by speech or signs, and they have been very serviceable. I still have them with me, and they are still of the opinion that I come from the sky, in spite of all the intercourse which they have had with me, and they were the first to announce this wherever I went, and the others went running from house to house and to the neighboring towns with loud cries of, "Come! Come! See the people from the sky!" They all came, men and women alike, as soon as they had confidence in us, so that not one, big or little, remained behind, and all brought something to eat and drink, which they gave with marvelous love. In all the islands they have very many *canoas* like rowing *fustes*, some bigger and some smaller, and some are bigger than a *fusta* of eighteen benches. They are not so beamy, because they are made of a single log, but a *fusta* could not keep up with them by rowing, since they make incredible speed, and in these they navigate all those islands, which are innumerable, and carry their merchandise. Some of these canoes I have seen with seventy and eighty men on board, each with his oar.

In all these islands, I saw no great diversity in the appearance of the people or in their manners and language, but they all understand one another, which is a very singular thing, on account of which I hope that Their Highnesses will determine upon their conversion to our holy faith, toward which they are much inclined.

I have already said how I went 107 leagues in a straight line from west to east along the coast of the island Juana, and as a result of that voyage I can say that this island is larger than England and Scotland together; for, beyond these 107 leagues, there remain to the westward two provinces where I have not been, one of which they call Avan,[9] and there the people are born with tails. Those provinces cannot have a length of less than 50 or 60 leagues, as I could understand from those Indians whom I retain and who know all the islands. The other, *Española*, in circuit is greater than all Spain, from *Colonya* by the coast to *Fuenteravia* in Vizcaya, since I went along one side 188 great leagues in a straight line from west to east.[10] It is a desirable land and, once seen, is never to be relinquished; and in it, although of all I have taken possession for their Highnesses and all are more richly supplied than I know or could tell, I hold them all for their Highnesses, which they may dispose of as absolutely as of the realms

9. *Auau* in the original Spanish edition, *Avan* in the 1497 Spanish edition, *Anan* in the Latin translation. Columbus meant *Avan*, the Arawak word for a Cuban region from which *Havana* is derived. Tailed men was one of the most popular yarns of Sir John Mandeville. Columbus and his men frequently inquired about such creatures and were "yessed" by the Indians, who probably thought they were talking about monkeys, not Cubans.

10. I.e., from Collioure, a port in the Gulf of Lyons that then belonged to Aragon, around the entire Spanish Peninsula to Fuenterrabia, the frontier town on the Bay of Biscay. Like his other estimates of land distances, this was greatly exaggerated.

of Castile. In this *Española,* in the most convenient place and in the best district for the gold mines and for all trade both with this continent and with that over there belonging to the Grand Khan, where there will be great trade and profit, I have taken possession of a large town to which I gave the name *La Villa de Navidad,* and in it I have built a fort and defenses, which already, at this moment, will be all complete, and I have left in it enough people for such a purpose, with arms and artillery and provisions for more than a year, and a *fusta,* and a master of the sea in all [maritime] arts to build others; and great friendship with the king of that land, to such an extent that he took pride in calling me and treating me as brother; and even if he were to change his mind and offer insult to these people, neither he nor his people know the use of arms and they go naked, as I have already said, and are the most timid people in the world, so that merely the people whom I have left there could destroy all that land; and the island is without danger for their persons, if they know how to behave themselves.

In all these islands, it appears, all the men are content with one woman, but to their *Maioral,* or king, they give up to twenty. It appears to me that the women work more than the men. I have been unable to learn whether they hold private property, but it appeared true to me that all took a share in anything that one had, especially in victuals.

In these islands I have so far found no human monstrosities, as many expected, on the contrary, among all these people good looks are esteemed;[11] nor are they Negroes, as in Guinea, but with flowing hair, and they are not born where there is excessive force in the solar rays; it is true that the sun there has great strength, although it is distant from the Equator twenty-six degrees.[12] In these islands, where there are high mountains, the cold this winter was severe, but they endure it through habit and with the help of food which they eat with many and excessively hot spices. Thus I have neither found monsters nor had report of any, except in an island[13] which is the second at the entrance to the Indies, which is inhabited by a people who are regarded in all the islands as very ferocious and who eat human flesh; they have many canoes with which they range all the islands of India and pillage and take as much as they can; they are no more malformed than the others, except that they have the custom of wearing their hair long like women, and they use bows and arrows of the same stems of cane with a little piece of wood at the tip for want of iron, which they have not. They are ferocious toward these other people, who are exceedingly great cowards, but I make no more account of them than of the rest. These are those who have intercourse with

11. *Mas antes es toda gente de muy lindo acatamiento.* The meaning is somewhat obscure; the Latin translator of the Letter thought that Columbus meant that the people were reverential.

12. *Veinte e seis,* a radical revision downward of the Admiral's two inaccurate calculations that the north coast of Cuba was in lat. 42° N and that of Hispaniola 34° N. Actually 21° and 20° are correct.

13. The Latin edition names this island *Charis,* i.e., *Caire,* the Carib name for Dominica. Note that the Admiral's captive Indians had given him the position of this island and that he steered for it on his Second Voyage.

the women of *Matremomio*,[14] which is the first island met on the way from Spain to the Indies, in which there is not one man. These women use no feminine exercises, but bows and arrows of cane, like the abovesaid; and they arm and cover themselves with plates of copper, of which they have plenty. In another island, which they assure me is larger than *Española*, the people have no hair. In this there is countless gold, and from it and from the other islands I bring with me *Indios*[15] as evidence.

In conclusion, to speak only of that which has been accomplished on this voyage, which was so hasty, Their Highnesses can see that I shall give them as much gold as they want if Their Highnesses will render me a little help; besides spice and cotton, as much as Their Highnesses shall command; and gum mastic, as much as they shall order shipped, and which, up to now, has been found only in Greece, in the island of Chios, and the Seignory[16] sell it for what it pleases; and aloe wood, as much as they shall order shipped, and slaves, as many as they shall order, who will be idolaters.[17] And I believe that I have found rhubarb and cinnamon, and I shall find a thousand other things of value, which the people whom I have left there will have discovered, for I tarried nowhere, provided the wind allowed me to sail, except in the town of Navidad, where I stayed [to have it] secured and well seated. And the truth is I should have done much more if the vessels had served me as the occasion required.[18]

This is enough. And the Eternal God, Our Lord, Who gives to all those who walk in His way victory over things which appear impossible; and this was notably one. For, although men have talked or have written of these lands, all was conjecture, without getting a look at it, but amounted only to this; that those who heard for the most part listened and judged it more a fable than that there was anything in it, however small.[19]

So, since our Redeemer has given this triumph to our most illustrious King and Queen, and to their renowned realms, in so great a matter, for this all Christendom ought to feel joyful and make great celebrations and give solemn thanks to the Holy Trinity with many solemn prayers for the great exaltation which it will have, in the turning of so many peoples to our holy faith, and afterward for material benefits, since not only Spain but all Christians will hence have refreshment and profit. This is exactly what has been done, though in brief.

14. Thus in both Spanish editions, *Mateunin* in the Latin, *Matinino* in the Journal for 15 January 1493. The French named it Martinique.

15. The first appearance in print of this name that Columbus gave to the natives of America.

16. The government of Genoa. Columbus as a young man had made a voyage or two to Chios.

17. I.e., the slave trade will be legitimate if not in Christians.

18. An oblique reference to the *Pinta*, or to the loss of the *Santa Maria*.

19. He probably had in mind *The Book of Ser Marco Polo*, which most of the learned in Europe regarded as fabulous.

Done on board the caravel off the Canary Islands,[20] on the fifteenth of February, year 1493.

At your service.

THE ADMIRAL.

Additional Note,[21] Which Came within the Letter.

After having written this, and being in the Sea of Castile, there rose up on me so great a wind south and southwest,[22] that I was obliged to ease the ships.[23] But I ran hither today into this port of Lisbon, which was the greatest wonder in the world, and whence I decided to write to their Highnesses. In all the Indies I have always found weather as in May; I went thither in thirty-three days and would have returned in twenty-eight but for these tempests which detained me twenty-three days, beating about in this sea. Here all the seafarers say that never has there been so bad a winter or so many losses of ships.

Done the fourteenth[24] day of March.

This letter Columbus sent to the Keeper of the Privy Purse[25] about the islands discovered in the Indies. Contained in another for their Highnesses.

2

PERO VAZ DE CAMINHA

While Columbus was determined to believe he had found a new sea route to the Indies, Pero Vaz de Caminha, who came to America only eight years later, already knew better. He visited Brazil briefly in 1500 with Pedro Alvares Cabral's expedition. His account of the discovery of that new land, also in the form of a letter, is as free of hyperbole and rhetoric as Columbus's is full

20. So in both Spanish editions; doubtless a misprint, as the *Niña* was already off Santa María of the Azores on the fifteenth, and Columbus knew perfectly well that he had been there before he sent the letter off. The Latin editions omit this line. See Señor Sanz's discussion in *La Carta de Colón* (folio, 1956) 25–8.

21. *Anima* (modern *nema*): a paper wrapped around a letter after its conclusion, and to which the seal is affixed.

22. *Sueste:* a misprint for *sudoeste*, as may be seen from the Journal.

23. Plural in both Spanish editions.

24. *Quatorze:* a misprint for *quatro*, for the *Niña* entered the Tagus on the 4th.

25. *El Escribano de Ración*, Luís de Santangel, Columbus's friend. The Latin editions name the recipient Gabriel (or Rafael) Sanxis, meaning Gabriel Sánchez, Treasurer of Aragon. It is probable that Columbus addressed another copy of the letter to him.

of them. His is a matter-of-fact presentation of the natives and their life and habits. Even when he wrongly decoded some of the signs (there is a comic confusion about the value of gold), his good sense finally took over. He described without any derogatory comment the natives' distaste for European food and drinks and seemed responsive to the physical beauty of the women. If he was a bit shocked by the Indians' nudity, and undoubtedly approved of the Captain's decision to cover them with clothes, he was also very observant of their fashions and sensitive to their innocence. His natives are almost as noble as Columbus's but more real.

His letter was never published during his lifetime (the first edition came out in 1817) and had no chance to fire the European imagination as Columbus's did. Perhaps it was better that way. The Renaissance appetite for the exotic and fantastic decisively favored hyperbole.

The Almost Noble Savage

From A Carta de Pero Vaz de Caminha, *Vaz de Caminha's letter of discovery from Brazil in 1500; especially translated by Thomas Colchie.*

At the Captain's order Afonso Lopez, our pilot in one of the smaller boats, being a fit and skillful man for such a task, boarded a skiff to enter and sound the harbor. And he seized from a canoe two of the young and huskier natives, one of whom was carrying a bow with six or seven arrows. And many more were standing on the beach with their bows and arrows but did not make use of them. That very night the same two were brought before the captain, where they were received with great pleasure and festivity.

They are darkish red in appearance with good-looking faces and well-shaped noses. They go naked without the slightest covering and pay no special attention to showing or not showing their shameful parts—and in this respect with as much innocence as they have in showing their faces. The lower lips of both natives were punctured and through each puncture a white bone was inserted: the length of the width of one hand and the thickness of a cotton spindle and pointed like a bodkin. They insert it from the inside of the lip, and the part of the bone which remains between lip and teeth is fashioned much like a chess rook. And they seem to place it somehow so that it never annoys them in any way or prevents their speaking or eating or drinking. Their hair is straight and they go with heads shaven nearly to the crown, where the hair grows quite long, and their faces are shaven clean to above the ears. And one of the two was wearing a kind of headdress, which extended from both temples around the back of the head and the ears. He had feather after feather stuck to his hair by means of a kind of smooth concoction, like wax but not; so that he had a very round and very full and very even headdress which was by no means small and was in fact a difficult thing to carry upright.

When the two came before the Captain, he was seated in a chair with a carpet at his feet for a dais and was well dressed with a great gold collar around his neck. And Sancho de Toar, Simão de Miranda, Nicolao Coelho, Aires Correa, and the rest of us there in the boat with the Captain were seated upon the carpet on the floor. We lit the torches and the two entered the cabin, but showed none of the usual courtesies nor spoke to the Captain or to anyone; but one of them noticed the Captain's collar and began to point with his hand to land and then to the collar, as if to say to us that there was gold on the land. And he also noticed a silver candleholder and, in the same way as before, pointed to land and then to the holder, as if there were silver there also. We showed them a gray parrot which belonged to the captain; they took it easily in hand and pointed to land, as if they had parrots there. We showed them a ram, but they made no mention of its being there also. We showed them a chicken; they were somewhat afraid of it and did not want to put a hand out for it, and they touched it, fearfully, only after a while. At that point we gave them bread and cooked fish, sweets, cakes, honey, and dried figs; they did not want to eat most of the foods and tried only one or two things and threw these down at once. We brought them wine in a cup; they barely touched it to their lips and did not like what they tasted or want any more of it. We brought them water in a waterskin; they each took a taste without swallowing any, only to wash their mouths and spit it out. One of them saw some white rosary beads, made signs for us to give them to him, and with these amused himself for quite a while, putting them around his neck and throwing them up in the air, getting them tangled around his arm. And he pointed to land and then to the beads and the Captain's collar, as if to give gold for the beads. Or rather we took this to be his meaning because we wished it to be so, while he really meant to say that he would take the beads and the collar together for himself; this we did not wish to understand because we did not have it to give. And after that he returned the rosary to the one who had given it, and then he and the other stretched out on their backs to sleep on the carpet without showing the least concern for covering their shameful parts, which were not circumcised and were shaven clean of any hair. The Captain ordered us to place pillows for each one beneath their heads and to be careful with the one's headdress, not to break it, and to throw blankets over both of them. And they consented to this and lay there and fell asleep.

3

AMERIGO VESPUCCI

Columbus discovered the New Indies for Europe, but it was the privilege of one of his countrymen, Amerigo Vespucci, to call it the New World and, eventually, to leave it his name. Born in Florence in 1454 (three years after Columbus was born in Genoa), Vespucci had the disadvantage of not being a navigator. But his education was good, and he could read for himself the new Latin cosmographies published by humanists and mapmakers. Thus, in his four voyages to the Indies he was able to measure the route more accurately and dared to pursue his explorations farther south. After his third trip (1501–1502), in which he discovered the River Plate estuary and almost reached what is now the Strait of Magellan, he become convinced that the Spanish Indies were not part of Asia but a vast unknown continent.

He wrote several letters about his explorations and discoveries, which were widely published and translated into Latin and the most important European languages of the day. They were read by Thomas More, who borrowed for his *Utopia* a few narrative touches (his Raphael is supposed to be one of Vespucci's companions) and some anthropological information (like the Indians, More's Utopians have no private property and pay little attention to gold). Another consequence of Vespucci's letters was even more momentous: in preparing his *Cosmographie Introductio* (1507), Martin Waldseenmüller wrote over the map of the New World the name "America," in honor of the learned explorer whose information he had used. Other cosmographers followed Waldseenmüller's lead. Since then, Vespucci's name has taken precedence over Columbus's. Unfortunately, he did not always fare well with later historians. In his own time he already stood accused by Las Casas of trying to steal Columbus's glory; some nineteenth-century critics went so far as to claim that almost all his letters were a tissue of fabrications and that he probably did not visit the New World four times. It is true that some of the letters have reached us in very imperfect copies. But they were published and circulated profusely during the sixteenth century without arousing any suspicion. The fact that they were deliberately vague and even evasive was perfectly understandable at the time: Vespucci was writing about voyages that in some respects were highly secret. Of his four explorations, the first two (1497 and 1500) were made for the King of Spain and involved mainly the part of the New World that Pope Alexander VI had reserved to Spain in his 1493 bull. The two last voyages (1501 and 1504) were financed by the King of Portugal, after Vespucci had left Spain secretly. He was probably commissioned by the Portuguese to find a western route to India. To do that, he had to navigate into Spanish waters. It is easy to understand his position if one considers the partial secrecy that even today clouds American and Soviet exploration of the solar system.

Nevertheless, Vespucci wanted the whole of Europe to get the gist of his discoveries. Thanks to his letters, the true dimensions of the New World became known. The 1503 letter reproduced here was called in its Latin version "Mundus Novus"; it presented his own observations of the land and the people of the New Indies. It is less hyperbolic than Columbus's. Like an early, untutored Malinowski, Vespucci registered with fresh astonishment the sexual lore of the new land; he acknowledged the beauty and appeal of the native girls, and their availability to the Europeans. A more realistic view of the New World now began to take form.

A New World

From El Nuevo Mundo, *edited by Luis Aznar (Buenos Aires: Nova, 1951); English translation of the letter* Mundus Novus *(1503) by George Tyler Northup, pp. 299–307,* Vespucci Reprints, Texts and Studies *(Princeton, 1916).*

AMERIGO VESPUCCI OFFERS HIS BEST COMPLIMENTS TO LORENZO PIETRO DI MEDICI

On a former occasion I wrote to you at some length concerning my return from those new regions which we found and explored with the fleet, at the cost, and by the command of this Most Serene King of Portugal. And these we may rightly call a new world.

Because our ancestors had no knowledge of them, and it will be a matter wholly new to all those who hear about them. For this transcends the view held by our ancients, inasmuch as most of them hold that there is no continent to the south beyond the equator, but only the sea, which they named the Atlantic; and if some of them did aver that a continent there was, they denied with abundant argument that it was a habitable land. But that this their opinion is false and utterly opposed to the truth, this my last voyage has made manifest; for in those southern parts I have found a continent more densely peopled and abounding in animals than our Europe or Asia or Africa, and, in addition, a climate milder and more delightful than in any other region known to us, as you shall learn in the following account wherein we shall set succinctly down only capital matters and the things more worthy of comment and memory seen or heard by me in this new world, as will appear below.

On the fourteenth of the month of May, 1501, we set sail from Lisbon under fair sailing conditions, in compliance with the commands of the aforementioned king, with these ships for the purpose of seeking new regions toward the south; and for twenty months we continuously pursued this southern course. The route of this voyage is as follows: Our course was set for the Fortunate Isles, once so called, but which are now termed the Grand Canary Islands; these are in the third climate and on the border of the inhabited west. Thence by sea we skirted the whole African coast and part of Ethiopia as far as the Ethiopic Promontory, so called by Ptolemy, which we now call Cape Verde and the Ethiopians Beseg-hice. And that region, Mandingha, lies within the torrid zone fourteen degrees north of the equator; it is inhabited by tribes and nations of blacks. Having there recovered our strength and taken on all that our voyage required, we weighed anchor and made sail. And directing our course over the vast ocean toward the Antarctic we for a time bent westward, owing to the wind called Vulturnus; and from the day when we set sail from the said promontory we cruised for the space of two months and three days, before any land appeared to us. But what we suffered on that vast expanse of sea, what perils of shipwreck, what discomforts of the body we endured, with what anxiety of mind we toiled, this I leave to the judgment of those who out of rich experience have well learned what it is to seek the uncertain and to attempt discoveries even though ignorant. And that in a word I may briefly narrate all, you must know that of the sixty-seven days of our sailing we had forty-four of constant rain, thunder, and lightning—so dark that never did we see sun by day or fair sky by night. By reason of this such fear invaded us that we soon abandoned almost all hope of life. But during these tempests of sea and sky, so numerous and so violent, the Most High was pleased to display before us a continent, new lands, and an unknown world. At sight of these things we were filled with as much joy as anyone can imagine usually falls to those who have gained refuge from varied calamity and hostile fortune. It was on the seventh day of August, 1501, that we anchored off the shores of those parts, thanking our God with formal ceremonial and with the celebration of a choral Mass. We knew that land to be a continent and not an island both because it stretches forth in the form of a very long and unbending coast, and because it is replete with infinite inhabitants. For in it we found innumerable tribes and peoples and species of all manner of wild beasts which are found in our lands and many others never seen by us, concerning which it would take long to tell in detail. God's mercy shone upon us much when we landed at that spot, for there had come a shortage of firewood and water, and in a few days we might have ended our lives at sea. To Him the honor, glory, and thanksgiving.

We adopted the plan of following the coast of this continent toward the east and never losing sight of it. We sailed along until at length we reached a bend where the shore made a turn to the south; and from that point where we first touched land to that corner it was about three hundred leagues, in which sailing distance we frequently landed and had friendly relations with those people, as you will hear below. I had forgotten to write you that from the promontory of Cape Verde to the nearest part of that continent is about seven hundred leagues, although I should estimate that we sailed more than eighteen hundred, partly through ignorance of the route and the shipmaster's want of knowledge, partly owing to tempests and winds which kept us from the proper course and compelled us to put about frequently. Because, if my companions had not heeded me, who had knowledge of cosmography, there would have been no shipmaster, nay not the leader of our expedition himself, who would have known where we were within five hundred leagues. For we were wandering and uncertain in our course, and only the instruments for taking the altitudes of the heavenly bodies showed us our true course precisely; and these were the quadrant and the astrolabe, which all men have come to know. For this reason they subsequently made me the object of great honor; for I showed them that though a man without practical experience, yet through the teaching of the marine chart for navigators I was more skilled than all the shipmasters of the whole world. For these have no knowledge except of those waters to which they often sailed. Now, where the said corner of land showed us the southern trend of the coast, we agreed to sail beyond it and inquire what there might be in those parts. So we sailed along the coast about six hundred leagues, and often landed and mingled and associated with the natives of those regions, and by them we were received in brotherly fashion; and we would dwell with them too, for fifteen or twenty days continuously, maintaining amicable and hospitable relations, as you shall learn below. Part of this new continent lies in the torrid zone beyond the equator toward the Antarctic pole, for it begins eight degrees beyond the equator. We sailed along this coast until we passed the tropic of Capricorn and found the Antarctic pole fifty degrees higher than that horizon. We advanced to within seventeen and a half degrees of the Antarctic circle, and what I there have seen and learned concerning the nature of those races, their manners, their tractability, and the fertility of the soil, the salubrity of the climate, the position of the heavenly bodies in the sky, and especially concerning the fixed stars of the eighth sphere, never seen or studied by our ancestors, these things I shall relate in order.

First then as to the people. We found in those parts such a multitude of people as nobody could enumerate (as we read in the Apocalypse), a race I say gentle and amenable. All of both sexes go about naked, covering no part of their bodies; and just as they spring from their mothers' wombs so they go until death. They have indeed large, square-built bodies, well formed and proportioned, and in color verging upon reddish. This I think has come to them, because, going about naked, they are colored by the sun. They have, too, hair plentiful and black. In their gait and when playing their games they are agile and dignified. They are comely, too, of countenance, which they nevertheless themselves destroy; for they bore their cheeks, lips, noses, and ears. Nor think those holes small or that they have one only. For some I have seen having in a single face seven borings, any one of which was capable of holding a plum. They stop up these holes of theirs with blue stones, bits of marble, very beautiful crystals of alabaster, very white bones, and other things artificially prepared according to their customs. But if you could see a thing so unwonted and monstrous, that is to say a man having in his cheeks and lips alone seven stones some of which are a span and a half in length, you would not be without wonder. For I frequently observed and discovered that seven such stones weighed sixteen ounces aside from the fact that in their ears, each perforated with three holes, they have other stones dangling on rings; and this usage applies to the men alone. For women do not bore their faces, but their ears only. They have another custom, very shameful and beyond all human belief. For their women, being very lustful, cause the private parts of their husbands to swell up to such a huge size that they appear deformed and disgusting; and this is accomplished by a certain device of theirs, the biting of certain poisonous animals. And in consequence of this many lose their organs which break through lack of attention, and they remain eunuchs. They have no cloth either of wool, linen, or cotton, since they need it not; neither do they have goods of their own, but all things are held in common. They live together without king, without government, and each is his own master. They marry as many wives as they please; and son cohabits with mother, brother with sister, male cousin with female, and any man with the first woman he meets. They dissolve their marriages as often as they please, and observe no sort of law with respect to them. Beyond the fact that they have no church, no religion and are not idolaters, what more can I say? They live according to nature, and may be called Epicureans rather than Stoics. There are no merchants among their number, nor is there barter. The nations wage war upon one another without art or order. The elders by means of certain harangues of theirs bend the youths to their will and inflame them to wars in which they cruelly kill one another, and those whom they bring home captives from war they preserve, not to spare their lives, but that they may be slain for food; for they eat one another, the victors the vanquished, and among other kinds of meat human flesh is a common article of diet with them. Nay be the more assured of this fact because the father has already been seen to eat children and wife, and I knew a man whom I also spoke to who was reputed to have eaten more than three hundred human bodies. And I likewise remained twenty-seven days in a certain city where I saw salted human flesh suspended from beams between the houses, just as with us it is the custom to hang pork. I say further: they themselves wonder why we do not eat our enemies and do not use as food their flesh, which they say is most savory. Their weapons are bows and arrows, and when they advance to war they cover no part of their bodies for the sake of protection, so like beasts are they in this matter. We endeavored to the extent of our power to dissuade them and persuade them to desist from these depraved customs, and they did promise us that they would leave off. The women as I have said go about naked and are very libidinous; yet they have bodies which are tolerably beautiful and cleanly. Nor are they so unsightly as one perchance might imagine; for, inasmuch as they are plump, their ugliness is the less apparent, which indeed is for the most part concealed by the excellence of their bodily structure. It was to us a matter of astonishment that none was to be seen among them who had a flabby breast, and those who had borne children were not to be distinguished from virgins by the shape and shrinking of the womb; and in the other parts of the body similar things were seen of which in the interest of modesty I make no mention. When they had the opportunity of copulating with Christians, urged by excessive lust, they defiled and prostituted themselves. They live one hundred and fifty years, and rarely fall ill, and if they do fall victims to any disease, they cure themselves with certain roots and herbs. These are the most noteworthy things I know about them.

The climate there was very temperate and good, and as I was able to learn from their accounts, there was never there any pest or epidemic caused by corruption of the air; and unless they die a violent death they live long. This I take to be because the south winds are ever blowing there, and especially that which we call Eurus, which is the same to them as the Aquilo is to us. They are zealous in the art of fishing, and that sea is replete and abounding in every kind of fish. They are not hunters. This I deem to be because there are there many sorts of wild animals, and especially lions and bears and innumerable serpents and other horrid and ugly beasts, and also because forests and trees of huge size there extend far and wide; and they dare not, naked and without covering and arms, expose themselves to such hazards. The land in those parts is very fertile and pleasing, abounding in numerous hills and mountains, boundless valleys and mighty rivers, watered by refreshing springs, and filled with broad, dense, and well-nigh impenetrable forests full of every sort of wild animal. Trees grow to immense size without cultivation. Many of these yield fruits delectable to the taste and beneficial to the human body; some indeed do not, and no fruits there are like those of ours. Innumerable species of herbs and roots grow there too, of which they make bread and excellent food. They have, too, many seeds altogether unlike these of ours.

They have there no metals of any description except gold, of which those regions have a great plenty, although to be sure we have brought none thence on this our first voyage. This the natives called to our attention, who averred that in the districts remote from the coast there is a great abundance of gold, and by them it is in no respect esteemed or valued. They are rich in pearls, as I wrote you before.

If I were to seek to recount in detail what things are there and to write concerning the numerous species of animals and the great number of them, it would be a matter all too prolix and vast. And I truly believe that our Pliny did not touch upon a thousandth part of the species of parrots and other birds and the animals, too, which exist in those same regions so diverse as to form and color; because Policletus, the master of painting in all its perfection would have fallen short in depicting them. There all trees are fragrant and they emit each and all gum, oil, or some sort of sap. If the properties of these were known to us, I doubt not but that they would be salutary to the human body. And surely if the terrestrial paradise be in any part of this earth, I esteem that it is not far distant from those parts. Its situation, as I have related, lies toward the south in such a temperate climate that icy winters and fiery summers alike are never there experienced.

The sky and atmosphere are serene during the greater part of the year, and devoid of thick vapors. The rains there fall finely, last three or four hours, and vanish like a mist. The sky is adorned with most beautiful constellations and forms, among which I noted about twenty stars as bright as we ever saw Venus or Jupiter. I have considered the movements and orbits of these, I have measured their circumferences and diameters by geometric method, and I ascertained that they are of greater magnitude. I saw in that sky three Canopi, two indeed bright, the third dim. The Antarctic pole is not figured with a Great and a Little Bear as this Arctic pole of ours is seen to be, nor is any bright star to be seen near it, and of those which move around of an orthogonal triangle, the half circumference, the diameter, has nine and a half degrees. Rising with these to the left is seen a white Canopus of extraordinary size, which when they reach mid-heaven have this form:

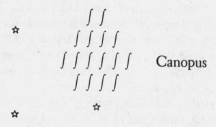

After these come two others, the half circumference of which, the diameter, has twelve and a half degrees; and with them is seen another white Canopus. There follow upon these six other most beautiful stars and brightest among all the others of the eighth sphere, which in the upper firmament have a half circumference, a diameter, of thirty-two degrees. With them revolves a black Canopus of huge size. They are seen in the Milky Way and have a form like this when observed on the meridian line:

I observed many other very beautiful stars, the movements of which I have diligently noted down and have described as beautiful with diagrams in a certain little book of mine treating of this voyage. But at present this Most Serene King has it, which I hope he will restore to me. In that hemisphere I saw things incompatible with the opinions of philosophers. A white rainbow was twice seen about midnight, not only by me but by all the sailors. Likewise we have frequently seen the new moon on that day when it was in conjunction with the sun. Every night in that part of the sky innumerable vapors and glowing meteors fly about. I said a little while ago respecting that hemisphere that it really cannot properly be spoken of as a complete hemisphere comparing it to ours, yet since it approaches such a form, such may we be permitted to call it.

Therefore, as I have said from Lisbon whence we started, which is thirty-nine and a half degrees distant from the equator, we sailed beyond the equator through fifty degrees, which added together make about ninety degrees, which total inasmuch as it makes the fourth part of a great circle according to the true system of measurement transmitted to us by our ancients, it is evident that we sailed over a fourth part of the world. And by this calculation we who live in Lisbon, thirty-nine and a half degrees north latitude this side of the equator, are with respect, to those fifty degrees beyond the same line, south latitude, at an angle of five degrees on a transverse line. And that you may the more clearly understand: A perpendicular line drawn, while we stand upright, from a point in the sky overhead, our zenith, hangs over our head; it comes down upon their side or ribs. Thus comes about that we are on an upright line, but they on a line drawn sidewise. A kind of orthogonal triangle is thus formed, the position of whose upright line we occupy, but they the base; and the hypotenuse is drawn from our zenith to theirs, as is seen in the diagram. And these things I have mentioned are sufficient as regards cosmography.

These have been the more noteworthy things which I have seen in this my last voyage, which I call my third chapter. For two other chapters consisted of two other voyages which I made to the west by command of the most Serene King of the Spains, during which I noted down the marvelous works wrought by that sublime creator of all things, our God. I kept a diary of noteworthy things that if sometime I am granted leisure I may bring together these singular and wonderful things and write a cosmographical or geographical work so that I may live with posterity and that the immense work of almighty God, partly unknown to the ancients, but known to us, may be understood. Accordingly I pray the most merciful God to prolong the days of my life that with His good favor and the salvation of my soul I may carry out in the best possible manner this my will.

The accounts of the other two journeys I am preserving in my cabinet, and when this Most Serene King restores to me the third, I shall endeavor to regain my country and repose. There I shall be able to consult with experts and to receive from friends the aid and comfort necessary for the completion of this work.

Of you I crave pardon for not having transmitted to you this my last voyage, or rather my last chapter, as I had promised you in my last letter. You have learned the reason when I tell you that I have not yet obtained the principal version from this Most Serene King. I am still privately considering the making of a fourth journey, and of this I am treating; and already I have been promised two ships with their equipment, that I may apply myself to the discovery of new regions to the south along the eastern side following the wind route called Africus. In which journey I think to perform many things to the glory of God, the advantage of this kingdom, and the honor of my old age; and I await nothing but the consent of this Most Serene King. God grant what is for the best. You shall learn what comes of it.

Jocundus, the translator, is turning this epistle from the Italian into the Latin tongue, that Latinists may know how many wonderful things are daily being discovered, and that the audacity of those who seek to scrutinize heaven and sovereignty and to know more than it is licit to know may be held in check inasmuch as ever since that remote time when the world began the vastness of the earth and what therein is contained has been unknown.

4

BARTOLOMÉ DE LAS CASAS

With Las Casas we have the darker side of the discovery and conquest: the ugly face of genocide is unmercifully presented in his pamphlets. He was the first to raise in Europe a voice for the poor, exploited, decimated Indians; the first to compile a vast catalogue of atrocities.

He was nineteen when he witnessed Columbus's triumphal return to Spain in 1493. Five years later he was even presented with an Indian as a slave. (Later, Queen Isabella ruled that all the natives had to be freed, and Las Casas' slave went back to America.) He was twenty-eight when he first came to the New World, as a teacher of Christian doctrine. Being a Spaniard, he was entitled to an *encomienda:* "a tract of land or village whose Indians were entrusted to a Spanish settler who, in return for instructing the Indians in Christian doctrine —or promising to instruct them—had the right to their forced labor in fields and mines." In fact, the Spaniards did not care about teaching any religious doctrine and merely used the Indians as slaves. When Las Casas saw what was happening, he reacted very strongly. He heard that some Dominican priests had come to the defense of the Indians. In 1514 he was converted to their point of view, resigned his *encomienda,* and began a tireless campaign. (Eventually, in 1522, he would became a Dominican himself.)

Although his conversion had been emotional, Las Casas would devote the best part of his remaining fifty-two years of life to a closely argued, theologi-cally based discussion of the rights of the Indians. He not only preached and wrote. He also traveled to Spain several times to talk to the King and his counselors. He even engaged in a debate in 1530 with the humanist Juan de Sepúlveda, who maintained that the Indians were not rational beings and could be made into slaves, according to Aristotle's doctrines. Against Sepúlveda, Las Casas contended that the Indians were rational beings and ought to be converted peacefully and actually paid for the work they did. The conclusion of the debate was indecisive, but Las Casas managed to persuade the Spanish Crown to uphold the new Laws of the Indies. Unfortunately, these Laws were hardly respected in America.

Unwittingly, Las Casas was also responsible for the Black Legend of Spanish Conquest, forcefully propagated by the competing empires of France, Holland, and England. One of his most damaging books, the *Very Brief Account of the Destruction of the Indies* (1552), was soon translated into six European languages. The truth about colonization, as Jonathan Swift pointed out in his *Gulliver's Travels,* IV, is that all conquest is brutal, all colonization is based on the destruction of the native society. At the time Las Casas was denouncing Spain's horrors, French, Dutch, Portuguese, and English conquerors and corsairs were demonstrating that no European nation had a monopoly on savagery, although very few had a Las Casas. (See selection 18 for a Spanish account of the English pirates.) Again, Las Casas' powerful and eloquent denunciations won the day.

His vivid documentation of genocide is still totally convincing. The three excerpts here presented belong to Las Casas' masterpiece, *The History of the Indies,* on which he worked from 1527 to 1564 and left unfinished at his death in 1566. It was not published until 1875, long after Spain had seen its vast American empire reduced to two islands in the Caribbean Sea—so long did the Spanish fear Las Casas' moral passion and rhetorical fire.

The Horrors of the Conquest

From Bartolomé de Las Casas: A Selection of His Writings, *translated and edited by George Sanderlin (New York: Knopf, 1971), pp. 60–66 (first excerpt: "The Conquest of Cuba") and pp. 80–85 (second excerpt: "Are Not the Indians Men?"); and a third excerpt, "The Angel of God," especially translated by Suzanne Jill Levine.*

The Conquest of Cuba

At this time, when it was known in the island of Jamaica that Diego Velázquez had gone to settle and pacify . . . the island of Cuba, Juan de Esquivel, the deputy in Jamaica, agreed to send one Pánfilo de Narváez, a native of Valladolid . . . with thirty Spaniards, to aid Diego Velázquez—or else they bestirred themselves and asked permission to go there. All were archers, with their bows and arrows, in the use of which they were more practiced than the Indians.

This Pánfilo de Narváez was a man with an air of authority, tall of stature, and rather fair-haired, tending toward red. He was honorable and wise, but not very prudent; good company, with good habits, valiant in fighting against the Indians and would perhaps have been valiant against other peoples—but above all he had this defect, that he was very careless. . . .

With his band of bowmen he was well received by Diego Velázquez. . . . Velázquez promptly gave them shares of Indians, as if these were heads of cattle, so that the Indians would serve them, although they had brought some Jamaican Indians to do that wherever they went. Diego Velázquez made this Narváez his chief captain and always honored him in such a way that, after Velázquez, Narváez held first place in that island.

A few days later I went there, the said Diego Velázquez having sent for me because of our past friendship in this island of Hispaniola. We went together, Narváez and I, for about two years, and secured the rest of that island, to the detriment of all of it, as will be seen.

[Las Casas tells how Velázquez terrorized the natives of eastern Cuba, near Cape Maisi, executed the chieftain Hatuey, and went on to Baracoa. Narváez landed at the Gulf of Guacayanabo, on the south coast near Maisi, and, on orders from Velázquez, invaded the province of Camagüey, in central Cuba.]

The Spaniards entered the province of Camagüey, which is large and densely populated . . . and when they reached the villages, the inhabitants had prepared as well as they could cassava bread from their food; what they called *guaminiquinajes* from their hunting; and also fish, if they had caught any.

Immediately upon arriving at a village, the cleric Casas would have all the little children band together; taking two or three Spaniards to help him, along with some sagacious Indians of this island of Hispaniola, whom he had brought with him, and a certain servant of his, he would baptize the children he found in the village. He did this throughout the island . . . and there were many for whom God provided holy baptism because He had predestined them to glory. God provided it at a fitting time, for none or almost none of those children remained alive after a few months. . . .

When the Spaniards arrived at a village and found the Indians at peace in their houses, they did not fail to injure and scandalize them. Not content with what the Indians freely gave, they took their wretched subsistence from them, and some, going further, chased after their wives and daughters, for this is and always has been the Spaniards' common custom in these Indies. Because of this and at the urging of the said father, Captain Narváez ordered that after the father had separated all the inhabitants of the village in half the houses, leaving the other half empty for the Spaniards' lodging, no one should dare go to the Indians' section. For this purpose, the father would go ahead with three or four men and reach a village early; by the time the Spaniards came, he had already gathered the Indians in one part and cleared the other.

Thus, because the Indians saw that the father did things for them, defending and comforting them, and also baptizing their children, in which affairs he seemed to have more command and authority than others, he received much respect and credit throughout the island among the Indians. Further, they honored him as they did their priests, magicians, prophets, or physicians, who were all one and the same.

Because of this . . . it became unnecessary to go ahead of the Spaniards. He had only to send an Indian with an old piece of paper on a stick, informing them through the messenger that those letters said thus and so. That is, that they should all be calm, that no one should absent himself because he would do them no harm, that they should have food prepared for the Christians and their children ready for baptism, or that they should gather in one part of the village, and anything else that it seemed good to counsel them—and that if they did not carry these things out, the father would be angry, which was the greatest threat that could be sent them.

They performed everything with a very good will, to the best of their ability. And great was the reverence and fear which they had for the letters, for they saw that through these what was being done in other, distant regions was known. It seemed more than a miracle to them. . . .

The Spaniards thus passed through certain villages of that province on the road they were taking. And because the folk of the villages . . . were eager to see such a new people and especially to see the three or four mares being taken there, at which the whole land was frightened—news of them flew through the island—many came to look at them in a large town called Caonao, the penultimate syllable long. And the Spaniards, on the morning of the day they arrived at the town, stopped to breakfast in a riverbed that was dry but for a few small pools. This riverbed was full of whetstones, and all longed to sharpen their swords on them [and did]. When they had finished their breakfast, they continued on the road to Caonao.

Along the road for two or three leagues there was an arid plain, where one found oneself thirsty after any work; and there certain Indians from the villages brought them some gourds of water and some things to eat.

They arrived at the town of Caonao in the evening. Here they found many people, who had prepared a great deal of food consisting of cassava bread and fish, because they had a large river close by and also were near the sea. In a little square were 2,000 Indians, all squatting because they have this custom, all staring, frightened, at the mares. Nearby was a large *bohio*, or large house, in which were more than 500 other Indians, close-packed and fearful, who did not dare come out.

When some of the domestic Indians the Spaniards were taking with them as servants (who were more than 1,000 souls . . .) wished to enter the large house, the Cuban Indians had chickens ready and said to them: "Take these— do not enter here." For they already knew that the Indians who served the Spaniards were not apt to perform any other deeds than those of their masters.

There was a custom among the Spaniards that one person, appointed by the captain, should be in charge of distributing to each Spaniard the food and other things the Indians gave. And while the captain was thus on his mare and the others mounted on theirs, and the father himself was observing how the bread and fish were distributed, a Spaniard, in whom the devil is thought to have clothed himself, suddenly drew his sword. Then the whole hundred drew theirs and began to rip open the bellies, to cut and kill those lambs—men, women, children, and old folk, all of whom were seated, off guard and frightened, watching the mares and the Spaniards. And within two credos, not a man of all of them there remains alive.

The Spaniards enter the large house nearby, for this was happening at its door, and in the same way, with cuts and stabs, begin to kill as many as they found there, so that a stream of blood was running, as if a great number of cows had perished. Some of the Indians who could make haste climbed up the poles and woodwork of the house to the top, and thus escaped.

The cleric had withdrawn shortly before this massacre to where another small square of the town was formed, near where they had lodged him. This was in a large house where all the Spaniards also had to stay, and here about forty of the Indians who had carried the Spaniards' baggage from the provinces farther back were stretched out on the ground, resting. And five Spaniards chanced to be with the cleric. When these heard the blows of the swords and knew that the Spaniards were killing the Indians—without seeing anything, because there were certain houses between—they put hands to their swords and are about to kill the forty Indians . . . to pay them their commission.

The cleric, moved to wrath, opposes and rebukes them harshly to prevent them, and having some respect for him, they stopped what they were going to do, so the forty were left alive. The five go to kill where the others were killing. And as the cleric had been detained in hindering the slaying of the forty carriers, when he went he found a heap of dead, which the Spaniards had made among the Indians, which was certainly a horrible sight.

When Narváez, the captain, saw him he said: "How does Your Honor like what these our Spaniards have done?"

Seeing so many cut to pieces before him, and very upset at such a cruel event, the cleric replied: "That I commend you and them to the devil!"

The heedless Narváez remained, still watching the slaughter as it took place, without speaking, acting, or moving any more than if he had been marble. For if he had wished, being on horseback and with a lance in his hands, he could have prevented the Spaniards from killing even ten persons.

Then the cleric leaves him, and goes elsewhere through some groves seeking Spaniards to stop them from killing. For they were passing through the groves looking for someone to kill, sparing neither boy, child, woman, nor old person. And they did more, in that certain Spaniards went to the road to the river, which was nearby. Then all the Indians who had escaped with wounds, stabs, and cuts—all who could flee to throw themselves into the river to save themselves—met with the Spaniards who finished them.

Another outrage occurred which should not be left untold, so that the deeds of our Christians in these regions may be observed. When the cleric entered the large house where I said there were about 500 souls—or whatever the number, which was great—and saw with horror the dead there and those who had escaped above by the poles or woodwork, he said to them:

"No more, no more. Do not be afraid. There will be no more, there will be no more."

With this assurance, believing that it would be thus, an Indian descended, a well-disposed young man of twenty-five or thirty years, weeping. And as the cleric did not rest but went everywhere to stop the killing, the cleric then left the house. And just as the young man came down, a Spaniard who was there drew a cutlass or half sword and gives him a cut through the loins, so that his intestines fall out. . . .

The Indian, moaning, takes his intestines in his hands and comes fleeing out of the house. He encounters the cleric . . . and the cleric tells him some things about the faith, as much as the time and anguish permitted, explaining to him that if he wished to be baptized he would go to heaven to live with God. The sad one, weeping and showing pain as if he were burning in flames, said yes, and with this the cleric baptized him. He then fell dead on the ground. . . .

Of all that has been said, I am a witness. I was present and saw it; and I omit many other particulars in order to shorten the account.

"Are Not the Indians Men?"

When Sunday and the hour to preach arrived . . . Father Fray Antonio de Montesinos ascended the pulpit and took as the text and foundation of his sermon, which he carried written out and signed by the other friars: "I am the voice of one crying in the desert." After he completed his introduction and said something concerning the subject of Advent, he began to emphasize the aridity in the desert of Spanish consciences in this island, and the ignorance in which they lived; also, in what danger of eternal damnation they were, from taking no notice of the grave sins in which, with such apathy, they were immersed and dying.

Then he returns to his text, speaking thus: "I have ascended here to cause you to know those sins, I who am the voice of Christ in the desert of this island. Therefore it is fitting that you listen to this voice, not with careless attention, but with all your heart and senses. For this voice will be the strangest you ever heard, the harshest and hardest, most fearful and most dangerous you ever thought to hear."

This voice cried out for some time, with very combative and terrible words, so that it made their flesh tremble, and they seemed already standing before the divine judgment. Then, in a grand manner, the voice . . . declared what it was, or what that divine inspiration consisted of: "This voice," he said, "declares that you are all in mortal sin, and live and die in it, because of the cruelty and tyranny you practice among these innocent peoples.

"Tell me, by what right or justice do you hold these Indians in such a cruel and horrible servitude? On what authority have you waged such detestable wars against these peoples, who dwelt quietly and peacefully on their own land? Wars in which you have destroyed such infinite numbers of them by homicides and slaughters never before heard of? Why do you keep them so oppressed and exhausted, without giving them enough to eat or curing them of the sicknesses they incur from the excessive labor you give them, and they die, or rather, you kill them, in order to extract and acquire gold every day?

"And what care do you take that they should be instructed in religion, so that they may know their God and creator, may be baptized, may hear Mass, and may keep Sundays and feast days? Are these not men? Do they not have rational souls? Are you not bound to love them as you love yourselves? Don't you understand this? Don't you feel this? Why are you sleeping in such a profound and lethargic slumber? Be assured that in your present state you can no more be saved than the Moors or Turks, who lack the faith of Jesus Christ and do not desire it."

In brief, the voice explained what it had emphasized before in such a way that it left them astonished—many numb as if without feeling, others more hardened than before, some somewhat penitent, but none, as I afterward understood, converted.

When the sermon was concluded, Antonio de Montesinos descended from the pulpit with his head not at all low, for he was not a man who would want to show fear—as he felt none—if he displeased his hearers by doing and saying what seemed fitting to him, according to God. With his companion he goes to his thatch house where, perhaps, they had nothing to eat but cabbage broth without olive oil, as sometimes happened. But after he departed, the church remains full of murmurs so that, as I believe, they scarcely permitted the mass to be finished. One may indeed suppose that a reading from the *Contempt of the World* was not given at everyone's table that day.

After finishing their meal, which must not have been very appetizing, the whole city gathers at the house of the Admiral, Don Diego Columbus . . . especially the king's officials, the treasurer and auditor, factor and comptroller. They agree to go rebuke and frighten the preacher and the others, if not to punish him as a scandalous man, sower of a new and unheard of doctrine which condemned them all. . . .

They call at the porter's box; the porter opens; they tell him to call the vicar and the friar who had preached such wild things. The vicar, the venerable Father Fray Pedro de Córdoba, emerges alone. They tell him, with more haughtiness than humility, to have the preacher called. Being very prudent, he replies that there was no need; that if his lordship and their worships command something, he was the superior of these religious and would respond. They insist violently that he have the preacher called; he very discreetly . . . excused himself and evaded their request.

Finally . . . when the Admiral and the others saw that the father vicar was not persuaded by arguments and words of high authority, they began to soften, to humble themselves, and to entreat him to order that the preacher be called because, with the vicar present, they wish to talk to them and ask why and on what grounds they had decided to preach something so novel and injurious, in disservice to the king and harmful to all the inhabitants of that city and of this whole island.

When the saintly man saw that they were taking another road and moderating the vigor with which they had come, he ordered the said Father Fray Antonio de Montesinos called. . . . After all were seated, the Admiral presents . . . their complaint. He asks why that father had dared preach things in such disservice to the king and so harmful to that whole land, by affirming that they could not possess Indians after the king, the lord of all the Indies, gave them to them—especially since the Spaniards had won those islands with great hardships and had subjugated the pagans who held them. And since that sermon had been so scandalous . . . they had decided that that father should retract everything he had said; if not, they would undertake to arrange a fitting remedy.

The father vicar replied that what that father had preached had been in accord with the vicar's own opinion and desire, and with that of all the others, and had had their assent, after being carefully considered. . . . They were obligated to this by divine precept, through their profession in baptism, first as Christians and afterward as friars-preachers of the truth. In this they intended no disservice to the king, who had sent them here to preach what they felt they should in accordance with the needs of souls, but they intended to serve him faithfully; and they considered it certain that as soon as His Highness was clearly informed of what was happening here, and of what they had preached about it, he would think himself well served and would thank them.

The speech and the reasons given by the saintly man availed little to satisfy them . . . for if they were deprived of their Indians, they would be defrauded of all their sighs and desires for riches. So each one there, especially the heads, said what he fancied to the purpose. All agreed that on the following Sunday that father should retract what he had preached; and they reached such a point of blind ignorance that they said if the friars did not do it, they should pack up in their little thatch houses and embark for Spain.

The father vicar replied: "Certainly, sirs, we will be able to do that with little labor." And it was so indeed, for their valuables were nothing but their coarse frieze habits . . . and some blankets of the same frieze. . . . Their beds were certain rods placed over some forked poles, called beds of branches, with some handfuls of straw over them. As for certain psalters and the things needed for Mass, room could perhaps have been found for all those in two chests.

Seeing how little God's servants feared all kinds of threats made against them, the officials softened again, beseeching them to reconsider the matter and, having carefully done so, to emend what had been said in another sermon—this to satisfy the community, which had been, and was, greatly scandalized. At last . . . in order to rid themselves of the officials and to put an end to their frivolous importunities, the fathers conceded that at a seasonable time it would be thus: the same Father Fray Antonio de Montesinos would return to preach the next Sunday and would go back to the subject and say what seemed best to him about it, and, as much as possible, would try to satisfy them and explain everything he had said. This having been agreed upon, the officials departed, happy in this hope.

They then proclaimed, or some of them did, that they had left with an agreement with the vicar and the others that on the following Sunday that friar would retract everything he had said. And to hear this second sermon no invitations were needed, for there was not a person in the whole city who was not found in the church on that day. . . .

When the hour for the sermon came, after Antonio de Montesinos ascended the pulpit, the text given as the basis of his retraction was a saying from Job, Chapter 36, which commences: "I will go back over my knowledge from the beginning, and I will prove that my discourse is without falsehood." That is, "I will go back to rehearse from the beginning my knowledge and the truths which I preached to you last Sunday, and I will show that those words of mine which embittered you are true."

Upon hearing this text of his, the most clear-sighted saw immediately where he was going to end, and it was misery enough to allow him to go on from there. He began to . . . corroborate with more arguments and texts what he had affirmed before, that those oppressed and exhausted peoples were held unjustly and tyrannically. He repeated his understanding that the Spaniards could certainly not be saved in the state they were in, and that therefore they should in time heal themselves. He made them know that the friars would not confess a man of them, any more than they would confess highway robbers, and that the Spaniards might proclaim and write that to whomever they wished in Castile. In all this, the friars considered it certain that they were serving God and doing the king no small favor.

After the sermon was finished, Antonio de Montesinos went to his house. And all the people in the church remained agitated, grumbling, and much angrier at the friars than before, finding themselves defrauded of their vain and wicked hope that what had been said would be unsaid—as if, after the friar made his retraction, the law of God which they disobeyed by oppressing and exterminating these peoples would be changed.

The Angel of God

One who was mainly responsible for the war was a dog called Little Calf, who could recognize Indian warriors and those who were not as if he were a person. Those Spaniards who ravaged the island of Hispaniola held this dog as an angel of God and believed that he performed miracles, which is why the Indians trembled when he went out with ten Spaniards, much more than if a hundred went out without him. His share of the spoils was one and a half, like an archer's, be it things to eat, or gold, or captured Indians made into slaves, from which his master benefitted. The Indians went out to kill him as if he were a principal enemy and finally did kill him with an arrow.

Only one thing they said about that dog do I wish to record here. In these Indies the Spaniards, when they brought dogs, would always throw the Indians they captured, men and women, to the dogs, for a pastime, or to make the dogs fiercer, or to put more fear into the Indians they tore to pieces. They decided once to throw an old woman to Little Calf, and the captain gave her an old piece of paper, saying, "Take this letter to some Christians," who were a league from there, to then let the dog loose after the old woman was on her way. The Indian woman took her letter happily, believing she could escape the hands of the Spaniards. And as soon as she was gone and far from any people, they let the dog loose. When she saw him come so fiercely toward her, she sat on the ground and began to talk to him in her language: "Master Dog, I'm taking this letter to the Christians, please don't hurt me, Master Dog," and put out her hand showing him the letter or paper. The dog stopped very tamely and began to sniff her and raised his leg and pissed on her, as dogs usually do to walls, and thus he didn't hurt her at all; the Spaniards, amazed at this, called to the dog and tied him, and freed the poor woman, so as not to be crueler than the dog.

5

GONZALO FERNÁNDEZ DE OVIEDO

A scholar, courtier, and soldier, Fernández de Oviedo (born in Spain, 1478) first came to the New World in 1513. He promptly developed an appetite for all things American, and began to compile *A General and Natural History of the Indies, Islands and Mainland of the Ocean Sea* (first part: 1535; second: 1557). The book was immediately recognized as the best and most entertaining written on the New World. Oviedo's was the official point of view on the conquest: he wrote to please the Emperor Charles V and accepted without discussion the "natural" inferiority of the Indians, as it had been defined by the humanist Juan de Sepúlveda (see selection 4). In dealing with Las Casas, he exaggerated rather casuistically the latter's ignorance of Latin. It is almost certain that Las Casas began his own *History of the Indies* when he heard Oviedo was writing his, and to set the record straight. But Oviedo's book was approved by the censors and published, while Las Casas' remained in manuscript until the late 1870s.

Like Columbus, but to a greater degree, Oviedo was familiar with the Renaissance epic and loved the fabulous romances of chivalry to the point of translating one himself, *Claribalte*, in 1519. Although he had a humanistic training, he refused to see in the Spanish conquest any sign of abuse and was ready, on the other hand, to admit the existence of prodigies, strange feathered monkeys, and griffins. In his shorter *Summary of the Natural History of the Indies* (1526), he was more the scholar and less the fiction writer. But today it is the latter that interests us most.

The Unique Monkey

From The Golden Land, *selected, edited, and translated by Harriet de Onís* *(New York: Knopf, 1948), pp. 7–8.*

It has been my habit in these accounts of mine to name the witnesses of those things I have not seen with my own eyes and which I have heard from others; and in connection with what I have said about griffins, I should like to mention something else I have heard of, which strikes me as being no less extraordinary than the griffins. It is said that in the southern land of Peru a monkey has been seen, one of those with long tails, the upper half of whose body, from its forepaws to its head, was covered with brown and different-colored feathers, and the other half, hindquarters and tail, with smooth, reddish fur, of a sort of fawn color. This monkey was very gentle and tame, and little bigger than a handspan in size. It belonged to an Indian princess, the sister of the Inca Amaro, brother to the great prince Atabalipa, and this sister, when she came into the power of the Spaniards, was married to a young man, the son of Baptista Armero, a skilled horseman, and in high favor at the court of His Majesty the Emperor. I am giving all these details because this youth is a person of standing. He asked his wife to give him this monkey to send to the Empress, our lady, of glorious memory, with Captain Per Ansurez, and she gave it to him. And this captain was taking it when, through the carelessness of certain of his servants, who were frolicking about, one of them, without meaning to, stepped on the monkey and killed it. I relate this misfortune as an example of the unhappiness of those eyes which had no opportunity to see this animal and give thanks to God who made it so different from all those that exist in the world. Men whose word may be credited have come to this city of Santo Domingo who say that they saw and held this monkey in their hands, and it was as I have described it, and had teeth. And no less to be wondered at than the foregoing is that the monkey, perched on the shoulder of the captain I have mentioned, or where he had it tied, would begin to sing when it felt like it, like a nightingale or a lark, first in a soft warble, and then gradually growing louder than either of these birds, and with as many or more modulations in its song. It was a great pleasure and delight to hear its sweet melody, which lasted for a long time, after the manner of singers. A gentleman named Diego de Mercado, from the city of Madrigal, and another hidalgo by the name of Tomás de Ortega, who made the trip with the aforesaid captain (and who, after they arrived here with fortunes, married in this city, and live here, and are persons whose word can and should be taken for this and much more), were eyewitnesses to what has been related, for they saw this monkey often and heard it sing.

There are those who say that this animal must have been born as the result of the adultery or miscegenation of a bird with a male or female monkey to engender a species of this sort partaking of the nature of both progenitors. But I do not hold with this opinion; and it is my belief (taking into account certain things that one cannot overlook regarding the dissimilarity of the generative organs of birds and monkeys) that this animal was not born as the consequence of such adultery, but belongs to a species of its own, as do the griffins, since the Lord of Creation has wrought other and greater works and wonders, may His name be praised and remembered forever and ever.

I greatly regret that this monkey did not reach this city alive, or dead either, for if I had seen it dead, I would have traded my cape for a little salt to cure it and preserve it so others could see it, too, to praise the wonders of God. And I believe that in Spain it would have been highly esteemed, and wherever there are men of wisdom. In this city of ours there are today four men who saw this monkey alive; and I would rather have seen it than all the rich emeralds I have beheld from those lands of Peru; and I will see as many more before another such animal is seen, unless, in accordance with the opinion I have expressed, others of its species are found in the course of time. I do not doubt that this will be the case, for this great world of our Indies is always revealing new things to those of us who are here, and those who will come after us to contemplate and admire the handiwork of God, to whom nothing is impossible. Therefore, let the Catholic reader recall the words of Hilary: "God can do more than the understanding of man can grasp."

6

ALVAR NÚÑEZ CABEZA DE VACA

If Columbus was the first European to register his astonishment at the nakedness of the Caribbean Indians, it fell to Alvar Núñez to astonish his readers with the story of his own misadventures and nakedness.

He was born in 1490 and was already thirty-seven when he joined Pánfilo de Narváez's expedition to explore Florida and the lands of the north. From the point of view of the conquest, the expedition would fail completely: of the six hundred men who left Spain in 1527, only four ever returned. But from the point of view of the exploration of the new lands, it was entirely successful: it proved beyond any doubt that the New World was not a group of islands but a wide continent, thinly populated by a great variety of Indian tribes.

The odyssey of Narváez's men and their almost unbelievable three-thousand-mile journey was told by Alvar Núñez in the first part of his *Narrative*, commonly called *The Shipwrecks*, which was published in 1542. (The second part deals with Alvar Núñez's less spectacular but highly dramatic exploits in South America.) The story he tells in the first part is one of failure, of death and violence, of incredible hardship. It is also a story of European men reduced to cannibalism in order to survive, forced to become slaves to Indians almost as poor and destitute as themselves. Those Spaniards, proud of their faith and of their country's power, had arrived fully equipped and brilliantly dressed for conquest. Suddenly, they were reduced to total, primeval nakedness: centuries of civilization were stripped off their backs. Alvar Núñez tells the story in simple and direct terms. The experience he records is as strange and overwhelming as the one conceived more than a century later by Calderón in his dramatic masterpiece, *Life Is a Dream*. Like Segismundo in his prison, Alvar Núñez discovered in the New World the depths of destitution and animality; like the prince, he also learned how to return from these abysses. After a long captivity, Alvar Núñez managed to recover some of his former rights as a free man; he even became a medicine man and was honored by the Indians and passed around, like their most valuable possession, from tribe to tribe. He and his companion traveled from Florida, through Louisiana and Texas, to California, and then to Mexico, already in the hands of the Spaniards.

His story (like Segismundo's) ends well, but its chronicle of hardships makes it one of the most extraordinary documents on the limits of human endurance. His *Narrative* also helped to discredit the myth that the New World was really the Garden of Eden. The excerpt presented here belongs to Chapters 10 to 12 of the original book and tells the fate of Narváez's men from the time they attempted to set foot on the coast (near Galveston, apparently) until they were made prisoners, and slaves, by the Indians.

The Naked Spaniards

From The Narrative of Alvar Núñez Cabeza de Vaca, *translated by Buckingham Smith (Washington, 1851), pp. 37–45.*

Of the Assault from the Indians

The morning having arrived, there came to us many Indians in canoes, asking us for their two companions who had remained in the boat as hostages. The governor said he would give them up when they should bring the Christians they had taken. With them had come five or six chiefs, who appeared to us to be the most comely persons, of more authority and condition, than any we had hitherto seen, although not so large as the others of whom we have spoken. They wore their hair loose and very long, and were covered with blankets of martens like those we had before taken. Some of them were made up after a strange fashion, having ties of lion skin that made them appear very brave. They entreated us to go with them and said that they would give us the Christians, and water, and many other things. They continued to collect about us in many canoes, attempting with them to take possession of the mouth of that entrance; and because of this, as well because it was hazardous to remain in that land, we went out to sea, where they remained by us until about midday. As they were not willing to deliver to us the Christians, for that reason we would not give up the Indians, and they commenced to throw clubs at us and to sling stones, making threats of shooting arrows, although among them all we had not seen more than three or four bows. While in this affray, the wind freshened, and they went back and left us.

So we sailed that day until the middle of the afternoon, when my boat, which was first, discovered a point made by the land, and against a cape opposite a broad river passed. I anchored by a little island which forms the point, to await the arrival of the other boats. The governor did not choose to come up, but entered a bay nearby, in which were a great many islets. We came together there, and took fresh water from the sea, for the stream entered it impetuously. To parch some of the corn we had brought with us, since we had eaten of it raw for two days past, we went on the island; but as we found no wood we agreed to go to the river behind the point, which was one league off. We were unable to get there by any efforts, so violent was the current on the way, which drove us from the land while we contended and strove to gain it. The north wind, which came from the shore, began to blow so strongly that it drove us to sea without our being able to overcome it. Half a league out we sounded, and found that with thirty fathoms we could not get the bottom, but we could not be satisfied that the river was not the cause of our failure to reach it. Toiling in this manner to fetch the land we navigated two days, and at the end of the time, a little while before the sun rose, we saw many smokes along the shore. While attempting to reach them, we found ourselves in three fathoms of water, and it being dark we dared not come to land; for as we had seen so many smokes we thought some danger might surprise us, and the obscurity leave us at a loss what to do. So we determined to wait until the morning. When it came, the boats had all lost sight of each other. I found myself in thirty fathoms, and keeping my course until the hour of vespers, I observed two boats, and as I drew near to them, I found that the first I approached was that of the governor, who asked me what I thought we should do. I told him that we ought to join that boat which went in the advance, and by no means to leave her, and the three being together that we should keep on our way to where God should be pleased to direct us. He answered me saying it could not be done, because the boat was far to sea, and he wished to reach the shore; that if I wished to follow him, I should order the persons of my boat to take the oars and work, as it was only by strength of arm that the land could be gained. He was advised to this course by a captain he had with him named Pantoja, who told him that if he did not fetch the land that day, in six days more they would not reach it, and in that time they must inevitably famish. I, seeing his will, took my oar, and the same did all who were in my boat, to obey it. We rowed until near sunset; but as the governor carried in his boat the healthiest men there were among the whole, we could not by any means hold with or follow her. Seeing this, I asked him to give me a rope from his boat, that I might be enabled to keep up with him; but he answered me that he would do no little, if they, as they were, should be able to reach the land that night. I said to him, that since he saw the little strength we had to follow him and do what he had commanded, he should tell me what he would that I should do. He answered me that it was no longer a time in which one should command another, but that each should do what he thought best to save his own life; that he so intended to act; and saying this, he departed with his boat. As I could not follow him, I steered to the other boat at sea, which waited for me, and having come up with her, I found her to be the one commanded by the captains Peñalosa and Tellez.

Thus we continued in company, eating a daily ration of half a handful of raw maize, until the end of four days, when we lost sight of each other in a storm; and such was the weather that it was only by Divine favor that we did not all go down. Because of the winter and its inclemency, the many days we had suffered hunger, and the heavy beating of the waves, the people began the next day to despair in such a manner that when the sun went down all who were in my boat were fallen one on another, so near to death that there were few among them in a state of sensibility. Among them all at this time there were not five men on their feet, and when the night came there were left only the master and myself who could work the boat. At the second hour of the night, he said to me that I must take charge of her, for that he was in such condition he believed that night he should die. So I took the paddle, and after midnight I went to see if the master was alive, and he said to me that he was better, and that he would take the charge until day. I declare that in that hour I would have more willingly died than seen so many people before me in such condition. After the master took the direction of the boat, I laid down a little while, but without repose, for nothing at that time was further from me than sleep.

Near the dawn of day, it seemed to me that I heard the tumbling of the sea; for, as the coast was low, it roared loudly. Surprised at this, I called to the master, who answered me that he believed we were near the land. We sounded and found ourselves in seven fathoms. He thought we should keep the sea until sunrise; and accordingly I took an oar and pulled on the side of the land, until we were a league distant, and we then gave her stern to the sea. Near the shore a wave took us that knocked the boat out of the water to the distance of the throw of a crowbar, and by the violence of the blow nearly all the people who were in her like dead were roused to consciousness. Finding themselves near the shore, they began to move on hands and feet, and crawled to land in some ravines. There we made fire, parching some of the maize we brought with us, and where we found rain water. From the warmth of the fire the people recovered their faculties, and began somewhat to exert themselves. The day on which we arrived here was the sixth of November.

Of What Befell Lope de Oviedo with Some Indians

After the people had eaten, I ordered Lope de Oviedo, who had more strength and was stouter than any of the rest, to go to some trees that were near, and having climbed into one of them to survey the country in which we were, and endeavor to get some knowledge of it. He did as I bade him, and made out that we were on an island. He saw that the ground was pawed up in the manner that the land is wont to be where cattle range, and hence it appeared to him that this should be the country of Christians; and thus he reported to us. I ordered him to return to examine much more particularly, and see if there were any roads in it that were worn, and without going far, because of the danger there might be.

He went, and coming to a path, he took it for the distance of half a league, and found some huts without any tenants, for the Indians had gone into the woods. He took from them an earthen pot, a little dog, and a few mullets, and thus returned. It appearing to us that he was long absent, we sent two others that they should look and see what might have befallen him. They met him nearby, and saw that three Indians with bows and arrows followed and were calling to him, and he in the same way was beckoning them on. Thus they arrived where we were, the Indians remaining a little way back, seated on the same bank. Half an hour after, they were supported by fifty other Indian bowmen, whom, whether large or not, our fears made giants. They stopped near us with the three first. It were idle to think that there were any among us who could make defense; for it would have been difficult to find six that could raise themselves from the ground. The assessor and I went and called them, and they came to us. We endeavored the best we could to recommend ourselves to their favor, and secure their good will. We gave them beads and hawk bells, and each one of them gave me an arrow, which is a pledge of friendship. They told us by signs that they would return in the morning and bring us something to eat, as at that time they had nothing.

How the Indians Brought Us Food

The next day at sunrise, the time the Indians had appointed, they came as they had promised, and brought us a large quantity of fish and certain roots that are eaten by them, of the size of walnuts, some a little larger, others a little smaller, the greater part of them got from under the water, and with much labor. In the evening, they returned and brought us more fish and some of the roots. They sent their women and children to look at us, who returned rich with the hawk bells and beads that we gave them, and they came afterward on other days in the same way. As we found that we had been provisioned with fish, roots, water, and other things for which we asked, we determined to embark again and pursue our course. We dug out our boat from the sand in which it was buried; and it became necessary that we should all strip ourselves, and go through great exertion to launch her, for we were in such state that things very much lighter sufficed to make us much labor.

Thus embarked, at the distance of two crossbow shots in the sea we shipped a wave that wet us all. As we were naked, and the cold was very great, the oars loosened in our hands, and the next blow the sea struck us capsized the boat. The assessor and two others held fast to her for preservation, but it happened to be for far otherwise, as the boat carried them over, and they drowned under her. As the surf near the shore was very high, a single roll of the sea threw the remainder into the waves, and left them half drowned on the shore of the island, without our losing any more than those the boat had taken under. Those of us who survived escaped naked as we were born, losing all that we had, and although the whole was of little value, at that time it was worth much. As it was then in the month of November, the cold severe, and our bodies so emaciated that the bones might have been counted with little difficulty, we had become perfect figures of death. For myself, I can say that from the month of May past, I had not eaten anything other than maize, and sometimes I found myself obliged to eat it unparched; for although the horses were slaughtered while the boats were being built, I never could eat of them, and I did not eat fish ten times. I state this to avoid giving excuses, and that every one may judge in what condition we were. After all these misfortunes, there came a north wind upon us, from which we were nearer to death than life. Thanks be to our Lord, that, looking among the brands that we had used there, we found sparks from which we made great fires. And thus we were asking mercy of Him, and pardon for our transgressions, shedding many tears, and each regretting not his own fate alone, but that of his comrades about him.

At sunset, the Indians, thinking that we had not gone, came to seek us and bring us food; but when they saw us thus, in a plight so different from what it was formerly, and so extraordinary, they were alarmed and turned back. I went toward them and called to them, and they returned much frightened. I gave them to understand by signs how that our boat had sunk, and three of our number been drowned. There, before them, they saw two of the departed, and those that remained were near joining them. The Indians, at sight of the disaster that had befallen us, and our state of suffering and melancholy destitution, sat down amongst us, and from the sorrow and pity they felt for us they all began to lament, and so earnestly that they might have been heard at a distance, and they continued so doing more than half an hour. It was strange to see these men, so wild and untaught, howling like brutes over our misfortunes. It caused in me, as in others, an increase of feeling and a livelier sense of our calamity. Their cries having ceased, I talked with the Christians, and said that if it appeared well to them, I would beg these Indians to take us to their houses. Some, who had been in New Spain, said that we ought not to think of it, for if we should do so they would sacrifice us to their idols. But seeing no better course, and that any other led to nearer and more certain death, I disregarded what was said, and besought the Indians to take us to their dwellings. They signified that it would give them great delight, and that we should tarry a little that we might do what we asked. Presently, thirty of them loaded themselves with wood and started for their houses, which were far off, and we remained with the others until near night, when, holding us up, they carried us with all haste. Because of the extreme coldness of the weather, lest any one should die or fail by the way, they caused four or five large fires to be placed at intervals, and at each one of them they warmed us, and when they saw that we had regained some strength and warmth, they took us to the next so swiftly that they hardly permitted us to put our feet to the ground. In this manner, we went as far as their habitations, where we found that they had made a house for us with many fires in it. An hour after our arrival, they began to dance and hold great rejoicing, which lasted all night, although for us there was no joy, appetite, or sleep, awaiting the time they should make us victims. In the morning, they again gave us fish and roots, and showed us such hospitality that we were reassured and lost somewhat the fear of the sacrifice.

7

BERNAL DÍAZ DEL CASTILLO

In Oviedo's *Natural History of the Indies* (see selection 5), one finds the point of view of the courtier. In Bernal Díaz's *True History of the Conquest of New Spain* one recognizes for the first time not only the common soldier's speech but also his own earthy and restricted vision. His is almost oral history: the true voice of Cortes's companions, a collective persona in which the "Us, poor soldiers" Archibald MacLeish would personify in his fine poem *Conquistador* is clearly audible.

Díaz was born in Spain around 1496 and was only twenty-three when he came to Mexico with Cortes's forces in 1519. (He had participated already in two previous attempts, which failed to secure a stronghold.) He fought in the long and exhausting campaign and had the honor to be counted among the "old conquistadores": those who twice entered the capital of the Aztecs and fought inch by inch with its fierce warriors.

After the conquest, he settled in Guatemala. He was already an old man when he first read Francisco López de Gómara's book *Conquest of Mexico* (1552), which gave all the credit to Cortes and forgot his companions. Gómara had never been in Mexico, and what he knew about the conquest was gathered from books or in conversation with Cortes, whose secretary he had been during the last six years of the conqueror's life. Being a priest and well trained in rhetoric, Gómara had a superiority over Bernal Díaz that is undeniable. But the soldier had been there, and remembered very vividly what had happened and how. Besides, he probably had rehearsed his narrative orally for the better part of fifty years. His incredible memory for detail, his capacity to record the haunting actuality of the past ("as I write, it all comes before my eyes as if it had happened only yesterday"), and the freshness of his style make his book one of the greatest historical narratives of the Renaissance.

It is not necessary to decide which of the two, Gómara or Bernal Díaz, is telling *the* truth. From a literary point of view it does not matter. Both have merit: Gómara for his skill as a biographer and historian; Bernal Díaz for his matchless reconstruction of a time and a place. He had the true eye and ear of the novelist. There is only one other work of the Spanish Golden Age to set next to (and perhaps before) his own: *Don Quixote.* In a sense, the narratives are very similar, and one may well wonder whether, *if* the Errant Knight had chosen the New World instead of La Mancha for his exploits, and *if* Sancho had known how to write, if then his chronicle would have closely resembled that of Bernal Díaz on Cortes. But Sancho did not know how to write, and Don Quixote remained in Spain, and Cervantes was a professional writer. His book was more fortunate than Bernal Díaz's; it was published in 1605 and immediately caught the imagination of Europe.

The True History, on the other hand, was to remain in manuscript until 1632, more than sixty years after Bernal Díaz sent a clean copy to Spain and fifty years after his own death. The first edition was heavily edited by a priest. Only in 1904 was the original manuscript published. From then on, the book became a classic. Bernal Díaz had a European point of view: he believed that the Spaniards had a religious mission to accomplish and that the Crown was right in conquering the Indians; he was opposed to Las Casas and thought that the *encomiendas* were devised to protect and not to exploit the Indians. But he was also aware of the abuses and argued against treating the natives as slaves.

Although he learned some Indian languages, he was not very conversant with the true meaning of their religion and mores. He was fond of legends, ready to believe that Montezuma ate the flesh of young boys, naturally censorious of human sacrifices, of polygamy and sodomy. On the other hand, he was the first Spaniard to present an Indian prince as equal in greatness to a Castilian conqueror. His dual portrait of Cortes and Montezuma is a masterpiece in dramatic confrontation. Although he had chosen the voice of the common man, he knew, like Bernard Shaw, how to present men as heroes. He was also responsive to the beauty and grandeur of Tenochtitlan, the capital of the Aztec empire, built like Venice on a lake and more splendid to this conqueror's eyes than any European city he had ever seen. Through his words, the fabled city remains intact, and alive.

The Entry of Cortes into Mexico

From The Conquest of New Spain, *translated by J. M. Cohen (New York: Penguin Books, 1963), pp. 216–41.*

Early next day we left Iztapalapa with a large escort of these great caciques, and followed the causeway, which is eight yards wide and goes so straight to the city of Mexico that I do not think it curves at all. Wide though it was, it was so crowded with people that there was hardly room for them all. Some were going to Mexico and others coming away, besides those who had come out to see us, and we could hardly get through the crowds that were there. For the towers and the *cues* were full, and they came in canoes from all parts of the lake. No wonder, since they had never seen horses or men like us before!

With such wonderful sights to gaze on we did not know what to say, or if this was real that we saw before our eyes. On the land side there were great cities, and on the lake many more. The lake was crowded with canoes. At intervals along the causeway there were many bridges, and before us was the great city of Mexico. As for us, we were scarcely four hundred strong, and we well remembered the words and warnings of the people of Huexotzinco and Tlascala and Tlamanalco, and the many other warnings we had received to beware of entering the city of Mexico, since they would kill us as soon as they had us inside. Let the interested reader consider whether there is not much to ponder in this narrative of mine. What men in all the world have shown such daring? But let us go on.

We marched along our causeway to a point where another small causeway branches off to another city called Coyoacan, and there, beside some tower-like buildings, which were their shrines, we were met by many more caciques and dignitaries in very rich cloaks. The different chieftains wore different brilliant liveries, and the causeways were full of them. Montezuma had sent these great caciques in advance to receive us, and as soon as they came before Cortes they told him in their language that we were welcome, and as a sign of peace they touched the ground with their hands and kissed it.

There we halted for some time while Cacamatzin, the lord of Texcoco, and the lords of Iztapalapa, Tacuba, and Coyoacan went ahead to meet the great Montezuma, who approached in a rich litter, accompanied by other great lords and feudal caciques who owned vassals. When we came near to Mexico, at a place where there were some other small towers, the great Montezuma descended from his litter, and these other great caciques supported him beneath a marvelously rich canopy of green feathers, decorated with goldwork, silver, pearls, and *chalchihuites,* which hung from a sort of border. It was a marvelous sight. The great Montezuma was magnificently clad, in their fashion, and wore sandals of a kind for which their name is *cotaras,* * the soles of which are of gold and the upper parts ornamented with precious stones. And the four lords who supported him were richly clad also in garments that seemed to have been kept ready for them on the road so that they could accompany their master. For they had not worn clothes like this when they came out to receive us. There were four other great caciques who carried the canopy above their heads, and many more lords who walked before the great Montezuma, sweeping the ground on which he was to tread, and laying down cloaks so that his feet should not touch the earth. Not one of these chieftains dared to look him in the face. All kept their eyes lowered most reverently except those four lords, his nephews, who were supporting him.

When Cortes saw, heard, and was told that the great Montezuma was approaching, he dismounted from his horse, and when he came near to Montezuma each bowed deeply to the other. Montezuma welcomed our Captain, and Cortes, speaking through Doña Marina, answered by wishing him very good health. Cortes, I think, offered Montezuma his right hand, but Montezuma refused it and extended his own. Then Cortes brought out a necklace which he had been holding. It was made of those elaborately worked and colored-glass beads called *margaritas,* of which I have spoken, and was strung on a gold cord and dipped in musk to give it a good odor. This he hung round the great Montezuma's neck, and as he did so attempted to embrace him. But the great princes who stood round Montezuma grasped Cortes's arm to prevent him, for they considered this an indignity.

*Actually a Cuban word; the Mexican word was *cactli.*

Then Cortes told Montezuma that it rejoiced his heart to have seen such a great prince, and that he took his coming in person to receive him and the repeated favors he had done him as a high honor. After this Montezuma made him another complimentary speech, and ordered two of his nephews who were supporting him, the lords of Texcoco and Coyoacan, to go with us and show us our quarters. Montezuma returned to the city with the other two kinsmen of his escort, the lords of Cuitlahuac and Tacuba; and all those grand companies of *caciques* and dignitaries who had come with him returned also in his train. And as they accompanied their lord we observed them marching with their eyes downcast so that they should not see him, and keeping close to the wall as they followed him with great reverence. Thus space was made for us to enter the streets of Mexico without being pressed by the crowd.

Who could now count the multitude of men, women, and boys in the streets, on the rooftops and in canoes on the waterways, who had come out to see us? It was a wonderful sight and, as I write, it all comes before my eyes as if it had happened only yesterday.

They led us to our quarters, which were in some large houses capable of accommodating us all and had formerly belonged to the great Montezuma's father, who was called Axayacatl. Here Montezuma now kept the great shrines of his gods, and a secret chamber containing gold bars and jewels. This was the treasure he had inherited from his father, which he never touched. Perhaps their reason for lodging us here was that, since they called us *Teules* and considered us as such, they wished to have us near their idols. In any case they took us to this place, where there were many great halls, and a dais hung with the cloth of their country for our Captain, and matting beds with canopies over them for each of us.

On our arrival we entered the large court, where the great Montezuma was awaiting our Captain. Taking him by the hand, the prince led him to his apartment in the hall where he was to lodge, which was very richly furnished in their manner. Montezuma had ready for him a very rich necklace, made of golden crabs, a marvelous piece of work, which he hung round Cortes's neck. His captains were greatly astonished at this sign of honor.

After this ceremony, for which Cortes thanked him through our interpreters, Montezuma said: "Malinche, you and your brothers are in your own house. Rest awhile." He then returned to his palace, which was not far off.

We divided our lodgings by companies, and placed our artillery in a convenient spot. Then the order we were to keep was clearly explained to us, and we were warned to be very much on the alert, both the horsemen and the rest of us soldiers. We then ate a sumptuous dinner which they had prepared for us in their native style.

So, with luck on our side, we boldly entered the city of Tenochtitlan or Mexico on the eighth of November in the year of our Lord 1519.

When the great Montezuma had dined and was told that our Captain and all of us had finished our meal some time ago, he came to our quarters in the grandest state with a great number of princes, all of them his kinsmen. On being told of his approach, Cortes came into the middle of the hall to receive him. Montezuma then took him by the hand, and they brought chairs made in their fashion and very richly decorated in various ways with gold. Montezuma requested our Captain to sit down, and both of them sat, each on his own chair.

Then Montezuma began a very good speech, saying that he was delighted to have such valiant gentlemen as Cortes and the rest of us in his house and his kingdom. That two years ago he had received news of a Captain who had come to Champoton, and that last year also he had received a report of another Captain who had come with four ships. Each time he had wished to see them, and now that he had us with him he was not only at our service but would share all that he possessed with us. He ended by saying that we must truly be the men about whom his ancestors had long ago prophesied, saying that they would come from the direction of the sunrise to rule over these lands, and that he was confirmed in this belief by the valor with which we had fought at Champoton and Tabasco and against the Tlascalans, for lifelike pictures of these battles had been brought to him.

Cortes replied through our interpreters that we did not know how to repay the daily favors we received from him, and that indeed we did come from the direction of the sunrise, and were vassals and servants of a great king called the Emperor Charles, who was ruler over many great princes. Having heard news of Montezuma and what a great prince he was, the Emperor, he said, had sent us to this country to visit him, and to beg them to become Christians, like our Emperor and all of us, so that his soul and those of all his vassals might be saved. Cortes promised to explain to him later how this could be, and how we worship the one true God and who He is, also many other good things which he had already communicated to his ambassadors Tendile, Pitalpitoque, and Quintalbor.

The great Montezuma had some fine gold jewels of various shapes in readiness which he gave to Cortes after this conversation. And to each of our captains he presented small gold objects and three loads of cloaks of rich featherwork; and to us soldiers he gave two loads of cloaks each, all with a princely air. For in every way he was like a great prince. After the distribution of presents, he asked Cortes if we were all brothers and vassals of our great Emperor; and Cortes answered that we were brothers in love and friendship, persons of great distinction, and servants of our great king and lord. Further polite speeches passed between Montezuma and Cortes, but as this was the first time he had visited us and we did not want to tire him, the conversation ended.

Montezuma had ordered his stewards to provide us with everything we needed for our way of living: maize, grindstones, women to make our bread, fowls, fruit, and plenty of fodder for the horses. He then took leave of us all with the greatest courtesy, and we accompanied him to the street. However, Cortes ordered us not to go far from our quarters for the present until we knew better what conduct to observe.

Next day Cortes decided to go to Montezuma's palace. But first he sent to know whether the prince was busy and to inform him of our coming. He took four captains with him: Pedro de Alvarado, Juan Velazquez de Leon, Diego de Ordaz, and Gonzalo de Sandoval, and five of us soldiers.

When Montezuma was informed of our coming, he advanced into the middle of the hall to receive us, closely surrounded by his nephews, for no other chiefs were allowed to enter his palace or to communicate with him except upon important business. Cortes and Montezuma exchanged bows and clasped hands. Then Montezuma led Cortes to his own dais, and setting him down on his right, called for more seats, on which he ordered us all to sit also.

Cortes began to make a speech through our interpreters, saying that we were all now rested, and that in coming to see and speak with such a great prince we had fulfilled the purpose of our voyage and the orders of our lord the King. The principal things he had come to say on behalf of our Lord God had already been communicated to Montezuma through his three ambassadors, on that occasion in the sandhills when he did us the favor of sending us the golden moon and sun. We had then told him that we were Christians and worshipped one God alone, named Jesus Christ, who had suffered His passion and death to save us; and that what they worshipped as gods were not gods but devils, which were evil things, and if they were ugly to look at, their deeds were uglier. But he had proved to them how evil and ineffectual their gods were, as both the prince and his people would observe in the course of time, since, where we had put up crosses such as their ambassadors had seen, they had been too frightened to appear before them.

The favor he now begged of the great Montezuma was that he should listen to the words he now wished to speak. Then he very carefully expounded the creation of the world, how we are all brothers, the children of one mother and father called Adam and Eve; and how such a brother as our great Emperor, grieving for the perdition of so many souls as their idols were leading to hell, where they burnt in living flame, had sent us to tell him this, so that he might put a stop to it, and so that they might give up the worship of idols and make no more human sacrifices—for all men are brothers—and commit no more robbery or sodomy. He also promised that in the course of time the King would send some men who lead holy lives among us, much better than our own, to explain this more fully, for we had only come to give them warning. Therefore he begged Montezuma to do as he was asked.

As Montezuma seemed about to reply, Cortes broke off his speech, saying to those of us who were with him: "Since this is only the first attempt, we have now done our duty."

"My lord Malinche," Montezuma replied, "these arguments of yours have been familiar to me for some time. I understand what you said to my ambassadors on the sandhills about the three gods and the cross, also what you preached in the various towns through which you passed. We have given you no answer, since we have worshipped our own gods here from the beginning and know them to be good. No doubt yours are good also, but do not trouble to tell us any more about them at present. Regarding the creation of the world, we have held the same belief for many ages, and for this reason are certain that you are those who our ancestors predicted would come from the direction of the sunrise. As for your great King, I am in his debt and will give him of what I possess. For, as I have already said, two years ago I had news of the Captains who came in ships, by the road that you came, and said they were servants of this great king of yours. I should like to know if you are all the same people."

Cortes answered that we were all brothers and servants of the Emperor, and that they had come to discover a route and explore the seas and ports, so that when they knew them well we could follow, as we had done. Montezuma was referring to the expeditions of Francisco Hernandez de Córdoba and of Grijalva, the first voyages of discovery. He said that ever since that time he had wanted to invite some of these men to visit the cities of his kingdom, where he would receive them and do them honor, and that now his gods had fulfilled his desire, for we were in his house, which we might call our own. Here we might rest and enjoy ourselves, for we should receive good treatment. If on other occasions he had sent to forbid our entrance into his city, it was not of his own free will, but because his vassals were afraid. For they told him we shot out flashes of lightning, and killed many Indians with our horses, and that we were angry *Teules,* and other such childish stories. But now that he had seen us, he knew that we were of flesh and blood and very intelligent, also very brave. Therefore he had a far greater esteem for us than these reports had given him, and would share with us what he had.

We all thanked him heartily for his signal good will, and Montezuma replied with a laugh, because in his princely manner he spoke very gaily: "Malinche, I know that these people of Tlascala with whom you are so friendly have told you that I am a sort of god or *Teule,* and keep nothing in any of my houses that is not made of silver and gold and precious stones. But I know very well that you are too intelligent to believe this and will take it as a joke. See now, Malinche, my body is made of flesh and blood like yours, and my houses and palaces are of stone, wood, and plaster. It is true that I am a great king, and have inherited the riches of my ancestors, but the lies and nonsense you have heard of us are not true. You must take them as a joke, as I take the story of your thunders and lightnings."

Cortes answered also with a laugh that enemies always speak evil and tell lies about the people they hate, but he knew he could not hope to find a more magnificent prince in that land, and there was good reason why his fame should have reached our Emperor.

While this conversation was going on, Montezuma quietly sent one of his nephews, a great cacique, to order his stewards to bring certain pieces of gold, which had apparently been set aside as a gift for Cortes, and ten loads of fine cloaks which he divided: the gold and cloaks between Cortes and the four captains, and for each of us soldiers two gold necklaces, each worth ten pesos, and two loads of cloaks. The gold that he then gave us was worth in all more than a thousand pesos, and he gave it all cheerfully, like a great and valiant prince.

As it was now past midday and he did not wish to be importunate, Cortes said to Montezuma: "My lord, the favors you do us increase, load by load, every day, and it is now the hour of your dinner." Montezuma answered that he thanked us for visiting him. We then took our leave with the greatest courtesy, and returned to our quarters, talking as we went of the prince's fine breeding and manners and deciding to show him the greatest respect in every way, and to remove our quilted caps in his presence, which we always did.

The great Montezuma was about forty years old, of good height, well proportioned, spare and slight, and not very dark, though of the usual Indian complexion. He did not wear his hair long but just over his ears, and he had a short black beard, well-shaped and thin. His face was rather long and cheerful, he had fine eyes, and in his appearance and manner could express geniality or, when necessary, a serious composure. He was very neat and clean, and took a bath every afternoon. He had many women as his mistresses, the daughters of chieftains, but two legitimate wives who were *caciques* in their own right, and when he had intercourse with any of them it was so secret that only some of his servants knew of it. He was quite free from sodomy. The clothes he wore one day he did not wear again till three or four days later. He had a guard of two hundred chieftains lodged in rooms beside his own, only some of whom were permitted to speak to him. When they entered his presence, they were compelled to take off their rich cloaks and put on others of little value. They had to be clean and walk barefoot, with their eyes downcast, for they were not allowed to look him in the face, and as they approached they had to make three obeisances, saying as they did so, "Lord, my lord, my great lord!" Then, when they had said what they had come to say, he would dismiss them with a few words. They did not turn their backs on him as they went out, but kept their faces toward him and their eyes downcast, only turning around when they had left the room. Another thing I noticed was that when other great chiefs came from distant lands about disputes or on business, they too had to take off their shoes and put on poor cloaks before entering Montezuma's apartments; and they were not allowed to enter the palace immediately but had to linger for a while near the door, since to enter hurriedly was considered disrespectful.

For each meal his servants prepared him more than thirty dishes cooked in their native style, which they put over small earthenware braziers to prevent them from getting cold. They cooked more than three hundred plates of the food the great Montezuma was going to eat, and more than a thousand more for the guard. I have heard that they used to cook him the flesh of young boys. But as he had such a variety of dishes, made of so many different ingredients, we could not tell whether a dish was of human flesh or anything else, since every day they cooked fowls, turkeys, pheasants, local partridges, quail, tame and wild duck, venison, wild boar, marsh birds, pigeons, hares and rabbits, also many other kinds of birds and beasts native to their country, so numerous that I cannot quickly name them all. I know for certain, however, that after our Captain spoke against the sacrifice of human beings and the eating of their flesh, Montezuma ordered that it should no longer be served to him.

Let us now turn to the way his meals were served, which was like this. If it was cold, they built a large fire of live coals made by burning the bark of a tree which gave off no smoke. The smell of the bark from which they made these coals was very sweet. In order that he should get no more heat than he wanted, they placed a sort of screen in front of it adorned with the figures of idols worked in gold. He would sit on a soft, low stool, which was richly worked. His table, which was also low and decorated in the same way, was covered with white tablecloths and rather long napkins of the same material. Then four very clean and beautiful girls brought water for his hands in one of those deep basins that they call *xicales*.* They held others like plates beneath it to catch the water, and brought him towels. Two other women brought him maize cakes.

When he began his meal they placed in front of him a sort of wooden screen, richly decorated with gold, so that no one should see him eat. Then the four women retired, and four great chieftains, all old men, stood beside him. He talked with them every now and then and asked them questions, and as a great favor he would sometimes offer one of them a dish of whatever tasted best. They say that these were his closest relations and advisers and judges of lawsuits, and if he gave them anything to eat they ate it standing, with deep reverence and without looking in his face.

Montezuma's food was served on Cholula ware, some red and some black. While he was dining, the guards in the adjoining rooms did not dare to speak or make a noise above a whisper. His servants brought him some of every kind of fruit that grew in the country, but he ate very little of it. Sometimes they brought him in cups of pure gold a drink made from the cocoa plant, which they said he took before visiting his wives. We did not take much notice of this at the time, though I saw them bring in a good fifty large jugs of this chocolate, all frothed up, of which he would drink a little. They always served it with great reverence. Sometimes some little humpbacked dwarfs would be present at his meals, whose bodies seemed almost to be broken in the middle. These were his jesters. There were other Indians who told him jokes and must have been his clowns, and others who sang and danced, for Montezuma was very fond of music and entertainment and would reward his entertainers with the leavings of the food and chocolate. The same four women removed the tablecloths and again most reverently brought him water for his hands. Then Montezuma would talk to these four old chieftains about matters that interested him, and they would take their leave with great ceremony. He stayed behind to rest.

As soon as the great Montezuma had dined, all the guards and many more of his household servants ate in their turn. I think more than a thousand plates of food must have been brought in for them, and more than two thousand jugs of chocolate frothed up in the Mexican style, and infinite quantities of fruit, so that with his women and serving maids and breadmakers and chocolate makers his expenses must have been considerable.

One thing I had forgotten to say is that two more very handsome women served Montezuma when he was at table with maize cakes kneaded with eggs and other nourishing ingredients. These maize cakes were very white, and

*Gourds.

were brought in on plates covered with clean napkins. They brought him a different kind of bread also, in a long ball kneaded with other kinds of nourishing food, and *pachol* cake, as they call it in that country, which is a kind of wafer. They also placed on the table three tubes, much painted and gilded, in which they put liquidamber* mixed with some herbs which are called tobacco. When Montezuma had finished his dinner, and the singing and dancing were over and the cloths had been removed, he would inhale the smoke from one of these tubes. He took very little of it, and then fell asleep.

I remember that at that time his steward was a great *cacique* whom we nicknamed Tapia, and he kept an account of all the revenue that was brought to Montezuma in his books, which were made of paper—their name for which is *amal*—and he had a great house full of these books. But they have nothing to do with our story.

Montezuma had two houses stocked with every sort of weapon; many of them were richly adorned with gold and precious stones. There were shields large and small, and a sort of broadsword, and two-handed swords set with flint blades that cut much better than our swords, and lances longer than ours, with five-foot blades consisting of many knives. Even when these are driven at a buckler or a shield they are not deflected. In fact they cut like razors, and the Indians can shave their heads with them. They had very good bows and arrows, and double- and single-pointed javelins as well as their throwing sticks and many slings and round stones shaped by hand, and another sort of shield that can be rolled up when they are not fighting, so that it does not get in the way, but which can be opened when they need it in battle and covers their bodies from head to foot. There was also a great deal of cotton armor richly worked on the outside with different-colored feathers, which they used as devices and distinguishing marks, and they had casques and helmets made of wood and bone, which were also highly decorated with feathers on the outside. They had other arms of different kinds, which I will not mention through fear of prolixity, and workmen skilled in the manufacture of such things, and stewards who were in charge of these arms.

Let us pass on to the aviary. I cannot possibly enumerate every kind of bird that was in it or describe its characteristics. There was everything from the royal eagle, smaller kinds of eagles, and other large birds, down to multicolored little birds, and those from which they take the fine green feathers they use in their featherwork. These last birds are about the size of our magpies, and here they are called *quetzals*. There were other birds too which have feathers of five colors: green, red, white, yellow, and blue, but I do not know what they are called. Then there were parrots with different-colored plumage, so many of them that I have forgotten their names. There were also beautifully marked ducks, and bigger ones like them. At the proper season they plucked the feathers of all these birds, which then grew again. All of them were bred in this aviary, and at hatching time the men and women who looked after them would place them on their eggs

*The gum of a native tree.

and clean their nests and feed them, giving each breed of birds its proper food.

In the aviary there was a large tank of fresh water, and in it was another type of bird on long stiltlike legs with a red body, wings, and tail. I do not know its name, but in Cuba birds rather like them are called *ypiris*. Also in this tank there were many other kinds of water birds.

Let us go on to another large house where they kept many idols whom they called their fierce gods, and with them all kinds of beasts of prey, tigers and two sorts of lion, and beasts rather like wolves which they call *adives*,* and foxes and other small animals, all of them carnivores, and most of them bred there. They were fed on deer, fowls, little dogs, and other creatures which they hunt and also on the bodies of the Indians they sacrificed, as I was told.

I have already described the manner of their sacrifices. They strike open the wretched Indian's chest with flint knives and hastily tear out the palpitating heart which, with the blood, they present to the idols in whose name they have performed the sacrifice. Then they cut off the arms, thighs, and head, eating the arms and thighs at their ceremonial banquets. The head they hang up on a beam, and the body of the sacrificed man is not eaten but given to the beasts of prey. They also had many vipers in this accursed house, and poisonous snakes which have something that sounds like a bell in their tails. These, which are the deadliest snakes of all, they kept in jars and great pottery vessels full of feathers, in which they laid their eggs and reared their young. They were fed on the bodies of sacrificed Indians and the flesh of the dogs that they bred. We know for certain, too, that when they drove us out of Mexico and killed over eight hundred and fifty of our soldiers, they fed those beasts and snakes on their bodies for many days, as I shall relate in due course. These snakes and wild beasts were dedicated to their fierce idols, and kept them company. As for the horrible noise when the lions and tigers roared, and the jackals and foxes howled, and the serpents hissed, it was so appalling that one seemed to be in hell.

I must now speak of the skilled workmen whom Montezuma employed in all the crafts they practiced, beginning with the jewelers and workers in silver and gold and various kinds of hollowed objects, which excited the admiration of our great silversmiths at home. Many of the best of them lived in a town called Atzcapotzalco, three miles from Mexico. There were other skilled craftsmen who worked with precious stones and *chalchihuites*, and specialists in featherwork, and very fine painters and carvers. We can form some judgment of what they did then from what we can see of their work today. There are three Indians now living in the city of Mexico, named Marcos de Aquino, Juan de la Cruz, and El Crespillo, who are such magnificent painters and carvers that, had they lived in the age of the Apelles of old, or of Michelangelo, or Berruguete in our own day, they would be counted in the same rank.

Let us go on to the women, the weavers and seamstresses, who made such a huge quantity of fine robes with very elaborate feather designs. These

*Bernal Díaz is mistaken here. This is an Arabic word for jackal, quite commonly used in Spain.

things were generally brought from some towns in the province of Cotaxtla, which is on the north coast, quite near San Juan de Ulua. In Montezuma's own palaces very fine cloths were woven by those chieftains' daughters whom he kept as mistresses; and the daughters of other dignitaries, who lived in a kind of retirement like nuns in some houses close to the great *cue* of Huichilobos, wore robes entirely of featherwork. Out of devotion for that god and a female deity who was said to preside over marriage, their fathers would place them in religious retirement until they found husbands. They would then take them out to be married.

Now to speak of the great number of performers whom Montezuma kept to entertain him. There were dancers and stilt-walkers, and some who seemed to fly as they leapt through the air, and men rather like clowns to make him laugh. There was a whole quarter full of these people who had no other occupation. He had as many workmen as he needed, too, stonecutters, masons, and carpenters, to keep his houses in repair.

We must not forget the gardens with their many varieties of flowers and sweet-scented trees planted in order, and their ponds and tanks of fresh water into which a stream flowed at one end and out of which it flowed at the other, and the baths he had there, and the variety of small birds that nested in the branches, and the medicinal and useful herbs that grew there. His gardens were a wonderful sight, and required many gardeners to take care of them. Everything was built of stone and plastered; baths and walks and closets and rooms like summerhouses where they danced and sang. There was so much to see in these gardens, as everywhere else, that we could not tire of contemplating his great riches and the large number of skilled Indians employed in the many crafts they practiced.

When we had already been in Mexico for four days, and neither our Captain nor anyone else had left our quarters except to visit these houses and gardens, Cortes said it would be a good thing to visit the large square of Tlatelolco and see the great *cue* of Huichilobos. So he sent Aguilar, Doña Marina, and his own young page Orteguilla, who by now knew something of the language, to ask for Montezuma's approval of this plan. On receiving his request, the prince replied that we were welcome to go, but for fear that we might offer some offense to his idols he would himself accompany us with many of his chieftains. Leaving the palace in his fine litter, when he had gone about halfway, he dismounted beside some shrines, since he considered it an insult to his gods to visit their dwelling in a litter. Some of the great chieftains then supported him by the arms, and his principal vassals walked before him, carrying two staves, like scepters raised on high as a sign that the great Montezuma was approaching. When riding in his litter he had carried a rod, partly of gold and partly of wood, held up like a wand of justice. The prince now climbed the steps of the great *cue*, escorted by many *papas*, and began to burn incense and perform other ceremonies for Huichilobos.

Let us leave Montezuma, who had gone ahead as I have said, and return to Cortes and our soldiers. We carried our weapons, as was our custom, both by night and day. Indeed, Montezuma was so used to our visiting him armed that he did not think it strange. I say this because our Captain and those of us who had horses went to Tlatelolco mounted, and the majority of our men were fully equipped. On reaching the marketplace, escorted by the many caciques whom Montezuma had assigned to us, we were astounded at the great number of people and the quantities of merchandise, and at the orderliness and good arrangements that prevailed, for we had never seen such a thing before. The chieftains who accompanied us pointed everything out. Every kind of merchandise was kept separate and had its fixed place marked for it.

Let us begin with the dealers in gold, silver, and precious stones, feathers, cloaks, and embroidered goods, and male and female slaves who are also sold there. They bring as many slaves to be sold in that market as the Portuguese bring Negroes from Guinea. Some are brought there attached to long poles by means of collars round their necks to prevent them from escaping, but others are left loose. Next there were those who sold coarser cloth, and cotton goods and fabrics made of twisted thread, and there were chocolate merchants with their chocolate. In this way you could see every kind of merchandise to be found anywhere in New Spain, laid out in the same way as goods are laid out in my own district of Medina del Campo, a center for fairs, where each line of stalls has its own particular sort. So it was in this great market. There were those who sold sisal cloth and ropes and the sandals they wear on their feet, which are made from the same plant. All these were kept in one part of the market, in the place assigned to them, and in another part were skins of tigers and lions, otters, jackals, and deer, badgers, mountain cats, and other wild animals, some tanned and some untanned, and other classes of merchandise.

There were sellers of kidney beans and sage and other vegetables and herbs in another place, and in yet another they were selling fowls, and birds with great dewlaps,* also rabbits, hares, deer, young ducks, little dogs, and other such creatures. Then there were the fruiterers; and the women who sold cooked food, flour and honey cake, and tripe, had their part of the market. Then came pottery of all kinds, from big water jars to little jugs, displayed in its own place, also honey, honey paste, and other sweets like nougat. Elsewhere they sold timber too, boards, cradles, beams, blocks, and benches, all in a quarter of their own.

Then there were the sellers of pitch pine for torches, and other things of that kind, and I must also mention, with all apologies, that they sold many canoe-loads of human excrement, which they kept in the creeks near the market. This was for the manufacture of salt and the curing of skins, which they say cannot be done without it. I know that many gentlemen will laugh at this, but I assure them it is true. I may add that on all the roads they have shelters made of reeds or straw or grass so that they can retire when they wish to do so, and purge their bowels unseen by passers-by, and also in order that their excrement shall not be lost.

But why waste so many words on the goods in their great market? If

---

*Turkeys.

I describe everything in detail I shall never be done. Paper, which in Mexico they call *amal,* and some reeds that smell of liquidamber, and are full of tobacco, and yellow ointments and other such things, are sold in a separate part. Much cochineal is for sale too, under the arcades of that market, and there are many sellers of herbs and other such things. They have a building there also in which three judges sit, and there are officials like constables who examine the merchandise. I am forgetting the sellers of salt and the makers of flint knives, and how they split them off the stone itself, and the fisherwomen and the men who sell small cakes made from a sort of weed which they get out of the great lake, which curdles and forms a kind of bread which tastes rather like cheese. They sell axes too, made of bronze and copper and tin, and gourds and brightly painted wooden jars.

We went on to the great *cue,* and as we approached its wide courts, before leaving the marketplace itself, we saw many more merchants who, so I was told, brought gold to sell in grains, just as they extract it from the mines. This gold is placed in the thin quills of the large geese of that country, which are so white as to be transparent. They used to reckon their accounts with one another by the length and thickness of these little quills, how much so many cloaks or so many gourds of chocolate or so many slaves were worth, or anything else they were bartering.

Now let us leave the market, having given it a final glance, and come to the courts and enclosures in which their great *cue* stood. Before reaching it you passed through a series of large courts, bigger I think than the Plaza at Salamanca. These courts were surrounded by a double masonry wall and paved, like the whole place, with very large smooth white flagstones. Where these stones were absent everything was whitened and polished, indeed the whole place was so clean that there was not a straw or a grain of dust to be found there.

When we arrived near the great temple and before we had climbed a single step, the great Montezuma sent six *papas* and two chieftains down from the top, where he was making his sacrifices, to escort our Captain; and as he climbed the steps, of which there were one hundred and fourteen, they tried to take him by the arms to help him up in the same way as they helped Montezuma, thinking he might be tired, but he would not let them near him.

The top of the *cue* formed an open square on which stood something like a platform, and it was here that the great stones stood on which they placed the poor Indians for sacrifice. Here also was a massive image like a dragon, and other hideous figures, and a great deal of blood that had been spilled that day. Emerging in the company of two *papas* from the shrine which houses his accursed images, Montezuma made a deep bow to us all and said: "My lord Malinche, you must be tired after climbing this great *cue* of ours." And Cortes replied that none of us was ever exhausted by anything. Then Montezuma took him by the hand, and told him to look at his great city and all the other cities standing in the water, and the many others on the land round the lake; and he said that if Cortes had not had a good view of the great marketplace he could see it better from where he now was. So we stood there looking, because that huge accursed *cue* stood so high that it dominated everything. We saw the three causeways that led into Mexico: the causeway of Iztapalapa by which we had entered four days before, and that of Tacuba along which we were afterwards to flee on the night of our great defeat, when the new prince Cuitlahuac drove us out of the city (as I shall tell in due course), and that of Tepeaquilla.* We saw the fresh water which came from Chapultepec to supply the city, and the bridges that were constructed at intervals on the causeways so that the water could flow in and out from one part of the lake to another. We saw a great number of canoes, some coming with provisions and others returning with cargo and merchandise; and we saw too that one could not pass from one house to another of that great city and the other cities that were built on the water except over wooden drawbridges or by canoe. We saw *cues* and shrines in these cities that looked like gleaming white towers and castles: a marvelous sight. All the houses had flat roofs, and on the causeways were other small towers and shrines built like fortresses.

Having examined and considered all that we had seen, we turned back to the great market and the swarm of people buying and selling. The mere murmur of their voices talking was loud enough to be heard more than three miles away. Some of our soldiers who had been in many parts of the world, in Constantinople, in Rome, and all over Italy, said that they had never seen a market so well laid out, so large, so orderly, and so full of people.

But to return to our Captain, he observed to Father Bartolome de Olmedo, whom I have often mentioned and who happened to be standing near him: "It would be a good thing, I think, Father, if we were to sound Montezuma as to whether he would let us build our church here." Father Bartolome answered that it would be a good thing if it were successful, but he did not think this a proper time to speak of it, for Montezuma did not look as if he would allow such a thing.

Cortes, however, addressed Montezuma through Doña Marina: "Your lordship is a great prince and worthy of even greater things. We have enjoyed the sight of your cities, and since we are now here in your temple, I beg of you to show us your gods and *Teules.*" Montezuma answered that first he would consult his chief *papas;* and when he had spoken to them he said that we might enter a small tower, an apartment like a sort of hall, in which there were two altars with very rich wooden carvings over the roof. On each altar was a giant figure, very tall and very fat. They said that the one on the right was Huichilobos, their war god. He had a very broad face and huge, terrible eyes. And there were so many precious stones, so much gold, so many pearls and seed pearls stuck to him with a paste which the natives made from a sort of root, that his whole body and head were covered with them. He was girdled with huge snakes made of gold and precious stones, and in one hand he held a bow, in the other some arrows. Another, smaller idol beside him, which they said was his page, carried a short

*Guadalupe.

lance and a very rich shield of gold and precious stones. Around Huichilobos's neck hung some Indian faces and other objects in the shape of hearts, the former made of gold and the latter of silver, with many precious blue stones.

There were some smoking braziers of their incense, which they call copal, in which they were burning the hearts of three Indians whom they had sacrificed that day; and all the walls of that shrine were so splashed and caked with blood that they and the floor too were black. Indeed, the whole place stank abominably. We then looked to the left and saw another great image of the same height as Huichilobos, with a face like a bear and eyes that glittered, being made of their mirror glass, which they call *tezcat*. Its body, like that of Huichilobos, was encrusted with precious stones, for they said that the two were brothers. This Tezcatlipoca, the god of hell, had charge of the Mexicans' souls, and his body was surrounded by figures of little devils with snakes' tails. The walls of this shrine also were so caked with blood and the floor so bathed in it that the stench was worse than that of any slaughterhouse in Spain. They had offered that idol five hearts from the day's sacrifices.

At the very top of the *cue* there was another alcove, the woodwork of which was very finely carved, and here there was another image, half man and half lizard, encrusted with precious stones, with half its body covered in a cloak. They said that the body of this creature contained all the seeds in the world, and that he was the god of seedtime and harvest. I do not remember his name.* Here too all was covered with blood, both walls and altar, and the stench was such that we could hardly wait to get out. They kept a very large drum there, and when they beat it the sound was most dismal, like some music from the infernal regions, as you might say, and it could be heard six miles away. This drum was said to be covered with the skins of huge serpents. On that small platform were many more diabolical objects, trumpets great and small, and large knives, and many hearts that had been burnt with incense before their idols; and everything was caked with blood. The stench here too was like a slaughterhouse, and we could scarcely stay in the place.

Our Captain said to Montezuma, through our interpreters, with something like a laugh: "Lord Montezuma, I cannot imagine how a prince as great and wise as your Majesty can have failed to realize that these idols of yours are not gods but evil things, the proper name for which is devils. But so that I may prove this to you, and make it clear to all your *papas*, grant me one favor. Allow us to erect a cross here on the top of this tower, and let us divide off a part of this sanctuary where your Huichilobos and Tezcatlipoca stand, as a place where we can put an image of Our Lady"—which image Montezuma had already seen —"and then you will see, by the fear that your idols have of her, how grievously they have deceived you."

Montezuma, however, replied in some temper (and the two *papas* beside him showed real anger): "Lord Malinche, if I had known that you were

*This was probably Tlaltecuhtli.

going to utter these insults I should not have shown you my gods. We hold them to be very good. They give us health and rain and crops and weather, and all the victories we desire. So we are bound to worship them and sacrifice to them, and I beg you to say nothing more against them."

On hearing this and seeing Montezuma's fury, our Captain said no more on the subject but observed cheerfully: "It is time for your Majesty and ourselves to depart." Montezuma replied that this was so, but that he had to pray and offer certain sacrifices on account of the great *tatacul*—that is to say, sin— which he had committed in allowing us to climb his great *cue* and in being instrumental in letting us see his gods and in the dishonor we had done them by our abuse. Therefore before he left he must pray and worship.

"If that is so, my lord," Cortes answered, "I ask your pardon." And we went down the steps, of which there were a hundred fourteen, as I said. As some of our soldiers were suffering from pustules, or running sores, their thighs pained them as they went down.

I will now give my impression of the *cue*'s surroundings. Do not be surprised, however, if I do not describe them as accurately as I might, for I had other thoughts in my head at the time than that of telling a story. I was more concerned with my military duties and the orders my Captain had given me. But to come to the facts, I think the site of the great *cue* was equal to the plots of six large town houses at home. It tapered from the base to the top of the small tower where they kept their idols. Between the middle of this tall *cue* and its highest point there were five holes like loopholes for cannon, but open and unprotected. But as there are many *cues* painted on the banners of the conquerors, including my own, anyone who has seen them can gather what a *cue* looked like from the outside. I heard a report that, at the time when this great *cue* was built, all the inhabitants of that mighty city placed offerings of gold and silver and pearls and precious stones in the foundations, and bathed them in the blood of prisoners of war whom they had sacrificed. They also put there every kind of seed that grew in their country, so that their idols should give them victories and riches and great crops. Some curious readers may ask how we came to know that they had thrown gold and silver and precious *chalchihuites* and seeds into the foundation of the *cue*, and watered them with the blood of Indian victims, seeing that the building was erected a thousand years ago. My answer is that after we conquered that great and strong city and divided the ground we decided to build a church to our patron and guide Saint James in place of Huichilobos's *cue*, and a great part of the site was taken for the purpose. When the ground was excavated to lay a foundation, gold and silver and *chalchihuites*, and pearls, seed pearls, and other precious stones were found in great quantities; and a settler in Mexico who built on another part of the site found the same. The officers of His Majesty's Treasury demanded this find as rightfully belonging to the King, and there was a lawsuit about it. I do not remember what the outcome was, only that they asked for information from the caciques and dignitaries of Mexico, and from Guatemoc, who was then alive, and they affirmed that all the inhabitants of Mexico had thrown jewels and other things into the foundations, as was recorded in their pictures and records of ancient times. The treasure was therefore preserved for the building of Saint James's church.

Let me go on to describe the great and splendid courts in front of Huichilobos, on the site where that church now stands, which was called at that time Tlatelolco. I have already said that there were two masonry walls before the entrance to the *cue,* and the court was paved with white stones like flagstones, and all was whitened, burnished, and clean. A little apart from the *cue* stood another small tower which was also an idol house or true hell, for one of its doors was in the shape of a terrible mouth, such as they paint to depict the jaws of hell. This mouth was open and contained great fangs to devour souls. Beside this door were groups of devils and the shapes of serpents, and a little way off was a place of sacrifice, all bloodstained and black with smoke. There were many great pots and jars and pitchers in this house, full of water. For it was here that they cooked the flesh of the wretched Indians who were sacrificed and eaten by the *papas.* Near this place of sacrifice there were many large knives and chopping blocks like those on which men cut up meat in slaughterhouses; and behind that dreadful house, some distance away, were great piles of brushwood, beside which was a tank of water that was filled and emptied through a pipe from the covered channel that comes into the city from Chapultepec. I always called that building Hell.

Crossing the court you came to another *cue,* where the great Mexican princes were buried. This also contained many idols and was full of blood and smoke. It too had doorways with hellish figures; and beside it was another *cue,* full of skulls and large bones arranged in an orderly pattern, and so numerous that you could not count them however long you looked. The skulls were in one place and the bones in separate piles. Here there were more idols, and in every building or *cue* or shrine were *papas* in long black cloth robes and long hoods.

To proceed, there were other *cues,* a short distance away from that of the skulls, which contained other idols and sacrificial altars decorated with horrible paintings. These idols were said to preside over the marriages of men. But I will waste no more time on the subject of idols. I will only say that all round that great court there were many low houses, used and occupied by the *papas* and other Indians who were in charge of them. On one side of the great *cue* there was another, much bigger pond or tank of very clean water which was solely devoted to the service of Huichilobos and Tezcatlipoca, and the water for this tank was also supplied by covered pipes that came from Chapultepec. Nearby were the large buildings of a kind of nunnery where many of the daughters of the inhabitants of Mexico dwelt in retirement until the time of their marriage. Here there were two massive female idols who presided over the marriages of women, and to which they offered sacrifices and feasts in order that they should get good husbands.

I have spent a long time talking about the great *cue* of Tlatelolco and its courts. I will conclude by saying that it was the biggest temple in Mexico, though there were many other fine ones, for every four or five parishes or districts supported a shrine with idols; and since there were many districts I cannot keep a count of them all. I must say, however, that the great *cue* in Cholula was higher than that in Mexico, for it had a hundred and twenty steps. The idol at Cholula, as I heard, had a great reputation, and people made pilgrimages to it from all over New Spain to obtain pardons. This was the reason why they had built it such a magnificent *cue*. It was differently planned from that of Mexico, but also had great courts and a double wall. The *cue* of the city of Texcoco was very high too, having a hundred and seventeen steps, and fine wide courtyards, again of a different shape from the others. Absurd though it was, every province had its own idols, and those of one province or city were of no help in another. Therefore they had infinite numbers of idols and sacrificed to them all.

When we were all tired of walking about and seeing such a diversity of idols and sacrifices, we returned to our quarters, still accompanied by the many caciques and dignitaries whom Montezuma had sent with us.

8

GASPAR DE CARVAJAL

Many of America's first visitors described prodigies they had only heard about. The Dominican friar Gaspar de Carvajal (born in Spain, 1504) was one of the few to believe he himself had seen one of these prodigies: the authentic Amazons of ancient lore and legend.

Carvajal was already thirty-one when he came to Peru and participated in Gonzalo Pizarro's fateful expedition to the Country of Cinnamon, one of the fabulous lost lands of the New World. (Other sources indicate that Pizarro was after another legend: the man covered with gold, or "El Dorado," The Gilded One, whose true story is told by Rodríguez Freile in his *Carnero;* see selection 12.) Before completing the first quest, Carvajal left Pizarro to follow Francisco de Orellana and his fifty-six companions in their search for the Atlantic Ocean, down the Amazon River. His *Relación,* or chronicle of this expedition (published in 1542), is a matter-of-fact minor epic; in some nine months of intolerable hardship they traveled more than two thousand miles, fighting almost every inch of the way with hostile Indians. Orellana's gross miscalculation of the river's length was less important to Carvajal than the prodigies he expected to see, and finally did see. With his mind conditioned (like Columbus's and Oviedo's) by Renaissance myths, he found it easy to identify with the fabled Amazons some fierce women warriors who attacked the expedition: "we saw [them] with our own eyes," he insisted. There is a certain symbolic irony in the fact that in the same fight he lost an eye to an arrow. Undaunted, Carvajal went right on taking notes. His credulous chronicle served to reinforce the European belief in the inexhaustible wonders of the New World.

Encounter with the Amazons

From The Golden Land, *selected, edited, and translated by Harriet de* Onis *(New York: Knopf, 1948), pp. 14–19.*

The following Thursday we passed by other small villages and did not bother to stop there. All these villages are fishing posts of tribes living inland. We were sailing along in this way looking for a pleasant spot to celebrate the feast of the blessed Saint John the Baptist, the harbinger of Christ, and God so willed it that as we came around a bend in the river we saw before us on the bank many and large villages, gleaming white. Here we came head on into the fair lands and domain of the Amazons. These villages had received word of our approach, and for this reason the inhabitants came out on the water to meet us, seeming well disposed. When they drew near, the Captain, wanting to make friends with them, began to speak and call out to them. But they laughed and made fun of us, and came closer and told us to go farther down the river and they would be waiting for us there, and they would take us all and carry us to the Amazons. The Captain, exasperated by their insolence, ordered us to fire on them with our crossbows and harquebuses to let them know that we had arms to attack them, and in this way we inflicted harm upon them, and they turned and went back to the village to tell what they had seen. We kept moving on and approaching the villages, and before we had traveled more than half a league, there appeared on the water many squadrons of Indians, and as we sailed ahead they assembled and drew near their settlements. In the middle of a village there was a great number of people, constituting a stout squadron, and the Captain ordered the brigantines to draw in where those people were to seek food, and as soon as we approached land, the Indians began to defend their village and shoot at us with arrows, and as there were so many, it seemed as though it were raining arrows. But our bowmen and harquebusiers were not idle; they did nothing but shoot, and although they killed many, it did not seem to matter, because in spite of all the harm we were doing them, some of them kept on fighting and others dancing. We were all on the verge of being lost there, because as so many arrows kept coming, our companions had all they could do to defend themselves from them and were unable to row, and for this reason they did us so much harm that before we could jump ashore they had wounded five of us, of whom I was one, for they got me in the side with an arrow that went through the hollow part of me, and if it had not been for the habit I was wearing, that would have been the end of me. When the Captain saw the danger we were in, he began to encourage and urge on the oarsmen to pull in to shore, and in this way, though with difficulty, we managed to touch bottom, and our companions leaped into the water, which reached to their armpits. There a great and fierce battle took place, because the Indians closed in on our Spaniards, who defended themselves so bravely that it was a wondrous thing to see. This fighting lasted for more than an hour, for the Indians were not dismayed, rather they seemed to take heart, although they saw many of their comrades dead, and advanced over their bodies, and fell back only to attack anew. I wish to tell the reason these Indians defended themselves so stoutly. It should be known that they are vassals and tributaries of the Amazons, and when our approach became known, they went to them to ask for aid, and as many as ten or twelve of those women came, and we saw them leading all those Indians in the fighting like captains, and they fought so boldly that the Indians did not dare fall back, and if one of them attempted to retreat before us, they killed him with blows of their clubs, and this is the reason why the Indians defended themselves so bravely. These women are very white and tall, and have very long hair, which they wear braided and wrapped around their head, and they are very strong and go naked except for their private parts, which are covered. With their bows and arrows in their hands they fight like ten Indians, and there was one among them who sent an arrow into one of the brigantines a handspan deep, and others less, so our boats looked like porcupines.

To return to the fight, Our Lord was pleased to give our companions strength and courage, and they killed seven or eight of these Amazons, which we saw with our own eyes, whereupon the Indians lost heart and were thrown back and scattered with heavy losses. But many reinforcements were coming from other villages, and they were sure to return, for they were sounding their war cries again, so the Captain ordered his men into the boats with all possible haste, for he did not want to put our lives in danger, and we went aboard, not without difficulty, for the Indians were attacking again, and besides a great fleet of canoes was coming over the water, so we set off downstream and left that land behind.

We had come a thousand and four leagues since we set out and left Gonzalo Pizarro, or probably more, and we did not know how far we were from the sea. In this village we have just spoken of we captured an Indian, a trumpeteer, who was about thirty years old, and after we had taken him he began to tell the Captain many things about the land in the interior, and he took him along with us.

Going downstream, as I have said, we let ourselves drift with the current, for our men were so weary that they had no strength to ply the oars. When we had gone about the distance of a bowshot, we saw a good-sized village where there seemed to be no one, and for this reason all the men asked the Captain to put in there, where we might find something to eat, for in the village we had just passed they had not allowed us to get any food. The Captain told them he would rather not, for even though it seemed to them that it was deserted, it would be safer to take more precautions here than in a place where we could see the people. But we all asked him again, and I with our other comrades, as a boon, and although we had already passed the village, the Captain, yielding to our wishes, ordered the ships to turn back to the village, and as we went skirting the shore, the squadrons of Indians, who were concealed among the trees waiting to take us in ambush, were able to attack us, and they began to shoot at us with such ferocity that we could not see one another for the arrows. But as our Spaniards, after the battle with Machiparo, had provided themselves with good shields, they did not do us as much harm as if we had not been armed with this defense. No one was wounded in this village except myself. I received an arrow in the eye which went in and came out on the other side, as a result of which I lost an eye, and I am not without suffering and pain, although Our Lord, not that I deserve it, chose to spare my life that I might mend my ways and serve Him better than I had before. In this brief time the Spaniards in the smaller boat had leaped ashore, and as the Indians were so numerous, they had surrounded them, and if it had not been for the Captain's coming to their help in the large brigantine, they would have been lost, and the Indians would have taken them prisoners. They would have done this anyway before the Captain arrived, had they not fought so skillfully and resolutely, but they were tiring and in great distress. The Captain rescued them, and when he saw that I was wounded he ordered the men into the boats, and so we went aboard, for the Indians were many and so fierce that our men could not withstand them, and the Captain was afraid of losing some of them, and he did not want them to run such risks, for he knew how necessary their aid was to him, as this land was thickly settled, and the lives of all of us had to be defended, for there was not half a league from one village to another, and still less all along the right bank of the river, which is to the south. Moreover, inland, some two leagues, more or less, great cities could be seen gleaming white, and the land is as naturally good and fertile as in our Spain, for when we came into it on Saint John's day, the Indians were already beginning to burn over the fields. It is a temperate land, where much wheat could be harvested and all kinds of fruit raised; besides it is very suitable for the raising of cattle because it has many of the same plants as in our Spain, such as wild marjoram, and thistles, some colored and striped, and many other very good plants; in the woods of these lands there are evergreen oaks, and cork oaks that have acorns, for we saw them, and other oaks; the land lies high and rolling, and is covered with grass that grows no higher than the knee, and there is game of all varieties.

Returning to our voyage, the Captain ordered us to make for the middle of the river to get away from the settlements, which were so numerous that we were filled with fear. We called this province the province of San Juan, because it was on his day that we came into it. I had said Mass that morning as we came down the river in honor of this glorious forerunner of Christ, and I am convinced that it was through his intercession that God spared my life.

That night we were past all the settlements, and we made camp in an oak grove that stood on a broad plain beside the river. We were fearful and alert, because the Indians came to spy on us, and inland there were many villages and roads leading to them, and for this reason the Captain and all of us were on watch against what might befall us.

At this camp the Captain talked with the Indian I mentioned above whom we had taken prisoner, because he could understand him with a vocabulary he had made, and asked him where he was from. The Indian told him he came from that town where we had captured him. The Captain asked him the name of the lord of that land, and the Indian told him he was called Couynco, and that he was a great lord, and ruler of the lands as far as we had come, which, as I have said, was one hundred and fifty leagues. The Captain asked him who those women were that had come to help them and make war on us; the Indian answered that they were women who lived seven days' march inland, and that as this Couynco was their vassal they had come to defend the shore. The Captain asked if these women were married, and the Indian said no. The Captain asked him how they lived; the Indian answered that, as he had said, they lived inland, and that he had been there many times, and had seen how they lived and their homes, for as a vassal of theirs, he had gone there to carry tribute to them when his ruler sent him. The Captain asked him if there were many of these women; the Indian said there were, and that he knew by name seventy villages, and he called them before those of us who were there, and said he had been in some of them. The Captain asked him if the houses were built of straw; the Indian said no, that they were built of stone and had doors, and that roads fenced in on both sides led from one village to the other, and every so often along these roads there were guards posted so no one could enter without paying toll. The Captain asked him if these women bore children; the Indian said they did. The Captain asked him how they conceived if they were not married and no man dwelt among them; he replied that these women had relations with Indians at certain times, and when that desire comes upon them, they assemble a large war party and go out to make war on a very great lord who lives and has his lands contiguous to those of these women, and they bring the men to their lands by force, and keep them with them as long as they want them, and after they have conceived, they send them back to their own land without doing them further harm. When their time comes, if they bear a son they kill him and send him to his fathers; if the child is a daughter they raise her with great care and teach her all the arts of war. He went on to say that among all these women there is one who holds all the others under her sway and jurisdiction, and this lady is known as Coñori. He said that they possess great wealth of silver and gold, and that all the leading women of rank eat only off dishes of gold and silver, and the women of lower class eat out of wooden dishes except for those in which they cook, which are of clay. He said that in the capital and principal city where the ruling woman lives, there are five great houses that are temples and houses dedicated to the sun, which they call Caranain, and that inside these houses there is wainscoting from the floor to half the height of a man, of thick gold panels covered with paintings of different colors, and many idols of gold and silver in the form of women, and many vessels of gold and silver for the service of the sun. The women wear clothing of finest wool, for in this land there are many sheep like those of Peru;

their dress is a blanket clasped below their breasts and reaching to the ground, and on top of this they wear a kind of cloak fastened in front with cords. They wear their hair, which reaches to the ground, loose, and on their head crowns of gold two fingers high. He said it was forbidden for any male Indian to remain in any of these cities after the sun had gone down; and he added that in many provinces bordering on theirs the Indians were subject to them and had to pay them tribute and serve them, while with others they carried on war, especially with the one we have already spoken of, and they bring them in to have relations with them. These men are said to be very large and white and numerous, and the Indian said that all he had described he had seen many times, as one who came and went every day. Everything this Indian told us, and more besides, we had heard when we were six leagues from Quito, for they were well informed about these women there, and many Indians traveled a thousand leagues down the river to see them. For this reason the Indians back there had told us that the man who wanted to go to the land of these women must start as a boy and would return an old man. He said the land was cold and that there is little wood there, and that it abounds in all kind of food. He told us many other things, and each day he reveals more, for he is an Indian of intelligence and very wise, as are all the others in this land, as we have observed.

9

ALONSO DE ERCILLA Y ZUÑIGA

Ercilla was a poet and a courtier; as a page to the young Prince Philip (the future King Philip II), he acquired a first-rate literary education and traveled widely in Europe. He was with the prince in England, in 1553, when news of the Araucan rebellion in Chile reached the court. Ercilla immediately volunteered to join the punitive expedition. He was then twenty-one. As "an obscure Spanish captain," he participated in all the battles and began on the spot to set down a verse narrative of the campaign, using all kinds of pieces of paper, soft hide, and (once, at least) the trunk of a tree to record his lines.

But instead of following the model of a chronicle, as had Bernal Díaz and Carvajal, Ercilla wrote an epic poem. To sing the exploits of a handful of Spaniards in a remote and obscure corner of the world, he decided to exalt not only his companions' courage but also that of the indomitable Indians. His contemporaries were quick to point out that his epic lacked a hero—and also that he had been less than fair to young García Hurtado de Mendoza, the Spanish commander. Ercilla had found him arrogant and quarreled with him, and still felt offended with the commander when he was forced to leave Chile for Peru in 1558 and finally to return to Spain in 1561.

In praising the enemy, Ercilla was observing the code of chivalry so vocally respected by the Spanish hidalgos. He admired the Araucans for their indomitable courage and upheld their right to fight to the death in defense of their native land. The conflict he described in such exalted verse was really a nasty little war, a guerrilla action the Araucans fought like masters. To win, the Spaniards had to resort to terror and genocide.

Long before James Fenimore Cooper, and with the authority of an eyewitness, Ercilla presented an idealized, noble version of these endless, dirty wars. In transforming the defeated Araucans into epic heroes, he was also following a model that harked back to Homer: Ercilla praised Caupolicán and Colocolo in the way the Greek poet praised Hector and Priam. His only departure from the classical tradition was to include himself as one of the warriors. Thus, his book kept some links with the chronicles of the conquest and even inspired some others. It also became the prototype of the historical epic: a detailed account of actual events somewhat modified or simplified by the devices and flourishes of Renaissance rhetoric. His chief models were Lucan's *Pharsalia* and Vergil's *Aeneid*, because they were less fabulous and imbued with a more patriotic spirit than Homer's poems. But he deplored Vergil's defamation of Dido and in one of his digressions came to the defense of that unfortunate queen. Although he attempted to resist the influence of the more sophisticated Italian epic, he also borrowed freely from Ariosto's dazzling devices.

While overall *The Araucana* is of uneven quality, Ercilla excelled in the description of physical action, in portraying fierce and violent characters, and in the inspired though purposefully anachronistic speeches he put into the mouths of his Araucans. In passages such as the one excerpted here, Ercilla proves himself a great poet. More than three centuries later, another great poet, Rubén Darío (Part Three, 4), would take the same episode as the theme of one of his Parnassian sonnets.

The Araucana took a very long time to complete. Ercilla lost his original enthusiasm for the task; he began to see that epic fight as only one, not the central, episode in Spain's conquest of the world, and started to wander far afield, from Chile to the Mediterranean (he included the battle of Lepanto) to the fields of Europe (the battle of San Quentin). The complete poem was published in three parts, in 1569, 1578, and 1589. Before his death in 1594, Ercilla added still more digressions to the last part.

Even in Ercilla's lifetime his great work came to be recognized as the best epic poem of Spanish letters, and it was praised even by rivals, such as the Gongorist Pedro de Oña, who wrote *The Arauco Tamed* (1596) in defense of Ercilla's enemy, Don García. *The Araucana* was the first literary text produced in the New World that was based on its own history. Today, it is considered

Chile's national epic. A poet born three centuries later, in the same fields and woods where the Araucans had made their defiant stand, was to echo to some degree, in his *General Song* (1950), the style and tone of Ercilla in telling over the story of this genocidal conquest (see Pablo Neruda, Four, 12).

An Election in Old Araucana

From The Historie of Araucana, *translated by George Carew and transcribed by Frank Pierce (Manchester: Manchester University Press, 1964), pp. 6–8.*

Being warm with drink, contention fell out among the Caciques as to who should be the general of the army. Thereupon such discord arose, as those who were sober had much pain to appease the dissension, every one of them prizing his own virtue above the rest. Tucapel (who disdained to obey) preferred himself to that dignity, thinking that his valor did deserve it and which he was ready to prove upon any man that dared oppose the contrary. Elicura and Ongolmo accepted his challenge, esteeming themselves to be worthier than he. Cayocupil condemned him, and Puren was as obstinate as he; Lemolemo gave place to none; and Lincoya despised them all. And they were ready to fall to blows.

Old Colocolo—who for his years and gravity was held in reverence—desired them to lay passion aside, and with patience to hear his advice. Thereunto they obeyed. "My Lords," said he, "I wonder what fury it is that misleads your judgments. We are here assembled for our common defense against the tyrants which oppress us, and the arms we bear are designed to that end. My spent days are many; long I cannot remain with you, yet while I live my love shall never fail to advise and counsel you the best I may. I beseech you, leave this contention for dignity, and let all our endeavors aim only to free us from bondage, wherein we are reduced by the Spaniard. Forbear your conceived furies; turn not your weapons upon your own bodies, but upon the Christians, by whom we must acknowledge we have been subdued. Let your valor be employed in shaking off the servile yoke we bear. I am not grieved to see your great spirits, but my fear is that if your valors be not governed, it will be the undoubted cause of our utter ruin.

"If my gray hairs cannot move you to be charitable to yourselves, and keep you from civil violence, let me entreat this pity from you: that I may first perish, and not see the ensuing calamities. You are all equal in valor, blood and descent. The least of your great minds is sufficient to govern a world, yet necessity enforces that one must command in chief, unto whom the rest ought to obey.

"Seeing we cannot without contention agree whom to elect, let us make choice of him whose force of body exceeds his fellows. The way of trial I wish to be a great piece of timber which every of you (one after another) may lay upon your shoulders, and that person which can stand most hours under that weight, let him be our general."

Against that kind of election many of the Caciques opposed, despising it as foolish, but the majority agreed to it. The first that proved his strength was Paycavi, who bore the log for six hours, not moving from his place. Cayocupil was next, and stood five hours. Gualemo and Louen followed, but they were soon weary. Angol bore it six hours; Puren half a day; Ongolmo longer time than he; Lebopia but four hours and a half; Lemolemo seven hours; Elicura nine hours; Tucapel fourteen hours. Lincoya took up the block at the sun rising, and bore until it was set. He then ran up and down with it, feeling no weariness, and cast it not from his shoulder until the next day's afternoon. Thereupon the assembly admiring and none daring to make further proof, they saluted him their chief, not thinking that any would attempt to contest for it.

But then, another warrior, Caupolican, who had missed all of this, came in unlooked for with his troops. He prayed that he might try his strength, whereat Lincoya waxed pale, for Caupolican was young and of great stature, and acknowledged besides for his wisdom, valor, descent in blood, austerity and justice. He was beloved and feared, though in his face Caupolican was somewhat deformed, for he was born blind in one eye, and the same of a ruby color.

Great joy was made at his coming, and his petition (though he was somewhat too late) was granted. When he was told of Lincoya's strength, he was unimpressed; with a lively spirit he took the piece of timber upon his shoulder, and without any show of fatigue or weakness he stood under it for three whole days and two nights. In the end, by common consent he laid it down, and was saluted and confirmed captain general, as most worthy to sustain the burden of state, the faculties of his mind answering his bodily strength.

There be some that make claim that this manner of election is but a poetical fiction. Let the reader give credit unto it, for nothing could be more true. This election was devised only by old Colocolo to appease the present dissension, and to win time that Caupolican might be the chief, who was then absent, and best suited to govern. To hasten his coming old Colocolo dispatched sundry messengers acquainting him with his stratagem and urging him to expedite his journey.

10

INCA GARCILASO DE LA VEGA

A half-caste and a bastard, Garcilaso Inca was the first American-born writer of real distinction. He was also one of the finest prose stylists of Spain's Golden Age. Son of a conquistador and an Indian princess (her father was one of the last Inca's brothers), Garcilaso was born in Cuzco in 1539. Being illegitimate, he did not carry his father's name, and was baptized Gómez Suárez de Figueroa. He got the best teaching that sad royal city could then provide. At the age of nineteen, after his father's death, he left for Spain to complete his education. He also hoped to persuade the authorities to recognize his rights to his father's confiscated fortune, but he never had a chance against the court bureaucracy. In 1561 he sought refuge in Montilla, Andalusia, where he lived under the protection of his paternal uncle.

By 1590 he had moved to Córdoba, where he participated actively in the city's literary and scholarly life. He had assumed his father's name, Garcilaso de la Vega (which was also the name of one of his relatives, a great Renaissance poet), but he added the "Inca" to honor as well his American heritage. With the utmost care and leisure, he produced three books: a translation into Spanish of the neo-Platonic *Dialoghi d'Amore*, written in Italian by the exiled Spanish Jew León Hebreo (1590); a historical narrative of Hernando de Soto's exploration of *La Florida* (1605); and his masterpiece, *The Royal Commentaries* (I, 1609; II, 1617).

Writing in Spanish and for Spaniards, Garcilaso was extremely cautious in preserving the conqueror's point of view. He also adopted a very orthodox stance in religious matters: for him, Spain had a transcendental mission to discover, conquer, and convert the New World.

In re-creating the past of his native land, however, he by no means relied on Spanish historians alone. Very discreetly, but firmly, he corrected some of their mistakes, especially those derived from their lack of familiarity with the Quechua language. Having been schooled in both Spanish and Quechua, he was the ideal interpreter. He did even more: out of the oral tradition devotedly preserved by his Indian relatives, the recollections of schoolmates he consulted by letter, and his own very vivid memories of places and people, of beautiful tales and myths, Garcilaso re-created the glory of the Inca empire and told of its tragic downfall. His was not, then, a purely historical work; it was also a defense of the Inca heritage and an exalted description of its originality and grandeur. True, he adopted perhaps too uncritically the Incas' version of their past; he accepted their division—more religious than factual—of their history into twelve kingdoms; he believed that theirs was the first civilization in old Peru. (In fact it was the last, and dated only from the twelfth century.) As a result, Garcilaso has been criticized by professional historians such as Prescott and Menéndez Pelayo, to name only two of the most distinguished. Modern archaeologists have proved he was mistaken about the superiority of the Inca culture to earlier ones.

His failings, however, seem less damaging if viewed in the context of sixteenth-century historiography. Many scholars and writers of the time shared his methods. The writing of history was regarded more as an occasion for teaching a useful moral or religious lesson than as an opportunity for the dispassionately factual reconstruction of events. Garcilaso's chief value as a historian, therefore, consists in his preservation of the Inca version of their people's past. And his work holds great psychological interest, besides, as a kind of symbolic autobiography. Having come to a full acceptance of his double origins, he was not shy in praising both the virtues of his royal ancestors and the dignity and courage of the Spanish conquerors. Very discreetly (a word that in his time also implied a keen intelligence) he wove into the historical narrative a symbolic portrait of his native land and of his own double self.

It was the exaltation of the Inca empire that especially troubled some of his Spanish readers. Even at the time the censors appreciated the dangers latent in a book that dared, however respectfully, to remind its audience that Peru had once been ruled by the Sons of the Sun. When the second part was published, the title had to be toned down to the less controversial *General History of Peru*. The censors' anxieties ultimately proved prophetic: In the eighteenth century, an Indian rebel who took the name of the last Inca and called himself Túpac Amaru II (see selection 22) found in Garcilaso's book the religious and political inspiration he sought. By a royal order of 1782, the book was silently sequestered, and no new editions were allowed to circulate in Spanish America. But the men who later made independence their business had read it: the Venezuelan Miranda used Roman and Inca institutions to create his model of a free continent; the Argentine San Martín started a popular subscription to reprint Garcilaso's book and distribute it to the whole continent; his countryman Belgrano presented a motion at the Congress of Tucumán, in 1816, to restore the Inca monarchy.

Garcilaso would have been proud of the posthumous success of his book. The three excerpts here presented cover different aspects of the *Commentaries*. The first shows vividly the book's oral sources and introduces Garcilaso himself as a privileged witness. The second is a long and tragic narrative of the oedipal feud between the Inca "Weeping Blood" and his courageous son, a story that has some undertones of the conflict Calderón presented in *Life Is a Dream*. The third excerpt is a true story, casually inserted in Book One and extraneous to the Inca history. It tells of the strange fate of Pedro Serrano, a Spaniard shipwrecked in the Caribbean Sea. Daniel Defoe may have seen it, since an English translation of the *Commentaries* was printed in 1626; if so, this might possibly explain the change of Robinson Crusoe's island from the Pacific (where the real Crusoe, Alexander Selkirk, was marooned) to the Caribbean—as Professor José Juan Arrom has suggested. Garcilaso's "Pedro Serrano" is a beautiful tale, one of the many in his vast, ambitious book. With *The Royal Commentaries* a truly Spanish American literature begins. Garcilaso is its founding father.

The Royal Commentaries of the Inca

From The Royal Commentaries, *Book 1, Chapter 19; Book 4, Chapters 16 and 20–24; and Book 1, Chapter 8; translated by Harold V. Livermore (Austin: The University of Texas Press, 1966).*

The Origin of the Inca Kings of Peru

After having prepared many schemes and taken many ways to begin to give an account of the origin and establishment of the native Inca kings of Peru, it seemed to me that the best scheme and simplest and easiest way was to recount what I often heard as a child from the lips of my mother and her brothers and uncles and other elders about these beginnings. For everything said about them from other sources comes down to the same story, as we shall relate, and it will be better to have it as told in the very words of the Incas than in those of foreign authors. My mother dwelt in Cuzco, her native place, and was visited there every week by the few relatives, both male and female, who escaped the cruelty and tyranny of Atahuallpa (which we shall describe in our account of his life). On these visits the ordinary subject of conversation was always the origin of the Inca kings, their greatness, the grandeur of their empire, their deeds and conquests, their government in peace and war, and the laws they ordained so greatly to the advantage of their vassals. In short, there was nothing concerning the most flourishing period of their history that they did not bring up in their conversations.

From the greatness and prosperity of the past they turned to the present, mourning their dead kings, their lost empire, their fallen state, etc. These and similar topics were broached by the Incas and Pallas on their visits, and on recalling their departed happiness, they always ended these conversations with tears and mourning, saying, "Our rule is turned to bondage," etc. During these talks, I, as a boy, often came in and went out of the place where they were, and I loved to hear them, as boys always do like to hear stories. Days, months, and years went by, until I was sixteen or seventeen. Then it happened that one day when my family was talking in this fashion about their kings and the olden times, I remarked to the senior of them, who usually related these things: "Inca, my uncle, though you have no writings to preserve the memory of past events, what information have you of the origin and beginnings of our kings? For the Spaniards and the other peoples who live on their borders have divine and human histories from which they know when their own kings and their neighbors' kings began to reign and when one empire gave way to another. They even know how many thousand years it is since God created heaven and earth. All this and much more they know through their books. But you, who have no books, what memory have you preserved of your antiquity? Who was the first of our Incas? What was he called? What was the origin of his line? How did he begin to reign? With what men and arms did he conquer this great empire? How did our heroic deeds begin?"

The Inca was delighted to hear these questions, since it gave him great pleasure to reply to them, and turned to me (who had already often heard him tell the tale, but had never paid as much attention as then) saying:

"Nephew, I will tell you these things with pleasure: indeed it is right that you should hear them and keep them in your heart" (this is their phrase for "in the memory"). "You should know that in olden times the whole of this region before you was covered with brush and heath, and people lived in those times like wild beasts, with no religion or government and no towns or houses, and without tilling or sowing the soil, or clothing or covering their flesh, for they did not know how to weave cotton or wool to make clothes. They lived in twos and threes as chance brought them together in caves and crannies in rocks and underground caverns. Like wild beasts they ate the herbs of the field and roots of trees and fruits growing wild and also human flesh. They covered their bodies with leaves and the bark of trees and animals' skins. Others went naked. In short, they lived like deer or other game, and even in their intercourse with women they behaved like beasts, for they knew nothing of having separate wives."

I must remark, in order to avoid many repetitions of the words "our father the Sun," that the phrase was used by the Incas to express respect whenever they mentioned the sun, for they boasted of descending from it, and none but Incas were allowed to utter the words: it would have been blasphemy and the speaker would have been stoned. The Inca said:

"Our father the Sun, seeing men in the state I have mentioned, took pity and was sorry for them, and sent from heaven to earth a son and a daughter of his to indoctrinate them in the knowledge of our father the Sun that they might worship him and adopt him as their god, and to give them precepts and laws by which they would live as reasonable and civilized men, and dwell in houses and settled towns, and learn to till the soil, and grow plants and crops, and breed flocks, and use the fruits of the earth like rational beings and not like beasts. With this order and mandate our father the Sun set these two children of his in Lake Titicaca, eighty leagues from here, and bade them go where they would, and wherever they stopped to eat or sleep to try to thrust into the ground a golden wand half a yard long and two fingers in thickness which he gave them as a sign and token: when this wand should sink into the ground at a single thrust, there our father the Sun wished them to stop and set up their court.

"Finally he told them: 'When you have reduced these people to our service, you shall maintain them in reason and justice, showing mercy, clemency, and mildness, and always treating them as a merciful father treats his beloved and tender children. Imitate my example in this. I do good to all the world. I give them my light and brightness that they may see and go about their business; I warm them when they are cold; and I grow their pastures and crops, and bring fruit to their trees, and multiply their flocks. I bring rain and calm weather in turn, and I take care to go around the world once a day to observe the wants that exist in the world and to fill and supply them as the sustainer and benefactor of men. I wish you as children of mine to follow this example sent down to earth to teach and benefit those men who live like beasts. And henceforward I establish and nominate you as kings and lords over all the people you may thus instruct with your reason, government, and good works.'

"When our father the Sun had thus made manifest his will to his two children he bade them farewell. They left Titicaca and traveled northward, and wherever they stopped on the way they thrust the golden wand into the earth, but it never sank in. Thus they reached a small inn or resthouse seven or eight leagues south of this city. Today it is called Pacárec Tampu, 'inn or resthouse of the dawn.' The Inca gave it this name because he set out from it about daybreak. It is one of the towns the prince later ordered to be founded, and its inhabitants to this day boast greatly of its name because our first Inca bestowed it. From this place he and his wife, our queen, reached the valley of Cuzco, which was then a wilderness."

The Foundation of Cuzco, the Imperial City

"The first settlement they made in this valley," said the Inca, "was in the hill called Huanacauri, to the south of this city. There they tried to thrust the golden wand into the earth and it easily sank in at the first blow and they saw it no more. Then our Inca said to his wife: 'Our father the Sun bids us remain in this valley and make it our dwelling place and home in fulfillment of his will. It is therefore right, queen and sister, that each of us should go out and call together these people so as to instruct them and benefit them as our father the Sun has ordained.' Our first rulers set out from the hill of Huanacauri, each in a different direction, to call the people together, and as that was the first place we know they trod with their feet and because they went out from it to do good to mankind, we made there, as you know, a temple for the worship of our father the Sun, in memory of his merciful beneficence toward the world. The prince went northward, and the princess south. They spoke to all the men and women they found in that wilderness and said that their father the Sun had sent them from the sky to be teachers and benefactors to the dwellers in all that land, delivering them from the wild lives they led and in obedience to the commands given by the Sun, their father, calling them together and removing them from those heaths and moors, bringing them to dwell in settled valleys and giving them the food of men instead of that of beasts to eat. Our king and queen said these and similar things to the first savages they found in those mountains and heaths, and as the savages beheld two persons clad and adorned with the ornaments our father the Sun had given them—and a very different dress from their own—with their ears pierced and opened in the way we their descendants have, and saw that their words and countenances showed them to be children of the Sun, and that they came to mankind to give them towns to dwell in and food to eat, they wondered at what they saw and were at the same time attracted by the promises that were held out to them. Thus they fully credited all they were told and worshiped and venerated the strangers as children of the Sun and obeyed them as kings. These savages gathered others and repeated the wonders they had seen and heard, and a great number of men and women collected and set out to follow our king and queen wherever they might lead.

"When our princes saw the great crowd that had formed there, they ordered that some should set about supplying open-air meals for them all, so that they should not be driven by hunger to disperse again across the heaths. Others were ordered to work on building huts and houses according to plans made by the Inca. Thus our imperial city began to be settled: it was divided into two halves called Hanan Cuzco, which as you know, means upper Cuzco, and Hurin Cuzco, or lower Cuzco. The king wished those he had brought to people Hanan Cuzco, therefore called the upper, and those the queen had brought to people Hurin Cuzco, which was therefore called the lower. The distinction did not imply that the inhabitants of one half should excel those of the other in privileges and exemptions. All were equal like brothers, the children of one father and one mother. The Inca only wished that there should be this division of the people and distinction of name, so that the fact that some had been gathered by the king and others by the queen might have a perpetual memorial. And he ordered that there should be only one difference and acknowledgment of superiority among them, that those of upper Cuzco be considered and respected as first-born and elder brothers, and those of lower Cuzco be as younger children. In short they were to be as the right side and the left in any question of precedence of place and office, since those of the upper town had been gathered by the men and those of the lower by the women. In imitation of this, there was later the same division in all the towns, great or small, of our empire, which were divided by wards or by lineages, known as *hanan aillu* and *hurin aillu*, the upper and lower lineage, or *hanan suyu* and *hurin suyu*, the upper and lower district.

"At the same time, in peopling the city, our Inca showed the male Indians which tasks were proper to men: breaking and tilling the land, sowing crops, seeds, and vegetables which he showed to be good to eat and fruitful, and for which purpose he taught them how to make plows and other necessary instruments, and bade them and showed them how to draw irrigation channels from the streams that run through the valley of Cuzco, and even showed them how to make the footwear we use. On her side the queen trained the Indian women in all the feminine occupations: spinning and weaving cotton and wool, and making clothes for themselves and their husbands and children. She told them how to do these and other duties of domestic service. In short, there was nothing relating to human life that our princes failed to teach their first vassals, the Inca king acting as master for the men and the Coya queen, mistress of the women."

The Peoples Subdued by the First Inca, Manco Cápac

"The very Indians who had thus been recently subdued, discovering themselves to be quite changed and realizing the benefits they had received, willingly and joyfully betook themselves to the sierras, moors, and heaths to seek their inhabitants and give them news about the children of the Sun. They recounted the many benefits they had brought them, and proved it by showing their new clothes they wore and the new foods they ate, and telling how they lived in houses and towns. When the wild people heard all this, great numbers of them came to behold the wonders that were told and reported of our first fathers, kings, and lords. Once they had verified this with their own eyes, they remained to serve and obey them. Thus some called others and these passed the word to more, and so many gathered in a few years that after six or seven, the Inca had a force of men armed and equipped to defend themselves against any attackers and even to bring by force those who would not come willingly. He taught them how to make offensive weapons such as bows and arrows, lances, clubs, and others now in use.

"And to cut short the deeds of our first Inca, I can tell you that he subdued the region to the east as far as the river called Paucartampu, and to the west eight leagues up to the river Apurímac, and to the south for nine leagues to Quequesana. Within this area our Inca ordered more than a hundred villages to be settled, the biggest with a hundred houses and others with less, according to what the land could support. These were the first beginnings of our city toward being established and settled as you now see it. They were also the beginnings of our great, rich, and famous empire that your father and his friends deprived us of. These were our first Incas and kings, who appeared in the first ages of the world; and from them descend all the other kings we have had, and from these again we are all descended. I cannot inform you exactly how many years it is since our father the Sun sent us his first children, for it is so long no one has been able to remember: we believe it is above four hundred years. Our Inca was called Manco Cápac and our Coya Mama Ocllo Huaco. They were, as I have told you, brother and sister, children of the Sun and the Moon, our parents. I think I have expatiated at length on your inquiry and answered your questions, and in order to spare your tears, I have not recited this story with tears of blood flowing from my eyes as they flow from my heart from the grief I feel at seeing the line of our Incas ended and our empire lost."

This long account of the origin of our kings was given me by the Inca, my mother's uncle, of whom I asked it. I have tried to translate it faithfully from my mother tongue, that of the Inca, into a foreign speech, Castilian, though I have not written it in such majestic language as the Inca used, nor with the full significance the words of that language have. If I had given the whole significance, the tale would have been much more extensive than it is. On the contrary, I have shortened it, and left out a few things that might have been odious. However, it is enough to have conveyed its true meaning, which is what is required for our history. The Inca told me a few similar things, though not many, during the visits he paid to my mother's house; these I will include in their places later on, giving their source. I much regret not having asked many more questions so that I might now have information about them from so excellent an archive and write them here.

The Seventh King, the Inca "Weeping-Blood": His Fears and His Conquests, and the Disgrace of the Prince

On the death of King Inca Roca, his son Yáhuar Huácac assumed the crown. He governed the kingdom with justice, piety, and mildness, caring for his subjects and doing them all the good he could. His desire was to sustain the property his forefathers had handed down to him without seeking new conquests or engaging in disputes, for owing to the ill omen of his name and the forebodings that daily surrounded him, he feared some untoward event and dared not risk trying his fortune for fear of provoking the anger of his father the Sun who might visit him with some grave chastisement, as the omens said. Fearing this, he passed some years, desiring peace and quiet for himself and his neighbors; and in order not to be idle, he visited his realms once, twice, and thrice. He sought to enrich them with splendid buildings. He favored his subjects in general and in particular. He treated them with greater affection and love than his predecessors had shown, as a result of the fear he felt. Thus nine or ten years passed by. But not to seem pusillanimous and to avoid being remembered among all the Incas as a coward who did not increase the empire, he resolved to send a force of twenty thousand soldiers to the southwest of Cuzco to the coast beyond Arequipa, where his ancestors had left unconquered a large though thinly peopled strip of land. He chose as commander-in-chief his brother Inca Maita, who, after being general of this expedition, was always known as Apu Maita, meaning Captain General Maita. He named four seasoned Incas as commanders. The Inca did not dare to take the field in person. Though he greatly desired to do so, he could not decide to go, for his evil omen concerning warlike deeds placed him on such stormy waves of doubt that when the swell of desire drove him forward the ebb of fear drew him back. Because of these fears he named his brother and officers, who completed the conquest briefly and with good fortune and added to the Inca empire everything from Arequipa to Tacoma, which is called Collasuyu and is the boundary and coastal limit of what is today called Peru. The land is broad and narrow and thinly populated, so that the Incas took longer to travel through it than to reduce it to their command.

When the conquest was completed, they returned to Cuzco and reported what had been done to the Inca Yáhuar Huácac. Encouraged by the successful outcome of this campaign, he determined to undertake a conquest of greater honor and fame by adding to his empire some large provinces still unconquered in the district of Collasuyu, by name Caranca, Ullaca, Llipi, Chica, and Ampara. These were both large and thickly populated with brave and warlike peoples. Consequently the previous Incas had not undertaken this conquest by force of arms, not wishing to destroy these untamed and savage tribes, but hoping that they would gradually become tamer and more civilized, and take to the rule and overlordship of the Incas after seeing from the experience of neighboring tribes that their rule was as mild, clement, and beneficial to their subjects as all those who made trial of it discovered.

The Inca Yáhuar Huácac was full of anxiety about the conquest of these provinces. Torn between fear and hope, he sometimes foresaw success such as had attended the expedition of his brother Apu Maita, and sometimes mistrusted the outcome because of his unlucky omen. On account of this he did not dare to risk the dangers of any military undertaking. Thus beset by worry and anguish, he turned his attention to other cares within his family circle, which for some time had caused him pain and grief. His eldest son, who would inherit his dominions, was of an unmanageable disposition. Since a child, he had shown himself harsh and cruel, ill-treating boys of his own age whose company he kept and showing signs of roughness and cruelty. Although the Inca made every effort to correct him, and hoped that he would develop self-control as he grew older and lose the wildness of his character, this hope seemed no longer justified, for as he grew older his disposition seemed more rather than less fierce. This caused the Inca, his father, very great anguish, for as all his ancestors had prided themselves on humanity and mildness, it was very grievous to him to see the prince so different. He tried to alter his son by persuasion and by reminding him of the examples of his forefathers, hoping he would come to admire them. He also upbraided the prince and showed him disfavor. But all this was to little or no purpose, for evil inclinations in the great and powerful seldom or never admit of correction.

Thus it happened that all the antidotes applied to the prince's evil disposition themselves turned to poison. His father the Inca saw this, and decided to disgrace him and banish him, with the object of disinheriting him if the disgrace did not bring about any improvement in his character, and choosing another of his sons who followed more after the pattern of his ancestors to succeed. He proposed in this to follow the custom of some of the provinces of the empire where the best-loved sons were those who succeeded; and he wished to apply this rule to his own case, though it had never been followed by the Incas. Consequently he ordered the prince, who was then nineteen, to be excluded from his house and court and taken to some fine pasture lands called Chita, just over a league to the east of the city: I have often been there. There were many flocks belonging to the Sun there, and the Inca ordered the prince to graze them with the shepherds. The prince had no recourse but to accept the banishment and disfavor visited on him to punish his wild and warlike spirit, and duly set about the task of tending the flocks with the other shepherds, and watched the flocks of the Sun, and the fact that they were of the Sun was a consolation to the sad Inca. The disgraced prince performed this task for three years and more, where we shall leave him to bide his time. He will give us much to relate, if we can tell the story well.

A Warning Given by an Apparition
to the Prince to Be Conveyed to His Father

The Inca Yáhuar Huácac had thus exiled his eldest son: the name of the latter while he was a prince is unknown, for the name he was later given completely expunged it, and as they had no writing, everything that was not entrusted to memory by tradition was completely forgotten forever. The Inca therefore decided to abandon all thought of war and the conquest of new provinces and attend only to the government and peace of his kingdom. He would no longer keep his son at a distance and out of sight, but have him at hand and try to improve his disposition, and if this did not avail, seek other remedies, though everything he could think of, such as confining him in perpetual imprisonment or disinheriting him and choosing another in his place, seemed violent and uncertain, owing to the novelty and importance of the case. Such solutions implied the loss of the divinity of the Incas, who were held to be divine children of the Sun, and his subjects would not have agreed to this punishment or any other against the prince.

In this state of anguish and care, which deprived him of rest and peace of mind, the Inca spent more than three years, during which time nothing of note occurred. He twice sent four of his kinsmen to visit the kingdom, assigning to each the provinces to be visited. He bade them see to the works that required to be done for the Inca's honor and the common benefit of his subjects—building new irrigation channels, erecting storehouses, palaces, forts,* bridges, roads, and other such works. But he himself dared not leave the capital, where he occupied himself with celebrating the festivals of the Sun and other annual events and in doing justice for his subjects.

At the end of this long spell, the prince one day shortly after noon entered his father's palace when he was least expected, alone and unattended as befitted one in disgrace. He sent to say that he was there and had a certain mission which he must discharge. The Inca angrily replied that he was to go away to his appointed place of residence, unless he wished to be put to death for disobedience to the royal command, for he knew that no one could disregard this, however trivial the thing commanded. The prince answered that he had not come to break his command but in obedience to another Inca as great as he, who had bidden him say certain things that it was of great importance he should know: if he wished to hear them, let him give permission for the prince to enter and tell them, if not, the latter would have fulfilled his mission by returning to the one who had sent him and reporting the answer.

The Inca, hearing mention of another lord as great as himself, ordered

*Reading *fuertes* for *fuentes*.

him to be admitted to see what nonsense this was and to find who it was who sent him messages by his exiled and disgraced son. He wished to investigate these new heresies and punish them. The prince, brought before his father, said:

"Sole Lord, know that as I was lying down today at noon, I do not know if asleep or awake, under a great rock there is in the fields of Chita, where by your bidding I tend the sheep of our father the Sun, a man appeared before me in a strange garb, and in features different from us, for he had a beard on his chin more than a palm long and his dress was long and loose and covered him down to his feet. He said to me: 'Nephew, I am a child of the Sun and brother to the Inca Manco Cápac and the Coya Mama Ocllo Huaco, his wife and sister, the first of your forefathers. I am therefore the brother of your father and of you all. I am called Viracocha Inca. I come from the Sun, our father, to bid you warn the Inca, my brother, that most of the provinces of Chinchasuyu subject to his empire and others not subject to him are in rebellion and have brought together many people to come with a powerful army and overthrow his throne and destroy our imperial city of Cuzco. Go then to the Inca, my brother, and tell him from me to prepare, forearm, and take the steps necessary to meet the emergency. In particular I tell you that in any adversity that may befall you, fear not that I shall fail you, for I will always succor you as my own flesh and blood. Therefore do not hesitate to undertake any deed, however great it seems, that befits the majesty of your line and the greatness of your empire, for I shall always be ready to favor and protect you, and will seek the aid you may need.' Having said these words," said the prince, "the Inca Viracocha disappeared, and I saw him no more. I took the road to Cuzco, to tell you what he bade me say."

The Discussions of the Incas About the Apparition's Message

The Inca Yáhuar Huácac was so angry and embittered against his son that he was unwilling to believe him. He told him that he was an arrogant madman who claimed that the nonsense he had imagined was a revelation of his father the Sun; let him return at once to Chita and never leave it again, under pain of his father's wrath. So the prince went back to guard his flocks, more deeply in his father's disgrace than ever. The Incas closest to the king, his brothers and uncles who had access to his presence, being much addicted to superstitions and auguries, especially dreams, took quite a different view of the prince's story, and told the Inca that the message and warning from his brother Inca Viracocha should not be disregarded, since he had said that he was a child of the Sun and brought the message from him. It could hardly be credited that the prince should have imagined such a speech taking the Sun's name in vain: it would have been sacrilege merely to imagine it, let alone recount it before his father, the king. They should therefore examine the prince's words one by one, make sacrifices to the Sun and take omens to see if they forbode ill or well, and take such steps as were necessary in so grave a matter. To leave it unheeded was not only to run a risk, but also to appear to scorn their common father, the Sun, who had sent the warning, and his son, the Inca Viracocha, who had brought it; it was in fact to heap error upon error.

The Inca, out of the hatred he bore his son for his ill disposition, was reluctant to accept the advice his kinsmen gave him. He declared that no notice ought to be taken of a raving madman's words: instead of mending his ways and checking the violence of his character, the prince had produced new follies. On this account and because of his oddness he deserved to be deposed and deprived of his rank as prince and heir to the kingdom, as the Inca had immediately thought of doing; and they ought to choose one of his brothers who could imitate their ancestors and merit the title of child of the Sun by his clemency, piety, and mildness. It was wrong that a madman with wrath and vengeance in his heart should destroy with the knife of his cruelty what all the past Incas had added to the empire with mildness and benefits; let them recall that it was more important to attend to this and seek a remedy than to attend to the foolish words of a raving lunatic, which were such as to show the source they came from. If his son had not obtained authority for his folly by saying that his mission was from a child of the Sun, he would have been beheaded for breaking the sentence of exile imposed on him. He therefore ordered them not to discuss the matter, but to keep perpetual silence about it, for it angered him even to remember the subject of the prince. He, the Inca, knew what was to be done with him.

On the orders of the king, the Incas were silent and spoke no more of the matter, though inwardly they continued to fear some untoward event. These Indians, like all heathens, were much addicted to auguries, and paid special attention to dreams, particularly if the dreams happened to be those of the king or the heir or the high priest, who were regarded among them as gods and great oracles. The diviners and wizards asked them to tell their dreams to be explained and interpreted, if the Incas themselves did not say what they had dreamed.

The Rebellion of the Chancas; Their Ancient Deeds

Three months after the dream of Prince Viracocha Inca—this name was afterward given to the prince on account of the apparition he saw—there came news, albeit unconfirmed, of the rising of the provinces of Chinchasuyu from Antahuailla onward. This is a distance of forty leagues to the north of Cuzco. The news came from no definite source, but as a confused and sinister rumor, as often happens in such cases. So although Prince Viracocha had dreamed it and the news corresponded to his dream, the king took no notice, regarding it as tittle-tattle and the memory of the past dream, which seemed almost forgotten. A few days later the same news circulated once more, still doubtful and confused, for the enemy had closed the roads with great care so that their rising should remain unknown and they could appear at Cuzco before their coming was known. The third rumor then arrived, and it was definite. The tribes called Chanca, Uramarca, Villca, Utunsulla, Hancohuallu, and others of their neighbors had rebelled and slain the governors and royal officials. They were coming against the city with an army of more than forty thousand warriors.

These tribes are the ones we have mentioned as having accepted the rule of King Inca Roca rather from fear of his arms than love for his government, and as we remarked, they preserved a hatred and rancor against the Incas which they were to reveal when the opportunity offered. Finding the Inca Yáhuar Huácac so unwarlike, but rather intimidated by the ill omen of his name and scandalized and bewildered by the cruel disposition of his son, Prince Inca Viracocha, and having learned something of the renewed displeasure of the king toward his son, though the cause was not known, and of the great disfavor into which the latter had fallen, they regarded it as the best occasion to show their hostility toward the Inca and the hatred they felt for his rule and dominion. So with the greatest possible speed and secrecy they sent out the summons to war and roused their neighbors. Between them all a powerful army of over thirty thousand warriors was raised, and it marched in the direction of the imperial city of Cuzco. The instigators of the rising who had stirred up the other lords of vassals were three leading Indians, the *curacas* of three great provinces of the Chanca tribe (many other tribes are included under the same name). The first was Hancohuallu, a youth of twenty-six, the next Túmay Huaraca, and the third Astu Huaraca. These last were brothers and relatives of the first. The ancestors of the three kinglets had been engaged in perpetual war before the time of the Incas against the neighboring tribes, and especially against the people called Quechuas, under which five large provinces are comprised. They had crushed these and other neighbors, and treated them roughly and tyrannically, for which reason the Quechuas were glad to become subjects of the Incas and accepted their rule readily and with affection, as we have said, in order to be rid of the insolence of the Chancas. The latter, on the other hand, regretted that the Incas had put an end to their doughty deeds, and had reduced them from lords of vassals to tributaries. They nursed the ancient hatred inherited from their fathers, and made the present rebellion, thinking that they could easily conquer the Inca because of the suddenness of the attack they had planned, and the state of unpreparedness they imagined they would find him in. They fancied he would be without warriors and that a single victory would make them masters, not only of their ancient enemies, but also of all the Inca empire.

With this hope they summoned their neighbors, both those subjected to the Incas and the rest, promising them a great share of the spoils. It was easy to persuade them, both because of the enormous prize that was offered and because of the ancient reputation of the Chancas as valiant warriors. They chose Hancohuallu as captain general. He was a valiant Indian. His two commanders were the two brothers, and the other *curacas* were leaders and captains of the host, which marched at all speed in search of Cuzco.

The Inca Abandons the City,
the Prince Saves It

Inca Yáhuar Huácac was bewildered by the confirmation that his enemies were on their way. He had never believed such a thing could happen. The experience of the Incas had always been that of all the provinces they had conquered and added to their empire none had rebelled from the time of the first Inca Manco Cápac till the present. Because of this uncertainty and because of his hatred for the prince, his son, who had foretold the rebellion, he had not wanted to believe it could happen or to take the advice of his kinsmen, since passion had blinded his understanding. Now he found himself submerged and had no time to call men together to go out against the enemy and no garrison in the city to hold them off until help arrived. He therefore decided to give way to the fury of the rebels and withdraw toward Collasuyu, where he knew his life would be safe because his subjects were noble and loyal. With this intent he withdrew with the few Incas who could follow him, and reached the ravine called Muina, which is five leagues south of the city. There he halted to discover what the enemy was doing on the road and how far he had advanced.

The city of Cuzco was defenseless in the absence of the king. No captain or leader dared even speak, much less consider defending it, but all sought safety in flight. Those who could scattered in various directions, according to what they thought would be most likely to save their lives. Some of the fugitives came upon Prince Viracocha Inca and told him the news of the rebellion of Chinchasuyu, and how his father, the Inca, had retreated toward Collasuyu, thinking there was no possibility of resisting the enemy because of the suddenness of their onslaught.

The prince greatly regretted that his father should have withdrawn and left the city unprotected. He ordered his informants and some of the shepherds he had with him to return to the city and tell all the Indians they met on the roads and those still left in the city that everyone who could was to try to follow the Inca their lord, with whatever arms they could find. He would do the same, and they must pass his order on from one to another. Having given this order, Prince Viracocha set out to follow his father by a short cut, without entering the city. Hastening, he came upon the Inca in the Muina ravine, for he had still not left the place. Covered with sweat and dust, with a spear he had snatched up on the way in his hand, he presented himself before the king and with a grave and sorrowful face said:

"Inca, why do you let news, whether true or false, that a few of your subjects have rebelled cause you to abandon your palace and court, and turn your back on enemies you have not even seen? How can you bear to deliver the house of your father, the Sun, to enemies who will tread in it with shoes on their feet and commit there the abominations your ancestors taught them to abandon, sacrifices of men, women, and children, and such bestialities and sacrileges? What regard have we for the virgins dedicated as brides of the Sun, with the observance of perpetual virginity, if we leave them unprotected for a brutal and bestial enemy to wreak his will upon them? What honor have we gained if we permit these iniquities to save our lives? I do not want to save my life, and therefore I shall return to take my stand before the enemy, and lose it before he enters Cuzco. I will not live to see the abominations the barbarians will commit in the imperial and sacred city the Sun and his children founded. Those who wish to follow me, come now, and I will show them how to exchange a shameful life for an honorable death."

Having said this with great grief and feeling, he retraced his steps toward the city, without stopping either to eat or drink. The Incas of the royal blood, who had set out with the king, together with their brothers and many nephews and cousins and many other relatives, to the number of over four thousand, all returned with the prince. Only the aged and incapable stayed with his father. On the way they came across many who were fleeing the city. They called on them to return, and encouraged them by telling them the prince Inca Viracocha had returned to defend the city and the house of his father the Sun. With this news the Indians so took heart that all those who were running away returned, especially the stouthearted. These called to others across the fields, passing the word from hand to hand that the prince had come back to hold the city. The news so stirred them that they returned with great relief to die by the prince's side. His courage and energy were such that they animated all his followers.

Thus he entered the city and ordered that the people who had collected should follow him at once. He marched on up the highway to Chinchasuyu, whence his enemies were coming, so as to take up a position between them and the city. His intention was not to resist them, for he thought his forces were insufficient, but to die fighting before the foe entered the city and trod its streets with their barbarian and victorious feet, without respect for the Sun, which was what touched him most deeply. And as Inca Yáhuar Huácac whose life we are recounting ended his reign here, as we shall see, I thought it right to cut the thread of this story to divide his deeds from those of his son Inca Viracocha. I shall insert information about the government of the empire to vary the story and prevent it from running all on one theme. This done, we will return to the deeds of Prince Viracocha, which were very great.

The Strange Adventure of Pedro Serrano

Serrana Island, which lies on the route between Cartagena and Havana, received its name from a Spaniard called Pedro Serrano, whose ship was wrecked near it, and he alone saved himself, being a great swimmer, and reached that island, which is uninhabited, uninhabitable, without water or wood, and by his courage and industry managed to live there for seven years. Before him this island was nameless; as he reported it, it has a circumference of two leagues. This is almost as it appears on mariners' maps, which show three tiny islands surrounded by sand shoals. These waters are full of them, and for this reason ships avoid them to keep from coming to grief.

It was Pedro Serrano's fate to be lost here, and he swam to the island, where he was overtaken by the greatest despondency, for he found there neither water nor wood, nor even grass that he could graze, nor anything else to keep him alive until some ship should pass and rescue him before he perished of hunger and thirst, a death more cruel than drowning, which is quicker. Thus he passed the first night, bewailing his misfortune, as unhappy as one may imagine a man would be in such a plight. When morning came he walked around the island again, and found some animals that had come up out of the sea, such as crabs, shrimps, and other vermin, of which he caught as many as he could, and ate them raw, because he had no fire to cook or roast them. In this way he managed to exist until he saw some turtles swim ashore, and when they were a distance from the sea, he caught one of them and turned it over on its back, and did the same thing with as many as he could, for it is hard for them to right themselves. With a knife he carried in his belt, and which saved him from death, he cut its throat and drank the blood instead of water. He did the same with the others, and put the meat in the sun to dry so he could eat it, and to have the empty shells in which to catch water when it rained, for, as is well known, this region has a heavy rainfall. In this way he kept himself alive the first days, killing all the turtles he could, and some of them were as big or bigger than the biggest shield, and others smaller, of all sizes. He was unable to turn the biggest ones on their back, for they were too strong for him, and even though he got astride them to tire them out and hold them down, it was no use, for even with him on their back they made for the sea. Experience taught him which turtles he should attack and which he should let go. In the shells he caught a great deal of water, because there were some that held as much as two arrobas. When Pedro Serrano saw that he had a sufficient supply of food and drink, it seemed to him that if he could get fire to cook his food and send up smoke signals when a ship came in sight, he would lack for nothing. With this thought, and being a man who had followed the sea, and these are superior at any task to others, he looked about for a couple of stones to serve as flint, for he planned to use his knife as a steel. And as he could find none on the island, for it was all covered with fine sand, he swam into the sea and dived to the bottom. Diligently seeking what he was looking for in one place and another, he finally found some pebbles and brought up as many as he could. He selected the best of these, and breaking them against each other so they would have edges against which to whet his knife, he tried his scheme. And when he saw that he struck sparks, he tore up a piece of his shirt, shredding it very fine until it was like carded cotton, to serve as tow, and by his persistence and skill, after many attempts, he got fire. When he found he had it, he considered himself very fortunate, and to keep it going, he collected the flotsam washed up by the sea, among which were seaweed, spars of ships lost at sea, shells, fish bones, and other things to sustain the fire. And so that the rain would not put it out, he built a hut of the biggest shells of the turtles he had killed, and with unrelaxing care tended the fire so it should not slip away between his fingers. At the end of two months, and even before, he found himself in the same state as when he was born, because the continual rains, the heat, and the dampness of the climate had rotted the few garments he had. The great heat of the sun made him suffer, for he had no clothes to cover himself, nor was there any shade where he could take refuge from it. When he was very tired he would get into the water until it covered him. With this struggle and effort he lived three years, and during that time he saw some ships go by; but even though he sent up his smoke signals, which on the ocean is the sign of shipwrecked castaways, they either did not see them or were afraid to approach for fear of running aground on the shoals, and they sailed by. Pedro Serrano became so disconsolate over this that he felt like dying and ending everything. Constant exposure to the weather had grown so much hair on his body that it looked like the pelt of an animal, and not just any kind of animal, but a wild boar. His hair and beard hung below his waist.

One afternoon to his great surprise, Pedro Serrano saw on his island a man who had been lost on the shoals the night before and had kept himself afloat on a plank of the ship. When morning came and he saw the smoke of Pedro Serrano's fire, suspecting what it was, he made his way toward it with the help of the plank and his swimming. When the two men came face to face, it would be hard to say which of the two was the more surprised. Serrano imagined that it was the Devil who had come to tempt him to some act of despair. The visitor thought Serrano was the Devil in person when he saw him covered with all that hair, and his long locks and beard. Each fled from the other, and Pedro Serrano called out as he ran: "Jesus, Jesus, save me, O Lord, from the Devil." When the other heard this, he took heart, and running after him, cried: "Do not run away, brother, I am a Christian like yourself." And to reassure him, as he ran, he recited the Creed in a loud voice. When Pedro Serrano heard this, he turned toward him, and they embraced each other with great affection and tears and sighs, seeing themselves as victims of a common misfortune and without hope of remedying it. Each recounted his past life briefly. Pedro Serrano gave his visitor to eat and drink of what he had, and this comforted him somewhat and he began to talk again about his misfortune. They arranged their life as best they could, spending the hours of the day and night looking for shellfish to eat, and seaweed and driftwood and fish bones and whatever else the sea washed up to keep the fire going. They had to keep continual watch over it, taking turns so it would not go out. Thus they lived for a number of days, but not many had gone by before they quarreled and separated and almost came to blows (proof of the slaves we are to our evil passions). The cause of the quarrel was that one said to the other that he was not taking care of things as he should, and this reproach, and the words in which it was voiced, gave rise to the quarrel, and they separated. But realizing what a foolish thing they had done, they asked each other's forgiveness, became friends again, returned to each other's company, and lived in this fashion four years more. During this time they saw other ships go by, and sent up their smoke signals, but the ships sailed on without taking notice of them, and the men were so disheartened they felt like lying down and dying.

After these long years a ship happened to sail so close that it saw the smoke and put a boat over the side to bring them in. Pedro Serrano and his companion, who was covered with a pelt like his, when they saw the boat approaching began to shout the Creed and call out the name of Our Redeemer in a loud voice, so that the sailors manning the boat would not think they were devils and flee from them. And their precaution served them well, for otherwise the sailors would surely have turned back, for they did not look like human beings.

Thus they brought them to the ship, and all who saw them and heard the trials they had endured were amazed. The companion died on the seas on the voyage back to Spain. Pedro Serrano arrived there, and went to Germany, where the Emperor was at the time. He left on the hair with which he was covered as proof of his years as a castaway and the sufferings he had undergone. He could have earned a great deal of money if he had wanted to exhibit himself in the towns he traveled through. Certain knights and gentlemen to whom he had shown himself gave him money for his expenses, and His Imperial Majesty, when he had seen and heard him, conferred upon him a pension of four thousand pesos, which amounts to four thousand, eight hundred ducats, in Peru. As he was coming out here to enjoy it he died in Panama, so he never even laid eyes upon it.

This tale, as told here, I heard from a gentleman called Garci-Sánchez de Figueroa, who had known Pedro Serrano. He said that he had heard it from his own lips, and that after Pedro Serrano saw the emperor he trimmed his hair and his beard, leaving the latter a little above his waist, and at night he braided it, otherwise it got all over the bed and disturbed his sleep.

11

FIVE MEXICAN BAROQUE POETS

Of the five poets chosen here to represent Mexican baroque poetry, only one is of the first rank: Sor Juana Inés de la Cruz; and she is also the least typical. In her poetry, Góngora's culteranism and Quevedo's conceptism are curiously and harmoniously blended. The other four are brilliant practitioners of a school that had already produced its best poetry in Spain but was to find a new vision and a universal scope in America (see Introduction to Part One). Together these five bring to the still a-borning literature of the New World the beauty and authority of a dazzling poetic tradition.

I / BERNARDO DE BALBUENA

Balbuena was Góngora's exact contemporary. Like him, he was born in Spain around 1561 and he died the same year: 1627. But his career was less brilliant, and had America as its setting. His family came to Mexico when he was only two years old; he lived in Guadalajara and Mexico City, where he studied theology and was ordained. From 1592 to 1604 he produced almost all his best poems. In 1606 he went back to Spain to complete his studies and obtain a degree of Doctor of Theology. He was appointed Abbot of Jamaica and later Bishop of Puerto Rico. Many of his manuscripts were burned at the time of the Dutch pirates' attack on the latter island (1625).

Of the surviving works—an epic poem to one of Spain's medieval heroes, a pastoral novel, a descriptive poem of Mexico City—only the third is undoubtedly a masterpiece. Published in 1604, under the title, *The Grandeur of Mexico,* it describes the imperial city as in a dream, with the poet guided by a nymph. The baroque conventions (classical mythology and imagery, wonders and marvels) allow him to indulge in a totally artificial language, yet the structure of his descriptive poem is not affected by it. Its simple and solid line proceeds step by step to its solemn culmination.

The first of a long chain of poets who attempted to celebrate the New World, Balbuena is the founder of a lineage that also includes Andrés Bello (see Part Two, 3, II), Rubén Darío (Three, 4), and especially Pablo Neruda (Four, 13).

Immortal Springtime and Its Tokens

From Grandeza Mexicana, *included in* Anthology of Mexican Poetry, *compiled by Octavio Paz, translated by Samuel Beckett (Bloomington: Indiana University Press, 1958), pp. 50–57.*

The bright rays of lofty Phaeton shine
upon the gold of Colchos and restore
to life the frozen and inanimate world.

The jasmine buds, the plants grow green again,
and lovely Flora with her garland sets
upon the heights their crown and ornament.

Amalthea scatters roses from her lap,
the limpid air sheds love and merriment,
·emerald and hyacinth deck the hills.

All things are redolent of summer, all
distill sweet vapors, all are saturate
with the fresh amber welling in their flowers.

And what though so it is in all the world,
yet in this paradise of Mexico
freshness has set its kingdom and its court.

Mistress, here it seems as though the hand
of heaven had stayed its choice on hanging gardens,
and heaven itself would fain be gardener.

Here May and April flourish all year long
in temperate pleasantness and grateful cool,
their zephyrs soft, their skies serene and bright.

Between the mount of Ossa and a spur
of towering Olympus there is spread
a valley full of freshness and of flowers,

whose beauty Peneus, with his grateless child,
increasingly enriches and augments
with leaves of laurel and with silver streams.

Here the sweet-smelling cyperus abounds,
sung by snowy swans who moist their wings
in the cold crystalline of sleeping meres.

Here midst grass and flower, shade and peace,
trembling waters lap against the sides
of dark caves murmurous with quiet winds.

The waves uprear their spume of pearly spray,
arching above the sand and grainy gold
whereon they break and washing glide away.

White shells re-echo to the plashing stream,
and by yon tangle of aspen, willow and sedge
greeny sea wrack coils a snaky tress.

Here the hart gambols, there the porcupine,
laden with strawberries and purple shells,
gives proofs sufficient of his industry.

The bird of Phasis cries, the nightingale,
deep in the tangles of an alder tree,
sings till the air is steeped in suavity.

To make an end, this human paradise,
so celebrated in Greek eloquence,
with more of wit and elegance than just cause,

is Tempe's spacious vale, by fancy held
to be the cradle of immortal summer,
without an equal, nay without a rival.

Dale most fair I doubt not, but withal
it is as nought, it is as jot and tittle
beside the flowering Mexican domain.

Henceforth its fame is sullied and obscured
increasingly: beside this deathless freshness
its grandeur were a sorry grandeur indeed.

Here midst devious streams the spring
enjoys her treasures in security.
her beauty never to be soiled by time.

She shelters in her kirtle pleasure's romps,
and in pellucid freshets, glassy cold,
perpetuates her mirrored youthfulness.

Here flourishes the laurel, shade and shelter
from all celestial rigor, solemn crown
of aged sages and of poets rare;

and the impetuous almond that proclaims
tidings of summer and, to make them known,
its blossoms jeopardizes and its life;

and the lofty pine exuberant
with pearls of lucent gum, and the vine
proffering its fresh grapes to the thirsty grasp;

brave water lilies, scenting of jessamine,
and the amorous ivy intertwined
with pretty tendril claws in beech and elm;

the cruel mulberry whose gloomy haunts
embower songs of love, the shady willow,
and the still unconquered Orient palm;

fair ornament of gardens, the funereal
cypress, and the stalwart silver tree
rearing its bulwark gainst the stormy main;

the glossy box, heavy, hard and trim,
the tamarisk close by the crystal wave,
the brazen oak, the poplar without flaw;

the knotty ilex with its rigid boughs,
the crimson cloth and the coral strawberry,
the lofty cedar reaching to the skies;

the gray walnut tree, the bitter fennel,
and it, befouled by the infernal fumes,
whose leaves enwreathe the brows of Hercules;

the snowy orange blossom that summer gives
to us in earnest of its bittersweets,
uncertain gage of dubious benefits;

among scarlet poppies the faint gleam
as if of grains of pearl upon the sand,
seen through the taintless water's limpid glass;

the rose half open and brimful of pearls,
the fresh carnation, bathed in cochineal,
green sweet basil, vervain, and sandalwood;

the amorous and tender clover grass,
the ever restless turnsole or marigold,
the tender jasmine, the crimson gillyflower;

the purple violet, the blue flower-de-luce,
the blithesome garden balm, the pointed thyme,
the bilberry, fresh myrtle and white musk rose;

flowering rosemary, the best of all
the herbs and flowers that the field could give,
red everlastings and rude calamint;

sweet garden broom imparting to its haunt
the scent of ambergris, and little pinks,
maidenly, with many-colored flowers;

green ferns and wild churlish camomile,
amorous jonquils, tender fodder grass,
flowery meadows and sweet-smelling pastures;

bitter cresses, all entanglement,
spangled over with little bells of gold,
scattering their freshness through this pleasant land;

and the Madonna lily that wittingly
I had forgot, sitting between thy brows,
whose whiteness it has borrowed for its own;

hyacinths and daffodils that were given
in earnest of thy coming to the orchards
and to be a promise of flowery boons;

joyous flowers, that in olden times
were monarchs of the world, shepherds and nymphs,
and dwell in bloom because in bloom they ceased;

birds of the air most beautifully hued,
various in plumage, various in song,
skylarks, popinjays, and nightingales,

that to the tumult of the wind and wave,
in most suave and sonorous harmony,
temper their unpremeditated strains;

and in the chilly pools above their beds
of shining glass, the nereids interlace
their graceful windings and lascivious coils;

some amid green sedges twine about,
others in the glittering crystal wave
weave and unweave their specious twists and turns.

The limpid waters shimmering far and wide,
troubled like to broken looking-glass,
dazzle the sight with trembling radiance,

and, impearled with blanching foam, reveal,
deep in their vitreous transparencies,
lovely naiads wrought in ivory.

They frolic, gambol, and with joyous starts
wanton on the yielding crystal sheen
in countless figures, miens, and attitudes.

One from the mantling wave strikes plumes of spray,
another glides along with sidelong stroke,
others course to and fro, or twist, or roll.

One, whose fairness is unparagoned,
with garlands of alternate gold and flowers
wreathes and embellishes her vaunted grace.

This loveliness, these beauties unconfined,
here dwell and take their pleasure all year long,
exempt from fear and discord and alarums,

in a royal plaisaunce which, in very truth,
exceeds in beauty Cyprus and in balm
of clime and excellence of site the world.

Woods dark with freshness, thickets fresh with shade,
whose immortal verdancy the brushes
of April and of May bedight with flowers.

In fine all things, orchards, gardens, nymphs,
crystal and palm, walnuts, ivy, elms,
pines and poplars, laurels and almond trees,

trellis and mulberry, cypress, cedar, beech,
box and tamarisk, ilex, oak and fir,
vine and arbutus, fennel and medlar trees,

orange blossom, poppies and carnations,
pinks and roses, lilies and irises,
musk and rosemary, sloe and gillyflower,

balm-gentle, clover, vervain, sandalwood,
myrtle and jessamine, marigold and broom,
bilberry and goldful camomile,

thyme and mead and tangling watercress,
narcissus and sweet basil and lady fern,
and as many flowers more as April strows,

here by the supreme giver one and all
in stintless grace and beauty are bestowed.
This is their dwelling, these their native fields,
and this the tide of spring in Mexico.

II / JUAN RUIZ DE ALARCÓN

Chiefly known as a playwright, Ruiz de Alarcón was born in Mexico in 1580, but his comedies were written for the Madrid stage and always had a Spanish setting. He was already twenty when he first visited Spain. Although he returned to his native land when he was twenty-seven and lived there for six more years, he went back to Spain for good in 1613. As a writer, he always pretended to be a bona-fide *Madrileño* and not an *Indiano*. Predictably, his colleagues never let him forget what he was: a Colonial, and a hunchback to boot.

Undaunted, Ruiz de Alarcón went on writing, in the most impeccable tradition of the Spanish drama, his cloak-and-dagger comedies. But if he externally conformed to the rules and upheld "honor" as did all the Castilian playwrights, he secretly undermined the same morality he was pretending to approve. In his best play, *The Suspicious Truth* (used by Corneille as a model for his *Le Menteur*), the protagonist, Don García, is criticized and punished not because he lies but because he does it so blatantly. The protagonist's father, Don Beltrán, is more concerned over the prospect that Don García's lies will prevent his marriage to a rich woman than with his son's offenses against truth. In uncovering the layers of deception on which society (any society) is based, Ruiz de Alarcón took revenge on the society that despised him as well as on the Colonial society from which he came— one as rooted in lies as that of the mother country.

The fragment chosen here is part of one of Don García's more elaborate fictions: his description of a feast given to a certain lady and which never took place. Baroque hyperbole suits the situation perfectly: everything here is surface, words are only signifiers with no real reference to anything, there is nothing signified but a pack of lies. All of Spanish society, both metropolitan and colonial, is laid bare in this beautiful sequence of empty images. If as a playwright Ruiz de Alarcón is among the best of the Golden Age, as a baroque poet he can be counted among the most successfully satirical, in a vein lighter but no less deadly than that exploited by Quevedo and Góngora.

Feast by the Manzanares

From Anthology of Mexican Poetry, *compiled by Octavio Paz, translated by Samuel Beckett (Bloomington: Indiana University Press, 1958), pp. 59–60.*

Midst the opacous gloom
and dense opacities
that with its elms the grove,
night with its shadows shed,
a table was ensconced,
square and clean and neat,
Italian in device,
Spanish in opulence.
Cloths and serviettes
in countless figures folded
were birds and beasts in all
but animation.
On four side tables, set
in quadrate symmetry,
stood silver plate and gold,
glasses and earthenware.
Scarce an elm with boughs
in all Sotillo stood,
for they had fallen to raise
the six tents here and there
disposed; four hid from view
four different quires; another,
first courses and desserts,
and the sixth the meats.
My lady came in her coach,
making envious the stars,
fragrant the ambient air,
joyful the riverbank.
The foot that I adore
had scarce to emerald turned
the grass, the stream to crystal,
the sand to pearls, when sudden
—with copious discharge,

of rockets, balls, and wheels—
the whole zone of fire
descended on the earth.
The sulphureous lights
still burning, those of four
and twenty cressets gan
the dimming of the stars.
First is heard the music
of the hautboys; then the viols
sound in the second tent;
from the third the flutes
with suavity are borne;
and in the fourth four voices
with harps and lutes resound.
The meantime have been served
full thirty banquet dishes,
first course and desserts,
all but as many, beside.
Fruits and wines in bowls
and goblets fashioned from
the crystal winter gives
and artifice preserves
are so deep frosted over
that Manzanares doubts
when through the Soto he goes—
he wends in the sierra.
Nor wants the sense of smell
when that of taste respites;
for with sweet-smelling spirits
of cassolettes and phials
and distilled essences
of perfumes, herbs, and flowers,
the Soto of Madrid

was as the Sheban realm.
Thrust in a man of diamonds
dainty shafts of gold,
in which my lady might view
her rigor and my resolve,
reft their pre-eminence
from willow, reed, and osier;
for when teeth are of pearl,
then haulms must be of gold.

And now, together mingled,
the four quires undertake
with separate accord
so to suspend the spheres
that envious Apollo
precipitates his course,
so the beginning day
may terminate the feast.

III / MIGUEL DE GUEVARA

The attribution to Miguel de Guevara of one of the most famous sonnets in the Spanish language (the first in this selection) is still very much a point of literary contention. The poem was found in the manuscript of a book by this Augustine priest, a manual for the study of one of the native Mexican languages. Spanish scholars have attributed this sonnet to poets as diverse as Saint Teresa of Jesus and Lope de Vega. The question need not, finally, be settled. Guevara (if he is in fact the author) was writing in a well-known poetic tradition, using the style of one of the baroque schools of the day, the so-called conceptist. The subtlety with which he plays with words and with their ambiguous meanings (or conceits) belongs to the school and not to any particular poet. Years later, Sor Juana Inés de la Cruz (see selection 11, v) would play with even subtler skill on the same instrument. This type of poetry is, in the best sense, a collective endeavor.

Three Sonnets

From Anthology of Mexican Poetry, *compiled by Octavio Paz, translated by Samuel Beckett (Bloomington: Indiana University Press, 1958), pp. 62–63.*

1
"I am not moved to love thee, my Lord God" . . .

I am not moved to love thee, my Lord God,
By the heaven thou hast promised me;

I am not moved by the sore-dreaded hell
to forbear me from offending thee.

I am moved by thee, Lord; I am moved
at seeing thee nailed upon the cross and mocked;
I am moved by thy body all over wounds;
I am moved by thy dishonor and thy death.

I am moved, last, by thy love, in such a wise
that though there were no heaven I still should love thee,
and though there were no hell I still should fear thee.

I need no gift of thee to make me love thee;
for though my present hope were all despair,
as now I love thee I should love thee still.

2
"Raise me up, Lord" . . .

Raise me up, Lord, who am fallen down,
void of love and fear and faith and awe;
I long to rise and in my place abide;
mine is the longing, mine the impediment.

I am, who am one only, cleft in twain;
I live and die, make merry and lament;
what I can do cannot by me be done;
I flee from evil and tarry in its toils.

I am so hardened in my obduracy
that spite the dread of losing me and thee
I never turn me from my wicked ways.

Between thy might and mercy I am torn;
in others every day I see amend,
in me I see fresh longing to offend thee.

3
"To crucify the Son" . . .

To crucify the Son and pierce his breast,
to sacrifice him that I might not die,
it is very sure proof, Lord, of love,
to show thyself so full of love for me.

So that—I God, thou mortal man—I should
give thee the godly being then were mine,
and in this my mortality lay me down
that of so good a God I might have joy.

And yet thy love received no recompense
when thou didst raise me up to excellency
of godhood, and to manhood God didst humble.

I owe and rightfully shall ever owe
the debt that by the Son upon the cross
was paid for me that thou mightst be requited.

IV / LUIS SANDOVAL Y ZAPATA

Very little but "ruins" is left of Sandoval y Zapata's works, according to the opinion of one of his critics. He was born in Mexico at an unknown date and flourished around 1645—that is all we know for certain. But his sonnets prove that he was one of the best of the American "Gongoristas." To an almost exhausted tradition he brought elegance, precision, and an uncanny ear.

Three Sonnets

From Anthology of Mexican Poetry, *compiled by Octavio Paz, translated by Samuel Beckett (Bloomington: Indiana University Press, 1958), pp. 72–76.*

1
**To the Admirable Transubstantiation of the Roses
into the marvelous image of Our Lady of Guadalupe . . .
the Roses Vanquish the Phoenix**

The Luminary of the Birds expires,
of the wind that winged eternity,
and midst the vapors of the monument
burns a sweet-smelling victim of the pyre.

And now in mighty metamorphosis
behold a shroud, with every flower more bright;

in the Cerecloth, reasonable essence,
the vegetable amber dwells and breathes.

The colors of Our Lady they portray;
and from these shades the day in envy flies
when the sun upon them shines his light.

You die more fortunate than the Phoenix, Flowers;
for he, feathered to rise, in ashes dies;
but you, Our Blessed Lady to become.

2
To Primal Matter

Within how many metamorphoses,
matter informed with life, hast thou had being?
Sweet-smelling snow of jessamine thou wast,
and in the pallid ashes didst endure.

Such horror by thee to thyself laid bare,
king of flowers, the purple thou didst don.
In such throng of dead forms thou didst not die,
thy deathbound being by thee immortalized.

For thou dost never wake to reason's light,
nor ever die before the invisible
murderous onset of the winged hours.

What, with so many deaths art thou not wise?
What art thou, incorruptible nature, thou
who hast been widowed thus of so much life?

3
To a Dead Actress

Here lies the purple sleeping and here lie
elegance and grace and loveliness,
and here that clarion of dulcitude
whose voice was lent to life's harmonious numbers.

Trumpet of love, no more thy clamant strain
with sonorous softness summons to the fray;
now in the tenebrous obscurity
with thine lies stricken many a tuneful soul.

Poesy thanks to thee was manifest
and with a fairer, surer life endued;
and—loving, cold, disdainful—thou didst feign

so well that even Death was unresolved
if thou didst simulate him as one dead
or didst submit to him as one alive.

V / SOR JUANA INÉS DE LA CRUZ

If Garcilaso Inca was the first great prose writer born in the New World, and Ruiz de Alarcón its first great playwright, Sor Juana was its first great poet. Born in 1651 to a noble Mexican family, Juana de Asbaje was sixteen when she chose to become a nun. Although she almost immediately returned to the viceregal court, where she was used to being feted and spoiled for her beauty and wit, the following year she went back to the convent and took vows as Sor Juana Inés de la Cruz, to remain there until her death in 1695.

Her adult life was a constant struggle against Colonial society. At court she discouraged her suitors with her wit. At the convent, she faced subtler opposition: those religious guides who wanted her to concentrate on her devotions and forget her scientific and poetic pursuits, unfit (they thought) for a woman and a nun. She fought for her rights. Sor Juana had been a child prodigy, and as a young woman she became a scholar and a humanist, a poet and a playwright. In an "apologetic" letter that she wrote to one of her superiors—who had chastised her under the guise of an older nun, Sor Filotea de la Cruz, but was really the Bishop of Puebla—Sor Juana gave free rein to her brilliant intellect and fine sense of irony in arguing for the rights of an independent spirit.

In her earlier poems she had followed the Gongorist tradition and written erotic poetry that was both flawless and impersonal. (It is doubtful that she herself was ever really in love.) With age, she became more and more ambitious, and wrote a philosophical poem, "First Dream," in which Góngora's imagery was at the service of an elaborate metaphysical theory. Her struggle against a stifling society lasted until she was forty. Then, apparently of her own free will, she gave up her studies, sold her famous library of some four thousand volumes (one of the best private libraries in Colonial Mexico), and devoted herself totally to the care of the poor. She died of a plague when she was only forty-four.

Her life, like her poetry, is surrounded with mystery. Was she really illegitimate? That would explain her rejection of the court's double standards and her choosing to be a nun. Was she a lesbian, or perhaps even bisexual? There is a tinge of hatred in one of her most famous poems, the one in which she scolds the "foolish men" who blame women for their erotic frailties at the same time that they profit from them. Her last decision to abandon her humanistic pursuits and her poetry is still unexplained. Even the most famous portrait of her (a beautiful young nun against the background of an impressive library) was done a century after her death, with the painter's daughter for a model. As a likeness the painting has little value, but as a symbol of Sor Juana's beauty and passion for study, the portrait is totally accurate. It is truer, in fact, than an accurate likeness would be, for it represents the Sor Juana still available in her unique texts.

Ten Poems

From Anthology of Mexican Poetry, *edited by Octavio Paz and translated by Samuel Beckett (Bloomington: Indiana University Press, 1958), pp. 78–79;* An Anthology of Spanish Poetry from Garcilaso to García Lorca, *edited by Angel Flores (New York: Doubleday, 1961), pp. 159–62.*

In Acknowledgment of the Praises of European Writers

Divine Oracles, tell me when,
when, most melodious of Swans,
when did my careless scrawls deserve
to occupy your thoughtful care?

And from what place does so much praise,
so many commendations, come?
Can it be distance that alone
added so much to my portrait?

What stature have you given me?
What great Colossus have you wrought,
entirely ignorant of height,
from this lowly original?

I am not what you think I am;
but over there you've given me
another being in your pens,
and other breath upon your lips,

and, different from what I am,
I walk beneath your pens, and am
not what I truly am, but what
you'd prefer to imagine me.

To rule by reputation would
not startle me so very much,
since I already have observed
affection magnifying sizes.

But if you actually saw
the humble features of my scrawls,
which in long-ago squandered time
formed careless recreations, then

what could have prompted you to this
poorly deserved applause? Is it
possible for the truth to be
so far dragged down by courtliness?

Is it to such an ignorant
woman, whose tutelage for the
exacting occupation never
passed beyond poorly chosen snatches;

to a base-born abortion of
some barren fields, that I have made,
by being born among them, more
burned out and barren than before;

to an uncultured education
which in its infancy took up
with these same cogitations all
the tutors' offices; is it

to this, that praises of the most
illustrious, venerated in
pulpits and schools by all the world
as sages, now direct themselves?

Which was the ascendant star
dominating the planets, that
made you incline toward me, and made
the foreordained voluntary?

What magical infusions, brewed
from herbals of the Indians
of my own country, spilled their old
enchantment over all my lines?

And how much distance is required
to modulate the sound of all
my doings, till it seemed to make
their dissonances harmonize?

What sinister perspectives give
apparent form and ornament
to a vague body outlined by
rough, ill-done sketches, nothing more?

How many times, how many times,
among the waves of so much praise,
none of it merited, and waves
of misdirected compliments;

how many times, dazzled and blind
in such tremendous seas of light,
would not Phaeton have died, or would
Narcissus have been endangered, had

I not possessed within myself
some homely antidote to hand,
like knowledge of myself, being
what ugly feet are to the peacock!

You have brought disgrace on me
in making me so famous, for
the light you shed reveals my faults
more clearly, making them stand out.

When the sun tries to penetrate
bodies impervious to light,
he who thinks that they benefit
should know the sun just injures them;

because dense objects and coarse things,
resisting, in the narrowness
and meanness of their crooked pores
the entrance of the rays of light,

and tolerating nothing more
than superficial contact, find
that in their case the brightness serves
only to create shadows. Thus,

it seems to me, under the light
of your most fulsome eulogies,
my obscure scribblings are bereft
of all but their deformities.

Your lofty compliments are but
the honorary sepulchers
of frozen corpses for my cold
spiritless notions: your praises

are elegant pantheons where
the jasper and the marble are
magnificent, superfluous
custodians of lifeless dust.

Everything that you receive
is not measured according to
its actual size, but, rather, that
of the receiving vessel. You

conceive of me in terms that are
your own, and I don't wonder at
the great thing: that these concepts must,
of course, be miracles. Because

the image of your own idea
is, after all, what you have praised;
and, being yours, it well deserves
your own approval and applause.

Continue then to celebrate
that simulacrum of your own
perceptions, that the laurel may
return to stay among yourselves.

Were it not that my sex, for once,
had made the great attempt, that thus
we unexpected ones had tried
to reach perfection's height at last;

if it were not for this, the joy
alone would be enough reward;
no need for squandering on me
such forced, unnatural compliments.

Whoever sees such judges stoop
to praise me so, what can he say
but that "good taste" has taken hold
of mere intelligence or wit? . . .

Verses Expressing the Feelings of a Lover

My love, my lord,
hearken to my weary plaints awhile
as on the wind I cast them,
that it may wing them to thine ears,
so be it scatter not,
even as my hopes, the grievous voice.

With thine eyes hear me,
thou whose ears are so removed
from my pen murmuring
the groaning woes of absence;
and since my rude voice cannot come to thee,
deafly hear me, who mutely mourn.

If the fields are pleasant to thee,
joy in their happy verdancy,
untroubled by these faint
vexatious tears;
for there, attentive, thou wilt see
ensample of my woes and weal.

If thou seest the prattling stream,
lover of the meadow flowers,
impart with amorous flattery
to all it looks on its desire,
there flow my tears that thou mayst know
its laughter at my sorrow's cost.

If thou seest the turtledove
plaintive on a green bough mourning
its withered hope,
let bough and dove remind thee of my grief,
for they set forth, in greenness and lament,
my hope and pain.

If thou seest the fragile flower,
the crag that proudly scorns
the spurning tread of time,

both image me, albeit differently,
that my contentment, this my obduracy.

If thou seest the wounded stag
that hastens down the mountainside,
seeking, stricken, in icy stream
ease for its hurt,
and thirsting plunges in the crystal waters,
not in ease, in pain it mirrors me.

If from the savage hounds
the timorous hare in terror flies
and leaves no trace, that it may live,
of its light feet,
so my hope, in doubting and misgiving,
is close pursued by cruel jealousies.

If thou seest the bright sky,
even such is my soul's purity;
and if the day, niggard of light,
wraps its radiancy in gloom,
its darkness and inclemency
image my life since thou art gone.

Thus, sweet Fabio,
thou mayst with tranquil mind
have tidings of my woes,
perusing nature's face,
and as to everything I fit my grief,
know my pain and still thy pleasure take.

But when alas! my glory, shall I have
my meed of joyance in thy tranquil light?
When will it be, the day
when thou shall put sweet end to so much pain?
When, dear enchantment, shall I see thine eyes
and tears desist from mine?

When will thy sounding voice
strike softly on mine ear,
and the soul that adores thee,
flooded with spate of joy,
to welcome thee with loving haste
shine forth dissolved in gladness?

When will thy fair light bathe
my sense in splendor?
And I, for happiness,
and soon to hold the guerdon of my tears,
count my vain sighs for nought?
—For such is joy and such the price of pain.

When shall I see the pleasant aspect
of thy gentle joyous face
and that unspeakable boon
no human pen can tell?
—For how should that which overflows the whole
of sense within the finite be contained?

Come then, beloved treasure,
for already my weary life is dying
of this sore absence;
come then, for while thou tarriest thy coming,
my hope, although its greenness cost me dear,
is watered by mine eyes.

Describes Rationally the Irrational Effects of Love

This torment of love
that is in my heart,
I know I feel it
and know not why.

I feel the keen pangs
of a frenzy desired
whose beginning is longing
and end melancholy.

And when I my sorrow
more softly bewail,
I know I am sad
and know not why.

I feel for the juncture
I crave a fierce panting,
and when I come nigh it
withholds mine own hand.

For if haply it offers
after much weary vigil,
mistrust spoils its savor
and terror dispels it.

. . . .

Now patient, now fretful,
by conflicting griefs torn,
who for him much shall suffer,
and with him suffer nought.

. . . .

On scant foundations
my sad cares raise
with delusive conceits
a mountain of feeling.

And when that proud mass
falls asunder I find
that the arrogant fabric
was poised on a pin.

Beguiled perhaps by grief
I presume without reason
no fulfillment can ever
my passion assuage.

. . . .

And though nigh disabused,
still the same grief assails me,
that I suffer so sore
for so little a cause.

Perhaps the wounded soul sweeping
to take its revenge
repents it and wreaks
other vengeance on me.

. . . .

In my blindness and folly
I, gladly deceived,
beseech disenchantment
and desire it not.

"Tarry, shadow of my scornful treasure" . . .

Tarry, shadow of my scornful treasure,
image of my dearest sortilege,
fair illusion for which I gladly die,
sweet unreality for which I painfully live.

To the compelling magnet of thy grace
since my breast as docile steel is drawn,
why dost thou with soft ways enamor me
if from me then in mockery thou must fly?

And yet thou mayst nowise in triumph boast
that over me thy tyranny has prevailed;
for though thou breakest, mocking, the narrow coil

that girdled thy fantastic form about,
what boots it to make mock of arms and breast
if thou art prisoner of my fantasy?

"Diuturnal infirmity of hope" . . .

Diuturnal infirmity of hope,
thou that sustainest thus my fainting years,
and on the equal edge of weal and woe
holdest in equilibrium the scales

forever in suspense, forever loath
to tilt, thy wiles obeying that forbid
the coming ever to excess of measure
either of confidence or of despair.

Who rid thee of the name of homicide?
For thou art crueler still, if well we mark
that thou suspendest the deluded soul

between a wretched and a happy lot,
not to the end that life may be preserved,
but to inflict a more protracted death.

"This colored counterfeit that thou beholdest" . . .

This colored counterfeit that thou beholdest,
vainglorious with the excellencies of art,
is, in fallacious syllogisms of color,
nought but a cunning dupery of sense;

this in which flattery has undertaken
to extenuate the hideousness of years,
and, vanquishing the outrages of time,
to triumph o'er oblivion and old age,

is an empty artifice of care,
is a fragile flower in the wind,
is a paltry sanctuary from fate,

is a foolish sorry labor lost,
is conquest doomed to perish and, well taken,
is corpse and dust, shadow and nothingness.

"Divine rose, that in a pleasant garden" . . .

Divine rose, that in a pleasant garden,
persuasive with sweet-smelling subtlety,
in crimson mastery impartest beauty
and snowy disciplines of loveliness.

Intimation of the human frame,
epitome of unavailing grace,
in whose being nature did unite
the joyful cradle and the fearsome tomb.

How haughty in thy pomp, presumptuous
and proud, thou dost disdain the threat of death,
and then, dismayed and humbled, showest forth

thy perishable being's withered marks!
Thus with learned death and ignorant life
living thou dost deceive and dying teach.

"Crimson lute that comest in the dawn" . . .

Crimson lute that comest in the dawn
with doleful ditty to thy cherished mate
and in the amber of the nutrient rose
stainest coral red thy golden beak.

Gentle goldfinch, birdling born to sorrow,
that scarce didst glimpse the lovely break of day
when, at the first note of thy melody,
thou wast by death received, by song abandoned.

In life there is no sure lot, verily;
with thine own voice thou callest on the hunter
that he fail not to strike thee with his shaft.

Oh dreaded destiny and yet pursued!
Oh passing belief that thine own life should be,
rather than silent, privy to thy death!

"Green enravishment of human life" . . .

Green enravishment of human life,
smiling frenzy of demented hope,
inextricable dream of them that wake
and, as a dream, of riches destitute.

Spirit of the world, robust old age,
imagination of decrepit vigor,
longing for the happy ones' today
and for the unhappy ones' tomorrow.

Let those who, with green glasses spectacled,
see all things sicklied o'er with their desire,
questing for thy light pursue thy shadow:

but I, more mindful of my destiny,
imprison my two eyes in my two hands
and see no other thing than it I touch.

"Amorous of Laura's loveliness" . . .

Amorous of Laura's loveliness
the heavens rapt her to their high abode,

it ill befitting her pure light to shed
its radiancy on these unhappy vales,

or to the end that mortal men, deceived
by the perfection of her bodily frame,
should not imagine, in their wonderment
at so much beauty, theirs a blessed lot.

Born where the red veil of the orient
falls from the dawning of the roseate face,
she died where the deep sea, with avid zest,

gives sepulcher to its effulgence;
it being ordained her godlike flight should cast,
even as the Sun, a girdle round the world.

12

JUAN RODRÍGUEZ FREILE

Unlike the other chroniclers and historians of the Spanish Indies, Rodríguez Freile (born in Santa Fe de Bogotá, in 1566) was more concerned with "la petite histoire" than with the epic of the conquistadors. He started to write a dutiful account of his native country's first one hundred years, but he lacked the training and discipline of a true historian. Instead, he let his chronicle drift into a report of all the gossip of the new settlement: duels over unfaithful women; tales of witchcraft, larceny, murder.

It was finished in 1636, when the author was seventy, but was never published during his lifetime. The first edition dates from 1859. The original manuscript (which has since disappeared) was entitled *The History of New Granada*, but it was generally known as *El Carnero* (The Sheep) for reasons still unclear: it might be an allusion to the original binding; it might contain a pun on the Latin word *carnarium*, a place where corpses are left to rot. Its strange name seemed to echo the strange fate of the book.

It is easy to understand why it was not published in the seventeenth century: it displayed, in elaborate detail, the dirty linen of some of the most important characters in town. In this respect, Rodríguez Freile's gossip is close to the most acerbic descriptions of Gregorio de Matos in

Bahia (see selection 17). Throughout his book, Rodríguez Freile claims he is using documents from judicial or administrative archives; always he protests he is telling nothing but the truth. His book is probably as accurate as Garcilaso's or Bernal Díaz's. But it really doesn't matter. Historians tend to fault him and catch him in errors, although he is a source of much of the information they have of the period. Today, his reputation as a storyteller is greater than his standing as a chronicler. He really belongs to literature, and especially to the development of the short story in Spanish America. He is one of the first and best of the local "cronistas": those writers who left a precise and naïve account of what life was like during the Colonial age in the marginal towns of the Spanish empire. In many respects he is closer to Bartolomé Arzáns de Orzúa y Vela, the chronicler of wealthy Potosí (selection 20), than to the more epical chroniclers of Mexico and Peru. His own attitude toward society was ambiguous: he claimed respectability, and insisted (though poor) on his Spanish ancestors and the purity of their blood. His mind was a conventional one. He devoted many pages to quotations from the Bible and classical writers that proved women unfaithful, treacherous, and prone to lead men to perdition. But he also admitted that he loved them and could hardly resist their charms. Like many of the best picaresque writers, he preached morality while exhibiting sin in the raw. He may well be called the first certified voyeur of the New World.

The ambiguous morality of his work is clearly apparent in the contrast between the first story in this selection, which reestablishes the historical truth about the ceremony of El Dorado (The Gilded One), and the second, in which he tells matter-of-factly a tall tale of witchcraft and adultery. Today, the world he chronicled seems subtly linked to the more hyperbolic exercises of another member of his literary tribe: Gabriel García Márquez, the fabulous chronicler of Colombia's "one hundred years of solitude."

Two Tales from Santa Fe

From The Golden Land, *pp. 60–62; and* The Conquest of the New Granada, *translated by William C. Atkinson (London: The Folio Society, 1961), pp. 70–74.*

El Dorado

In my youth I left this kingdom for those of Castile, and there I spent six years. I returned, and have traveled widely in this land, and among the many friends I have had here was Don Juan, the cacique and lord of Guatavita, a nephew of the one the conquistadors found in power when they entered this kingdom, who later succeeded his uncle and who told me all these old tales and those that follow.

He told me that at the time the Spaniards entered by way of Vélez, upon the discovery of this kingdom and its conquest, he was fasting in preparation for occupying the throne of his uncle, for among them the power passed to a nephew, the son of a sister, and this custom continues until our own days. When he entered upon his fast he already had had knowledge of women, and the fast and ceremonies were as follows:

It was the custom among these Indians for the successor and heir to the power or lordship of the uncle he was succeeding to fast for six years, living in a cave that was designated for this purpose, and in all this time he must have nothing to do with women, or eat meat, salt, or hot peppers, or do other things that were forbidden. Among these were that during the fast he must never see the sun; only at night was he permitted to emerge from the cave and see the moon and stars, but he had to return to the cave before the sun should see him. When this fast and ceremonies were over he took possession of the *cacicazgo*, or lordship, and the first trip he had to make was to the great lake of Guatavita to make offerings and sacrifice to the devil, whom they held to be their god and master.

The ceremony consisted in making a great raft of reeds, which they prepared and decked out as beautifully as they knew how. They set upon it four lighted braziers in which they burned *moque*, which is the incense they used, and turpentine, and many other different perfumes.

On this occasion the lake, which was very large and deep enough so seagoing ships could sail upon it, was completely surrounded by Indians, men and women, decked out in feathers, and breastplates and crowns of gold, and with bonfires burning all around it. At the same time that the fuming began on the raft, they lighted the fires on land, and so dense was the smoke that it clouded the light of day.

Thereupon they stripped the clothing off the heir, leaving him completely naked, and smeared him over with a sticky mud, and then they dredged him with gold dust and ground gold, so that he was completely covered with this metal. They put him on the raft, standing erect, and at his feet they placed a great heap of gold and emeralds as an offering to their god. Four chieftains, his most important vassals, got on the raft with him, naked too, and adorned with feathers, gold coronets, bracelets, breastplates and earrings of gold, each with his offering.

As the raft moved away from the land the instruments began to resound, horns, conch-shell trumpets, and other instruments, and along with these such yells and cries as deafened the hills and valleys, and continued until the raft reached the middle of the lake, when a flag was hoisted as a signal for silence.

The gold-covered Indian made his offering, throwing all the gold in the pile at his feet into the middle of the lake, and the other chieftains who accompanied him did the same. When this was concluded they lowered the flag that had been flying all during the ceremony, and as the raft started back toward land, the shouting, the trumpets, the horns, began again with dances such as they used. In this fashion they received the newly elected and recognized him as their prince and sovereign.

This is the ceremony that gave rise to that celebrated name of *El Dorado*, which has cost so many lives and fortunes. It was in Peru that the word was first heard. It fell out that after Quito had been conquered, Sebastián de Benalcazar, in the course of his wars and conquests, met an Indian of these of the kingdom of Bogotá, who told him that when they chose a king in his country, they took him to a great lake and covered him all over with gold, and with great ceremonies made him king. As a result of this Don Sebastián said: "Let us go find this golden Indian."

The news spread to Castile and the rest of the Indies, and incited Benalcazar to set out to look for him, and for that reason he had a share in the conquest and foundation of this city.

A Tale of Witchcraft

The second incident also originated in Santa Fé. The reader will recall the paper that appeared one day, years before, on the walls of the city hall concerning the deaths of the two *oidores* with the foundering of the flagship off Bermuda. It was a long story, that began with one of the fleets sailing to Castile after Montaño's arrest, in which there took passage a resident of this city anxious to put his money into buying goods in Spain. He was married to a young and pretty wife, and she, in her husband's absence, preferred to enjoy her beauty rather than watch it go to seed. Making a slip, she found herself with child, but reckoned there was no hurry and that she would still be able to put the matter to rights. Before her time was up, however, news came knocking on the door that the return fleet had arrived at Cartagena. This threw the poor lady into a commotion, and she tried all she knew to bring about a miscarriage, but without success.

She took her problem to a friend, one Juana García, a freed Negress who had come up to New Granada with two daughters in the train of Governor Luis de Lugo. The daughters trailed dresses of silk and gold here in Santa Fé and had men at their heels. The mother, as events proved, was something of a witch. The wife told her her troubles and how desperate she was to end her pregnancy, and asked her help. "But who said your husband was with the fleet?" She replied that she took it so because he had assured her he would come back without fail at the first opportunity. "It could be," said the gossip, "but do nothing until I have made sure. I will soon know whether he has arrived or not."

During the night she applied herself to the business, and next day was back with the answer. "Good friend," she said, "I have made my inquiries. The fleet lies in truth in Cartagena harbor, but I find no news of your husband, nor anyone to confirm that he sailed with it." The other was still greatly distressed, and again besought her aid to get rid of the unwanted child. "That you must not," she said, "not until we know for certain if he has come. What you can do is this.

You see that small green tub?" The woman nodded. "Well, fill it with water and put it in your room, and then prepare a meal. I'll bring my daughters, and we'll enjoy ourselves. And afterwards we will think of something for your need."

When night had fallen all three turned up at the woman's home. She meanwhile had invited other girls nearby to join the company. All had arrived, and the girls were singing and dancing, when she said to her gossip, "I've got such a pain in my middle. Would you come and look at it for me?" She picked up a candle, led the way to her room, shut the door, and said, "Gossip, there is the tub." "Good: take the candle and see if you see anything in the water." She looked: "I see a country I don't recognize, and there is my husband, sitting on a chair. There is a woman standing by a table, and a tailor with scissors in his hand cutting out a scarlet dress." Said the gossip, "Let me see." And when she looked she saw just as the other had said. "What country is that?" the wife asked. "Hispaniola, Santo Domingo."

Just then the tailor snipped out with his scissors a piece of cloth for a sleeve and threw it across his shoulder. Said the gossip, "Would you like to see me take that piece of cloth away from him?" "You can't do that?" "If you want it," she said, "I can take it." "Take it, my friend; take it by all means." Scarcely were the words out of her mouth when the other said, "Here it is," and gave her the sleeve. They continued to watch until the tailor had finished cutting out the dress. Then, in a second, the whole scene vanished, leaving nothing but the tub and the water. "Now," said the gossip, "you can see what a hurry your husband is in to get back to you. You needn't worry about being with child. You have time for another one for that matter." The other, much relieved, threw the sleeve into a trunk she kept by the bed, and they went back to join the company.

The husband, meantime, on his arrival in Seville, had met with friends and relations come from Santo Domingo who talked about the wealth there and suggested he accompany them back and trade his purchases in the island. He took their advice, went to Santo Domingo, and was lucky. He returned to Spain, bought more goods, and took ship a second time to Santo Domingo. It was on this trip that the incident took place of the scarlet dress. Having again sold his merchandise he returned yet a third time to Spain, renewed his stock, and this time came home to New Granada. By now the infant had grown into a child, and was living with its mother under guise of being an orphan.

Husband and wife had a fond reunion, and for some days their happiness and amity were unclouded. Then she started asking for this present and for that, and into the asking there crept wisps of jealousy, until the husband grew tired of it. Ill temper at lunch became anger by dinner, for now the wife had passed to veiled hints at the affair in Hispaniola, arousing in him the suspicion that some friend in the island had been telling tales. At length he gave in and began pampering her, in the hope of discovering who had betrayed him. There came a night when, as they sat dining together in genial mood, his wife asked him to treat her to a new green skirt with trimmings. This was too much, and he began making excuses, at which she remarked, "I bet if it were a present for the lady in Santo Domingo, like the scarlet dress, you wouldn't be making a fuss."

Confirmed in his fears and anxious now to know all, he gave her the skirt and other bits of finery, which made her well content. At length, one afternoon when both were again in good mood, he said to her, "Tell me, wife, who told you I had given a scarlet dress to a lady in Hispaniola." "You are not going to deny it, are you?" she replied. "You tell me the truth, and I'll tell you how I know." "Wife, it is true. When a man is far from home and in a strange land, he must have some amusement. I did give a lady such a dress." "And tell me," she asked him, "when the tailor was cutting it out, was there a sleeve missing?" "Why, so there was. He forgot to cut one sleeve, and had to get an extra piece of material." "Would you know the sleeve again if you saw it?" "Have you got it?" asked the husband. "Come with me and you'll see." They went to the trunk, and from the bottom of it she took out the sleeve. "Is this it?" "Indeed, wife, it is. And I swear to God I'm going to find out who brought it from Hispaniola to Santa Fé."

He took the sleeve and went off with it to the bishop, he being also chief inquisitor, and told him the whole story. The bishop called the wife before him and took from her a declaration, in which she confessed frankly to the incident of the tub of water. Juana García the Negress likewise confessed everything, and told in addition how it was she who had put up the notice about the drowning of the two *oidores*. Her statement implicated various other women, and report had it that quite a number were caught in the net, ladies of quality among them. In the end Jiménez de Quesada himself waited on the bishop with other citizens of rank and besought him to quash the proceedings, saying that the kingdom was still in its infancy and they must not cast a slur on its fair name.

Such was their insistence that the bishop gave way, refusing only to absolve Juana García. On her he imposed as penance that she stand on a raised platform in Santo Domingo church at the hour of high mass with a halter round her neck and a lighted candle in her hand. And there she lamented amid her sobs, "We were all in it, all of us, and I alone am made to pay!" She and her daughters were forbidden to set foot more in New Granada. In her confession she had revealed that when she went to Bermuda, at the time of the sinking of the flagship, she took wing from the hill behind the church of Nuestra Señora de las Nieves, where the cross stands; and for long afterward this was known as Juana García Hill.

13

JUAN DE MELÉNDEZ

If Sor Juana Inés de la Cruz can be seen as representing the New American Woman, so far in advance of her times, Saint Rose of Lima, on the contrary, represents the submissive female, the culmination of centuries of Christian womanhood. She was the first saint to be born in the New World, and a proof for the faithful that God also dwelt on this side of the Atlantic. She was born in 1586 and died in 1617. Her external life was nothing. Everything was in her inner struggle to conquer flesh, in her total devotion to the main task of giving testimony, through the most exquisite pain, to God's grace. She used her poor tortured body as a stage for the continuous performance of a solipsistic play: The Imitation of Christ.

But it is not her "real" life that must concern us here: it is her life as seen by the eyes of Juan de Meléndez, a seventeenth-century Peruvian friar who left in a book of prodigies, *True Treasures of the Indies,* the chronicle of her sufferings and eternal glory. It is Meléndez's pious text that introduced Saint Rose of Lima into Spanish American literature and transformed the real saint into a medieval character, freshly copied from the Golden Legend. In retelling her life, Meléndez accepted, matter-of-factly, the marvelous (mosquitoes that avoid biting her flesh or making any noise to disturb her meditations) and even the miraculous. In his text, if not in real life, sadism and masochism combine to produce beatitude.

Saint Rose of Lima

From The Green Continent, *edited by Germán Arciniegas, and translated by Harriet de Onís (New York: Knopf, 1967), pp. 184–93.*

That the city of Lima, the mart and metropolis of the vast and powerful kingdoms of Peru, might have nothing to envy the rest of the world, there was born there around the year 1586 one of the most extraordinary women the New or the Old World has ever seen: Rosa de Santa Maria. The Church was then under the rule of His Holiness Sixtus V, and the Kingdom of Spain under His Majesty Philip II.

She was born in the month of April, the month of the joys of spring, when the flowers unfasten the green button that has been holding them close, to adorn and celebrate May. This Rose was born to be the ornament of the May of the Church of my religion and of its blossoming and pleasant gardens. Her felicitous birth took place on the twentieth of April, when the heavens and the stars are in their most peaceful and auspicious conjunction and the waters flow most crystalline and clear, the winds are most gentle and restrained, when the earth brings forth new plants and flowers, and the heat of the fire on high is still tempered.

Her parents were Gaspar Flores and Maria de la Oliva. Her father was born in the city of Puerto Rico of the Windward Islands, in the domain of Hispaniola; her mother, in the city of Lima itself. They were of respectable and honest origin, though not overblessed with worldly goods. But by the designs of Providence they were endowed with far greater riches, with the incomparable treasure and priceless jewel of such a daughter.

Close beside the Hospital of the Espíritu Santo, in Santo Domingo Street, lived her father when the Virgin Rose was born. Here we see the happy augury of the ardent spirit she was to inherit from her glorious father Santo Domingo, which would enable her to achieve thirty-three years of triumph over nature, with the help of grace, in silent struggles between the spirit and the flesh, following from so early an age the path of such extreme perfection; treading the straight road of virtue with all the power and breath of her life, with that joy and happiness in its progress which we shall contemplate and admire.

From childhood everything in the Virgin Rose was love, and for this reason she went to the lengths she did. She had no fear of suffering, because she had no fear of loving. She began her discipline with the severity with which others end, because she began with a love which is to be found in few. She grew in years and in love, in fasting, mortification, and penitence. When she entered upon her new obligations in the Third Order of Santo Domingo, she employed new forms of discipline. Out of two iron chains she made a scourge, and to follow in the steps of our Father Santo Domingo, she flagellated herself every night until her blood watered the ground. She followed a plan in these bloody scourgings, setting forth the end for which they were employed: one night for her many and great sins, providing they were not mortal or among the graver venial sins; another night for public calamities, to appease the wrath of God, temper His justice, and implore His mercy; another night, and this most frequently, for the misfortunes of the Church, offering herself as the victim, being merciless with herself so that God might take pity on the state of the Church and cure its wounds with hers.

Another night for the kingdoms of Peru and her beloved natal city of Lima, in the hope that the Divine Bridegroom, beholding her back bathed in blood, would remember that He had suffered likewise for us, and that His mercy, which the many sins of its dwellers had benumbed, would be aroused at the sight of the severity of her discipline and He would not visit His wrath upon the city. Another night for the souls of the departed in Purgatory, in the hope that her blood might slake that raging, devouring fire. Her love and discipline were spurred on by the desire to bring them some comfort in their burning torment, and she poured out streams of blood in the hope that the great quantity of blood might extinguish the great fires.

Another night for the dying, so that in that dangerous but inevitable transaction they might have the aid and succor of Heaven, which all those in that state so greatly need, for all eternity hangs on a moment's repentance. Another night for those in mortal sin, that God might give them light and knowledge of their miserable and perilous state, the more perilous because they are sure to be lost and their souls lost if they are not reconciled in time to God. She asked this with many voices because her desire was so great, and to this end she furrowed and laid open her flesh with the greatest severity until she was become Job the patient and Lazarus the beggar, without friends to console her or dogs to lick her wounds. What pious impiety! To endanger her life to win souls for God, seeking their conversion with her own blood! The scourgings she gave herself were cruel, and applied with greatest harshness to those parts of her body most sensitive to pain.

The Crown of Thorns

In order to know many kinds of suffering, the Virgin Rose tried to make herself a crown; and as all the just seek, with pious ambition, a crown of thorns in this life, leaving the crown of gold for the other, this aspiration, which is fortuitous in others, was very natural to our Rose. Because what rose is there, or has there ever been, that is not crowned with thorns? The rose and the thorns that are to crown it are born together. The thorns remain blunt until the rose bursts its green bud. Little by little it breaks through the narrow prison cell of its leaves, and the thorns grow finer and sharper. The Virgin Rose was born and at the same time the blunt thorns of the Rose; she began to free herself from the first afflictions of nature and began to give off the sweetest fragrance of virtue. The thorns grew and the Rose grew because with the passing of the years her penitence increased. She had come to love crowns since once when her friends had put a garland of flowers upon her head; she put a pin in it, so the Rose might never be without thorns, and the pin pierced her brow. From that time she vowed in her heart to make a crown that should serve as a penitence, because the one she put on that time had done very well. These desires had been engendered by experience and love; and her grief at beholding a sorrowful image of an *Ecce Homo* so strengthened them that she immediately put them into effect. She looked at the image, pity filled her and sorrow and gratitude, and her heart was afflicted to see that precious head pierced with thorns. And she said with great emotion: "Why should I be so delicate a member, when Thy head is so severely wounded and pierced?" And moved by this tender consideration, she made herself a crown of tin, interlaced with string to which she tied some little nails on the side that was to rest against her head. She put it on, the nails pierced her temples, and it pleased her so much that she never again took it off—if not this same one, another like it—from the day she put it on until she died. Death took away her life and her crown, so that God might crown her life with a better life, and her crown with a better crown.

As tin is a soft metal, and obedient to the hands, it lacked that firmness that the Virgin Rose needed to hold the nails in place, for they would come loose and not wound her as she wanted them to do. She decided to make one of harder, stronger metal and found silver to be the best, both because of its cleanliness as well as for the purpose she had in mind. She ordered a narrow strip of silver to be beaten out and three rows of nails to be soldered into the strip itself. Each row was to have thirty-three nails to commemorate the years of Christ Our Lord, making ninety-nine nails all together, and this crown she wore with great delight of her heart.

And because her hair might interfere and prevent the nails from piercing her head as she wished, she shaved off all her hair, and this she did whenever it grew back, leaving a few locks on her forehead to cover the crown, for the rest of it was covered by her wimple, so she was a crowned victim under the folds of her wimple. It is difficult to understand or even conceive the pain and suffering she underwent with this strange penitence. How it wounded her delicate head! How sharply the nails pierced her! If one alone was more than enough to pierce her brain, what would so many do and so close together? It was not as though the pain were confined to her temples, forehead, and brain, for as all the senses and acts of the body are dependent upon that higher force by which they are governed, all the members and parts of the body feel the pains suffered by the head. From this fact comes the proverb that when the head suffers, all the body suffers. Her eyes felt it most because of their proximity; then her mouth, talking or eating; her breast when she coughed; so that every natural movement she made was one of torture and martyrdom.

Ninety-nine strong immovable nails pierced her delicate head day and night; and to this cruel martyrdom she added still another.

Every day she changed the crown around so the nails would open new wounds each day. On Fridays she pushed it toward the back so it would encircle her ears, which, after her eyes, were the most sensitive part, and there she would leave it until Sunday, thus accompanying the Blessed Virgin, the mother of anguish and suffering, who lies pierced with grief at the foot of the cross. A tender and devout meditation for the day! She kept this mortification hidden from the eyes of her parents, her brothers and sisters, and the other members of the household for a long time, for it did not occur to them that under the folds of her wimple the prudent virgin had such a fierce torment concealed. Only her confessor knew about the crown, but he did not know what kind of crown she wore. He did not know about the nails or the things she thought of to make the pain of her penitence greater. She never gave him a clear account of it nor did she explain how she had come to make such a strange invention. But Divine Providence, whom every creature obeys, did not permit silence to lock away a thing so marvelous and rare; and breaking down the walls that imprisoned it, let it be known of all for its own honor and glory and the great credit of its omnipotence.

Fervent Exercise of Prayer

In her early years, when the only study of children of that age is how to amuse and entertain one another, since it is the natural condition of childhood to play together, for this is all their concern and occupation, the neighbors of the Virgin Rose came with their dolls and played with them and dressed and undressed them, with that instinct for beautification they display so early. They called to the Blessed Girl and coaxed her to bring hers out; she excused herself, saying she had none, nor did she want them, either. "But why don't you want them?" asked one of her neighbors. And she answered: "Because they say the Devil sometimes talks through the mouth of dolls." And this was true, because most of the idols worshiped by the Indians look like dolls. All the little girls in the neighborhood were absorbed in playing with their dolls while the wise little Rose thought only of how to slip away from them and withdraw to the secret place of her house where she could pray and commend her soul to God. Her brothers and sisters, who amused themselves and played with the other children of their age, often missed her. One of them, seeing that she had slipped away from the games and was not to be found anywhere, went to look for her. He found her in a room full of dust and rubbish in the cellar, where she sat in a corner by herself praying. He began to laugh at her and tease her, saying: "Sister, is it better to sit amongst this rubbish and dirt, alone and hidden, than to play with the other girls with your dolls?" To this she answered with a prudence and judgment not to be expected of one of her tender years: "Leave me alone here with my God, for I know that He is here, and I do not know whether He would like to be where the dolls are."

Solitude

This tender love of solitude grew in her as she grew in years. She was now older, and was entering upon new obligations, free now from those of childhood. She asked an older brother, called Fernando, to build her a shrine and a little altar among some banana trees that grew in the garden beside the walls that encircled it. But it was to be done so secretly that the family should neither see it nor know about it. He told her he would and immediately set to work at it as his sister had desired and requested, covering it all over with banana fronds, and this was easy to do, for the altar was small and the leaves are so large that they are sometimes two yards long and two-thirds of a yard wide. He put a cross on it painted in many colors, and beside it many pictures of saints to keep it company, and he arranged it so it could be used as an oratory in keeping with the wishes of his sister Rose.

It seemed to her that in this little piece of ground which she had consecrated to her solitude all the pleasures and delights of the world were to be found. She did not want to leave it all day long. All the time she had left from her work, her duties in the house, and sleep she spent in the garden, at the altar praying, and this was her conversation, her play, and her amusement. She lived apart from all, yet living with all; like David, who being with many was with none, and, like an angel in human flesh, praised God at all hours. She grew so fond of this little retreat that it became her center of existence and she was ill at ease, as though lost, when she was not there. She knew no greater moment of pleasure than when she was at prayer in her shrine. "If you want to find Rose go look for her in the garden," her family would say; you will not find her anywhere else because the Blessed Girl was nowhere else.

Rose and the Mosquitoes

At night, especially when the sky was serene and the wind blew stronger after the sun had departed from the horizon, many more mosquitoes came, seeking refuge in her cell. But the senseless little beasts were so polite that they made no noise nor bit her.

If her mother or some other visitor came to see her they bit their hands and faces so much they had to go home, so much did they suffer from the bites and the swelling they caused. They were amazed to see that in spite of the army of mosquitoes by which she was surrounded, Rose had no marks on her hands or face. They spoke of this to her and she smiled and answered: "When I moved into this house the mosquitoes and I made a friendly agreement: I would not bother them or drive them away and they would not bite me or make a noise; and we live in such friendship that they neither bite nor annoy me; on the contrary, they help me to praise the Lord with the hum of their buzzing." And this really took place, for as the first rays of dawn appeared, she would open the door and window and say to all the mosquitoes: "Come, my friends, let's praise God, let's praise God."

They would come out, obedient to the Virgin Rose's voice, and grouping their squadrons as in a choir, some of them would intone a gentle buzzing and others would answer them, and the sound of their buzzing made so gentle and pleasant a music that it seemed as though they had the gift of reason. She sent them out to seek their food, the choir and the music ceased, and they departed. They would return in the evening and she would say to them: "Now, friends, it would be good for you to sing God's praises with me before we go to bed, for He has cared for you today and He cares for us all." They formed a choir the same as in the morning and began the sonorous music of their noisy buzzing, but in such perfect time and rhythm that it seemed as though they were trying to make a most agreeable harmony. Then she would tell them to be quiet and go to sleep; they would obey without making another sound all night.

Rose's Birds

Accustomed now to the plants' obeying her, submissively doing as she bid them, she wanted the birds to obey in the same way. It was easy for her to achieve this, for all animals render obedience to whoever serves the Lord truly and with a pure and perfect heart, as the ardent voice, aflame with charity, of Saint Francis of Paul asserts. A year before she died, being a guest of the Treasurer, Don Gonzalo de la Maza, this singular thing happened throughout one Lent: She would sit with her work beside a window which overlooked the greater part of the beautiful garden of the Treasurer, in which there was a huge tree that gave it shade. Every night, an hour before evening prayers, a bird came and sat on a branch in view of Rose, whetting its beak, fluttering its wings, and breaking into gentle warblings. Rose left her work and sang to it:

> Come, little nightingale,
> Let us praise the Lord.
> Raise a song to your Creator,
> I shall sing unto my Savior.

The stanza had metrical defects, but although many saints have composed elegant verse, the ardor of the spirit often pays little attention to the correction of the syllables but seeks the harmony of the feelings. The spirit does not work for the perfection of the meter, but only that the words may tell its love.

The Saint Sings

The Virgin Rose sang and sang well, for she had an excellent voice and could modulate it in trills, arpeggios, and changes of tone. When she stopped, the nightingale began. For this bird not only sings, but has taught human beings its art, for it loves them tenderly and only displays the full gamut of its talents when it knows they are listening. When the nightingale had completed its harmony, the Rose entered, breaking her silence, and they sang to each other in turn, so beautifully and rhythmically that all who heard them marveled. This sweet melody of music and singing lasted for a whole hour, because it began when the sun was going down. As night closed in, the nightingale departed, and the Virgin Rose closed her window, a mourning dove that before was a gay linnet, pouring forth sad lamentations to the Lord:

> How shall I love You, my God
> When I am but Your creature
> And You my Creator?

In gentle lament she poured forth the burning desires of her heart to His Majesty, to whom the music and concert were directed every afternoon, for the nightingale came daily to help her sing, obedient to her command, like the trees and the flowers. And the lamentation and pleasure went hand in hand, for even in the most spiritual persons, like this one, joy is never complete and as a rule sorrow walks beside delight. And she bemoaned the absence of those divine ardors with which to follow the ascent of love until she should be consumed in them. But she contemplated her lowliness, the lowliness of a being whose love, however much it ascends, has limits beyond which it cannot pass. She longed to love God with the love with which His Divine Majesty loves Himself, and she piteously lamented this impossible struggle, seeing how her love was finite and that of God infinite.

Then she turned to those who had been drawn by the new music, who were the members of the household and many from outside, gathered together by this unusual prodigy, and continued her laments:

> The little bird departs and leaves me,
> Flying away in the night,
> But my God remains beside me,
> Blessed be His name.

Then she withdrew to continue in sweet colloquies the occasion of her song and her sad lament in the oratory, toward which all her thoughts and actions were directed. She pondered greatly how a little bird without the gift of reason praised its Creator, and accompanied her with its music, merely because she told it to do so; and how men, supposedly endowed with reason, persuaded and obliged by all the tongues God has given them and the manifold reasons for praising Him, neither heed the one nor fulfill the other, deaf to the example and exhortation of creatures devoid of reason. As she burned in a fire of divine love, she would have burned the hearts of all, like the seraphic virgin Saint Catherine, so that they might serve, praise, and glorify Him who by so many rights deserves to be served and reverenced.

14

FRANCISCO NÚÑEZ DE PINEDA Y BASCUÑÁN

Pineda was the son of a Spanish conquistador. He was twenty-two when he was captured by the Araucans in Chile in 1629, and for several months he was in the hands of those fierce warriors of whom Ercilla had sung in his epic poem (see selection 9). Unexpectedly, Pineda was treated well by the Indians: he was exhibited in several places as a prized possession and eventually was ransomed. Unlike many of his contemporaries, he came to admire and respect his captors. Perhaps his schooling with the Jesuits had prepared him for this understanding, which one century earlier was achieved by only Las Casas and Ercilla. But in the seventeenth century, as Father Vieira's *Sermons* prove (see selection 16), the Jesuits had come to the defense of the Indians.

Twenty years after Pineda was ransomed, he wrote the book of his experiences, *The Happy Captivity and the Reasons of the Numerous Wars of Chile.* (It was not published until 1863.) Although the adventures he was telling had really happened to him, by the time Pineda started writing, fiction had taken over completely. The protagonist is presented according to the heroic prototype of the popular romances of chivalry. The Araucans are also cast in the same mold. Dialogues are elaborated in a literary fashion and without any attempt to present the way real Indians talked. The narrative is closer to Ercilla's epic poem than to a purely historical chronicle. Recalling his adventures, Pineda describes in this fragment how he escaped, thanks to divine inspiration, a fate worse than death. His testimony runs quite counter to the normal attitude of Spaniards toward native women. They generally did not refuse them in the honorable terms Pineda did; rather they were known for seeking them under any pretext. Even priests were susceptible to their rustic charms, and in one of the chronicles of the Spanish settlements in Paraguay, a virtuous witness went so far as to call the country "Mohammed's Paradise," for the polygamous life the Spaniards had established. But Pineda's narrative bears testimony that at least one Spaniard in thousands was truly chaste.

The Happy Captivity

From Spanish American Literature in Translation, *edited by Willis Knapp Jones, and translated by Connie Wick (New York: Frederick Ungar, 1966), I, pp. 79–81.*

That night was given over to dancing and festivities with which they are accustomed to follow their plowing and their planting, and since the sun had set, my companion remained with us. The chief, Quilalebo, who was giving the feast, celebrated his arrival with more than usual ceremony, because he was truly ostentatious and gallant in his actions. After we had feasted splendidly, the old chiefs, the one from Villarrica, and I went to the fire where the dance had already begun. The chiefs begged me to dance with them, and I did so to please them. In the midst of this entertainment, Quilalebo, my new friend, brought his daughter to me, who was among those dancing. He brought her and some of the other girls to where we were watching and told her to take my hand and dance with me because he had given her to me as my wife. The rest of the chiefs chose among those girls who had accompanied Quilalebo's daughter and began dancing hand in hand with them. At the persuasion of her father and the rest of the ancient chiefs, I did the same thing after the girls toasted us. That is what the unmarried girls are accustomed to doing when they want the unmarried men to dance with them, or when they wish to flatter the old chiefs. And in this way they frequently find husbands at these feasts and dances, which they call "gnapitun."

On this occasion the girl's mother came to where we were standing, and engaged in conversation. She offered me a jar of clear, sweet corn liquor from the earthen jugs that Chief Lepumante had sent for me. She treated me as her son-in-law, signifying that she was happy that her husband, Quilalebo, had given her daughter to me. She was one of the principal ladies of Valdivia, and said her child was the granddaughter of one of the ancient conquistadors. At that time she told me his name, but since it did not matter to me that she had been involved with one of those barbarians, I did not try to remember the name. I took advantage of the occasion to tell her about the obstacles which prevented my marrying her daughter. I gave her polite and agreeable reasons, repeating what I had previously told the girl. Since she was an understanding woman, even though primitive in language, dress, and customs, she told me that my reasons seemed just, but nevertheless, her husband had wanted me to entertain and dance hand in hand with his daughter. The old lady took one of her daughter's hands and one of mine, and between the two of them, showing my excitement and happiness, I did what the rest of the people were doing. And although I was present in body, because I could not help it, in the midst of these dancers, my spirit and heart remained in God's presence as I sought His help and guidance which He bestows mercifully to those who fear and love Him. For this is the doctrine of Saint Paul.

15

JUSTO MANSILLA and SIMÓN MACETA

Less well known than the Spanish conquistadors or the North American pioneers, the Brazilian bandeirantes deserve, for better or for worse, at least the same ambiguous reputation. They were men that followed the flag, or ensign *(bandeira)*, and opened up in the late sixteenth and early seventeenth centuries the vast interior of Brazil. In achieving their aims, they extended the Portuguese domains into the Spanish heart of the continent. They clashed not only with the Spanish settlers but with the Jesuits, who had already started to organize the Indians in missions *ad majorem Dei gloriam.*

The Jesuits did not accept the bandeirantes' sense of destiny; they saw them as brutal and greedy spoilers. According to them, the bandeirantes were forcing the Indians into slavery (which was forbidden by both Spanish and Portuguese law) and drastically uprooting them from their natural habitat to resettle them in São Paulo and on the Atlantic coast. Like Las Casas, the Jesuits wrote passionate pleas in defense of the Indians.

The document here transcribed was addressed in 1629 to Philip IV of

Spain by two priests: Justo Mansilla van Tuerck, a Fleming, and Simón Maceta, an Italian. They had been appointed by their superior, Antonio Ruiz de Montoya, to accompany the bandeirantes and their several thousand captives to São Paulo to dispute the mass kidnapping with the Portuguese authorities of the colony. For a less critical view of the bandeirantes than that presented here, it is possible to invoke later testimonies, such as the one written by a Benedictine friar, Brother Gaspar da Madre de Deus, that absolves the bandeirantes and in turn accuses the Jesuits themselves of tyrannizing the Indians under the pretext of saving their souls. Brother Gaspar's arguments found later comic echoes in Chapter 14 of Voltaire's *Candide* (1759). From a modern point of view, and with tongue somewhat in cheek, Professor Morse has observed: "On anthropological grounds one can argue indeed that the nomadic life of the hundreds, even thousands of Indian slaves and servants who might accompany a bandeira conformed more closely to their aboriginal ways than did their regulated existence in the Jesuit stockades, engaging in intensive agriculture, learning the catechism, and, it is said, being awakened at night by the church bell to perform their conjugal duties."

Atrocities of the Bandeirantes

From The Bandeirantes, *edited and translated by Richard M. Morse (New York: Knopf, 1965), pp. 82–91.*

An account of the injuries perpetrated by certain citizens and inhabitants of the town of São Paulo de Piratininga of the captaincy of São Vicente of the state of Brazil in plundering the settlements of the Fathers of the Company of Jesus in the mission of Guairá and Plains of the Iguaçu in the jurisdiction of Paraguay with exceeding contempt for the Holy Gospel in the year 1629.

Rendered by the Fathers Justo Mansilla and Simón Maceta of the Company of Jesus, who were in these very settlements when they were plundered by the Portuguese, and who accompanied them to São Paulo, following their parishioners, and continued to Bahia, where they pleaded for the latter's liberty and for redress in the future before the Governor General Diogo Luís de Oliveira.

For forty years the inhabitants of São Paulo have flouted the laws of the King Our Lord with no regard for them, nor for their great offense against God, nor for the punishment they deserve. In their raids they continually capture and carry off by force of arms free and emancipated Indians, whom they keep for their own slaves or sell. Lately their boldness has been even greater than in years past, and for two principal reasons: first, this time they have gone out in greater numbers than ever, emboldened by the little or no punishment inflicted on them for their continual and unjust entradas in the past; second, they have assaulted the reductions of the Fathers of the Company of Jesus of the Province of Paraguay and taken all the people whom we were instructing.

With regard to the first point: In the beginning of the month of August 1628, some nine hundred Portuguese left the town of São Paulo with muskets, swords, cotton armor, bucklers, machetes, and much ammunition of shot and powder, and other arms. They were accompanied by two thousand two hundred Indians, unjustly taken captive on previous occasions, and also among them were the two judges of the same town of São Paulo, Sebastião Fernandes Camacho and Francisco de Paiva; two aldermen, Maurício de Castilho and Diogo Barbosa; the Procurator of the Town Council, Cristóvão Mendes; and the son, son-in-law, and brother of Amador Bueno, the senior judge of the town. And from the town of Santa Ana de Parnaíba, which is seven leagues from São Paulo, came Captain André Fernandes and the judge Pedro Álvares, his son-in-law. Thus there remained in São Paulo only twenty-five men who could bear arms, not counting the old men who could not go because of their age.

Dividing all these men into four companies, their captains and other officers of war hoisted their flags as if they had arisen and mutinied against your Royal Crown. The flags which they carried did not bear the arms of the King, but different insignia. Antônio Rapôso Tavares was declared captain major of the Company, and he took Bernardo de Sousa as his lieutenant and Manuel Morato as his sergeant, and for captain of his advance guard he took Antônio Pedroso and of his rear guard Salvador Pires. The captains of the other companies were Pedro Vaz de Barros, Brás Leme, and André Fernandes.

As field master of all the companies went Manuel Prêto, author of all these raids. . . .

With regard to the second point: The men of the company of Antônio Rapôso Tavares, who committed these injuries which we are recording here, had said many times before setting out from São Paulo that they had decided to plunder and destroy our settlements, and thus they purposely took the route to the Plains of the Iguaçu. Here, far removed from the towns of the Spaniards and isolated in these lonely regions, where twelve reductions or Indian settlements have already been built and others, for lack of priests, merely planned, we were settling and instructing the Indians in their own lands with infinite toil and lack of necessities, being content to carry on for the love of God and for the salvation of those heathen. We suffered the poverty of the land in food and dress, planting vineyards and sowing wheat so as to have the host and wine for saying Mass.

When these bandits, then, had crossed the River Tibajiva on the eighth of September of that same year 1628, they built their palisade or fort of wooden stakes close by our villages. And—to show clearly the intention they had from the beginning—Antônio Pedroso, Captain of the advance guard of this Company, as soon as he arrived in these parts chanced upon some seventeen Christian

Indians from our settlement of Encarnación on the Ñatingui, who had left their wives and children in the village under the protection of the Fathers and gone to the woods to collect mate, which they drink with warm or cold water after grinding it into powder. Pedroso seized them and carried them all off. . . .

Thereafter, although they continued most cruelly to capture the heathen who, for lack of Fathers, had not yet been settled in reductions, wounding, killing, and mangling many old caciques and unbaptized children, they left us in peace with our wards for four months; and we treated them with friendliness, for in this way, although we could not arrest the many evils they were committing, we at least protected our reductions as best we could and those Indians who were again coming to us. And when it was necessary to dispatch some Indians of our village elsewhere we simply gave them a note begging the Portuguese to let them pass as our own sons; thus we treated the thief as a loyal friend, and they let them pass. Furthermore the Fathers went now and again to their palisade and baptized the children and the sick (for there were many afflicted with pox) to save them from eternal captivity since they could not be saved from the temporal one. The Portuguese themselves also sent for Father Pedro [Mola], who was in the village of San Antonio, a day's journey from their palisade, to confess a Portuguese who was dying, although God would not allow it, depriving him of speech and reason the whole time the Father remained with him.

This false peace lasted until a very great cacique called Tatabrana who had many vassals—and whom Simão Álvares, a citizen of São Paulo, had unjustly captured a few years previously but who, desiring his freedom, soon fled and returned to his lands—came to deliver himself with all his people to the same Father Mola. They were Christians whom we had won over, shortly before the Portuguese entered those parts, by gifts and celebrations given in their honor when they entered our villages to see us, attracted by the good word which had gone forth concerning the peace and contentment enjoyed by the Indians who lived in them with us.

Then the Portuguese, thinking that they now had some pretext to carry out their wicked intention, sent to ask the Father for Tatabrana. And as the Father replied that he could not be turned over to them since he was free and in his own lands, they advised Captain Major Antônio Rapôso Tavares requesting his approval, and then, on the thirtieth of January, 1629, they came to take by force not only Tatabrana but also all the others whom the Father was instructing in the village of San Antonio. Thus, as they themselves admit, they took from it four thousand Indians or burden bearers along with a crowd of others, and they destroyed the entire village burning many houses, plundering the church and the Father's house, and desecrating an image of Our Lady. With great violence they removed the Indian men and women who had taken refuge in the Father's house, and they killed an Indian at the very door of the house, as well as another ten or twelve persons in the same village. They took most of the Father's meager belongings, including a few shirts, two blankets, shoes, hats, napkins, tablecloths, spoons, knives, ten or twelve iron wedges, and six or seven chickens that he had. They killed one of three cows they found, and took other small things. . . .

What is of gravest concern in this whole affair is that the Holy Gospel is now so disesteemed and its Preachers so discredited that—with the door now completely closed to the preaching of the Gospel among all those heathen—the Indians imagine and repeat that we did not gather them to teach them the law of God, as we told them, but to deliver them by this subterfuge to the Portuguese. They also say that we tricked them by telling them so often that they were safe with us and that the Portuguese, being Christians and vassals of the same king, would not touch nor harm those who were with the Fathers, for they were then Christians and children of God. Therefore, since an action so atrocious goes unpunished and with no effective remedy, it seems to me that we shall be forced to abandon all these heathen, whom year after year we have been gathering together and instructing by order of His Holiness and His Majesty with so much labor and hardship. . . .

And so that the multitude of the infidels which was already disposed to settle with the Fathers and embrace the Holy Faith may be better appreciated: In the village of Jesús María alone, Father Concovado had almost five thousand warriors not counting their crowd of women and little ones. Besides this, the caciques of Caayu . . . saw that because of the lack of Fathers (who, in villages as densely populated as those, were almost all distributed one by one) they could not achieve their good hopes of having priests in their lands to instruct them; so they themselves with their vassals went to the village of San Antonio, just recently plundered, to be there with the Father. They had not known of the shameless action of the Portuguese there, but when they saw the village destroyed, the houses burned and so many killed, they returned to their lands and now, from what they have seen, imagine that we are traitors and deceivers, and that we have secret intelligence with these Portuguese. And therefore, as some Indians who met these people on a journey have affirmed to us, many of them are now traveling in a band looking for Fathers to kill them. . . .

What we saw along the route [to São Paulo] was the inhumanity and cruelty with which [the Portuguese] treated the Indians. For the poor creatures were overworked and sick at heart to find themselves slaves with little hope of regaining their liberty. Against their will and resistance they were leaving their lands where they had lived most contentedly and amid great plenty; and they now had to cross many rivers, swamps, lakes, and mountains, making this long march on forty consecutive days from the palisade to São Paulo, carrying their little ones on their backs, seeing them turn sick and die from hunger, cold, exertions, the maltreatment of the Portuguese, and the rigors of the journey. They ate only the little that the Portuguese sometimes gave them, stolen from their own farms and plots, or else what they themselves had to search for in the forests and woods, fatigued from the day's journey—although not all were permitted to do this for fear they would escape. Besides all this, the Portuguese loaded them with their burdens, and many caciques as well as vassals (especially those from our reductions) were taken in chains to São Paulo. All day they were scolded and at night the Portuguese kept them from sleeping, wearing them out with constant shouting and sermonizing which they themselves did or ordered their Tupi to do, or else some of the recently captured caciques. The latter were on the one hand promised, to discourage their escaping, that they would have a very good life, both temporal and spiritual, with their houses and lands in São Paulo (as if perpetual captivity could be designated a life), and, on the other hand, the Indians were threatened that if they fled they would be killed, and in fact when someone did run away they sent their Tupi after him, and when he was brought back he was cruelly whipped. . . .

Two Indians whom the Portuguese released to us after persistent importunities assert that when the Portuguese left the palisade they set fire to the huts and settlements, burning with them some of the aged and infirm, and, if some did manage to escape so as not to die in the flames, the Tupi in the presence of their masters forced them to return to the fire to expire in it. In this regard we might say here that the cruelty of the Tupi was no less than that of their masters and that they no less deserve to be punished than the Portuguese. . . .

But let us return to the Portuguese and consider the wiles they employ to deceive the courts and avoid the punishment which they deserve. This does not require much effort, for they have as companions in crime not only all the people of São Paulo but also the very judges and administrator of the council of this same town. However, so that they might have a way of deceiving the higher magistrates of the state (if it can be called deceit, against persons who witness enough cases of the constant entradas, carried out with so many wrongs and cruelties, to have no illusions about such clear and open deceits), they requested I know not what sort of legal writs. Thus Pedro Vaz de Barros obtained one to pursue some who had already set out to capture Indians and to make them return. But this was only so that he and his companions might accompany them under this pretext.

André Fernandes, a great killer and flayer of Indians, carried a similar license. Judge Francisco de Paiva obtained another writ from the Holy Office of the Inquisition authorizing him to search for a heretic who he said had taken refuge in those wilds. And in this highhanded manner he accompanied Pedro Vaz de Barros as if this were the real matter at hand, and taking advantage of this trick he had it announced that all the members of this entrada carried a license from the inquisitor.

All of them are well aware, and confess it, that what they do is against the law of God and of His Royal Majesty, who has prohibited it so many times by his laws and ordinances under threat of most severe penalties.

But to excuse themselves they say that it is the custom in São Paulo to capture and sell Indians, and that King Dom Sebastião has awarded these Indians as slaves, as evident in his law which he passed at Évora on the twentieth of March, 1570 (although this is very far from the truth, for he awarded as slaves only those who might be taken in a just war and by his license). And they say that now the King, because he was ill informed, declared them free men and emancipated, and that it seems that in this matter the magistrates dissemble, for the punishments set by the laws are never exacted. On the contrary, they say that all of them receive pardon from Bahia whenever they go out to capture Indians.

And they said that this is also the case now, and that they had pardon for all the soldiers by paying His Majesty with one Indian of every six. However, the captains are to appear in Bahia until they obtain another more favorable decision, which, as they said, they would soon receive.

. . . In past years there were governors of this state who instead of punishing the culprits, as they were obliged to do, ordered them to set aside the royal fifth, as if the captives were gold taken from His Majesty's mines. . . . In São Paulo when they returned this time we saw that each one went to make an agreement with the official of the region and to offer him some of the Indians brought as captives. And thereupon, after committing so many abominations, they were well received. For if this were not the case it would not be possible, not only for Christians or those who call themselves Christians, but even for Turks or Moors or infidels, to dare to act against the laws of their king with such liberty and audacity as do the inhabitants of São Paulo. Certainly no one could imagine such a thing if he did not see it with his own eyes, for the whole life of these bandits is merely going to and returning from the sertão, going and bringing captives with all that cruelty, death, and pillage and then selling them as if they were pigs. . . . These bandits have other pretexts, and say that they bring the Indians into the church, as if God wished any infidel to be forced or captured to become a Christian. And they readily declared that their intention was merely to bring the Indians into the church when they took them from our reductions, where some were already Christians and others were catechumens receiving our Holy Faith in order to be baptized. Another more deceitful pretext is that they bring them to perform necessary service, and that they know they do wrong bringing them in the manner they do; but they say that there is no other remedy in this land, and that after the Indians arrive they keep them in their houses and on their farms, not as slaves but as free men. The matter would be less serious if it were as they say, and if they did not go about selling them for a bottle of wine or something else for them or their wives and children to eat or wear, as is common knowledge to everyone of this state. However, the truth is that the Indians whom they have in their houses have liberty in name only, and they are used accordingly, as though they were slaves from Guinea. The situation would be quite different in this land if each were content to live according to his condition, and if all did not wish to be hidalgos supporting themselves, their wives, and children with this infamous merchandise acquired by so much theft and pillage. They also offer as a pretext for having plundered our villages this time that the Indians whom we were instructing were subjects of the Crown of Portugal, to which we reply that although the Spanish have more basis for their belief that they belong to the Crown of Castile, since they are close to the Spanish towns of Guairá and Villa Rica and for other reasons, we do not establish our arguments on this point, nor do we attempt to define the limits or boundaries of realms. We merely gather and instruct the Indians in their own lands where we find them, and if they belong now to the Crown of Spain and now to that of Portugal, we do not take them from one to the other. And, all the more, if these Indians belong to the Crown of Portugal as the Portuguese claim, why do they dare to capture them in defiance of so many and such explicit laws of His Majesty and the previous kings of Portugal . . . in which it is forbidden to capture the Indians of the state of Brazil or to carry them off by force? And these laws declare all men, Christians and infidels alike, and even those not yet gathered in reductions, to be free and emancipated, as they are by nature. . . .

What we aspire to and came to seek on such long and wearying journeys by land and sea, with such toil and hardship, is some effective remedy for the past and for what is to come. For the past, we feel that there can be no proper satisfaction unless all the captured Indians are given their freedom, and unless all or most of them are returned to their lands and the reductions. In this way they can bear witness to those of their lands that we are innocent, that we did not deliver them to the Portuguese, and that we took measures here to try to secure their freedom. And moreover they can remove the bad opinion which the infidels not yet in reductions have already formed of us of the Company, that we are traitors and deceivers, and thus we would regain the credit which we enjoyed with them and without which it seems impossible to convert them to Our Holy Faith. As for the future, let some very exemplary punishment be fixed, or in some other fashion let an order be given that extortions and enslavements such as the men of São Paulo have carried on for so many years be henceforth prevented. . . .

It is said that simply the band of Antônio Rapôso Tavares, which plundered our villages, carried away as many as twenty thousand souls, and it is therefore certain that if a very genuine remedy is not supplied in the briefest time, they will soon destroy everything and depopulate these populous lands as they have done in most of the state of Brazil. . . .

There were those who for five, and others . . . who for seven continuous years, and even those who for eighteen years neglected their salvation and remained in those wilds capturing Indians and living in concubinage with as many Indian women as they wished. They lived like beasts without thinking of their homes and legitimate wives or hearing Mass or confessing or taking communion in all this time. Those who went on this most recent entrada spent nine months without observing Advent, Lent, and Resurrection, or fulfilling their obligations to Our Holy Mother Church. Therefore if some remedy is not found to halt these entradas, it appears that we might as well forget all of our remaining reductions and all those numerous and countless heathen for whose conversion the King Our Lord not only sends us from Europe with so many expenses but also sustains us among the Indians with his royal alms. . . .

In this City of Salvador Bahia de Todos os Santos, October 10, 1629.

16

ANTÔNIO VIEIRA

Father Antônio Vieira, a baroque counterpart of Las Casas, came strongly to the defense of the Brazilian Indians in some of his most eloquent *Sermons* and *Letters*. Like his Spanish predecessor, Vieira was born in Europe (Lisbon, 1608) but had, perhaps, a touch of the New World in his blood: one of his grandmothers was a descendant of a black slave brought to Portugal from either Africa or Brazil. He was only six years old when his family moved to Bahia, then the administrative center of the colony. He attended the Jesuit school and soon was singled out by his teachers. He was sixteen when the Dutch, expanding their attacks on the Portuguese empire, occupied Bahia in 1624. This terrible experience fortified Vieira's determination to defend his native country and its prized colonies against Protestant invaders. He was ordained a priest in 1634.

From the very beginning of his career, he had been deeply interested in the peaceful conversion of the natives. He studied their general language (Tupí-Guaraní) and went on a mission among their tribes. Like Father Mansilla and Father Maceta, he was horrified by the brutality of the Portuguese settlers toward the Indians. Yet he accepted, as a lesser evil, the exploitation and slavery of blacks. This distinction was normal for his time; even Las Casas had held such a view—its rationale being that the blacks had been, allegedly, sold to the Europeans by their kings, and therefore were "legitimately" in slavery. Only quite late in his career, in a letter addressed to the King of Portugal (April 20, 1657), did Vieira indicate that he was also opposed to the injustice done to the blacks.

The settlers, however, never bothered to make any such distinction: they were determined to exploit both Indians and blacks impartially, and fought the Jesuits as fiercely as did the bandeirantes (see selection 15).

In 1641, Vieira went back to Portugal to plead his cause in a higher tribunal. He soon became famous as a preacher, and King João IV made him a royal counselor. He was sent on a number of diplomatic missions to Paris and Rome, and also became involved in the founding of a company of the Western Indies, whose main purpose was to protect Portuguese trade against Dutch corsairs.

Upon his return to Brazil, in 1652, Vieira started a mission to the Maranhão. He was called by the natives *Payassu* (Big Father). On two other occasions he was to return to Portugal to pursue his campaign against the settlers. But he had already lost favor at court. Unable to preach in either Portugal or Brazil, and prevented from participating in public affairs by a royal order, he devoted the best part of his time to the preparation of a complete edition of his *Sermons* (1679–1710, in 14 volumes). Before the work was completed, he went back to Bahia, to die obscurely at the Quinta of the Jesuits, on the outskirts of the city (1697).

Vieira's influence as a preacher had no parallel in the Iberian world of his time. His *Sermons* and *Letters* circulated in pamphlet form all over Latin America and Europe. A learned commentary on one of his sermons, done by Sor Juana Inés de la Cruz, was the occasion of a witty exchange of letters between the Mexican nun and the Bishop of Puebla. At the time Vieira was living in Rome (1669–1675), his *Sermons* in Italian attracted the attention of the learned Queen Christina of Sweden, who appointed him her confessor. Although Vieira's theology was considered unorthodox—he was suspected of heresy and the Inquisition forbade him to preach—his impact on his own time was principally due to the incisiveness and eloquence of his preaching. Some of his more imaginative works, such as *History of the Future* (posthumously published in 1718), may have indeed departed widely from orthodox views. But Vieira's "heresy" was basically political. For the structure of his *Sermons* he followed the tenets of classical rhetoric very closely. He explicitly declared his dislike of the useless affectations of the Góngora school of preaching, which he characterized as a "xadrex de palavras" (a "word chess-playing"); but he was deeply influenced by baroque poetics. In the fabric of his *Sermons*, in its dazzling network of interlaced imagery and Biblical quotations, as well as in the complex musical structure of his speeches, it is easy to recognize the underlying tensions of baroque thought and its obsessive *topoi*—All the World Is a Stage, Life Is a Game, Time and Death Erode Human Nature, etc. The Brazilian critic Eugenio Gomes has suggested a comparison with John Donne.

How to Save Both Souls and Bodies

From Sermões, *especially translated by Thomas Colchie.*

From the Sermon on the First Sunday of Lent, in the City of São Luis in Maranhão, in the Year 1653, by Father Antônio Vieira

I see what you tell me: "That would be fine, had we some other remedy; but we wish to defend ourselves with the same Gospel. Which was the severest temptation: the first or the third? We know it was the first, because in the first instance Christ had been without food for forty days and the Devil offered bread to him. In the third instance he offered Him kingdoms and monarchies; and a man can live without kingdoms or empires. But without bread to put into his mouth, he cannot live. And we ourselves live in such extremity. This people, this republic, this State, cannot sustain itself without Indians. Who is to fetch us a jug of water, a bundle of firewood? Who is to dig us our manioc beds? Should our women go do it? Should our children go do it?"

First of all, these are not the extremities into which I would place you; but when necessity and conscience oblige as much, then I say yes, and I say yes again: that you, that your women, that your children, and that all of us sustain ourselves by our own hands: for it is better to sustain oneself by one's own sweat than by the blood of others. Oh! lands of Maranhão, if those cloaks and mantles were wrung, what blood would pour out of them. The Samaritan went with her pitcher to fetch water from the fountain, and she was blessed, as we know. Jezebel was the wife of King Ahab, queen of Israel, and she was eaten by the dogs and entombed in Hell, because she took from Naboth a vineyard which she could not manage to obtain freely. I ask, then, which is better: to carry the pitcher to the wellspring, and to go to Heaven like the Samaritan woman; or to be mistress, well served, and queen, and to go to Hell like Jezebel?

Adam was our better, and offended God with fewer transgressions; and he owed to the work of his hands the morsel of food which he put to his mouth. Christ was the Son of God, and he earned his keep with a work-tool by which he sustained a life that later he was to give up for our sake. God himself does this for us; and we, are we too arrogant to do as much, to abide by the law?

You will say that your so-called slaves are your feet and hands; and you might also say that you love them greatly, because you have raised them like your own children and because they have also raised your own. True enough. Yet Christ has already answered to such a plea: *Si oculus tuus scandalizat te, erue eum; et si manus vel pes tuus scandalizat te, amputa illum* (Matthew V, 29–30). Christ does not mean us to pluck out our eyes, nor to cut off our feet and hands; he means, rather, that if we are given cause for scandal by that which we love like our eyes and by that which we need like our feet and hands, then we should cast them from us, even if it cause us pain as if we had cut them off from us.

Who is there who does not greatly love his arms and his hands? But if they should break out with herpes, you will let them be cut off to save your life. The merchant or traveler who comes from India or from Japan greatly values the potions which cost him so much there. But if his life be endangered, he will throw them all overboard to save that life. I say the same in our case. If to satisfy one's conscience and to save one's soul, it were necessary to lose all and to become like Job, then lose all.

But be at peace, my friends, for it is not necessary to go that far, nor even very far at all. I have studied the matter with all due consideration and with all due sympathy; and, following the most generous and the most favorable opinions, I have managed to simplify things to a point at which I know that, with very little temporal loss, the consciences of all the inhabitants of this state can be satisfied, and their wealth can be increased with very great benefits in the future. Give me your attention.

All the Indians of this State either serve as slaves or are free inhabitants of the King's settlements or live in the backlands in a more natural and even greater state of liberty. These last are bought or "ransomed" (as they say, giving the pious name of "ransom" to a sale so forced and violent that it is perhaps effected at gunpoint).

As for those who serve you, all of them in this territory are inherited, obtained and kept in bad faith, on account of which they will be doing no little thing (even though they will do it easily enough) by pardoning you all their past servitude. Nevertheless, if after they are informed of their free condition they spontaneously and voluntarily wish to serve in your houses and to remain there, at least the most domestic ones—because of having been raised in your houses and with your children—none of them, inasmuch as they so desire, shall be taken from your service.

And what shall be done with those who do not wish to continue in such a state of subjection? These will be obliged to do service in the King's settlements, where they will also serve you in the manner that we will shortly specify.

Access to the backlands shall be permitted annually, at which time those Indians may be actually ransomed who are (as they say) at the end of a rope, about to be eaten, and such a cruel fate will thus be commuted to perpetual servitude. Also to be captives are all those who without violence were sold as slaves of their enemies, taken in just war, which shall be judged by the Governor of the whole State, the Justice of the Peace, the Vicar of Maranhão or of Pará, and the Prelates of the four religious Orders—Carmelite, Franciscan, Mercy, and Company of Jesus. All those who are in this way judged to qualify as actual captives will be distributed among the inhabitants of the State for the same price at which they were purchased.

And those who are not regarded as having been taken in a just war, what shall be done with them? All will be placed in new settlements, or divided among the present settlements, where, employed by the same inhabitants along with the other Indians from those settlements, they will give service for six months of the year, every other month in alternation, so that the other six months remain for them to take care of their crops and their families.

In this way, therefore, all the Indians of this State will serve the Portuguese, either as captives properly and entirely (meaning those at the end of a rope, those from a just war, and those who freely and voluntarily wish to serve, as we have said in the first instance), or as half-captives, which means all those from the old and new settlements, who for the well-being and preservation of the State, as I have shown, will, though free, subject themselves to serving us and helping us for half the span of their lives.

It only remains to know what will be the price of those whom we have designated as half-captive, or half-free, the price to be paid for their labors. It is a matter that would bring laughter in any other nation in the world, and only in this territory is not wondered at. Money in this territory consists of cotton; and the ordinary price for the service of these Indians, and for which they will serve each month, is two yards of this cloth, which is worth all of a few nickel coins! From which it follows that an Indian will serve each day for less than seven copper cents; such a thing is unspeakable in itself, and what is yet more unspeakable is that, by not paying even such a small price, men of understanding and of Christian belief still want to damn their own souls and go straight to Hell.

From the Sermon for Sexagesima Sunday,
Preached in the Royal Chapel, Lisbon,
in the year 1655, by Father Antônio Vieira

Might it perchance have to do with the style which is today employed in the pulpits? A style so twisted, so laborious, so affected, a style so antithetical to all art and to all nature? There is reason enough in this as well. Style should always be very simple and very natural. That is why Christ has compared the preacher's task to the task of sowing: *Exiit qui seminat, seminare.* So does Christ compare preaching to sowing, because sowing is a skill less akin to art than it is to nature. With other arts, all is art: with music, all is built upon rhythm; with architecture, all is built to scale; with arithmetic, computation; with geometry, measure. Such is not the way with sowing. It is an artless art: fall where it will. Remember our husbandman from the Gospels and how he sowed. Wheat fell upon thorns and sprouted forth: *Aliud cecidit inter spinas, et simul exortae spinae.* Wheat fell upon stones and sprouted forth: *Aliud cecidit super petram, et ortum.* Wheat fell upon good soil and sprouted forth: *Aliud cecidit in terram bonam, et natum.* Thus the wheat: falling and sprouting forth.

So likewise should it be with preaching. Things should fall and things should sprout forth; as naturally as they go falling, so opportunely will they come sprouting forth. How different the violent and tyrannical style which is employed today. Let us watch the sad steps of the Scriptures, approaching as if invested with martyrdom: some are carted along; some are dragged; some, distended; others, twisted; and others come broken; only the properly bound together fail to make an appearance. Is there such tyranny then? And in the midst of all this martyrdom, how lofty seems that previous falling. Substance is not to be uplifted, but must be allowed to fall: *Cecidit.* Not here an allegory peculiar to our language. The wheat of the sower, even though it has fallen four times, sprouts forth only three; for the sermon to begin to sprout forth, it should fall in three fashions. It should fall with the proper effect, it should fall with the proper inflection, it should fall with the proper feeling. The effect is with respect to the substance, the inflection is with respect to the words, the feeling is with respect to the spirit. The effect is for the substance, since it must come about appropriately and in its place: it must have effect. The inflection is for the words themselves, since they must be neither scabrous nor dissonant: they must have the proper inflection. The feeling is for the spirit, since it must be natural and unaffected enough to seem feeling and not effort: *Cecidit, cecidit, cecidit.*

While I am speaking against modern styles, I wish to adopt for myself the style of the oldest preacher in the world. And who is that? The oldest preacher in the world is Heaven itself. *Caeli enarrant gloriam Dei, et opera manuum ejus annuntiat firmamentum,* says David (Psalm XIX, 1). Now if Heaven is to be seen as a preacher, then Heaven must have sermons and it must have words. And so it has, the same David tells us (Psalm XIX, 3)—words and sermons and, even more, the power to be heard: *Non sunt loquellae, nec sermones, quorum non audiantur voces eorum.* And what are these sermons and these words of Heaven? The words are the stars, the sermons are the composition—the order, course, and harmony—of those stars. See how the style of Heaven preaching addresses us, with that style which Christ taught us here on earth? Preaching should be in the manner of him who sows, and not in the manner of him who lays tile or brick. Ordered, but in the manner of the stars: *Stellae manentes in ordine suo* (Judges V, 20). All the stars are in their appropriate order, but it is an order that impels, not an order that ornaments. God made not Heaven into a checkerboard of words. If in one part it be white, in another there must be black; if in one part it be day, in another there must be night; if in one part it say light, in another there must be darkness; if here it say "descended," in another part there must be "risen." Does it suffice that we never see two words at peace in a sermon? Must all words always be at odds with their counterparts? We learn from Heaven itself the style of the spirit, and that of words as well. How should words be? Like the stars. The stars are quite clear and quite distinct. And yet for all that, you do not fear for any lowliness of style; the stars are quite distinct and quite clear, and yet the quintessence of loftiness. Style can be quite as clear and quite as lofty—so clear that it may be understood by those who do not know, and so lofty that it may challenge the understanding of those who do know. The rustic finds lessons in the stars for his husbandry, and the sailor for his navigation, and the mathematician for his observations and and judgments. In this way the rustic and the sailor, who have never learned to read or write, understand the stars; and the mathematician who has read as much as has ever been written fails to understand all that is contained therein. Thus let a sermon be: stars, which are seen by all and measured by very few.

From the Letter to King Afonso VI of Portugal From Father Antônio Vieira, April 20, 1657

Senhor.—Divine Providence, which in its loftiest judgment has placed the scepter of Portugal in the hands of Your Majesty at such a tender age, will bestir itself to comfort and enlighten the soul of Your Majesty with the special support of its spirit and grace, as necessitates the burden of so extensive a kingdom, in such circumstances as the present. And we, the monastic brothers of this Mission of Your Majesty, shall not cease to thus continually beseech God, offering to that end and for the sake of the life and happiness of Your Majesty all our sacrifices, prayers, and labors.

Senhor, kings are the vassals of God, and, if kings fail to castigate their vassals, still God castigates his own. The principal cause of crowns failing to perpetuate themselves in the same nations and families is one of injustice, or rather injustices, as it says in the Holy Scriptures. And among those injustices none clamors so much before Heaven as the taking away of the liberty of those who were born free, or as the failure to pay for the sweat of those who labor; and these are and always have been the two sins of this State, which still claims so many defenders. The loss of the late king Don Sebastião in Africa, and the seventy years of captivity which resulted for the whole kingdom, was expiation (as the scribes of that time noted) for that enslavement which on the coast of that same Africa our first conquistadors began to effect, with so little regard for justice (as can be seen in those same histories). But the injustice and the tyranny which have been inflicted on the natives of the present territory far exceed that which was carried on in Africa. In the space of forty years, along the coast and in the backlands, more than two million Indians have been killed and more than five hundred settlements the size of large cities have been destroyed, and for this no punishment has ever been noted. In the year 1655, some two thousand Indians were captured along the Amazon River, many of whom were friends and allies of the Portuguese, and vassals of Your Majesty, all in violation of the provisions of the law which in that same year had been delivered to this State, and this was done at the instigation of those who had the greatest responsibility to enforce that same law—and again there was no punishment. And not only do they demand, before Your Majesty, total impunity for such crimes, but even license to continue them!

It is with a great deal of pain, and a great deal of fear about reminding Your Majesty, that I say what I am about to say; but God wills that I say it. Upon King Pharaoh, because he had consented in his reign to the captivity of the Hebrew people, God wrought great punishments, and one of these was to take from him his firstborn. In the year 1654, on the advice of the trustees of this State, a law was passed conferring such excessive license with respect to the enslavement of the Indians that later, Your Majesty being better informed, it would have been wiser to have revoked it, and it has been noted that in that same year God took the firstborn of sons and the firstborn of daughters from Your Majesty. Senhor, if someone asks or counsels Your Majesty to grant greater licenses than that which exists today in this respect, then take him, Your Majesty, for an enemy of the life, the posterity, and the crown of Your Majesty.

They will say perchance (and they do say) that upon such enslavement, in the manner in which it has been effected, depend the preservation and the expansion of the State of Maranhão. That, Senhor, is heresy. If, in order not to commit even a venial sin, it should be necessary to lose Portugal, lose it, Your Majesty, and consider well chosen such a Christian and glorious loss; but I say it is heresy even politically speaking, because nothing is either secure or permanent when founded upon injustice. And experience has shown just that, in this same State of Maranhão, in which so many governors have acquired great wealth, but none of them has enjoyed it nor was it ever maintained by them. Nor is there anything acquired on this island that ever lasts, as the very inhabitants themselves confess: nothing which moves ahead, no business which succeeds, no ship constructed here which comes to any good end; because everything is tinged with the blood of the poor, who are always crying out to Heaven.

If the blood of one innocent raised such an outcry to God, what will be the result of so many more? And Abel, *Senhor,* was saved, and is now in Heaven. And if one soul which is saved calls out for vengeance, then what vengeance will so many thousands and millions of souls, which because of the injustices of this State are burning in Hell—despite its being Portugal's just obligation to guide them to Heaven—what vengeance will they cry out for to God? And that being so, *Senhor,* yet only those who defend justice are persecuted; only those who are busy saving souls are affronted; only those who have taken seriously this great service to God have all men here set against them. Your Majesty would do well to begin to reflect that as long as such tyrannies have been committed in Maranhão there has been no one, ecclesiastical or secular, to administer healing or salvation to these souls; and whenever someone has finally assumed responsibility for one or another of God's labors, immediately there have been so many zealots who take up arms against such service—a clear indication of all this being the mark, and at the instigation, of the devil, in order to impede the spiritual well-being of every Portuguese as well as Indian—that both the one and the other were doomed to Hell. And it would be a disgrace, terrible to behold, if the ministers of the devil should prevail over those of Christ, in a kingdom as Christian as Portugal. The other kingdoms of Christendom, *Senhor,* must work for the preservation of their vassals, for the sake of their temporal felicity in this world and of eternal felicity in the other; the kingdom of Portugal, in addition to this purpose common to all, has as its own particular aim the propagation and extension of the Catholic faith to the lands of the gentiles, it being for that purpose that God has instituted and exalted this kingdom. And the more Portugal concerns itself to this end, the more certain and secure it may be of its preservation; and the more it strays from that course, the more doubtful and hazardous will be the same.

With the return voyage of Your Majesty's dispatches I hope that Your Majesty will have ordered the implementation of all the recommendations that I sent by last year's ships. And since I can not know what may have happened in the meantime, I shall summarize here once again everything that at present is necessary for the preservation, increase, and tranquility of this Christian State. They are principally the four points which follow:

First: that with respect to the law and regulation of Your Majesty concerning the Indians and the missions, nothing be altered, and to this end nothing be given or granted to petitions to the contrary.

Second: that the governors and provincial captains who come to this State be men of conscience; and, since such men are not accustomed to come here, that they at least be made aware of the fact that they will truly suffer punishment, if in any way they should break said law and regulation.

Third: that the heads of the Religious Orders be men concerned to make their members conform to their discipline and commands, that they do not consent to any contravening of them in public or in private; and if there be any disobedient member of an Order in these regions, that he be sent away from Maranhão.

Fourth: that Your Majesty send here a greater number of Jesuit Fathers to help carry on what we who have been here have already begun, because it is the only way (since there is so much work for so few brothers) that the number of heathen can be reduced by conversion.

And since news has reached us that, against us, missionaries who in this State serve God and Your Majesty, and against the government of the said mission, there have been presented to Your Majesty a number of complaints, we humbly beg Your Majesty that Your Majesty be so good as to send us all such to look at, even if they be ones which concern the State, because we hope to satisfy all complaints in such a way that it will become known, with absolute clarity, how useful the missionaries of the Company of Jesus are, not only with respect to the spiritual betterment of the Portuguese and the Indians, but even with respect to the temporal well-being of all.

To the most high and most powerful person of Your Majesty, God keep, as all of Christendom and the vassals of Your Majesty have need.
Maranhão, April 20, 1657.   *Antônio Vieira*

17

GREGORIO DE MATOS

Gregorio de Matos was a popular poet in the rakish vein of François Villon, a ruffian and a scoundrel. He was so influential in his native Bahia that Father Vieira once admitted the poet's satires had a more chastening effect on their contemporaries than his own missions. Much contradictory information has been gathered about his life and writings. Even the date of his birth is uncertain. He was born in Bahia, sometime between 1623 and 1633. His father, a prosperous Portuguese settler, owned a sugar mill and had one hundred thirty black slaves. Like his elder brothers, de Matos attended the same Jesuit college Father Vieira had attended. The difference in age prevented any friendship at that time, although it is known that one of de Matos's brothers became Vieira's friend and colleague.

To complete his law studies, Gregorio went to Lisbon. He got his degree in 1661. For several years he practiced in Lisbon, among the poor, learning from firsthand experience how the destitute lived. His reputation for drunkenness and scandal was already solidly established when he was forced to return to Bahia in 1681. There he was protected by the Archbishop, who appointed him General Vicar and Treasurer, but his main interest did not lie in Church affairs. Instead, he devoted the best part of his time to writing, singing, and whoring. His satirical poems circulated orally in the proud city. They spared no one: governors and nuns, adulteresses and merchants, pimps and widows were endlessly paraded in his verses. A tropical Juvenal, de Matos exposed the fabric of lies and pretensions that constituted the Colonial establishment. He was skillful in all genres and even wrote many moving religious poems, but his real Muse was to be found walking the streets. Playing a guitar made out of a pumpkin, he sang poems that blended the baroque style of the Spanish models (Quevedo, Góngora) with the most popular vein of the anonymous jugglers. If his rhetoric had impeccable academic origins, his vocabulary and rhythms reflected the oral literature of his day. He liked to include Indian and black expressions in his poems; and he followed the Brazilian pronunciation of Portuguese, already distinct from the peninsular. His contemporaries called him *Boca do Inferno* (Hell's Mouth) because of his sharp and sometimes near-blasphemous wit. (One of his poems comically tells of his finding all the ladies he was then courting in bed with their monthlies.) It has been said that many of the most important people in Bahia called themselves his friends to avoid being the object of his satires.

His last years were spent outside his native town: first in harsh exile in Angola (1686–1695), later in Recife, where he was sent upon his return to Brazil and where he died, poor and alone, in 1696.

After his death, his reputation suffered a long eclipse. While in Portugal, he had never bothered to collect his works; in Brazil, there were no printing presses at the time. His poems circulated orally or in manuscript copies made by admirers. Not until 1831 were any of his poems printed, when some were included in Januario da Cunha Barbosa's *Parnaso Brasileiro*. The first collection of his *Obras Poeticas* is dated 1882; the last, *Crônica do Viver Bahiano* (in seven volumes), was published in 1969, and its editor was still unable to separate definitively what he actually wrote from the anonymous productions of his contemporaries.

Despite all such difficulties, de Matos's works survived to constitute one of the most original bodies of baroque poetry in Latin America. They are also the foundation of a truly national Brazilian poetry. Some of his echoes can be found today in João Cabral de Melo Neto's hard and brilliant works (see Part Five, 8, ıı) or in the young and irreverent authors of the Protest songs.

The Satirical and Popular Muse

From Crônica do Viver Bahiano, *especially translated by Thomas Colchie.*

Pretending to applaud the integrity of the city, the poet begins to do justice to its inhabitants, by illustrating the vices with which some of them have debased themselves.

Such an illustrious city,
such an honorable people
see themselves one day esteemed,
the rich and the indigent,
each in his own coin;
but if the devil incites me,
in trying to do her justice,
to set some petticoat on the block,
they cannot deny me
that by law, and by rights,
such is but justice, bidden by the King.

The Gentleman of the manor
pretends to be embarrassed
at borrowing a bit of money
to provide for his paunch:
he maintains, steal he would rather
to preserve his black honor,
than submit to the dishonor
of someone's refusing him perhaps;
but if you spot him in his galley chains
with the dignity of a Viceroy about him,
such is but justice, bidden by the King.

The Maiden muffled up,
badly dressed and poorly fed,
wants more than anything in life
to have her dress and not her honor:
vaunting her concubinage
to bolster her black little pride,
and if a neighbor knows about it
and the clergy should overhear,
they meet her down in her dungeon,
and the price of the law is paid:
such is but justice, bidden by the King.

The Wife with fancy clothes
and the Husband poorly dressed,
believe me, that very Husband
his peruke of cuckold displays:
if you tell by his demeanor
that he suffers like Father Two-face,
he does so, his honor to uphold;
wait for the ax to fall,
with his Inquisitional dunce cap

he will make Viceroy in Angola:
such is but justice, bidden by the King.

The Educated Coxcombs,
citing the same Authority
to turn Author into Defendant,
try to straddle both sides of the fence:
if within their secret assemblies
they admit to prevarication,
the excuse that they offer
is their family honor,
and so must the plaintiffs
flee from this infamous parish:
such is but justice, bidden by the King.

The presiding Clergyman,
who judges the case so shamelessly,
failing to notice that I might see
the error of the Law and its Authority:
when they see from the Monsignor
the Sentence Overruled,
from knowing it was purchased
with money or a kiss,
the answer comes from the vagrant Judge,
my honor is unto itself the Law:
such is but justice, bidden by the King.

The money-grubbing Merchant,
when he extends his cash in hand,
be it what he buys or sells,
he takes two hundred percent;
no ass is he not to think
that in a place like Lisbon
they would throw him in the clink;
but once his money is gone,
says he, honor means more
and so does respect for the Law:
such is but justice, bidden by the King.

The trustworthy Widow,
who possesses not a dime,
because her goodly Husband
mortgaged off the home:
here brings a fresh load of friars;
like ants in a swarm, they chorus

that if they go homing
'tis only to honor the home;
if you see it burst into flames,
you can be sure 'tis only honor's ardor:
such is but justice, bidden by the King.

Adonis in the morning,
Cupid all day long,
leading the life of a Vagabond
with sweet greetings from Venus:
and if they clip his wings,
he says he always wanders there
well dressed and well groomed,
all for the sake of his honor;
yet I might catch him so disheveled
I could expose to you his shoulders:
such is but justice, bidden by the King.

If you should see some Master Abbot
so passionate in the pulpit,
call him not a Brother,
rather pronounce him Friar:
and if the said Paternity
filches the rents of the Monastery,
to contribute to the upkeep
of his whore, and the pittance
it takes to evade suspicion
of Vicar-General or Viceroy:
such is but justice, bidden by the King.

. . .

The poet defines his city:

Of two *f*'s, as I see it,
is this city composed,
one *fraud*, the other *fornication.*

The law was once epitomized,
and the one who epitomized it
with two *f*'s had it characterized
as being *fashioned* in the best *fashion:*
to be well Digested, as well as Comprehensive,
only the two *f*'s will do the job,
and thus anyone who takes a look

at the situation herein contained
has to agree, that of two *f*'s
· is this territory now composed.

If of two *f*'s the city
of Bahia is composed,
the error of orthography
to great danger is exposed:
I wish to make a wager,
and I wish to lose my dime
because, as I see it,
there has to be something strange,
if *fraud* and *fornication*
are not the two *f*'s
which the city contains.

I will now prove my conjecture
and do it aptly with a trick:
Bahia has five letters,
which are B-A-H-I-A:
now no one will dare to quip
that two *f*'s can be found,
since not a one is around,
except if in point of fact
we consider the two *f*'s of the city,
one *fraud*, the other *fornication*.

.   .   .

The poet describes the city of Recife in the State of Pernambuco:

Between the Sea and the River Beberibe
On sandy ground, coarse and mudded,
Sits Recife, the half-breed city,
which Belgian tyranny has constructed.

Its People are scarce, and scarcely civilized,
who live at the mercy of sausage meats,
of tasteless razor clams to eat,
and sickly prawns all their lives.

Its courtesan Damsels, with eyes
swollen and infected, with pestilences,
by purgations never purified, go by.

But the fault lies with your reverences,
since, vanquished and defiled, you draw them nigh
with your scapulars, cordons, and indulgences.

18

CARLOS DE SIGÜENZA Y GÓNGORA

Englishmen's versions of their buccaneering exploits, in the Caribbean or elsewhere, always portrayed the Spaniards as clumsy and cowardly villains. In Sigüenza y Góngora's *Misadventures of Alonso Ramírez* it is possible to see the other side of the coin. A Jesuit, and a man of rare learning, the Mexican author really believed the English pirates were heathen, and he did not spare any detail to prove their brutality, their lust for blood, their pleasure in genocide and massacre. His account coincides in general with the more detailed and overwhelming one published by Exquemelin (Amsterdam, 1678) under the title *The Buccaneers of America.* (There is a Spanish translation, 1681, also printed in Amsterdam, which Sigüenza y Góngora might have seen.)

Although *The Misadventures* follows the fictional scheme of a first-person narrative, it is actually based on a true story: Alonso Ramírez did exist, and he told Sigüenza y Góngora his life. In writing it, the Mexican author managed to be at once direct and elegant. Published originally in 1690, when the author was forty-five, the book was soon accepted as one of the best examples of Colonial narrative. With it, Sigüenza y Góngora crowned rather unexpectedly a scientific and literary career that had been long and (to the taste of his time) entirely successful.

As a poet, Sigüenza y Góngora belonged to the baroque school that flourished in Mexico in the seventeenth century (see selection 11). Although he did his best to out-Góngora Góngora (his distant relative), he did not succeed. Today he is mainly read as a prose writer of curious lore.

The Misadventures of Alonso Ramírez is his masterpiece, and the prototype for many later narratives of its kind. In our time, the Colombian Gabriel García Márquez has written *The Shipwrecked's Story* (1958), reviving the same fictional device: a first-person narrative of somebody else's adventures.

The chapter reproduced here is the third: it tells the story of Alonso Ramírez from the moment he is captured by English pirates near the Philippines to the time they reach the coast of Brazil, after a long and murderous journey westward. Upon entering the Caribbean, he will be set free with some companions on a boat and eventually, after many hazards, will reach Yucatán. But it is in the vivid account of the pirates' Asian exploits that Sigüenza y Góngora's narrative is at its best.

Living with English Pirates

From The Misadventures of Alonso Ramírez, *translated by Edwin H. Pleasants (Mexico, 1962), pp. 29–48.*

Knowing that the ship had been in my charge, I was placed on one of the larger pirate vessels, where the captain received me with false hospitality. He immediately promised me my freedom in return for news about which of the islands were more wealthy and if one could expect much resistance from them. I answered that I had left Cavite only to visit Ilocos and so could not satisfy his desire for information. He insisted on asking me if the island of Caponiz, which at a distance of fourteen leagues is northwest southeast with respect to Marivelez, would be safe for his ships and if there would be obstacles to face there. I told him that there was no village there at all and that I knew of a bay where he could easily secure what he needed. It was my intention, if he should go there, that he should be seized unexpectedly not only by the natives but by the Spanish who serve on the prison staff of that island. At about ten in the evening they anchored where they thought best and between this question and others the night passed.

Before setting sail they put my twenty-five men on board the flagship. It was commanded by an Englishman called Master Bel. It had eighty men, twenty-four pieces of artillery, and eight stone mortars all bronze. Captain Donkin was master of the second ship, and he had seventy men, twenty pieces of artillery, and eight stone mortars. In both there were a great many shotguns, cutlasses, axes, grenades, and pots full of various foul-smelling ingredients besides grappling irons.

In spite of every effort on my part I never discovered their route to the sea except that they went south through the strait of Mayre and that when they found it impossible to rob the coasts of Peru and Chile, which was their intent (because of a vehement storm from the east which lasted eleven days), they left that meridian by five hundred leagues. It not being easy to return, they decided to take advantage of India to rob a richer country.

I found out also that they had been in the Marianas and that battling tempests and heavy seas, doubling the capes of Engaño and Boxeador, and having before seized some Chinese junks and sampans belonging to the Chinese and the Indians, they reached the mouth of Marivelez, where they came upon us.

Turning the frigates toward Caponiz with mine in tow, they began with pistols and cutlasses in hand to examine me again and even to torture me. They tied me and a companion of mine to the main mast, and as we did not answer their questions to their liking about where to find gold and silver, they laid hands on Francisco de la Cruz, a half-breed Chinese trader and companion of mine, and whipped him until he fainted on the deck almost lifeless.

They put me and my companions in the hold, where we could hear above much shouting and the report of a blunderbuss. I noticed the blood on the deck after they let us out, and showing it to me they said it was that of one of my men who had died and that the same thing would happen to me if I did not respond properly to questioning. I told them humbly that they could do what they wanted with me because I had nothing to add to what I had already said.

Careful then to find out which of my companions had died, I checked and found the number the same as before, which puzzled me. I found out much later that what I had seen was the blood of a dog and that the whole episode had been feigned.

Not satisfied with what I had said, they began asking questions again in a solicitous manner of my boatswain, who being Indian could not be expected to do things properly, and they discovered from him that there was a village and prison on the island of Caponiz, which I had stated previously to be uninhabited.

With this news and more that they discovered for themselves such as the sight of two horsemen along the shore to which they added the lie that I had never left Cavite except for Ilocos, they fell upon me with cutlasses unsheathed and much shouting.

Never had I feared death more than at that moment, but they commuted it with kicks and blows on the neck until they left me unable to move for many days.

They anchored off land from a direction where they expected no trouble from the islanders and leaving on shore the Indians who were the owners of a junk which they had seized the previous day, they headed for Pulicondon, an island populated by Cochin Chinese on the coast of Cambodia. There they found a port and transferred to their two frigates everything they found in mine and set it on fire.

Arming the canoes with sufficient men they made for land and found the inhabitants friendly. They told the islanders they only wished a safe harbor for the ships so as to add provisions and fruit, which they lacked.

Either through fear or for other motives which I did not learn about, the poor barbarians agreed to this. They received clothes which had been stolen in return for pitch, fat, salted turtle meat, and other items.

Because of a lack of clothing on that island or the pent-up emotions of the pirates, nakedness and curiosity forced them to commit the most shameful disgrace which I ever saw.

The mothers brought the daughters and even the husbands their wives and delivered them to the English with the recommendation that they were beautiful, for the vilest price of a blanket or some such trifle.

Such an ugly convenience made their stay of four months at the island tolerable, but since they felt they were not living if they were not stealing and since their ships were ready to navigate, they placed on board all the supplies they could in order to depart.

Consulting over the price they should give the islanders for their hospitality, they settled it the same day they set sail by attacking at dawn those who were sleeping without precautions, and putting everyone to the knife, even the women they had left pregnant. Setting fire to the village and then hoisting colors, they boarded their ships with great rejoicing.

I was not present at this base cruelty but fearing that someday the same would come to pass in my case, I watched from the flagship where I was kept and saw the flames and heard the shots.

If they had carried out this abominable victory after consuming quantities of the brandy they use, it would not be important to keep silent about this deed, but having seen the incidents which I saw, how could I fail to mention them without suffering pangs of conscience at remaining silent?

Among the things which they brought from the village which they had given in payment of the women and the supplies was a human arm from one of the victims of the fire. From this each one cut a small slice and praising the quality and flavor amid repeated toasts they finished it off.

I was watching dismayed and scandalized at such bestial conduct when one of them approached me with a piece and insisted that I should eat it. When I rejected it, he said, "Being Spanish it follows you are a prude and a coward unequal to men of valor." He insisted no further in order to respond to a toast.

On the third day they noticed the continental coast of Cambodia and, touching along the shore from place to place, they captured a sampan full of pepper; they did with them what they did with me and seizing the silver and other valuables and ignoring the pepper, they removed the helm and sails so that it drifted off to be lost.

Having dropped off the people from the sampan on solid ground, they visited the uninhabited island of Puliubi, where they found coconuts and ñames in abundance, and since they were sure that neither I nor my companions could flee to safety in such a place, they took us off the ships to twist ropes. The material we used was similar to wicker, and we were without the use of our hands for many days for having finished the work in a few.

The prizes they secured during the course of this stop were of high value although but three in number, since of these, one belonged to the King of Siam and the others to the Portuguese of Macao and Goa. In the first ship was an ambassador of that king sent to the governor of Manila, and for this purpose he carried with him a gift of jewels of great esteem and many fruits and precious goods from that land.

Interest in the second ship was much greater because it contained exclusively richly woven silks from China and a quantity of gold in filigree, which was being sent to Europe by way of Goa.

The third belonged to the Viceroy of Goa with an ambassador from the King of Siam on board.

I know not how, but a Genoese had not only gained the ear of the king but was made his deputy at his main port. Puffed up with so much authority he had the hands of two Portuguese gentlemen cut off for slight cause. News of this reached the Viceroy of Goa, who sent to ask satisfaction and even to ask that they deliver up the Genoese to be punished.

The gift which was sent to gain over the king seemed of such value as to be outside the realm of possibility. I saw and touched with my hands a piece of workmanship like a tower or castle thirty-three inches high of pure gold sprinkled with diamonds and other precious stones and, though not of equal value, of equal interest were many silver jewels, a quantity of camphor, amber, musk, and other things which were to be traded in that kingdom.

When the pirates had removed all valuables they set fire to the ships. They left the Portuguese as well as the Siamese, together with eight of my men, on that island without inhabitants and sailed for Cianton, a place inhabited by Malayans, whose garments did not reach above the waist and whose weapons consisted of daggers.

Here they took on some goats, coconuts, oil for cooking and lighting, and other refreshments. Subjecting the poor barbarians to a dawn attack, after killing some and robbing the others, they turned their vessels toward Tamburlan.

There live the Macazares, and when the English did not find there what they had found in other places, they set fire to the village when the inhabitants were sleeping and went on to the great island of Borneo. For fourteen days they plied to the windward along the western coast without finding spoils until they approached the port of Cicudana on the same island.

In this territory they found many precious stones and especially large diamonds. These had aroused the greed of the English that live in India to ask King Borney (through the governor which he had in Cicudana) if they might have a trading post at that place.

The pirates set to work in their canoes to sound the river bar, not only to see if larger ships might enter but to plan an attack. They were interrupted in this by a coastal sampan in which were representatives of the authorities of the place, who had come to reconnoiter. The pirates answered that they were from the English nation and were loaded with noble and exquisite goods to be exchanged for diamonds.

As they had received friendly treatment from this nation and saw the rich samples from the ships captured at Puliubi, they granted a license to trade. They gave a generous gift to the governor and received permission to go up river to the town, a fourth of a league from the sea, whenever they wished.

During the three days we were there, our captors found the place to be undefended and open on all sides. Telling the Cicudanes that they could not stay for long and that they should collect their diamonds in the governor's house, where there would be a fair, they left us on board under guard and went up river at midnight well armed. They attacked the village by surprise, advancing first on the governor's house. There they sacked the building for the diamonds and other precious stones gathered there and then proceeded to do the same with other houses, which they put to the torch together with some boats they found there.

On board we could hear the clamor of the village and the shots; the mortality, as they bragged later, was considerable. This detestable treachery being carried out without injury to themselves, they brought the governor as a prisoner together with other leaders on board with great speed, and raising the anchor they sped away. Never has there been pillage to compare to this in the high price received for so little effort. Who can say what it was worth? I saw Captain Bel with the crown of his hat heaped full of diamonds.

In six days we had reached the island of Baturiñan, which they left behind as unprofitable, and went on to Pulitiman, where they found fresh water and wood. Putting the governor and his principal advisers from Cicudana on land, after treating them badly and feeding them little, they turned toward Bengal, where more boats plied the seas. In a few days they captured two large vessels belonging to black Moslems and found on board satin, elephants, herons, and sarampures. After despoiling them of their cargo, they burned the boats while many of the Moors were put to death in cold blood. Those that remained were given small launches that they themselves had brought along so that they might depart.

Up until now they had not met any ship that was capable of opposing them. But now in this locale, either by accident or because news of such famous thieves was spreading so that I believe people had put out to punish them, four ships of war with artillery came into view, all of them, it seemed, being Dutch.

They were to the leeward so the pirates, having gotten as much as possible and aided by the obscurity of the night, changed direction for Pulilaor for supplies and water. Not feeling secure now in these parts and fearful of losing the inestimable riches which they had found, they determined to leave that archipelago.

In doubt as to whether to come out through the straight of Sunda or that of Singapore, they elected the latter as closer though more tedious and difficult, rejecting the other although shorter and easier as too distant, or what is more likely, as being more frequented by ships that go and come from New Batavia.

Entrusting themselves to a pilot familiar with the strait, and aided by breezes and currents, with Dutch flags flying and well armed for any eventuality, they awaited a lugubrious night and entered into the strait in desperate resolution. They ran the strait almost to the end without encountering more than a single boat the second day.

This was a frigate with a forty-foot keel carrying a load of rice and a fruit called bonga. As they attacked it (in order not to lose the habit of robbing even when they were in flight), the Malayans on board abandoned ship and leaped into the sea, swimming to land to save their lives.

Happy at having found a ship which would relieve them of much of their cargo, they put seven men from each of their ships with all their arms and ten pieces of artillery with ammunition on the captured vessel and continued their voyage about five o'clock in the afternoon; that same day they sailed out of the strait. About that time five of my men disappeared and I assume that they took advantage of the nearness of land to gain their freedom swimming.

After twenty-five days we spied an island, whose name I don't recall, and which we avoided because it was inhabited by Portuguese and headed for New Holland, a land not yet fully explored by the Europeans, and owned, it would seem, by barbarians, a land which we reached after more than three months.

They disembarked on the coast to find evidences that in former times people had lived there, but the winds were adverse and strong and the anchorage poor, which caused them to move on to an island of flat land. Shelter for the ships was available there and a brook of sweet water as well as many turtles and no inhabitants. They busied themselves careening the ship while my men and I mended the sails and prepared meat.

In about four months we were ready to sail for Madagascar or San Lorenzo and with an east wind aiding us we reached there in twenty-eight days. The Negroes who lived there supplied them with chickens, goats, and cows and, receiving news that an English merchant vessel was about to enter the port to trade with the Negroes, they determined to await it.

From their actions and conversation I expected them to try to seize the ship; however, when it appeared, they noticed how well armed it was and well manned, so they exchanged salutes and friendship. The merchant seamen gave brandy and wine to the pirates and they responded with what they had stolen in abundance.

Not being able to capture the ship by force, which was impossible, Captain Bel left no effort untried to become master of the ship by stealth. But what he had in thievery and greed, the captain of the merchant ship had in vigilance and wisdom. Although the pirates with much insistence and invitations tried to get the merchant captain on board their ship, he turned them down and proceeded about his business with prudence.

The caution of Bel and Donkin was not less in keeping secret from the merchant seamen the business in which they were involved. To this purpose they ordered me and my companions, whom they suspected, that under pain of death we were not to speak to the merchant seamen except to say that we were voluntary seamen and that they paid us.

Two of my men violated this order by speaking to a Portuguese who was on the merchantman. The pirates took pity on the two by not taking their lives immediately but condemning them to receive four lashes from each of the pirates. Since there were a hundred and fifty of them, the blows would be many. In fact, the whip was such and the impulse behind the blows so violent that the poor men were dead by dawn of the following day.

They tried to leave me and the few companions that were left on that island; but considering the barbarity of the black Moors that lived there, I knelt down and kissing their feet in complete submission and reminding them of how much I had served them, offering to assist them on their voyage as if I were a slave, I managed to get them to take me with them.

They proposed to me as they had before that I should swear to accompany them always and they would give me arms. I thanked them for their favor, but reflecting upon the obligations of my birth, I told them with affected humility that it were better to serve them than to fight others since the fear I had of guns, being a cowardly and chickenhearted Spaniard, made me unworthy of being one of them, and they did not insist.

We bid farewell to the merchantman and, well supplied with provisions, sailed toward the Cape of Good Hope on the coast of Africa, and after two months of navigating, including five days plying to the windward, we finally passed in front of it. From there for a space of a month and a half we sailed along the coast to the Isla de Piedras, where we took on water and wood and then turned westward. With swift breezes we sighted the coast of Brazil in twenty-five days.

During the two weeks we paralleled the coast, the mountains dropping in altitude, we twice put six men on shore in a canoe and having spoken with who knows what Portuguese and buying refreshments, we went on until finally we reached a broad river in whose estuary anchor was dropped to a depth of five fathoms and which I presume was the Amazon, if I am not mistaken.

19

JOSÉ GUMILLA

Although he spent thirty-five years in "the green hell" of the Orinoco jungles, Frey José Gumilla never once abandoned his European point of view. He observed, very accurately, American nature; he was able to describe with precision the way the Indians lived; he collected an immense amount of scientific data. His book, *The Orinoco Illustrated*, is a mine of firsthand information on the region and its inhabitants. Throughout, however, his judgments and perceptions are conditioned by European assumptions and values.

He was eighteen when he first set foot in Bogotá, in 1705. Until he was twenty-eight, he remained there, completing his ecclesiastical training. When he went into the jungle, he already had a theory about the origin of the American Indians: they were the ten lost tribes of Israel. He was not the first to think so, but he probably was one of the few who, after a long sojourn in the New World, continued to believe it.

In the excerpt presented here, he describes in detail how the Indians make the lethal poison curare, and with the same conviction states that the Devil himself taught them. It is not surprising that curare should have so had the power to fire his imagination—in a later time, none other than Sherlock Holmes was called on to do battle against a criminal who made use of it.

How the Indians Make Curare

From The Golden Land, *pp. 31–35.*

The cursed serpent, not satisfied with having infected the whole of mankind with his foul and mortal poison from the days of the Garden of Eden, never wearies or abates his sinister designs, spewing forth new forms of death for sin-ridden souls and bodies in the poisons with which he tempts persons of reason and judgment, and with the hidden venoms he discovered and revealed to the blinded natives of the Orinoco and others like them. I say this in all seriousness and sincerity, for when, from my own observation, I compare the mysterious secrets of some of these poisons with the limited capacity and complete lack of reasoning power of those ignorant Indians, I come to the conclusion, which I think is warranted, that the knowledge and process of manufacture of these poisons cannot have come from their feeble intelligence or their rude industry. These deadly weapons proceed from the implacable hatred with which our common enemy regards the human race, whose complete destruction would be his greatest joy. The demonstration of the fact will be the best proof of my assertion.

The Caberres, the most inhuman, brutish, and bloodthirsty of all the tribes that inhabit the valley of the Orinoco, have a monopoly of the most deadly poison, in my opinion, to be found on the face of the globe. This tribe alone holds the secret, and it manufactures it, and receives a rich income from the other tribes who themselves, or through some third party, come to buy the curare, which is the name by which it is called. It is sold in little pots or vessels of clay. The largest of these holds about four ounces of this poison, which is similar in color to boiled honey. It has no taste, nor is it especially bitter. It can be taken into the mouth and swallowed without any danger, provided there is no open wound on the gums or in any other part of the mouth, for all its activity and strength is directed against the blood, to such an extent that for it to touch one drop of blood and curdle all the rest in the body with the speed of lightning is all one. It is amazing to see how a wound from an arrow dipped in curare, even though the scratch is no bigger than that of a pin, will make all the person's blood clot, and he dies before he can say the name of Jesus three times.

A soldier, who was later an officer of the guard of our missions, from Madrid, by the name of Francisco Macías, a brave, courageous man, a great student of the nature and properties of plants and animals, and even of insects, was the one who first told me of the instantaneous action of curare. I withheld judgment, and waited to see for myself. It happened that a band of yellow monkeys soon came along, which the Indians consider very good eating and which are known in their language as *arabata*. All the Indians got ready to shoot as many as they could. I called one Indian aside and asked him to shoot a monkey that was standing on a palm frond, holding onto the leaf above it with its left paw. It raised its right paw in a movement to try to pull out the arrow (as they do when these are not dipped in curare), but even as it made the gesture, without time to get its paw on the arrow, it dropped dead to the foot of the palm tree. I ran over, and, although it was not far away, all the warmth had departed from the outside of the body. I asked to have it cut open from the breast down, and I could find no trace of warmth, not even in the heart itself. Around this organ there was a large quantity of coagulated blood, dark and cold; there was hardly any blood in the rest of the body, and the little I found in the liver was like that around the heart. The outside of the body was covered with an orange-covered cold foam, and I came to the conclusion that the intense cold induced by the curare instantly chills the blood, and that this seeks refuge in the heart; not finding sufficient warmth there, it clots and freezes, and this causes the victim to die more quickly, as the heart is smothered.

While I was watching, the Indian cut the monkey into pieces, put it into a pot, and set it to cooking, and the other Indians did the same with their monkeys. My amazement did not come from the fact that they ate that flesh, or because it was a monkey, or because it had been killed by poison. What astounded me was that those clots of blood that contained all the force of the poison also went into the pots and afterwards into the stomachs of the Indians. I asked them a number of questions, and so satisfied was I with their answers that that same day I ate the liver one of them was cooking (and it is as delicious as that of the tenderest suckling pig, unless my hunger deceived me), and from then on, whenever there was a similar encounter with monkeys, I always asked for a liver as my share of the spoils.

I saw the same instantaneous effect of curare on jaguars, deer, pumas, and many other wild animals and birds. So powerful is it that an Indian is not frightened even when he comes on a jaguar face to face. Calmly he takes out his arrow, takes aim, and shoots, certain that he will not miss his mark, and even more certain that he has only to wound the animal lightly on the tip of the nose or in any other part of the body and it will give one or two leaps and drop dead.

In view of this unheard-of and deadly poison, and the ease with which all the tribes along the Orinoco and its broad basin manage to secure it, I cannot refrain from giving praise to the infinite providence of the Almighty and calling upon all to bless His fatherly mercy for having so arranged things that those savages should not be fully aware of the invincible weapon they have in their curare. Which missionary, which Spaniard, which soldier, could live among them if they did not prefer to the silent fury of their arrows and curare the contingent noise of a gun? I say contingent, because of the flint that may not strike; of the aim that is not certain; because of the rain that may put it completely out of condition, when, on the contrary, for the curare-dipped point, there is no antidote, no cure, not even time to commend one's soul to God. I say without cure or antidote, because even though an innocent boy revealed to Father Juan Rivero that if one has salt in his mouth curare cannot harm him, which he found to be true by performing several experiments on animals, this remedy is not practical for men, because how can they stand salt in their mouth for a long time? And if they have it in their knapsack, the poison does not give them time to get it out.

We have seen, not without astonishment, the unerring power of curare. Now let us see the strange process of its preparation. All the poison of curare comes from a root by the same name, and such a strange, unique root that it is only root, never producing leaves or stalk, and although it grows, it is always hidden, as though it were afraid to show its secret malignance. And the better to hide itself, it has sought, or the Creator has assigned it, not such soil as other plants commonly grow in, but the fetid, rotten slime of those bayous that have no outlet and whose waters are never drunk except in case of dire necessity, because they are heavy, dark, foul-tasting, and equally malodorous. In the putrid slime upon which these pestilential waters rest, there comes into being and grows the root of the curare, a fit offspring of such foul origins. The Caberre Indians dig up these roots, which are brownish in color, and after washing them and breaking them into pieces, they pound them up and put them into large pots over a slow fire. For this task they select the most useless old woman of the tribe, and when she drops dead from the effects of the fumes given off by the brew, as generally happens, they pick another like her in her place. These women make no protest about the work, nor does the community or their relatives object; they all know that this is what old women are for. As the water grows warmer, the poor old woman kneads her death, going from pot to pot and squeezing and stirring the macerated roots, so they can the more freely yield up their poison, and the juice begins to color the water, which must remain tepid, until it is the shade of light honey. Then the old woman, with such feeble strength as she possesses, squeezes the last juice from the roots into the brew and throws them away, useless now, and then adds wood to the fire, and the brew begins to boil hard. After the pots have boiled for a little while, she drops dead, overcome by the fumes, and the second one takes charge. Sometimes the latter escapes with her life, sometimes not.

When the brew has cooked down to its proper consistency and concentration, which is when about one third of the liquid has evaporated, the unfortunate cook calls out, and the chief, accompanied by his captains and all the other people of the village, hastens up to examine the curare and see if it is ready or not. (And this is the most astonishing thing about this whole strange operation.) The chief dips the end of a stick in the curare, and at the same time one of his braves, with the point of a sharp bone, cuts himself in the leg, thigh, or arm (wherever he feels like), and when the blood begins to flow from the wound, the chief holds the point of the stick dipped in curare near it. He does not touch it, or bring the curare in contact with the blood; he just puts it near it, because if he should touch the blood and it should shrink back, it would infect all the veins and the patient would die at once. If the blood that was about to flow out draws back, the poison is ready; if it remains at the mouth of the wound and does not draw back, it is almost ready; but if the blood flows out, as it naturally would, it needs more cooking. In this case they order the poor old woman to continue with her deadly task, and then they test it again until the blood's drawing back violently from its enemy gives them proof that the curare has reached its maximum strength.

If some famous botanist had discovered this root and learned its secret malignancy, it would be nothing to wonder at. If the famous Tritemio or Borri or one of those learned inventors of chemistry, as a result of their experiments and studies, had finally hit upon this singular process, they would deserve great praise, and it would be looked upon as the outcome of their cultivated understanding. But who can believe that all this should be the invention of the most uncouth and barbarous tribe of the whole Orinoco River without admitting that the whole thing, from the discovery of the root to the completion of the poison, was the work of the devil? This is what I believe.

It is also worth remarking how this poison preserves its properties, the obstinacy with which it maintains all its vigor and strength until it is completely used up, even though the Indians take no special precautions with it, not even covering the little pots in which they buy it, and it does not evaporate or lose one iota of its mortal powers. This is surprising, but, after all, as it is there together, and in concentrated form, it is not so strange that it should preserve all its potency. What is most remarkable is that once the arrow points are daubed with it, even though the amount used is so small that each tip receives no more than a smear, yet that small quantity maintains and preserves all its strength for many years, as many as it takes the owner of the arrows to use them up. Until now, so far as is known, no matter how many years these poisoned arrows lie exposed without any protection, the strength of the deadly curare does not abate. I noticed one thing, however, on several of my trips through those jungles, and this was that when the Indians took their arrows out of their quivers to kill a monkey or a wild boar, or in case of sudden attack, they always put the poisoned tip in their mouth before fitting the arrow to the bow. When I asked them the reason for this (impelled by my insatiable and natural curiosity), they always answered that with the warmth of the mouth and the moisture of the saliva the powers of the curare were activated and the effects of the shot surer, which struck me as being very natural.

20

BARTOLOMÉ ARZÁNS DE ORZÚA Y VELA

Like Rodríguez Freile in his *El Carnero* (see selection 12), the author of *History of the Imperial Town of Potosí* was really more interested in local history than in History. His was the day-by-day chronicle of a town which for more than a century and a half was the center of the silver industry of the Spanish empire. Haphazardly sprawled over the side of a 2,000-foot mountain called by the Indians "Potosí" (probably meaning "high place"), the town dated its origins from the day in 1545 the Spaniards were told of the mountain's fabulous silver lode. Some sixty years later, it was a boom town of 160,000 inhabitants who came from all over Spanish America and Europe to participate in the silver rush. In 1611, Potosí was not only the largest city in the New World, but larger than most of the urban centers of Europe and Asia, as R. C. Padden has pointed out. The town's name became synonymous in Spanish with immense wealth. Potosí became the real El Dorado that explorers had been trying to locate all over the New World, and had now finally succeeded in finding in the high, windy, mercilessly cold plateau of today's Bolivia. This land of wealth, whose tribute in silver made possible the Spanish empire, was also the wildest frontier in America, as the *History* minutely documents. Nevertheless, and for all it was worth, the strictest Spanish code of honor still functioned there. The story reproduced here from the vast repertory of anecdotes that constitutes the book tells of a Gothic revenge that continues after death, and of cannibalism, transforming the victim's remains into a sadistic fetish.

Little is known about the author of the *History*. Until quite recently not even his name was correctly spelled. The manuscript was never published in his lifetime. It was first rescued from oblivion by a Bolivian bibliophile, who published a selection in Paris in 1872. In 1941, a second selection was published by a Bolivian historian on the basis of a manuscript found in the National Library in La Paz. But it was not until 1965 that Lewis Hanke and Gunnar Mendoza were able to produce a complete text in a scholarly edition in three volumes, which subsequently became the basis of an anthology in English, *Tales of Potosí* (1975).

From these sources some information about Bartolomé Arzáns can be gathered. He was a native of Potosí and lived there his entire life. (His father was a Spaniard who somehow failed to become rich in that land of riches.) Born in 1676, Bartolomé Arzáns had little formal education but was an avid reader. Eventually he became a teacher and devoted a great part of his energy to collecting the information for his monumental *History*. But lacking, like Rodríguez Freile, the training of a historian, he settled for a year-by-year chronicle of events, with the emphasis more on the private lives of the Potosinos than on the public life of the town. He was very pious, and loved to quote church authorities. He believed every miracle and reported them all with untiring wonder. He was also sympathetic to the Indians, who suffered the most brutal exploitation in the mines. Being cautious not to look like a dissident, Arzáns used to quote Las Casas with approval (see selection 4). Like a true American-born Spaniard, he resented the tyranny of the Spanish-born authorities. When he started writing his book, at the beginning of the eighteenth century, Potosí was already in decline—its population reduced to 60,000, and only half of the boom-times refineries still working. Arzáns recorded all this with grief and frustration. Given the *History*'s revelations about the injustices, violence, and corruption of the Colonial administration, it may be safely assumed that the book (like *El Carnero*) received no encouragement. The authorities, in fact, did their best to keep it out of circulation. As a result, we in our time are practically the first readers of Arzáns de Orzúa y Vela.

The Wicked Hermit

From Tales of Potosí, *Edited by R. C. Padden. Translated by Frances M. López-Morillas (Providence, R.I.: Brown University Press, 1975), pp. 37–39.*

The Lord says: "Be ye not like the hypocrites who make show of what they are not and use tricks to make it seem that they fast and, feigning sanctity, secretly give rein to vice." O monstrous tricksters, hermits in appearance and devils in deed! How well was it said by the poet who compared you to the prodigious mountain of Catania [Mount Etna] in the following lines:

> Hypocritical Mongibello,
> Displaying snow, hiding your fire,
> If mountains can dissemble,
> What cannot humans hide?

And that is what hypocrites are: mountains (like Mongibello) covered with the white snow of feigned virtue; but within, what are they? Let that mountain speak, for it is a mouth of hell according to its acts. The following case is also an illustration of this, an example of how a rancorous breast can hide its terrible and abominable deeds.

In the year 1625 there died in this city of Potosí a man who was well known as a hermit and who for twenty years had wandered through its streets dressed in a sack or tunic, wearing a long beard and carrying a skull in his hand.

To all he gave the impression of being a good and penitent man, and such was he held to be and as such was he venerated. Since he always walked with the skull in his hand and sometimes stopped and looked at it very fixedly, all supposed that he was contemplating the fact of death. His usual dwelling place was among some dilapidated buildings behind the parish church of Santiago.

As I have said, his life came to an end, and he died provided with all the sacraments of the Church. After he had expired, those who were with him took up the skull as he had requested, and inside it they found a paper on which was written in his own hand the following message:

> I, Don Juan de Toledo, a native of this city of Potosí, son of a gentleman of very good repute in this realm ever since he came from Spain in an official capacity, wish to make known to all who have known me through sight and speech in the city and to all who would like to know about me in the future that I am the man whom all took to be a hermit because they saw me always clothed in a sack, and the more intelligent considered me to be virtuous and weary of the things of this world; and I was generally acclaimed in all this city as a just man.
>
> I am none of these, for I am the most evil of all the wicked men that have ever been in the world. Know that my garb was not the mark of virtue but of damnable malice. And so that you may all know of it I will say that a little more than twenty years ago, because of grievous wrongs inflicted on me by the Spaniard Don Martín de Salazar, in which he defamed all or at least the greater part of the honor God had given me, I stabbed him to death; after he was buried I found a way to enter the church by night, open his tomb, and take out his body, and I opened his breast with a dagger, took out his heart, and ate it (oh, my enormity!). After this I cut off his head and skinned it, and having reburied the body, carried off the skull. I donned a sack such as you have all seen me wear, and taking the skull in my hands I have walked about with it for nearly twenty years, never letting it out of my sight either on my table or in my bed.
>
> Everyone has taken me for a good and penitent man, but I deceived them when I gazed upon the skull, for they supposed that I was contemplating death; but, indeed, it was the opposite, for just as men become beasts through sin, I became the most terrible beast of all, a fierce and cruel crocodile. They say this beast groans and weeps over the skull of some unhappy victim whose flesh it has devoured, not because it has killed him but because it cannot eat him again; thus did I (more bloodthirsty than the very beasts) contemplate the skull of my enemy whose life I had taken, and I was sorrowful to see him dead, for had he risen again a thousand times I would have killed him again as many times. And I have lived with this cruel rancor for twenty years without ever being able to abandon

my vengeance and have pity on myself up to this very moment, which is the last of my life; but in this moment I repent of what I have done and pray God to pardon me and implore all to ask pardon for me from that Father of Mercies who prayed for those who crucified Him.

Such was the content of the letter. Take note, O Christian reader, of this terrible case!

21

CONCOLORCORVO (ALONSO CARRIÓ DE LA VANDERA)

Now that the gaucho has become the national hero of both Argentina and Uruguay, it is hard to remember that in the eighteenth and early nineteenth centuries the citizens of Buenos Aires and Montevideo had a completely different opinion of him. For them, the gaucho was the representative of "barbarism": at best, a lazy, asocial individual; at worst, an outlaw, a rapist, a killer. The radical change that ensued in the gaucho myth—from outlaw to epic hero—would take the best part of the nineteenth century and would only be completed in this century.

One of the first authentic descriptions of the gaucho, or *gauderio,* as he was then called, can be found in *The Guide for Blind Travelers,* surreptitiously published in Lima around 1775. The author was Alonso Carrió de la Vandera, a Spaniard who had been commissioned to inspect and reorganize the postal service in South America. Carrió de la Vandera, having been born in 1715, obviously knew well that part of the Spanish empire. He preferred to ascribe the authorship of his book to one of his aides, the half-caste Calixto Bustamante Carlos Inca, and further, to give him the pen name of Concolorcorvo (literally, "The Dark-Colored"). Even the book's place of origin was disguised: it is represented as having been printed in Spain, and two years earlier than in fact (Gijón, 1773). All these precautions indicate a strong conviction on Carrió's part that the book would never be approved by the Colonial authorities.

Under the fictional guise of a journey overland from Montevideo to Lima, Carrió describes and criticizes the Spanish administration. The book pretends to be a guide for the untutored (or "blind") traveler, and through anecdotes, descriptions, and assorted gossip, it presents a detailed picture of everyday life in some of the more God-forsaken provinces of the empire. In writing about the gauchos, Carrió displayed the same prejudices that some decades later would be shown by Argentine writers as important as Echeverría (see Part Two, 4) and Sarmiento (Two, 5). On the other hand, his description did accurately capture the unique way of life and customs of these skilled riders of the Uruguayan hills and Argentine plains. What he did not see was what would also escape the eyes of Echeverría and Sarmiento: that the economic exploitation of the gauchos by the landowners and the traders was the real cause of their "barbarism."

In quoting examples of their favorite songs, Carrió demonstrates that their folkways were rooted in a solid Spanish tradition dating from the Middle Ages. Theirs was not the kind of poetry that in the nineteenth century would be called "Gauchesca," which was actually written by citizens of Montevideo and Buenos Aires and pretended to imitate the gauchos' peculiar way of speaking. The gauchos did talk in a kind of dialect, but when they sang, they sang like their Spanish masters.

An Unflattering Glimpse of the Gauchos

From El Lazarillo de Ciegos Caminantes, *especially translated by Irving A. Leonard.*

These inhabitants of the plains are lads born in Montevideo and in nearby localities. Dressed in very tattered shirts and extremely worn garments, they try to supplement their apparel by a poncho or two, which, added to the saddlecloths of their horses, serves also as bedding while a saddle acts as a pillow. On small, poorly mastered guitars they strum badly bungled ballads and out of their own heads make up songs—mostly about love affairs—which they sing quite off key. They freely roam all around the countryside, living off and eating at the expense of the remarkably compliant and half-civilized settlers, meanwhile spending whole weeks stretched out at their ease on hides, strumming instruments and singing. If their horse is lost or stolen, they are either given another mount or they catch one on the plains by lassoing it with a very long rope called a *rosario* (rosary). They also have another rope with two billiard-sized balls—often merely round stones encased in leather—attached at the end. They hurl the latter so as to trip the horse. Another kind with three balls at the end and called *ramales* can cripple an animal enough to render it useless—a consequence that bothers the lads and the owners of the horses not at all.

Quite frequently these individuals get together in groups of four or five, sometimes more, and head into the country to amuse themselves; for their needs they take along only their lassos, ropes with *bolas,* and knives. They may decide to feed on the rump of a cow or a steer, in which case they lasso it, throwing it to the ground, and then tie its four legs together tightly; while it is still alive, they cut off its hindquarters, hide and all. They slice off pieces of flesh from the flank, barely brown it, and then consume it half raw, seasoned only by a pinch of salt if, by chance, they happen to have it. Or they may slaughter a cow or a steer solely for the meat between the hide and the ribs; then again they may just cut out the tongue and broil it over hot coals. Sometimes they may fancy the *caracuses,* which are the bones with marrow cooked on a revolving spit, and they feast on that substance. But the most extraordinary sight of all is to see them slaughter a cow, remove the entrails and all the fatty matter from the belly, and then set fire to the fat with only a live coal or a bit of dry cow dung. As soon as the fire starts and spreads to the fatty substance and bones, it burns brightly. Then, after it is restored to the cavity of the cow, the beast gives the appearance of breathing fire and smoke through its mouth and nostrils. It cooks in this fashion the whole night and a good part of the day until it is thoroughly done. Then in the morning or the afternoon the people gather around it, and each one hacks off whatever part he happens to like with his knife, and eats it without bread or anything else. When appetites are appeased, everyone abandons all the rest except one or more who carry off pieces to their rustic sweethearts.

Now let the London newspapers try to awe us with the size of the beef at state dinners in that capital! If the biggest beef there that the two hundred lordly banqueters feast on weighs two hundred pounds, here a five-hundred-pound one serves just seven or eight of these plains people, who usually invite the cow's or the steer's owner to come and partake, and he, in turn, usually considers himself well treated thereby! But enough about these inhabitants of the plains, for I perceive that our travelers are anxious to be off to their destinations by way of Buenos Aires.

. . . It is thus that a small number of settlers are content to live in a primitive manner, subsisting on meat and drinking their aloja, a beverage made of the carob bean and honey, in the shade of the thick, wide-spreading trees that produce this fruit and where they customarily concoct it. There they have good times together, bandying verses back and forth and with their rustic sweethearts, and lampooning each other in bits of song to the accompaniment of poorly strung and badly tuned guitars. If propriety and good taste permitted, I would write down here some of the rather off-color songs that they improvise after getting drunk on one aloja after another, though such intoxication is not usual among the younger fellows.

With due allowance for their crude and coarse ways, their songs are well harmonized, at the beginning, anyway, because they are improvised and learned from some droll wag. One afternoon when the inspector wanted to take a little ride on his horse, he and his guide led us into one of these thick groves where a sizable group of these inhabitants of the plains, both male and female, were gathered. He warned us to laugh along with them but not to join in their banter lest they start swinging their bolas at us. The inspector, as the most experienced among us, was the first to approach the gathering and he greeted them according to their own fashion. Then he asked if he and his companions, who were wearied by the hot sun, might rest a while in the cool of those wide-spreading trees. These picnickers welcomed all of us heartily, bringing us drinks of aloja. The inspector drank his and the rest of us, trusting his good judgment and example, did the same. Four of the young louts got up from a log where they were seated, and gallantly offered their seats to us. Two buxom young females were moving backward and forward on a swing formed by two tightly tied ropes suspended from two stout trees. Some other women, about a dozen in number, were busy squeezing juice to make drinks and slicing melons. Two or three men were occupied in heating pieces of half-dried meat and some bone marrow over coals, while still others were getting guitars ready by adjusting worn strings. An old man who looked about sixty years old but who was actually one hundred four, was stretched out beneath a shady beech tree, giving orders. As he deemed that it was now time to eat, he sat up and asked the women when they expected to feed their guests. The women answered that they were waiting for some cheese and honey from the house. The old fellow then remarked that that seemed all right to him.

The inspector, who is little inclined to warm his seat for any length of time, promptly told the old man that *he* didn't think that it was a good idea at all "and so, Señor Gorgonio, please have the lads and lassies sing a few songs that they like, accompanied by their tuneful instruments."

"So be it," said the venerable old man. "Have Cenobia and Saturina come and sing first of all with Espiridion and Horno de Babilonia." The individuals named stepped forward briskly and asked the aged fellow whether they should repeat the verses that they had sung during the day or some others out of their own heads.

At this point the inspector spoke up and said, "I like the latter ones, for they'll surely be very funny." They then sang some twenty perfectly awful verses, as the good-natured old man characterized them. At that moment the mother Nazaria and her two daughters Capracia and Clotilde put in an appearance, much to the joy of Pantaleon and Torcuato, who came running up with the scorched meat. But by now the inspector had taken out his watch twice, by which we all knew that he wanted to take his leave. But the old man, who recognized this at once, instructed Rudesinda and Nemesio to sing three or four quatrains composed by a friar who had been along that way the week before.

The inspector cautioned us to pay close heed and for each of us to make note of the verses that we liked best. The first ones sung contained nothing really noteworthy, but the last four stanzas happened to strike me as worthy of print because of their bizarre nature, so I am going to write them down here for the record:

THE WOMAN: I know your wily ways
and your many crooked deals.
You eat the choicest melons,
and leave us the chalk for the cheese.

THE MAN: Cut out that sham and nonsense!
Nobody gets me with that,

for my belly's already rubbed raw,
from crawling about on all fours.

THE WOMAN: You're just a great big dud,
and only aloja can get you moving.
At the sixty-ninth swallow,
the big row begins.

THE MAN: Get out of here, all of you!
including that big old blow-hard!
And everyone else get out who wants to,
so that I can wipe my tail!

"That's enough!" exclaimed the inspector, "and before the bolas come flying at us, because they've no rocks to throw, let's get back to our outfit!" And so we took our leave, to the considerable regret of the younger fellows who wanted to see the last of the fun, even if we stayed up all night. But the inspector did not consider it advisable, on account of all the drinking that had gone on. We really believed that the joke about substituting chalk for cheese or, more literally, catmeat for hare, was the friar's invention. The inspector told us, however, that it was a common expression in Paraguay and in the province of Buenos Aires, though not much used in Tucumán. But the original verses, he added, were quite as good as those sung by the ancient shepherds of Arcadia, despite the lyric embellishments of the later poets Garcilaso de la Vega and Lope de Vega.

The bizarre names of the men and women greatly surprised us, but the good-natured old man told us that they were those of new saints that the learned Cosme Bueno had introduced into his calendar. New saints, in general, performed more miracles than did the older ones, who just got tired of beseeching God in behalf of men and women sinners. We all laughed at this bizarre notion, but we did not try to disabuse them of it because the inspector, placing his index finger across his mouth, made the perfect sign of the cross. Although the young chaps called each other and every passer-by *macho*, or "tough guy," we did not mind it much, but it did seem wrong to call the young women *machas*. The inspector explained, however, that in describing themselves in this way, they were merely imitating that great Spanish satirist Francisco de Quevedo, who humorously and appropriately used the terms *pobre* and *pobra* to define the poor and wretched, male and female. Hence, these people here used *machos* and *machas*, but applied these designations just to their own members, male and female.

22

[TÚPAC AMARU]

In the life of Saint Rose of Lima (see selection 13) the New World had the first taste of the legend of Christian martyrdom. In the rebellion of Túpac Amaru can be found the nucleus of another legend: that of the revolutionary martyr. José Gabriel Condorcanqui (Peru, 1740–1781) was probably a half-caste, but a man of wealth and education, as contemporary accounts describe him. He was a descendant of the last Inca and took the name of Túpac Amaru II to lead his people in one of the most daring attempts ever made to free them from exploitation.

Túpac Amaru's reading of Garcilaso Inca's *Royal Commentaries* (selection 10), together with the living memory of his ancestors, helped him to rally under his banner a considerable part of the native population: he was seen by the Indians as the reincarnation of their Sun Kings. But he also sought to attract to his cause the American-born Spaniards, or *criollos*. To this end, he refrained from openly preaching rebellion against the Colonial administration, but concentrated his attack instead on the economic exploitation embodied in the institution of the *Corregidores*. These officials were responsible for distributing among the Indians the goods imported from Spain. As there were practically no local industries, they arbitrarily overpriced everything, from a knife to a pair of scissors, cloth fabrics and mirrors, glasses and playing-cards.

Túpac Amaru ultimately failed in his challenge to Colonial rule, and was executed in a very cruel manner in Cuzco's main square. But he was to become a symbol for all the patriots who in the early part of the nineteenth century finally achieved independence. In Bolivia and North Argentina, in Ecuador and Uruguay, in Colombia, the rebels rallied under his name. They were called "Tupamaros" by the Colonial authorities, or they proudly invoked the title themselves. Even today, the urban guerrillas who for several years successfully challenged the Uruguayan government claimed Túpac Amaru as their spiritual ancestor.

The official documents transcribed here show the extent of the authorities' alarm and fear. In the first, Juan Manuel, Bishop of Cuzco, accuses Túpac Amaru of being against religion, against the native Spaniards, and against the Crown, and justifies the Church in taking arms against him. In the second, the rebel leader is described as having next to him "two fair men, of goodly aspect, who looked as though they might be English." As the Spanish authorities believed, or pretended to believe, that England was backing the rebellion, this reference amounted to accusing Túpac Amaru of treason. In all the documents, he is presented as an upstart driven by overweening ambition, making boastful claims to be the only legitimate sovereign of Peru. In the last document, a touch of superstition alters the rather bureaucratic presentation of his execution. The

Inca cannot be quartered properly, as if made of iron; the Devil himself has prevented his followers from attending the execution; a strong unexpected wind forces everybody to run for cover. All these portents introduce magic into the ghastly account of the ceremony. Once more, imagination takes over—a demonstration of Colonial literature's faithfulness to its fabulous origins.

Rebellion and Death of Túpac Amaru

From The Green Continent, *pp. 195–203.*

The Uprising

The public funds were gone, because all the money in the royal treasury had been taken to Lima a little while before. The citizens were impoverished, and those who had means found all sorts of excuses to refuse to contribute to the daily upkeep of the troops. There was no gunpowder or other ammunition in the stores, for the thought of a catastrophe of this sort had never entered anyone's mind. And since it was imperative to supply this help at once, it seemed proper to me to assemble the clergy and the priors of the various religious orders and lay before them the need of raising a subscription to attend to the needs of the country and the King, and I set an example by subscribing 12,000 pesos in my name and in that of three convents, and the other groups did the same, according to their means, so that we raised close to 30,000 pesos, besides 14,000 in church funds which I borrowed without interest, and the priest of San Jeronimo gave 40,000.

The enemy had the advantage over us, for our forces were weak, and the members of the so-called Council of War spent their time fighting with one another, arguing over everything and deciding nothing. If, by chance, they agreed upon some measure that would have been helpful, it was never carried out. And so, to leave no stone unturned to help our country and put down the rebellion, I became a soldier myself, without ceasing to be a bishop, and when things looked blackest for us I armed the regular and the secular clergy, and, as a last resort, appointed the dean of my cathedral, Don Manuel de Mendieta, commander of these church troops, set up barracks, and formed the priests and the students of the two seminaries into four companies, with their respective officers, with arms and munitions which I provided, and they began their military training and drill under the command of an army officer. And there Your Reverence has the clergy of Cuzco, armed with sword and rifle, waiting every moment to meet the attack of the rebel Túpac-Amaru on state, religion, and crown. They have already appeared in the market-place, under the sign of the banner of the Christ of the Earthquakes, the image of the Virgin of the Rosary, the portrait of the King and his arms, prepared to lend their assistance to the regular troops in the first encounters with the Indians at Chita, three miles from the city. They have conducted themselves like seasoned veterans, and by their example have put heart into the masses and a different attitude into the nobles and raised the spirits of our scanty troops.

At the same time that they were lending this aid, the clergy stood watch in the towers, patrolled the streets, guarded the most dangerous posts, without omitting the most routine duty of the soldier, as they stood guard, night and day, with their arms in their hands, over the convents of nuns. I devoted my attention to all this, untiringly, for this was my rest.

Critics have not been lacking who have frowned upon this determination I took, and to justify their defamations they have circulated among the people a letter, purporting to come from Your Reverence's hand, saying that, even in the case of an insurrection, the clergy must not take up arms. I have paid no attention to this imposture, which brought forth a statement from the University of Lima that in such circumstances the clergy could and should take up arms; this is based on the doctrines of the greatest authorities in canon law, but apparently the impostor lacked this knowledge, and even that supplied by history. There have been many popes, since the days of Saint Gregory, who have taken up arms, not in defense of the faith, but for purely temporal motives, even against Catholics. We have the case of Julius II leading an army, not for religious reasons, but to defend his states; Cardinal Cisneros directing the campaign for the conquest of Orán; Juan Caramuel, Suffragan Bishop of Prague, conducting the defense of that city in 1648, and, before that, against the French and the Dutch; and if we want to go back to more remote times, we see Prince Sancho of Aragon, son of King Jaime, a member of the Order of La Merced, and later Archbishop of Toledo, who raised an army and went to Andalusia to fight the Moors, and as he was killed in battle the historians of his order consider him a martyr. And, leaving aside other examples of prelates and friars who have commanded armies, and have died with them, we have the case of Don José Dávila Falcón, judge of the ecclesiastical tribunal of the see of Lima, who, at the orders of the royal council of that city, raised a troop of eight hundred fifty clergymen when the capital was threatened by the English.

This bloody conflict has made it plain that the Indians are Christians only superficially, or as a mere rite, and that, if the truth be told, they are hardly less barbarous than their ancestors, though more cruel; and at the same time they have shown themselves to be irreconcilable enemies of the Spaniards. Therefore if it is not wrong for a priest to kill to defend an innocent person when there is no other way of saving his life, as Covarrubias, Lecio, Suárez, Bonocina, and others have held to be just, legitimate, and holy, as proved by Deuteronomy, chapter ix, verse 23, where Moses kills the Egyptian, how much more justified was the clergy of Cuzco in taking up arms against the Indians, who, aside from having given indubitable proof of their hostility to religion, were savagely attacking so many innocent persons, without sparing even the children. Besides, as I have pointed out, theirs was only a secondary aid, for the occasion never arose for them to take the field.

And what would Your Reverence say if he knew that in addition to all these cares I have laid upon me one which is far greater, and superior to my strength, which is that of preventing the inhabitants of the towns from fleeing, and making them remain where they are, as happened in Calca, Colla, Lamay, Pisac, San Salvador, etc., to guard the bridges and accompany the priests on their expeditions of spiritual reconquest, for the commanders of the troops have advised me that the people do not feel safe or respectable without the comfort of the divine services. All this fell upon me, and the most trying thing of all was safeguarding the town of Urubamba and its surrounding villages, because of the reckless order that had been issued to burn its bridge of withes, which was its only means of communication with the neighboring provinces. I opposed this order, determined to station members of my army to guard it, because if that had ever been done, the enemy would have been left in undisputed possession of the impregnable fortress of Vilcabamba in the province of Abancay and of all the others as far as Lima, and all this help would have been lost if we had destroyed the bridge, as Túpac-Amaru planned to do; and once Urubamba was in his hands, Cuzco would have been left without the abundant supply of grain from its fertile fields and exposed to frequent attack.

It is common knowledge how the priests of that valley of Urubamba worked to defend it from the raids of the enemy; for although they reached the neighboring village of Incay, they were thrown back with heavy losses and were unable to penetrate into the rest of the province. The zeal of the priests of Cotabambas is equally praiseworthy; they worked hard to strike at the root of the evil that was spreading through all that province and the bordering one of Chumbivilcas; for when the sacrilegious Bermúdez and Parbina, Tupac-Amaru's principal lieutenants, had been defeated and killed, the evil disappeared completely. Neither were the clergy of Paucartambo contaminated by this evil; they took up arms and strengthened the ranks of the inhabitants of that rich settlement, without excepting the women, who also served, thus throwing back Diego Túpac-Amaru, a cousin of José's, who tried to overcome it with a powerful army in order to go to the help of the rebel, who was laying siege to Cuzco, an attempt that was unsuccessful although the first time he besieged it for more than three months, in which time there were more than sixteen combats. I shall omit giving you further details about the priests and ecclesiastics of the rest of the diocese, because the account would be too long.

> *(From Juan Manuel, Bishop of Cuzco, to the Reverend Gregorio Francisco, Bishop of La Paz)*

Portrait of Túpac Amaru

Some of those who have recently fled here from the province of Azangaro say that when the rebel entered that province he was accompanied by four masked men who had nothing to do with any of the others, and this piece of news has been repeated by many, and it agrees with that given by Zavala, which is as follows: "The army was very large, and, besides the infantry, there were a thousand cavalry troops, Spaniards and mestizos, all armed, and on Túpac-Amaru's right and left two fair men, of goodly aspect, who looked as though they might be English. Túpac-Amaru was riding a white horse, with handsome trappings, and had two blunderbusses, a pair of pistols, and a sword. He wore a suit of blue velvet, embroidered in gold, a red cloak of the same material, a gold galloon about his forehead, a three-cornered hat, and, over all his clothing, a surplice like that of a bishop, without sleeves, richly embroidered, and around his neck a golden chain and, hanging from it, a sun of the same metal, the insignias of his princely ancestors."

(From a newspaper of Arequipa)

The Defeat of Túpac Amaru

The night of the seventh of the present month [April], a little before eight o'clock, we received reliable word of the capture of the rebel José Gabriel Túpac-Amaru, with his wife and children, who were accompanying him, and who have been with him throughout the war he has been making on us. It would be too long to give you a detailed account of the engagements between our troops and the rebels, nor have I time, for a soldier is leaving on horseback in a few minutes, at the order of the circuit judge, to carry these glad tidings to the capital, so I shall give you only the principal facts.

On March 31 the heads of two of the rebel's famous captains, called Porvida and Bermúdez, were brought to this city. They had been killed in a battle between our men and a rebel column of from five to six thousand men. Over a thousand of these were killed and the rest completely defeated. These two captains fought so fiercely that they died beside the cannon which they were firing upon us. This action took place in the province of Chumbivilcas, near Tinta. The commander of our troops, who was marching along another road to this province with a considerable force, which was to be joined by four other columns near Tungasuca, where the rebel had set up his court, entered the town of Quiquijana with an army of sixteen thousand men, and there took prisoner the rebel's chief justice and another chief, named Pomiaca, who were both hanged immediately. From there we marched toward Tungasuca, and on the outskirts of the town the rebels came out to meet us and give battle. But it was one of the showy sort he fights, with great uproar and movement, and the six cannon and other firearms he shot off were so badly handled that they killed only three men of our regiment. One of ours, comprising from three hundred to four hundred men, which was closest to the enemy, attacked them with such fury that they completely routed them, with such slaughter that Túpac-Amaru was horrified. His consternation grew when he saw that they captured his cannon, supplies, munitions, equipment, and all the booty he had stolen. He managed to escape without being taken prisoner because of the fine horse he was riding, and when he saw that all was lost, he sent word to his wife and children to flee as best they could, and he plunged into a swiftly flowing river and managed to swim across. But when he got to the other side the man he had made colonel of Langui took him prisoner in the hope of saving his own skin, and turned him over to our men, and the same thing happened with his wife, children, and other allies. Tomorrow our commander will leave this city to bring back the prisoners so that they may receive their just reward.

At six o'clock this morning Francisco Túpac-Amaru, the uncle of José, together with another chief named Torres, both famous captains of the rebels, were brought in prisoners. The first wore the royal garments the Incas used, with the arms of Túpac-Amaru embroidered in silk and gold on the corners.

This city is in a state of wild excitement over the capture of Túpac-Amaru and his family. The bells are pealing and the common people of the city are rejoicing, although two trunks of papers that were found among the rebel's possessions will keep some folks from sleeping soundly at night. Among the treasures that have been captured with the rebel are twelve coffers of embossed silver, many jewels of gold and diamonds, and many other things that cannot be listed here, for they say the inventory will take many days.

> *(From the Journal of the Army that left Cuzco to fight Túpac-Amaru under the command of Field Marshal José del Valle)*

The Death of the Rebel Leader

On Friday, the eighteenth of May 1781, the soldiers of this city of Cuzco were formed in a hollow square around the plaza, with their lances and their shotguns, and the four-sided gallows was surrounded by a squad of mulattoes and Indians, all with fixed bayonets. Nine prisoners were led forth, who were the following: José Verdejo, Andrés Castelo, a half-breed, Antonio Oblitas (who was the executioner of General Arriaga), Antonio Bastidas, Francisco Túpac-Amaru, Tomasa Condemaita, the woman chieftain of Acos, Hipólito Túpac-Amaru, the son of the traitor, Micaela Bastidas, his wife, and the rebel José Gabriel. They were all brought out together, their hands and feet shackled, in big baskets of the kind they use to bring maté leaves from Paraguay, and dragged along behind a harnessed horse. Accompanied by priests to administer the last rites to them and by guards, they were brought to the foot of the gallows, and two executioners meted out the following deaths to them:

Verdejo, the half-breed Castelo, and Bastidas were hanged. Francisco Túpac-Amaru, the rebel's uncle, and Hipólito, the rebel's son, had their tongues cut out before they were thrown down the steps of the gallows. The Indian woman of Condemaita was garroted against a post that had been fixed up with an iron screw for this purpose, which was something that had never before been seen in these parts. And Túpac-Amaru and his wife saw these torments with their own eyes, even that of their son Hipólito, who was the last to go to the gallows. Then the Indian woman Micaela was taken up to the scaffold, where, in the sight of her husband, her tongue was cut out and she was garroted, and her sufferings were unspeakable, because as her neck was very slender the screw was not able to strangle her, and the executioners had to tie ropes around her neck, and each pulled in a different direction, and with kicks in the stomach and breast they finally killed her. The spectacle ended with the death of José Gabriel. He was brought into the middle of the square and the executioner cut out his tongue. Then they unshackled his hands and feet and laid him on the ground. They tied four ropes to his hands and feet and fastened the ropes to the girths of four horses, and four mestizos led them in four different directions, a sight this city had never before beheld. Either because the horses were not very strong, or because the Indian was really of iron, they could not possibly tear him apart, even though they tugged at him for a long time so that he was stretched in the air in a way that looked like a spider. Until finally the commander, moved to compassion, to end the miserable wretch's sufferings, sent word to the executioner that he was to cut off his head, and this was done. Then his body was laid under the gallows and his hands and feet were cut off. The same was done with the women, and the heads of the others were cut off and they were sent to different towns. The bodies of the Indian and his wife were taken to Picchu, where a huge fire was built and they were thrown into it and reduced to ashes, which were thrown into the air and the stream that runs through there. And this was the end of José Gabriel Túpac-Amaru and Micaela Bastidas, whose pride and arrogance were so great that they called themselves King and Queen of Peru, Chile, Quito, Tucumán, and other regions, even including the Great Paititi, and other follies of the same sort.

A great many people had gathered that day, but nobody uttered a cry or spoke a word. Many observed, and I among them, that in all that assembly there were no Indians to be seen, or at least not in their customary garb; if there were any, they were disguised in capes or ponchos. Sometimes things happen in such a way that it seems the Devil must have a hand in them to confirm these Indians in their abuses, beliefs, and superstitions. I say this because, although the weather had been fine and dry, that day dawned overcast, without a sign of the sun, and threatening rain; and at twelve o'clock, when the horses were tugging at the Indian, a strong wind arose, followed by a sudden downpour, so that everybody, even the guards, had to run for shelter. As a result of this the Indians are saying that the heavens and the elements were lamenting the death of the Inca whom the cruel, impious Spaniards were putting to death so inhumanely.

(From a contemporary account)

Part Two

THE REDISCOVERY OF AMERICA

In freeing themselves from Spanish rule after 1810, the new Spanish American nations had a major problem to solve: how to maintain the cultural unity of the New World. For almost a century, the continent was plagued by political divisions, by local feuds and civil wars, by revolutions and the endless fight for power among petty chieftains. All these helped enormously the successful efforts made by the more imperialistic European states (England and France, joined later in the century by an emerging international power, the United States) to perpetuate the Balkanization of what had once been the proud Spanish empire. Against these forces, the unity provided by a common language, a common religion, and a common body of traditions was essential. In political terms, Spanish America was truly divided and weak, and it was in the maintenance of this cultural unity that there lay the only hope for future integration.

One of the first to discern this problem, and to analyze it in all its aspects and implications, was the Venezuelan Andrés Bello (selection 3). In 1823, while still living in England, he began to publish a sequence of poems, *The American Odes*, in which he not only besought the Muse of Poetry to leave decadent Europe and settle once and for all in the New World but also admonished the Spanish Americans against the lasting damage of war and division, exhorting them to work rather for peace and unity. Bello was a kind of Vergil for his time; he fought all his life to make the cultural integration of Spanish America a reality. Having lived in England, moreover, and so had the opportunity to observe the Industrial Revolution at its height, he was able to act as a mentor for Spanish Americans in the great task of entering the modern world, at the same time as he encouraged them to hold on to what was best in their past. From Chile, where he settled in 1829, he taught a whole continent how to preserve and update a living tradition. His work was later to be continued by men as diverse as the Argentine Sarmiento (selection 5), the Uruguayan Rodó (Part Three, 8), and the Mexicans Alfonso Reyes (Three, 19, v) and Octavio Paz (Five, 1).

At the time of the wars for independence, Latin America was still reacting and adjusting to the teachings of the Enlightenment; neoclassicism was still prevalent in its poetry. Romanticism did not settle in the New World until the late 1830s. This delay of almost fifty years had enormous consequences. It completely distorted the evolution of Latin American literature and prolonged almost until the end of the century the life of a movement that in Europe had already exhausted its vitality by the 1850s.

The official date of the arrival of romanticism in Spanish America (the Brazilians underwent a parallel but separate evolution) is 1832, when the Argentine poet Esteban Echeverría (Part Two, 4), after a prolonged visit to Paris (1825–1830), published *Elvira, or The Bride of the River Plate,* a collection of bad romantic verse. This date, however, does not take into account the preromantic and even romantic poets who were active in the northern part of South America long before the return of Echeverría. Actually, the earliest romantic poets depended less on French models, and were directly inspired by contact with Anglo-Saxon culture. In the 1820s, the Ecuadorian Olmedo (selection 3, I), the Venezuelan Bello, and the Cuban Heredia (3, III) had shown diverse but unmistakable signs of romanticism in many of their best poems. Olmedo, like Bello, had lived in England, and both were familiar with the English preromantic poets and with some of the romantics. Heredia lived in New York for two years and even published there, in 1825, a slim volume of Spanish verse in which traces of Byron's influence were easily detectable. These poets were the first to introduce romanticism as a countervailing tendency to the rather stilted and traditional poetry that had been written in Spanish America thus far.

Even in the River Plate area, romantic themes and ideas had arrived before Echeverría's return, thanks to the now almost forgotten metropolitan-Spanish poet José Joaquín de Mora, who settled in Buenos Aires in 1827. He had come from England, where he had sought refuge for political reasons. In the first quarter of the nineteenth century, England became a haven both for Spaniards escaping the tyranny of Ferdinand VII and for the Spanish Americans seeking an ally in their struggle against the mother country. Some publishers had started to cater to the New World market, publishing collections of poems, popular fiction, and cheap editions of texts of study. Several periodicals were also founded in the 1810s and 1820s. With this very important movement Bello had been associated almost from the moment of his arrival in London in 1810. Mora also became one of the leading publicists of the Hispanic colony; he translated some of Walter Scott's novels, wrote pious sentimental poems to accompany a Spanish edition of Blake's engravings, and produced with great rapidity diverse kinds of educational materials. Mora even preceded Bello's return to Spanish America. In Buenos Aires, he began a much-needed updating of the educational system; later he went successively to Chile, Peru, and Bolivia, to accomplish similar tasks. And everywhere he went, he planted the first seeds of romanticism. Thus, the actual introduction of romanticism in the River Plate area had been anticipated by a man whose models were basically Anglo-Saxon.

If, then, it is an error to make the year 1832 the official date for the introduction of romanticism in Spanish America, its selection as a landmark can nonetheless be defended from a different point of view. After the publication of *Elvira,* Spanish American poetry began to show everywhere signs of acute contamination by romantic themes and exalted visions. From the very beginning the new literary movement was associated with the fight for freedom both from Spain and from local tyrants. One of the forerunners of romanticism, Rousseau, was also the main source for the political ideology of the newly created countries. Whereas in Europe some of the most distinguished romantics were (or eventually became) conservatives, in the New World romanticism and revolution were tightly linked. Taking Byron and Victor Hugo as models not only of poetic style but also of a committed political attitude, the Spanish American poets attempted to change both society and literature. Thus, some of the early romantics (like Heredia and Echeverría) were forced into exile because of their political convictions. From a purely literary point of view, the movement was based on French letters. Of the great English romantics, only Scott (as novelist) and Byron were widely read, and generally in French translation; of the Germans, only Goethe, Schiller, and Heine, and very few Italians, with the exception perhaps of Manzoni and Leopardi. But the influence of French authors permeated all genres: Lamartine, Hugo, and Musset were the most quoted, translated, and imitated—sometimes to the point of plagiarism. The fact that French romanticism was itself largely dependent on German and Anglo-Saxon models only gave it a more international appeal. From the romantic vogue onward, the development of Latin American literature would be closely linked to changes in the French literary scene.

As compensation for its lateness in arriving, romanticism was slow in leaving, and it took almost the best part of the nineteenth century to disappear completely. Some poets, like the Brazilian Castro Alves (3, IV), or the even later Uruguayan Zorrilla de San Martín (who wrote the best narrative poem of the movement, *Tabaré*, in 1888), were still composing romantic verse at a time when, in Europe and the United States, the new schools of realism and naturalism on the one hand, and Parnassianism and symbolism on the other, were already flourishing. A polemic between Sarmiento and some of Bello's disciples, which took place in Chile in 1842, not only challenged the validity of neoclassicism and urged the adoption of romanticism, but even went so far as to proclaim that romanticism as such had already been replaced in Europe by socialism. This controversy, despite all its confusions, accelerated the diffusion of romanticism and oriented both writers and readers to a less sentimental and more sociological approach to literature. To this movement, Sarmiento contributed a masterpiece, the biography of an Argentine Gaucho chieftain, *Facundo* (1845). In the following decades, romanticism would be slowly contaminated by realism. But it was not exclusively the influence of French models that brought about the change. In attempting a more accurate description of Latin American reality—that is, in rediscovering America in literary terms—the new writers were also returning to a tradition of Spanish realism that was as old as Spanish literature. Thus, it is not accidental that one of the first novels to be published in the nineteenth century was a picaresque account of the life and times of *The Itching Parrot*, by the Mexican Fernández de Lizardi (selection 2), and that the brilliant *Memoirs* of Friar Servando Teresa de Mier (1) were also in a picaresque vein. In other genres, the same Hispanic tradition of realism could be recognized. The gauchesco poetry that was developed in the River Plate area during the nineteenth century had its roots in Spanish ballads and popular songs. It presented the realities of rural life in its contrasted states of pastoral and civil war. In the second half of the nineteenth century, poetry gave way to prose, and the best gauchesco writing was done in novel form (selections 4–8).

Other tendencies also mixed romanticism with realism. An Indianist movement achieved notable success during the nineteenth century. It drew its inspiration from sentimental narratives on the order of Chateaubriand's *Atala*, but it managed to produce at least one masterpiece of the historical novel: *Enriquillo*, by Manuel de Jesús Galván (9). Another such tendency was mainly devoted to re-creating the old traditions of Spanish American society through the presentation of daily life in the capitals and the provinces. This school was allied with the work of such gossipy old chroniclers of earlier times as the Colombian Rodríguez Freile (One, 12) and the Bolivian Bartolomé Arzáns (One, 20); and it produced at least two genuinely great figures: the Peruvian Ricardo Palma and the Colombian Tomás Carrasquilla (Two, 10, 11). The new chroniclers infused and blended the old realism with an exalted romantic vision while achieving at the same time greater discipline and control in their work. Through the work of all these schools, Spanish American artists in prose and verse were discovering their own unique forms of expression.

The Brazilian novel had a less adventurous development. Mirroring the stability of Brazilian society—independence had come to Brazil at the hands of a Portuguese prince—it developed more harmoniously and coherently than the Spanish American. From José de Alencar's romances (in which regionalism and Indianism were blended) to Machado de Assis' urban and psychological realism; from Manuel Antônio de Almeida's picaresque account of Rio de Janeiro's lumpenproletariat to Raul Pompéia's elegant dissection of obscure adolescent impulses in a private boarding school, the Brazilian novel of the nineteenth century solidly established a narrative tradition that in the course of its evolution in the next century would continue to produce some of the best Latin American writers.

1

FRAY SERVANDO TERESA DE MIER

Like one of Byron's damned souls, Fray Servando spent most of his life in bitter exile, in dark prisons, trying to escape from forces (the Church, the Inquisition, the Crown) that were fated to crush, humble, and finally destroy him. But unlike the Corsair or Childe Harold, Fray Servando had no horrid secret to hide. Born in Monterrey, Mexico, in 1763, he entered the Dominican order, and in 1780 received a degree in theology. Nothing eventful might ever have happened to him if he had not decided, on December 12, 1794, to preach a sermon against a popular belief of the time: that the Virgin Mary had appeared to the poor Indian Juan Diego at Guadalupe and left her painted image on his cape as a sign of her concern for the conversion of the natives.

According to a theory Fray Servando borrowed from José Ignacio Borunda, it was rather on Saint Thomas's cape that the Virgin had left her miraculous imprint. Here he was alluding to another widely held belief—namely, that Saint Thomas, one of the Twelve Disciples of Christ, had come to America and preached there many centuries before the arrival of the Spaniards. By a characteristic process of syncretism, the Indians had come to identify the saint with, and to worship him as, the indigenous Mexican divinity Quetzalcóatl, the Plumed Serpent. Saint Thomas's cape with the Virgin's imprint had only later, Fray Servando argued, been presented to Juan Diego.

Borunda's theory, or at least Fray Servando's version of it, was in fact a rather farfetched attempt to merge two different legends: the allegedly overseas origin of the Mexican god, and the miracle of the Virgin of Guadalupe. In his sermon, the friar was not only challenging the deep popular belief in the Virgin's miracle, which the Spanish Church tolerated, but was also seeking to give a solid theological foundation to the theory that the Gospel had been preached in the New World before the conquest. From the Spanish standpoint, however, the theory had dangerous implications, in that it undermined their claim to a providentially assigned role as missionaries to the indigenous peoples. Fray Servando —who had always sympathized with Las Casas' spirited defense of the Indians (see Part One, 4)—apparently failed to foresee the disastrous consequences his exposition of such ideas could, and did, have for himself. For the Church authorities perceived at once the danger that the theory represented, and they reacted promptly and vigorously: Fray Servando was sent to Spain for trial, and was condemned to ten years in prison. For the next twenty-odd years, he was forced to live in Europe, persecuted by the Church and the omnipresent Spanish bureaucracy, imprisoned in all kinds of dungeons, escaping from one only to be recaptured and immured in another, in an endless succession of adventures that took him not only to all parts of Spain, but also to France, Italy, and England. Those two decades saw the collapse of the Spanish Empire in America, the first wars of independence in Mexico and South America, and the redesigning of the map of Europe by the Napoleonic armies.

Amidst this ongoing political cataclysm, Fray Servando pursued his private war against very specific and almost allegorical enemies. (His major foe was called León, or Lion.) He never got tired of dank, rat-infested prisons, or of jumping from high windows, or of walking across hostile frontiers. Even when he managed to extricate himself at last from the claws of the Spanish Church and returned to his native land in 1817, as a revolutionary priest, the dungeons of the Mexican Inquisition were waiting for him. The government of the self-proclaimed Emperor Iturbide had no place for Fray Servando. Somehow, he survived and even died peacefully in the Convent of Saint Domingo, in 1827.

But yet stranger adventures ensued. His mummified body was first shown publicly in 1842, as a relic of the convent; later, in 1861, it was sold to an entrepreneur, who carried it in and out of the New World. He ended up by being billed as a "Victim of the Inquisition" in a Brussels exhibition in 1882.

In a sense, the label was correct. But Fray Servando had also been a victim of his own insatiable appetite for adventure. Wrongly cast into the role of heretic and revolutionary, Fray Servando was actually a very conservative man who was pushed to excesses by his own exalted sense of the dramatic. He was a true creature of his time—a time when every young man thought he could reach the highest places, the time of Napoleon and Bolívar. Fray Servando belonged to the generation that destroyed the *ancien régime* on both sides of the Atlantic. But his was not a heroic or tragic life. He belonged more to the picaresque than to the epic. In the various autobiographical accounts he left (only recently collected under the general title of *Memoirs*, 1946), he was mainly concerned with setting the record of his life straight. But, like Rousseau or Casanova, he also wrote to fulfill a deeply narcissistic need: to leave behind a record of his dashing, brilliant, beautiful self.

The fragment here presented shows Fray Servando at his best: escaping into revolutionary France, being sought after by learned rabbis and beautiful Jewesses. Fray Servando had no reticence whatsoever in talking about his attractive appearance (at thirty-eight) and high moral qualities. What he lacked in discretion he compensated for in verve. He was obviously very much in love with himself, and like Rousseau he claimed to be of such a tender nature that he could not even bear to step on an ant. Reading this lively text, it is hard to realize that it was first set down on paper some twenty years after the events described, and in the absence of any documents to refresh the author's memory. At the time of writing, Fray Servando was imprisoned in a cellar and suffering from a liver condition. But he seems not to care, and writes as if he were showing off in a Paris salon. Some hundred fifty years later, a young Cuban novelist, Reinaldo Arenas, was to write a fictional account of Fray Servando's life (see Five, 20). The book, *Hallucinations*, is one of the best of the New Latin American novels and a perfect homage to this flamboyant priest.

The Flight into Revolutionary France

From Memorias, *especially translated by Suzanne Jill Levine.*

I certainly no longer considered submitting to the iniquities of the Council or the whims of León, whose only interest was to gain time. To promise me justice after making me carry out the archbishop's sentence was a mockery. But I didn't have money to live on. The Council, because of the Royal decree, ordered the attorney of my province to provide for my wants while in Salamanca and to arrange for my trip, giving me the necessary money for expenses. To pick up this allowance, I made an agreement with a coachman, who went with me to the attorney; I made believe I was leaving early next morning, left my cell in the Indies quarters of the San Francisco convent, received an ounce of gold from the attorney, and went into hiding. But the coachman was smarter; he discovered my lodging and demanded the money which, he said, they had asked him to get. How could they ask him for something they hadn't given to him? Fearing, nevertheless, that he would betray me, I gave him twelve duros, which was all I had left at the end of four days. He probably took them, since he told the attorney that I, telling him I had some business to attend to, had made him wait all day long; which I found out because afterward León used that lie against me. This is the only scheme that I've ever attempted in this life, and, as you can see, it was a failure. My candor excludes all deceit. In vain my friends have always urged me to have a little Christian roguery in me, as they would say. But it is not in my power to be malicious.

Uncertain about my destiny, I kept myself hidden with the help of some of my countrymen, until I learned that the Council had consulted the Ministry on what to do when they found me, and that León, to turn Minister Caballero against me, told him that I was plotting to kill him. Imagine, poor me, why when I see ants on the road, I hop around them to avoid squashing their little bodies! And to save mine, which I could not hide for long, I got on a mule and set out for Burgos, to see if among the friends I had there I could gather some money and go to France. All I could secure was an ounce of gold, and two days later I decided to go on to Agreda, where there was a French clergyman smuggler, who was also a friend and could help me with the money and resources that I needed to get to France and then on to Rome, with the purpose of leaving the cloth. As long as I wore the cloth, they would be kicking me around like a ball, because in Spain they look upon friars with the utmost contempt, as upon the scum of the earth: their honor has no importance, and the worse you treat them the more highly you're regarded. Their only problem in storing them away is to find the means of providing for their maintenance, and if they have some province to take care of that, the oppressors are free to do what they like.

Just as I was ready to get on the mule, the mayor of Burgos overtook me at the inn. There was a lot of caution with travelers then, since the plague had taken Andalusia, and as the damned innkeeper saw that I only went out at night, because I was well known in Burgos, he had reported that I was suspect. This left me speechless thinking he had brought some warrant; my fear and my answers made the judge suspicious, he grabbed my papers, found the Council's order to go to Salamanca, and while he informed the court he sent me to the San Francisco convent. As I was leaving for the convent I told the boy, who brought me the ounce of gold from Madrid, not to go, because I would leave the convent that night and we would go together to Agreda. He told the mayor, who then imprisoned me in a cell of the said convent. Since I was highly esteemed in Burgos, this caused a great scandal.

The next day, a priest offered to help me jump out the window to the courtyard below. But I didn't let him, because, always candid and simple, I still didn't know León and I thought he would be satisfied with making me go to Salamanca, I having declared to the mayor that I had only come to Burgos for a short while, to secure some money with which to set up my cell in Salamanca and to buy some utensils. But the fierce León, who again saw me in his clutches, returned to his favorite theme: that I must carry out every bit of the archbishop's sentence, and he sent the order to take me to Las Caldas and bury me there in a dungeon for the four remaining years of the sentence.

One of the ministers told the secret to my friend Don Juan Cornide, and he sent me the news through a Burgos businessman, who delivered the letter to me, despite the convent warden, who intercepted my mail, because friars have no scruples in these matters. Thunderstruck, my powers and senses were paralyzed for four hours. Well, if we're going to lose everything, I said to myself as I came to, we must risk everything; and I began to figure out ways of escaping. My first thought was to fly down under my umbrella, whose tips I would be tied to, to the bottom of a square patio which was lined on three sides by cells and where a door could be seen. But I was too high up; below, enormous stones would receive me and my flight would be as successful as Simon Magus's. I went back to the priest who had offered to take me out from the start, but he was already afraid, having seen the care with which they guarded me, taking turns day and night to watch me. He suggested, however, that I could climb down with the rope that formed the web of my bed.

With that tied to the window I began to climb down at the stroke of midnight, the moment when the friar on guard retired to attend matins; and while there were windows to prop myself on, I went down well; but then, the weight of my body made me cut my hands, and, without realizing it, I went down faster that I would have wanted to. When for the same reason I thought I'd find myself splattered on the ground, I instead found myself hanging on the end of the rope, which was knotted. I ended my flight rather damaged, and went through a door that led to a yard; it was closed, but had a crack through which I squeezed with great effort. I got outside the yard and ran a quarter of a mile from Burgos, where the hospital of the king's *comendadores* is; they hid me that day.

There I hung the cloth out of necessity, and with a hunter's pouch filled with some provisions and eight duros, I left at eight at night for Madrid, on San Francisco's coach, as they say. It would take a long time to tell of the troubles I had, resting in the day, walking at night, jumping off the road at any sound, fighting with the dogs that fill the villages in battalions, and trembling for fear of the thieves who, led by Chafaldin, desolated Old Castile. This was my first experience of traveling on foot, and my feet and legs swelled so that after two nights of walking, it took almost a day for me to walk a mile—until, reaching a village three miles from Torquemada, I began to weep. A muleteer who was on his way to this town took pity on me, put me on a donkey, and took me to stay at the house of a good man, his benefactor.

For my money this man gave me a mule, with a boy who would take me to Valladolid. On the road we met up with some people who were going to Burgos, and they said, "That's the Father who was in San Francisco's," which made me quicken my pace, since through them my course could be known in Burgos and a warrant might catch up with me. In Valladolid, I was given shelter by two men who had been my students in rhetoric in Burgos. To be careful, I would go into the country on the days the mail came from that city, in case there was some news, and not come back till they called me for dinner. There I learned that in Burgos León had asked for all my papers that the mayor had taken from me; the rest had remained in my trunk in Madrid. This was one of León's goals: to take my papers and documents away from me, and then attack me when I was empty-handed, or find some material among them with which to incriminate me. There he has the titles of my orders, my degrees, my defense, etc.; and he didn't deposit them in the secretary's office, because afterward I asked Don Zenon to look for them, and they weren't there.

After resting eight or ten days in Valladolid, I continued my journey, in a Catalonian cart, a very uncomfortable vehicle that almost drove me mad. I identified myself, as always, as an émigré French clergyman. Arriving in Madrid, I went to the house of Don Juan Cornide, who lived with Filomeno, now the attorney general of Havana, his native city. They informed me that León, furious that his prey had escaped his clutches, had ordered the arrest of the whole San Francisco convent of Burgos; but the mayor had reported that the priests made him see the bloodprints of my hands on the wall, which proved that I had escaped without their help. Also, I found out that León had ordered warrants issued against me throughout Spain. Can you believe such excesses? Wouldn't you judge, in view of these scandals, that I was some murderer, highway robber, or hardened criminal? León was to accuse me as such, basing his accusation solely on the archbishop's report that I had been tried by two viceroys, although León had in his possession the letter in which the count of Revillagigedo refuted the archbishop. All this was, of course, the wrongdoing of this wicked minister.

The one from Mexico, Don Zenon, sent me word that he had exempted Catalonia from the warrant on purpose, so that I could escape through there to France. In that country, however, I would be totally without resources. The shortage of money was what put me in greatest danger. My good brother, Don Froilán, may God keep him, kept writing from Monterrey that money orders could not be sent from Mexico to Spain, but that I should borrow money here in his name. It is even more difficult to find someone who will lend money in Spain, to then be paid in America; and in time of war, like the one that has been going on with England since I've been in the Peninsula, it's almost impossible. Spain lives off America, as Rome the Papal bulls, and as soon as the merchant ships are obstructed, only hunger and misery are to be found in Spain. When Bishop Espiga was sent hastily to Havana because he had been found guilty of being a Jansenite and a friend of Urquijo, he had to borrow money at 200 percent in order to be able to assume his bishopric. How was *I* going to find money!

In Navarre I could resort to the French clergyman-smuggler who was in Agreda. He was also a friend of Don Juan Cornide, who had relatives there, since his brother Don Gregorio was vicar general in France. He suggested, then, that I travel with some muleteers from Agreda, and he and Filomeno got me out through the gate of Fuencarral, in a hackney coach, making a lot of noise when passing through so that the guards would not be suspicious. A quarter of a mile away they left me with the muleteers, who already had my trunk; and for my credentials as an émigré French clergyman, Cornide gave me those of the late Dr. Maniau, whose testament he had executed. They suited me in every way, since he was my age and rank. The new Maniau got on a mule, and at night we stopped to rest in the muleteers' inn outside Alcalá de Henares.

That evening at eight a tumult frightened me, and it was none other than Cornide and Filomeno, who having received a copy of the warrant from Don Zenon, came to change my appearance. And indeed they diabolically transformed me, to the point of putting a mole on my nose and another on my lip with a charcoal crayon. My own mother wouldn't have recognized me. And not only that, but since León said in the warrant that I was good-looking, cheerful, and friendly, they urged me to look taciturn, sad, and ugly. So when I'd see guards, I'd grimace, cross my eyes, and literally carry out the last cry of the Portuguese army: "Show the enemy your fiercest face." Nevertheless, we didn't dare enter through the gate of Agreda, where there were two warrants—the government's and another from the mayor of Burgos—and the muleteer took me through a side door to his house.

He was one of the confidants of my clergyman-smuggler, who then came to see me. I handed my trunk over to him, which he still has in his possession, and he left me in the hands of another confidant who would take me to Pamplona, recommending me to a French business firm, with which I was also acquainted, that would get me into France. Upon leaving Aragon for Navarre, I had a view of Spain's despotism and ruinous extravagance, since they search you more rigorously for the money you carry from province to province than on the borders. Although my baggage was reduced to a little sack of clothes, which the guards spilled onto the floor, and also eight *duros,* which I had declared, they also went through my prayerbook with an awl, in case I was hiding some gold there.

I reached Pamplona four days after Urquijo's arrival as a prisoner in the fortress, and from the tavern I went to the French businessman's house. "Don't go back to the inn," he said to me, "because they've just taken two men, believing them to be you and Cuesta, the archdeacon of Avila, fugitive because of the learned pastoral he had presented and that his bishop published." All this happened at the critical time of Godoy's persecutions (the same Godoy who on this account was called, in a brief from Rome, a *pillar of religion*) of the Jansenites. "Jansenites" is what they call in Europe all the men solidly instructed in religion and friends of the ancient and legitimate discipline of the Church.

Immediately, my Frenchman called for a muleteer who had taken many clergymen over the Pyrenees to France. He came with his mule, and as we followed him out, the businessman handed the guards a few pesetas. I got on the mule at the end of the Paseo de la Taconera, and he instructed us to get as far into the Pyrenees as possible that same night—as we did, walking till two in the morning, when we reached Hostiz, frozen stiff. The next day we crossed the valley of Bastan, and on the third we slept in Cincovillas, from where you can see the sea, Bayonne, and its outskirts, bleaching in the country like a drove of cows. I was not much at ease in the inn, because there were guards there and they had a warrant; but the muleteer, well known there, declared that I was a French clergyman, which was confirmed by my physiognomy, hair, moles, and Mexican accent (which they said was foreign: in Andalusia, Mexicans pass for Portuguese or Castilians, and in Castile for Andalusians); all this put me in the clear.

The next day we went through Ordaz, the last little stop in Spain on that side, and my only desire was to know where the border with France was. "This is it," the muleteer said to me, pointing to a very little and shallow stream. I crossed it, got off, and lay face down on the ground. "What are you doing?" he asked.

"I've crossed the Rubicon," I answered. "I am not an émigré, but a Mexican, and I have only this passport (it was Maniau's) from Mexico to Spain."

"It doesn't matter," he said. "The gendarmes don't understand Spanish, and they will think you so distinguished that they will doff their hats to you as to an important person." And that's exactly what happened.

We slept in Añoa, the first place in France—that is, of the Basques or French Biscayans, because Biscay is part of Spain and part of France, and from either one they come to America as Spaniards, just as from French and Spanish Catalonia. The next day, to enter Bayonne, a walled city, the muleteer made me get off the mule and mix with the people on the avenue, where for the first time I saw carriages pulled by oxen. That measure was useless because the guard spotted me as a stranger, with my boots, and all covered with dust as I was from the road. He took me to the town hall, where I presented my Mexican passport, and since they didn't understand it, they gave me my security card or ticket. All this was very necessary in those times because of the still not completely quenched turbulence of the Republic. It still was one, although governed by consuls, Bonaparte being the first. That day was Good Friday of the year 1801. What could I do for a living, being so punctilious, as befits my origins, and incapable not only of begging but even of showing my misery? I, instead, suffered deathly pangs, and I wouldn't have gone through them if I had been an atheist. By chance I entered, unknowingly, the synagogue of the Jews of the Sancti Spiritus quarter. They were singing the Psalms in Spanish and preaching in Spanish. All the Jews in France, and almost all of them in Europe, except Germany, are Spaniards by origin, and many of them, natives. I saw them arrive in Bayonne to be circumcised: all of them, men and women, speak Spanish; their Bibles are in Spanish, all their prayers in Spanish, and they are so punctilious about this, that although the marriage contract for a German Jew marrying in Bayonne, who didn't understand Spanish, was put into Hebrew so that he'd understand it, it was first read in Spanish, and it was this version that he signed. And they still preserve their Spanish customs in everything, and do most of their business with Spain, which they have all visited. The cause of such determination to preserve everything Spanish is that, they say, those who came to Spain by order of the emperor Hadrian are from the tribe of Judah.

When I entered the synagogue, the day after arriving, it happened to be the Passover of the unleavened bread and the lamb. The rabbi preached, proving as they always do on that Passover that the Messiah had still not come, because the sins of Israel detain him. Leaving the synagogue they all surrounded me, wanting to know what I thought of the sermon. They had already spotted me, because I wore the ecclesiastic collar, and had taken off my hat, when on the contrary all of them wear it in the synagogue, and the rabbis conducting the services wear a sash on their heads besides. The greatest show of respect in the Orient is to cover your head. Only in the cadí, or commemoration of the dead, which an orphan always recites, do they uncover their heads in the synagogue. And their way of finding out if someone is Jewish is to ask him in Hebrew: What's your name? I tore down in a minute all the rabbi's arguments, and they challenged me to a public dispute. I accepted, and as I had at my fingertips Bishop Huet's evangelical arguments, I was so brilliant in the dispute that they offered me in matrimony a beautiful and rich young woman named Raquel, and in French *Fineta*, because they all use two names, one for the community and another for the public; and they even offered to pay for my trip to Holland, to marry there, if I didn't want to do it in France.

As you can imagine, I rejected their offer; but I remained in such good standing among them from that day on that they called me Jajá, that is to say, wise man; I was the guest of honor in all their services; the rabbis would consult me on their sermons, so that I would correct their Spanish, and they made me a new suit. When I went out of curiosity to the synagogue like other Spaniards, the rabbis made me take a seat in their tribune or pulpit. And the evening service over, I would stay alone with the rabbi, to watch him study what he was going to read the next day. He would then take out the law of Moses, which when the people are present is taken out with great ceremony and veneration, all of them leaning toward it. It is written in scrolls, with only consonant letters, and the rabbi would study it, I reading it in the Bible with the vowels. And then I would put out the candles, because they cannot do it, nor light fire to make food nor warm themselves on Saturdays. They use Christian maids for all this, and I told them that for that very reason their religion could not be universal.

As I was still youthful-looking, I didn't lack candidates among the young Christian women either. They have no trouble in expressing themselves, and when I'd answer that I was a priest, they'd say that was no problem if I wished to leave the Church. The multitude of priests who, because of the revolutionary terror, had married out of necessity, removed these women's scruples. In Bayonne and in all the province of the Low Pyrenees to Dax the women are white and pretty, especially the Basques; but I was never more impressed by the influence of climate as when I was traveling toward Paris and saw that from Montmarsan, eight or ten miles from Bayonne, to Paris the men and women were dark, and the latter ugly. Frenchwomen on the whole are ugly; they look like frogs. Bad figures, stumpy, wide-mouthed, and slanty-eyed. They look better toward the north of France.

In order to live in Bayonne, I went for help to the French clergymen whom I had helped when they were émigrés in Spain. In compliance with the French government an order was issued in 1797 demanding that the poor French priests leave Spain for the Canary and Balearic Islands, and those of Burgos were ordered to the port of Coruña to carry this out. I had sent in their name a petition to the Burgalesian clergy to help them make their journey. It pleased the clergy so much that they went out enthusiastically into the streets with trays to make a collection, and got together enough to decently transport sixty priests, who, in my honor, departed from San Pablo's convent, where I then was staying. The poor things sent me forty francs to Bayonne, with which I determined, after two months, to travel into France. What I needed was a passport; but the Jews brought to my attention that in the Mexican one I had for Spain, this last word was abbreviated and a blank space followed at the end of the line. There I put "and France," and I embarked on the river for Dax, four miles away.

From there I continued on foot to Bordeaux, more than thirty miles away, in the company of two Spanish deserters, shoemakers by profession. Since the way there is through sand, I suffered infinitely, and I would never have reached Bordeaux, because of my swelling feet, had I not embarked on another river. My shoemakers began working immediately, and they made money like dirt, while I, full of theology, was dying of hunger and envy. Then I realized the good parents could do in teaching their children, even the most noble, some craft in their childhood, especially one so easy and so necessary everywhere. This means providing them with bread through all the ups and downs of life.

I had received a letter from the Spanish ambassador in Paris, Don Nicolás Azara, and another from the botanist Zea, because in the midst of all my labors and miseries I always received attention and correspondence from the scholars of Europe. In view of these letters, the Spanish consul, who needed the ambassador to approve his budget, gave his secretary orders to lodge me. This was a Spaniard who was determined to make me an atheist through the works of Freret, as if an Italian wouldn't have reduced his sophisms to dust. I have observed that people read impious books with pleasure, because they encourage the passions, and not only do they not read the refutations, but they despise them, because the self-confident boasting and satisfied tones of unbelieving authors pass on to the spirit of the readers. And the truth is that such boasters are the ignorant ones and the impostors. They speak with the satisfaction which they don't have within themselves to prevail, and if they have it, it is because of their own ignorance. *Qui respicit ad pauca, de facili pronuntiat.*

As soon as said secretary learned that I had money, he faked an order from the consul and made me pay twenty duros for my lodgings, which he pocketed. The money had come from the generosity of Don José Sarea, count of Gijón, native of Quito, who disembarked in Bordeaux and brought all his money in sugar from Havana, from the sale of which he planned on earning a great deal. And, in fact, there wasn't any sugar then in Bordeaux. I urged him to visit Paris before going to Spain, and he took me as an interpreter. He threw away money as if he were in America, and I, figuring that he would reduce himself to poverty in Europe, where they all conspire to strip the newly arrived Americans, stopped his hand, even when he wanted to spend for my sake. He was angry at this and abandoned me almost as soon as we reached Paris. He was very sorry afterward, because he was overwhelmed with the troubles I had predicted. Instead of selling the sugar immediately, the Bordeaux businessman, on whom he relied, waited for the market to overflow with sugar from other sources, a result of the peace of Amiens, and then sold it for nothing, or pretended to sell it, keeping the money in payment for the storage. The count recognized my gentlemanly honesty in the end, and I haven't had a better friend since.

I don't want to omit that a Frenchman in the service of Spain, who became my friend in Bayonne, successfully recommended me from Bordeaux to his brother, who occupied a place of influence in Paris, because *even though he's a priest,* he said of me, he is a *gentleman.* He showed me this phrase and told me it was necessary, because all of them were atheists. Then I saw that it was the common phrase in the recommendation of a priest. The unbelievers had declaimed so much against religion, and called its ministers impostors, that they finally impressed the people, who went out to hunt them in the forests, where they fled the revolution, saying they were going to kill black beasts.

If the Frenchman had known that I was a true believer, he wouldn't have recommended me, because the condition of friar made me unacceptable. Among Catholics as well as unbelievers it is an ignominy, or rather, the epitome of all ignominies, and just by calling you that, they believe they have exhausted all insults. Friar is the equivalent of a man who is low, mean, ill-bred, lazy, beggarly, ignorant, an impostor, a hypocrite, a liar, fanatic, superstitious, capable of all baseness and incapable of honor and of being a gentleman. It seems incredible, and it is the truth. Even in Catholic ships one must not admit that one is a friar; if there is some storm they throw him in the water, as has happened several times. That's why in Spain they killed off the French friars remorselessly, in and out of the convents. That's why they almost don't exist in Spain. Joseph Napoleon had persecuted them to extinction in Spain, and the Courts did the same. Where there are still some left they are looked upon with the greatest contempt, and they are not allowed into any decent house. I happened to visit the daughter of the trader Terán in Madrid, as she was my countrywoman, and after I had given my name, she answered that I write to her explaining my business. The worst is that priesthood leaves an indelible mark. There is no use leaving the cloth or becoming a bishop or Pope. They always friar him contemptuously, and in Rome, to scorn the Pope, or some decree of his, men and women alike say, "Oh, è un frate."

JOSÉ JOAQUÍN FERNÁNDEZ DE LIZARDI

Until the advent of independence, fiction was not allowed to circulate freely in the New World. The Colonial authorities had banished all novels, although some romances of chivalry and *Don Quixote* were regularly smuggled in. But with independence, fiction writing was legally authorized for the first time. Paradoxically, the first Latin American novelist of some importance was a writer who, like Henry Fielding, resorted to this genre only because political censorship prevented him from continuing to write satirical commentary.

Lizardi was born in Mexico in 1776 and had a good though incomplete education: he entered the Jesuit College of San Ildefonso in 1793 but left sometime after 1798 before getting a degree. He worked in some bureaucratic position and was Assistant Justice in picturesque Taxco, in 1811, when the revolutionaries sacked the town. He was accused of having helped them and was taken prisoner to the capital, judged, and finally exonerated. It was Lizardi's only direct contact with the independence movement. Although he was a liberal and had absorbed some Enlightenment ideas, he was a sincere Catholic and believed in reform rather than revolution. Yet he was very much against the excessive power of the Mexican Church, defended a representative system of government in which women would have the right to vote, and once even dared to praise the Masons. For this, he was promptly excommunicated in 1822.

As soon as the Colonial authorities relaxed their political censorship, Lizardi founded the first of his five periodicals, *The Mexican Thinker* (1811–1812). The journal's title became his pseudonym. It espoused a complete program of action. Over the following fifteen years, Lizardi became, in effect, Mexico's conscience. An endless outpouring of journals and pamphlets attested to his preoccupation with public affairs and morals. When censorship was again reinstated in 1815, Lizardi had recourse to novel-writing. A mere four works, hastily written over some four years, comprise the sum of his production in the sphere of fiction. As soon as the Constitutional Government, which took over from the Spaniards, restored freedom of the press, in 1820, Lizardi deserted literature and went back to political journalism. Eventually, in 1825, he became publisher of the *Official Gazette*, and held this post until his death in 1827.

Lizardi's four novels constitute the foundation of the Spanish American novel of today. They are odd, strangely anachronistic books. As a professional writer, Lizardi was addressing an audience of old-fashioned tastes, which he had to entertain if he would instruct. To achieve this twofold purpose, he resorted to an old formula: a mixture of wild adventures and sentimental preachings. At least two of his novels followed more or less the picaresque model that had ceased to be in fashion in Spain some hundred fifty years before. But Lizardi's *Itching Parrot* and *Don Catrín de la Fachenda* were perhaps closer to the *Bildungsroman* and the edifying novel of the eighteenth century (Richardson, Fielding, Gold-smith, Rousseau), or to the neopicaresque works of Dickens such as *Pickwick Papers, Oliver Twist,* and even *David Copperfield,* than to the old Spanish originals. Half of *The Parrot* is unreadable today because of its banal digressions. *Don Catrín* fares better from this point of view (it is mercifully shorter), but its hero's adventures are less comic.

Lizardi's two other novels—*The Quijotita and Her Cousin* and *Gloomy Nights and Happy Days*—are more indebted to the sentimental-cum-preaching fiction of the day. The first is a good satire on women's education in Old Mexico; the second, a tear-jerking rewriting of Young's *Night Thoughts* and the Spanish Cadalso's imitation of the former, *Lugubrious Nights.*

Today, however, Lizardi's literary reputation rests almost exclusively on *The Parrot.* Katherine Anne Porter's translation is a masterpiece. She edits the sermons out and frees the narrative from all cant, in this way emphasizing what a good storyteller Lizardi could be. The excerpt here presented corresponds to four chapters of the original and covers some of the hero's wildest activities. He is seen first as a rash barber, then a murderous druggist's assistant, and finally a self-appointed physician. The novel's title comes from a schoolboy's pun on his name, Pedro Sarmiento. In Spanish, the nickname for Pedro is Perico, which also means parrot; the surname, Sar*m*iento, was changed into Sar*n*iento because Pedro had caught a *sarna* (itch). The "Stewpot" mentioned at the beginning of the excerpt is a lawyer who had befriended the Parrot and has been duly betrayed by him.

Today Lizardi's moralizing liberalism seems extremely tame. We know that some of his Rousseauesque ideas were acquired through a laundered version of Jean-Jacques produced by a Jesuit priest, Father Blanchard. But in Lizardi's own time, not even the cloak of fiction prevented him from being censored. The last part of *The Parrot* was published posthumously in 1830–31 because the censors had objected to a chapter in which Lizardi openly criticized slavery. A similar fate befell the two last parts of *The Quijotita,* in which he attacked the popular though not canonic belief in the capacity of saints to perform miracles. His last novel, *Don Catrín,* was published only posthumously in 1832. A liberal Catholic thinker was an extremely dangerous person in those revolutionary days.

The Itching Parrot

From The Itching Parrot, *translated and edited by Katherine Anne Porter* *(New York: Doubleday, 1942), pp. 128–170.*

The ground a coward can cover when running away is unbelievable. It was twelve o'clock sharp when I left Stewpot's house in the Street of the Ratas, and I ran with such good will that I awaited the quarter bell in the Alameda. I was terrified and covered with sweat, hatless, my head was broken, I was torn to rags and dying of hunger; but even so, I considered my escape from Stewpot cheaply bought. I feared his scurrilous pen even more than his club, for if he had got me in his clutches, not only would he have beaten me, but he would have cooked up slanderous charges, and sent me to dive for mother-of-pearl at San Juan de Ulua island.

A venerable old man and a boy were busy catching leeches in a basket in the nearby ditches. Going about this work, the old man greeted me, and I answered him politely. On hearing my voice, he peered up at me sharply and, after hesitating a moment, jumped the ditch, threw his arms about my neck, and said, "Pedrito, my soul! Is it possible I see you again! What has happened to you? What is the meaning of these rags and these bloodstains? How is your mother? Where do you live?" I could not answer a word, surprised to have a man I did not know speak to me familiarly by name.

Guessing the cause of my confusion, he said, "Then you do not remember me?"

"No, sir," I responded, "except to serve you."

"Well, I remember you; I know your parents and owe them a thousand favors. My name is Agustín Chinscraper. I shaved the late Don Manuel Sarmiento, your father, for many years, so I knew you quite well, my son, quite well. I can say I saw you born, and don't think I didn't. I loved you very much and played with you when your father came to be shaved."

"Well, Agustín," I said, "now I begin to remember these things a little."

"What are you doing here, my son, and in this condition?" he asked.

"Oh, sir," I responded, shedding widow's tears, "I have had the most miserable luck. My mother died two years ago; my father's creditors threw me out into the street and attached everything in the house. I have supported myself by serving first this man and then another; and today my master, because the cook ladled out his soup cold and I carried it so to the table, threw it at me and broke my head with the plate; then, his anger not satisfied with this, he grabbed up a knife and chased me, and had I not got a start on him I would not now be telling you my troubles."

"Imagine!" cried the simple barber. "Who is this cruel master?"

"Who, sir," I said, "but the great Marshal Mouse."

"Who? What are you saying?" said Chinscraper. "That cannot be, for there is no such name in the world. It must be some other."

"It is true, sir; I have forgotten my master's name and title because I was scarcely two days in his house; but it does not matter whether I remember his right title or give him a comedy title, for if we look at it seriously, what title is there in the world that is not comedy? According to my way of thinking, it matters not whether I remember or forget the title of the master who beat me. What I will not forget are his cursed acts, for these are, after all, what stick in men's memories, to be damned and resented; but not so the titles and dictates that die with time and are confounded with the dust of tombs."

The innocent barber listened to me astonished, thinking I must be a learned, virtuous man, and, feeling sorry for me, took me home, where a good old woman named Aunt Casilda and a boy apprentice received me with sweetest hospitality. I supped that night better than I had hoped for, and the next day the master said to me, "My son, although you are already big for an apprentice" —I was about nineteen or twenty years old and he spoke rightly—"if you wish, you may learn my trade. It is not one of the most favored, but at least it brings in enough to eat; and so, if you apply yourself, I will give you a home and a mouthful, which is all I can afford." I accepted, because it was convenient for the moment, and set myself to play at washing towels, holding the basin, and doing whatever I saw the other apprentice do.

Once when the master was away, I made an experiment to prove whether I had progressed in my trade. With the help of the apprentice, I caught a dog and, binding its feet, front paws, and muzzle, we sat it in a chair and tied it in. We laid out a little rag to clean the blades and I began shaving. The miserable animal raised his whines to heaven as I nicked him from time to time with the razor. The operation was finally finished and the poor animal was fit to sit for his portrait. As soon as we freed him, he ran for the street like a soul pursued by devils, and I, puffed up over this first trial, determined to make another on a poor Indian who came to be shaved for a penny. With great care, I tied the towels around him, had the apprentice bring the basin of hot water, sharpened the razors, and gave him such a punishment of scratching and cutting that the unhappy man, unable to endure my harsh hand any longer, got up, shouting, "Let me go, Christian, let me go!" So I gave him his penny back and he went away half shaved.

Not satisfied with these experiments, I dared to take out a tooth for an old woman who came in raving with a fierce toothache. I made her sit down and deliver up her head to the apprentice to hold. He did his work well. The miserable old woman opened her desert of a mouth after having shown me the tooth that hurt her; I took the scraper and began to cut off slices of her gum happily. The miserable old woman, seeing a bowl of blood in front of her, said, "Young master, for God's sake, when will you finish scraping?"

"Don't worry, auntie," said I, "and have a little patience, it's only a little way now to the jawbone." Finally, after I had cut out enough meat for the house cat to breakfast on, I took hold of the tooth with the proper instrument and gave a hard jerk, but awkwardly, and so I broke the tooth, hurting her terribly.

"Oh, Jesus," cried the old woman, "you've torn out my jawbone, you devil!"

"Don't talk, auntie," I said, "or the air will get into your mouth and rot your jaw."

"Rot yourself, you devil!" said the poor woman: "Oh, Jesus, oh, oh, oh!"

"Now there, there, auntie," said I, "open your mouth. Let's finish taking the root out. Don't you see it's rotten?"

"Rot in hell, you botcher, you worthless fool!" said the old woman.

Without paying any attention to her insults, I said, "Come, auntie, come on now, and open your mouth. Let's finish getting out that damned tooth. You'll see how one pain stops another. Come, even though you do not pay me."

"Curse you," said the old woman, "go pull teeth out of the drunken sow who bore you! You swinish chinscrapers are not so much to blame as we who put ourselves in your hands." Continuing these praises, she went out of the shop without even looking back at the place of sacrifice.

I pitied her for her suffering, and the boy rebuked me for my stupid obstinacy, saying, "Poor old soul! What pain she must be in! And the worst of it is, what will the master say if she tells on us?"

"Let him say what he likes," I responded. "I did it to help him earn his bread. Besides, you can learn only by experience." I explained to the mistress that the disturbance was all due to the old lady's money tricks, because she had a rotten tooth that could not be pulled out at first haul, a thing that happens only in the best cases.

I stayed with Don Agustín four months and a half, and went on with my devilish capers, for which my clients paid sometimes in money, sometimes in abuse. This long stay was due partly to my fear of Stewpot and partly to my lack of a better asylum; for in that house I ate, drank, and was treated with respect and attention by the master. I was lucky enough not to have to run errands or do anything but look after the barbershop and misbehave whenever I had a chance, for I was an honorary apprentice, so spoiled and such a big numbskull that, although I had no shirt, there was still someone to envy me my fortune.

This was Andrés, the apprentice, who, talking one day while we were waiting for a customer willing to try out for a martyr, said, "Sir, who wouldn't be like you!"

"Why, Andrés?" I asked.

"Because," said he, "you are already a man, your own master, with no one to order you about, while I have many to scold me and do not know what it is to have a penny in my pocket."

"But as soon as you finish learning the trade," I said, "you'll have money and be your own master."

"What a dream that is!" said Andrés. "I have been here apprenticed for two years already, and know nothing."

"Nothing, man?" I asked, much surprised.

"Just that. Nothing," he answered. "But since you came I have learned something."

"What have you learned?" I asked.

"I have learned," he responded, "to shave dogs, flay Indians, and break old women's jawbones, which is not little. May God reward you for teaching me. For the rest, my whole day goes in running errands here or for Tulita, my master's daughter; and in her house it's even worse, for they make me carry the baby, scrub diapers, run back and forth to the barbershop, wash dishes, and put up with as many disagreeable chores as they like. With all that to do, how can I learn the trade?

"We're running into the third year, and still the master shows no sign or intention of teaching me anything."

"Then why didn't you apprentice yourself to a tailor?" I asked Andrés.

"Oh, sir! To a tailor? They sicken of the lungs," he said.

"Or to a tinsmith?"

"No, sir; for they get cut on the tin and burnt with their irons."

"Why not to a carpenter?"

"Oh, no; because they suffer great harm to their chests."

"To a coachmaker, or a blacksmith?"

"May God forbid. Indeed, they are like devils when they are at the forge beating the iron."

"Well, son of my soul, Pedro Sarmiento II, brother of my heart," I said to Andrés, getting up from my seat. "You are indeed my little brother; yes, we are twins, doubles. Give me a hug. From today on I shall love you more than ever before, for your way of thinking is so like my own it could be mistaken for the original; in fact, we are identical, you and I. You are as lazy as my own mother's son. The trades do not attract you because of the discomforts that go with them; nor does it please you to serve because masters scold. But it does please you to eat, drink, idle, and have money for little or no work. The same thing goes for me! You can see how I have plenty of reason to like you."

"That is to say," replied Andrés, "that you are a lazy fellow, and I am, too."

"You are right, my boy," I answered.

"Well, if that is your reason," said Andrés, "you ought to find many brothers in this world, because there are many lazy fellows with our very tastes. Still, you should know that it is not the trade that troubles me, but two other things: One is that they teach me nothing, and the other is the mean disposition of that damned old woman, the mistress. Except for these, I would be contented in this house, because the master could not be bettered."

"It is true," I said, "the damned old woman is the very devil, quarrelsome and stingy as Judas. What else do you expect from her, with her face like a wrinkled sheet and her mouth like an old slipper?"

The shop opened directly on the street, with a little upstairs, the kind we call cup-and-saucer, and we forgot that the mistress was listening, as she always did listen to our talk, until I began these praises of her. Justly irritated against me, in perfect silence she caught up a pot of hot water she had on the brazier and dumped it on my head, saying, "You dirty ingrate, get out of my house, for I won't put up with such devil-possessed fellows as you, who come here to talk about me."

I do not remember whether I answered or not, for I was deaf and blind with pain and rage. Andrés, fearing another worse bath, and taking warning from my scalded head, fled into the street. I, raving and skinned all over, dashed up the little staircase with the intention of knocking the breath out of the old woman, and then escaping, like Andrés. But the cursed old woman was brave and determined; when she saw me coming up, she seized a knife from the brazier and went after me with the greatest courage, stuttering in fury, "Ah, you idiot, you dare! I'll teach you!" I did not wait to learn what she meant to teach me, but turned tail instantly and fled with such unlucky haste that I stumbled over a little dog and went down the stair more quickly than I had gone up, headfirst, smashing my ribs. The old woman was hot after me. She had no pity and did not stop at my misfortune, but bolted down with the knife in her hand, so determined that even now I believe if she had caught me she would have killed me. As always, I had wings on my heels when danger threatened, and in four jumps I put four squares between me and her fury.

In its untimeliness, this leavetaking was like the one from Stewpot's house. For the rest, it was worse, because I left not only pursued, hatless, but dripping and scalded. So I found myself about eleven in the morning on the Tlaxpana highway. I sat in the sun to dry my poor clothing, which day by day went from bad to worse, for I had no change. At three in the afternoon, it was entirely dry, dust-dry, and I in a bad condition, for hunger beset me with all its strength. My shoes were so worn they had stayed on my feet until then out of mere compliment and abandoned me finally in my flight. I could imagine the weird figure I must make without them, because my ragged stockings showed all the dirt and patches of the linen linings, so I took them off and threw them away, leaving my feet and legs bare. To top off my disgrace, fear overcame me when I wondered where I would pass the night. I could not decide whether I should remain in the country or go back to the city, for I found insuperable obstacles to either choice. In the country I feared hunger, inclement weather, and the darkness of the night; and in the city I feared jail, an unlucky meeting with Stewpot, or the Master Barber; but finally, at vespers, I overcame the lesser fear and returned to the city. At eight I was at the Flores portal, dying of hunger, which had increased with so much walking. I had nothing on my person of any value except a little silver medal I had bought for five reals when I was in the barbershop. It cost me trouble to sell it at that hour, but finally I found someone who would give me two and a half reals for it, of which I spent a real for supper and a half real for cigarettes.

My stomach filled, it remained but to decide where to spend the night. I walked through street after street without finding a place, until, passing by the Inn of the Angel, I heard the sound of gambling and, remembering Long John's trestles, said to myself, "There is no help for it. I have a real in my pocket for the keeper; here I stay this night." Said and done, I went into the gambling den. Everyone stared at me, not because of my shabbiness, but because of my fantastic appearance. I was unshod; drawers I had not and my outside breeches were black wool, patched and torn; my shirt, besides being worn out, was almost black with dirt; my waistcoat was calico with big red buttons; my hat had been left in the house; and, added to such ostentatious rags, I had an extravagant face, for it had blistered and my eyes were half hidden within the puffs raised by the boiling water. Everyone continued to stare, but their attention did not matter to me: I would have suffered any offense in exchange for not having to stay in the street.

At nine o'clock they all stopped playing and everyone began to leave, except myself. I set about putting out the candles at once; which did not displease the keeper, who said, "Little friend, God reward you for that, but it is late and I am going to close, so you must go."

"Sir," I said, "I have nowhere to stay. Do me the favor of letting me pass the night here on a bench. I will give you a real I have, and if I had more I would give it."

"Keep your real, my friend. Stay and welcome. Have you supped?" he asked.

"Yes, sir," I responded.

"So have I. Let us go to bed," he said. He got out a blanket for me and while we undressed he asked me who I was and the reason for my being in so sad a state. I told him a thousand pathetic lies instantly. He took pity on me and told me he would speak to a druggist friend who had no servant and see if he would accommodate me in his place. I accepted the favor, thanked him, and we went to sleep.

The following morning, in spite of my laziness, I got up before the keeper, swept, dusted, and did everything I could to win his good will. He paid me for this and said, "I am going to see the druggist. But what shall we do about a hat for you? As you are, you look very suspicious." "I do not know what I will do," I said, "because I have not enough money to buy one. But by the time you do me the favor of going to see this druggist, I shall come back."

Saying this, I went away, breakfasted, and in a portal took off my waistcoat and traded it in a secondhand shop for the first hat offered me, although I felt I was cheating the shopkeeper. The hat was nothing but a wornout one cleaned up, so what must the waistcoat have been? When I made the exchange I remembered the old verse about

> Montalvo of Segovia, lately wed,
> Was much dissatisfied.
> He had crosseyes, lame back, bald head,
> So try to imagine the bride!

Happy about my hat and feeling myself disguised in my own odds and ends of clothing, the son of Don Pedro Sarmiento converted into a servant for hire, I set out to look for the keeper, who told me that everything was arranged, but that my shirt looked like a winding sheet and I must go wash it at the canal; poverty was one thing and filth another: the former provoked pity but the latter disdain and contempt: I should remember the proverb that says as I see you I judge you: and at noon he would take me to my new job.

I stayed two months as servant, grinding bark, skinning snakes, fanning the fire, running errands, and helping wherever I was needed or ordered, to the satisfaction of the master and his assistant. As soon as I had got eight pesos together, I bought stockings, shoes, jacket, waistcoat, and neckerchief; all second-hand, but serviceable. I brought everything to the house secretly and on Sunday dressed myself up like an alderman. My master did not know me at first, and then, gladdened at my metamorphosis, he said to his assistant, "You see, it's clear this poor boy is the son of good parents and was not brought up to be a pharmacy servant. That's the way, son; always show your good beginnings even if you are poor, for one of the signs of good parentage in a man is his dislike of being ragged and dirty. Do you know how to write?"

"Yes, sir," I responded.

"Let us see your hand," he said. "Write on this."

Wishing to show off a little and confirm the master in the good opinion he had formed of me, I wrote the following: *"Qui scribere nesciunt nullam putant esse laborem. Tres digiti escribunt, caetera membra dolent."*

"Well!" said my master, admiringly. "The boy writes well, and in Latin! Now, do you understand what you have written?"

"Yes, sir," I said. "It says those who do not know how to write think it no work, but although only three fingers write the whole body is uncomfortable."

"Very well," said the master, "then you must know what the label on that flask means."

I read *"Oleum vitellorum evorum"* and said, "Oil of the yolk of eggs."

"So it is," said Don Nicolás; and putting out cans, flasks, bottles, and boxes, he continued asking me, "What does this say here?"

As he asked, I answered, *"Oleum escorpionum:* Oil of scorpions. *Aqua Menthae:* Peppermint water. *Aqua petrocolini:* Parsley water."

"Enough," said the master, "from today on you are an apprentice. You will work here with Don José and go with him into the laboratory to learn, although you know something already, from what you have said. Study and apply yourself, for you will find it to your benefit."

From that moment, the assistant no longer called me plain Pedro, but Don Pedro. I was proud of my change of luck and my important-sounding title of pharmacy apprentice, not knowing then the common proverb that says, careless as a student, a sacristan, or a pharmacist. I did not intend to apply myself to learning chemistry and botany; my studies were limited to mixing a few evil-tasting beverages, to learning a few technical terms, and to taking care of the customers; but I was such a good hypocrite that I won the assistant's confidence and affection—my master himself was seldom in the pharmacy—and within six months I was already such a help to Don José that he had time to go for promenades and even to sleep away from the shop. For my last three months with them, he had paid me eight pesos a month; I would have turned out an assistant with much higher pay if chance had not caused me to leave that place.

But before I relate this adventure, you need know about some other things. At that time in this capital there was an old physician nicknamed Doctor Physic, because he invariably prescribed a purge to every one of his patients, no matter what their illness might be. This poor old man was a good Christian, but a bad doctor and theorist. He did not hold by Hippocrates, Avicena, Galen, and Averroes, but to his own caprices. He believed that no sickness came of anything but an abundance of vicious humor; and he maintained that by evacuating this the cause of the sickness was removed. He might have been enlightened by the number of victims he sacrificed on the altar of his ignorance, but he never admitted he was human; he believed himself incapable of making a mistake, and so did great harm. This doctor was in a kind of partnership with my master. That is, my master, Don Nicolás, sent Doctor Physic as many patients as he could; and Doctor Physic sent all his patients to our pharmacy: My master told them there was no better doctor than the old man; and the Doctor assured them there was no better pharmacy than ours. Between us, we did very well; and the shame of it is this case is not fictitious and has innumerable originals.

This Doctor knew me well; he came into our pharmacy every night. He liked my handwriting and disposition—for when I liked I could deceive the devil—and often said, "My son, when you leave here, advise me, for you will never lack something to eat and something to wear in my house." The old man wanted to set up a pharmacy of his own and hoped to have in me a trained assistant at small cost. I thanked him for his offer, saying I would accept it if I fell out with my master, but at the time I had no reason for leaving.

I was, in fact, living a famous life, such a life as a lazy man longs for. My duty was to see that the boy cleaned the pharmacy in the morning and kept the water bottles filled with distilled and infused water. I did not care a whistle about all this: the well saved me the trouble of distilling water, and I said, "If the labels are different, even if the water is the same it does not matter, for who will know? The very doctor who prescribes probably does not know them apart except by name; the sick man who takes them knows less, and has usually lost his sense of taste: So this deceit is a safe one."

There was another very pernicious abuse in the pharmacy where I worked, and it is common in all others: As soon as it became known that some drug was scarce, Don José put up the price to the extreme of refusing to sell less than a real's worth, and because of this abuse—we can call it covetousness without the least scruple—the miserable man who had but a half real and needed a little bit of some drug, let us say camphor, to cure himself, could not obtain it from Don José even in the name of God and all His Saints; as if Don José could not have given for a half or quarter real the half or quarter part of what he gave for a real, little though it might be. The worst of it is there are many pharmacists of Don José's way of thinking, thanks to the indifference of the Tribunal of Physicians.

At night I had more freedom, because the master came only for a little while in the morning, collected the sales of the day before, and then did not return at all. The assistant, knowing this, when he saw I could dispatch prescriptions, at seven o'clock took his cloak and went to pay compliments to his lady, although he had to be careful to be in the pharmacy early in the morning. I was in my glory. Certain fellows at once made themselves my friends, came there to visit with me, and we ate together merrily, sometimes playing games at two, three, or four reals, all at the expense of the money drawer, against which I held an open draft.

Some months passed this way, and then the master decided to strike a balance. He found that although there was no loss of any importance—few pharmacists ever lose—the profit was scarcely perceptible. Don Nicolás was surprised to find a deficit and when he took Don José to task the latter explained it by saying the year had been a healthy one and such years were lamentable, at least not profitable, for doctors, pharmacists, and priests. The master was not content with this answer and with a grave face said, "The lack of profit must be due to something other than the temperate seasons this year, for even in the best there are always sicknesses and deaths." From that day on he began to watch us distrustfully and was not absent many hours from his shop. Within a little while, the pharmacy began recovering profit; the drawer suffered fewer evacuations; Don Nicolás did not leave until late at night and when he did carried off the money. If a friend invited him to some amusement, he excused himself, saying he thanked him, but could not abandon his attention to the business, for the man who has a shop must attend to it. We were soon tired of this; the assistant could not go out and the apprentice could not tipple, play, or loaf at night.

During this time, over I know not what question, my master quarreled with the Doctor and broke off their agreement and friendship. How true it is that most friendships are sustained out of selfish interest! For that reason there are so few that last.

I thought of leaving the place, for I was angry now at his supervision and the little chance I got of handling the money drawer with the liberty I had before, but I stayed on because I had nowhere else to go, and nothing to eat if I went. One day it happened that I set about to dispatch a prescription that called for a small dose of magnesia. I poured the water in the bottle; then the syrup; and, meaning to take the magnesia box, I picked up the arsenic and mixed the required dose. The miserable man, I afterward learned, confidently drank it down and the women of the house stirred up the dregs in the glass with a spoon, telling him he should take them because the powders were the most beneficial. Soon he began to froth, writhing in the infernal pains that tore at his entrails. The household was alarmed; they called the doctor and told him that the moment the man took the medicine ordered for him, he began to suffer uneasiness and pain. The doctor asked for the prescription, put it safely away, had the bottle and glass brought, looked at the powder still in them, tasted it, and cried out in alarm, "The sick man is poisoned. This is not magnesia, it is arsenic. Bring warm oil and milk, a great deal, and quickly." Everything was brought instantly, and with these and other remedies the sick man was saved. As soon as the doctor saw he was out of danger, he asked from what pharmacy the dose had been brought. They told him, and he notified the Tribunal, offering his prescription, the testimony of the servant who went to the pharmacy, and the bottle and glass, as credible proofs of my stupidity. The judges commissioned another doctor, who, accompanied by the scrivener, came to our shop. My master was surprised to see such visitors. The commissioner and the scrivener briefly and summarily stated the case, as though I were already confessed and convicted. They wanted to take me to jail, but when they were informed that I was not an assistant but only a raw apprentice, they left me in peace, charging my master with all the blame. He suffered as penalty the payment of two hundred pesos fine, in the act, and threat of embargo in case of delay in payment. The commissioner notified him on the part of the Tribunal, under penalty of closing the pharmacy, that he should never again put apprentices to dispatching, for what had just happened was not the first nor the last calamity that would be wept over because of the stupidities of attendants. There was no help for it. My poor master got into a coach with these gentlemen, glaring at me with the highly indignant face of a badly paid blacksmith, and told the coachman to drive to his house, where he had money to pay the fine.

The coach had gone but a little way when I went back into the pharmacy to get my cloak and hat. I said to the assistant, "Don José, I am going now, because if the master finds me here he will kill me. Give him my thanks for the good he has done me and ask his pardon for my devilish mistake; it was really an accident." No persuasion on Don José's part was enough to detain me. I hastened on, regretting my disgrace, but consoling myself that at least I had come out of it better than I had from Stewpot's and Don Agustín's houses.

Stopping one day in this gambling den, another in that, some twenty days passed, and I was once more without cloak or jacket. Not wishing to see myself again without shoes or in even worse state, I resolved to go as servant to Doctor Physic.

3

A SAMPLE OF ROMANTIC POETRY

It is well known that romantic poetry does not always travel well. Wordsworth's lyrics are as untranslatable as the Spanish Bécquer's subtle *Rhymes;* the best of Hölderlin or Nerval is perhaps lost in translation. Latin American romantics are no exception to this rule. Their verses are too much the product of a certain time, a certain atmosphere, a certain tone and diction. In trying to be fair to them it is better to reduce the selections to a few.

The four poets presented here cover practically the whole span of the movement. The first two, Olmedo and Bello, are essentially neoclassicists who were moved by the wars of independence and by exile to accept some romantic postulates without really renouncing their basic outlook. The third is a younger Cuban poet who had a very romantic life (in exile, first in Mexico, later in New

York, again in Mexico for the rest of his life) and who wrote perhaps the best romantic poems in Spanish American literature. The fourth is a late romantic, a Brazilian poet who came after the first great wave of Brazilian romanticism but who, both in his short life and in his work, embodied the movement in its entirety. Through the works of these men, with their exalted tone and noble feeling, it may perhaps be possible to grasp what the romantic movement meant to the newly liberated lands.

I / JOSÉ JOAQUÍN DE OLMEDO

The names of José de Olmedo and Andrés Bello are closely linked. Although they first met in 1825–26, and in Europe, when both were in their middle forties (Bello was one year younger), a community of taste and training, as well as deep mutual affection, united both their lives and their poetry.

Olmedo was born in Ecuador in 1780 and received a thorough classical education. He was attracted to the cause of independence and served his country well as a diplomat and public official. As a poet, he belonged to the period of transition between neoclassicism and romanticism. He was not very prolific (ninety poems in some forty years), and he believed in the Horatian precept of letting a manuscript rest for a time in a drawer. Some rested too long and were never finished. With Bello's encouragement, he completed the translation of the first three epistles of Pope's *Essay on Man*, but like his friend and mentor, he was never a full-time poet.

His most famous work is "The Victory at Junín," a poem written in 1825 to celebrate the battle which liberated Peru and precipitated the total collapse of the Spanish army in South America. The poem was written at Bolívar's suggestion, although the hero did not ask specifically for a song to him. To avoid outright flattery, Olmedo placed the victory in a larger context. Using a well-known rhetorical device which had already served Ercilla's similar purpose in *The Araucana* (see Part One, 9), Olmedo introduced the ghost of the last Inca, Huayna Cápac, to announce in the day of Junín, the future and more decisive victory of Ayacucho, won by General Sucre, one of Bolívar's lieutenants. The apparition was widely discussed in its time. Bello approved of it as a poetical figure, but some saw in it an allusion to the idea held by some Latin American leaders of restoring the Inca empire. (See "Rebellion and Death of Túpac Amaru," Part One, 22.)

From a purely literary point of view the poem blended a traditional, neoclassical style with some elements already unmistakably romantic. Olmedo described American nature, exalted the independence cause, offered a new concept of New World man, and resorted to native words and to what was then called "local color." Only once after this poem did Olmedo achieve the same heights—when, in 1835, he wrote the great ode "To General Flores, Victor at Miñarica." But his name is preeminently associated with the earlier song.

It is a long poem (more than nine hundred verses); here only an excerpt is presented. As Henríquez Ureña once indicated, the initial metaphor of thunder is reminiscent of Horace, but the general tone of the excerpt, its movement, and its diction are already pointing toward romanticism.

The Victory at Junín: Song to Bolívar

From Canto a Bolívar, *especially translated by Donald Walsh.*

The horrendous thunder that crashing bursts
and swells in muffled rumbles
throughout the flaming globe
announces to God that He reigns in Heaven.

And the thunderbolt that in Junín breaks and scatters
the Spanish throng
that fiercer than ever threatened
with blood and fire eternal servitude,
and the song of victory
that in a thousand echoes flows deafening
the deep valley and the craggy peak
proclaims Bolívar on the earth
the arbiter of peace and war.

The proud pyramids that to Heaven
bold human art once raised
to speak to the centuries and the nations,
temples, where the hands of slaves
deified with pomp their tyrants,
are a mockery of time, which with its feeble
wing touches them, and knocks them to the ground,
after the fleeting wind in wanton play
has blotted out their lying inscriptions;
and confused beneath the rubble
in the shadow of eternal oblivion
oh example of ambition and misery!
the priest lies, the god and the temple;

but the sublime mountains, whose brow
is raised to the ethereal region,
that see storms at their feet
flash, roar, break, dissolve;
the Andes . . . the enormous, stupendous
mounds resting upon golden bases,
earth with its weight equilibrating,
will never move. They, mocking the fury
and power of alien envy
and perverse time, will be eternal
heralds of Liberty and Victory,
that with deep echo
will to the world's last age thus speak:
"We saw the battlefield of Junín;
we saw that, upon the unfurling of
the banners of Peru and Colombia,
the haughty legions are confused,
the fierce Spaniard flees in terror,
or, submissive, begs for peace.
Bolívar conquered: Peru was free;
and in triumphal pomp sacred Liberty
was placed within the Temple of the Sun."

II / ANDRÉS BELLO

To discuss Bello exclusively as a poet would be like discussing Emerson or Matthew Arnold only as a poet. Even more perhaps than his North American and English counterparts, Bello was an all-round intellectual. He was born in Venezuela in 1781, and received a sound traditional education in his native Caracas. In 1810, he went to London as Simón Bolívar's secretary, and at the conclusion of this mission, stayed on there instead of returning home. He remained in England for nearly two decades, in the service not only of his own country but of other Latin American nations as well.

Bello's sense of mission, however, was not confined to diplomatic affairs. A man of encyclopedic interests and learning, he assumed a major role in the monumental task of bringing the newly created Latin American nations into the modern world. During his stay in London, he made ample use of the facilities of the British Museum, and from 1814 to 1829 was a regular visitor to its Reading Room. He eventually made himself equally at home in both classical and medieval philology. The scholarly projects in which he participated ranged from the revision of a Spanish translation of the Bible, on the one hand, to the editing of Jeremy Bentham's manuscripts, on the other. In addition, he produced a splendidly authoritative edition of the first Spanish epic, the *Poem of El Cid*, and wrote the best Spanish grammar of his time.

In 1829 Bello retired to Chile, there to complete, in the remaining thirty-five years of his long life, the great work of building a nation. There he founded the university (in 1843), wrote the Chilean civil code, the prototype for all Latin American nations, and became an expert in international law, helping to solve some of the problems involved in establishing borders between the new countries. In the intervals of this very active life, Bello wrote poems and literary criticism, edited two encyclopedic reviews (*Biblioteca Americana*, 1823; *Repertorio Americano*, 1826–27, both in London) and a newspaper, *El Araucano* (Chile, 1830–1853), and taught seminars on subjects as varied as Latin and poetics.

The few poems he wrote are among the best of his time. The most famous is the "Ode to the Agriculture of the Torrid Zone." It was written and published in London, the second of the two odes he meant to be part of a long descriptive poem on the New World. He never completed the project, but what he wrote showed his mastery. A walk in the early 1820s along the docks of London, where ships were discharging their load of tropical species, activated Bello's sensitivity. Like Baudelaire and Proust, he found a stimulus to his poetic imagination in the fragrances of his faraway country. Months or years later, Bello converted his sensations and subconscious feelings into the most elegant and precise series of metaphors. Although there were many classical reminiscences in the poem (Lucretius, Vergil, Horace), Bello eliminated all allusions to classical mythology and concentrated his vision on the fragrant native fruits and the majestic American landscape. A second part embodied a typically Horatian moral reflection: the poet recommended peace and its fruitful labors to men divided and exhausted by the wars of independence.

At the end a very delicate reference to the victories already achieved by the American armies contained the only allusion to Bolívar. Less direct and obsequious than his friend Olmedo (selection 1), Bello nevertheless admired Bolívar's military genius. The poem belonged to the descriptive-and-didactic classical tradition, which was revived by the Renaissance humanists, imported by the Jesuits to Latin America (see Balbuena, Part One, 11, 1), and later developed by the encyclopedists and naturalists in the eighteenth century. Into this long tradition Bello incorporated the subtlest romantic touches.

Some fifteen years later, he became involved in a series of chaotic polemics on romanticism. While in London he had had the opportunity to have a firsthand acquaintance with the English and French romantics; in Chile he had even translated some of them (Byron, Lamartine, Hugo). But in 1842, he was accused by the fierce Sarmiento of having formed a generation of poets too respectful of neoclassical rules and too ignorant of the new romantic freedom. Bello did not participate in the resulting polemics except once, to clarify some points of grammar and style. The outcome of this discussion, however, was that his name became associated exclusively with neoclassicism and Sarmiento's with romanticism. Today, Bello is seen in a totally different light. He was one of the first explorers of modern Europe, the Europe of the Industrial Revolution, a man who introduced into Latin American letters the best of romanticism at a time when very few were really at all acquainted with it. The "Ode" is perhaps the only Latin American poem of his period to have survived intact. Its echoes can be found in the later poetry of Darío (Three, 4), Neruda (Four, 12), and Ernesto Cardenal (Five, 11, vɪ).

Ode to the Agriculture of the Torrid Zone

From "Oda a la agricultura de la zona tórrida," especially translated by Donald Walsh.

Hail, fecund zone,
that dost circumscribe the enamored sun's
vague course and dost conceive every being
that stirs in every varied clime
caressèd by its light!
Thou weavest summer's garland,
from thy fair groves
no hue is missing; and therein drinks
the wind a thousand fragrances
of pomegranate tassels; thou givest
the grape to the seething cask,
not of purple fruit, or red, or yellow,
and flocks go without number
grazing thy verdure, from the plain
that has the horizon for its edge,
as far as the uplifted mountain
of inaccessible and everwhite snow.
    Thou givest the beautiful cane
whence honey is refined,
because of whom the world disdains the honeycombs;
thou in coral urns dost thicken the almond
that in the foaming jug runs over;
in thy prickly pears boils living carmine
that would be a rival to the purple of Tyre
and the generous ink of thine indigo
emulates the sapphire's light;
the wine is thine, which the wounded maguey
pours for the sons

of happy Anáhuac; and the leaf is thine
that, when from gentle
smoke in errant whirls it flees,
fastidium will solace the tedium of inert idleness.
Thou dost dress in jasmine
the coffee plant,
and thou givest it the perfume that in feasts
will temper Bacchus' wild fever,
for thy sons the lofty palm
its varied fiefdom grows,
and the pineapple seasons its ambrosia;
the yucca its white bread,
the potato trains its blond apples;
and the cotton unfolds to the faint dawn
the golden roses and the snowy fleece.
Stretched out for thee the fresh passionflower
in bowers of luxuriant verdure
hangs from its climbing shoots
nectareous globes and fringéd flowers;
and for thee the maize, haughty chieftain
of the tasseled tribe, swells its grain;
and for thee the banana tree
swoons under the weight of its sweet burden;
the banana, first
of all the fine gifts granted
by Providence with a generous hand
to the people of the happy Equator.
No more by human arts obliged
the fruitful prize it yields;
not to the pruning knife, not to the plow
is it indebted for its racime;
scant industry suffices it, such as
a slavish hand can steal from his tasks;
it grows swiftly, and when it ends exhausted
adult progeny succeed it all about.
      But if, just as thy soil
yields, oh fertile zone, to no other soil,
and as it has been the special care of Nature,
so would it were of thy indolent inhabitant!
Oh, if to the deceptive noise
that calls to him from his threshold
he had the wisdom to prefer the true happiness
of the simple farmer,
far from the silly, vain
pomp, the false glitter,

the pestilent idleness of the city!
By what dismal illusion
do those whom Fortune made lords
of such happy and abundant and varied earth
abandon the native estates
to care and mercenary faith,
and in blind tumult imprison themselves
in wretched cities,
(bathing it in blood!) its right hand unarmed;
and if the innate gentleness sleeps,
awakes it in the American breast.
The verdant heart
disdained by a happy obscurity,
that in the bloody chance of combat
beats with joy,
and covetous of power or fame,
loves noble dangers;
let it esteem alone vituperation and affront
the honor that it receives not from the fatherland,
the liberty more gentle than the empire,
and the olive branch more beautiful than the laurel.
Citizen soldier,
cast aside the livery of war;
let the branch of victory
be hung from the altar of the fatherland,
and glory be the sole adornment of merit.
Of its triumph, then, my fatherland,
peace will see the longed-for day;
peace, at whose sight the world is filled
with soulful serenity and rejoicing,
man returns inspired to the task,
the ship hoists anchor, joyfully
wishing breezes to her friends,
the workshop swarms, the farmhouse seethes,
and the sickle is not enough for the ears.
      Oh, young nations, who raise
above the astonished occident
your heads girt with early laurels!
Honor the field, honor the simple life
of the farmer, and his frugal plainness.
Thus liberty will have in you
a perpetual dwelling,
ambition a restraint, and law a temple.
People on the path
of immortality, arduous and rough,

will take heart, citing your example.
He will emulate it zealously,
your posterity and new names
adding fame
to those whom he now acclaims:
"These are the sons, sons
(he will preach to mankind)
of those who as victors conquered
the peak of the Andes;
sons of those who in Boyacá, those who in the arena
of Maipó, and in Junín, and in the glorious
campaign of Apurima
did humble the lion of Spain."

III / JOSÉ MARÍA DE HEREDIA

If Olmedo and Bello reached romanticism after a long and fruitful practice of neoclassicism, Heredia, more than twenty years younger, was almost from the very beginning a romantic in both his life and his poetry.

Heredia was born in Cuba in 1803 and was already an exile at nineteen. The Spanish authorities expelled him for having conspired against them, and he then found refuge first in Mexico and later in the United States. Although he had already started writing some romantic verses, it was his two-year stay in New York that helped him to get in close contact with the work of Ossian and Byron.

His first book, *Poems,* was published in New York in 1825, when he was only twenty-two. One of the first critics to recognize in Heredia's verses the influence of Byron's "genius and style" was Andrés Bello. Reviewing the book in London, he called attention to the predominant melancholy, verging on misanthropy, that he detected in the poems. Later critics confirmed this judgment. After the publication of his book, Heredia returned to Mexico, where he eventually settled. In the last years of his life (he died in 1859) he turned against romanticism. Nevertheless, his name is securely linked to the foundation of that movement in Hispanic letters.

The "Ode to Niagara" is the most famous of his poems. Heredia did visit the falls in 1824, but apparently he had already begun the poem before the visit, and the actual contemplation of that mighty spectacle merely helped to give the poem its final form. The splendor of untamed nature contrasted forcefully with the author's own dark moods. Although he was overwhelmed, he could not help longing for the softness of tropical palms and for his lost mistress. In a sense, the "Ode" is a successful summation of all the typical romantic *topoi.*

The translation was done in 1827. Bryant might have known Heredia when the latter was living in New York, although there is no record of their having met. At the time, Spanish was more widely known among English and American writers than today, and Bryant translated some other poems by Heredia as well. His rendering of "Niagara" conveys the tone and style of the original very faithfully.

Heredia's reputation in the Hispanic world is still strong, but outside that linguistic area he tends to be confused with his cousin and namesake, José María de Heredia, who spent practically all his life in France, wrote in French, and is one of the most important poets of the Parnassian movement. Even the catalogue of the New York Public Library has not succeeded in distinguishing the two. It is not such a difficult feat to manage: A check of the chronology will show that the younger Heredia was only seventeen when his cousin died in Mexico. He himself lived until 1905.

Ode to Niagara

From "Oda al Niágara," translated by William Cullen Bryant.

My lyre! Give me my lyre! My bosom finds
The glow of inspiration. Oh, how long
Have I been left in darkness, since this light
Last visited my brow! Niagara!
Thou with thy rushing waters dost restore
The heavenly gift that sorrow took away.
Tremendous torrent! for an instant hush
The terrors of thy voice, and cast aside
Those wide-involving shadows, that my eyes
May see the fearful beauty of thy face!
I am not all unworthy of thy sight,
For from my very boyhood have I loved,
Shunning the meaner track of common minds,
To look on Nature in her loftier moods.
At the fierce rushing of the hurricane,
At the near bursting of the thunderbolt,
I have been touched with joy; and when the sea
Lashed by the wind hath rocked my bark, and showed
Its yawning caves beneath me, I have loved
Its dangers and the wrath of elements.
But never yet the madness of the sea
Hath moved me as thy grandeur moves me now. . . .
The hoarse and rapid whirlpools there! My brain

Grows wild, my senses wander, as I gaze
Upon the hurrying waters, and my sight
Vainly would follow, as toward the verge
Sweeps the wide torrent. Waves innumerable
Meet there and madden—waves innumerable
Urge on and overtake the waves before,
And disappear in thunder and in foam. . . .
What seeks thy restless eye? Why are not here,
About the jaws of this abyss, the palms—
Ah, the delicious palms—that on the plains
Of my own native Cuba spring and spread
Their thickly foliaged summits to the sun . . . ?
But no, Niagara—thy forest pines
Are fitter coronal for thee. The palm,
The effeminate myrtle and frail rose may grow
In gardens, and give out their fragrance there,
Unmanning him who breathes it. Thine it is
To do a nobler office. Generous minds
Behold thee, and are moved, and learn to rise
Above earth's frivolous pleasures; they partake
Thy grandeur, at the utterance of thy name.
God of all truth! in other lands I've seen
Lying philosophers, blaspheming men,
Questioners of thy mysteries, that draw
Their fellows deep into impiety;
And therefore doth my spirit seek thy face
In earth's majestic solitudes. Even here
My heart doth open all itself to thee. . . .
I see thy never-resting waters run
And I bethink me how the tide of Time
Sweeps by eternity. So pass, of man—
Pass, like a noonday dream—the blossoming days,
And he awakes to sorrow. I, alas!—
Feel that my youth is withered, and my brow
Plowed early with the lines of grief and care.
Never have I so deeply felt as now
The hopeless solitude, the abandonment,
The anguish of a loveless life. Alas!
How can the impassioned, the unfrozen heart
Be happy without love? I would that one
Beautiful, worthy to be loved and joined
In love with me, now shared my lonely walk
On this tremendous brink. 'Twere sweet to see
Her sweet face touched with paleness, and become

More beautiful from fear, and overspread
With a faint smile, while clinging to my side.
Dreams—dreams! I am an exile, and for me
There is no country and there is no love.
Hear, dread Niagara, my latest voice!
Yet a few years, and the cold earth shall close
Over the bones of him who sings thee now
Thus feelingly. Would that this, my humble verse,
Might be, like thee, immortal! I, meanwhile,
Cheerfully passing to the appointed rest,
Might raise my radiant forehead in the clouds
To listen to the echoes of my fame.

IV / ANTÔNIO CASTRO ALVES

Unlike Heredia, the Brazilian Castro Alves never left his native land. But he shared with the Cuban poet the very Byronic feeling of being a pilgrim, a soul seeking in vain for a long-lost peace.

He was born in 1847 on a ranch close to Bahia. If he borrowed from Byron the pilgrim's cloak and the liberal commitment, from de Musset he copied the intensity and unconventionality of his love affairs. For two years Castro Alves lived openly with the Portuguese actress Eugênia Câmara and wrote for her a play, *Gonzaga, or The Revolution of Minas Gerais* (1867), which exalted a failed independence movement of the late 1780s. The play is almost unreadable today, but it achieved a contemporary success in both Bahia and São Paulo.

Castro Alves's life was intense and short: he was only twenty-four when he died of (naturally) tuberculosis. In his poems he defended all the ideals set in motion by the French Revolution, ideals that were not extremely popular in Brazil's Second Empire. He made the abolition of slavery his cause and wrote a series of poems, grandly modeled after Victor Hugo's epic *La Legende des Siècles,* to further the cause. One of them, "The Slave Ship," was immensely popular. But he did not live to see the book completed (it was published in 1883), or the cause won. Slavery was not abolished in Brazil until 1881. To the same collection belongs a poem on Lincoln's assassin, which carries a predictable epitaph from Byron's dramatic poem *Cain.*

When Castro Alves began to write, romanticism was firmly established in Latin American letters. He actually belonged to the second Brazilian generation and was already contemporary with the new realist and Parnassian poets. But he was faithful to romanticism and became the most exalted representative of the movement. Although in some of his poems he shared their excesses and could even be included in the group scornfully called "condoreiristas" (those who soar like condors), in the best of his lyrics it is possible to recognize a deep feeling for Brazilian nature and a subtle emotional music. One of the most outstanding examples is undoubtedly "Twilight Upcountry." It condenses most effectively Castro Alves's feelings for the untamed tropical landscape of his native country, for its grandeur and its somewhat sinister beauty.

Twilight Upcountry

From "Crepusculo Sertanejo," especially translated by Thomas Colchie.

Evening expired! Across the turbid waters
Long shadows fell from the banks.
From the uppermost reaches of dry trees
Came a sad crying of arapunga birds.

Evening expired! . . . Out of the branches,
Twigs, stones, lichen, ivy, and thistles,
The black, cruel leopards crept away
To crouch in the low-lying penumbra.

Evening expired! A galled branch of mimosa
Washed deeper into the waters. . . .
The wild palm snapped in creaking rhythm
To the cold shudder of rattling winds.

Impenetrable rustling! Colossal agitation!
Silence!—perhaps . . . Perhaps—a crescendo!
From the leaf, the calyx, the wings, the insects. . . .
From the mite—to stars . . . from the worm—to forests!

Herons tucked their crimson beaks under wing,
—Away from the buffeting breeze.
And earth, in the blue wash of the infinite,
Covered her head with the feathers of night!

But at times, out of the jungles
Along the enormous gulfs in that region,
—Surprised, apprehensive—a savage bull
Would lift its head covered with slime.

Then the widgeon, drifting about, arched
Fearfully in their flight, to scatter. . . .
And the timid flock, seeking faraway strands,
Passed over the canoe . . . with their cry!

4

ESTEBAN ECHEVERRÍA

In his lifetime, Echeverría was widely recognized as the man who
introduced romanticism to Argentina—the first poet to write a volume of unmistakably romantic verse, *Elvira* (1832; see Introduction to Part Two). Today his
poetry is scarcely read, and there is general agreement that it is banal, farfetched,
and hollow (to select a few epithets from one of his critics). Fortunately for
Echeverría, his reputation has another basis on which to rest. If his claims to fame
as a poet are unfounded, his accomplishments in prose, at least, have proved quite
durable.

He was born in Argentina in 1805 and as a very young man sowed the
proverbial wild oats. But he reformed, and in 1825 was sent to Paris to study
economics and business management. Instead, however, he became a spectator
of the romantic scene, an avid reader and follower not only of the young French
masters (Lamartine, Hugo, Vigny) but also of the German and English poets
(Goethe, Schiller, Byron) and of the ideologues of romanticism—Herder, the
Schlegels, Savigny, Leroux, Guizot, Cousin. When he returned home in 1830,
he carried with him not only the romantic germ but a new ideology as well, an
ideology with which he attempted to reshape his country. Unfortunately, the
times were not propitious.

In 1835, a wealthy landowner, Juan Manuel de Rosas, took power, and
for the next seventeen years ruled Argentina with a very stern hand. His rule was,
in fact, a reign of terror. To fight Rosas, Echeverría and some friends founded
in 1838 the Association of May (named after the month in which the independence movement started in 1810). Echeverría contributed a pamphlet, *The
Socialist Dogma*. Despite its title, it does not preach an economic and social
upheaval of society but presents a liberal program of social reform. The dictator
did not take the Association lightly. In 1840 Echeverría had to emigrate to
Uruguay. He died there, poor, sad, and disillusioned, in 1851, a year or so before
Rosas' downfall.

Among the papers left unpublished in his desk, the collector of his

Complete Works (1870–1874) found the draft of a story, "The Slaughterhouse," a brilliant and violent tale of Rosas' Buenos Aires. It was probably written around 1838; apparently Echeverría never decided to publish it. It might have been only a prose draft for a narrative poem like the ones he had written before, of which "The Captive" (1837) is the best known.

Like many sketches of the Old Masters, this draft is better than anything else Echeverría ever wrote. It is a brutal, detailed description of a slaughterhouse that supplied meat to Buenos Aires in Rosas' time. It begins with a panoramic presentation of the day-to-day activities and, through carefully selected episodes, gradually focuses on the more brutal of the workers. The tale culminates with an incident involving a young and elegant citizen who happens to pass by and who is first ridiculed and finally tortured to death by the mob. The romantically emphasized details, the brutal tensions of the story, and the hyperbolic ending show Echeverría's mastery. The story can also be read allegorically: Buenos Aires is the slaughterhouse; the mob that tortures the young man is the so-called *mazorca* that Rosas incited to terrorize and execute his political enemies. It is the single most effective piece of political propaganda of its time— and one of the best Latin American short stories of any time.

The Slaughterhouse

From "El matadero," translated by Angel Flores (New York: Las Americas Publishing Co., 1959).

Although the following narrative is historical, I shall not begin it with Noah's ark and the genealogy of his forebears as was wont once to be done by the ancient Spanish historians of America who should be our models. Numerous reasons I might adduce for not pursuing their example, but I shall pass them over in order to avoid prolixity, stating merely that the events here narrated occurred in the 1830s of our Christian era. Moreover, it was during Lent, a time when meat is scarce in Buenos Aires because the Church, adopting Epictetus's precept —*sustine abstine* (suffer, abstain)—orders vigil and abstinence to the stomachs of the faithful because carnivorousness is sinful and, as the proverb says, leads to carnality. And since the Church has, *ab initio* and through God's direct dispensation, spiritual sway over consciences and stomachs, which in no way belong to the individual, nothing is more just and reasonable than for it to forbid that which is both harmful and sinful.

The purveyors of meat, on the other hand, who are staunch Federalists and therefore devout Catholics, knowing that the people of Buenos Aires possess singular docility when it comes to submitting themselves to all manner of restrictions, used to bring to the slaughterhouse during Lent only enough steers for feeding the children and the sick, whom the Papal Bull excused, and had no intention of stuffing the heretics—of which there is no dearth—who are always ready to violate the meat commandments of the Church and demoralize society by their bad examples.

At this time, then, rain was pouring down incessantly. The roads were inundated; in the marshes water stood deep enough for swimming, and the streets leading to the city were flooded with watery mire. A tremendous stream rushed forth from the Barracas rivulet and majestically spread out its turbid waters to the very foot of the Alto slopes. The Plata, overflowing, enraged, pushed back the water that was seeking its bed and made it rush, swollen, over fields, embankments, houses, and spread like a huge lake over the lowlands. Encircled from north to east by a girdle of water and mud, and from the south by a whitish sea on whose surface small craft bobbed perilously and on which were reflected chimneys and treetops, the city from its towers and slopes cast anxious glances to the horizon as if imploring mercy from the Lord. It seemed to be the threat of a new deluge. Pious men and women wept as they busied themselves with their novenaries and continuous prayers. In church preachers thundered and made the pulpit creak under the blows of their fists. This is the day of judgment, they proclaimed, the end of the world is approaching! God's wrath runs over, pouring forth an inundation. Alas, you poor sinners! Alas, you impious Unitarians who mock the Church and the Saints and hearken not with veneration to the word of those anointed by the Lord! Alas, you who do not beg mercy at the foot of the altars! The fearful hour of futile gnashing of teeth and frantic supplications has come! Your impiety, your heresies, your blasphemies, your horrid crimes, have brought to our land the Lord's plagues. Justice and the God of the Federalists will damn you.

The wretched women left the church breathless, overwhelmed, blaming the Unitarians, as was natural, for this calamity.

However, the torrential rainfall continued and the waters rose, adding credence to the predictions of the preachers. The bells tolled plaintively by order of the most Catholic Restorer, who was rather uneasy. The libertines, the unbelievers—that is to say, the Unitarians—were frightened at seeing so many contrite faces and hearing such a clamor of imprecations. There was much talk about a procession which the entire population was to attend barefoot and bareheaded, accompanying the Host, which was to be carried under a pallium by the bishop to the Balcarce slope, where thousands of voices exorcising the demon of inundation were to implore divine mercy.

Fortunately, or rather unfortunately, for it might have been something worth seeing, the ceremony did not take place, because the Plata receded and the overflow gradually subsided without the benefit of conjuration or prayer.

Now what concerns my story above all is that, because of the inundation, the Convalescencia Slaughterhouse did not see a single head of cattle for fifteen days and that, in one or two days, all the cattle from nearby farmers and water carriers were used up in supplying the city with meat. The unfortunate little children and sick people had to eat eggs and chickens, and foreigners and heretics bellowed for beefsteak and roast. Abstinence from meat was general in the town, which never was more worthy of the blessing of the Church, and thus it was that millions and millions of plenary indulgences were showered upon it. Chickens went up to six pesos and eggs to four reals and fish became exceedingly expensive. During Lent there were no promiscuities or excesses of gluttony, and countless souls went straight to heaven and things happened as if in a dream.

In the slaughterhouse not even one rat remained alive from the many thousands that used to find shelter there. All of them either perished from starvation or were drowned in their holes by the incessant rain. Innumerable black women who go around after offal, like vultures after carrion, spread over the city like so many harpies ready to devour whatever they found edible. Gulls and dogs, their inseparable rivals in the slaughterhouse, emigrated to the open fields in search of animal food. Sickly old men wasted away for the lack of nutritive broth; but the most remarkable event was the rather sudden death of a few heretic foreigners who committed the folly of glutting on sausages from Extremadura, on ham and dry codfish, and who departed to the other world to pay for the sin of such abominations.

Some physicians were of the opinion that if the shortage of meat continued, half the town would fall in fainting fits, since their stomachs were accustomed to the stimulating meat juice; and the discrepancy was quite noticeable between this melancholy prognosis of science and the anathemas broadcast from the pulpit by the reverend fathers against all kinds of animal nutrition and promiscuity during days set aside by the Church for fasting and penitence. Therefore a sort of intestinal war between stomachs and consciences began, stirred by an inexorable appetite and the not less inexorable vociferations of the ministers of the Church, who, as is their duty, tolerated no sin whatsoever which might tend to slacken Catholic principles. In addition to all this, there existed a state of intestinal flatulence in the population, brought on by fish and beans and other somewhat indigestible fare.

This war manifested itself in sighs and strident shrieks during the sermons as well as in noises and sudden explosions issuing from the houses and the streets of the city and wherever people congregated. The Restorer's government, as paternal as it is foreseeing, became somewhat alarmed, believing these tumults to be revolutionary in origin and attributing them to the savage Unitarians, whose impiety, according to Federalist preachers, had brought upon the nation the deluge of divine wrath. The government, therefore, took provident steps, scattered its henchmen around town, and, finally, appeasing consciences and stomachs, decreed wisely and piously that without further delay and floods notwithstanding, cattle be brought to the slaughterhouses.

Accordingly, on the sixteenth day of the meat crisis, the eve of Saint Dolores's day, a herd of fifty fat steers swam across the Burgos pass on their way to the Alto Slaughterhouse. Of course this was not much, considering that the town consumed daily from two hundred fifty to three hundred and that at least one-third of the population enjoyed the Church dispensation of eating meat. Strange that there should be privileged stomachs and stomachs subjected to an inviolable law, and that the Church should hold the key to all stomachs!

But it is not so strange if one believes that through meat the devil enters the body and that the Church has the power to conjure it. The thing is to reduce man to a machine whose prime mover is not his own free will but that of the Church and the government. Perhaps the day will come when it will be prohibited to breathe, to take walks, and even to chat with a friend without previous permission from competent authorities. Thus it was, more or less, in the happy days of our pious grandparents, unfortunately since ended by the May Revolution.

Be that as it may, when the news about the action of the government spread, the Alto Slaughterhouse filled with butchers, offal collectors, and inquisitive folk who received with much applause and outcry the fifty steers.

"It's surely wonderful!" they exclaimed. "Long live the Federalists! Long live the Restorer!" The reader must be informed that in those days the Federalists were everywhere, even amid the offal of the slaughterhouse, and that no festival took place without the Restorer—just as there can be no sermon without Saint Augustine. The rumor is that on hearing all the hubbub the few remaining rats dying in their holes of starvation revived and began to scamper about, carefree, confident, because of the unusual joy and activity, that abundance had once more returned to the place.

The first steer butchered was sent as a gift to the Restorer, who was exceedingly fond of roasts. A committee of butchers presented it to him in the name of the Federalists of the slaughterhouse and expressed to him, *viva voce*, their gratitude for the government decree and their profound hatred for the savage Unitarians, enemies of God and men. The Restorer replied to their harangue by elaborating on the same theme, and the ceremony ended with *vivas* and vociferations from both spectators and protagonists. It is to be assumed that the Restorer had special dispensation from His Most Reverend Father, excusing him from fasting, for otherwise, being such a punctilious observer of laws, such a devout Catholic, and such a staunch defender of religion, he would not have set such a bad example by accepting such a gift on a holy day.

The slaughtering went on, and in a quarter of an hour forty-nine steers lay in the court, some of them skinned, others still to be skinned. The slaughterhouse offered a lively, picturesque spectacle even though it did contain all that is horribly ugly, filthy, and deformed in the small proletarian class peculiar to the River Plata area. That the reader may grasp the setting at one glance, it might not be amiss to describe it briefly.

The Convalescencia, or Alto Slaughterhouse, is located in the southern part of Buenos Aires, on a huge lot, rectangular in shape, at the intersection of two streets, one of which ends there while the other continues eastward. The lot slants to the south and is bisected by a ditch made by the rains, its shoulders pitted with ratholes, its bed collecting all the blood from the slaughterhouse. At the junction of the right angle, facing the west, stands what is commonly called the *casilla*, a low building containing three small rooms with a porch in the front facing the street and hitching posts for tying the horses. In the rear are several pens of ñandubay picket fence with heavy doors for guarding the steers.

In winter these pens become veritable mires in which the animals remain bogged down, immobile, up to the shoulder blades. In the casilla the pen taxes and fines for violation of the rules are collected, and in it sits the judge of the slaughterhouse, an important figure, the chieftain of the butchers, who exercises the highest power, delegated to him by the Restorer, in that small republic. It is not difficult to imagine the kind of man required for the discharge of such an office.

The casilla is so dilapidated and so tiny a building that no one would notice it were it not that its name is inseparably linked with that of the terrible judge and that its white front is pasted over with posters: "Long live the Federalists! Long live the Restorer and the Heroine Doña Encarnación Escurra! Death to the savage Unitarians!" Telling posters, indeed, symbolizing the political and religious faith of the slaughterhouse folk! But some readers may not know that the above-mentioned Heroine is the deceased wife of the Restorer, the beloved patroness of the butchers, who even after her death is venerated by them as if she were still alive, because of her Christian virtues and her Federalist heroism during the revolution against Balcarce. The story is that during an anniversary of that memorable deed of the *mazorca,* the terrorist society of Rosas' henchmen, the butchers feted the Heroine with a magnificent banquet in the casilla. She attended, with her daughter and other Federalist ladies, and there, in the presence of a great crowd, she offered the butchers, in a solemn toast, her Federalist patronage, and for that reason they enthusiastically proclaimed her patroness of the slaughterhouse, stamping her name upon the walls of the casilla, where it will remain until blotted out by the hand of time.

From a distance the view of the slaughterhouse was now grotesque, full of animation. Forty-nine steers were stretched out upon their skins and about two hundred people walked about the muddy, blood-drenched floor. Hovering around each steer stood a group of people of different skin colors. Most prominent among them was the butcher, a knife in his hand, his arms bare, his chest exposed, long hair disheveled, shirt and sash and face besmeared with blood. At his back, following his every movement, romped a gang of children, black and mulatto women, offal collectors whose ugliness matched that of the harpies, and huge mastiffs which sniffed, snarled, and snapped at one another as they darted after booty. Forty or more carts covered with awnings of blackened hides were lined up along the court, and some horsemen with their capes thrown over their shoulders and their lassos hanging from their saddles rode back and forth through the crowds or lay on their horses' necks, casting indolent glances upon this or that lively group. In mid-air a flock of blue-white gulls, attracted by the smell of blood, fluttered about, drowning with strident cries all the other noises and voices of the slaughterhouse, and casting clear-cut shadows over that confused field of horrible butchery. All this could be observed at the very beginning of the slaughter.

But as the activities progressed, the picture kept changing. While some groups dissolved as if some stray bullet had fallen nearby or an enraged dog had charged them, new groups constantly formed: here where a steer was being cut open, there where a butcher was already hanging the quarters on the hook in the carts, or yonder where a steer was being skinned or the fat taken off. From the mob eyeing and waiting for the offal there issued ever and anon a filthy hand ready to slice off meat or fat. Shouts and explosions of anger came from the butchers, from the incessantly milling crowds, and from the gamboling street urchins.

"Watch the old woman hiding the fat under her breasts," someone shouted.

"That's nothing—see that fellow there plastering it all over his behind," replied the old black woman.

"Hey there black witch, get out of there before I cut you open," shouted a butcher.

"What am I doing to you, ño Juan? Don't be so mean! Can't I have a bit of the guts?"

"Out with the witch! Out with the witch!" the children squalled in unison. "She's taking away liver and kidneys!" And with that, huge chunks of coagulated blood and balls of mud rained upon her head.

Nearby two black women were dragging along the entrails of an animal. A mulatto woman carrying a heap of entrails slipped in a pool of blood and fell lengthwise under her coveted booty. Farther on, huddled together in a long line, four hundred black women unwound heaps of intestines in their laps, picking off one by one those bits of fat which the butcher's avaricious knife had overlooked. Other women emptied stomachs and bladders and after drying them used them for depositing the offal.

Several boys gamboling about, some on foot, others on horseback, banged one another with inflated bladders or threw chunks of meat at one another, their noise frightening the cloud of gulls which celebrated the slaughtering in flapping hordes. Despite the Restorer's orders and the holiness of the day, filthy words were heard all around, shouts full of all the bestial cynicism which characterizes the populace attending our slaughterhouses—but I will not entertain the reader with all this dirt.

Suddenly a mass of bloody lungs would fall on somebody's head. He forthwith would throw it on someone else's head until some hideous mongrel picked it up as a pack of other mongrels rushed in, raising a terrific growl for little or no reason at all, and snapping at one another. Sometimes an old woman would run, enraged, after some ragamuffin who had smeared her face with blood. Summoned by his shouts, his comrades would come to his rescue, harassing her as dogs do a bull, and showering chunks of meat and balls of dung upon her, accompanied by volleys of laughter and shrieks, until the judge would command order to be restored.

In another spot two young boys practicing the handling of their knives slashed at one another with terrifying thrusts, while farther on, four lads, much more mature than the former, were fighting over some offal which they had filched from a butcher. Not far from them some mongrels, lean from forced abstinence, struggled for a piece of kidney all covered with mud. All a representation in miniature of the savage ways in which individual and social conflicts are thrashed out in our country.

Only one longhorn, of small, broad forehead and fiery stare, remained in the corrals. No consensus of opinion about its genitals had been possible: some believed it to be a bull, others a steer. Now its hour approached. Two lasso men on horseback entered the corral while the mob milled about its vicinity on foot or on horseback, or dangled from the forked stakes of the enclosure. A grotesque group formed at the corral's gate: a group of goaders and lasso men on foot, with bare arms and provided with slipknots, their heads covered with red kerchiefs, and wearing vests and red sashes. Behind them several horsemen and spectators watched with eager eyes.

With a slipknot already around its horns, the angrily foaming animal bellowed fiercely; and there was no demon strong or cunning enough to make it move from the sticky mud in which it was glued. It was impossible to lasso it. The lads shouted themselves hoarse from the forked stakes of the corral and the men tried in vain to frighten it with blankets and kerchiefs. The din of hissing, hand clapping, and shrill and raucous voices which issued from that weird orchestra was fearful.

The witty remarks, the obscene exclamations traveled from mouth to mouth, and either excited by the spectacle or piqued by a thrust from some garrulous tongue, everyone gratuitously showed off his cleverness and caustic humor.

"So—they want to give us cat for rabbit!"

"I'm telling you, it's a steer—that's no bull!"

"Can't you see it's an old bull?"

"The hell it is—show me its balls and I'll believe you!"

"Can't you see them hanging from between its legs? Each one bigger than the head of your roan horse. I guess you left your eyes by the roadside!"

"It's your old woman who was blind to have given birth to a chump like you! Can't you see that the mess between its legs is just mud?"

"Bull or steer, it's as foxy as a Unitarian!"

On hearing this magic word "Unitarian," the mob exclaimed in unison: "Death to the savage Unitarians!"

"Leave all sons of bitches to One-Eye!"

"You bet, One-Eye has guts enough to take care of all the Unitarians put together!"

"Yes, yes—leave the bull to Matasiete, the beheader of Unitarians. Long live Matasiete!"

"The bull for Matasiete!"

"There it goes!" shouted someone raucously, interrupting the interlude of the cowardly mob. "There goes the bull!"

"Get ready! Watch out, you fellows near the gate! There it goes, mad as hell!"

And so it was. Maddened by the shouts and especially by two sharp goads which pricked its tail, the beast, divining the weakness of the slipknot, charged on the gate, snorting, casting reddish, phosphorescent glances right and left. The lasso man strained his line taut, till his horse squatted. Suddenly the knot broke loose from the steer's horns and slashed across the air with a sharp hum. In its wake there came instantly rolling down from the stockade the head of a child, cut clean from the trunk as if by an ax. The trunk remained immobile, perched in the fork of a pole, long streams of blood spurting from every artery.

"The rope broke and there goes the bull!" one of the men shouted. Some of the spectators, overwhelmed and puzzled, were quiet. It all happened like lightning.

The crowd by the gate trickled away. Some, clustered around the head and palpitating trunk of the beheaded child, registered horror in their astonished faces; others, mostly horsemen, who had not witnessed the mishap, slipped away in different directions in the tracks of the bull. All of them shouted at the top of their voice: "There goes the bull! Stop it! Watch out! Lasso it, Sietepelos! It's coming after you, Botija! He's mad, don't get too close! Stop it, Morado, stop it! Get going with that hag of yours! Only the devil will stop that bull!"

The hubbub and din was infernal. A few black women who were seated along the ditch huddled together on hearing the tumult and crouched amid the intestines which they were unraveling with a patience worthy of Penelope. This saved them, because the beast, with a terrifying bellow, leaped sideways over them and rushed on, followed by the horsemen. It is said that one of the women voided herself on the spot, that another prayed ten Hail Mary's in a few seconds, and that two others promised San Benito never to return to the damned corrals and to quit offal-collecting forever and anon. However, it is not known whether they kept their promises.

In the meantime the bull rushed toward the city by a long, narrow street which, beginning at the acutest point of the rectangle previously described, was surrounded by a ditch and a cactus fence. It was one of the so-called "deserted" streets because it had but two houses and its center was a deep marsh extending from ditch to ditch. A certain Englishman, on his way home from a salting establishment which he owned nearby, was crossing this marsh at the moment on a somewhat nervous horse. Of course he was so absorbed in his thoughts that he did not hear the onrush of horsemen or the shouts until the bull was crossing the marsh. His horse took fright, leaped to one side, and dashed away, leaving the poor devil sunk in half a yard of mire. This accident did not curb the racing of the bull's pursuers; on the contrary, bursting into sarcastic laughter—"The gringo's sunk. Get up, gringo!"—they shouted and crossed the marsh, their horses' hoofs trampling over his wretched body. The gringo dragged himself out as best he could, but more like a demon roasting in the fires of hell than a blond-haired white man.

Farther on, at the shout of "the bull! the bull!," four black women who were leaving with their booty of offal dived into a ditch full of water, the only refuge left them.

The beast, in the meantime, having run several miles in one direction and another, frightening all living beings, got in through the back gate of a farm and there met his doom. Although weary, it still showed its spirit and wrathful strength, but a deep ditch and a thick cactus fence surrounded it and there was no escape. The scattered pursuers got together and decided to take it back convoyed between tamed animals, so that it could expiate its crimes on the very spot where it had committed them.

An hour after its flight, the bull was back in the slaughterhouse, where the dwindling crowd spoke only of its misdeeds. The episode of the gringo who got stuck in the mud moved them to laughter and sarcastic remarks.

Of the child beheaded by the lasso there remained but a pool of blood: his body had been taken away.

The men threw a slipknot over the horns of the beast, which leaped and reared, uttering hoarse bellows. They threw one, two, three lassos—to no avail. The fourth, however, caught it by a leg. Its vigor and fury redoubled. Its tongue, hanging out convulsively, drooled froth, its nostrils fumed, its eyes emitted fiery glances.

"Knock that animal down!" an imperious voice commanded. Matasiete dismounted at once from his horse, hocked the bull with one sure thrust, and, moving on nimbly with a huge dagger in his hand, stuck it down to the hilt in the bull's neck and drew it out, showing it smoking and red to the spectators. A torrent gushed from the wound as the bull bellowed hoarsely. Then it quivered and fell, amid cheers from the crowd, which proclaimed Matasiete the hero of the day and assigned him the most succulent steak as his prize. Proudly Matasiete stretched out his arm and the bloodstained knife a second time, and then with his comrades bent down to skin the dead bull.

The only question still undecided was whether the animal was a steer or a bull. Although it had been provisionally classified as a bull because of its indomitable fierceness, they were all so fatigued with the long-drawn-out performance that they had overlooked clearing up this point. But suddenly a butcher shouted: "Here are the balls!" and sticking his hands into the animal's genitals he showed the spectators two huge testicles.

There was much laughter and talk and all the aforementioned unfortunate incidents of the day were readily explained. It was strictly forbidden to bring bulls to the slaughterhouse, and this was an exceptional occurrence. According to the rules and regulations this bull should have been thrown to the dogs, but with the scarcity of meat and so many hungry people in town the judge did not deem it advisable.

In a short while the bull was skinned, quartered, and hung in the cart. Matasiete took a choice steak, placed it under the pelisse of his saddle, and began getting ready to go home. The slaughtering had been completed by noon, and the small crowd which had remained to the end was leaving, some on foot, others on horseback, others pulling along the carts loaded with meat.

Suddenly the raucous voice of a butcher was heard announcing: "Here comes a Unitarian!" On hearing that word, the mob stood still as if thunderstruck.

"Can't you see his U-shaped side whiskers? Can't you see he carries no insignia on his coat and no mourning sash on his hat?"

"The Unitarian cur!"

"The son of a bitch!"

"He has the same kind of saddle as the gringo!"

"To the gibbet with him!"

"Give him the scissors!"

"Give him a good beating!"

"He has a pistol case attached to his saddle just to show off!"

"All these cocky Unitarians are as showy as the devil himself!"

"I bet you wouldn't dare touch him, Matasiete."

"He wouldn't, you say?"

"I bet you he would!"

Matasiete was a man of few words and quick action. When it came to violence, dexterity, or skill in the handling of an ox, a knife, or a horse he did not talk much, but he acted. They had piqued him; spurring his horse, he trotted away, bridle loose, to meet the Unitarian.

The Unitarian was a young man, about twenty-five years old, elegant, debonair of carriage, who, as the above-mentioned exclamations were spouting from these impudent mouths, was trotting towards Barracas, quite heedless of any danger ahead of him. Noticing, however, the significant glances of that gang of slaughterhouse curs, his right hand reached automatically for the pistol case of his English saddle. Then a side push from Matasiete's horse threw him from his saddle, stretching him out. Supine and motionless he remained on the ground.

"Long live Matasiete!" shouted the mob, swarming upon the victim.

Confounded, the young man cast furious glances on those ferocious men and hoping to find in his pistol compensation and vindication, moved toward his horse, which stood quietly nearby. Matasiete rushed to stop him. He grabbed him by his tie, pulled him down again on the ground, and whipping out his dagger from his belt, put it against his throat.

Loud guffaws and stentorian *vivas* cheered him.

What nobility of soul! What bravery, that of the Federalists! Always ganging together and falling like vultures upon the helpless victim!

"Cut open his throat, Matasiete! Didn't he try to shoot you? Rip him open, like you did the bull!"

"What scoundrels these Unitarians! Thrash him good and hard!"

"He has a good neck for the 'violin'—you know, the gibbet!"

"Better use the Slippery-One on him!"

"Let's try it," said Matasiete, and, smiling, began to pass the sharp edge of his dagger around the throat of the fallen man as he pressed in his chest with his left knee and held him by the hair with his left hand.

"Don't behead him, don't!" shouted in the distance the slaughterhouse judge as he approached on horseback.

"Bring him into the casilla. Get the gibbet and the scissors ready. Death to the savage Unitarians! Long live the Restorer of the laws!"

"Long live Matasiete!"

The spectators repeated in unison "Long live Matasiete! Death to the Unitarians!" They tied his elbows together as blows rained upon his nose, and they shoved him around. Amid shouts and insults they finally dragged the unfortunate young man to the bench of tortures just as if they had been the executioners of the Lord themselves.

The main room of the casilla had in its center a big, hefty table, which was devoid of liquor glasses and playing cards only in times of executions and tortures administered by the Federalist executioners of the slaughterhouse. In a corner stood a smaller table with writing materials and a notebook and some chairs, one of which, an armchair, was reserved for the judge. A man who looked like a soldier was seated in one of them, playing on his guitar the "Resbalosa," an immensely popular song among the Federalists, when the mob rushing tumultuously into the corridor of the casilla brutally showed in the young Unitarian.

"The Slippery-One for him!" shouted one of the fellows.

"Commend your soul to the devil!"

"He's furious as a wild bull!"

"The whip will tame him."

"Give him a good pummeling!"

"First the cowhide and scissors."

"Otherwise to the bonfire with him!"

"The gibbet would be even better for him!"

"Shut up and sit down," shouted the Judge as he sank into his armchair. All of them obeyed, while the young man standing in front of the Judge exclaimed with a voice pregnant with indignation:

"Infamous executioners, what do you want to do with me?"

"Quiet!" ordered the Judge, smiling. "There's no reason for getting angry. You'll see."

The young man was beside himself. His entire body shook with rage: his mottled face, his voice, his tremulous lips, evinced the throbbing of his heart and the agitation of his nerves. His fiery eyes bulged in their sockets, his long black hair bristled. His bare neck and the front of his shirt showed his bulging arteries and his anxious breathing.

"Are you trembling?" asked the Judge.

"Trembling with anger because I cannot choke you."

"Have you that much strength and courage?"

"I have will and pluck enough for that, scoundrel."

"Get out the scissors I use to cut my horse's mane and clip his hair in the Federalist style."

Two men got hold of him. One took his arms and another his head and in a minute clipped off his side whiskers. The spectators laughed merrily.

"Get him a glass of water to cool him off," ordered the Judge.

"I'll have you drink gall, you wretch!"

A Negro appeared with a glass of water in his hand. The young man kicked his arm and the glass smashed to bits on the ceiling, the fragments sprinkling the astonished faces of the spectators.

"This fellow is incorrigible!"

"Don't worry, we'll tame him yet!"

"Quiet!" said the Judge. "Now you are shaven in the Federalist style —all you need is a mustache, don't forget to grow one! . . . Now, let's see: why don't you wear any insignia?"

"Because I don't care to."

"Don't you know that the Restorer orders it?"

"Insignia become you, slaves, but not free men!"

"Free men will have to wear them, by force."

"Indeed, by force and brutal violence. These are your arms, infamous wretches! Wolves, tigers, and panthers are also strong like you and like them you should walk on all fours."

"Are you not afraid of being torn to pieces by the tiger?"

"I prefer that to having you pluck out my entrails, as the ravens do, one by one."

"Why don't you wear a mourning sash on your hat in memory of the Heroine?"

"Because I wear it in my heart in memory of my country which you, infamous wretches, have murdered."

"Don't you know that the Restorer has ordered mourning in memory of the Heroine?"

"You, slaves, were the ones to order it so as to flatter your master and pay infamous homage to him."

"Insolent fellow! You are beside yourself. I'll have your tongue cut off if you utter one more word. Take the pants off this arrogant fool, and beat him on his naked ass. Tie him down on the table first!"

Hardly had the judge uttered his commands when four bruisers bespattered with blood lifted the young man and stretched him out upon the table.

"Rather behead me than undress me, infamous rabble!"

They muzzled him with a handkerchief and began to pull off his clothes. The young man wriggled, kicked, and gnashed his teeth. His muscles assumed now the flexibility of rushes, now the hardness of iron, and he squirmed like a snake in his enemy's grasp. Drops of sweat, large as pearls, streamed down his cheeks, his pupils flamed, his mouth foamed, and the veins on his neck and forehead jutted out black from his pale skin as if congested with blood.

"Tie him up," ordered the judge.

"He's roaring with anger," said one of the cutthroats.

In a short while they had tied his feet to the legs of the table and turned his body upside down. In trying to tie his hands, the men had to unfasten them from behind his back. Feeling free, the young man, with a brusque movement which seemed to drain him of all his strength and vitality, raised himself up, first upon his arms, then upon his knees, and collapsed immediately, murmuring: "Rather behead me than undress me, infamous rabble!"

His strength was exhausted, and having tied him down crosswise, they began undressing him. Then a torrent of blood spouted, bubbling from the young man's mouth and nose, and flowed freely down the table. The cutthroats remained immobile and the spectators, astonished.

"The savage Unitarian has burst with rage," said one of them.

"He had a river of blood in his veins," put in another.

"Poor devil, we wanted only to amuse ourselves with him, but he took things too seriously," exclaimed the judge, scowling tiger-like.

"We must draw up a report. Untie him and let's go!"

They carried out the orders, locked the doors, and in a short while the rabble went out after the horse of the downcast, taciturn judge.

The Federalists had brought to an end one of their innumerable feats of valor.

Those were the days when the butchers of the slaughterhouse were apostles who propagated by dint of whip and poniard Rosas' Federation, and it is not difficult to imagine what sort of Federation issued from their heads and knives. They were wont to dub as savage Unitarians (in accordance with the jargon invented by the Restorer, patron of the brotherhood) any man who was neither a cutthroat nor a crook; any man who was kindhearted and decent; any patriot or noble friend of enlightenment and freedom; and from the foregoing episode it can be clearly seen that the headquarters of the Federation were located in the slaughterhouse.

5

DOMINGO FAUSTINO SARMIENTO

If Echeverría is remembered more today for his political significance than for the several volumes of romantic verse he wrote, Sarmiento, who was a full-time politician, is mainly remembered for his powerful writings. Although he devoted the best part of his long life and immense energy to shaping the destinies of his country, Argentina, he really belongs to literary history.

Born in 1811, in the remote province of San Juan, Sarmiento was too poor to receive a complete education, but he was determined to have one. He was self-taught, and at fifteen was already teaching at an elementary school. All he learned, and he learned a great deal, was through avid reading of anything he came across: the Bible and Benjamin Franklin's *Autobiography* (a book he loved), the Spanish classics and a second-rate French encyclopedia, poets and thinkers of all persuasions, the trashy serial novels of the time, and the most abstruse sociologists and economists. He did not begin to write steadily until, at twenty-eight, he became the editor of a short-lived political journal, *El Zonda.* He had to teach himself journalism. But the times were not propitious. In 1831 his journal was destroyed by his political adversaries and he was exiled to Chile. (He would return to Argentina in 1837, only to be exiled a second time in 1840.) The exile, however, was a blessing in disguise: he had left Rosas' tyranny behind.

In Chile he found the first, and one of the better-organized, of the new Latin American democracies. Education and culture were under the guiding hand of Andrés Bello. Neoclassicism was still in fashion, although Bello was subtly leading his disciples into romanticism. Sarmiento admired Bello, but could not accept the slow pace he had established. Like a tornado he swooped down on Chilean culture and attracted the best of the young to his banner. In two memorable polemics with some of Bello's disciples (1842), Sarmiento placed romanticism in the foreground. A lot of what he was saying was old hat, and he marred his arguments with faulty scholarship, but his general position was correct. Even Bello came to admire him, and in 1843 he invited Sarmiento to join the staff of the newly created university.

While fighting for a new concept of education and literature, Sarmiento remained very active in his war against Rosas. He wrote several works against the dictator, but the best was a long biography of one of the gaucho leaders, Juan Facundo Quiroga, a former associate of Rosas whose death was probably ordered by the latter. *Facundo* (as the book came to be known), hastily written and published serially in 1845 in a Chilean newspaper, transformed the protagonist into a symbol of all the dark forces that were then tearing apart the fabric of Argentina's political life. The book presented Facundo as a rougher version of Rosas. Through him, Sarmiento aimed directly at the dictator. To place the character in the proper setting, Samiento began the book with a sweeping geosociological description of Argentina, and particularly the Pampas. (He had never been there, and based his account on those of other visitors, especially of English travelers.) The land and the men, the fierce gauchos, were brilliantly evoked. Then Sarmiento moved swiftly to Facundo's life and re-created the leader in his romantic mixture of cruelty and heroism. The last chapters brought the action back to the present. In a prophetic vein, Sarmiento predicted Rosas' downfall seven years before it happened.

The political impact of the book was enormous: it ran into several editions, and was even translated into English in 1868 by Mrs. Horace Mann, whom Sarmiento had met in the United States. In its political views, the book prefigured Sarmiento's future course of action. He returned to Argentina in 1851 to participate in the final struggle against Rosas. Later, as congressman and eventually president (1868–1874), he fought for the extinction of the barbarism the gauchos had represented. Like his North American counterparts, he was also in favor of the total extermination of the Indians. He promoted the immigration of European settlers, the fencing of the wide Pampas, and the creation of a vast railroad system. He had visited Europe and the United States in 1845–48; he would return to the latter several times. In the success of that nation he found the model for the Argentina of the future.

Today Sarmiento's vision of an epic struggle between civilization and barbarism seems greatly exaggerated. He himself came to realize that it was wrong to equate all that was good in Argentina with the city (Buenos Aires, Córdoba, etc.) and all that was wrong with the gauchos and the pampas. But he was, like a true romantic, fascinated by the utopian ideal of a powerful, developed, civilized Argentina. His vision was popular among the ruling classes in nineteenth-century Latin America. Echoes of it can still be found in José Enrique Rodó's *Ariel* in 1900 (Part Three, 8) and Euclides da Cunha's 1902 masterpiece, *Os Sertões* (Part Two, 16).

But if *Facundo* presented a wrong, or at least a faulty vision, as a narrative it was unique. For the first time, a book was written in a style that was totally free of allegiance to Spain's obsolete academic rules; it was a book that dared to borrow openly from French romantic writers and thinkers, but was also faithful to the colorful vernacular of provincial Spanish America. Sarmiento was accused in his time of using too many "Gallicisms"; he retorted, rightly, that his writing was closer to the colonial Spanish he had learned in his native San Juan. The energy and vitality of his writing were unsurpassed. It would be necessary to wait until Martí's appearance on the literary scene to find an equally vital prose (see Part Three, 1).

The chapter from *Facundo* presented here is the first of the biographical part of the book. It is a portrait in which the contradictory aspects of its subject's personality are brilliantly displayed through a collage of anecdotes. Sarmiento shared with Milton and Byron the power of portraying evil without making it look unattractive. Up to a point he even admired Facundo, and once admitted that he had something of the gaucho in himself. It is that quality of deep empathy for its protagonist that makes the portrait so outstanding.

In later years, Sarmiento published some other important books: *Travels* (1849), a vivid account in letter form of his first impressions of Europe and the United States; *Memories of Provincial Life* (1850), a delightful recollection of his native town and family life; *Life of Dominguito* (1886), a moving biography of his only son, killed in the war against Paraguay. But none were so essential to the new literature that was being produced in Latin America as was *Facundo*. In it, Sarmiento achieved the perfect romantic narrative—a unique mixture of fact and fiction, of history and romance—and created the prototype of a literature to come.

A Portrait of Facundo

From Life in the Argentine Republic in the Days of the Tyrants, *translated by Mrs. Horace Mann (New York: Hafner, 1868), pp. 73–90.*

Between the cities of San Luis and San Juan lies an extensive desert, called the Travesia, a word that signifies *want of water*. The aspect of that waste is mostly gloomy and unpromising, and the traveler coming from the east does not fail to provide his *chifles* with a sufficient quantity of water at the last cistern that he passes as he approaches it. This Travesia once witnessed the following strange scene. The consequences of some of the encounters with knives so common among our gauchos had driven one of them in haste from the city of San Luis and forced him to escape to the Travesia on foot, and with his riding gear on his shoulder, in order to avoid the pursuit of the law. Two comrades were to join him as soon as they could steal horses for all three. Hunger and thirst were not the only dangers which at that time awaited him in the desert; in these regions, where man must contend with the tiger for dominion over nature, the former sometimes falls a victim, upon which the tiger begins to acquire a preference for the taste of human flesh, and when it has once devoted itself to this novel form of chase, the pursuit of mankind, it gets the name of *man-eater*. The provincial justice nearest the scene of his depredations calls out the huntsmen of his district, who join, under his authority and guidance, in the pursuit of the beast, which seldom escapes the consequences of its outlawry.

When our fugitive had proceeded some six leagues, he thought he heard the distant roar of the animal, and a shudder ran through him. The roar of the tiger resembles the screech of the hog, but is prolonged, sharp, and piercing, and even when there is no occasion for fear, causes an involuntary tremor of the nerves as if the flesh shuddered consciously at the menace of death. The roaring was heard clearer and nearer. The tiger was already upon the trail of the man, who saw no refuge but a small carob tree at a great distance. He had to quicken his pace, and finally to run, for the roars behind him began to follow each other more rapidly, and each was clearer and more ringing than the last. At length, flinging his riding gear to one side of the path, the gaucho turned to the tree which he had noticed, and in spite of the weakness of its trunk, happily quite a tall one, he succeeded in clambering to its top and keeping himself half concealed among its boughs, which oscillated violently. Thence he could see the swift approach of the tiger, sniffing the soil and roaring more frequently in proportion to its increasing perception of the nearness of its prey. Passing beyond the spot where our traveler had left the path, it lost the track and, becoming enraged, rapidly circled about until it discovered the riding gear, which it dashed to fragments by a single blow. Still more furious from this failure, it resumed its search for the trail, and at last found out the direction in which it led. It soon discerned its prey, under whose weight the slight tree was swaying like a reed upon the summit of which a bird has alighted. The tiger now sprang forward, and in the twinkling of an eye its monstrous forepaws were resting on the slender trunk two yards from the ground, and were imparting to the tree a convulsive trembling calculated to act upon the nerves of the gaucho, whose position was far from secure. The beast exerted its strength in an ineffectual leap; it circled around the tree, measuring the elevation with eyes reddened by the thirst for blood, and at length, roaring with rage, it crouched down, beating the ground frantically with its tail, its eyes fixed on its prey, its parched mouth half open. This horrible scene had lasted for nearly two mortal hours; the gaucho's constrained attitude, and the fearful fascination exercised over him by the fixed and bloodthirsty stare of the tiger, which irresistibly attracted and retained his own glances, had begun to diminish his strength, and he already perceived that the moment was at hand when his exhausted body would fall into the capacious mouth of his pursuer. But at this moment the distant sound of the feet of horses on a rapid gallop gave him hope of rescue. His friends had indeed seen the tiger's footprints and were hastening on, though without hope of saving him. The scattered fragments of the saddle directed them to the scene of action, and it was the work of a moment for them to reach it, to uncoil their lassos, and to fling them over the tiger, now blinded by rage. The beast, drawn in opposite directions by the two lassos, could not evade the swift stabs by which its destined victim took his revenge for his prolonged torments. "On that occasion I knew what it was to be afraid," was the expression of Don Juan Facundo Quiroga, as he related this incident to a group of officers.

And here ends the private life of Quiroga, in which I have omitted a long series of deeds which only show his evil nature, his bad education, and his fierce and bloody instincts. . . . The fault is not his that thus he was born. In order to contend with, rule, and control the power of the city, and the judicial authority, he is willing to descend to anything. If he is offered a place in the army, he disdains it, because his impatience cannot wait for promotion. Such a position demands submission, and places fetters upon individual independence; the soldier's coat oppresses his body, and military tactics control his steps, all of which are insufferable! His equestrian life, a life of danger and of strong excitements, has steeled his spirit and hardened his heart. He feels an unconquerable and instinctive hatred for the laws which have pursued him, for the judges who have condemned him, and for the whole society and organism from which he has felt himself withdrawn from his childhood, and which regards him with suspicion and contempt. With these remarks is connected by imperceptible links the motto of this chapter, "He is the natural man, as yet unused either to repress or disguise his passions; he does not restrain their energy, but gives free rein to their impetuosity. This is the character of the human race." And thus it appears in the rural districts of the Argentine Republic. Facundo is a type of primitive barbarism. He recognized no form of subjection. His rage was that of a wild beast. The locks of his crisp black hair, which fell in meshes over his brow and eyes, resembled the snakes of Medusa's head. Anger made his voice hoarse, and turned his glances into dragons. In a fit of passion he kicked out the brains of a man with whom he had quarreled at play. He tore off both the ears of a woman he had lived with, and had promised to marry, upon her asking him for thirty dollars for the celebration of the wedding; and laid open his son John's head with an axe, because he could not make him hold his tongue. He violently beat a beautiful young lady at Tucuman, whom he had failed either to seduce or to subdue, and exhibited in all his actions a low and brutal yet not a stupid nature, or one wholly without lofty aims. Incapable of commanding noble admiration, he delighted in exciting fear; and this pleasure was exclusive and dominant with him to the arranging all his actions so as to produce terror in those around him, whether it was society in general, the victim on his way to execution, or his own wife and children. Wanting ability to manage the machinery of civil government, he substituted terror for patriotism and self-sacrifice. Destitute of learning, he surrounded himself with mysteries, and pretended to a foreknowledge of events which gave him prestige and reputation among the commonalty, supporting his claims by an air of impenetrability, by natural sagacity, an uncommon power of observation, and the advantage he derived from vulgar credulity.

The repertory of anecdotes relating to Quiroga, and with which the popular memory is replete, is inexhaustible; his sayings, his expedients, bear the stamp of an originality which gives them a certain Eastern aspect, a certain tint of Solomonic wisdom in the conception of the vulgar. Indeed, how does Solomon's advice for discovering the true mother of the disputed child differ from Facundo's method of detecting a thief in the following instances:

An article had been stolen from a band, and all endeavors to discover the thief had proved fruitless. Quiroga drew up the troops and gave orders for the cutting of as many small wands of equal length as there were soldiers; then, having had these wands distributed one to each man, he said in a confident voice, "The man whose wand will be longer than the others tomorrow morning is the thief." Next day the troops were again paraded, and Quiroga proceeded to inspect the wands. There was one whose wand was, not *longer*, but *shorter* than the others. "Wretch!" cried Facundo, in a voice which overpowered the man with dismay, "it is thou!" And so it was; the culprit's confusion was proof of the fact. The expedient was a simple one; the credulous gaucho, fearing that his wand would really grow, had cut off a piece of it. But to avail oneself of such means, a man must be superior in intellect to those about him, and must at least have some knowledge of human nature.

Some portions of a soldier's accounterments having been stolen and all inquiries having failed to detect the thief, Quiroga had the troops paraded and marched past him as he stood with crossed arms and a fixed, piercing, and terrible gaze. He had previously said, "I know the man," with an air of assurance not to be questioned. The review began; many men had passed, and Quiroga still remained motionless, like the statue of Jupiter Tonans or the God of the Last Judgment. All at once he descended upon one man and said in a curt and dry voice, "Where is the saddle?" "Yonder, sir," replied the other, pointing to a thicket. "Ho! Four fusiliers!" cried Quiroga. What revelation was this? That of terror and guilt made to a man of sagacity.

On another occasion, when a gaucho was answering to charges of theft which had been brought against him, Facundo interrupted him with the words, "This rogue has begun to lie. Ho, there! A hundred lashes!" When the criminal had been taken away, Quiroga said to someone present, "Look you, my master, when a gaucho moves his foot while talking, it is a sign he is telling lies." The lashes extorted from the gaucho the confession that he had stolen a yoke of oxen.

At another time he was in need of a man of resolution and boldness to whom he could entrust a dangerous mission. When a man was brought to him for this purpose, Quiroga was writing; he raised his head after the man's presence had been repeatedly announced, looked at him, and returned to his writing with the remark, "Pooh! That is a wretched creature. I want a brave man and a venturesome one!" It turned out to be true that the fellow was actually good for nothing.

Hundreds of such stories of Facundo's life, which show the man of superior ability, served effectually to give him a mysterious fame among the vulgar, who even attribute superior powers to him.

6

ESTANISLAO DEL CAMPO

The gauchos suffered from a negative image in Argentine literature for quite some time: Concolorcorvo (see Part One, 21) presented an unflattering first glimpse of them as outlaws and idlers; Echeverría (Two, 4) and Sarmiento (5) exaggerated their barbarism and saw them basically as brutal instruments of Rosas' tyranny.

But a completely different version of the gauchos had already been growing in the River Plate area since the beginning of the independence wars. Realizing their value in the fight for freedom, educated poets like the Uruguayan Bartolomé Hidalgo (1788–1823) had borrowed their language and poetic diction to create very successful patriotic dialogues. The gauchesco poetry thus founded was different from the actual gaucho poetry, which was more traditional and followed the pattern of Spanish folklore, as can be seen in the samples quoted by Concolorcorvo. Gauchesco poetry was instead a form of pastoral created by cultivated men, and endowed with explicit political connotations. After Hidalgo, the Argentine Hilario Ascasubi (1807–1875) enlarged and perfected the genre, not only writing political songs and dialogues against Rosas but also producing a complex narrative poem on the gaucho minstrel Santos Vega. Following their footsteps, Estanislao del Campo managed to produce a poem, *Faust* (1866), that soon became a classic of gauchesco poetry.

Born in Buenos Aires in 1834, del Campo began his poetic career imitating the romantics and producing undistinguished verses. He participated in the civil wars that followed Rosas' defeat in 1852. After 1857 and with the limited experience of gaucho life he got in his military campaigns, del Campo started writing in imitation of Ascasubi. Even the pseudonym he chose, "Anastasio the Chicken," was a tribute to his master's "Aniceto the Rooster."

Like many practitioners of pastoral poetry, del Campo was imitating, not reality, but a poetical version of it. From Hidalgo he took the idea of presenting Buenos Aires from a gaucho point of view, but instead of merely following his model, he complicated matters by using parody. His Anastasio attended a performance of Gounod's *Faust;* later he would tell a gaucho friend, Laguna, in his own peculiar style, his interpretation of the opera.

If del Campo lacked originality, he more than compensated for it by the vigor of his comic genius. Even the structure of his dialogue, a parodic narrative inside a dialogue inside a narrative, came from Hidalgo. But he added a new perspective by contrasting the natural setting of the friend's dialogue with the trappings of the stage version of *Faust.* The interplay of imitation and parody remained del Campo's major achievement. Although the poem followed closely the phonetic peculiarities and specific archaisms and native words that seasoned the gauchos' language, it was easily accessible to educated readers. *Faust* became an instant success in Buenos Aires and Montevideo.

Doctor Faust in the Pampas

From The Golden Land, *translated by Walter Owen, pp. 117–22.*

I had bare sat down and looked around,
When the band with a bang let go,
Behind a fence, down on the ground
Where the stage was, for the show.

And a big tarpaulin they gave a haul,
With such a rush, I tell you true,
Would have bowled you over, horse and all,
If it caught you goin' through.

And behind the screen a chap appeared,
A doctor by vocation,

Called Fowst, it seems—for so I heer'd—
And well known by reputation.

—It's Curnel Fowst, I understand,
Or my mem'ry's gettin' dim;
The Uruguayan—no doctor him—
Why, I served in his command!

—Oh shucks! I knew the Curnel good;
He's cold meat now, God save him;
It's many the time he cinched his wood
On a chestnut hoss I gave him.

To find two broncs the same hair and size,
Ain't nothin' unheard of, brother,
Don't trouble the Fowst that's in Paradise;
I'm talkin' about this other.

—I never knew gaucho wag his chin
As smart as you, *aijuna!*
—Just give me a swig at that crock of gin,
Before I go on, Laguna.

Well, this doctor comes on, as I said before,
And begins a long oration,—
Confidin' the crowd that he's feelin' sore,
And the why of his tribulation.

He told us that all the pile of books
He had read till his eyes were dim,
Weren't helping his case with a goldy-locks
That hadn't no use for him.

He kept snoopin' around her grazin' patch,
Neglectin' his sleep and food,
And bleatin' all night outside her thatch,
But it didn't do no darn good.

When at milkin'-time that gal came out,
As dainty and fresh as dew,
He hobbled the cow, and stood about;
But nix!—So, says he, I'm through!

It wasn't worth livin' life that way,
She'd not see his face again;

He'd pizen himself that very day—
He was checkin' out there and then.

Then he sloshed his hat on the floor and fell
To cussin' worse than double,
And wound up by callin' the Fiend of Hell
To fix his particular trouble.

He should have thought twice! He'd barely spoke,
By Christ, what a scare I got!
For there in a cloud of stinkin' smoke,
The Devil was on the spot!

Yes, crossin' yourself won't harm you, pard,
At the time I did it too.
—Why didn't the doc start trackin' hard?
—That's just what I'm askin' you!

You ought to have seen the Devil, my word!
Skin and bone, in a flappin' coat,
A hat with a feather, cats' claws, a sword,
And a beard like an old buck goat.

He was rigged for legs like a bloomin' stork,
With socks right up to his very fork,
For eyes, in his face he had two black holes,
With sparks inside like burnin' coals.

Said the Devil—"I'm at your service, doc,
Just order yours most truly."
But the doctor was showin' signs of shock,
Like his wits were goin' woolly.

—"I'm aimin' to help," said the Evil One;
"There ain't nothin' to be afraid of;
Whatever you order's as good as done—
I'll show you the stuff I'm made of."

The doc was scared, and he asked him quick,
To get goin' for good,—and pronto;
And wasn't he wise?—You betcha, Chick,
—But the Devil he didn't want to.

He claimed that in trackin' into town,
He'd had travelin' expenses,

And ended by calmin' the doctor down,
And makin' him lose his senses.

—But how could the Devil drop his rope
On a doctor with all that learnin'?
—Once you listen to Satan, there ain't no hope,
The next thing you know, you're burnin'.

Then the Devil again says most polite,
"Now what can I do for you?
There ain't the least call for takin' fright;
Call your orders—I'll put them through.

If you want *dinero*—I don't talk rash—
But I'll do you proud and proper;
When I'm done with fixin' you for cash,
Anchorena'll look a pauper."

—Says Fowst: " 'Tain't because I ain't livin' rich,
That right now I'm feelin' hurt;
I'm wantin' something beside of which
Gold's just so much yellow dirt."

"Whatever you like," says the King of Hell;
"I reckon that's what you heard;
D'you want the Government? Good and well,
You're it, if you say the word."

" 'Tain't power nor money I'm pinin' for,"
Says Fowst; "let's quit palaver;
I'm nuts on a gal, my good señor,
And my trouble's that I can't have her."

So soon as those words the Devil hears,
He busts loose with such ugly laughter,
That it kept on ringin' in my ears
The rest of the evenin' after.

He stamps the floor, and the solid wall
Cracks open top to bottom,
And standin' there was the doctor's gal—
I guess the doc thought he'd got 'em!

—By cripes! Is all I'm hearin' true?
You ain't aimin' at kiddin' me?

—I ain't one, Laguna, to fib to you.
Half the town was there to see!

That gal was a topper for looks, my son,
Pure peach, with locks like flax;
I thought I was settin' eyes on one
Of them Virgins they make from wax.

She'd a blue dress on—no frills or frays,
Just tucks around the hem—
And her hair was gold like the beard of maize,
That's fresh plucked off the stem.

She'd skin like curds of cream, old pard,
When the cow food's lush and rich;
Beside a Madonna 'twould have been hard
To pick out which was which.

She'd teeth like pearls fresh from the sea,
Two mornin' stars for eyes,
And a red rosebud where her mouth should be—
No, chum, I'm not tellin' lies.

The doctor gave hisself his head,
Makin' tracks in her direction;
But Satan headed him off, and said:
"Not so fast!—she's in my protection.

"If you're ready, I'll only be too pleased
To put things in black and white.
You give me your soul; and you'll find all greased
For smooth-workin' . . . you got me right?"

"Okay," says the doctor on the spot,
"Just show me where I sign."
And the Devil flips out a bill he'd brought,
And gets Fowst on the dotted line.

—A doctor!—and signin' a bond like that!
—Do you wonder he met disaster?
"Diamond cut diamond" fits here just pat;
For the Devil's the lawyer's master.

You must know that the doc hadn't seen his youth
For a longish interval,

And a trifle shaky and long in the tooth
To go pawin' around a gal.

So he says to the Devil with a wink,
As he hands back the contract, signed,
"Can't you fix me up with some witchin' drink?
You know what I've got in mind . . ."

The Devil was hot stuff, I'll allow,
Old Fowst had no sooner said it,
Than the Devil did somethin'—don't ask me how—
And Gee!—it's hard to credit . . .

Did you ever chance to see a grub
Turn into a butterfly?
That's somethin' how as Old Beelzebub
Made over that crocked old guy.

Old bag-coat, nightcap, and silvery hair,
Went poof! and no more were seen;
And there was the doctor, standin' there,
As good as he'd ever been.

—Am I hearin' right? What's that you said?
The doctor got back his youth?
—Listen matey; may lightnin' strike me dead,
If it ain't pure gospel truth.

The Devil then waved the gal to quit;
And with some kind of magic knack,
He mended the wall where he'd busted it . . .
And they pulled the tarpaulin back.

And now, please pass that talkin' juice;
My talk box is gettin' wheezy.
—Here you are; give your pipes a double sluice.
And go on when they work more easy.

7

JOSÉ HERNÁNDEZ

Writing only a few years after *Faust* was published, Hernández took a completely different, harder, and more political line in his *Martín Fierro* (1872). He did not believe the gauchos should be made into figures of fun, no matter how brilliantly done. He came ardently to their defense. He did not see them as the barbarians at the service of a tyrant that Echeverría and Sarmiento (see selections 4, 5) had portrayed. Instead, he identified them as an exploited minority, the highly skilled workers of the pampas, caught between greedy ranch owners and unscrupulous small-town politicians. He knew they were being used against their will in the Indian wars. The new Argentina that Sarmiento was finally shaping as president was totally hostile to them: it curtailed their legendary freedom with fences and railroads; it made them completely obsolete by the importation of new techniques of cattle-raising and by opening the vast hinterland to the industry of millions of European immigrants. *Martín Fierro* talked about all this; it was a political tract, though it was also more than that.

Hernández was particularly qualified to write of the gauchos. Born on a farm on the outskirts of Buenos Aires in 1834, he had the experience of real gaucho life that del Campo so conspicuously lacked. He spent his childhood and early youth in the pampas, and even traveled south to have a direct glimpse of the fierce Indian tribes. In later years he became involved, as del Campo did, in the civil wars that followed Rosas' downfall, but he fought on the other side. Although he was a federalist, he was never a Rosist. But the distinction was lost on his enemies. This explained Sarmiento's hostility to Hernández.

In choosing a character like Martín Fierro as his protagonist, Hernández wanted to show what made an honest gaucho into an outlaw. He underlined the abuses of authority committed by the justice of the peace and the sheriff in Fierro's home district, and by the commander of the military garrison where Fierro is sent for failing to support the government in the elections. The brutality of army life and the constant danger of being killed by the better-armed and more skillful Indians force Fierro into desertion. Returning home, he finds only the ruins of his small ranch, his wife and children gone. He then becomes an outlaw and gets involved in two duels, killing his rivals.

Fierro tells this sad story in his own words and thus becomes a representative of another gaucho prototype, the minstrel. The tradition goes back to Ascasubi's *Santos Vega*, but Hernández managed to improve considerably on it. His Fierro is one of the best characters in Latin American fiction. Hernández found for him the most persuasive tone of voice and the exact diction to communicate the pathos and energy of his adventures. Occasionally, he even hit on the right comic note to relieve the tension of some particular episode.

Seven years after the publication of *Martín Fierro*, Hernández published a second part, *The Return* (1879), different from the first in being more episodic and with the narrative divided among several voices. At its end, the protagonist makes his peace with society. Many things had changed in these seven years: Sarmiento was no longer in power; Hernández himself had come to realize that the new Argentina had another destiny, and that the gauchos as a group were doomed. He now believed they had to make an honest pact with society. *Martín Fierro*'s success was enormous. The same gauchos that the protagonist represented became the book's most avid consumers. Cheap copies of the poem were sold in general stores to be read aloud to them.

The educated public took longer to discover its real merit. For many years it was the prevailing view that del Campo's *Faust* was superior. By the end of the century, however, things had begun to change. Two distinguished Spanish critics—Unamuno in 1894, and Menéndez Pelayo in 1895—praised it without reservation, emphasizing the very Spanish diction of the poem in spite of the local vocabulary and idioms. In 1916, the Argentine poet Leopoldo Lugones (Part Three, 5) devoted to it a long panegyric in which he discovered, or invented, the poem's epic nature. Later writers like Borges or Ezequiel Martínez Estrada have disagreed with Lugones on this point, but have agreed with him on the poem's exceptional quality. Now *Martín Fierro* is Argentina's national classic.

The excerpt here presented belongs to the final pages of the first part. Martín Fierro is being chased by a police patrol. In the fight, Sergeant Cruz, impressed by his courage, joins forces with him. After the fight is over, they decide to seek refuge in the desert, among the Indians. The episode is beautifully told and, as Borges has pointed out, very strange. In the middle of the night, Cruz discovers simultaneously a friend and his real vocation as an outlaw. Inspired by this curious change of heart, in 1944 Borges wrote a short story, misleadingly entitled "The Life of Tadeo Isidoro Cruz (1829–1874)," and later included in *The Aleph* (1949). In his story he unraveled some of the labyrinthine threads of Hernández's tale. It is one of the most extraordinary tributes ever accorded this exceptional book.

The Gaucho Martín Fierro

From The Gaucho Martín Fierro, *translated by Frank G. Carrino, Alberto J. Carlos, and Norman Mangouni (New York: State University of New York, 1974), pp. 61–68.*

So, one night I found myself
gazin' at the stars,
which look more beautiful

the worse you feel;
God must've created 'em
so we can console ourselves.

A man feels good about them
and it always makes him happy
to see the Three Marys come out,
since in a clear sky after a rain
the stars are the guide
for the gaucho in the pampas.

Know-it-alls are losers here:
only experience counts;
here they'd see how little they know,
those who think they know so much,
because this lock takes a different
    key
and the gaucho knows which one it
    is.

Out here in the plains it's sad
to spend the whole night long
watchin' the moves
of the stars that God made,
without any more company
than your loneliness and the wild
    beasts.

Like I said, one night I was
in that lonely place,
with all that darkness,
complainin' to the wind
when the *chaja* bird
made me prick up my ears.

Like a worm I flattened myself
on the ground to listen;
soon I felt the poundin'
of horses' hoofs;
there were a lot of riders,
I could tell right away.

When a man's in danger
he shouldn't be too sure of hisself;
stretched out on my belly,
I gave all my attention
and pretty soon I heard
somethin' like the clank of a sword.

They were comin' up so quiet
that I got my guard up;
maybe they'd spotted me
and were coming for me;
but I wouldn't run off
since that's only for yellow gauchos.

Right away I crossed myself
and took a swig of gin,
making like an armadillo
curled around the jug:
"If they're gonna give me a lick or
    two,"
I said, "this is as good a time as
    any."

I slipped off my spurs,
so I could fight easier;
I rolled up my pants
and made my sash good 'n' snug;
and on a tuft of grass
I tested the edge of my knife.

Just so I'd have him handy,
I tied my horse to a clump of grass,
fixed his cinch,
and in that moment of danger,
backed up against him
and waited for 'em real quiet.

When I felt them close by
and knew they'd come to a stop,
my hair stood on end,
and even though I couldn't see a
    thing,
"You're not gonna die of a whim,"
I said, as they moved up.

I wanted to let them know
that there was a real man there;
I knew what they wanted
and just because of that
I beat 'em to the draw,
and didn't wait for the call to give up.

"You're a gaucho outlaw,"
said one, acting tough,
"You killed a black man
and another guy in a bar,
an' this here's the police
that's come to settle accounts;
we're gonna get you good
if you put up a fight."

I said, "Don't come to me
with stories about dead people;
that doesn't matter a damn;
come and get me, if you can,
since I'm not about to give up,
even if you come at me all at once."

But they didn't wait any more
and they tumbled off their horses;
like I was a wild dog
they surrounded me;
I put myself in the hands of the
    saints
and grabbed hold of my blade.

And then I seen this flash
from a rifle shot,
but the bad luck
of that spineless coward made him
    miss me,
and right there I lifted him
on my knife just like a sardine.

Another one was hurrying
to land a bola shot,
and I went for him just once
and let him feel some steel,
and away he went like a dog
whose tail's been stepped on.

They were so worked up
and so hot to get me,
that they all came at me,
just where I was waitin' for 'em:
they were fallin' all over one another,
blind with excitement.

Two of them who had swords,
were more confident and bold;
with ponchos wrapped around their
    arms,
they came up right in front of me
and lunged for me at the same time
like a couple of dogs on the loose.

I pulled the trick of backin' up
and droppin' my poncho in front of
    me,
an' soon as he puts his foot on it,
this one stupid guy,
I give it a sudden jerk
and sent him flat on his ass.

When he saw he was alone,
the other one backed off;
then I went for him,
without giving him a chance to
    catch his breath,
but he didn't care to fight
and took off like a bitch in heat.

One of them had a cane
with a shears blade tied to it
and he came at me like I was
a hitching rail for calves,
but I give him two well placed jabs
and he took off howlin'.

At that moment, by luck,
daylight was coming
and I said, "If I'm saved
this time by the Virgin,
from now on, I swear
I'll live a good life."

I waded amongst 'em
and began to tangle unafraid;
I stayed in a low crouch
as a pair of 'em came at me,
while along the ground I drew the
    tip
of my knife to lead 'em on.

The first glutton for punishment
came down on me with a slash;
I pushed it aside with my arm,
since if I hadn't, he'd 'uv killed my
　　lice;
before he could take another step
I threw dirt in his two eyes.

And while he was shakin' his head
and rubbin' his eyes,
I went straight for him
and gave it to him fast;
"May God help you," I said,
as I dropped him with a backhand
　　slash.

But right then
I felt along my ribs
a sword was ticklin' me,
and my blood ran cold.
From then on
I was a wild man.

I backed up a few steps
to get some footing;
in front of me I was tradin'
jabs and slashes with a *criollo;*
suddenly he stepped in a hole,
and to The Hole I sent him.

In his heart, maybe,
a blessed saint touched
one of the gauchos, who cried
　　out
and said: "Cruz won't stand
for this! I won't let you bastards
kill a brave man like this!"

And so then he joined with me,
and fought against the police;
I charged at them again,
and between the two of us it was a
　　steal;
this guy Cruz fought like a wolf
defendin' his den.

He sent off to hell one
of the two who rushed him;
the rest of them went into a spin,
since we were gettin' the upper
　　hand,
and in a little while they scattered
like a bunch of worms.

There, stretched out before us was
the ones whose snouts we'd stiffened;
to another one who was wobblin' off,
Cruz shouted from behind:
"Get some more police to come
with a cart and haul 'em away."

I gathered up the bodies,
knelt and said a little prayer for 'em;
I made a cross from a little stick
and begged my merciful God
to pardon me for the crime
of havin' killed so many people.

We stacked up in a pile
the poor fellows who died;
I don't know if they ever came for
　　them—
because we went away—
or if maybe the vultures
ate them up right where they were.

8

EDUARDO ACEVEDO DÍAZ

While Hernández came to the defense of the Argentine gauchos when they were already almost extinct as an influential element in the national life, Acevedo Díaz had the difficult task of writing about them when they were still shaping the destiny of Uruguay.

He was born on the outskirts of Montevideo, in 1851, while the war against Rosas was still undecided. It ended the following year with the tyrant's defeat. Enduring peace failed to come to Uruguay. For the next fifty years, the country was torn by civil strife between two political parties—the Blancos (Whites), who had been on the side of Rosas, and the Colorados (Reds). (An imaginative Italian historian, Cesare Cantú, misinterpreted these terms as indicating "white men" and "red skins.") Not until 1910 was democracy really established.

It is against this background of chronic civil war that the life and work of Acevedo Díaz must be placed. He was an intellectual by temperament, a gifted writer and orator. He began by studying law at the University of Montevideo, but before he had a chance to get a degree he became involved in the 1870 revolution of Timoteo Aparicio, a White gaucho leader. For Acevedo Díaz, who was only nineteen, it was the first opportunity to see action. He was very impressed by the skill and bravery of the gauchos.

From then on, although he returned to Montevideo and got a degree, he became actively engaged in politics. He contributed articles to several newspapers and became the most brilliant orator of the White party. In 1875 he participated in another revolution; in 1884 he was exiled to Buenos Aires. His political career had ceased for the time being; he resorted to writing historical novels in which the origins of the contemporary civil wars could be examined.

The historical genre was still flourishing in Latin American letters. In Brazil, José de Alencar (see selection 12) had written several, the most successful of which was *The Guaraní* (1857), about the adventures of a noble Indian in the early seventeenth century. In Spanish America, some of the most ambitious works of fiction were then being prepared or written by novelists as diverse as the Dominican Manuel de Jesús Galván (selection 9), whose *Enriquillo* came out in two parts in 1878 and 1882, and the Chilean Alberto Blest Gana, whose masterpiece, *At the Time of the Reconquest,* would be published in 1897.

But Acevedo Díaz had greater ambitions than any of his colleagues. In quick succession he wrote and published three novels (*Ishmael,* 1888; *Native,* 1890; *The Battle-Cry of Glory,* 1893) and probably also sketched a fourth (*Spear and Sabre,* completed only in 1914). The novels covered Uruguayan history from the beginnings of the war of independence (1808–1811) to the first civil war

(1834–1838), with the fight against the Portuguese and Brazilian occupation as the narrative's centerpiece (1823–1827).

Like Luis María Berón, the hero of the two central novels, Acevedo Díaz was an educated man who fought side by side with the gauchos because for him they represented the true national cause. But the author's fight was fiercer and uglier. While Berón was facing a foreign enemy, Acevedo Díaz was involved in a fratricidal civil war. In 1895 he returned from Argentina and participated in the 1897 revolution of Aparicio Saravia. But he no longer believed in armed rebellion, and in 1903 he deserted his party to support the Colorado candidate —an act that amounted to political suicide. He had to leave the country for the last time, his exile disguised as a series of diplomatic missions in Europe and Latin America. Far from the political strife he managed to complete the last of his historical novels. He died in Buenos Aires in 1921, almost completely forgotten.

In recent years, his novels have begun to be read not just as examples of a genre once important and now obsolete, but as symbolic explorations of the roots of Uruguayan nationality. In spite of everything, Acevedo Díaz had managed to complete one of the best, if not the best, historical cycle in Latin American literature. Scott's and Dumas's novels were undoubtedly his models. Although he followed these exemplars in devising intricate plots filled with unexpected revelations of kinship and overwhelming sentimental attachments, his true concern lay in the exploration of the epic and political implications of his narrative. With uncanny poetic insight, he delineated the many threads that created the complex fabric of Uruguayan nationality. Yet he was a contemporary of Zola and the naturalists, and incorporated into his romances touches of stark realism.

"The Battle of the Ruins" is perhaps his best short story, a genre he cultivated but little, yet one in which he was a master. It was written in 1889 and, from the point of view of his subject, can be placed in the interval between the first and the second novels of the historical cycle. It presents very graphically the horrors of the Portuguese invasion. The fate of the small group of gauchos and their women can be seen as symbolic of the whole country's. In presenting their plight, Acevedo Díaz avoids abstraction and makes the struggle brutal and unbearable.

The Battle of the Ruins

From "El Combate de la Tapera," especially translated by Carlos Hortas.

It was after the Catalan disaster, more than seventy years ago.
A tenuous radiance on the horizon was all that was left of the daylight.

The journey had been hard, without rest.

Shafts of breath issued out of the sweating horses' nostrils, and their flanks heaved in and out as if all the air they pulled in were not enough to satisfy the anxiety of their lungs.

A few of these kind brutes showed large wounds on their necks and chests, lacerations caused by lances and sabres.

The mud from brooks and marshes had splattered onto the torn pieces of skin and had stopped the flow of blood.

They resembled the nags used in bullfights, gouged and mistreated by the bulls. Besides their rider, two or three of them carried men on their croups and displayed on their rumps one or another red furrow, as if drawn by an iron whip, which were fresh impressions of the bullets received in flight.

A few others seemed to be almost on the point of collapse under the weight of their load, and began to fall behind, heads downcast, insensible to the spur.

Noticing this, Sergeant Sanabria shouted vigorously, "Halt!"

The detachment stopped.

It was made up of fifteen men and two women; muscular men, long-haired, taciturn, untamed; dragoon-women, their hair tied in kerchiefs, carrying sabres and barefoot.

Two large mastiffs with muddy tails and tongues hanging out panted under the bellies of the horses, turning to look back at the dark and sinister landscape of the depths whence they came, as if they still felt the heat of the gunpowder and the clamor of war.

Nearby, ahead of them, some ruins could be seen among the shadows: two mud walls reinforced by horizontally placed bamboo poles, perforated and partly demolished. The front and back walls, as well as the roof, had disappeared.

As for the rest, there were a few piles of rubbish overgrown with weeds and, on the sides, forming an incomplete square, half-filled ditches from whose depths emerged alder and hemlock plants in flexible canes adorned with black clusters and white flowers.

"Let's regroup inside the ruins," said the sergeant with an imperious gesture. "The rear guard and the women, get something to eat. . . . Corporal Mauricio! Have five shooters lie down flat on their bellies, behind the hemlock bushes. . . . The others inside the ruins to load the carbines and blunderbusses. Dismount, dragoons and stay sharp, damn you!"

The sergeant's voice sounded harsh and energetic in the stillness of the place.

No one answered.

Everyone went over the ditch and dismounted, regrouping little by little.

The orders were carried out. The horses were led behind one of the dry mud walls, and next to them the panting mastiffs lay down.

The shooters threw themselves on the ground behind a depression covered by weeds, holding their cartridge bags in their teeth; the rest of the strange troop distributed itself within the interior of the ruins, which offered a goodly number of holes through which the firearms could be aimed. The women, instead of accompanying the worn-out beasts, began to untie the sacks of munitions or kerchiefs full of mixed cartridges that the dragoons carried tied to their waists in place of cartridge belts.

Squatting down, leaning on the men's legs, they were laboriously starting to sort the cartridges when night began to fall.

"Don't anybody smoke," said the sergeant. "Load without much noise and conserve the blunderbusses until I tell you. Corporal Mauricio! Make sure that those good-for-nothings don't fall asleep unless they want me to shoot a few hairs off their heads. Keep your eyes open and ears sharp!"

"Don't worry, sergeant," answered the corporal hoarsely. "The warning's unnecessary; we've got more heart here than a frog's throat."

Some brief moments of silence elapsed.

One of the dragoons, who had his ear to the ground, raised his head and murmured softly, "Sounds like a good-sized party. . . . It's probably cavalry advancing."

A muffled rumbling of many hoofs on the carpet of short grass began to be distinctly heard.

"Load your muskets and wait; there come the Portuguese. Your skin is riding on this, damn it! And we've got to bide our time until we hear their horses. Ciriaca, have you got any liquor left in the canteen?"

"It's half full," answered the one spoken to, a heavy-set creole woman dressed like a man, with her braids tied up and hidden under a colorless hat with a worn leather chin strap. "Look, it'd be a good idea if you gave the men a drink."

"Give some to those in the forward positions, woman, and don't hold back on them."

Ciriaca took off at a hop, avoiding the men's spurs; she squatted down and began to pass the bottle around from mouth to mouth.

While she was so occupied, the dragoon on one side of her caressed her legs and another tickled her breasts, if he wasn't pinching a still fleshier part, saying, "Full moon."

"It'll shine on your dead body, you nut!" she answered one laughing, and to the other she said, "Let go of what's not yours, you unworthy slob," and to still another one, "Loosen your grip on the bottle, you infant!"

And she distributed slaps to everyone.

"Watch your step," yelled the sergeant in a powerful voice. "We're on the verge of dying and you sweeties can think of nothing else but making love. Move away, Ciriaca; pretty soon only the bullets will be whistling at you!"

Just then the muffled rumbling grew louder and a volley of shots rang out amidst savage shouts.

The platoon responded vigorously.

The ruins were enveloped in a dense cloud of smoke and burning plugs, an atmosphere that dissipated very quickly and then formed once again among new volleys of fire and harsh clamorings.

II

Between explosions and shots, the mad furious barking of the mastiffs seemed to echo the curses and crude swearing of the men.

A semicircle of flashes indicated clearly that the enemy had advanced in a half-moon formation so as to dominate the ruins with their continuous fire.

In the midst of all the shooting, Ciriaca rushed out with a string of cartridges, in search of Mauricio.

On all fours, among sinister whistlings, she crossed the short space that separated him from the ruins.

The shooters crawled among the grasses like snakes, loading and reloading their weapons.

One of them was motionless, facing the ground.

The girl pulled him by the hair and noticed it was soaked in a warm liquid.

"Look," she exclaimed. "It's hit him in the head."

"He's not swallowing," added the corporal. "Didya bring the gunpowder?"

"Here it is, and bullets for the Portuguese to swallow. It's a shame that it's so dark. . . . Those cowards can really shoot!"

Mauricio unloaded his carbine.

While he was extracting another cartridge from his small bag, he said, biting it, "Instead of this kind, I'm sure they'd prefer another type of heat. Ah, if they should get their hands on you, Ciriaca! It's sure they'll punish you like they did Fermina."

"Let them come get their meat!" the girl muttered.

And saying this, she grabbed the dead man's carbine and began to load it with great skill.

"Fire!" the voice of the sergeant roared out. "Whoever lets up, I'll cut his head off with the notched knife!"

III

The bullets that penetrated the walls of the ruins had already felled three men. Perforating the weak mud wall, some had wounded and dropped a few of the worn-out horses.

When the fire that came from within, through the improvised gunholes, increased, the second of the creole girls, a companion of Sanabria named Catalina, slunk out like a tiger through the bushes, holding on to the carbine of one of the dead men.

It was Cata, as she was called, a well-built and beautiful woman, copper-skinned, with very black eyes screened by thick eyelashes, red, swollen lips, abundant hair and a body of extraordinary vigor. She was hard and fearless, and her moves were sure and quick. She wore a blouse and chiripá and carried her sable across her back.

The night was very dark, full of stormy clouds; but great flashes of lightning—"red snakes of the skies," as the country people called them—sufficed to illuminate the semicircle that the gunfire made in the darkness.

The brightness of the lightning allowed Cata to observe that the enemy troops had dismounted and that the soldiers were firing their shots from behind their horses, exposing no other target than their heads.

A few bodies lay spread out here and there. A dying horse, hoofs in the air, thrashed about convulsively on top of his dead rider.

Once in a while a bugler suddenly blared out a call to attention or to advance, sometimes nearby, then far away, depending on the position of the commander.

One of those times, the bugle sounded very near.

From its echo, it seemed to Cata that the bugler was short of breath, and that he was afraid.

At that moment an especially bright flash of lightning bathed the bushes and the side of the hill, and allowed her to see, a few meters away, the leader of the Portuguese detachment. Mounted upon a gray horse, he was personally directing a charge against their flank.

Cata, who was crouching down among the elder trees, recognized him instantly.

It was the man himself, Captain Heitor, wearing a helmet with a tuft of blue feathers, a short braided jacket, long wolfskin boots, black saddlebags, and catskin holsters.

Tall, wiry, a curved sabre in his right hand, he sat high in the saddle and made his gray horse move from side to side, so as to push the soldiers back into their lines and keep them from breaking ranks.

Seemingly infuriated, he threatened the men with his sabre and hurled insults at them.

His men, without letting go of the horses' halters, and suffering the wrenching and jerking of the frightened steeds, redoubled their efforts, some crawling on their knees, others shielding themselves behind their horses.

The flint in the firearms sparkled along the front line, and not a few of the bullets fell harmlessly a short distance away, next to the burning plugs.

One of them grazed Cata's head, not hurting her but felling her on her side.

In that position, without uttering a cry, she began to drag herself among the weeds toward the dense part of the thicket, where Heitor commanded his group.

A ditch covered with brambles favored her movements.

In her catlike advance, Cata managed to place herself behind the troops, almost on top of their leader.

She heard distinctly the voices of command, the laments of the wounded, and the choleric utterances of the soldiers, proffered before an unexpected resistance, as vigorous as it was firm.

In the depths of the darkness, she saw the even darker shape that the ruins formed, from which came continuous crackling of fire and mournful whistlings that seemed to prolong themselves in space, passing with the deathly bullets over the thicket. At the same time, within her reach, she could make out the assault group in the brightness of their own shots, moving in an orderly fashion, advancing or retreating, according to command.

IV

From the ruins jets of fire kept gushing out into a thick cloud of smoke that impregnated the air with a strong smell of gunpowder.

The drama of the nocturnal battle, with its heroic episodes and details, as in the ancient tragedies, had a strange chorus, full of profound echoes, like those that can come only from wounded innards. To the crackling of the guns were joined death cries, the shouting of men and women united by the same rage, the muted hoarseness of frightened horses, the furious barking of dogs; and when the electric radiation spread its intense light over the scene, tinting it with a bright yellowish color, it revealed the eye of the assailant; in the middle of a dense landscape, two sharp, black points from which lead issued, and deformed shapes that stirred continuously as if involved in a hand-to-hand struggle. The flashes of lightning without echo, like gigantic heads of fire spreading their strands of hair in dark space, contrasted by their silence with the red puffs of smoke of the weapons followed by strong blasts. The thunder did not accompany the chorus, nor the lightning—heaven's ire—the rage of the men. On the other hand, a few dense drops of hot rain struck the sweating faces at intervals—not, however, attenuating the fever of the struggle.

The continuous barrage of projectiles had finally worn away one of the dry clay walls, already weakened and unstable because of the pounding of men and beasts, thereby opening a wide breach through which the bullets entered from an angle.

The small force had only six soldiers in shape to fight. The rest had fallen one after another, or rolled wounded into the ditch at the back, without enough strength to handle weapons. There were few cartridges left in the small bags.

Sergeant Sanabria, a blunderbuss in hand, commanded the firing to stop, ordering his men to fall on their bellies in order to take advantage of their last shots when the enemy advanced.

"Soon as those are used up," he added, "get on a horse if you can and ride over by the side of the hill. . . . But before that, don't anybody move unless you want to come face to face with my blunderbuss. And what's happened to the women? I don't see Cata."

"Here's one," answered a hoarse voice. "She's got her head broken and she's already gotten a little stiff."

"It's probably Ciriaca."

"Judging by her kinky hair, it's her, for sure."

"Shut up!" said the sergeant.

The enemy had also stopped firing, suspecting an escape, and advanced toward the "ruins."

The noise of horses nearby could be felt, as well as the clashing of sabres and the creaking of musket-locks.

"They're not on foot," said Sanabria. "Renew your fire."

The shooting broke out anew.

But those who advanced were many, and the resistance could not be prolonged.

It was necessary to die, or else look for salvation in the shadows and in flight.

With a roaring cry, Sergeant Sanabria discharged his blunderbuss.

A volley of bullets whistled at the front; the Portuguese carbines appeared almost on top of the ditch like huge clubs, and a dense cloud of smoke surrounded the "ruins," which were covered with flaming plugs.

All at once the firing ceased.

The vigorous shooting was followed by confused movement within the assaulting troops; clashes, voices, commotion, cracking of whips in the darkness, as if a sudden panic had taken hold of them; and, after that awful confusion, some pistol shots and frenetic running, as of those who rush out to escape pursued by vertigo.

Then a profound silence. . . .

Only the ever-more-distant sounds of flight could be heard in those deserted places that had minutes before been animated by the clamor of battle. And men and cavalry seemed pulled by an invisible windstorm that squeezed them with creaking and gnashing between its powerful rings.

V

A gray, ash-colored dawn was breaking; the sun was needed to break the dense barrier of stormy clouds, when a woman made her way out of the neighboring thicket, dragging herself on her hands and knees; and now on its edge, which she climbed with some effort, she stopped—no doubt to regain her breath—and looked around her searchingly at the desolation before her.

Riders and mounts among pools of blood, carbines, sabers, and helmets fallen here and there, plugs still smoldering, lances with their streamers in shreds thrust at an angle into the soft floor of the ravine, a few wounded turning over in the grass, livid, weak from loss of blood, without breath to raise their voices: such was the scene in the field that the enemy occupied.

Captain Heitor lay face down next to a thick patch of thistles.

An accurate bullet fired by Cata had felled him from the back of his horse right in the middle of the assault, the shot and the fall causing confusion and a sense of defeat among his troops, who in the darkness thought themselves attacked from the rear.

Madly fleeing, filled with a sudden fear, those that could fired their guns out over the brambles, and one of the projectiles hit Cata in the middle of the chest.

From that spot a thick thread of black blood oozed.

The captain was still moving. For brief moments he twitched violently, raising himself on his elbows, to once again become rigid. The bullet had passed through his neck, which was completely red and covered with thick blood.

Lying with his clothes in disorder and his spurs tangled in the brambles, he was the objective of the fierce and sinister eye of Cata, who approached him dragging herself, catlike, with a horn-handled knife in her right hand.

Farther ahead, one could see the ruins, which were now clumps of earth, the ditch with the bushes plastered down by the weight of the dead bodies; and toward the back, where the horses had been tied up, a shapeless pile in which one could only make out heads, arms, and legs of men and horses in lugubrious disorder.

The field was empty. Two or three of the horses that had escaped the slaughter, withered, with their sides sunken in and their gear in disorder, tried to chew the blades of grass in spite of the bridle. Next to the bit, bubbles of bloody foam oozed out.

On the other flank, rose a hill of tala trees covered at the base with thorny bushes.

On its perimeter, as if watching their prey, with their snouts to the wind and their nostrils wide open, avid for a scent, half a dozen wild dogs came and went restlessly, emitting muffled growls once in a while.

Catalina, who had hastened her advance, arrived next to Heitor, quiet, panting, with her long hair loose like a dark frame for her bronzed face: she got up on her knees again, letting out a hoarse breath, and with the fingers of her left hand she searched for the neck of the Portuguese officer, pushing away the coagulated liquid from the lips of the wound.

Had he seen those fixed, dark eyes, that hairy head leaning toward him, that hand armed with a knife, and felt that broken breathing in whose warmth the instinct whistled like a branded reptile, the spirited soldier would have shuddered with fright.

Upon feeling the pressure of those hard, clawlike fingers, the captain shook, letting out a type of bellowing that must have been a cry of anger; but she, mute and implacable, introduced the knife there, dug it in with a look of hideous rage, and then she cut with all her strength, pinioning under her knees the hand of the victim, who tried to rise convulsively.

"It's no use!," roared the she-dragoon with redoubled ire.

Tissues and veins opened under the iron blade up to the trachea, the head rose up and then kissed the ground twice, and from the wide rent the blood spurted out in a thick gush, accompanied by hoarse sounds.

That warm and fuming rain bathed Cata's bosom and ran down to the ground.

Motionless she endured it, breathing harshly, arrogantly, savagely; and finally, when the muscular body of the captain stopped shaking and shrank down, contracted, with the nails dug into the ground, the face turned upward with the mouth open and the eyes out of their orbits, showing the angry frown of the final moment, she passed her closed fist up and down her bosom with an expression of disgust, until she caused the coagulated blood to splash away from her, and she shouted with unspeakable rage, "Let the dogs lick it up!"

Soon afterward she went down on her belly and continued dragging herself toward the ruins.

Just then the wild dogs crowned the rise, spread out, moving like beasts, stretching out as far as they could their bristle-haired necks as if to better draw in the strong vapors of the slopes.

VI

A few large crows, quite black, bald-headed and hook-beaked, with their wings extended and motionless, were beginning to circle in space at a low height, emitting their lewd and anxious cries like a funereal note.

A wild dog with his snout and chest bloodied could be seen near the ditch. He wore red boots, since he seemed to have sunk his front feet in the belly of a corpse.

Cata extended her arm and threatened him with the knife.

The dog growled, showed his fangs, his hair bristled on his back and, lowering his head, he readied himself to charge, seeing no doubt that his enemy dragged herself along devoid of strength.

"Come, Canelón!" shouted Cata angrily, as if she were calling an old friend. "Get him, Canelón."

And she fell to the ground in a faint.

There, a short distance away, among a pile of bodies perforated by wounds, dusty, motionless with the profound stillness of death, lay a lion-skinned mastiff as if guarding his master.

A projectile had run through the upper part of his legs, and he seemed prostrate and in pain.

Even more so was his master. It was Sergeant Sanabria, lying on his back with his arms over his chest, in whose dilated pupils still flickered a spark of life.

His appearance was terrible.

The hard, strong, brown beard, which his soldiers compared to the end of a bull's tail, was tinted black and red.

His jaw was broken, and two fragments of the broken bone jutted outward among crushed flesh.

In his chest, another wound. The bullet had passed through his body and destroyed a spinal vertebra.

The powerful body agonized without moving.

When he heard Cata's cry, the mastiff next to Sanabria seemed to come out of his stupor; he began to rise shakily, as if numbed; he took a few unsure steps out of the bush and stuck out his head.

The wild dog lowered his tail and went away licking his whiskers, slowly, thinking more about the feast than the fight. Marauder of the brambles, companion of the crow, he came to root in the fresh entrails, not to test himself in the fight.

The mastiff returned to his place, and Cata managed to cross the ditch and dominate the gloomy landscape.

Her black, feverish eyes came to a stop when she saw Sanabria, stretched out in front of her, on a bed of brambles. She looked at him with an intense expression of love and anguish.

And still dragging herself along, she reached him, lay down by his side, caught her breath, sat up again with a moan, kissed him noisily, pushed his hands away from his chest, covered his wound with her two hands, and remained looking at him fixedly, as if she were observing how life escaped from him and from her also.

The sergeant's pupils were clouding over, and Cata felt that within her the fire in her entrails grew worse.

She looked around her with her already failing eyesight, almost dead, and was able to make out a few steps away a disheveled head that showed its brains hanging over its eyelids like a horrible head of hair. The body was hidden within the brambles.

"Ah! Ciriaca!" she exclaimed as she belched forth blood.

Just then she stretched out her arms and fell heavily on Sanabria.

His body trembled, and suddenly the pale shimmer of his eyes went out.

They ended in the shape of a cross, both lying on the same puddle, which Canelón sniffed at once in a while between deep moans.

9

MANUEL DE JESÚS GALVÁN

Born fifteen years earlier than Acevedo Díaz, Galván shared with the Uruguayan writer a similar preoccupation with his country's traditions and destiny. But while Acevedo Díaz had a novelist's imagination and generally presented the historical characters only in secondary roles, Galván was in thrall to historical fact. His *Enriquillo,* translated into English as *The Cross and the Sword,* belonged more to fictionalized history than to historical fiction.

He was born in Santo Domingo in 1834, at the time when the country was occupied by Haiti, and always saw the Spaniards as allies against the rule of their black neighbors. In 1861 he supported, if not inspired, the decision to return to Spanish rule. But in 1865, the independence party won the day, and Galván went into exile, returning to the island only in 1876 to collaborate with a new administration. The political crisis he had witnessed convinced him of the need to defend Santo Domingo's double heritage. He wanted to exalt its Indian roots but without renouncing Spain's cultural and religious legacy. To this end he conceived the idea of a historical novel based on one of the earliest and most successful Indian uprisings.

The action of *Enriquillo* takes place from 1502 to 1533, at the time when Diego Columbus, the admiral's son, was in charge of the island. The hero of the novel was an Indian chieftain who had been brought up as a Christian under Father Las Casas' guidance (see Part One, 4), and who had been driven to rebellion by Spanish brutality and treachery. Galván began his novel shortly after the publication in 1875 of Las Casas' long-suppressed *History of the Indies.* The compassionate Dominican friar's description of Enriquillo was closely followed by Galván, who gave the friar a major role in the novel. He even quoted verbatim some of his speeches and discourses.

But Galván not only followed Las Casas as a historian; he also adopted his point of view about the excesses of the conquest. He sided with the friar in the way some Spanish liberals like Quintana did. The latter's *Life of Las Casas* (1807) was one of Galván's acknowledged sources. By his words and actions, Las Casas had proved not only the horrors of genocide but also that not all the Spaniards were indifferent to the Indians' fate. Thus, Galván made his work at once an attack on and a defense of the Spanish conquest. It is this two-sided viewpoint that gives *Enriquillo* its dramatic tension.

Following the historical documents very closely, Galván left himself very little room for invention. He created only one major character, the archvillain Mojica, though this is one of the book's best portraits. He tampered just a little with his hero's family connections to make him more interesting. He imagined a love affair between two secondary characters (the chaste María de Cuéllar and the unfortunate Grijalva), of which there is no historical record; with it he tried to add some romantic interest to a rather boring second part. But the little he invented did not take him too far from his sources. The best parts of the book, however, are those in which he does not romanticize, especially the last section, in which he describes Enriquillo's successful guerrilla campaign. It comes out strongly in Robert Graves's excellent translation, as is shown here by the excerpt of Chapters 42 to 45 of the third part. If Galván did not succeed in writing a great historical novel, as some have claimed, he proved to be a master at re-creating some decisive incidents in his country's long-remembered origins. The book was published in two parts (1878 and 1882); since then it has become the Dominican Republic's national classic.

Enriquillo, the Indian Rebel

From The Cross and the Sword, *translated by Robert Graves (Bloomington: Indiana University Press, 1954), pp. 315–30.*

The next afternoon, Vasa, one of Enriquillo's lesser caciques, gazing at the distant summits of the Bahoruco mountains clearly outlined against the blue of the western sky, reined in his horse and, pointing toward them, said solemnly, "Yonder lies liberty!" His companions, much moved, echoed his words mechanically, and tears of joy filled their eyes. Enriquillo said:

"Yes, friends; yonder lies liberty, yonder lies a life fit for men. How different from the life that slaves lead! Yonder lies the duty to fight boldly in defense of that life and that liberty—gifts for which, as good Christians, we must give thanks to the Lord God Almighty."

They listened to him with religious devotion, realizing instinctively that their most urgent need was for a leader whom they could obey: that this leader must be Enrique Guarocuya, by right of birth and by merit of a moral and intellectual superiority which they could not ignore. Vasa and the other caciques of the convoy were qualified by their courage and intelligence to assume independent commands; but they had all adopted old Antrabagures's proposal, which was to swear an oath to obey him in everything.

At twilight they reached a rugged defile, which led up into the mountains between sheer precipices and gloomy chasms and wore a terrifying aspect. Mencia's blood chilled and her scalp crawled, as she heard the stones which her bearers' feet dislodged rattle down the darkness, but Enriquillo, who had dismounted and ordered a young servant to take charge of his horse, followed on foot behind the litter. Seeing with what sure-footed agility he sprang from rock to rock, she soon ceased to be afraid.

At last they stopped at a group of mountain cabins in a small, narrow plain and made ready to pass the night there. A fire was lit, supper eaten, prayers said; then Mencia and Anica wrapped themselves in the woollen and cotton blankets which they had brought, and the rest lay down on the bare ground. Soon all were asleep.

At dawn they resumed their journey to the interior of the mountains; by midday they had reached the banks of a small river, which wound between enormous rocks. After fording it, they climbed a hill and found themselves in a fertile valley shaded with palms and other tall trees. Thence could be seen a wide panorama of bare mountain slopes, colored here and there with patches of green tillage. Here Enriquillo decided to make their first settlement, and told the caciques that his plan was to make numerous similar ones throughout the wide range in whatever fertile but inaccessible spots offered themselves. They could thus be sure of food: for if one settlement were denied them they could always pass on to another.

Everyone approved of this wise decision, and set to work with enthusiasm. Before the day was over a spacious and comfortable hut had been built for Enriquillo and his wife. Several others soon appeared round it, and well-organized parties then set to work in the maize fields; some clearing and fencing the plots, others hoeing them and sowing different sorts of grain. They were favored by magnificent weather.

That night Enriquillo assembled all the Indians at the door of his house and repeated the Rosary of the Virgin; a service which thenceforth became an established custom and from which nobody was allowed to absent himself. The next two days were similarly spent in regularizing the life of that active and willing colony. More Indians flocked in; first, those who had escaped to the mountains beforehand, next fresh refugees from La Maguana, finally men from different localities in the south and west of the island who had been specially summoned by Enriquillo or his companions to come and enjoy liberty in the Bahoruco, or who had been otherwise informed of the exodus.

By the third day there were a hundred Indians of all ages and both sexes in the settlement. At first Enriquillo could count on only twenty-seven fighting men, including eleven caciques armed with lances and swords. They carried daggers, axes, crossbows (which they did not yet know how to use), pikes, or lances tipped with the sharp spines of the sting ray. But this force was soon increased when Tamayo arrived with his ten men and Galindo, bringing with them half a dozen muskets and other captured arms. Enriquillo strongly disapproved of Tamayo's act of arson, which had not entered into his calculations, but Tamayo could point to his bloodless victory and the presence of Galindo—whom Enriquillo embraced effusively—and was forgiven.

Enriquillo was sure that the authorities of La Maguana would now be roused to swift action and prepared to act at once. He ordered his scouts to be on the alert, and report on all movements in the foothill villages.

On the afternoon of the fourth day, Luis de la Laguna and his two fellow caciques arrived with the mastiffs. They brought definite news: Andrés de Valenzuela and Mojica had left San Juan that same day at the head of a band of horsemen and foot soldiers.

On learning that his enemies were after him, Enriquillo at once established a line of communication between the settlement and the foot of the mountains, with scouts and lookout men well posted and ready to take cover at any alarm. Vasa was chosen by Enriquillo to command this outpost detachment. Enriquillo then returned to the camp and calmly prepared to face the threatened attack. He divided his fighting men into companies and exhorted them to do their duty, keeping fifteen men, most of them caciques, under his immediate command, and putting the remainder under that of Tamayo and Matayco, whom he instructed to work either together or independently according to the circumstances.

The ancient caciques Incaqueta and Antrabagures, who were experienced physicians, had been provided with balsams and herbs, and remained at the dressing station in charge of the women and noncombatants. Galindo, whose wounded hand had not yet healed, was obliged to stay with them.

After all these detailed preparations had been made, Enriquillo fenced with Tamayo to make sure that he had not forgotten his swordmanship, and then made first the caciques and then the other fighters try their skill at arms. When night put an end to these exercises, he felt by no means discontented with his people's aptitude for war.

The other arrangements which Enriquillo made during the night justified the blind confidence in his leadership which all his men showed him. The mastiffs, led by the caciques who had trained them, went to reinforce Vasa's detachment, and messengers arrived at regular intervals from the foot of the mountains to report events. Toward morning, Enriquillo knew for certain that the troops from San Juan had passed the night at the village of Careybana, and would resume their march to the mountains at dawn. From Careybana three defiles led to the settlement, all of much the same length. Which would be chosen? Until he had the answer to this, Enriquillo could not commit his forces to any one defensive position but he expected the enemy to take the easiest route, which was the one Vasa was watching, and he soon proved to be right.

It was nearly midday before runners arrived to report that the troops had actually entered the main defile. Enriquillo then addressed his comrades, again exhorting them to fight boldly for their freedom, and hastened with his bodyguard to reinforce Vasa.

As they descended the slope by the stream, they heard a distant barking: it was Luis de la Laguna's mastiffs giving warning of the enemy's approach. A little later, several harquebus shots rang out, and Enriquillo had reached the opposite hillside when he was mortified by seeing the greater part of the outpost detachment fleeing in disorder like a frightened flock of sheep. He halted them with a shout and a gesture, reproved their cowardice, and asked where Vasa was. Nobody could tell him, but he followed the road and soon found Vasa lying on the ground with a leg wound. Luis de la Laguna stood by with his three mastiffs; he had helped him there and was begging him to exert himself and escape.

From beyond a sharp bend of the defile came the shouts of the enemy. They were encouraging one another as they climbed in pursuit of the Indians whom they had so easily dislodged from their advance positions. Enriquillo saw at a glance the advantage of that narrow passage; he quickly distributed his small force among the rocks to left and right of the road, and posted himself just behind the bend at the head of five caciques armed with lances and swords.

An instant later Andrés de Valenzuela and Mojica arrived with their troops—all on foot, for they had not been able to bring their horses up the steep slope. Encouraged by the easy success of their first assault, and believing that the Indians would not again dare face them, they kept shouting, "Where is that dog Enriquillo?"

Even as they spoke they were confronted not by a dog, not by a serf whom they had despised as a vile coward, but by a transfigured Enriquillo—imposing, haughty, and terrible. Indomitable valor shone in his eyes, inflexible resolution showed in his bearing; and at the sight of his intrepid approach—for he took no precautions against harquebus shots and seemed to think himself invulnerable—they suddenly felt their courage fail, fell silent, and took a few paces backward.

"Here is the man whom you seek," he cried in a voice of thunder. "Here is the lord of these mountains, who is sworn to live and die free from hateful tyranny!"

Then, seeing the enemy troops hasten up to support their leaders, he turned to his comrades and cried, "At them, comrades!"

With him they hurled themselves like a torrent on the disordered Spaniards, and so violently that some of them rolled down the slope with their victims transfixed on their lances. Enriquillo, going like a lion in search of Pedro de Mojica, who tried to elude him, broke through the ranks of soldiers as though through a rotten fence, and managed at last to inflict a deep sword thrust on Mojica's face. But the coward fled at breakneck speed with the rest of his men and got away.

As Andrés followed in the ruck, Tamayo dealt him a swinging blow with the butt of his broken lance, which opened his head and sent him sprawling. He was about to kill him where he lay, but Enriquillo darted forward and held his arm.

"Do not kill him," he said. "Remember Don Francisco de Valenzuela."

"You are a coward, Enriquillo," answered Tamayo angrily. "To each what he deserves. Don Francisco is in Heaven; let this knave go to Hell!"

"No, Tamayo: today I must pay my debt to that noble soul."

And lifting the confused and wounded Andrés from the ground, he examined his wound, saw that it was not serious, and spoke these simple words to him: "Be grateful, Valenzuela, that I do not kill you. Go, and never return here again."

Tamayo stamped with fury: then, as though a sudden idea had occurred to him, struck his head with his hand. Seeing that Enriquillo was busy helping to carry Vasa back to the camp, he waited behind with six or seven companions until the party was out of sight; then rushed down the defile and reached the foot of the mountain just as Mojica, unarmed, hatless, his face covered with blood, had mounted his horse with the help of two men and gone off at a gallop. Tamayo let out a roar at the thought of his escape; but then he saw five or six chargers, already saddled and with their bridles hanging from the saddletrees, which had not yet been retrieved by their owners. He quickly mounted the nearest one, and set off in pursuit. The horse, urged forward with cries and blows, covered the distance with such speed that Tamayo felt certain of success; and looking more closely at its wavy mane, he found to his joy that it was Enriquillo's own mare, Azucena.

Mojica, who had recognized Tamayo, plunged the rowels of his spurs deep in his horse's sides; but it could not compete with Azucena, and half dead with terror he saw the distance between himself and his pursuer lessen every moment. Overcome by fear rather than by fortune, he decided to surrender at discretion.

"Tamayo," he pleaded, slackening the pace, "what do you want of me? Here I am: help me to escape from this plight and I will give you whatever you ask."

Tamayo reined in the excited mare, which was covered with froth, and taking hold of Mojica's arm, said with a fierce smile, "Yes, here you are, man, evil man, son of the Devil! What is this about giving me whatever I ask? I only want your life, and I would not exchange it for all the gold you have ever stolen."

And threatening him with his fist, he ordered him to dismount.

Mojica obeyed, trembling, and mumbled more pleas for mercy, mixed with offers of ransom and appeals to the Virgin and all the saints. The implacable Tamayo, removing his sword-belt—he had lost his sword as he ran down the slope —tied Mojica's hands tightly with it, and waited for the arrival of his companions, who were hurrying up, some on horseback and others on foot.

When they arrived, the terrified Mojica resumed his lamentations and prayers.

"Do not kill me, dear lads!" he besought them. "I will be your best friend; I will see that they pardon you and allow you to live in freedom. I will give you all I have; only save my life, in the name of Jesus Christ, of the Sacred Virgin, and of San Francisco!"

"The grotesque figure carved in La Higuera, eh?" replied Tamayo, whom Enriquillo had told of Mojica's scurrilous remarks in the tribunal. "Do not worry, you shall pay for your heresies. The Saint has delivered you into my hands!"

And without more ado, he cut the bridle of the nearest horse, knotted one end into a running noose, and slipped this over Mojica's head.

"Pray!" he said.

"What shall I pray?" asked Mojica in horror.

"Whatever you please." He told his men, "Hold him well."

"I do not know how to pray," cried Mojica, hoping to gain time.

"So much the worse for you!" answered Tamayo harshly. "Off you go to Hell!"

With these words, he tightened the noose around Mojica's throat, pressing a foot against his back and hauling on the rein with both hands. Mojica closed his eyes, then opened them wide. His face grew livid; the blood ceased to flow from the wound in his face and a convulsive shudder shook his body. They hanged him on the nearest tree.

Tamayo watched until his limbs had ceased to twitch and then said coldly, "He is dead now and well dead. The greatest villain in all La Maguana. May God forgive me! Now I can once more believe in Him and in His justice."

Then, patting Azucena's arched neck, he remounted and returned to the camp, followed by his men.

"And here is another proof of God's justice," he ruminated. "How happy Enriquillo will be to recover his beautiful mare."

A man came stumbling down the defile. When he saw the group of Indian horsemen, he tried to conceal himself in a thicket, but too late. He was seized, and Tamayo recognized in that crestfallen, defeated figure, wearing blood-stained clothes and with his head roughly bandaged, the proud tyrant, Andrés de Valenzuela.

Valenzuela looked at him miserably, and asked resignedly, "What do you want of me?"

"Your comrade Mojica asked me the same question a little while ago," replied Tamayo pitilessly, "and I have just told him, and told him very well. But I confess, I do not know what I want of you. Evidently San Francisco has delivered you too into my hands. But Enriquillo has granted you his pardon."

He spoke indecisively, for he had a burning desire to make an end of Andrés, as he had done with Mojica; but did not dare to go so far in violation of his leader's wishes.

Suddenly he turned his mare around, and said to Valenzuela, "Follow me: I do not want much of you."

They went to where Mojica was hanging; Andrés could not at first recognize the swinging corpse.

"Do you see, your friend, your associate in crime and sacrilege?" cried Tamayo, his voice like the hissing roar of a hurricane. "Enriquillo is worth a thousand of you, and he pardoned you. I, who am not worth so much, also pardon you for his sake. But listen well, Valenzuela! Forsake your evil ways; do not afflict the wretched; do not dishonor helpless women; be a good Christian, as your father was! Else I swear I will put an end to you, wherever you may be." He ended vehemently: "Now go, go! And never come back here again."

Valenzuela, confused, terrified, more dead than alive, heard Tamayo's words like a funeral warning from Heaven, and stumbled on his way, hardly able to set one foot before the other.

Careybana was the first village of any importance on the road from the Bahoruco to La Maguana. There the broken remnants of the punitive force stopped for shelter and rest. Andrés arrived at nightfall, and after assuaging his hunger with what little food he found, and dressing his broken head more carefully, slept, worn out, until late the next morning.

He tried to buy a horse to carry him back to San Juan but was unable to procure one at any price. In his pain and weakness, he could not decide what to do and felt incapable of walking even so much as a league; but at last a farmer from La Maguana, one of his comrades in misfortune, rode up on Azucena. He told Andrés, "I was captured yesterday afternoon while wandering on the mountain. This morning the cacique released me on condition that I gave you this." He handed him a note, which ran as follows:

"Though I much regret, my lord Andrés, the outrage committed by Tamayo, I heartily agree with the advice which he tells me he gave you. May God touch your heart and make you follow it. Keep the mare in my memory and that of your good father, for I can now freely offer her to you, having ceased to be what I was by the recovery of my natural freedom. If you are true to your word and marry Doña Elvira, let this be my wedding gift, and may it bring you happiness! Bestow Mencia's estates, which have brought her only ill fortune, upon Don Diego Velázquez in our name. It will be a payment of the debt that I owe him for his care. Farewell! Enrique."

News of the disastrous defeat suffered by the troops from San Juan spread rapidly throughout the island and astonished all hearers. "Enriquillo has rebelled!" "The Indians have defeated the Spaniards in the Bahoruco!" Rumors ran from mouth to mouth, with ever fresh exaggerations and distortions. Badillo thought that here was a magnificent chance to cover himself with glory at little cost. He called to arms all Spaniards in La Maguana capable of bearing them, summoned help from Azúa, and little more than a week later had assembled two hundred fifty soldiers, well armed and equipped. How could the rebels of Bahoruco resist so powerful a force? Badillo, full of martial illusions, marched his men off in good order, undecided only about one thing: what sort of punishment to inflict on Enriquillo and his men when he laid his hands on them.

But the Indian army had swelled remarkably. Victory had given courage to the timid, and every day fresh bands of serfs reached the Bahoruco in search of liberty. One of the first of these new arrivals, a cacique, Romero by name, was even younger than his cousin Enriquillo, but yielded nothing to him in courage or tactical skill. Of this he soon gave proof; as also of his loyal obedience to orders.

Enriquillo might have done nothing else in his life but practice the art of war, to judge by the forethought and ability with which he organized his reinforcements. He seemed to divine at first sight each new recruit's special capacity and assigned him the task most suited to it. He organized a corps of scouts and lookout men, who never worked singly but always in groups of two or three, taking turns to sleep and watch; and a corps of skirmishers, consisting of the strongest and most agile men, who practiced for several hours a day climbing seemingly inaccessible peaks and precipices. These men could jump like does from crag to crag, or like serpents swarm up and down the creepers that hung from the sheer rocks, and in short perform all the operations necessary to assure the insurgents complete command of that craggy wilderness.

Exercises in the handling of the lance, sword, sling, and crossbow also occupied a great part of the army's time. Enriquillo had captured some harquebuses in his first engagement but because of the great scarcity of powder could use them only on rare occasions, as signal guns. But more formidable than the artillery of that time was the practice of rock-toppling: heavy fragments broken from the sharp mountain summits were poised above the narrow passes through which the enemy would try to force his way, and could be released in a moment by cutting the cords which held them there.

Next, Enriquillo appointed a body of captains and caciques to act both as a senate and town council, and attend to the daily needs of his small republic. But he was careful to keep the supreme authority in his own hands, realizing that only so could he secure unity among his scattered people, and that on unity depended their successful defense against the hazards of a perilous situation.

Among the arms and armor of which some of the rebel caciques had managed to deprive their masters were two magnificent coats of mail, one of which was presented to Enriquillo. This gave him the idea of manufacturing sword-proof cuirasses from tightly twisted cords of pita, sisal, and majagua, varnished on the outside with resin. By providing his best men with these, he increased their boldness in battle, and some time later improved on his invention by manufacturing legpieces and armpieces in the same style. It was a little time before the Indians grew accustomed to this rough armor, but when they did, they looked and behaved like professional soldiers and Enriquillo's military power became more formidable than ever.

When he received news that Badillo was leading an army against him, he harangued his men briefly but sufficiently, swearing to honor and reward the brave but to inflict exemplary punishment on all cowards.

He then covered each of the three principal approaches to the mountains with a strong advance guard. The commanders, Tamayo and two other trusted caciques, were given great mother-of-pearl conches, called *lambios* by the Indians, the sound of which was louder than any trumpet; and were told what calls to blow on them for warning, or summons, or reassurance. Romero, with a striking force of seventy men, was to come to reinforce whichever of the three advance guards bore the brunt of the attack, and Enriquillo would hold the rest in reserve until the right moment came to fall on Badillo's rear.

The Spaniards reached the foothills and again made for the main defile, the defense of which had been confided to Tamayo. He and his men were holding a height which seemed to rise to a sheer peak; nobody could have guessed that it served at once as observation post, arsenal, and fortress to a great number of men. Calmly he waited until the San Juan militia had advanced some distance up the ravine and then let fall an avalanche of enormous rocks, which not only crushed many of them but also blocked their advance and thoroughly disorganized their ranks. Tamayo's conch sounded, and several others replied from the distance, passing on the news that the action had begun and summoning all forces to converge on the main defile. Badillo, seeing that the rain of rocks was causing him severe casualties, gave the order to advance and force the pass; but soon found that this only made matters worse, because there was now room for only two men to advance abreast, and the rocks continued to fall as thickly as ever. Having no military experience, he then lost his head and, not knowing what else to do, sounded the retreat and ran like a madman to direct it.

His army was now in utter confusion: those most exposed to Tamayo's battering fought violently with their own comrades, each trying to be the first to escape. At this critical moment Romero's men appeared on the flank, and fell resolutely with lance and sword upon the disordered rabble. A hand-to-hand battle ensued. Some Spaniards defended themselves bravely, and Badillo was heartened to see that the fall of stones had stopped and that only a small force of the enemy had dared commit themselves to cold steel. But his satisfaction was short-lived; Tamayo's mountaineers clambered down from their peak, armed with swords, and charged to Romero's assistance, shouting vociferously.

Suddenly the mountains re-echoed with the metallic notes of a hunting horn sounding a solemn toccata, which caused panic among the boldest of the Spaniards and chilled Badillo's heart. It announced the arrival of Enriquillo. The Indians acclaimed him enthusiastically, and "Enriquillo!" was a war cry to infuse new spirit into the already triumphant Indians, and make them resolve on the complete overthrow of the invaders.

Tamayo, the ardent and indefatigable Tamayo, pressed hard on the retreat. Badillo, whose vainglory and negligence had caused the disaster, fled hastily along a footpath after the huntsmen who had acted as his guides. Every man saved himself as best he could, and many were killed while trying to scale the precipitous sides of the defile.

Again the raucous conches blew, this time giving the order to rally and break off the pursuit. Much blood had flowed, and Enriquillo magnanimously decided to spare the survivors. But Tamayo was already far ahead and either did not hear, or did not want to hear, the merciful signal. After waiting for him a quarter of an hour or more, Enriquillo and many of his warriors decided to descend the steep slope down which Tamayo had run after the main body of the fugitives, like a wild beast let loose. Near the foot of the mountain, a few steps from the path, he at last came upon Tamayo and his men, all busied with a strange task. There was a cave screened by trees, and in front of it a great pile of brushwood and fallen branches had been heaped, almost blocking the mouth. Tamayo's men were grouped in a semicircle about it and he had just applied a resinous torch to the dry leaves at the edge. Already the flame was spreading voraciously in all directions, and a thick cloud of smoke arose. It eddied here and there, but the wind blew most of it into the cave. Tamayo stood contemplating his work with grim satisfaction.

"What is this?" cried Enriquillo, hurrying up.

"Watch, cacique," replied Tamayo. "We are fumigating the men inside."

These brutal words were hardly out of his mouth when Enriquillo leaped on him, pushed him to one side, and began to stamp out the blaze and toss the burning pieces of wood far away. His soldiers hurried to help him.

"Barbarian!" he cried indignantly. "Is this how you interpret my instructions?"

And he shouted into the cave, "Come out of there, Spaniards! You need have no fear. Enriquillo pledges his word that your lives will be spared."

The unfortunate men, who were already convinced that their refuge would prove their sepulcher, came out one by one, choking, and half blinded.

Enriquillo counted seventy-two of them.

"Return in peace to La Maguana," he bade them, "or wherever you please. Inform the tyrants that I and my Indians know how to defend our liberty; but that we are neither executioners nor villains. You, Martín Alfaro," he said, turning to a benign-looking Indian at his side, "escort these men to the plain and let them go in safety. You will answer for their lives with your own."

Preserved from certain death, the Spaniards clasped their hands in gratitude, and blessed Enriquillo's name. One of them went up to him, kissed his right hand with deep emotion, and said, "Hear me, my lord Enriquillo. In my tribulation I vowed to God that, if you saved me, I would devote the rest of my life to His service. I will keep my vow, and pray daily for your well-being."

Feeling wonderfully relieved, the prisoners set off under the protection of Martín Alfaro and his escort. Enriquillo then turned to Tamayo who, motionless and in an ugly frame of mind, stood sullenly watching everything from where he had been pushed.

"I told you the other day, Tamayo," he said severely, "that we must not offend God with such inhumanities as you practiced on Mojica. It is not right for those who fight for justice to murder their prisoners."

"I can see, Enriquillo," answered Tamayo fiercely, "that if this sort of thing continues you and I must quarrel. Steel or fire is all that our enemies deserve, and you would give them sweetmeats and flowers when they come to kill us."

"You are mistaken, Tamayo. This is a war of freedom, not of purposeless cruelty. Come, let us return to the camp; we will eat and rest a little until the moon rises and then you can take your men down to the plain and bring back all the cattle you can find between here and Careybana."

Tamayo heaved a sigh of satisfaction; the task was much to his taste. His ill humor disappeared as if by magic, and he promised to obey Enriquillo's instructions to the letter.

But when he returned the following afternoon with more than a hundred head of cattle, Enriquillo was horrified to see that he was wearing a necklace of six human ears. They belonged to three cattle owners of Careybana, who had boldly resisted his seizure of their property.

Enriquillo was disgusted with Tamayo's cynical ostentation of his cruelty and instead of congratulating him, as he perhaps expected, reproved him with sincere sorrow. Tamayo listened impatiently and, when he had done, said haughtily, "I shall go away and make war on my own."

"Go, as soon as you please," answered Enriquillo in exasperation, "and take with you all who are as bloodthirsty as yourself. I am a Christian and do not have this madness in my heart."

"Very well, Enriquillo," replied Tamayo. "It is better that I go. Tomorrow I shall leave the Bahoruco with any companions who wish to follow me, and will wage war as the Christians of Spain taught me how to wage it."

"You are your own master, Tamayo. Go, and when you have finished with your evil work, return to the Bahoruco, to fight in the way I fight—namely in resistance to tyranny, not in joy of bloodshed."

Badillo's defeat provided the Indians with numerous arms and horses of which Enriquillo made good use: for many days the Bahoruco cavalry were masters of the neighboring plains, and the fame of Enriquillo spread far and wide, enhanced by this second victory. The authorities in Santo Domingo were taken aback by the astonishing news. The Jeronymite fathers had already returned to Spain, and the Judges of Appeal, with the Royal Officers, who now held the seals of government, ordered a general levy of troops: all contingents were to converge on the Bahoruco simultaneously and extinguish the rebellion in blood.

These orders were about to be carried out when the Viceroy suddenly returned from Spain. He was followed a few days later by Father Las Casas, who was on his way to the American mainland, to attempt the peaceful colonization of the Cumaná coast. The corrupt authorities of Hispaniola naturally put as many obstacles as possible in the way of his pious projects; and to extricate himself from the heat and malevolence which they stirred up, he resolved to come to an agreement with them, and offer them shares in his venture. Then, of course, he was given every facility and left Santo Domingo well equipped; he called this "having to buy the Gospel, since they do not wish to give it free."

On his arrival at Hispaniola, he met Camacho who, after Badillo's defeat, had been treated with such great suspicion in San Juan that he had gone away to Santo Domingo; and heard from him, with great sorrow, of the events leading up to Enriquillo's rebellion. A little later Andrés de Valenzuela also arrived at Santo Domingo, where the Viceroy imprisoned him and drew up a criminal case against him, charging him with having provoked the revolt by his tyrannies. In memory of good old Don Francisco, Father Las Casas managed to smother the anger and aversion which he felt for the wretch and went to see him in prison, hoping that the moral lesson which Fortune was giving him would perhaps make him behave better in future. Much to his surprise, he did not find the proud, swaggering Andrés whom he remembered, but a sick and defeated Andrés who threw himself at his feet and, weeping contritely, blessed him for having come on so charitable a mission, and acknowledged that the misfortune was well deserved. Father Las Casas, moved to his very soul by this wholly unexpected action, consoled the penitent as best he could, reminding him of God's extraordinary mercy in the Day of Judgment, and offering to plead for him with the Viceroy and the other authorities.

Bit by bit, Andrés related all the circumstances of his defeat in the Bahoruco; of his shame to find himself conquered and pardoned by Enriquillo, upon whom he had been accustomed to look with more disdain than on the dung in the fields; of the horror which the sight of Mojica hanging from the tree had caused him; of Tamayo's cruelty as contrasted with Enriquillo's generosity. He expressed his conviction that all these things, but especially Tamayo's severe admonition on that fearful occasion, constituted a warning from Heaven to forsake the way of perdition in which he had so long persisted. The final shock had come when Enriquillo's generous note reached him in Careybana, with the gift of Azucena and the suggestion that he should keep his promise of marriage to Doña Elvira. His heart had suddenly returned to divine grace, and he sincerely repented of his sins; being now resolved to reform, to do as much good as he possibly could, and to offer to marry Elvira if she would still have him.

Las Casas was delighted, and not only exhorted Andrés to continue on this praiseworthy course but said that he would help him to do so; and, indeed, he worked so hard that three days later, with the cooperation of Doctor Alonso Zuazo and others, he had Andrés released, and two weeks later, with the Viceroy and Vicereine acting as his sponsors, Andrés married Elvira Pimentel. They decided to reside in Santo Domingo, because Andrés did not want to return to La Maguana and the memories of his dissipation which the place evoked. He afterward tried to deed Mencia's estates to Don Diego Velázquez, as Enriquillo had charged him to do; but, as Governor of Cuba, Velázquez was now so rich that he refused the offer, excusing himself by a reference to the famous laws of Toro. Thus Andrés continued to manage the estates until his death.

Whether the Supreme Judge of Heaven and Earth punished Andrés's sins in the afterworld, or whether his marriage with the featherbrained Elvira was considered sufficient punishment, is a theological question which we shall not attempt to discuss, for want of sufficient data. All we know is that after his marriage he lived a Christian life, humble in heart and a friend to the unfortunate, as Don Francisco had been in his time; and, as a partaker of eternal bliss, Don Francisco must have congratulated himself that the seed of his own good example had germinated, though somewhat late, in his son's heart.

10

RICARDO PALMA

Like Rodríguez Freile (see Part One, 12), one of his acknowledged models, Ricardo Palma wanted to write history but succeeded instead in creating the most delightful historical fiction.

He was born in Peru in 1833. He quickly outgrew the romantic style and themes, after leaving behind him three volumes of bad poetry, some awful plays, and very naïve tales. Palma had always been attracted to Peru's colorful past, which encompassed the time span between the fabulous Incas and the no less fabulous viceroys of the Spanish Empire. He once attempted an important historical work on the Inquisition of Lima (1863), but was soon compelled to recognize that this kind of writing was not his forte. He found his real vein, instead, in the short, light narratives on historical matters he was already publishing in the newspapers. With his first collection of these pieces, published in 1872 under the title of *Peruvian Traditions*, he may with some justice be said to have invented a new genre. It is true, strictly speaking, that "traditions" had been written in both Spain and Latin America before Palma (even Sarmiento authored some), but it was Palma's genius to give this species of writing a completely new look. Until eight years before his death in 1919, he continued to issue volumes of these short and witty tales, which had become his distinctive literary enterprise. (He even prepared a volume of "blue" *Traditions*, collected in 1901 and only recently published.)

To write his tales, Palma ransacked libraries, avidly chasing manuscripts, and exhausted convents' records and provincial archives. He was indefatigable, always willing to distill the essence of a four-hundred-page dossier into a five-page story. The success of his traditions depended not only on his swift comic evocation of Peru's past but also on his skill in blending historical facts with gossip, the stiff language of the documents with the vivid speech of the oral witnesses.

The best of his traditions are set in naughty eighteenth-century Lima, at a time when Micaela Luján, La Perricholi (The Indian Bitch), reigned undisputed as concubine of the viceroy. Celebrated by Palma, she had already been immortalized by Prosper Mérimée in *The Coach of the Holy Sacrament* (1829), and was later used in Thornton Wilder's novel *The Bridge of San Luis Rey* (1929) and in Jean Renoir's film *The Golden Coach* (1953).

In his own time, Palma was accused of being too much in love with the past, and a very reactionary past at that. Younger liberal writers attacked his devotion to tradition and his nostalgia for the viceroyalty. But if Palma had a bit of the snob about him, he also had a very sharp eye for any phoniness. His Lima was not only a beautiful and proud city; it was also the center of the grossest intrigues, the most appalling debaucheries and brutal murders.

The gilt of many a coat of arms was constantly exposed by Palma's mischievous narrative. In the best tradition of his irreverent masters—from Rabelais and Voltaire to the Balzac of the *Droll Tales*—Palma laughed at the antics and pretensions to nobility of his very greedy, vulgar characters. He exposed them with a laugh. Palma himself had been born illegitimate and never knew who his real mother was. He was brought up by his father in a lower-middle-class family. But he managed to become Peru's most respected writer, Director of the National Library, correspondent to the Spanish Royal Academy, and what not. Under an impeccably respectable façade, Palma maintained the privileges of satire, even if he made it more palatable to his very conventional readers by an ambiguous smile. Today he is still the most widely read of his country's writers, the one who encompassed in his work the widest human panorama. To represent Palma's range accurately, it would have been necessary to select at least twenty of his best *Traditions*, including the long one on La Perricholi. What is offered here is only a sample of the variety and wit of a work that is counted among the very best produced in nineteenth-century Latin America.

Three Peruvian Traditions

From The Golden Land, *pp. 138–40; and* The Knights of the Cape, *translated by Harriet de Onís (New York: Knopf, 1945), pp. 224–29 and 165–69.*

The Goblins of Cuzco

There stands in the city of Cuzco a magnificent house known as the "house of the admiral." It seems that the admiral in question was as much of a sailor as some I can think of who have seen only pictures of the sea. The fact is that the title was hereditary and was handed down from father to son.

The house was a striking edifice. Two of its most notable features were the water drains and the sculpted beams of the roof, on one of which was carved the head of the admiral who built the house.

That four admirals lived in Cuzco is borne out by the family tree that in 1861 was presented to the Congress of Peru by Don Sixto Laza in a petition to have himself declared the sole and legitimate heir of the Inca Huascar and thus entitled to an income from the guano beds, the duchy of Medina de Rioseco, the marquisate of Oropesa, and several other tidbits. We were going to have to pay dear for the honor of having a prince of our own! But it is on record, against the day we tire of the Republic, theoretical or factual, and for a change decide to install the monarchy, absolute or constitutional, for anything can happen, by the grace of God and at the pace we are going.

According to this genealogy, the first admiral was Don Manuel de Castilla, the second, Don Cristobal de Castilla Espinosa y Lugo, who was succeeded by his son, Don Gabriel de Castilla Vázquez de Vargas, and the fourth and last was Don Juan de Castilla y González, whose descendants were all female.

It is told of the Castillas, to show how proud they were of their lineage, that when they recited the Hail Mary they employed this wording: "Holy Mary, mother of God, our relative and lady, pray for us. . . ."

The arms of the Castillas were a trouçonné shield, the dexter quarter in gules with a castle of gold on azure, the sinister in silver, with a lion rampant on a field of gules and a sinople bend with two dragons also in sinople.

It would be difficult to decide which of the four admirals is the hero of this tradition, and in view of this doubt the reader can make any one of them the scapegoat in the assurance that he will not come back to complain if there has been a mistake.

The admiral in question was prouder than Lucifer, vainer of his pedigree than a peacock, and stiffer than his starched ruff. In the courtyard of the

house stood a magnificent stone fountain to which the people of the neighborhood used to come for water, taking at its face value the saying that nobody was
ever refused water or fire.

But one morning His Excellency got up in a devil of a bad humor and
gave his servants orders to beat to a jelly any of the trash that ventured to cross
his threshold in search of the liquid that cools but does not intoxicate.

One of the first to receive this punishment was a poor old woman, and
the news of the outrage caused general indignation.

The next day the woman's son, a young priest attached to the parish
of San Jerónimo, a few leagues distant from Cuzco, came to the city and
learned of the affront his old mother had suffered. He went immediately to the
house of the admiral; and the owner of the bearings and quarterings called him
a son of a goat and a *vela verde,* and that aristocratic mouth spewed forth verbs
and gerunds, toads and snakes, and he wound up by giving the priest a terrific
beating.

The excitement the attack gave rise to was tremendous. The authorities
were afraid openly to take a stand against a person of the admiral's rank, and they
let time go by, hoping it would take care of things, as it generally does. But the
clergy and the populace declared the haughty admiral excommunicate.

The insulted priest, a few hours after the outrage, made his way to the
cathedral and knelt in prayer before an image of Christ, a gift to the city from
Charles V. When his prayer was finished he left at the feet of the Supreme Judge
a petition stating his complaint and demanding divine justice, for he was sure he
would not receive it at human hands. It is said that he returned to the temple
the next day and picked up his complaint, on which there had been written in
the margin: "Petition noted. Justice will be done."

And so three months went by, when one morning a gallows was seen
standing before the house of the admiral and dangling from it the body of the
excommunicate. Nobody was ever able to discover the authors of the crime, in
spite of the fact that suspicion naturally fell upon the priest. But he had many
witnesses to testify to his whereabouts and was able to establish an alibi.

At the inquest that followed, two women of the neighborhood stated
that they had seen a group of "little men with big heads," generally known as
goblins, setting up the gallows, and that when it was ready they had knocked three
times at the door of the house, and at the third knock it opened. In a little while
the admiral, in ceremonial dress, came out surrounded by the goblins, who
without further ado strung him up like a bunch of grapes.

With testimony of this sort, justice was left completely in the dark, and
since it was impossible to lay hands on the goblins, it was decided that the best
thing to do was to bring in a verdict of "death at the hand of person or persons
unknown."

If the people accept as an article of faith that it was the goblins who
brought the excommunicated admiral to his end, it is not a poor chronicler's place
to wear himself out trying to find another explanation, no matter how much the
incredulous folk of the time whispered that it was all the work of the Jesuits, to

insure that those of the sacerdotal order were treated with the respect that was their due.

The mayor and the magistrates of Cuzco reported what had happened to the viceroy, who after reading the lengthy report said to his secretary, "A nice theme for a ballad! What is your opinion of this, my good Estuñiga?"

"That Your Excellency ought to give those stupid magistrates a piece of your mind for not being able to discover those guilty of the crime."

"But then the affair would lose its poetry," answered Esquilache, smiling.

"That is true, sir; but justice would have been done."

The viceroy remained pensive a few seconds; then, getting up from his chair, he laid his hand on his secretary's shoulder.

"My friend, what has been done has been well done; and the world would be better off if, in certain cases, instead of sly, tricky lawyers and other ravens of Themis, it were goblins who meted out justice. And now good night and may God and the Virgin Mary watch over us and keep us from goblins and remorse."

Fray Gómez's Scorpion

In diebus illis—that is to say, when I was a boy—I often heard old women say, in praising the beauty or value of a piece of jewelry, "It's as valuable as Fray Gómez's scorpion."

I've got a little girl who is a treasure, everything that is winning and delightful, with a pair of eyes that are more roguish and mischievous than a couple of notaries:

> A girl that is like
> The morning star
> At the break of day.

In my paternal besottedness I have nicknamed this flower of mine "Fray Gómez's little scorpion." And now I am going to explain the old wives' saying and the tribute to my Angélica by relating this tradition.

I

Once upon a time there was a lay brother who lived at the same time as Don Juan de la Pipirindica, the silver-tongued, and San Francisco Solano. This lay brother lived in Lima, in the convent of the Franciscans, where he performed the duties of refectorian in the nursing home or hospital of the devout friars. The people called him Fray Gómez, Fray Gómez he is called in the conventual records, and tradition knows him as Fray Gómez. I believe that in the petition for his beatification and canonization that was sent to Rome this is the only name he is given.

Fray Gómez performed miracles right and left in my land, without even knowing that he was working them, and as though against his will. He was a born miracle-worker, like the man who talked in prose without suspecting it.

One day the lay brother happened to be crossing a bridge when a runaway horse threw its rider on the flagstones. The poor fellow lay there, stiff as a board, his head as full of holes as a sieve, and blood gushing from his mouth and nose.

"He's fractured his skull. He's dying. Go quick and bring a priest from San Lázaro to administer the last rites." The noise and confusion were indescribable.

Fray Gómez walked calmly over to the fallen man, touched his mouth with the cord of his girdle, pronounced three blessings over him, and without further doctoring or medication the dying man got to his feet as though nothing had happened.

"A miracle! A miracle! Long live Fray Gómez," shouted the multitude that had witnessed the scene. And in their enthusiasm they wanted to carry the lay brother in a triumphal procession. But the latter, to avoid this demonstration, started off at a run for his convent and shut himself up in his cell.

The Franciscan chronicle gives a different version of what happened at this point. It says that Fray Gómez, to escape from his admirers, rose in the air and flew from the bridge to the belfry of his convent. I neither deny nor affirm this. Perhaps he did, perhaps he didn't. In questions of miracles I do not intend to waste ink either defending them or refuting them.

That must have been Fray Gómez's day for working miracles, because as he came out of his cell on his way to the hospital, he found San Francisco Solano stretched out on a bench with a terrible sick headache. The lay brother felt his pulse and said to him, "Father, you are very weak and you ought to have something to eat."

"Brother," answered the saint, "I'm not the least bit hungry."

"Make an effort, reverend father, and take something, even if it's just a bite."

And the refectorian kept at him so long that the sick man, to stop his nagging, hit upon the idea of asking him for something that it would have been impossible even for the viceroy to get, because it was out of season then.

"Well, brother, the only thing I'd like to eat would be a couple of smelts."

Fray Gómez put his right hand into the left sleeve of his habit and pulled out a pair of smelts that were as fresh as though they had just come out of the water.

"There you are, father, and let's hope they make you feel better. I'll cook them for you right away."

And the fact of the matter is that the blessed smelts cured San Francisco like a charm.

These two little miracles I have mentioned just in passing do not seem to me chaff. And I am leaving in my inkwell many others this lay brother performed, because I do not propose to relate his life and miracles. Nevertheless, to satisfy the demands of the curious, I shall jot down that over the door of the first cell of the small cloister that is still used as a hospital, there is an oil painting depicting the two miracles I have described, which bears the following inscription:

"The Venerable Fray Gómez. Born in Extremadura in 1560. Took the habit in Chuquisaca in 1580. Came to Lima in 1587. Was a nurse for forty years, displaying all virtues, and was endowed with celestial gifts and favors. His life was a continuous miracle. He died on May 2, 1631, and was held to be a saint. The following year his body was laid in the chapel of Aranzazú, and on October 13, 1810, was placed beneath the high altar in the same vault where the remains of the priors of the convent are interred. Doctor Don Bartolomé María de las Heras was a witness to this transfer. This venerable painting was restored on November 30, 1882, by M. Zamudio."

II

Fray Gómez was in his cell one morning, given over to meditation, when a couple of timid knocks sounded on his door, and a plaintive-toned voice said, *"Deo gratias. . . .* Praised be the Lord."

"Forever, amen. Come in, brother," answered Fray Gómez.

And the door of the humble cell opened to admit a ragged individual, a *vera efigies* of a man crushed by poverty, but whose face revealed the proverbial forthrightness and honesty of the Old Castilian.

The entire furnishings of the cell comprised four rawhide chairs, a table that had seen better days, a cot without mattress, sheets, or blankets and with a stone for a pillow.

"Sit down, brother, and tell me frankly what brings you here," said Fray Gómez.

"Well, father, I want to tell you that I am an honest and decent man . . ."

"That is plain, and I hope you will continue that way, for it will give you peace of heart in this life, and bliss in the next."

"You see, I am a peddler, and I have a big family, and my business does not prosper because I am short of capital, not because of laziness or lack of effort on my part."

"I am glad, brother, for God helps a man who works as he should."

"But the fact of the matter is, father, that so far God hasn't heard me, and He is slow in coming to my help. . . ."

"Don't lose heart, brother, don't lose heart."

"But the fact of the matter is that I have knocked at many doors asking for a loan of five hundred duros and I have found them all locked and bolted. And last night, turning things over in my mind, I said to myself, 'Come, Jerónimo, cheer up and go ask Fray Gómez for the money, for if he wants to, a mendicant friar and poor as he is, he'll find a way to give you a hand.' And so here I am because I have come, and I beg and request you, father, to lend me that trifling sum for six months, and you can be sure that it will never be said of me:

> The world is full of folks
> Who reverence certain saints,
> But whose gratitude ends
> When they've answered their plaints."

"What made you think, son, that you would find such a sum in this poor cell?"

"Well, father, the fact is that I wouldn't know how to answer that; but I have faith that you will not let me leave empty-handed."

"Your faith will save you, brother. Wait a minute."

And running his eyes over the bare, whitewashed walls of the cell, he saw a scorpion that was crawling calmly along the window frame. Fray Gómez tore a page out of an old book, walked over to the window, carefully picked up the insect, wrapped it in the paper, and, turning to his visitor, said, "Take this jewel, good man, and pawn it; but don't forget that you are to return it to me in six months."

The peddler could hardly find words to express his gratitude; he took his leave of Fray Gómez and like a flash was on his way to a pawnbroker's shop.

The jewel was magnificent, worthy of a Moorish queen, to say the least. It was a brooch in the shape of a scorpion. A magnificent emerald set in gold formed the body, and the head was a sparkling diamond, with rubies for eyes.

The pawnbroker, who understood his business, greedily examined the jewel and offered the peddler two thousand duros on it; but the Spaniard insisted that he would accept only five hundred duros for six months, at a Jewish rate of interest, of course. The papers or tickets were made out and signed, and the moneylender comforted himself with the hope that after a time the owner of the jewel would come back for more money, and that with the compound interest that would pile up, he would be unable to redeem it, and he would become the owner of a jewel so valuable in itself and because of its artistic merit.

With this little capital the peddler's affairs went so well that, when the time was up, he was able to redeem the jewel, and wrapping it in the same paper in which he had received it, he returned it to Fray Gómez.

The latter took the scorpion, set it upon the windowsill, blessed it, and said, "Little creature of God, go your way!"

And the scorpion began to crawl happily about the walls of the cell.

11

TOMÁS CARRASQUILLA

A writer even more tradition-bound than Palma was the Colombian Tomás Carrasquilla. Born in the remote province of Antioquia, in 1858, he spent almost all his life writing in deliberate isolation. He refused to participate in the literary life of Bogotá, the capital; he rejected the fashions of the day; he published practically all his books in his native province.

His literary career began by accident. A friend found out that he had written some fiction and asked him to read it in a literary center recently founded at Medellín. Carrasquilla accepted, and at thirty-two entered the life of letters with a reading of "Simon Magus." Forty-five years later he had completed and published three full-length novels, five shorter ones, and five volumes of short stories. The publication of his last volume of stories, in 1936, coincided with the first prize he had ever won. He was already seventy-eight and had only five more years to live.

Carrasquilla always wrote about the small towns of his province and the small people who lived there and the small lives they led. But he completely refused to sentimentalize his subjects. Although a devout Catholic, he knew how to expose the hardness and meanness of the most devoted parishioners. He portrayed the poor with sympathy but without sentimentality. At the time Carrasquilla began to write, romanticism was still very much alive in Colombia. Even the genre he most successfully practiced, the regionalist story, had had its heyday a few decades before. But he never indulged in romantic flights of rhetoric—he was a realist, in the vein of Flaubert and the Russians he admired. "To describe man in his milieu" was his professed aim. He carefully avoided all overstatement or vehemence, never raising his narrative voice. He was concerned always with a minute observation of reality, and he excelled in an almost understated irony. These qualities placed him in opposition to the excesses of romanticism but also to the new school, modernism, that became prevalent in Spanish American letters at the turn of the century. He found it too precious.

Although as a novelist he failed repeatedly to achieve a major work, his short stories are among the best in the genre. The one selected here is a masterpiece. It blends very smoothly a vivid autobiographical evocation of childhood with comic exploitation of folklore. The characters, especially the old black nanny, are beautifully observed. Carrasquilla avoided the traps of nostalgia by an effective use of distance: everything is seen from the vantage point of mature recollection. Not until the appearance of García Márquez (Part Five, 14) would a more skillful narrator emerge on the Colombian literary scene.

Simon Magus

From The Golden Land, *pp. 146–63.*

Among my critical, literal-minded fellow citizens it is accepted as an article of faith that my parents, by their sternness and their firm belief in the maxim "Spare the rod and spoil the child," managed to curb the terrible temper of our family to a degree. Whether this opinion has any foundation or is mere speculation, the fact is that if the authors of my days did not manage to bring up their offspring in the way they should go, it was not for lack of trying. They certainly put their hearts into it.

There is no end to the tales my sisters tell about being shut up all day in that dark pantry closet, where they nearly died of fright. My brothers still wince as they recall the smart of a three-thonged rawhide or my father's riding whip against their bare skin. They tell of my mother that she always carried at her waist, in the manner of a sword, a cat-o'-nine-tails, and not as an ornament. When it was least expected, and without warning, she laid it about her, and let the chips fall where they would. Not to mention those small, excruciatingly painful pinches with which she drove home the point of every reprimand.

Thanks be to God, this parental severity did not extend to me. Only once in my life did I taste the bitterness of the lash. The fact that I was the youngest of the children, and small and puny into the bargain, explains this forbearance.

Everybody in the house adored me; I was the idol and the family treasure, but it was hard for me to reciprocate this general affection when all mine was devoted to Frutos.

When I came of an age to realize that I was a person like anybody else who could love and be loved, there at my side I found Frutos, who, more than all the others, and as her sole occupation, seemed to me to have only one purpose in life: to like what I liked and to do everything I wanted.

Frutos was in charge of the cleanliness and care of my person; and so deft and gentle were her hands that neither the rubbings of the damp cloth, as she washed "that face like a sun," bothered me, nor did I go into a tantrum when she combed my hair, nor did she hurt me when, with a needle and without shedding a drop of blood she dug out of my feet things . . . that I am ashamed to speak of.

Frutos taught me to pray, put me to bed, and watched over me while I slept. In the morning she woke me up with my cup of chocolate. What else did she do? When I came home from school for lunch, there was Frutos waiting for me with my corn cake, my meat, my fried plantain. The best of those delicate dishes in whose preparation Frutos had a hand was for me. These were generally chocolate ground without the addition of even a pinch of flour, fig preserves, sausages.

And the tricks she knew! Dear Lord! She would sprinkle bran around the foot of the orange tree; then she would prop a little trough over the bran with a stick; to this she would tie a long string and, holding the other end, hide behind a clump of cane to wait until the sparrow came down to eat. The poor thing had no more than taken its first peck when Frutos pulled the string, and bang! Under the trough was a bird for me.

Out of a broomstick, a piece of rag, some thread, with a stitch here, a bit of stuffing there, she would make me a horse with fiery white eyes, long mane, reins and all, which made the other boys turn green with envy. Any bit of board, with a few horsehairs or wires, in her hands became a guitar that tinkled faintly, and I strummed away on it all day long.

And the drums out of old tin cans! And the kites with fancy tails!

With a wit and grace I found incomparable, she told me the famous adventures of Pedro Rimales—Urde, they call him now—making me laugh until I was weak. She transported me to the "Land where you go and don't come back," following the mysterious bird of "the seven-colored feather," and en-chanted me with the marvelous feats of "Patojito," which I took to be the gospel truth, as I did the tale of "Sebastian de las Gracias," a romantic folk hero who with equal ease intoned a ballad to the accompaniment of his guitar or dispatched a sinner to the other world with a knife thrust. Half the charm consisted in not having the verses or the music to which they were sung vary in the least from one time to the other, or the effect was spoiled.

In her cracked voice, and solely for my pleasure, Frutos sang me certain native airs—they were called *corozales*, she said—which transported me out of this world, so beautiful and melodious did they seem to me.

My "most-favored-nation" status was respected by everyone in the family. To have attempted anything different with Frutos around would have been like running head-on into a stone wall. To my mother's complaint: "That boy is spoiled to death," Frutos's answer was: "Everyone is picking at the poor lamb." "What he needs is a whipping," growled my father, to which Frutos's reply was: "Not as long as I live," and taking me by the hand, she went off with me. And when this happened, she sulked all day; and everyone kept out of her way.

And when I told her that I had been punished at school! Holy Mother! The things that mouth spewed forth against that Jew, that hangman of a school-teacher; against Mamma, who had no more backbone than a snail, and was foolish, into the bargain, to tolerate such things; against my father, who wasn't man enough to go and give that old devil a couple of good punches. On the occasion of one of these punishments, Frutos got so hot under the collar that she waited at the house door for the teacher to come by, and as soon as she set eyes on him, she ran up to him, and shaking her fist under his nose, shouted at him furiously: "Oh, you devil! What you did to that child! Like Our Redeemer on the road to Calvary! If only he were mine, I would pull out every one of your goat whiskers." The teacher, who outside the classroom was a summer zephyr, took no notice of her; and I played up my sufferings for all they were worth, for on the days when there had been strap or rod, I was repaid with usury. Frutos gave me every tidbit she could lay her hands on, and cosseted me in every way she could think of. I was not "the child," but her "grain of gold," her "little king," and other things in the same vein.

Nobody in the family had as many clothes as I, because Frutos was always bemoaning the fact that "the child" was naked, and she worried my mother and sisters until, whether they wanted to or not, they had to buy or make me new clothes. And not just any kind, but to suit Frutos's taste.

The result of all this was that I wallowed in that love, till I needed nothing in the world but Frutos. Frutos was my life, my all, and the other members of the family, even my parents, meant absolutely nothing to me.

What could Frutos have seen in a snot-nose of eight years to idolize in that fashion? I don't know. All I can say is that Frutos seemed to me an extraordinary being, a kind of guardian angel, something that could not be defined or explained, but superior to anybody else.

And now let's see what Frutos was.

She—her name was Fructuosa Rua—at that time must have been in her sixties. She had been a slave of my maternal grandparents. When slavery was abolished she left the house, to enjoy, no doubt, those fine and entertaining privileges of the free. But either she did not feel sure of herself or she had a bad time of it, for some years later she came back somewhat disillusioned. Though she did say that she had known the world and, according to her, had had a wonderful time.

Finding my mother, whom she had raised, married and the mother of several children, she came to work for us in the care and upbringing of the small fry. For many years she held this post, with certain attributes in the kitchen in the preparation of special dishes. She kept my mother severely in her place, though in her own way she was very fond of all the family and had a great respect for my father, whom she called "my master."

My mother liked her and overlooked her temper and bad humor.

Frutos had had children of her own, but at the time I was in her charge they were not with her, and she did not seem to care much for them and paid little attention to them when they happened by to visit her. As a result of the gout that afflicted her, she had practically retired when I was born, and in taking charge of the Benjamin of the household, she was really assuming a heavier load than she could carry. If it had not been for the way she set her heart on me, she could never have stood all the trouble I gave her.

Frutos was pure Negro by race. I never knew anyone so black, of a soft, shimmering blackness, with lips that stuck out a mile, especially on the days she was in a bad humor, which was most of the time. I don't know if women in those days used, as they do now, that thing that sticks way out behind. I think they must have, and of course Frutos did too; and the size of her was such that her skirt of purple percale, which touched the ground in front and got entangled in her splay toes, was so short in the back that her white petticoats showed through.

A low-necked, ruffled shirt comprised her bodice, and her rough, thick arms were completely bare. She covered her woolly hair with a brilliant bandanna, which she tied in front like an Oriental turban. Only when she went to church did she wrap herself in a shawl that time had turned green. When out for a walk or on any everyday occupation, she used no wrap. But tidy and neat as a new pin, for no one was cleaner about her person than Frutos.

Very black and very ugly, wouldn't you say? Nevertheless, she had the most aristocratic prejudices and was class-conscious to a far greater degree than many whites. She would not let me play with colored children, because she said they would not respect me as they should when I was a man. She would never let me stay in her room, even when she was suffering from gout, "because a white child that stays in colored folks' rooms gets silly and turns into a ninny." She alleged similar reasons for not letting me go to the kitchen, and that was a spot that fascinated me. Only on Christmas Eve was I allowed to stay there as long as I liked, and even to stick my dirty little paw into everything. But this was because on such days the whole family went into the kitchen. My father and my older brothers, with the solemn air of persons of consequence, made their appearance there, to lift out of the boiling kettle with the skimmer a golden doughnut, a cake of crisp, feathery puff paste, or take a turn at stirring the caldron of custard, which as it bubbled and popped made craters the size of thimbles.

The time that I was in school, which was Frutos's hours of leisure, she spent weaving, an art at which she was very deft; but as soon as the scholar appeared on the scene, spindle, cotton, and thread went into a corner. "The child" came ahead of everything else; only "the child" put her in a good humor; only "the child" brought a laugh to those lips that were the normal abode of angry words and growls.

My mother, amazed at this phenomenon, used to say, "The Lord must intend this boy for a saint, to let him perform such miracles as a child."

With a wall like this at my back, I developed such a touchy disposition, such a temper, that nobody could come near me with a four-foot pole. If I did not get my own way, I threw myself on the floor, hitting my head against everything around me; or I let out howls to raise the dead, accompanied by tears and sobs, not to mention breaking anything I could get my hands on and biting.

Aunt Cruz, a very timid and circumspect person, took the liberty of saying one day in front of Frutos when I was having one of my tantrums that "the child" was spoiling for a whipping. It would have been better if she had been struck dumb. Frutos called her everything she could lay her tongue to, and took such a dislike to her that every time she laid eyes on her she snorted with rage.

My father, seeing the turn things were taking, complained and went so far as to mention a thrashing. But Mamma quieted him down, saying, as she clapped her hand to her brow: "Don't touch him! For Heaven's sake, don't touch him! There'll be no living with Frutos."

And as I had a rare facility for grasping everything bad, I realized that I had them in a forked stick and I worked my advantage to the limit. Whenever the storm began to seem really menacing I took to my heels and sought refuge in Frutos's arms. Out to the garden we went, the site of our conversations, and, once there, we might have been in the moon.

As I grew, Frutos's tales and narrations grew to match. Frutos's specialty was the lives and miracles of the saints, the doings of the souls of the departed, and this so entranced me that I could have listened forever. The gift of gab she had! My faith and admiration were boundless; I came to believe that Frutos represented the sum of the wisdom of the universe. Every word that fell from her lips was gospel to me.

In the course of her narrations we finally got around to tales of witchcraft and goblins, and here I reached my seventh heaven. Everything I had heard before, which had so enchanted me, now seemed trumpery. Witches! That was the real thing. Here was something worthwhile to which one could devote oneself body and soul for all one's life!

Until then my ambition had been to be a clown or the chief of police. But from then on I said to myself: "Clown, nothing! I'm going to be a witch."

Everything daring, stupendous, useful seemed to me comprehended in witchcraft. I was feverish with enthusiasm.

By making Frutos tell her stories over and over again, I managed to engrave them in my memory to the last trivial detail.

From the stories we went on to the commentary.

"Catching witches?" she said to me once. "The easiest thing in the world! All you have to do is take a handful of mustard and sprinkle it around the room, and at night when the good-for-nothings come into the room, they start to scrape up the mustard. And while they are bent over doing this, all you have to do is throw Saint Augustine's girdle over them, and there you have them lassoed hand and foot. A priest of Tunja used to catch a lot of them like that, and he tied them to the leg of the table; but his cook was so silly that she gave them soft-boiled eggs, and they sailed away in the shell. The foolish thing! Why, you can't even speak about an eggshell in front of witches, because the next minute they have shrunk to the size of an ant's eye, and off they go."

"Oh-ho. And how can they fit in an eggshell?"

"Heavens," answered Frutos, "that's nothing. They make themselves any size they want to in the eggshell."

"Can't you kill them?" I inquired.

"You can, but it's not so easy. If you give them a good stab they die; but as they are so smart, they give themselves another stab, and that way it's a tie and they're even and they get well again."

"And what happens when you do kill them?"

"Silly boy. They only die of the stab once in a great while. You have to run the knife right through them at the start to kill them. But with our Father Saint Augustine's girdle, their tricks are no good to them."

"Where do you get that?" I interrupted.

"The girdle?" replied my interlocutor, with the air of one speaking of the well-nigh impossible. "That's very hard to get. The bishop sometimes lends it to the real good priests."

"Maybe Mamma could borrow it from him," I exclaimed excitedly.

"Ave Maria, child! What are you going to do with the girdle?"

"What am I going to do? Catch witches and tie them to the trees!"

In spite of the difficulties in the way of getting hold of the girdle, I went to my mother with my plan. She was very much engrossed in a card game she was playing with some of her friends.

"Mamma," I said to her, "I want to talk to you just a minute." And putting my mouth against her ear, I made my request in that high-pitched whisper children use.

The ladies, who were not deaf, let out a peal of laughter.

"Get away, you nuisance," exclaimed my mother. "Where in the world does this child get such crazy notions?"

I slunk away, red with embarrassment and grumbling to myself.

For days I thought of nothing but how I could get hold of the girdle. My "witch mania" had taken such a hold on me that I wanted to talk of nothing else.

"Who has stuffed you full of all this nonsense?" my sister Mariana, the learned member of the family, once asked me. "There's no such thing as witches. That's old Frutos's humbug! And you believe it!"

"You're a liar! You're a liar!" I raged at her. "There are too. Frutos told me so!"

"And if Frutos said it, it must be so—as though Frutos were the Mother of God! You big fool!"

"Freckle-face, freckle-face!" and I rushed at her with every intention of biting her.

She caught me by the shoulders and gave me a good shaking.

"I'm going to tell Papa on you, so he'll give you a good hiding, for that's what you need, you spoiled brat. Nobody can stand you any more."

I rushed off to find Frutos, and choked with sobs, I cried, "What do you think, Frutos! That stupid Mariana told me that there weren't any witches and that you were just telling me stories."

With a horrified expression on her face, she dried my tears, and taking me gently by the hand, led me in silence to a bench beside the kitchen door.

"Look, my child," she began, "there is no doubt that there are witches. What an idea! Certainly there are. But—you mustn't believe in them."

My eyes, dry by this time, must have opened to the size of saucers. I couldn't understand, but Frutos had said it, and it must be so.

We discussed the topic at length, and as I let no opportunity go by to delve deeper into the matter, I asked her, "Tell me, Frutos, are witches people that become witches, or is it God that makes them that way?"

"Don't be foolish. My God makes nobody but Christians. The ones who want to become witches."

"And are there men witches too?"

"Of course there are. Don't you remember? I told you about it. But as they don't have long hair, they can't go way up in the air and have to fly low."

"And how do you learn to be a witch?"

She was quiet for a little while, and then with the air of one who bares his innermost heart, she said to me in a low voice, "People can turn themselves into witches very easily. The way they do it is like this: you rub all your joints real good with oil; you take off everything but your undershirt, and then go up to some high place; when you're way high up, you spread your arms wide, as though you were going to fly, and then you say, but really meaning it: 'I don't believe in God or the Blessed Virgin!' three times, one right after the other, without breathing, and then you take off into the air and fly through space."

"Don't you fall?"

"Of course not. That is if the oil is the right kind, and you say things right."

A shiver ran through me. I must not have known that kneeling was a sign of adoration, for if I had, I would have been at Frutos's feet. She had made me the happiest soul in the world.

That night after I had said my prayers I got into bed and said in a very low voice, "I don't believe in God or the Blessed Virgin! I don't believe in God or the Blessed Virgin! I don't believe in God or the Blessed Virgin!" I had a little trouble getting to sleep after this declaration of atheism.

Early the next morning I was running down the hall with arms spread wide as though flying, and repeating the prescribed formula. Mariana heard me and called out, "Mamma, just come here and see what this good-for-nothing is saying." But my mother did not manage to "see" my words, because before she got there, I was out in the street on my way to school. I couldn't say why, but I was not anxious to have my mother see me doing such things.

When I got home Frutos was not waiting to meet me. I had to go to look for her, and for the first time I found her in a rage with me. Mamma had practically eaten her alive on account of the things she was telling and teaching me, and it was all my fault for being a tattletale, and I had better not come around bothering her any more, asking her to tell me stories, because with a blabber-mouth like me—

At lunch my father scowled at me as he said, "Young man, any more nonsense out of you like this morning, and you'll be sorry!"

I was dumfounded. My father threatening me! Frutos refusing to have anything to do with me! And just when there were so many things I had to ask her! I did not know what to do about the long hair, or what kind of oil to use!

For three days I implored Frutos to tell me just those two little things, and gave her my word of honor that I wouldn't open my mouth. I might have been talking to the wall. Not a word could I get out of her.

And the worst of it was that what had begun as a fancy, a whim, in the face of difficulties and opposition was becoming an obsession, an irresistible desire.

To be a witch! To be able to fly at night over the housetops, over the church-spire, "into the blue"! Was there anything in the world to compare with it? What would they say at home when I said to them, "Anything you want from Bogotá? I'm going there tonight"?

And Mamma would answer: "Bring me some apples." And before you knew it, I would be back with a beautiful branch loaded with them which I had just broken off. Or just to start soaring like a hawk, up, up—

I had to be a witch. There were no two ways about it. I felt smothered down on the ground. I needed air. "I don't care," I thought to myself, "let them scold me. Even if Frutos won't talk, I'll know what to do. Who taught the first person that became a witch? I can always get hold of oil, even if I have to use castor oil. But that long hair, like a woman's—where do I get that?"

I scratched my head.

I, who from the last amen of evening prayers until six in the morning slept like a log, began to lie awake at night. In the nervous excitement of my insomnia I saw marvels that seemed entirely feasible: twice I saw myself gently flying around, higher, higher, and below I saw the towns, the fields like a picture on paper.

Pepe Ríos, the son of a neighbor, was my bosom friend; and I finally decided to take him into my confidence and tell him my plans. At first he did not seem to share my enthusiasm, and he came out with that same nonsense about there being witches, but one must not believe in them, which served to strengthen my conviction, seeing that he was in complete agreement with Frutos. But I painted the plan in such glowing colors that he finally caught my enthusiasm.

Pepe was not one of those who drown in a spoonful of water. His inventive mind found a solution for everything.

"Look," he said to me. "Tomorrow there is going to be a *Salve* at church, and I'm one of the altar boys. I know where the sexton keeps the oil, and when I go in to get dressed I'll steal some. You get a good bottle, and we'll fill it up."

"And what do we do for hair?" I asked. "Because we want to fly good and high. It's no fun just flying above the ground like the goblins."

"That's as easy as pie," answered Pepe. "My sisters and my mother have false hair, and we'll steal it. What difference does it make if it isn't our own hair? Just so it's long and plenty of it, that's enough."

"What a boy!" I thought to myself as I stood there gaping-mouthed. "What a team he and Frutos would make!"

The next day, pretending we were looking for a parrot that had got lost, Pepe and I invaded the bedrooms of the Ríos girls. Poking about here, looking there, we finally came upon a big box with a mirror on it, and in it a trove of hair of every color, some in coils, some in curls, some in braids covered with a net, some straight and smooth, some wavy, and all mixed with snaggle-toothed combs and hairpins. A little bottle of red liquid attracted my eye, and as I was about to lay covetous hands on it, Pepe said, "Don't touch that. It's for Mamma's cheeks. Why, she might even kill us!"

Very little hair was left in the box after we had made our selection.

"Now, listen," he warned, as he handed it over to me, "you hide this carefully in your house. Don't let them smell a rat. If they catch us . . . And don't say one word about what we're going to do. You talk so much."

"That's what you think," I answered him with great solemnity. "Don't you worry about me saying anything."

From that day we were inseparable. To be sure, Frutos was not in the least pleased at this sudden intimacy with "that Caiphas," the name she applied to Pepe.

That night I informed the family that I didn't intend to go to bed until the grownups did, because I was almost ten years old. And I didn't. To pass the time, I fluttered about the candles like a moth, lighting papers or trimming the wick, with which I greatly annoyed Mariana, who was the only one in the family that stood up to me.

"You pest," she grumbled, "not even at night are we to have a little peace. Go on to bed, nuisance!"

But I was so pleasantly employed that I did not even bother to answer her, just sticking my tongue out, or crossing my eyes at her.

"Devil!" shouted Mariana. "If Papa doesn't give you a thrashing—I'm going to get hold of you, and I'll pound you to a jelly!"

I crossed my eyes still more.

Doña Rita, Pepe's mother, and her daughters used to come over to play lotto occasionally in the evening, and Pepe always came along; but after the formation of our alliance, he sacrificed the pleasure of calling the numbers to go off with me. In this way we were free to discuss our plans at length, and the "elevation" was set for the following Sunday night.

Two days to go! What excitement! I even lost my appetite; I even forgot about Frutos, who was having an attack of gout.

"Now, what devilment are they up to?" she would mutter gloomily as we went by her room.

Finally the eagerly awaited Sunday dawned. From noon on, we were out in the back yard getting the hair ready. We had got hold of an old umbrella, and out of the cover, as best we could, we made ourselves wigs, with the help of God, some black sealing wax, and string.

When we had finished the complicated job we tried them on in front of Mariana's mirror, which we had sneaked out of her room. They looked wonderful! How beautifully the long locks snaked down!

We hid everything carefully away and went out in the street to play so nobody would suspect anything. But we were seething inside.

After a day that seemed as though it never would end, evening came and Pepe appeared with his mother. As soon as the lotto game was under way we slipped off to the back yard.

A violent argument broke out between us as to which was the best spot from which to take off in flight. Pepe was in favor of the oven, which was on the back porch; I insisted that the stone fence was the best place, because the oven was not very high, and besides it was under the eaves, and we would have to fly at an angle and could not mount high enough. We finally settled on the pigpen, which seemed to have everything. From there we would fly to the Alto de las Piedras, which overlooked the town to the south, and once there, we would launch ourselves into the blue. We would take off simultaneously.

Although there was a moon, we had taken along a piece of candle, and by its light we began our "witching" toilette in the dining room. We hung our linen suits on a chair, rolled up our shirts, and each provided with a chicken feather, we began our anointing. Dear Heaven, the smell of that oil!

When the bottle was empty and our joints were as sticky as taffy, we adjusted our wigs, securing them with a chin strap of rope.

Tremulous with emotion, we slipped into the back yard, with the air of circus acrobats coming out to greet their public.

At the farthest end of the yard, behind the rustling foliage of the banana grove, where the ground sloped down, was the pigpen, built of stout logs, with a fern-thatched roof. The water drained down that slope to form a black, malarial pool that fertilized the volunteer tomatoes and mullein weeds that had sprung up around it.

The outraged grunts of the pig, protesting at having her privacy invaded at such hours, were frightening, but they did not daunt us. We simply ignored them.

Pushing ahead of Pepe, I did not stop until I had my foot on the top rail. Holding fast to one of the uprights on which the roof rested, like another Girardot with his flag, I paused for a second. My eyes were filled with the immensity of space.

I expended all my pent-up faith in that instant, and almost choking with fear of failing to observe the inviolable rule by an inopportune breath, I repeated, "I don't believe in God or the Blessed Virgin, I don't believe in God or the Blessed Virgin, I don't believe in God or the Blessed Virgin," and took off.

Something strange was happening. I did not seem to be flying upwards as I had planned. I was cold, my head felt funny, and—that was all.

I opened my eyes. Someone was laying me down on a floor. I felt something like blood on my face; I looked at myself: I was almost naked and covered with mud. From the disorder of the furniture, from the lotto cards and numbers scattered about the floor, from the general atmosphere of alarm, I suspected what had happened. A chill as of ice congealed my heart; I closed my eyes not to see myself, not to look upon something dreadful that I was sure was going to happen.

"Toñito! Antoñito! Did you fall? Are you hurt?" Everyone was talking at the same time.

They were feeling me, bringing a candle close to my face.

"It's nothing. He's all right."

"It's nothing. He's just stunned."

"He's opening his eyes. Antonio! Antoñito!"

"Calm yourself, calm yourself, Miss Anita! Nothing has happened!"

The sound of teeth grinding together struck me to the heart. I opened my eyes, and saw my mother stretched out in a chair, her arms rigid, her hands clenched, her face livid and twisted to one side, her eyes rolled up in her head, her nostrils dilated as though she could not breathe. She was trying to scream, but no sound came out of her throat, as she shuddered in the throes of a convulsion. Some of the women were holding her down, sprinkling water on her, rubbing her hands, holding smelling salts under her nose. My sisters were crying.

I jumped up off the floor screaming, "Mamma, mamita!"

"He's all right," they all began to shout, "he's all right. He's not even hurt."

"What happened, for Heaven's sake? How did you get yourself into such a mess?"

"He has hurt his face. Toñito, keep away. Just look at him."

In horror of myself I tried to run away, but they cut me off at the door with a tub of warm water. The cook lifted me into the middle of the steaming bath, and I offered no resistance. She stripped off my filthy shirt, and as I stood there, naked as our first father, she began scrubbing me with the help of some of the ladies.

"But what has this child got into? It won't come off," said one.

"What a stench!" answered another, covering her nose with her handkerchief.

"Give me the soap and let's see if I can get it off."

I was soon a mass of lather. "My dears," observed the soaper, "this is palm oil, and not dirt from the pigsty."

"So it is! So it is!" the others answered in chorus.

"But where on earth did it come from?"

I was lifted out of the tub onto the floor, and wrapped in a bath towel. Mariana, herself again, brought a nightshirt, and was about to put it on me when a crowd of people burst into the room. My father was one of them.

"Is he dead?" he asked in a voice I had never heard before.

Without waiting for an answer, he went out. Hardly a second had elapsed till he was back with a strap.

"Don't whip him," came a chorus of feminine voices.

"Poor lamb," said the soaper. "It's not his fault."

"Papa, it's not fair. Look, he's hurt," lamented the members of the family.

Papa paid no attention to any of them. Taking me by the arm with one hand, he raised the doubled strap in the other and said in an unsteady voice, "I have put up with your nonsense for a long time, but this is one too many. Take that, you good-for-nothing, and see if it teaches you a lesson." The strap cracked across my bare skin.

A cry like the howl of an animal filled the room: it was Frutos.

"Master, master!" she sobbed, trying to pull the strap out of his hand and putting herself between him and me. "Master, in the name of God, don't whip him, for the sake of our Redeemer who died on the Cross!" and she knelt before him, clasping his knees, almost making him fall. "It's not his fault, it's not his fault!"

My father pushed her aside, but Frutos got to her feet, and, standing in front of me, she wrapped her skirts about me.

"You old witch!" shouted my father, pulling off her bandanna and grabbing her by the hair. "Get away from here or I'll kill you." With one hand he pushed her aside, while with the other he pulled me out of the protecting wrapper.

"Take her away from me before I kill her," he shouted in fury.

Raising the strap again and counting one—two—up to twelve, he brought it down on my bare body, which jerked from side to side like a dummy.

Frutos straightened up and then like a lifeless bundle fell back on the floor uttering strange noises.

Not one cry did I let out—I, who used to raise the roof off the house if a fly settled on me.

Frutos lay writhing on the floor; suddenly she raised herself up and then fell back again, flinging herself about in shameless disorder, pushing aside people, and knocking against the furniture. Some of the people tried to take hold of her, but she drove them back with blows, kicks, and bites. Finally she managed to bring out with a voice that was dreadful to hear, "Let me out of this damned house right away."

All the men grabbed her, and after a struggle punctuated by groans and blows, they managed to get her out in the hall. In the confusion I caught a glimpse of her, and in spite of my love for her, she struck me as a diabolical being. Her hair was standing out around her head, her eyes were staring and bloodshot, and foam was coming from her mouth.

The doctor came in and examined me. He said I had no broken or dislocated bones, not even a sprain. He looked at the scratch on my cheek, took out an instrument, and without hurting me extracted a splinter from the scratch. He gave me something to drink that had brandy in it; took a cup, held a lighted paper in it, and applied the cup to different places on my back, raising up the flesh in painful tension. Feminine hands, wet with camphorated brandy, rubbed me all over, and finally they tied bits of rag dipped in a yellowish liquid on me at various spots.

While they were in the midst of these operations, there came the sound of hurrying steps accompanied by the rustle of starched skirts. Doña Rita appeared in the door with one of the wigs in her hand.

"I can't tell you how sorry I am," she exclaimed, all out of breath and her face working. "I have just made de Ríos give Pepe such a thrashing. Look what those devils were doing"—here she held up the wig for all to see—"they were being witches. That is where they got the idea of flying. What do you think of that? And this is the hair we had for the wig of Jesus!"

Everybody gathered around to examine it and exclaim over it. The doctor took it in his hands and laughed until the tears ran down his cheeks.

"Ave Maria, doctor!" went on Doña Rita. "Don't you see? It was a miracle, nothing but a miracle, that these fiends didn't break their necks. Did you ever hear the like, doctor? Jumping off that high pigpen! And a fall like that! Fortunately he fell in the mud, and that bush broke the fall. Otherwise he would have been dead when they picked him up. We were in here having such a nice game of lotto; I had just filled three rows, doctor, when—we heard mine call out, 'Hurry, hurry, Antonio has killed himself.' Doctor, I thought I was going to drop dead right where I was. They all ran out with candles, and in a few minutes they carried him in with nothing on but his undershirt, covered with pig filth up to his eyes, and gushing blood. Just as though he had been killed, exactly. Mine was saved, because as he is so lazy, he wouldn't jump first. But, would you believe it, doctor, the scamps had covered themselves all over with palm oil that they had stolen from the sexton. They say you have to use it to be a witch. But, believe me, he got a first-class hiding. I tell you I think these children today learn from the Old Nick himself."

"It's not Old Nick," interrupted my father, coming in from the adjoining room. "It's that devil of a Frutos whom Anita has put up with all these years that put that stuff in their heads. And don't think this boy has gotten off so easy. He may die of the effects. He's had a bad fall."

"The danger is remote, and there are no alarming symptoms about the case," the doctor answered. "I haven't even had to give him any special treatment."

"I hope you're right," said my father. "It's all that damned Frutos's fault. From the minute they called me and told me he'd fallen off the top of the pigpen, I knew just what had happened. Well, he's had a lesson he won't forget."

He went on to tell about my attempts to fly through the hall, and my blasphemous incantations.

When the mystery was cleared up, everybody broke into comments and questions.

Their talk brought me out of my somnambulistic state. I felt myself the unhappiest person in the world. "What do I care if I die," I said to myself, "now that Frutos had fooled me with lies, and is so bad, and a person can't fly? And now Mamma is dead"—for I firmly believed she had died—"and Papa has whipped me in front of all these people—and they all saw me with my clothes off—and Pepe has gone and told everything—"

I felt as though all the springs of my soul had been broken, and I was left without faith, without illusions. I closed my eyes tight, the quicker to die and rest, but it was no good. Terrible visions kept going through my head, and sigh after sigh escaped my breast.

Very late that night, after everyone had left, I finally went to sleep. It would have been better to stay awake. I saw Frutos flying about, laughing at me, making faces at me. I heard the bells tolling sadly, so sadly, and I caught the smell of cypress and burning wax, and saw my mother in a black coffin—so black. Then

I was in a swamp, buried up to my neck, and I tried to get out, I tried to scream, but I couldn't.

Finally with one supreme effort I managed to free myself. I gave a scream and woke up, trembling from head to foot, my hair standing on end, and drenched in cold sweat. There was a light in the room, and my mother had me by the hands and was shaking me.

"Toñito—Toñito," she called. "Don't be afraid, darling. It's just a bad dream."

"Is Mamma alive," I thought to myself, "or am I still dreaming?"

She picked me up as though I were a baby, and, hugging me to her breast, she kissed me on the forehead, and her tears wet my face.

"See what you did, my child, to make Papa punish you! And what if you had killed yourself? What would I have done?" And the tears kept rolling down her cheeks.

"Mamita dear! You're not dead, are you?"

"No, my lamb. Don't you see that I am here with you? I just fainted with fright. But I'm all right now. Take another sip of this medicine the doctor left. It's good!"

She was alive! I sat up to take the glass, and saw my father sitting at the foot of the bed. He was crying too. He put his hand on my forehead, felt my pulse, and then said in a very sad voice, "He's got a high fever. Awfully high."

And he went to call the doctor, who was sleeping in the next room. They gave me some drops in sugar water.

I calmed down, and cried and cried, but they were tears of happiness.

I was in bed for six days, listening to the comments of Doña Rita and other callers, some funny, some lugubrious, on my adventure. I learned from them that Frutos had left the house and had sent for her belongings. Days before, this would have driven me out of my mind, but now it had no effect on me.

Don Calixto Muñetón, the luminary of our town, who always spoke on Independence Day and when the bishop paid us a visit, who read a great deal, and who had composed a novena for the Holy Child, was among those who came to call. Without its being the twentieth of July, he unleashed his eloquence on the subject of my fall. He held forth on human frailties, excoriating the sin of ambition. And when he was ready to leave, with his bamboo cane in his left hand, and holding up his right like a signpost, he turned to me with a pitying glance and summed up his remarks in these words:

"And so, my young friend, remember: anyone who tries to fly too high generally lands in the pigpen!"

12

JOSÉ DE ALENCAR

Before Alencar, many writers had attempted to create a truly Brazilian novel, but he was the first to succeed, paving the way for a long line of distinguished successors. The vast scope of his production made him the founding father of Brazilian fiction.

Alencar was born in Ceará in 1829 and, like Acevedo Díaz (see selection 8), had strong political ambitions. His father had been a senator and leader of the independence movement. Alencar studied law in São Paulo, where he graduated in 1850. He entered politics with two learned pamphlets against the Emperor, Pedro II. Dom Pedro, as he was called, modeled himself on the eighteenth-century enlightened despots. He was a man of letters, a distinguished amateur in the arts and sciences. But he was also a prince, and never took any attack lightly. In 1868 Alencar became Minister of Justice, but his political career was cut short in 1870 by the Emperor's decision to exclude him from the senate despite the large number of votes he had.

Alencar's devotion to his political career does not seem to have impeded his literary fecundity. His published work comes to two volumes of poems, nine plays, and, most importantly, fourteen full-length novels. At the time he began writing, romanticism was still an influential force in Brazilian letters. In some of his earlier narratives, he paid homage to Chateaubriand and his idyllic view of the Indians as "noble savages." He also favored the then very popular historical romances in the vein of Scott and Cooper, and on several occasions tried his hand at the regionalist novel. One of his most interesting efforts, *The Gaucho*, 1870, was published immediately after the political crisis that cut short his career.

In the last years of his life, he wrote some of his best urban novels. It was a genre he had practiced from the very beginning of his career. It required a more realistic eye, a sharper style, but Alencar rose to the occasion. In his lifetime the Brazilian reader preferred novels like *The Guaraní* (1857), later turned into a very popular opera by Carlos Gomes, or *Iracema* (1865), both sentimentalized and romantic portrayals of the Indians. Today, however, Alencar's urban novels have undergone a critical reappraisal. The best is *Senhora* (Madame), originally published in 1875. It presents a very grim view of marriage in the bourgeois society of the Second Empire. The protagonist, Aurélia, is a beautiful, wealthy young woman. Madly in love with a man she takes to be unworthy and greedy, she chooses an unexpected revenge: to marry him but to keep total control of her bed and purse. A duel between husband and wife ensues, elegantly controlled but savage.

In the chapter here presented, Aurélia is discussing with her tutor, a venal man, the stiff terms under which she will buy herself a husband. In this novel—reminiscent of some of George Sand's and Balzac's—Alencar concentrated the experience of a lifetime as a politician and observer of the mores of the Second Empire. He died of tuberculosis only two years after the publication of this masterpiece. Already his most brilliant successor, Machado de Assis (selection 14), was at work.

A Marriage of Convenience

From Senhora, *especially translated by Jack E. Tomlins.*

Anyone seeing Aurélia at that moment could not have failed to note the new expression that animated her face and was immediately communicated to the very attitude of her body.

It was a cold, deliberate, and inflexible expression that lent a certain opaque quality to her beauty, with the concomitant frigidity one usually associates with statues. But in the flash of her large brown eyes the light of a keen intellect gleamed. Some rebellion was at work in her. The focal point of woman's vital essence, the heart, had been dislocated and had taken up new residence in the brain, the customary location of man's speculative faculties.

On those occasions her mind acquired such lucidity that it struck a chill in Lemos's faint heart, giving the lie to the massive back with which nature had provided the plump old fellow's torso.

To be absolutely truthful, the perspicacity with which the eighteen-year-old girl answered the knottiest of questions had always astonished strangers and alarmed her tutor. She revealed a thorough knowledge of business affairs and absolute facility in reckoning up sums, often from memory, no matter how difficult or intricate the operation might be.

Nonetheless, there was in Aurélia not the slightest trace of that ridiculous pedantry so often observed in certain young ladies who have garnered a few vague snippets of information from their superficial reading and thereafter take to prattling about any subject whatever that might enter their empty heads.

Quite the contrary, she stored away her experiences and drew on their account at a later date when her own interests required it of her. Beyond that, no one ever heard her utter a syllable about business affairs or offer an opinion regarding anything that might not have been proper for a young unmarried girl.

Lemos was out of sorts; he had lost that bounding joviality which always lent him a jesting air of popcorn popping. In the unaccustomed gravity of that interview, he who was a wise and experienced man glimpsed serious complications.

He was, therefore, all ears, absorbed in the girl's words.

"I took the liberty of disturbing you, uncle, in order to speak with you regarding a matter of extreme importance for me."

"Oh, 'extreme importance,' indeed," the old man repeated, tapping his head.

"My marriage!" Aurélia said with the greatest of *sang-froid* and serenity.

The old man sprang from his chair like a rubber balloon. To conceal his agitation he rapidly rubbed his hands together, a gesture by which he indicated his extreme mental anguish.

"Do you not think that I have reached the proper age to entertain such thoughts?" the girl asked.

"Of course! Eighteen . . ."

"Nineteen."

"Nineteen! I had not realized you had celebrated your nineteenth birthday. Many girls marry at that age, some even younger; but those are cases when the girl has a father or a mother to make a good match for her and ward off certain adventurers. A girl who is an orphan and inexperienced, I would not advise her to marry until she had reached her majority and knew more of the world and its ways."

"I know more than enough now," the girl countered in the same serious tone.

"Then you have made up your mind?"

"So much so that I have requested this conference with you."

"I know. You wish me to suggest someone. You wish me to arrange a fiancé for you, properly set up. That is difficult, not an easy matter to find a personage well enough situated to seek the hand of a young lady like you, Aurélia. But I assure you I shall make every effort!"

"You need not bother, uncle. I have already found such a person!"

Lemos suffered another alarm, which caused him to leap anew from his chair.

"What? You have someone in your sights?"

"Forgive me, uncle, I do not understand your figurative language. I am telling you quite simply that I have chosen the man whom I shall marry."

"I understand. But mark you well, as your tutor I shall have to give my approval."

"Of course, dear tutor; but you will surely not be so cruel as to withhold your approval. If you do, as I hope you will not, the orphans' magistrate will grant his approval in your stead."

"The magistrate, indeed? Who has put such nonsense into your head, Aurélia?"

"Senhor Lemos," the girl said unhurriedly as she pierced the perplexed gaze of the old man with a frigid glance, "I am now nineteen years of age. I can petition for an age supplement showing that I possess the capacity to direct my person and my property. With right on my side I shall obtain from the magistrate, in spite of your objection, a judicial permit to marry whom I please. And if these judicial arguments do not satisfy you, I shall present you one that is closer to me."

"We shall see," the old man answered to break the silence.

"It is my will. You do not know the strength of my will, but I swear to you that, in order to carry out my own wishes in this matter, I shall not hesitate for one moment to sacrifice the inheritance of my grandfather."

"The ways of youth! One entertains such notions only when one is nineteen."

"You forget that of those nineteen years I lived eighteen in extreme penury and but one of them in the lap of luxury in which I was all too suddenly set down. I have learned two great lessons from the world: poverty and opulence. Formerly I knew money as a tyrant; today I know it as a submissive captive. As a consequence I must be older than you, who have neither been as poor as I was nor as rich as I now am."

Lemos stared in shock at the young lady who spoke to him, with such knowledge of the world, of a strange philosophy totally unknown to him.

"It would not be worth the while to have so much money," Aurélia continued, "if it did not allow me to marry at my pleasure, even if I have to squander a few wretched contos to have whom I will."

"There's the rub," interjected Lemos who for some time had been preparing an objection. "You well know, Aurélia, that, as your tutor, I cannot spend one red cent without the magistrate's authorization."

"You refuse to understand me, dear tutor," the girl answered with a slight trace of impatience in her voice. "I know that and I know many other things which no one suspects. For example: I know the dividend on the shares, the interest rate, the market quotations, and I am well aware that I can compound interest with quite the same degree of exactitude one finds in the real-estate listings."

Lemos's head was swimming.

"And in the last instance I know that I have a record of all my grandfather's possessions, written by his own hand and given to me by none other than himself alone."

At this point the old gentleman, who was of a normally florid complexion, went pale, the terrifying symptom of the total fullness of his flesh, of such massive girth that it gave his emigrant's trousers and black cutaway the appearance of being padded like a quilt.

"This means that should I have a tutor who displeased me and fell into my disfavor, on the occasion of my majority I should not release him from my service without first making a thorough examination of the accounts of his handling, for which purpose I fortunately do not stand in need either of lawyers or accountants."

"Yes, my lady, you are indeed within your rights to take such steps," the old man added with contrition.

"As, however, I have the good fortune to possess a tutor who is also my friend and follows my bidding, as you indeed do, uncle . . ."

"That is most assuredly so!"

"In that case, instead of trying my patience and troubling myself with legal documents and accounts, I hereby consider the matter felicitously closed. And in addition, I am aware that you have tutored me totally without recompense, and that is not done so properly when orphans have more than they require with which to repay the annoyance they cause."

"Come now, Aurélia. This charge is a sacred duty that I honor in the memory of your mother, my good and ever-lamented sister . . ."

Lemos dabbed at the corner of his eye to catch a tear that he had successfully shed, if indeed he had not invented the entire gesture, which seems the more probable. And the young lady, in tribute to the memory of her mother which the old man had called forth, rose to her feet for an instant on the pretext of glancing through the window. When she returned to her place, Lemos had regained his composure after the shock he had been forced to suffer, and he returned to his normal attitude: lively, excitable, and jovial.

"Then we are in agreement?" the girl asked with the prudent dignity she had maintained throughout this entire conversation.

"You are a little sorceress, Aurélia; you do with me as you will."

"Consider well, dear uncle. I am going to entrust my secret to you, a secret that has never been confided to anyone in this world. It is known to God alone. If, after you have heard it, you do not wish to continue in my service, then I shall never forgive you."

"You may entrust your secret to me, Aurélia, and rest at peace. I shall prove myself worthy of your confidence."

"I believe you, Senhor Lemos. To relieve you of any scruples that may vex you, I swear to you on the memory of my mother that if there is to be any happiness for me in this world, it is this happiness that you alone can give me."

"Put yourself totally in my hands."

Aurélia paused for a second.

"Are you acquainted with Amaral?"

"Which Amaral?" the old man asked, somewhat timidly.

"Manuel Tavares do Amaral, in the employ of the customhouse," the girl answered, consulting her notebook. "Please take note. He is not a man of great wealth, but he does have some funds at his disposal. He arranged the marriage of his daughter Adelaide to a young man at the time absent from Rio de Janeiro, and he offered him a dowry of thirty contos."

As she said these words, the girl's voice, which was usually so clear, assumed a fleeting tremor and soon thereafter it became positively raspy.

Lemos, customarily florid, went perfectly purple. To disguise his vexation he shook his head, considerably disquieted, and his finger tugged at his collar as if it were stifling him.

Aurélia rested her frigid gaze for an instant on the old man. Then, looking serenely away, she stared at the page of her open notebook, thus giving her uncle time to compose himself. He did so with dispatch. Lemos was experienced in the ways of the world.

"Thirty contos?" he observed. "That is not a bad beginning!"

Aurélia continued, "As soon as possible we must break off this marriage engagement. Adelaide must marry Dr. Torquato Ribeiro, whom she loves. He is penniless, and that is why her father has rejected him. However, if you should assure Amaral that the young man can count on fifty contos of his own, do you think Amaral would refuse?"

"And supposing I did make such an assurance. Whence would come such a sum?"

"I shall give it him with the greatest pleasure."

"But, my dear child, why are we to introduce ourselves into the private affairs of others?"

"You are sufficiently perspicacious to perceive that which I should try in vain to conceal from you. I find it preferable to confide in you without any reservations." The girl spoke with exertion. "That young man who is engaged to Adelaide Amaral is the man whom I have chosen for my husband. Obviously he cannot belong to two women at once. I must, therefore, seek to win him for myself."

"You may trust me in this!" the old gentleman retorted, wringing his hands as if he could foresee the benefits that such a love held out for a tutor with his expertise.

"That young man . . ."

"His name?" the old man asked as he dipped the quill of his pen into the inkwell. Aurélia indicated with a nod that he should be patient.

"That young man arrived only yesterday. Naturally he is busy with the preparations for a marriage that has been arranged now for nearly a year. You must seek him out as soon as possible . . ."

"This very day."

"And make your proposal to him. These arrangements are quite common in Rio de Janeiro."

"They occur every day."

"You know better than I how to dispatch these commissions between the parties of an engagement."

"Come, come!"

"I must charge you, however, never to allow my name to slip into this affair."

"Ah, you wish to remain incognito."

"Until the very moment when we are introduced. However, feel free to say whatever you must so that it will not be presumed that I must be either ancient or crippled."

"I understand," the old man exclaimed with a laugh. "A marriage of the heart!"

"No, my good man. Please do not exaggerate. You have permission to say no more than this: the prospective bride is neither old nor ugly."

"Do you want to prepare the surprise?"

"Perhaps. The terms of the proposal . . ."

"With your kind permission! Since you desire to remain incognito, should not I be the one to make the contact?"

Aurélia reflected for a moment.

"I do not wish this affair to go beyond you. Should he recognize you as my uncle and tutor, could you perhaps not convince him that I am totally free of all responsibility in this matter, that it is a family affair or an arrangement made by my relatives?"

"Excellent idea! I shall see to it. Do not fret."

"The terms of the proposal should be as follows, mark you well: the family of the said mysterious young lady wishes to marry her with separation of property, granting to the groom the sum of one hundred contos as dowry. If this sum is not sufficient and *he* demands more, the dowry shall rise to two hundred contos . . ."

"One hundred will suffice, rest assured."

"At any rate I wish you to understand perfectly the nature of my thoughts on this subject. Obviously, I wish to attain my purpose, and as inexpensively as possible. But the importance lies in the attainment. I shall give up to one half of all I possess and raise no question. I am determined to purchase my happiness."

These last words were spoken by the girl with an expression that defied description.

"Will it not be very expensive?"

. "Oh, no matter," Aurélia exclaimed. "I would give all my fortune for it. Others have their happiness free of charge, directly from heaven, so to speak. However, I cannot complain, for if that benefice was denied me, God did indeed deem to take pity on me and send me—when I least expected it—a sizable inheritance that I might fulfill my life's aspiration. Are they far from the mark who say money brings all good fortune?"

"The greatest good fortune that money brings, child, is the possession of it. All the others are secondary," Lemos said with the conviction of one who knew well what he spoke.

Aurélia had been briefly carried away by her sentiments, but she soon returned to the cold, intentional tone with which until that moment she had discussed the matter of her future.

"I still must recommend one small point to you, dear uncle. Words may be forgotten as well as twisted. Would it not be possible to make all arrangements in writing?"

"Have the fellow sign a contract? Of course. But if he reneges, there is no legal way to force him into matrimony."

"No matter. I prefer to entrust myself to his sense of honor, rather than to the courts. I shall be quite pleased if he merely gives his word."

"That shall be arranged."

"That is all I hope from your friendship, dear uncle."

Lemos allowed the irony which accented the word *friendship* to pass, and he stretched out perpendicularly the sheet of paper on which he had jotted his notes.

"Let us see! . . . Tavares do Amaral, employee of the customhouse . . . the daughter Dona Adelaide . . . thirty contos . . . Dr. Torquato Ribeiro . . . guarantee fifty . . . the other one . . . from one hundred to two hundred. I lack only the name."

Aurélia tore the calling card from the notebook and presented it to her tutor. As he was preparing to repeat the name aloud, she cut him short with the crisp word of command which sometimes twisted her lips.

"Write!"

The old gentleman copied the information from the card and returned it to the girl.

"Nothing else?"

"Nothing, except to repeat to you once again that I have placed in your hands the sole happiness which God has reserved for me in this world."

The girl spoke these last words with such profound conviction that it touched the old fellow's good-natured skepticism.

"You shall be happy indeed, I promise you."

"Give me this happiness that I so long for; I shall give to you all the joy that I have left over."

"You may depend on me, Aurélia."

The old man clasped the girl's hand. She had touched his heart with this last promise. Then he left.

When he reached his house, Lemos's head was still reeling from the shock he had undergone.

13

MANUEL ANTÔNIO DE ALMEIDA

To find a Spanish American equivalent of Almeida's only novel, *Memoirs of a Militia Sergeant,* it is necessary to look back to Fernández de Lizardi's *Itching Parrot* (Part Two, 2). Both books belong to the tradition of the picaresque novel, so popular in Europe some two centuries earlier. But Almeida's narrative set a less frenetic pace than was customary for the genre, and incorporated as well a vein of near-Dickensian nostalgia.

Almeida was born in Rio in 1831 of Portuguese parents. He was too poor to get a regular education, so, being a gifted draftsman, he began his studies at the School of Fine Arts; later he switched to the medical school. Although he did graduate as a doctor, he could never afford to have a clinic of his own, and he finally settled for journalism. In 1858, Almeida became the Administrator of the National Printing House, and in that capacity had the opportunity to help his younger colleague Machado de Assis (selection 14). His last attempt to embark on a profitable career of his own, and his life, was abruptly cut short when he drowned in a shipwreck in 1861, just as he was beginning his first political campaign.

 Memoirs, the novel that made him famous, was published serially and anonymously in a newspaper in 1853; it was successful enough to justify publication in book form in 1854–55 and even a pirate provincial edition (Pelotas, 1862). It was based on the recollections of an older friend, a Portuguese journalist, Antônio César Ramos, and thus had a partial foundation in fact; but Almeida felt free to embroider and enlarge, using some of the classics of the Spanish picaresque novel as models. What he achieved was a vivid presentation of Rio during the last years of Portuguese rule: "the King's times," as he indicated at the beginning of his narrative. In contrast to Alencar and Machado de Assis, who in their urban novels concerned themselves mainly with the upper and middle classes, Almeida was almost exclusively interested in the lower classes.

 In the chapter here presented, Leonardo, the protagonist, has barely escaped from one danger when he faces another. This time he will brave the wrath of his commanding officer, Major Vidigal (a character taken from real life), to protect Teotônio, a notorious scoundrel, but a good friend of his family. The narrative follows the realistic conventions of the picaresque with a few well-placed touches of local color and some grotesqueries. All this is hardly new. What makes the book unique is (as noted above) its subtle tone of nostalgia. He was not writing about the Rio where he had been born and which he knew so well but about an earlier and rougher, a freer city. The Second Empire added to that city a façade of respectability that obviously bored Almeida. In the *Memoirs* he managed to recapture a time and place irretrievably lost, and one, moreover, that he had never really known himself.

Fresh Mischief

From Memoirs of a Militia Sergeant, *especially translated by Barbara Shelby.*

 To the astonishment of all and particularly of himself, Leonardo was let off lightly and his escapade was allowed to go unpunished. Whether it was because this was the first time he had fallen from grace, having until then performed all his duties with the utmost punctiliousness, or whether the very audacity of the deed had predisposed Major Vidigal to treat him with indulgence, the fact remains that except for the laughter and teasing of his fellow soldiers, and the anguished half hour he had spent swaddled in the shroud, he was called upon to endure nothing further. This was seen as an amazing proof of unwonted benevolence on the part of the major. Leonardo went about abashed and pensive for several days as if crushed by the weight of his remorse; and his comrades made the most of this occasion to make merry at his expense and saw to it that he never had a minute's peace.

"He still has one foot in the grave," one of them would remark, going up and peering at him closely.

"One foot nothing," another would retort. "He's already on the other side."

"Papai lêlê, saeculorum," intoned the others in chorus.

To none of these gibes did Leonardo pay the slightest heed, and in this he showed good sense; for he thus deprived his pitiless companions-in-arms of fresh fuel for mockery. Once the novelty of the thing had worn off it was soon forgotten, and barracks life flowed back into its accustomed well-worn channel.

One day the major announced that he had a very important mission to carry out. For some time he had had his eye on a certain convivial rascal, the perfect type of ne'er-do-well of the age, but so far the sly fellow had contrived to escape his clutches. The scoundrel's real occupation was a puzzle and a mystery to many; nevertheless, he always seemed to have a few coins to jingle in his pocket, though all he possessed of any real value was a voluminous cape in which he went constantly wrapped, and a guitar that he never laid aside. He enjoyed the reputation of being a very amusing fellow, and no entertainment was complete without his presence. All his time was spent in fulfilling his social obligations. He customarily greeted the dawn on a spree that had begun the evening before, a birthday party, for instance; on leaving that, he would go to a christening dinner, and in the evening would attend a wedding feast. He owed his reputation as a wag, which enabled him to pass his days so pleasantly, to certain social talents, in one of which in particular he had no peer. He played the guitar and sang ballads in a mellow voice, he danced the *fado* to perfection, he could talk like a darky and sing like one, too; could pretend to be crippled in any part of his body with consummate naturalness; could imitate perfectly the speech of country bumpkins and their offspring; he knew thousands of conundrums, and finally—and this was his rarest talent—he could twist his face into the most incredible grimaces ever seen on a human countenance. Consequently he was always in demand among the lively circles in whose society he moved. The host who wished to ensure a large and congenial gathering at his home had only to spread the word that Teotônio (that was the fellow's name) would be among the guests.

As to Teotônio's occupation or means of livelihood, which, as we have said, was an impenetrable mystery to many, by dint of long and patient investigation the major at last discovered what it was: on certain days of the week a group of men met stealthily in the attic where Teotônio lived and remained there until late at night. In a word, the attic was a gambling den and Teotônio was the banker.

Now all the major had to do was catch him in the act. He attempted to do so for a long time without success, for his vigilance was always cheated by the gamblers' continually changing the day of the week on which they met. He was nonetheless determined to lay hands on Teotônio by hook or by crook, and through him to capture the others.

As the reader will recall, Leonardo the elder—that is, Leonardo-Pataca —was then living with the *comadre*'s daughter, by whom he had had a baby daughter whose birth we have already described. Now, in spite of the fact that a considerable time had passed, the baby was not yet baptized. At the urging of the *comadre*, who was very uneasy in her mind at the delay, Leonardo-Pataca finally set a day for the infant to be made a Christian. The family gave a christening party in accordance with immutable custom; and, also in accordance with custom, Teotônio was invited. The major had got wind of the affair and had made up his mind to catch Teotônio there and pounce on him. Thus the announcement made to his guardsmen to which we have already referred.

It was the major's misfortune to be an eternal wet blanket; and it is the misfortune of the writer of these lines to repeat the same scenes monotonously with but slight variations. His only excuse is that fidelity to the age whose customs he is attempting to sketch obliges him to do so.

The major arrived at Leonardo-Pataca's house at the appointed time. As there was not the slightest reason to expect violence, for the most perfect harmony prevailed, he went in alone, having obtained the previous consent of Leonardo-Pataca (the host) to watch the festivities. As luck would have it, when the major appeared Teotônio was holding forth. Having already exhausted his gamut of skills he was preparing to offer the *pièce de résistance:* his cleverness at making faces. Here it should be noted that Teotônio's art was not limited to mere grimacing at random; he could imitate the expressions of people known to his audience, and it was this talent above all that convulsed his audiences with laughter.

The guests were seated in an expectant circle around Teotônio, who stood in the middle of the room. Turning to one of them he displayed the countenance of an old man, then whirled around to face another, suddenly changing his expression to that of an idiot and accompanying the gesture with a burst of doltish laughter. He kept up the performance for some time, showing a different face to each person in the room. Finally, his inventiveness exhausted, he ran into a corner where he could be seen by all the guests at once, and showed them the last funny face of the evening. The onlookers burst into a concerted roar of laughter and pointed to Major Vidigal. Teotônio had reproduced the long, lean countenance of the major to the life.

The major bit his lip at the jest. If he had had interesting plans for Teotônio before, he conceived even better ones then.

The laughter was slow in dying down, and the major, unable either to face it with equanimity or take violent action—since, as we have explained, he had no plausible motive for doing so—thought it most prudent to take his leave, find a strategic spot in which to lie in wait for the party to break up, and then invite Teotônio to make faces at the grenadiers in the guardhouse. In some confusion, then, he beat a retreat.

Going up to his grenadiers, who had remained a short distance away, he addressed Leonardo and told him he was bound and determined to lay hands on Teotônio that very evening, come what might; that he had reason to suppose that the other guests suspected as much and might find some means of aiding Teotônio to escape; that he therefore needed some person to keep an eye on Teotônio: namely, Leonardo.

"But I'm not welcome in my father's house," that young man objected.

"Today's a good day for a reconciliation."

"But they may not let me in."

"Your godmother's there, isn't she?"

"Yes, but so is her daughter, and that woman can't stand the sight of me. She's a regular viper, sir."

"Viper or not, off you go. That's an order! I won't have that scoundrel making me a laughingstock by taking my face for a model."

The grenadiers, who were acquainted with the gifted Teotônio, guessed from the major's words what had happened and burst out laughing in their turn. Leonardo, heeding the major's appeal to obedience and discipline, with which he had been on pretty uneasy terms since the night of Papai Lêlê, mastered his initial repugnance at the thought of carrying out the mission with which the major had entrusted him and set off for his father's house.

He went up to the door and knocked. No sooner did those inside see his military cap and the color of his uniform than they set up a cry of fright and blew out all the candles at once as though by prearrangement (the major had been right!). Such confusion prevailed that one would have thought a brawl had suddenly broken out.

This was not a very promising start, but Leonardo could not help being amused at the fright he had caused. He spoke up from outside the door to calm the fears of the company.

"This is a fine welcome for a son in his own father's house! You'd think it was Ash Wednesday—all that's missing are the wooden rattles."

The *comadre,* recognizing her godson's voice, burst out laughing and exclaimed, "Why, it's Leonardo! There now, look how he's fooled us all! Light the candles, friends, and don't be afraid; the corporal of the guard is a good friend of ours."

"The nincompoop," grumbled old Leonardo, "still up to his old tricks. Look what a scare he's given all our friends. Come on down, Teotônio; it was only a false alarm."

By the glimmer of the first candle to be lighted, Teotônio could be seen clambering down through a trap door in the ceiling of the room, which led to an attic where he had taken refuge. When his feet touched the ground he made an expressive grimace of terror that provoked another explosion of laughter. Guests began to emerge from every corner of the house, and as Leonardo looked on the merrymaking began anew.

Some few of the guests had lingering suspicions at Leonardo's uniformed presence on such an occasion, so soon after the major's departure; but the *comadre* laid their suspicions to rest by assuring them that Leonardo was not on duty at the barracks that day and had asked for leave to celebrate his little sister's baptism with the rest of the family.

"He's a harebrained lad, it's true," she told all the guests in turn, "but he's a good son and never forgets his family."

Leonardo did all he could to bear out his godmother's avowals of his innocence and gradually entered into the festivities. Contrary to his expectation, he had met with a cordial welcome. As he warmed to the pleasure of the *fado* and the singing, remorse began to steal over him at the Judas role he was playing at the feast. Every time he looked at Teotônio, who had made him laugh so heartily from the moment he had entered the house, his heart smote him at the thought that he, Leonardo, must betray Teotônio to the major. More than once he was on the verge of offering to help the fellow escape; but thoughts of duty and Papai Lêlê held him back, and he could not make up his mind to do so.

As he hesitated, a prey to conflicting thoughts, he cast repeated glances in Teotônio's direction. The latter, who was no fool, suspected something; instinct warned him of Leonardo's thoughts, and he put himself on guard.

All at once Leonardo made up his mind.

"Discipline be hanged!" he said to himself. "I'll get the man away somehow, see if I don't!"

He called out from where he was sitting, "Oh, Mr. Teotônio, I have news for you! If you so much as put one foot outside that door, the major'll grab you. He's lying in wait for you this very minute; that's why he sent me in here."

"The devil you say!" the guests exclaimed in chorus.

"Don't you worry, now; I'll get him out of here some way or other if it's the last thing I do."

"Now, don't you play the fool, boy," his godmother warned him in a whisper. "The major's got no use for that kind of trick, and you'll be in trouble if you don't watch out."

"Aw, I feel sorry for Teotônio. All he did was make faces."

And so Leonardo and Teotônio put their heads together and devised a plan by which the latter might escape the major without compromising the former. The hour was advanced when the two conspirators arranged matters so that a large number of guests trooped out in a body, preceded by Leonardo, who went running to the major.

"Major, major, here he comes, sir!"

"Close in, men!" the major ordered, and each man went to his post. The major stationed himself in a nearby doorway and kept his eyes open.

A figure approached, calmly whistling the refrain of a popular ballad. When the man was a short distance away the major sprang at him and held him fast. A feeble cry of protest was heard, "Let me go! What do you want with me?"

Major Vidigal took a closer look. The voice was not Teotônio's and the major saw that he had laid violent hands on a poor hunchback who was crippled in the right leg and the left arm to boot.

"Oh, go to blazes!" said the major. "What the deuce is a freak like you doing out on the street at this time of night? Be off with you, I say!"

The cripple lost no time in obeying. Quickly shaking off his fright he went limping off, whistling his refrain. Deep silence fell, and Major Vidigal saw no other passers-by except a party of stragglers from the christening. Teotônio was not among them. The major's temper flared up again. Calling the grenadiers to him he said reproachfully to Leonardo, "He didn't come out."

"Why, yes he did, sir," Leonardo replied. "I can even tell you just what he was wearing: a white jacket and a straw hat. Why, Major, I saw him make a beeline straight for the door where you were standing."

"You say he was wearing a white jacket and a straw hat?"

"Yes, sir, and black pantaloons. I didn't grab him because I could see he wasn't going to escape you, sir."

"Ah, the cheating scoundrel," growled the major, "I've never been so taken in in my life. So it was that confounded crippled hunchback!"

"He knows how to play the cripple or the hunchback, I can vouch for that," a grenadier spoke up. "I saw him do it once, and you couldn't tell him from a real one."

The reader will have guessed that Teotônio was indeed the cripple the major had laid violent hands on.

Leonardo laughed in his sleeve at the clever trick he had played on the major. It was not long, alas, before the young man's glee turned sour, when the major discovered his part in that night's charade.

14

JOAQUIM MARÍA MACHADO DE ASSIS

Five major novels, several collections of outstanding short stories: such is the corpus of Machado de Assis' fiction, one unrivaled in Latin American letters.

Machado, as he is usually called in Brazil, was born in Rio de Janeiro in 1839, the son of a Brazilian mulatto and a Portuguese woman from the Azores. The family was poor and Machado attended only primary school. He was always an avid reader and educated himself by spending his free time at the Library of the Portuguese Cabinet of Reading. Very early in his life he began a bureaucratic career that brought him the security and status he needed for writing. From the modest position of apprentice typographer at the National Printing House, where he was a protégé of Manuel Antônio de Almeida, he rose to become in 1897 the first president of the Brazilian Academy of Letters (a position he kept until his death) and, in 1902, General Director of Accounts in the Department of Public Roads.

Although he was in origin a mulatto and lived in a society based on slavery, he conformed to the "rules of the game" and wrote as if that society were color-blind. He never wrote like a black writer, a categorization that he probably would have rejected; in his fiction he was as white as his protagonists and readers. He even married a Portuguese lady, a few years his senior, and led a quiet, almost boring, life with her.

A master of realistic and accurately detailed portrayal, Machado nevertheless so subtly distorted the image that this proud Brazilian society had of itself that it has taken the best part of a century to discover the sharpness of his critical eye. In presenting the follies and foibles of his contemporaries, he was not only a faithful portraitist; like Goya in his capacity as court painter, he was also a judge.

He began his literary career at sixteen by writing poems in the romantic fashion; at twenty-five he published a first volume of verse, *Crisálidas* (Chrysalises). He was to continue to write poems, more or less successfully, and even tried his hand at drama, but he soon realized that he had more talent for narrative. When he was already forty-two, and after several novels, he published his first important one, *Memorias póstumas de Brás Cubas* (*Epitaph for a Small Winner*, 1881). In the next twenty years he would complete a kind of trilogy by adding *Quincas Borba* (badly translated as *Philosopher or Dog?*, 1891) and *Dom Casmurro* (1900) to the canon. Before his death in 1908 he completed two extremely subtle novels, *Esau and Jacob* (1904) and *Memorial of Aires* (1908).

In a sense, his narrative work can be seen as a continuation of Alencar's cycle of urban novels. But at a time when Alencar was still struggling very hard to free himself of romantic attitudes and methods—using George Sand and Balzac as models for a more realistic presentation of Second Empire society—Machado, quickly and with apparent ease, left romanticism, and Alencar, behind in his achievement of the incredible maturity of *Brás Cubas*. Whereas his master presented the clash and conflict of strongly delineated characters, in concretely detailed settings and in a series of well-staged confrontations, Machado developed the art of ambiguity and understatement. Even the urban landscape of Rio he knew so well was reduced to a few spare touches. Instead of the social criticism that in Alencar bordered at times on satire, he chose irony. His characters are always tormented by their own demons; they are caught in a web of their fears and dreams; their vision of reality is entirely subjective.

In the way Machado handled the realistic novel he proved to be a true contemporary of Henry James, although they apparently never heard of each other. But they did have some common models. Machado was deeply indebted, for example, to such English writers as Laurence Sterne. In his major works, the story is never presented directly to the reader, but always through a first-person narration by the protagonist. Being generally the main actor as well as the teller of the story, the narrator becomes an unreliable witness. He is also so much taken by an urge to discuss his own version of the facts that the novels became exercises in a new type of fiction: the one that talks about itself. Thus, the text itself ultimately emerges as the protagonist.

The best example of this technique (which anticipated by several decades similar experiments of Borges) is perhaps *Dom Casmurro*. The protagonist has been given this nickname (his real name is Bento) because he is morose and tight-lipped. He is writing a memoir of his life. As an adolescent, Bentinho falls in love with a beautiful girl, Capitú. Although his mother wants him to become a priest, with the help of Capitú he eventually escapes that fate and becomes a lawyer, marries Capitú, and fathers a son, Ezekiel. Many years later, Bento will discover (or believe he has discovered) Capitú's infidelity with a close friend of his school days, Escobar. He is even convinced that Ezekiel is not his own son. Escobar dies in an accident, and to avenge himself on the adulterous wife and the bastard son, Bento will separate them forever.

Dom Casmurro can be read as a variation on the Othello theme. To underline the similarity, Bento is even made to attend a performance of the play. But his own story represents a witty variant on the theme: here the protagonist is his own Iago. As Machado was in real life very jealous, critics have tended to read *Dom Casmurro* as a kind of confession. From a purely biographical point of view, this may be true (although Machado had no children) and his personal experience may well have proved of value in the writing of this novel. The novel, however, is *not* about Capitú's real or imaginary infidelity, as some critics have maintained, but rather about her husband's version of it. The book is really about the writing of a book. The fact that Dom Casmurro is the only source we have for the story removes the question of truth or fact to the realm of mere hypothesis. Everything becomes fiction. Besides, Dom Casmurro is more obsessed with discussing his own presentation of the facts than in setting the record straight. The gap in years between the protagonist as a young man (Bentinho) and the narrator as an old man (Dom Casmurro) not only creates a conflict of ages and points of view, but also focuses the reader's attention on the narration as such, on the telling of the story rather than the story. The book turns over on itself: the writing becomes a mirror for the act of writing.

In the excerpt here presented, almost half of a very short chapter is devoted to the discussion of the order in which the narrative ought to have been told; the next chapter is even entitled "Anterior to the Anterior." It is a typical example of the very involved and ironical way of writing that constitutes Machado's mature style. Not until the present century would Latin American narrative offer anything similar.

Dom Casmurro

From Dom Casmurro, *translated by Helen Caudwell (New York: The Noonday Press, 1953), pp. 250–64.*

One Day

One day Capitú wanted to know what made me so silent and gloomy. She suggested Europe, Minas, Petropolis, a series of balls, a thousand of those remedies prescribed for the melancholy. I did not know how to answer her; I declined the diversions. Since she insisted, I replied that business had been going badly. Capitú smiled to cheer me. And what if it had? It would improve, and until then her jewels, objects of any value, would be sold, and we could go and live in some alley. We would live quietly, forgetting and forgotten; later we would rise to the surface again. The tenderness with which she said this would have moved a stone. But *I* was not moved. I answered drily that there was no need to sell anything. I remained silent and gloomy. She proposed a game of cards or checkers, a walk, a visit to Matacavallos; and, as I would have none of them, she went into the living room, opened the piano, and began to play. I availed myself of her absence to take my hat and leave.

. . . Pardon me, but this chapter ought to have been preceded by another, in which I would have told an incident that occurred a few weeks before, two months after Sancha had gone away. I will write it. I could place it ahead of this one before sending the book to the printer, but it is too great a nuisance to have to change the page numbers. Let it go right here; after that the narration will proceed as it should right to the end. Besides, it is short.

Anterior to the Anterior

The truth was that my life was once again sweet and placid. The law paid me well enough. Capitú was more beautiful. Ezekiel was growing up. We were entering the year 1872.

"Have you noticed that Ezekiel has an odd expression about the eyes?" asked Capitú. "I've seen only two other people with the same expression, a friend of Papa's and poor Escobar. Look, Ezekiel, look straight, there, look at Papa— you needn't roll your eyes, there, there. . . ."

It was after dinner. We were still at table. Capitú was playfully teasing her son, or he her, or each the other, for they were truly very fond of each other —but actually, he was even fonder of me. I drew closer to Ezekiel; I found that Capitú was right. They were Escobar's eyes, but they did not seem odd to me for that reason. After all there are probably not more than a half-dozen expressions in the world, and many resemblances occur naturally. Ezekiel did not understand, he looked in startled amazement from her to me, and finally jumped up and threw his arms around my neck:

"Let's go for a walk, Papa?"

"Presently, my son."

Capitú, unmindful of either of us, was staring at the other side of the table. But when I told her that for beauty, Ezekiel's eyes resembled his mother's, Capitú smiled and shook her head with an air I have never found in another woman, probably because I never loved the others half as much. People are worth the value that our affection sets on them, and it is from this that we get the adage, "Ugly is fair to a lover." Capitú had half a dozen gestures that were unique on this earth. This one went straight to my heart—which explains why I ran to my wife and darling, and covered her face with kisses. But the second incident is not fundamentally necessary to the comprehension of the last chapter nor of those to follow. Let us stay with Ezekiel's eyes.

The Sketch and the Color

Not only his eyes, but the remaining features also, face, body, the entire person, were acquiring definition with the passage of time. They were like a rough sketch that the artist elaborates little by little. The figure begins to look out at you, smile, throb with life, almost speak; at length the family hangs the picture on the wall in memory of what was and can be no longer. In this case, it could be and was. Habit helped conceal the change; nevertheless, the change occurred. It happened not in the manner of the theater, but like the day, which appears slowly, so slowly that at first a letter can scarcely be read, and then, behold, the letter may be read in the street, in the house, in the study, without opening the windows; the light filtering through the Venetian blinds is sufficient for distinguishing the words. I read the letter, uncertainly at first, though not all of it; later I was able to make it out more surely. True, I refused to read it, shoved the paper into my pocket, ran home, shut myself in, refused to open the blinds, even closed my eyes. When I opened my eyes again, letter and writing were clear—the message crystal clear.

Escobar emerged from the grave, from the seminary, from Flamengo; he sat at table with me, welcomed me on the stairs, kissed me each morning in my study or asked for the customary blessing at night. All this repelled me; I endured it so as not to be revealed to myself and to the world. But what I could conceal from the world I could not conceal from myself—I was closer to myself than anyone. When neither mother nor son was with me, my desperation was extreme, and I would vow to kill them both, suddenly or slowly—slowly, so as to transfer into their dying all the moments of my dulled, agonized life. When I returned home and saw waiting at the head of the stairs the little child so devoted to me, I would be disarmed and would defer the punishment from day to day.

I shall not record here what passed between Capitú and me during those dark days; such a record would be too repetitious. Now, so long after the events, I would be unable to recall them without omissions or weariness. But I shall relate the most significant thing. The most significant thing was that the storms had now become continuous and terrible. Before discovering that evil land of Truth, we had had other storms, but of short duration—before long the sky would be blue, the sun bright, and the sea smooth, and we would again unfurl our sails, and they would carry us to the fairest islands and coasts of the universe before another squall blew down everything, and we lay to, waiting for another calm; it would not be slow in coming, nor would it be doubtful, but rather complete, near at hand, and sure.

Forgive these metaphors; they savor of the sea and of the tide which brought death to my friend, my wife's lover, Escobar. They savor also of Capitú's eyes, eyes like the tide when the undertow is strong. And so, though I have always been a landsman, I tell this part of my life as an old sailor recalls his shipwreck.

The only thing lacking between us now was the final word. We read it, however, in each other's eyes, vibrant and decisive. Whenever Ezekiel approached, he only drove us apart. Capitú suggested placing him in a boarding school, from which he would only come home weekends. It was difficult for the little boy to accept this situation.

"I'll go with Papa! Papa must go with me!" he shouted.

And it was I who took him, one Monday morning. The school was in old Lapa Square, not far from our house. I went on foot, taking him by the hand; my same hands had taken away the other's coffin. The little boy accompanied me, crying and asking questions at every step . . . Would he return home? . . . When? . . . Would I come to see him? . . .

"I will."

"You won't come, Papa."

"Yes, I will."

"Swear it, Papa!"

"Of course."

"Papa, you didn't swear to it."

"I swear it."

I brought him there and left him. The temporary absence did not eliminate the evil, and all Capitú's artful attempts to attenuate it were to no purpose: I grew steadily worse. The new situation itself aggravated my torture. Ezekiel was no longer constantly present; but his return on weekends—either because I was no longer accustomed to him or because time was completing the resemblance—was the return of Escobar, only more alive and noisier. After a while, even the voice seemed the same. On Saturdays I avoided dining at home and would not return until he was asleep; but there was no escaping him on Sundays as I sat over newspapers and legal work in my study. Ezekiel would enter, boisterous, expansive, smiling and full of love, for the little devil kept growing fonder of me. I, on the contrary, now felt an aversion, an aversion I could scarcely conceal from Capitú and the others. Since I could not completely hide my state of mind, I kept out of his way as much as possible. Either I would have work which obliged me to lock my study door, or on Sundays go out and I would promenade my secret misery through the city and its environs.

An Idea

One day—it was a Friday—I could endure no more. A certain idea, which took black form within me, opened its wings and began to flap from side to side, as ideas do when they wish to be free. That it was Friday, I believe, was chance, but it could also have been design. I was brought up in terror of that day. I had heard ballads sung at home, ballads from the plantation and the old country in which Friday was a day of foreboding. Still, as there are no almanacs in the brain, it is probable that the idea would not have beat its wings except for its need to get out and breathe the air of life. Life is so beautiful that even the idea of death must be born before it can be realized. You must already understand. Now read another chapter.

Witches' Sabbath

The idea finally freed itself from my brain. It was night, and I could not sleep, however much I tried to shake it from me. Yet no night ever passed so swiftly. It began to grow light. And I had thought it no more than one or two o'clock. I went out, intending to leave the idea at home; it accompanied me. Outside, it had the same dark color, the same tremulous wings, and though it flew, it was as if fixed, and I carried it on my retina—not that it hid external objects from me, but through it they were paler than usual, and fleeting. Nothing remained.

I do not much remember the rest of the day. I know I wrote some letters, bought a substance, which I shall not name in order that I may not awaken the desire to try it. The pharmacy has failed, it is true; the owner became a banker —his bank prospers. When I found myself with death in my pocket I felt as if I had just drawn the grand prize—no, greater joy; for a lottery prize fades away, but death does not. I went to my mother's house to say farewell, but under pretext of paying a visit. Whether it was really so or an illusion, everything there seemed better that day: my mother less sad, Uncle Cosme unmindful of his heart, Cousin Justina of her tongue. I passed an hour in peace. I even considered relinquishing my project. What would I need in order to live? Never leave that house again, or engrave that hour within myself. . . .

Othello

I dined out; went to the theater in the evening. They happened to be playing *Othello*, which I had never seen or read. I was familiar only with its theme, and rejoiced at the coincidence. I watched the Moor rage because of a handkerchief—a simple handkerchief!—and here I furnish material to be considered by psychologists of this and other continents, since I could not escape the observation that a handkerchief was enough to kindle the jealousy of Othello and fashion the most sublime tragedy of this world. Handkerchiefs have passed out of use; today one must have nothing less than sheets, at times it is not sheets but only shirts that matter. These were the vague and muddled ideas that passed through my mind as the Moor rolled convulsively and Iago distilled his calumny. During the intervals between the acts I did not leave my seat. I did not wish to risk meeting someone I knew. Most of the ladies remained in the boxes, while the men went out to smoke. Then I asked myself if one of these women might not have loved someone who now lay quiet in the cemetery; and there came to me other incoherencies, until the curtain rose and the play went on. The last act showed me that not I, but Capitú ought to die. I heard the prayers of Desdemona, her pure and loving words, the fury of the Moor, and the death he meted out to her amid the frantic applause of the audience.

"And she was innocent!" I kept saying to myself all the way down the street. "What would the audience do if she were really guilty, as guilty as Capitú? And what death would the Moor mete out to her then? A bolster would not suffice; there would be need of blood and fire, a vast, intense fire to consume her wholly, and reduce her to dust, and the dust tossed to the wind, in eternal extinction. . . ."

I roamed through the streets the rest of the night. I had supper, it is true, a trifle, but enough to live on till morning. I saw the last hours of night and the first hours of day. I saw the late strollers and the first sweepers, the first carts, the first noises, the first white streaks of day, a day that came after the other and would see me depart never to return. The streets I roamed seemed to flee from me of themselves. I would never again contemplate the sea beyond Gloria, nor the Serra dos Orgãos, nor the fortress of Santa Cruz, and the rest. There were not so many people on the street as on weekdays but there were quite a number off to tasks they would do again; but I would never do anything again.

I reached home, opened the door very slowly, climbed the stairs on tiptoe, and let myself into my study. It was almost six. I took the poison out of my pocket, sat in my shirt sleeves and wrote one more letter, the last, directed to Capitú. None of the others were for her. I felt the necessity of writing some word which would leave her remorseful for my death. I wrote two versions. I burned the first, thinking it too long and diffuse. The second contained only what was necessary, clear and brief. It did not remind her of our past, nor of the struggles we had had, nor of any joy: it spoke only of Escobar and of the necessity of dying.

The Cup of Coffee

My plan was to wait for my morning coffee, dissolve the drug in it, and gulp it down. Meanwhile, I had not wholly forgotten my Roman history, I remembered that Cato, before he killed himself, read and reread a book of Plato. . . . I did not have Plato by me; but an odd volume of Plutarch which related the life of the celebrated Roman would suffice to occupy the little remaining time. To imitate him in all points, I stretched out on the settee. Nor was it only for the purpose of imitating him; I had to arouse in myself the same courage, just as he had required the thoughts of the philosopher to die intrepidly. One of the evils of ignorance is being without this remedy at the final hour. There are many people who kill themselves without it, and expire nobly; but I believe more people would put a term to their days if they could find this sort of moral cocaine in good books. Nevertheless, as I wished to avoid all suspicion of imitation, I remember distinctly that in order that the book of Plutarch might not be found beside me and mentioned in the newspapers, along with the color of the trousers I was wearing at the time, I planned to put it back in its place before drinking the poison.

The butler brought the coffee. I rose, put away the book, and went to the table where the cup of coffee stood. They were already stirring in the house; it was time to make an end of myself. My hand trembled as I opened the paper wrapping of the drug. Even so I was courageous enough to empty the substance into the cup and begin to stir the coffee, my eyes wandering, my thoughts on the innocent Desdemona. The play of the evening before was obtruding itself upon the reality of the morning. But the photograph of Escobar gave me the courage I lacked: there he was, with his hand on the back of the chair, gazing into the distance. . . .

"Let us make an end of this," I thought.

As I was about to drink, I reflected whether it would not be better to wait for Capitú and the boy to leave for Mass; I would drink it then, that would be better. This settled, I began to pace the study. I heard Ezekiel's voice in the hall, I watched him come in and run to me, shouting, "Papa! Papa!"

Reader, at this point there was a gesture that I will not describe because I have completely forgotten it, but, believe me, it was beautiful and tragic. Practically speaking, the appearance of the little boy made me retreat until I knocked against the bookcase. Ezekiel threw his arms around my knees, perched on tiptoe as if he wanted to climb up and give me the usual kiss, and kept repeating as he pulled at me, "Papa! Papa!"

Second Impulse

If I had not looked at Ezekiel, it is probable that I would not be here writing this book, because my first impulse was to run to the coffee and drink it. I went so far as to lift the cup, but the little boy was kissing my hand, as he always did, and the sight of him, as well as the gesture, gave me another impulse which it is painful for me to record; but, oh well, let everything be told. Let them call me assassin if they like; I am not the one to gainsay them or contradict them. My second impulse was criminal. I bent down and asked Ezekiel if he had already had coffee.

"Yes, Papa; I am going to Mass with Mamma."

"Have another cup, just a half cup."

"And you, Papa?"

"I'll ring for more. Go on, drink it!"

Ezekiel opened his mouth. I brought the cup to his lips, with such trembling that I almost spilt it, but ready to pour it down his throat in case the taste or the temperature was repugnant to him—for the coffee was cold. . . . But I felt something, I do not know what, that made me draw back. I set the cup on the table, and found myself wildly kissing the child's head.

"Papa! Papa!" exclaimed Ezekiel.

"No, no, I am not your father!"

Enter Capitú

When I raised my head, I was looking straight at Capitú. Here is another stroke which smacks of the theater, and yet it is as natural as the first one, seeing that the mother and son were going to Mass, and Capitú never left the house without speaking to me. By now it was a brief, cold word; and usually I did not even look at her. She always looked, and waited hopefully.

This time, as I faced her, I do not know whether my eyes deceived me, but Capitú appeared livid. There followed one of those silences which can, without exaggeration, be called an age. Such is the extension of time in great crises. Capitú regained her composure, told her son to go outside, and asked me for an explanation. . . .

"There is nothing to explain," I said.

"There is everything to explain. I don't understand your tears, nor Ezekiel's. What took place between you?"

"Didn't you hear what I said to him?"

Capitú answered that she had heard weeping and the murmur of voices. I believe that she heard everything clearly, but to admit it would mean losing the hope of silence and of reconciliation. Therefore, she denied hearing and admitted only seeing. Without relating the episode of the coffee, I repeated to her the words at the end of the last chapter.

"What?" she asked, as if she had not correctly heard.

"That he is not my son."

Capitú's stupefaction, and the succeeding indignation, were both so natural they would confuse the finest eyewitnesses of our courts. I have heard that there are such available for all kinds of cases—question of price. I do not believe it, particularly since the person who told me this had just lost a suit. But, whether or not there are witnesses for hire, mine was genuine. Nature herself took the stand in her own behalf, and I would not care to doubt her. Thus, without marking Capitú's words, her gestures, the pain that racked her, or anything, I repeated the words I had twice spoken, with such resoluteness that she wilted. After several moments she said to me:

"This unjust abuse can only be explained by sincere conviction; and yet you, who were so jealous of the least gesture, never showed the slightest shadow of distrust. What has given you this idea? Tell me," she continued, when I made no reply, "tell everything. After what I have heard, I can hear the rest—it can't be much. What has now given you such conviction? Come, Bentinho, speak! Send me away, but first tell me everything."

"There are certain things one does not say."

"Which one does not leave half said; but now that you have said half, say all."

She sat in a chair near the table. She may have been a trifle confused; her bearing was not that of an accused person. I begged her once more not to insist.

"No, Bentinho, either tell the rest, so that I may defend myself—if you think that there is any defense possible for me, or I beg you for an immediate separation; I can endure no more!"

"The separation is a foregone conclusion," I retorted, seizing upon her words. "It would have been better to part with half words or in silence; each would leave with his own hurt. Seeing, however, that you insist, senhora, here is what I can say, and it is everything."

I did not say everything. I could scarcely allude to the affair with Escobar without mentioning his name. Capitú could not help laughing, a laugh which unfortunately I cannot transcribe. Then in a tone half ironic, half melancholy:

"And even dead men! Not even the dead escape your jealousy!"

She fastened her little cape and stood up. She sighed, I believe she sighed, while I, who would have liked nothing better than her complete justification, uttered some words or other to this purpose. Capitú looked at me disdainfully, and murmured:

"I know the reason for this: it is the chance resemblance. . . . The will of God must explain everything. . . . You laugh? It is natural; in spite of the seminary, you do not believe in God; I believe . . . But let's not speak of this. It is best to say no more."

The Photograph

Truthfully, I was on the brink of believing myself victim of a grand illusion, a phantasmagory of hallucination; but the sudden entrance of Ezekiel shouting, "Mamma! Mamma! It's time for Mass!" restored me to a sense of reality. Capitú and I, involuntarily, glanced at the photograph of Escobar, and then at each other. This time her confusion was pure confession. They were one; there must have been some photograph of Escobar as a little boy which would be our little Ezekiel. With her lips, however, she confessed to nothing; she repeated her last words, pulled away her son, and they went off to Mass.

15

RAUL POMPÉIA

Pompéia, like Manuel Antônio de Almeida (see selection 13), is known today exclusively as the author of one book, although he wrote several. He was born in a small town close to Rio de Janeiro in 1863 and followed in Alencar's footsteps, studying law in São Paulo. After graduation, he returned to Rio not to practice law but to become a successful political journalist. He also held several official positions, the most important being that of Director of the National Library. A very high-strung person, Pompéia began his literary life by writing poems, short stories, and even novels, but he succeeded in attracting attention only with *The Atheneum*, published in 1888.

It was the time when realism and naturalism were being replaced by decadentism. A certain Wildean preoccupation with style and with the expression of refined sensations—the impact of the Goncourts' theories about art for art's sake—was at the back of the mind of every young writer of the period. In a sense, Pompéia became the most impressive representative of this movement in Brazilian letters.

His novel is the chronicle of two years in the life of Sergio, the protagonist, a student at a boarding school called O Atenéu, presided over by the autocratic professor Aristarco. The names chosen for the school and its master —the Atheneum was a temple for the goddess of learning; Aristarchus was an Alexandrian critic famous for his scholarship and severity—allude ironically to the classical aspirations of Brazilian culture. They also give away the satirical undertone of the book. In it, Pompéia was only barely disguising his own recollections of life at the Colegio Abilio, owned by Professor Abilio César Borges. Like his fictional counterpart, Professor Abilio was apparently a hypocrite who covered with a veneer of classical learning the cruel emptiness of his teaching. In the novel, the college is presented as a somber place. Sergio is the object of homosexual advances by Sanches, one of his eldest colleagues, but instead of yielding, he rejects him, nauseated.

If one compares this book with its strict Argentine counterpart, Miguel Cané's delightful *Juvenilia* (1884), the darkness of Pompéia's vision comes out very strongly. While the Argentine's work is a poetic evocation of long-lost youth, *The Atheneum* is a chronicle of a descent into Hell. All the author's frustrated rage against his father, the person solely responsible for putting him in the Colegio Abilio, is transferred in the novel to the master and some of the students. In a brilliant and anguished reconstruction, Pompéia managed thus to evoke and pass judgment on the most traumatic experience of his life.

The book was so much in advance of its time that to find a Spanish American equivalent one must look ahead to the 1960s. Only then did the Peruvian Mario Vargas Llosa, in *The Time of the Hero* (1963) (Part Five, 17), and the Cuban Lezama Lima, in his *Paradiso* (1966) (Part Four, 15), dare to deal with the perversities of similar initiations. But one must remember that Pompéia was only twenty-five when he wrote *The Atheneum* in the Victorian society of Brazil's Second Empire. Seven years later, unable to cope any longer with his emotional problems, he committed suicide.

The Initiation

From O Atenéu, *especially translated by Jack E. Tomlins.*

If as a child I had been goaded by a single spark of shining prudence to such an extent that while others were vigorously attacking their ball games I had applied myself to the gentler task of inventing autobiographical documents and the concomitantly opportune confection of one more *enfance célèbre,* of a certainty I should not have thought to include among the incidents of my charmed childhood the banal affair of the swimming pool, an affair which moreover held dire consequences for me and served as the source of the bitterest vexations I had known till then.

By "swimming pool" we denominated our bathing tank, constructed on a plot of land that housed the Atheneum's outbuildings. Otherwise it was a great sheet of water at ground level, thirty meters long by five wide, fed by large faucets and draining into the Comprido River. The tile bottom, which was not visible, sloped gently from one end to the other. The difference in depth was made the more evident by two steps conveniently placed so that the smaller children might touch the bottom as did the older boys. At one spot the water was deep enough to cover a man's head.

During the intense heat of February and March and year's end we were allotted two baths a day. Every bath was a delight in that oily water, brackish from the perspiration of the preceding class, since the restricted dimensions of the tank did not allow for proper renewal of the water supply. It was a turbulent froth of naked bodies, tightly cinched into their bright-striped knit trunks. The boys slithered together like eels, some diving under the water while others bobbed up again, their eyes bloodshot and their hair streaming down their faces. Others sported welts on their skin from the unintentional scratches of their playmates' fingernails, and the air was filled with cries of delight, fright, and terror. The smaller boys bunched together at the shallow end and held hands out of fear when one of their rougher companions approached.

Some among the older lads indeed posed a frightening prospect as they plowed the water with vigorous overarm strokes and broke the force of the waves with the sheer might of their shoulders. There were others who dived headlong into the bath, wriggling their feet in the air as though they were the tail of a fish, paying no heed to the luckless fellow on whom they happened to land. Bubbling and gushing about the bodies of the swimmers, great billows crashed over the edge of the pool, thoroughly flooding the periphery.

Along the tank ran the fence beyond which stood the principal's private cottage. In the distance one could discern the windows in a part of the house where students would be lodged from time to time when they were taken ill. Its green louvers were always closed.

Every afternoon the Canary Islander, Angela, came to observe the daily bath. She would climb onto the wall and sit half concealed by a bamboo thicket and ivy branches. She would throw small stones at the boys, and they in turn blew kisses to her and dived under the surface to retrieve the pebbles. Angela, nervously wringing her hands, would lean backward and laugh crazily, revealing a red blossom burgeoning through white teeth.

I was terrified by the bustling confusion of my first bath in that tank. I sought out the corner where the younger boys were huddled together. Our exercises were determined by the division of the bathers into three classes according to age. However, owing to an oversight in the inspection, the three classes mingled together; and the supervisor, cane on the ready for stragglers, had withdrawn a bit and was observing the scene from one side, so that the weaker lads were exposed to the abuses of their burlier companions whose misdeeds were hidden by the spraying water. I had scarcely entered the tank when I felt two hands clutch at my ankles and knees from the bottom. Wrenched violently I lost my balance and tumbled backward. The water stifled my cries and engulfed my eyes. I felt myself being carried away. Desperately gasping for breath, I knew I was going to die. I did not know how to swim and could only believe that I had been abandoned at the moment of utmost peril. My arms were flaying aimlessly as I grew faint beneath the water. Then suddenly someone came to my rescue. One of the larger chaps lifted me by one shoulder and deposited me over the edge, where I lay vomiting water. It took some time before I realized what had happened. I rubbed my eyes at last and realized that it was Sanches who had saved me. "You were about to drown," he said, supporting my head as I wiped my streaming hair from my eyes. Still half stupefied with fright I told him at length what they had done to me. "Monsters," my friend observed with pity in his voice, and he blamed the brutality on some pest who had fled in the flurry of the swimmers. His solicitude was boundless as he sought to allay my fears. Later I had good reason to believe that the monster and pest had been none other than Sanches himself, intending as he did to turn a profit on his good deed.

Nonetheless, the immediate consequence of the ordeal was that I hid the revulsion which Sanches inspired in me and feigned the deepest gratitude to him and pretended that we were the closest of friends. Strange and checkered was to be that adventure of mine in friendship and confidence.

In the Atheneum we did everything two by two: in pairs we performed our gymnastic exercises, attended chapel, went to the dining hall and to class, responded to the noonday Angelus bell, received our dry bread after choral practice. Out of respect for the regimentation of military organization, the three hundred students were subdivided into groups of thirty under the immediate command of a decurion or tutor.

As Aristarco had it, the tutors were selected from the aristocracy. A tutor was Malheiro, the daredevil on the trapeze; likewise Ribas, the most talented vocalist in the glee club; a tutor was Mata, a wizened little hunchback with a broken spine, nicknamed the "peddler," honey-tongued in his dealings with others, never punished, no one knew why exactly, considered to be a superior student because it never occurred to anyone to verify how Rebêlo recorded the marks as the chief of the principal's secret police; a tutor was Saulo, who had chalked up three distinctions in the public school; a tutor was Rômulo, dubbed "master cook," a great outsized beast, always the last in gymnasium owing to his flaccid corpulence, low man in his classes, excused from glee club because of his high-pitched cracking voice, but performing the complex and delicate duties of the bass-drum player in the band purely because of the prominent breadth of his incapacity. I do not know whether it was this particular talent for the drum, augury in musical form, or the famous inheritance which Rômulo expected to receive from well-to-do relatives: the truth is that Rômulo was chosen from the lot by Aristarco for the enviable privilege of becoming his future son-in-law.

Several tutors numbered among these, selected according to a criterion that allowed the fellow chosen for his skill at the horizontal bar to come off rather sadly at his marks; vice versa, another like Ribas, at the top of his class, was thin and drained and could just barely execute the simplified acrobatics of the vertical fall. Sanches was also a tutor.

These subordinates of the school militia became martinets delegated by the supreme dictator. Armed with wooden swords with leather handles, they assumed the responsibilities of their command with all seriousness and generally operated with lovable savagery. The swords summarily punished all infractions of discipline in the ranks: remarks merely whispered in close file, too slow a gait in the march, a noticeable deviation in the line formation. Utterly Siberian discipline, clearly, from which derived the high regard of the underling for the tutor.

In the particular case of our fortuitous friendship, the considerable importance of the tutor Sanches within the school hierarchy could not fail to influence my life. However, other circumstances determined my new condition, a fact which became evident after the incident of the bath.

It was now proper time for me to be considered an initiate into the intimate familiarity of the school. Put to the test by Mânlio, I made myself liked and gained for myself a certain aura which favored me for some time. I had a run-in with Barbalho. I scratched his cheeks with my nails, and thereafter he avoided me. At recess I committed the injustice of forsaking Rebêlo. Moreover, that gracious comrade suffered from halitosis, a drawback that seriously prejudiced the purity of his counsel. In addition to that, when he engaged another in conversation, he had the mania of gripping his fellow with pincer-like fingers, all the while firing off aphorisms at close range. On his part the venerable colleague responded to the bustle by bumping into me, which was an annoyance. During classes, in which we sat near to one another, he was desperately absorbed in his own affairs, as if he were miles away. If, however, he felt some urgent need to speak to me, he did so with the habitual affability of a young priest.

I was acclimated, but I had become so out of hopelessness, like a prisoner in his cell. After I shook off the hobble of my ingenuous ideals, I felt myself bereft of spirit; I had never before been so aware of the imponderable spirituality of the soul. The vacuum dwelled inside me. I was oppressed by the power of things, and I felt myself unnerved. I had forgotten Rebêlo's manly lesson: to dispense with protectors. I wanted a protector, someone who would come to my aid in those strange and hostile surroundings. I wanted direct help, something stronger than words.

If I had not forgotten Rebêlo's good advice as well as his personal assistance, I would perhaps have realized that I was gradually being invaded, as he had observed, by the morbid effeminacy that plagues boarding schools. But theory is fragile, and it falls asleep like delicate larvae when the weather turns cold. Moral lethargy was weighing me down. And as if the soul of a child, like his physique, were waiting for the days to pass in the determination of his individual sexual conformation, I felt myself possessed by a certain listless need for assistance, a voluptuousness of weakness quite out of keeping with the male character. Convinced that the campaign of study and moral energy was not precisely a daily cavalcade, spurred on by the clarion of rhetoric, as on feast days, and by the emphatic verses of the hymnal, I was saddened by the prospect of harsh reality. I was disillusioned by the theatrical stage setting of the glorious parade, once I had seen it from the inside. Not every day of the military life is decked out with the hurly-burly of assault and triumphal return. I was demoralized by the stagnant routine of the peaceful barracks, the elemental prosaism of fatigue duty.

Along with this crisis of sensibility went the fear that the microcosm of the Atheneum inspired in me. Everything is a threat to the defenseless. The riotous unrestraint of one's companions at play, the easy manner of carrying out one's assignments seemed to me signs of shattering superiority. I was shocked by the liveliness of the little ones, so small some of them were! The arm of Sanches came to save me from drowning a second time, coming to my aid as I floundered in the vertigo of that particular moment.

I did not study. My marks, however, remained good, owing to a series of fortuitous elements. My situation at school was fair owing to a happy coincidence of events: my teachers were all kindly disposed, I had received a good recommendation addressed to Professor Mânlio, and on my side I also had the slight learning I had brought with me. I maintained a fair average, but the risk of degenerating was constantly with me. The method was my worst obstacle; without the aid of someone more practical I was lost. Sanches would no doubt help me with his ability as a splendid student, especially with the engaging goodwill that he unselfishly exhibited. Not to mention the boon I realized from his friendship, as he took up his terrible tutor's sword on my behalf, the one with the leather handle!

As a matter of fact, it was not long before he lent me his hand, like Fénelon's gentle Minerva. I took to geography as to my own habitat. The unevenness of a continent's outlines was undone on my maps, to make my work the briefer; rivers had to do without their complicated meandering as they flowed into my brain, abandoning the natural slope of their watershed; mountain ranges like immense troops of trained elephants were arranged in highly simplified systems of orography; the number of the principal cities of the world was reduced as they were swallowed up by the earth so that I would not be forced to memorize so many names; the assessment of population was rounded off and bothersome fractions were dropped in detriment to the census and to the greater burden of the nation's uteruses; a felicitous mnemonics taught me how to enumerate the states and provinces. Thanks to Sanches's cleverness, no incident studied on the face of the earth failed to stick in my brain, as if the inside of my head were the exact reproduction of the physical contours of the globe.

In its turn grammar opened up to me like a bag of holiday confections, all sugar and azure satin. With delight I randomly selected the adjectives like almonds frosted in adverbial complements of the most delightful variety. And the lovely nouns fluttered about my head, common and proper, like dear creatures of winged icing. Etymology, syntax, prosody, and orthography: four equal degrees of sweetness.

At first, grammatical exceptions and irregular verbs merely irritated me, like those ugly chocolate crispies so delicious when plopped onto the tongue.

The history of Brazil delighted me to the utmost. From the colonial missionaries with their catechisms who came to meet me in the company of Father Anchieta, all of them visions of goodness, reciting selected strophes from the gospel of the jungle as they directed the natives forward, happy in their floral headdresses, along the wide roadway of glistening sand, apprentices as they were in the faith and Western civilization, marching along with the savage multitude all of them the color of tree bark, festooned in plumes, daubed in a thousand colors in respectful contrition for their recently abandoned fetishism, looming up from the heart and depths of the dreary forest like a fantastic march of tree trunks. Down to the period of national independence, a complex evocation of confusion commemorative of the dawns in the Lisbon Rocio and the ill-defined yearnings of youthful patriotism: the forging of a prince, riding over a date, showing the flag with the official legend of the Ipiranga to the people; farther down, punctuated by the salvos of Santo Antônio, the acclamations of an alienated people that allowed Tiradentes to die in order to wear themselves out cheering Domitila's coffee branch.

Every page was a delight, prefaced as it was by the affable explanation of my colleague. Thanks to the ability of his presentations, I shook hands with the most truculent figures of the past, the most powerful. Antônio Salema, the cruel, smiled at me; Vidigal was gracious; Dom João VI

left snuff on my fingers. I learned to recognize Mem de Sá on sight, also
Maurice of Nassau; I saw the hero of Minas Gerais pass by serenely, his
hands tied behind him like Christ, the flowing beard of the apostle to the
people, a sunbeam glittering on his wide, smooth brow, balded by fate in order to receive the better crown of martyrdom.

Sacred history revealed this epic hero to me—who would have thought
it?—this Canon Roquette! I imbibed the musical rapture of the chapters like the
solemn plainsong of the cathedrals. I heard Faith sigh, the idyl of the Garden
of Eden, the primitive love of Genesis envied by the very angels under the gaze
of gentle lions. I heard the touching lamentation of the first couple banished to
grief and travail: Adam shamefully girding on the fig leaves of the first modesty,
Eve concealing her youthful lily-white nakedness beneath the golden tunic of her
tresses, her hands covering her belly, the obscenity of all mothers, stigmatized
by the very curse of God.

And the music of the chanting of the entire tradition of human suffering superseded by the Divinity. The harmony was intoned in sweet warbles,
singing the exaltation of the Psalms, the sensual ecstasy of the Song of Songs in
the mouth of the Shulamite maiden, and the seduction of Boaz snared by the
honest trap of tenderness, and the tragic melancholy of Judith, and the serene
glory of Esther, the beloved princess.

Suddenly the musical portrait opened to make way for the sudden
entrance of the chorus of lamentations. The last strains of David's harp trailed
off in the air like dying fireflies. The final antistrophe of Solomon echoed away
in the distance. The picture of Ruth, the golden sheaf of wheat in her arms,
disappeared at the far end of a field. The shadowy Hebrew woman entered
Halophernes's tent, bearing on her lips the murderer's kiss. The shining apparition of Esther was covered with the sleep of Mordecai's night. The sorrowful
gamut of terror. The curses of the Flood were called down, the desperation of
Gomorra; the sword of the angel of Sennacherib flamed in the firmament. The
supplication of Egypt, the wail of Babylon, the cursed stones of Jerusalem chatted
in mournful concert. The murky gloom of the preachments of the prophets cried
out. In vain the splendor of transfigurations, like the livid lightning flash, opened
wide and dazzling over the storm of night; Ezekiel had a vision of the Eternal;
Elijah visited the Mystery in a flight of flame. Nothing. The solemn music was
the Miserere. Neither the brilliance of the dawn of Bethlehem of Judea could
overcome the shadows, nor the living illusion of Tabor. The epic agonized as the
world rolled on, echoed in a cave which contained a tomb. It roared in triumph
for a moment over the Resurrection of the Just One and slowly, slowly died with
the prayers of the martyrs in the amphitheater, with the distant subterranean
prayers of the fugitives in the catacombs.

Christian doctrine, annotated by the proficiency of the explicator, was
the occasion for redoubled ardor in teaching, which greatly interested me. It was
Heaven opened up, surrounded by altars, to all creations sanctified by the faith.
Strange to face the greatness of the Most High. But there were also windows that
opened onto Purgatory; their view was far more seductive, and Sanches and I

peeked through them together. The tutor had a touch of unction in his voice and in his manner, the haughtiness of a spiritual director who speaks of sin without defiling his mouth. He delivered his exposition almost contritely, staring at the ceiling, snapping his fingers nervously, carried away as he was by religious abstraction. He delivered his exposition, dragging out certain incidents, the most horrific manifestations of Satan loose in the world. Nor indeed did he make any attempt to gild Old Ned's horns to make him less frightening to me. On the contrary he seemed to take especial delight in shocking me with his fantasies of Evil and Temptation, and according to Sanches's description the devil's tail was perhaps two meters longer than in reality it was. And to tell the truth he once insinuated that the "old boy" was not so ugly as they said he was.

The catechism began to fill me with the terror-stricken fright of the ancient and obscure oracles. I did not wholly believe, of course. In fact, I thought that at least half of all that was the wicked invention of Sanches himself. And when he took to telling of chastity—paying no attention to the stupidity of the substance of the theological precept—another man's wife, the Immaculate Conception of the Virgin, outcries to Heaven over sensuality against nature, the moral advantages of matrimony, and flesh, the innocent flesh which I knew to be condemned only by keepers of Lent and monopolists in the cod trade, poor beef flesh was an enemy of the soul; when I corrected my error to the effect that flesh was something quite other—and especially so when roasted, and most especially when carved—I chewed a bit of indignation over the slander against the holy primer of my devout creed. But, really, it was an interesting subject, and I was collecting snippets of information so that I might later sort out the lot and judge for myself.

With the multiplication tables and sketching I dispensed with the services of my elder colleague, because I found it amusing to trace the capricious strokes and dally with the geometrical figures tiny as toys. I did not require the services of a tutor because where sums and the metrical system were concerned I no longer held out any hope of surpassing my mediocrity and advancing to gymnast of calculation. I decided to leave to Maurílio—or to anyone at all—primacy in the area of numbers.

In two months we had mastered all the materials of the course; and with this preparation, I was smiled upon by the portent of a brilliant future when fate stepped in to bring it all to ruin. I have mentioned that Sanches absolutely inspired a stomach-turning repugnance in me. After the incident in the bath my gratitude predominated over my revulsion, and I permitted the solicitudes which my companion showered on me. However, at last the old instinctive revulsion came back to separate me from the other youth.

As I was dubious of the whole concept of school paternity, the personification of which seemed to me to be Barbalho, I was frightened by the rowdiness of the play periods. One measure of prudence consisted of remaining behind in the classroom. I used the required recreation hours to improve myself in my studies. At any rate, during these moments of extra application when we were left alone, the larger boy and myself, I realized what had been all along the basis for the antipathy that had made me so apprehensive. The openness of our close companionship increased imperceptibly from day to day. We would take our places on the same bench. Then Sanches began to sit closer to me. From there he took to leaning against me. He would close his own book and read from mine, breathing against my face the breath of fatigue. To explain something he would sit back a short distance. Then he would grasp my fingers and crush them with such force that it made my hand ache as if it were clay, all the time staring at me with unjustified rage. Then as suddenly he would return to words of affection, and the reading would proceed as he slipped his arm around my neck like the warmest of friends.

I permitted it all, pretending not to notice, although I conceived the plan of breaking off the relationship. But I was incapacitated by a want of courage. Surely there could be no fault in these expressions of friendship; I merely found them inopportune and impertinent, especially as I never made the slightest move to return the affection.

I noticed that he would adjust himself whenever a tutor showed his head at the doorway of the classroom or when he sought to inform me of some extraordinary regulations. Then my strange master took on an air of the severest and most distant gravity. This inconstancy alarmed me. It was, after all, a kind of pastime. Often I lost the thread of my reading to pay closer heed to the wiles of this newest of charades.

On one very warm day he had just explicated like a priest a page of religion, the diverse acts of Contrition, Attrition, Faith, Hope, and Charity, when he suggested that I should repeat these matters to him seated at his knee. I found that cozy arrangement totally unnecessary, and I said my lesson as I strolled about the room. Good Lord, the fellow wanted to deal with me once and for all as if I were a baby! A little more and he would be offering to change my diapers! If I had still been in possession of the spunk that I had brought with me when I left home for school, no doubt I would long since have sent Sanches packing, along with his primer. But I had changed. My will vegetated in me like a tender, ductile sprout, after the annihilation of my first disenchantment. I continued to postpone open conflict with Sanches.

Sometimes my passive resistance disappointed my tutor. He would stare at me in a furor as if to say, "Just try to do without protection and see how well you fare!" Or he would conceal his evil thoughts under a sickly grin and otherwise put on an abstract expression which was none other than the *facies* of an *idée fixe*.

We did our exercises in the afternoon one hour after dinner, a propitious time, for it taught us to keep our food down as we performed on the parallel bars and executed our turns. I discovered the handsome parade grounds when I went there the first time after matriculation. I missed the pennants waving over the green turf. But even with the counterfeit gaiety of the parade dismantled, the field was still a very pleasant place. Open to the sky as it was, it seemed airier than elsewhere, and there I expanded my lungs after the oppressive regime of indoor study.

After our exercises were over, Master Bataillard left, and watched over by two proctors, Silvino and João Numa, or João Numa and old Margal, the venerable and sickly Spaniard whom we all loved, or Margal and the *Counsellor,* we students enjoyed a period of recreation until nightfall.

One time, as it was growing dark, I was walking in silence beside Sanches, who also said nothing. We were watching the daylight expire beyond the mountains, and I heard my companion mumble a question. He spoke absent-mindedly, admiring the dusk with his brow furrowed, in the half-abstraction that was his customary grimace. We had reached the far side of the pathway that went around the parade ground, opposite the gate where the proctors were chatting. My colleagues were playing ball in the grass or they amused themselves at leapfrog, stationed at distant points. Since I did not understand the question, Sanches repeated it. Without wishing to, I allowed a laugh to escape my lips. I was faced with the very strangest sort of suitor! I laughed openly but I was bewildered. Sanches's extravagances were truly original! Today he is an engineer for a railroad in the South. A very serious engineer, indeed. . . . Seeing that we could not reach a satisfactory arrangement, the brilliance of the sunset took its stand between us, and we resolved our embarrassment by expressing a unanimous opinion on the subject.

During the days that followed this incident, Sanches was cold and distant. I was afraid I had lost his protection. He gave me my lessons without a single one of his usual unpalatable signs of affection. He spoke to me only in short sentences, half peevish, half melancholic. I suspected that he might have undergone a drastic change of temperament, and I reached the conclusion that I might have found what I most urgently required: a temperate friend who would protect me from the annoyances of school life in the lower grade. However, that was not the situation. Sanches had understood that his candor had undermined all the fervor of his teaching. He maneuvered then to return to his duties as quickly as possible. To that end he took especial care to insist on my edifying preparation.

He invented an analysis of *The Lusiads,* a text on which we were to be examined, the difficulty of which he could not stress enough. He led me to the Ninth Canto as to a disreputable back street. I took criminal delight in my fear of the unknown. My mentor carried me beyond the stanzas, revealing on the noble face of the poem views of the brothel glimpsed through a lavender haze. The beast! There was a thin veil of modesty over the bare truth of the word. He crudely ripped those delicate tunics apart, from top to bottom. He turned the graceful artistry of each verse into an offensive crudity. I followed him without remorse, vaguely feeling that I was a victim; and I submitted to the cruelty, lulled by the advantage gained by my own submission. His analysis spurred the rhymes onward, and the rhymes passed, leaving behind a recollection of some shameless concupiscence. And the stern expression on the face of an imperturbable Sanches.

He casually took apart each sentence, each clause, with the sober manner of the anatomist: subject, verb, complements, subordinate clauses; then the meaning, bang!, an incision with the scalpel and the phrase rolled over dead, repulsive, with its entrails falling out in loathsome putrefaction.

In the same way he initiated a colorful course on the dictionary. The dictionary is the universe. It prides itself on enlightenment, but on first sight it dumfounds like the excitement of great and strange cities. Names with the numerous progeny of their derivations were strangely grouped together on the large pages or the gallicisms appeared alone like foppish *petits-maîtres;* proud dandies were those words of Albionian provenance. They irritate us with their supercilious air because we are not acquainted with them. Their meanings trail on endlessly, crisscrossing in a confused topographical network. The neophyte cannot progress by a single step in this gigantic capital of words. Sanches knew his way around. He went with me to the farthermost hostelries of the metropolis, down to the very sewer of indecent expressions. He stripped the magisterial discretion of the lexicon down to its skeletal caricature for my delectation, as he had besmirched the Parnassian elegance of the poem.

I felt myself crushed beneath the weight of these new revelations. I was horrified by this knowledge of things I had never before dreamed. My honorable spiritual director perceived that I was beginning to bend under the first signs of his authority over me. He began to look me straight in the eye, and he often burst out in malicious laughter. After days of icy reserve he came back with all the assurance of his firm possession of my will. I went about in wretched spiritual disorder. From time to time Rebêlo would obliterate me through his blue glasses with a look of despisal or of sympathy, which would degrade me even more. My father came to see me every week; I would show him the awards I had won for my diligent study, I talked with him about affairs at home, and the rest I kept to myself. As I was always suspicious and fearful of others, Sanches was practically my sole companion. We were always together, he and I. Inside the Atheneum it was general knowledge that he was my tutor; they even imagined that he was paid for his services. No one was shocked by our closeness.

Nevertheless, Sanches avoided the crowded places, as do all those of evil intention. He liked to wander about with me in the evening before dinner, time and again crossing the dark courtyard, clutching me nervously and often holding me so tight that he lifted me off the ground. I tolerated it all as I recalled in resigned silence the artificial sex of the weakness that Rebêlo had explained.

Stimulated by this abandon, which he took for tacit consent, Sanches precipitated a denouement. One rainy afternoon we were straggling about the entrance to the washrooms. It was dark and humid and smelled of dank towels and toothpaste: suitable seclusion rendered the more favorable by enormous square pillars which supported the edifice just as they cut off the view of possible spies. All of a sudden my companion brought his mouth close to my face and whispered something to me.

His voice alone, the simple cowardly sound of his voice—groveling and clinging as if every syllable were as long as a legend—made my flesh crawl as though in contact with some foul instrument of torture. I pretended that I had not heard him; but inside me I felt the explosion of all my revulsion toward such a person, and very calmly looking aside I made up the excuse that I needed a handkerchief because the chilly weather had given me a cold. And I left to fetch one.

Once outside the magnetic field where my good friend held me captive, my weakened instincts of revulsion came back to life, and Sanches simply became a stranger to me. My friendship with him ended in a flash. At the same time I lost my tutor and bodyguard. It was a stroke of high heroism on my part. The first time we met each other after our break, he saw clearly that the whole affair was definitely ended. He took to lurking about in my footsteps. When he looked at me, I clearly discerned the glint of the stiletto blade in the thrust of his gaze.

It was not the best possible time for open conflict. For reasons of expediency Professor Mânlio's class had been divided into two sections, and I had been included in the group placed under the tutelage of Sanches, who was considered a highly capable assistant. The outcome was what it had to be. Maltreated and reprehended by the assistant, so terrified that I tested out very badly in the examinations to which the professor subjected me, and demoralized by solemn reprimand, much to Sanches's delight, I vowed vengeance. I would scandalize the whole school with a kind of idleness they had never even dreamed of! I rushed through all my lessons as a mockery of study. That, however, might not be enough. Let it be enough! was my motto. And things went from bad to worse. My marks were lower than Barbalho's, too low to be considered passing, in other words. They were even lower than Álvares's. I was the low man in the class! Not bad results, considering the labors of what little spirit I was beginning to muster.

At about the same time, taking the cue from all the troubled philosophers of the past, I sought the sweet consolation of the stars. Aristarco had initiated a night course in cosmography. The stars were decidedly his field. The noble instruction. No teacher in the school would have dared to attempt to fill his astrologer's shoes for fear of expulsion. You should have seen him at the window, indicating the constellations, impelling them through the night skies with his pointing finger! We students, of course, could see nothing, but we gaped in admiration. It was quite enough for him deftly to outline a star cluster in the heavens, and each one of us in his turn felt more *a quo*. And we were wafted away dodging the phosphorescent stardust.

As for me, I especially marveled at the courage with which Aristarco picked out the heavenly bodies, because everybody knows that pointing at stars will cause warts. Once, in a flurry of enthusiasm, our illustrious master showed us the Southern Cross. A little later, whispering over what little we knew of the cardinal points, we discovered that the window faced the north, but we gave no indication. Aristarco realized that he had made a slip, but he refused to go back on his word. And there the Southern Cross reluctantly remained, imprinted on the hemisphere of the North Star.

I fell in love with space and eagerly studied the mechanics of the infinite as recorded in Abreu's textbook. On overcast nights Aristarco produced his gadgets. Numberless mechanisms for teaching astronomy, exemplifying the solar system, the theory of eclipses, the gravitation of satellites, concentric spheres, terrestrial and celestial, the inner one made of shiny cardboard, the outer made of glass. On the table an indescribable clutter of stars and twisted wires, wheels with brass teeth, dim naphtha lamps parodying the sun. Aristarco turned the crank and everything whirled. His pince-nez with thick tortoise-shell frames poised at the tip of his nose, he controlled the tumult of the worlds.

"See," he would say as he explained the workings of nature, "see my hand here?" He indicated his right hand, cranking as if at a hurdy-gurdy, a splendid huge hairy paw that would have done credit to Esau himself: "Behold the hand of Providence!"

16

EUCLIDES DA CUNHA

Although da Cunha's purpose in writing his great work, *Os Sertões (Rebellion in the Backlands)*, was to re-create the peasant revolt against the recently proclaimed republic in primarily historical and sociological terms, the book was soon acclaimed as a masterpiece of literature as well. It was also recognized as one of the most effective attempts ever made to probe beneath the surface of Brazilian reality and to expose the hidden forces at work.

Da Cunha was born in the outskirts of Rio de Janeiro in 1866. He was attracted to the army, but was finally unable to accept its discipline completely. He studied at the Military School, left it in 1888 as a consequence of his then-current political activities, and returned to the army one year later after having completed his training as an engineer at the Polytechnic School. In the army he rose to the rank of first lieutenant (1892), but finally resigned in 1896 to devote himself to engineering and journalism.

As a correspondent for the newspaper *O Estado de São Paulo*, he was assigned in 1897 to cover the last stages of the rebellion, centered in the deserted hinterland of the Northeast. At this point the conflict between the peasant rebels, led by a mystic named Antônio Conselheiro, and the local authorities had been in a state of stalemate for a year or more. Conselheiro's followers had founded a number of small communities, which became refuges for outlaws and in which free love was openly practiced; they had raided neighboring ranches and had refused to pay any taxes or respect the local churches. When the local militias proved ineffectual in quashing the rebellion, the army was called in. Three expeditionary forces failed to destroy the rebels' last stronghold, Canudos; the fourth succeeded. Before reaching Canudos, da Cunha read avidly about the causes and origins of the rebellion, which had been caricatured in the Brazilian press. When he arrived at his destination, he was well prepared not only to report but also to interpret what he saw. The brilliant accounts he sent to his newspaper became the basis for a book in which he later attempted to delineate the tragedy in its full dimensions.

After the fall of Canudos, da Cunha went to São Jose do Rio Pardo to build a bridge. In his spare time, and with the help of books lent by learned friends, he wrote *Os Sertões*, which he published in 1902. In his effort to place the rebellion in its proper context, da Cunha not only reconstructed in the most vivid way the three expeditions he had not participated in but also began his work by offering a detailed description of the land and the people. In this he was clearly guided by the example of Sarmiento's *Facundo* (see selection 5), and he even took from his Argentine predecessor the image of an epic conflict between civilization and barbarism. And, in line with certain positivistic notions concerning the "degeneration" of the races in America, he presented a dark prognosis for the future of the human community produced by miscegenation. At the same time, he was a firm believer in the great myth of unceasing progress so characteristic of the period—a notion reflected in the motto on the national flag ("Ordem e Progresso")—and was thus prepared to see the rebels simply as reactionaries. (They even wanted a restoration of the Empire!)

And yet, despite all his theoretical preconceptions, da Cunha saw that not all the barbarism lay on the side of the rebels, and that civilization had to mean something more than the political and military establishment of Brazil. He recognized the grandeur of the charismatic Antônio Conselheiro. In reconstructing Conselheiro's career, he pointed out, to be sure, the excesses the rebel leader had committed and the flaws in his beliefs, but gave him the tragic stature that was his due. Da Cunha also exposed the bureaucratic incompetence of the government and the incredible lack of professionalism within the army. As a witness of the last episode of the civil war, he had seen the senseless killing and the genocidal furor, and he was able to reconstruct the whole campaign in the most horrifying details.

Perhaps the book's principal flaw lies in its failure to recognize the economic context of the events it describes. Da Cunha did not see how the roots of the rebellion lay in the feudal social structure of the Northeast, which made this sort of desperate revolt not only possible but inevitable. (In a later book— a collection of essays entitled *Contrasts and Confrontations*, 1907—he discussed the socialist interpretation of history.)

Whatever its shortcomings, *Rebellion in the Backlands* has the advantage of being a first-rate narrative, written in a powerful idiosyncratic style. As an introduction, da Cunha devised a lengthy description of the land, in which minute details suddenly give way to visionary overviews. He also achieved brilliant portraits of the different types of character produced by this tragic land. In this regard, he covered some of the same ground already explored in a romantic vein by Alencar's regionalist novels (see selection 12). But da Cunha's vision was less idyllic. Without diminishing the stature of his characters as prototypical figures, he managed to portray them convincingly as real human beings.

The third part of the book achieves a kind of epic grandeur. The portrait of Antônio Conselheiro here excerpted shows da Cunha at his best. Like Sarmiento, he was both attracted and repelled by a man so totally different from himself. It is this passionate ambivalence that gives the portrait its unusual dimensions. In the last part of the book he describes Conselheiro's body, which he actually saw exhumed after the killing had stopped at Canudos.

The success of *Rebellion in the Backlands* was immediate and strengthened da Cunha's resolution to pursue this type of study. Unfortunately, he did not have much longer to live: he was killed in 1909 in a street confrontation with a man who was probably his wife's lover. But the book has continued to live and to influence Brazilian culture. It is the chief root source for the Brazilian novel of the Northeast and evoked more directly a narrative reply on a grand scale, Guimarães Rosa's *Grande Sertão: Verédas* (*The Devil to Pay in the Backlands* is the English translation's title, in an obvious reference to da Cunha's book; see Part Four, 22). The New Cinema in Brazil can also claim *Os Sertões* as a source book.

Antonio Conselheiro, the "Counselor"

From Rebellion in the Backlands, *translated by Samuel Putnam (Chicago: University of Chicago Press, 1944), pp. 127–42.*

And there appeared in Bahia that somber hermit. He was terrifying to behold, with his hair hanging down to his shoulders, a long, unkempt beard, a face like a death's-head, glittering eyes, garbed in a habit of blue cotton, and in his hand the classic pilgrim staff.

For a long time nothing was known of his existence. An old *caboclo* who was imprisoned in Canudos during the later days of the campaign gave me a little information about him, but vague and imprecise. The *sertões* of the inland of Pernambuco knew of him a year or two after he left Crata. From the words of this witness I came to the conclusion that while still a young man, Antonio Maciel had made a vivid impression on the imagination of the dwellers of that region. He appeared among them without any definite purpose, a wanderer. He made no reference to his past. He rarely spoke, and when he did, it was in brief phrases or monosyllables. He roved about aimlessly, from one ranch to another, indifferent to life and danger, eating poorly and irregularly, sleeping in the open air beside the road, in a prolonged, severe penance.

He gradually became something supernatural or bewitched to the minds of those simple people. When this strangely aged man, who was only a little more than thirty years old, appeared among the cattle herders, their songs ceased and their guitars were silenced. It was only natural. He suddenly loomed up—squalid and emaciated—in his long, plain blue habit, silent, like a specter, from the wasteland inhabited by ghosts.

He went on his way leaving the superstitious countryfolk awed and apprehensive.

He acquired an ascendancy over them without making any effort to do so. In a primitive society in which, by reason of its racial composition and the influence of the nefarious "holy missions," life rested on a basis of miracles they could not fathom, his mysterious mode of life began to create an atmosphere of supernatural prestige about him which, perhaps, aggravated his deranged temperament. Little by little all this domination which he unintentionally exercised on others seemed to have taken hold on him. All the conjectures and legends by which he was soon surrounded stimulated the growth of his aberration. His madness acquired outward form. He saw it reflected in the intense admiration and unquestioning respect that in a short time made his word law in all disputes and quarrels and converted him into the supreme authority in all decisions. This attitude on the part of the multitude spared him the ordeal of trying to understand his own mental state, the painful effort of self-analysis and that obsessive introspection which drives an unhinged mind to madness. The multitude recast him in its own image, created him, enlarged him beyond all human proportions, and launched him upon a sea of errors two thousand years old. It needed someone who should translate its own vague idealism and guide it along the mysterious paths that lead to heaven. The evangelist emerged, but inhuman, an automaton. This agitator was a puppet. He acted passively, like a sleepwalker. But in his behavior he reflected the obscure, formless aspirations of three races.

And he acquired such dimensions that he projected himself into history.

From the *sertões* of Pernambuco he proceeded to those of Sergipe, appearing in the city of Itabaiana in 1874.

He arrived there, as everywhere, unknown and arousing distrust by reason of his strange attire: a long, unbelted tunic, a hat with a wide, drooping brim, and sandals. On his back hung a knapsack in which he carried paper, pen, and ink, and two books, a *Brief Missal* and *The Hours of Mary*.

He begged his bread, but he always refused to take more than he needed for the day. He sought out the loneliest ranches. He never accepted any bed but the bare boards or, lacking this, the hard earth. He wandered about like this for a long time until he appeared in the *sertões* to the north of Bahia. His fame was growing. He no longer traveled by himself. The first of the faithful were following him on his uncharted route. He did not call them. They came of their own free will, happy to share with him his life of privation and suffering. For the most part they were the dregs of humanity, of doubtful antecedents, averse to work, a troupe of life's outcasts, adept in the ways of laziness and thievishness.

One of the disciples carried on his back the only temple that then existed of this puny new religion: a roughly carved cedar altar on which was an image of Christ. When they stopped along the roadside they hung it from the branch of a tree, and there they knelt in prayer. As they entered the hamlets and villages they bore it triumphantly aloft, intoning a chorus of litanies.

In 1876 the Counselor, as he was known, appeared in the town of Itapicuru de Cima. His fame had become widespread. A document published that year in the capital of the Empire bears witness to this:

> There has appeared in the *sertão* of the north a man who calls himself Antonio the Counselor and who exerts a great influence on the lower classes, utilizing for this end his mysterious aspect and his ascetic habits, which make a great impression on the ignorance of these simple-minded people. He has let his hair and beard grow long, he wears a cotton tunic and eats very little, looking almost like a mummy. He goes about in the company of two women converts, and he spends his life praying and preaching and giving advice to the multitudes that gather to hear him wherever the priests permit it. By playing on their religious sentiments he attracts the people and does what he likes with them. He shows himself to be a man of intelligence, though devoid of culture.

These remarks, which were the exact truth, published in a journal hundreds of miles away, are eloquent testimony to the fame he was acquiring.

Meanwhile in this town of Itapicuru his extraordinary career almost came to an end. That same year, to the consternation of the faithful, he was arrested. This came about as the result of a false accusation that his strange life and past domestic difficulties justified to a certain point. He was said to have killed his wife and his own mother.

It was a gruesome tale. It was said that his mother hated her daughter-in-law and set about to work her ruination. With this in mind she told her son that his wife was unfaithful to him; and as he demanded proofs of her guilt, she proposed to supply them without delay. She advised him to pretend that he was going away on a trip, but to remain in the neighborhood and at night he would see the seducer who was dishonoring his home. The poor wretch, following her advice, rode several miles away from the town and then, taking a roundabout lonely route back, hid in a place he had selected where he could see what took place and act quickly.

There he remained hidden for hours until, late in the night, he saw a shadowy figure approach his house. He saw it creep up and climb into one of the windows. Before it could get through he felled it with a shot.

With one bound he was in the house and with another shot he killed his wife, who was asleep.

Then he turned back to discover the identity of the man he had killed. And he saw, to his horror, that it was his own mother, who had disguised herself as a man to carry out her diabolical plan.

Aghast, crazed, he immediately fled, leaving everything he owned, to the *sertões* of the interior.

The popular imagination had begun to create a legend about his life, giving it a vigorous touch of tragic originality.

Nevertheless the fact remains that in 1876 the law laid hold of him just as the evolution of his spirit had reached its climax and he was sunk in a dream from which he was never again to awaken. The ascetic was emerging, full stature, from the rude discipline of fifteen years of penance. He had reached perfection in his apprenticeship of martyrdom, a profession so highly recommended by the old Church fathers. It was the result of brutally binding himself over to hunger, thirst, fatigue, and every form of pain and misery. There was no suffering he did not know. His leathery skin was stretched over his insensible flesh like a battered and cracked coat of mail. It had been anesthetized by its sufferings. It was lacerated and scarred by disciplines more severe than a hair shirt; it had been dragged over the stones of the road, it had been charred by the blazing heat of the drought, numbed by the cold morning dew, had known only momentary rest in the bone-breaking beds of the rough hills.

His prolonged fasts brought him many times to the brink of death. The perfection of his asceticism would have surprised Tertulian, that gloomy advocate of the slow elimination of the flesh, "ridding himself of his blood, that heavy, importunate burden of the soul eager to flee. . . ."

For a person undergoing this training in suffering, that prison order was but a trifling incident. He received it with indifference. He forbade his followers to defend him. He gave himself up. He was taken to the capital of Bahia. There his strange appearance, his corpselike face, as rigid as a mask, expressionless and unsmiling, his eyelids drooping over his sunken eyes, his strange garb, his revolting appearance, that of an unburied corpse, in the long tunic like a dark winding sheet, and the lank, dusty hair falling about his shoulders, mingling with the unkempt beard, which hung to his waist, made him the object of general curiosity.

As he was led through the streets, people exclaimed and made signs to ward off the evil eye, while devout old women crossed themselves and fell back in fear.

The judges questioned him in amazement. He was accused of old crimes he had committed in his native region. He listened to the questions and accusations without answering a word, in stony silence. It was later learned that the guards who had brought him in had beaten him on the road. He did not voice the slightest complaint. His was the lofty indifference of a stoic. Only on the day he was to be embarked for Ceará—and I have this from a person of complete reliability—did he ask the authorities to protect him from the curiosity of the crowds, the only thing that bothered him.

On reaching his native town the charges against him were proved to be groundless and he was placed at liberty. And that same year he appeared in Bahia once more among his followers, who had been waiting for him. His return, on the very day he had prophesied when he was arrested, so it was said, assumed the character of a miracle. His influence became thrice what it had been.

Then for a time (1877) he wandered about the *sertões* of Curaca, making his headquarters in Chorrochó, a village of a few hundred inhabitants, whose lively fair attracted the majority of the people of that region of San Francisco. A beautiful chapel, still standing, tells of his stay there. And perhaps more deserving of veneration is a little tree at the entrance to the village which for a long time was the object of extraordinary devotion. It was a sacred tree. Its shadow cured the ills of the faithful; its leaves were an unfailing panacea.

The multitude vouched for a great series of miracles to which the unhappy wretch probably had never given a thought.

From 1877 to 1887 he wandered about those *sertões,* from one end to the other, even reaching the seacoast, in Villa do Conde (1887). There is probably not a city or village in this whole region where he did not make his appearance. Alagoinhas, Inhambupe, Bom Conselho, Geremoabo, Cumbe, Mucambo, Massacara, Pombal, Monte-Santo, Tucano, and other settlements saw him arrive, accompanied by the troupe of the faithful. In nearly all he left a trace of his passage: in one the rebuilt walls of a ruined cemetery; in another a restored church; farther on, a chapel, always beautiful.

His entrance into the towns, followed by the contrite multitude, in silence, bearing images, crosses, and banners of the Lord, was solemn and impressive. The people deserted their shops and farms. They swarmed into the place where he was, and for a time, overshadowing the local authorities, the humble, wandering penitent took command, became the sole authority.

Sheds covered with branches were erected in the public square, and in the afternoon the faithful intoned their prayers and litanies; and when the gathering was great a platform was constructed in the middle of the market place so the words of the prophet could be heard from all sides and edify the faithful.

There he stood up and preached. It was an extraordinary experience, according to witnesses who are still living. It was a barbarous, hair-raising oratory, made up of fragments from *The Hours of Mary,* disconnected, abstruse, with astounding Latin quotations, pouring forth in disjointed phrases a confused, tangled mixture of dogmatic advice, commonplace precepts of Christian morality, and weird prophecies.

It was grotesque and terrifying. Imagine a clown carried away by a vision of the Apocalypse!

Using few gestures, he would talk for a long time, his eyes fixed on the ground, without looking at the multitude, which was spellbound by the rush of words, which varied from nerve-racking exhortations to a wearisome singsong.

It would appear that he was often bemused by the effect of some significant phrase. He would pronounce it and then become silent, raising his head and suddenly opening his eyelids wide; then his deep, black, shining eyes could be seen, and the brilliant glitter of his glance. Nobody dared to look upon him. The crowd, overawed, lowered its eyes, under the strange hypnotic spell of that terrible insanity.

It was on such occasions that this tormented wretch performed his only miracle: he managed not to make himself ridiculous.

In his preaching, in which he successfully competed with the wandering Capuchin fathers of the missions, he upheld a vague, incongruous system of religion. Whoever heard him could not avoid suggestive historical comparisons. On rereading the unforgettable pages of Renan's *Marcus Aurelius,* in which he brings to life, through the power of his style, the mad leaders of the religious sects of the first centuries of Christianity, one can see in the Counselor's teachings the complete revival of their extinct aberrations. It would be impossible to find a more faithful reproduction of the same system, the same metaphors, the same hyperboles, almost the same words. It is a beautiful example of the similarity of evolutionary phases among peoples. This retrograde of the *sertão* is the living copy of the mystics of the past. One can experience, looking at him, the marvelous effect of a perspective of centuries.

He does not belong to our time. He belongs with all those stragglers whom Fouillée, in a felicitous phrase, calls the "runners on the field of civilization who fall farther and farther behind."

He was a dissenter cast in the same mold as Themison. He rose in rebellion against the Church of Rome, and he hurled invectives against it, employing its own arguments: it had forsaken its glory and was following Satan. His moral teaching was an interlinear translation of that of Montanus: chastity carried to the point of utter horror of woman, while at the same time there was absolute tolerance for free love, leading almost to the extinction of marriage.

In the Phrygian, as perhaps in the man from Ceará, this was the result of an unhappy conjugal experience. Both severely forbade the young women to do anything that enhanced their beauty. They fulminated against fancy wearing apparel, and both of them, above all, against elaborate hairdressing; and what is very curious, they both fixed the same punishment for this sin, the demon of the hair: a piercing crown of thorns for the offenders.

Beauty was to them a snare of Satan. The Counselor missed no opportunity to show his invincible repugnance for it. He never looked at a woman. He talked with his back turned even to pious old women who would have exercised a restraining influence on a satyr.

This similarity with the past grows even more impressive as one examines the absurd concepts of this mad apostle of the *sertões.* Like his predecessors, he appeared when it was believed that the world was coming to an end, that the millennium was at hand; and he had the same terror of the antichrist, whose presence could be felt in the universal collapse of life. The world was approaching its close.

The faithful were to abandon all their possessions, all that might defile them with the slightest trace of vanity. As all worldly goods would be engulfed in the imminent catastrophe, it would be rash folly to treasure them. Let them give up their fleeting pleasures and make their lives a stern purgatory, unsullied by the sacrilege of a smile. The Judgment Day was at hand.

He prophesied years of disaster to follow one after another:*

*These prophecies were written out in a number of little notebooks that were found in Canudos. These I have quoted were copied from one of them that belonged to the adjutant of the officer in charge of the campaign.

. . . In 1896 a thousand flocks will flee from the meadows to the desert, and then the desert will become a meadow, and the meadow a desert. In 1897 there will be much pasture and little stubble, and a single flock and a single shepherd. In 1898 there will be many hats and few heads. In 1899 the waters will turn to blood, and a planet will appear in the east with a ray of sun that the branch will confront on the earth, and the earth in some spot will be confronted by the heavens. There will come a great rain of stars, and that will be the end of the world. In 1900 the lights will go out. God says it in the Gospels: I have a flock that is wandering outside the fold, and it must be brought together so there will be but one flock and one shepherd.

Like those of old he believed he had been sent to do the will of God, and that it was Christ Himself who had prophesied his coming:

In the ninth hour, as He sat resting upon the Mount of Olives one of the disciples asked Him: "Master, what shall be the sign of the end of the world?" And He answered: "There shall be many signs in the Moon and the Sun and the Stars. And an angel will be sent forth by My eternal Father, preaching at the gates, building towns in the desert, building churches and chapels, and giving advice. . . ."

Through all this wild maundering, together with the religious Messianic concept, there was the Messianism of the race, urging him on to rebellion against the republican form of government:

Verily, verily I say unto you, when nation shall rise against nation, Brazil against Brazil, England against England, Prussia against Prussia, from the depths of the sea Don Sebastian will come forth with all his army.

From the beginning of the world which he enchanted with all his army and restored in war.

And when he was enchanted he buried his sword in a rock, up to the hilt, and said: "Farewell, World."

Until a thousand and so many to two thousand years you will not come.

On that day when he comes forth with his army, he will put all those of this play republic to the sword. The end of this war will come in the Holy House of Rome and the blood will run loin deep.

Prophecy had, as can be seen, the same accent in him as when it first appeared in Phrygia, moving westward. It foretold the same Last Judgment, the downfall of the mighty, the destruction of the godless world, and the coming of the millennium.

Is there not to be seen in all this a marked trace of Judaism? It seems indubitable. This return to the golden age of apostles and prophets, this revival of old illusions, is nothing new. It is the ever-recurring return of Christianity to its Hebrew cradle. Montanus is reproduced throughout history, changed in this respect or the other, depending on the character of the different nations, but revealing in his very revolt against the ecclesiastical hierarchy, in his approach to the supernatural, in his vision of heaven, the outlines of the primitive dream of the old religion, before it had been distorted by the canonized sophists of the Church councils.

Following the example of his predecessors in the past, Antonio Conselheiro was a pietist, waiting for the coming of the reign of heaven on earth, which had been promised, ever delayed, and finally completely forgotten by the orthodox Church of the second century. His creed had little to do with Catholicism, which he hardly understood.

In keeping with the mission he had taken upon himself, after delivering these homilies, he ordered penances, which were generally to the benefit of the locality. Neglected churches were restored; abandoned cemeteries were repaired; beautiful new edifices were built. The stonemasons and carpenters worked for nothing; stores donated the materials; the multitude brought in the stones. For days on end the workmen busied themselves with their pious tasks, and their wages were credited to them in heaven.

When the work was finished, the messenger of God suddenly departed —whither? Anywhere, taking the first road deeper into the *sertões*, over the endless plains, without even looking back at those who followed him.

He was unperturbed by the hostility of his dangerous adversary, the priest. According to reliable testimony, the clergy, in general, encouraged or at least allowed him to practice, without return of any sort, all those acts from which they derive their income: baptisms, confessions, feasts, and novenas. They showed indulgence toward the absurdities of the possessed saint, who at least helped them to eke out their meager sustenance. In view of this, the archbishop of Bahia, in 1882, to bring to an end this tolerance, not to say barely disguised protection, sent out a circular to all the priests of his see:

> It has come to our knowledge that a person known as Antonio Conselheiro is going about among the parishioners of this see, preaching to the people who flock to hear him superstitious doctrines and excessively rigid moral concepts with which he is disturbing the consciences and undermining, not a little, the authority of the clergy in those regions. Therefore we order Your Reverence not to tolerate this abuse among your parishioners, advising them that we absolutely forbid them to gather to hear his preachings, for in the Catholic Church it is the mission of the ministers of religion alone to instruct the people, and a layman, however learned and virtuous, has no authority to do this.
>
> Meanwhile let this serve to increase your zeal in the exercise of your preaching duties so that your parishioners, properly

instructed, will not be swept off their feet by every passing wind of doctrine. . . .

But the intervention of the Church was futile. Antonio Conselheiro continued his mad apostolate without let or hindrance through the *sertões*. And as though he wished to keep green the memory of the first persecution he had suffered, he always came back to Itapicuru, where the police authorities finally appealed to the government in a report which, after giving a brief summary of the antecedents of the agitator, says:

> . . . He made his camp in this vicinity and soon he was building a chapel at the expense of the town.
>
> Although this work may be an improvement, even a necessary one, for the town, it is not worth the agitation and unrest; and from the state the people are in, the apprehension of great disturbances is more than justified.
>
> In order that you may judge what Antonio Conselheiro is, I need only tell you that he is followed by hundreds and hundreds of people who listen to him and follow his orders in preference to those of the parish priest.
>
> There are no limits to their fanaticism, which is so great that it may be affirmed without fear of error that they adore him, as though he were a living God.
>
> On the days of sermons, prayers, and litanies, over a thousand people come together. In the building of this church, which involves weekly wages of almost a hundred thousand milreis, ten times the amount that should be paid, people from Ceará are employed, to whom he gives his absolute protection, tolerating and covering up their violations of the law, and this money comes from the credulous and ignorant, who not only do not work, but sell what little they have, and even steal so that nothing may be lacking, without mentioning the large sums that have been collected for other buildings in Chorrochó, in the region of Capim Grosso.

Then it goes on to describe the latest outrage of the fanatics:

> Owing to a misunderstanding between Antonio Conselheiro's followers and the priest of Inhambupe, they have armed themselves as though they were going into battle, alleging that they believe the priest is going to the place called Funco to kill him. It frightens those who have to go by to see those scoundrels armed with clubs, knives, daggers, shotguns, and God help anyone who is suspected of being hostile to Antonio Conselheiro.

As far as can be gathered, this report, couched in such alarming terms, received no answer. No measures were taken until the middle of 1887, when the diocese of Bahia intervened once more, the archbishop writing to the governor of the province to urge that measures be taken to curb "a person known as Antonio Vicente Mendes Maciel who is preaching subversive doctrines, and doing great harm to religion and the state, distracting the masses from their religious duties and dragging them after him, trying to convince them that he is the Holy Ghost, etc."

In the face of this complaint, the governor of that province addressed himself to one of the ministers of the empire, asking that the madman be confined in an insane asylum in Rio. The minister answered the governor, adducing the extraordinary argument that there was no vacancy in that institution, and the governor, in turn, communicated this cogent decision to the archbishop.

This was the beginning and the end of the legal measures taken during the empire.

The Counselor continued his demoralizing apostolate without interference, acquiring an ever greater hold on the popular imagination. The first legends began to crop up. I shall not give a complete list of them.

He founded the settlement of Bom Jesus; and the astounded people told that on a certain occasion, when they were building the beautiful church that is there, ten workmen were struggling in vain to lift a heavy beam into place; whereupon the Chosen One climbed upon the wood and then ordered just two men to raise it up; and that which so many had been unable to do was done by the two quickly, without any effort. . . .

Another time—and I heard this strange tale from persons who had not fallen under his spell—he came to Monte-Santo and ordered that a pilgrimage be made to the top of the mountain, where there was a little chapel. The ceremony began in the afternoon. The multitude laboriously toiled up the steep slope, chanting hymns of praise, stopping at the Stations of the Cross, imploring forgiveness. He marched at the head of the procession, grave, awe-inspiring, his head uncovered, the wind blowing his long hair about, supporting himself on his inseparable staff. Night fell. The penitents lighted torches, and the procession formed a luminous pathway along the ridge of the mountain. When they reached the cross at the summit, Antonio Conselheiro, panting, sat down on the first step of the rude stone stairway and fell into an ecstasy, raptly contemplating the sky, his gaze lost in the stars. . . .

The first wave of the faithful crowded into the little chapel, while the rest remained outside kneeling upon the jagged rocks.

Then the dreamer got to his feet, showing signs of great fatigue. Between the respectful rows of the faithful he made his way into the chapel, his head bowed in humility, drawing his breath with difficulty.

As he approached the altar he raised his pale face, framed by his disheveled hair. A shudder ran through the astounded multitude. Two tears of blood rolled slowly down the immaculate visage of the Blessed Virgin. . . .

These and other legends are still related in the *sertões*. It is only natural. Antonio Conselheiro summed up in his mad mysticism all the errors and superstitions that form the lowest common denominator of our nationality. He attracted the inhabitants of the *sertões*, not because he dominated them, but because they were dominated by their own aberrations. He was favored by his surroundings, and at times, as we have seen, he even achieved the absurdity of being useful. He was serving the ends of old, irresistible ancestral impulses; and dominated by them, he revealed in all his acts the placable disposition of an incomparable evangelist. In fact, his neurosis was benumbed by an astonishing placidity.

One day the priest of a congregation of the *sertões* saw arrive at his door a man, thin to the point of emaciation, exhausted, with long hair falling about his shoulders and a long beard down his breast: the traditional figure of the pilgrim, lacking neither the traditional cross hanging from the rosaries at his belt, the worn, dusty cloak, the canteen of water, nor the long staff. . . .

The priest offered him food; he accepted nothing but a piece of bread. He offered him a bed, but he preferred a board, on which he lay down without blankets, dressed, without even untying his sandals.

The next day this strange visitor, who until then had spoken few words, asked the priest to allow him to preach on the occasion of a feast that was to be held in the church.

"Brother, you are not ordained; the Church does not permit you to preach."

"Then let me perform the services at the Stations of the Cross."

"I cannot do that either," answered the priest. "I am going to do that."

At this the pilgrim looked at him fixedly for a while and, without speaking a word, took from beneath his tunic a cloth. He brushed the dust from his sandals and departed.

It was the classic reproach of the apostles. . . .

Meanwhile the growing reaction he was encountering began to eat into his soul. Completely masterful by nature, he began to show irritation at the slightest obstruction.

Once, in Natuba, in the absence of the priest, with whom he was not on good terms, he ordered stones to be brought to repair the church. The priest arrived, saw that his sacred domains had been invaded, and in exasperation decided to put a stop to the infringement of his authority. Being a practical man, he appealed to the people's selfishness.

A few days before, the town council had ordered the inhabitants to pave the walks of their houses. The priest told the people they could use the stones that had been brought up for that purpose.

This time the Counselor did not limit himself to brushing the dust off his sandals. At the gates of the ungrateful city he uttered his first curse and departed.

Some time later, at the request of this same priest, a local political figure sent for him. The church was falling into ruin, the cemetery was overgrown with weeds; the parish was poor. Only one who controlled the credulous as did the Counselor could repair this state of affairs. The apostle accepted the invitation, but he laid down his own terms, recalling with a haughtiness in contrast to his former meekness the affront he had received.

He was growing bad.

He looked upon the republic with evil eyes and preached rebellion against the new laws. From 1893 he assumed a belligerent attitude that was completely new. It began with a matter of slight importance.

The autonomy of the municipalities having been established, the town councils of the interior of Bahia posted on bulletin boards, which took the place of newspapers, edicts regarding the levying of taxes and so forth.

When these innovations were introduced, Antonio Conselheiro was in Bom Conselho. The imposition of the tax exasperated him, and he planned an immediate answer to it. He gathered the people on a holiday and, amidst seditious shouting and volleys of rifle fire, he ordered the bulletin boards burned in a bonfire in the public square. His voice was heard above the "auto-da-fé," which the authorities were too pusillanimous to interfere with, openly preaching rebellion against the laws.

Later he realized the gravity of what he had done. Leaving the town, he took the Monte-Santo road to the north.

The event produced a strong effect in the capital, and a considerable force of police was sent out to apprehend the rebel and dissolve the rioting groups, whose number at this time did not exceed two hundred. The police overtook them in Massete, a desolate desert spot between Tucano and Cumbe in the foothills of the mountains of Ovo. The thirty members of the pursuing force attacked the crowd of miserable-looking penitents, certain of dispersing them with their first shots. They were dealing, however, with the fearless *jagunços*. They were completely routed and took to flight, their commanding officer in the lead.

Unfortunately this little battle was to be repeated on a larger scale many times later.

After their victory the faithful resumed their march, following the prophet in his hegira. They did not seek the towns as before. They made for the desert.

The rout of the troops would be followed by more vigorous persecutions, and with the protection of the wilderness they counted on being able to defeat their new adversaries by drawing them on into the hills. Without loss of time eighty soldiers of the line set out from Bahia. But they did not proceed beyond Serrinha, where they turned back without venturing into the desert. Antonio Conselheiro did not build up false hopes with this inexplicable retreat that saved him. He led the horde of the faithful, which was joined every day by dozens of proselytes, along the paths to the *sertão*, following a fixed route. He came to know the *sertão* well. He traveled it from one end to the other in an uninterrupted pilgrimage that lasted twenty years. He knew of hidden refuges where he would never be found. Perhaps he had marked them out earlier, foreseeing future vicissitudes.

He headed straight for the north. The faithful went with him. They did not ask where he was leading them. And they crossed steep sierras, sterile plateaus, and bare hills on the march day after day, in time to the chanting of hymns and the slow step of the prophet.

Part Three

THE RETURN OF THE GALLEONS

The romantics had tried very hard to create a new independent literature to match the political independence of their new countries (see Introduction to Part Two). Many succeeded, and thanks to their efforts the language and letters of the New World began to move toward original expression. But their efforts were largely uncoordinated, and generally did not transcend the geographical boundaries of each country. Very few Argentine writers were read in Mexico and Cuba; the River Plate area, in turn, knew very little about Caribbean or Andean writers. The names of truly international significance—such as Bello, Sarmiento, Palma (Part Two, 3, 5, 10)—were few. Only with the advent of modernism did a general Spanish American literature begin to emerge out of separate strands of development. Writers began to circulate all over the continent; for the first time their works were published and discussed outside their native countries, and achieved fame even in Spain and France.

The individual most responsible for the new international appreciation of Spanish American literature was Rubén Darío (selection 4). Born in Central America, his first important book was published while he was living in Chile in 1888; his second, while he was residing in Buenos Aires, in 1896. He completed the conquest of the Hispanic world in two successive trips to Spain in the late 1890s. His work achieved recognition everywhere, and he began to influence young poets on both sides of the Atlantic. Through him, modernism was implanted in the old mother countries. For the first time in Hispanic history, the tide of influence was reversed. The galleons of the conquest were (as the Venezuelan Manuel Díaz Rodríguez phrased it) returning home, this time not with the gold of the Indies but with the silver of the new poetry.

The development of modernism took place almost simultaneously in several countries in the northern part of Spanish America around the last quarter of the nineteenth century. In these countries, newly emergent capitalistic societies were producing a more sophisticated audience, conversant with the latest developments in European (especially French) literature and culture; newspapers and magazines were proliferating in the rapidly expanding cities, and for the first time there existed a solid middle-class reading public capable of sustaining and encouraging a substantial body of professional literary work. This was most notably the case in such centers as Mexico City, Havana, and Bogotá in the north, and Santiago de Chile, Buenos Aires, Montevideo, and Rio de Janeiro in the south. Poets like the Mexicans Salvador Díaz Mirón (selection 2) and Manuel Gutiérrez Nájera, the Cubans José Martí and Julián del Casal (1 and 3), the Salvadoran Francisco Gavidia, and the Colombian José Asunción Silva had already by the 1880s produced a notable transformation in Spanish language and literature—a transformation that prepared the ground for the great work of Rubén Darío.

At first, the modernists consisted only of a small number of isolated individuals who had grown dissatisfied with romanticism and realism and were groping, initially with only intermittent success, for new forms of poetical expression. In their search, they went directly to French sources. Although only one of them actually visited France (Martí in 1873), they were all in touch with French literature through the careful reading of books and periodicals. While Salvador Díaz Mirón was echoing Baudelaire's most "wicked" verses in his own lyrics, Julián del Casal was engaged in a correspondence, in French, with Joris Karl Huysmans, the high priest of decadentism. Living in the United States, Martí was familiar with all the new literary fashions through the well-informed North American press, and he even covered the first New York impressionist exhibition for some of the most important Latin American journals. The consequence of this massive exposure to the transnational culture then being created in France (Paris was then the only true cosmopolis) was of decisive importance. The Spanish American modernists discarded completely the ponderous, "uncouth," traditional manner in Spanish prose and began to write in a more direct, elegant, supple style. In poetry, they followed both the Parnassians in their quest for perfection of form and sculpted imagery and the symbolists in their exploration of musical possibilities in verse. Paul Verlaine's "Music above all" was to become their watchword. And they found another source of inspiration in the medieval masters of their own Hispanic tradition. Martí, for one, excelled in blending old and new in some of the most revolutionary verse of the time.

It was not, however, until Darío emerged on the literary scene that modernism really found a name and became a continental movement. In his early poetical statements, he claimed to be the founder of modernism. He was not, of course. But he was the one who dutifully propagated and developed the new gospel. By the time he began to publish his most revolutionary work, all the first modernists were already dead—del Casal in 1893, Martí and Gutiérrez Nájera in 1895, Asunción Silva in 1896—or had already written, like Díaz Mirón, their best poetry. Nonetheless, Darío's role as the pivotal figure of the new movement cannot be denied. He was to become the recognized leader of the new poets in Chile, Argentina, and Uruguay. Modernism as it is known today was created by him in Buenos Aires and Montevideo, its diffusion promoted by the influential journals that were published there. If in his first important collection of poetry (*Profane Proses*, 1896), Darío had proved to be too much under the spell of Verlaine's music, in his later work he would show himself a discriminating reader of Baudelaire's and Mallarmé's more complex verses. Like some of his predecessors, he found fresh inspiration in earlier masters of Spanish verse—the medieval Berceo, the baroque Góngora and Quevedo. Darío was interested in experimenting with all kinds of meters and rhythms, and he transformed Spanish verse so decisively that to find an equivalent to the revolution he carried out, it is necessary to hark back to Spain's Golden Age. His discoveries were soon adopted in Buenos Aires and Montevideo by the most adventurous of the new poets: the Argentine Leopoldo Lugones (selection 5), the Uruguayans Julio Herrera y Reissig (6) and Delmira Agustini (7). They developed and extended his experiments and helped prepare the way for the poetry of the avant-garde. Later, in Spain, Darío would rally under his banner the best of the young writers: Salvador Rueda, Manuel and Antonio Machado, Valle Inclán, and Juan Ramón Jiménez.

A reaction against some aspects of modernism, in both Spain and Spanish America, would later attempt to rewrite the story of those days. The revisionists would claim that Darío's influence was superficial, that the Spaniards soon found in native masters (Unamuno, Baroja, Azorín) their true leaders, and that even some of his disciples (Antonio Machado, Valle Inclán, Jiménez) had later deserted him. Perhaps so. But not before everyone had assimilated Darío's teachings and discarded the traditional verse and prose styles of the nineteenth century. Darío also visited Paris on several occasions and even had the chance to meet Verlaine. (The poet was drunk and repeated monotonously one word: *merde.*) On the eve of the 1914 war Darío founded in Paris a magazine in Spanish, called *Mundial,* which attempted to do for the modernists what Bello's two London reviews had done for the writers of the early nineteenth century. With his books and literary enterprises, Darío contributed to the truly international poetical revolution, centered in Paris, which was to produce the avant-garde movement of the early twentieth century. His name is hardly ever mentioned when calling the roll of distinguished foreigners who lived and worked in Paris during those decisive years, but he ought to be included as one of the most truly creative.

By 1900 a reaction against some of the more decadent aspects of modernism was beginning to emerge in Spanish American literature. The writer who best represented this reaction was the Uruguayan José Enrique Rodó (selection 8). Although an early admirer of Darío—he had written one of the most perceptive critical analyses of *Profane Proses* in a booklet published in 1899—Rodó soon became disillusioned with the frivolous aspects of that poetry, and its lack of commitment to the cause of Latin America. In his *Ariel* (1900), he attempted to create a different image of its culture. He made use of Shakespearean symbolism in exhorting Latin American youth to reject imitation of the materialistic United States (Caliban, in his imagery) and to follow "Ariel," that is, to seek a spiritual harmony between ethics and aesthetics. In a sense, Rodó was continuing the task initiated by Bello in London in 1823. By the time Rodó's *Ariel* became popular all over Latin America and Spain, Darío himself was also tired of Verlaine's Versaillesque poetry and had assumed the persona of a truly Spanish American poet, writing to censure Teddy Roosevelt or to celebrate the new countries. A new Latin Americanism emerged from their common efforts. It was not the opposite of modernism but its ideological complement.

Because modernism produced such outstanding poetry, it has generally been forgotten that it produced some very important fiction as well. Martí and Darío had already effected a profound renovation in Spanish prose and written a number of stories in a completely new style. Following Darío's lead, Rodó achieved perfection in a kind of disguised fiction he called "parables," short didactic tales that were very popular in his lifetime. But it was among the naturalist writers that modernism would find its best storytellers. As part of the complex set of influences that were integrated into modernism, naturalism came into Latin American letters mainly through the work of the Goncourts, Maupassant, Zola, Chekhov, and Gorky. Their influence helped to purge Latin American literature of the lingering remnants of romantic heroism and sentimentality and directed writers' attention to the more sordid or lurid aspects of reality. Some of the best Spanish American naturalists came from the River Plate area. The Uruguayan Javier de Viana (selection 9) was one of the masters of the rural tale and a true follower of the school, although in his later work he showed the influence of less dogmatic models. Another master was Horacio Quiroga, who soon transcended the limitations of naturalism and, with his short stories set in the jungles of northern Argentina, founded a new school of narrative. The Argentine Ricardo Güiraldes (13) escaped from naturalism and used avant-garde techniques to express a radically new vision of gaucho life, a theme so amply exploited by both romantics and realists during the greater part of the nineteenth century (Part Two, 5–8). A concern for the life and destiny of the peasants, the exploited workers of plantations and mines, the isolated inhabitants of the pampas or the Andean countries, began to emerge in what was then called the "Novel of the Earth." It dealt with social injustice and political revolution but also with the fight against an implacable Nature. Some of the best writers came out of Mexico (Mariano Azuela and Martín Luis Guzmán, 10 and 14), Venezuela (Rómulo Gallegos and Arturo Uslar Pietri, 11 and Part Four, 4) and Colombia (José Eustasio Rivera, 12). They were very successful in both Latin America and Spain, and their work paved the way for the extraordinary explosion of narrative creativity in Latin American literature in the middle of the twentieth century.

If Brazilian literature did not produce any outstanding poet in the 1880s and 1890s—the equivalent to Spanish American modernism is the movement called Parnassianism—it did produce very important novelists. They continued and broadened the exploration of Brazilian reality begun earlier in the century by José de Alencar and Machado de Assís, Manuel Antônio de Almeida and Raúl Pompéia (Part Two, 12–15). Perhaps the best of the naturalists was Lima Barreto (Three, 15), a writer who has only quite recently been recognized as a major novelist. Very soon, younger writers were expanding the scope and depth of the Brazilian novel. Like their Spanish American counterparts, the "Novelists of the Earth," Graciliano Ramos, Lins do Rêgo, and Jorge Amado (16–18), refined the naturalistic tradition and re-created in their novels the tragic world of the Northeast: a world Euclides da Cunha had so dramatically portrayed in his masterpiece, *Rebellion in the Backlands,* published in 1902 (Two, 16). But their vision was radically different: instead of attributing the backwardness of the region to some native inferiority of the Brazilian "race" (as da Cunha did), they revealed the economic roots of the problem. Their novels were not only works of fiction but documentary studies of a feudal world, and they prepared readers for the complex works produced by João Guimarães Rosa (Four, 22) in the 1940s and 1950s, which brought the Brazilian novel to a level worthy of consideration by a demanding international audience.

1

JOSÉ MARTÍ

Martí has been called the last of the great Latin American writers who was also a great political figure. Like Bello and Sarmiento, Acevedo Díaz and Alencar (Part Two, 3, 5, 8 and 12), Martí devoted the best of his energies to political activities and wrote only in the intervals permitted him by his chief life's work: the liberation of his native country from Spanish rule.

In the second half of the nineteenth century, Cuba and Puerto Rico were the only parts of the New World that still belonged to the old and crumbling Empire. It was a state of affairs Martí could not endure. He was born in Havana in 1853, to Spanish parents of limited means, who lacked the resources to educate him adequately. He found a patron and guide in the poet Rafael María de Mendive, who sent him to the Institute of Havana. At fifteen, Martí founded, with Mendive's help, a political newspaper, *The Free Fatherland.* The Spanish authorities were not amused by the poetry he was then writing and put him in prison. After six months, and with his health permanently damaged, he was exiled to Spain. There he completed his education and got a law degree but had little chance to practice.

While in Spain he did not stop his political activities. In 1871 he published a pamphlet on *The Political Prisons in Cuba.* After the proclamation of the first Spanish Republic in 1873, he tried to interest the new authorities in the freedom of Cuba. He failed and decided to return to the island. He traveled via Paris (where he met the elderly Victor Hugo and visited the tomb of Abelard and Heloise), Mexico, and Guatemala, where he fell in love with a girl. In Cuba he was again sent to prison and subsequently had to take the path of exile. This time he chose New York. He was determined to devote himself completely to the cause of Cuban independence. He managed to survive by writing regularly for the big South American newspapers (mainly in Buenos Aires and Caracas), serving as a representative of various Latin American countries (Uruguay had the honor to have him as consul), and lecturing extensively. He soon became the chief organizer of the new revolution and persuaded Generals Maximo Gómez and Antonio Maceo to join him.

In the meantime, there flowed from his feverish pen the best prose in Spanish since Sarmiento's. He wrote on every subject that came before his eyes: on Grant's tomb and on old Walt Whitman, on the first French impressionist exhibition in New York, as well as on the treacherous murder of Jesse James. Chiefly, however, he wrote about "Our America," as he called Latin America in a memorable essay of 1891. At the same time, he was writing the most experimental poetry of the time in Spanish. Two collections were produced in those years: *Ismaelillo* (Little Ishmael, 1882), mainly devoted to his young son, whom he had hardly ever seen; and *Simple Lyrics,* his most important book, published in 1891.

But he was unable to continue to develop his poetic career. In 1892 he was proclaimed leader of the Cuban Revolutionary party. When the revolutionaries landed in Cuba in 1895, Martí was in the first rank. He might have stayed in New York, using his extraordinary talents as orator and fund-raiser to support the campaign. But he preferred to participate directly in the action. He was killed that same year in Dos Ríos.

Martí's death made him the martyr of Cuban independence and his country's national hero. Even today he is honored as precursor of the new socialist regime. In a sense, this view of him is correct. He was a firm anti-imperialist and once wrote about the United States: "I know the monster; I have lived in his entrails." Martí was fully aware of the importance of Marx's economic theories, and on the occasion of Marx's death, he attended an enthusiastic socialist rally. Still, it seems excessive to portray him as a Marxist. He died at a time when formal Marxist ideology was still largely unknown in Latin America.

As a writer, Martí actively participated in another, wider and more continental revolution—one that brought about a profound upheaval in Hispanic language and literature and freed them, once and for all, from the tutelage of the mother country. This was the literary movement known as modernism.

To this movement, Martí contributed his prose and verse. When he began writing, romanticism was still very much alive. He admired the French romantics and even imitated them, but he remained deeply rooted in Spanish literature. He read and reread the classics, especially Saint Teresa, Quevedo, and Gracián; he admired Spanish American writers, like the Puerto Rican Hostos or the Ecuadorian Montalvo, who belonged to the same tradition. Very soon he discovered in this tradition a line of simplicity, elegance, and subtle tension that suited him splendidly. He also admired some of the new writers France was producing as a reaction against romanticism: the Parnassians and early symbolists. Blending what he took from the classics with inspiration he drew from his nineteenth-century masters, Martí produced poetry that bears his own unique stamp: low-keyed and understated on its surface, popular and at the same time brilliant, very concise but capable of sudden baroquisms. He learned to move from the utmost simplicity of such lyrics as "I am a sincere man" (which was later incorporated into the revolutionary version of "Guantanamera") to the deceptive spareness of a composition like "The Girl from Guatemala." The latter poem was based on a real love affair he had had while visiting that country; but Martí so condensed and refined the story as to make it a tale of legend, one as popular and simple as the ballads that all Hispanic people have sung since the Middle Ages.

Simple Lyrics

From Versos sencillos, *especially translated by Donald Walsh.*

I

I am a sincere man
from where the palm tree grows;
and before I die I want
to loose my verses from my heart.

I come from everywhere,
and I go everywhere:
I am art among the arts;
in the hills, I am a hill.

I know the strange names
of the grasses and the flowers,
and of mortal deceits
and of sublime griefs.

I have seen in the dark night
rain over my head
the rays of pure fire
of divine beauty.

I saw wings born on the shoulders
of beautiful women,
and butterflies come flying
from the rubbish.

I have seen a man live
with a dagger in his side,

without ever saying the name
of the woman who killed him.

     Swift, like a flash,
twice I saw the soul, twice:
when the poor old man died,
when she bade me farewell.

     I trembled once—at the grille,
at the entrance to the vineyard—
when the barbarous bee
stung my girl on the forehead.

     I was happy once, in a way
that I've never since been happy: when
the sentence of my death
was read by the weeping warden.

     I hear a sigh across
the lands and the sea,
and it is not a sigh, it is
that my son is going to wake.

     If they say: from the jeweler,
take the best jewel,
I take a sincere friend
and put love aside.

     I have seen the wounded eagle
fly to the tranquil blue,
and the poisonous viper
die in its lair.

     I well know that when the world
yields, livid, to rest,
over the profound silence
the gentle brook murmurs.

     I have placed a daring hand,
stiff with horror and jubilation,
upon the extinguished star
that fell in front of my door.

     I hide in my wild breast
the sorrow that wounds it:

the son of an enslaved people
lives for it, is silent, and dies.

All is beautiful and constant,
all is music and reason,
and all, like the diamond,
before it is light is coal.

I know that the fool is buried
with great luxury and great weeping,
and that there is no fruit on earth
like that of the burial ground.

I am silent, and I understand, and I doff
the pomp of the rhymer;
I hang from a withered tree
my doctor's hood.

VII

For Aragon, in Spain,
I have in my heart
a place all Aragon,
frank, fierce, faithful, without cruelty.

If a fool wants to know
why I have such a place, I tell him
that there I had a good friend,
that there I loved a woman.

There, in the flowering plain,
plain of heroic defense,
to defend what they think
people gamble their lives.

And if a mayor besets him,
or a sullen king annoys him,
the peasant puts on his cloak
and goes with his gun to die.

I love the yellow earth
that the muddy Ebro bathes,
I love the bluish Pillar
of Lanuza and Padilla.

I honor him who with a blow
casts a tyrant to the ground;
I honor him if he is Cuban;
I honor him if he is Aragonese.

I love the dark courtyards
with embroidered staircases;
I love the silent naves
and the empty convents.

I love the flowering earth,
Musulman or Spanish,
where the scanty flower of my life
burst its corolla.

IX

I want, in the shadow of a wing,
to tell this flowery tale:
the girl from Guatemala,
the one who died of love.

The flowers were lilies
and the trimmings were mignonette
and jasmine: we buried her
in a casket of silk.

. . . She gave the forgetful one
a fragrant pillow;
he came back, came back married;
she died of love.

She was borne in triumph
by bishops and ambassadors;
behind went the people in shifts,
all laden with flowers.

. . . She, to see him again,
went out to the watchtower to look:
he came back with his wife:
she died of love.

Like candent bronze
at the farewell kiss
was her brow: the brow
that I have loved most in my life!

. . . She entered the river at dusk,
the doctor brought her out dead:
they say that she died of the cold:
I know that she died of love.

There, in the icy crypt,
they laid her on two benches:
I kissed her slender hand,
I kissed her white shoes.

Silent, at nightfall,
the gravedigger called me away:
nevermore have I seen
her who died of love!

XXIII

I want to leave the world
by the natural gate:
in a cart of green leaves
they are to take me to die.

Don't put me in the dark
to die like a traitor:
I am good, and like a good man
I shall die facing the Sun!

XXV

I think, when I rejoice
like a simple schoolboy,
of the yellow canary—
whose eye is so black!

I want, when I die,
without country, but without master,
to have on my gravestone a bouquet
of flowers—and a flag!

XXXIV

Sorrows! Who dares to say
that I have sorrows? Afterward,
after the thunderbolt, and the fire,
I'll have time to suffer.

I know of a deep regret
among the nameless sorrows:
the slavery of men
is the great sorrow of the world!

There are mountains, and one must climb
the high mountains; afterward
we shall see, my soul, who it is
that has put me upon you in death!

2

SALVADOR DÍAZ MIRÓN

Among the early modernist poets—those who, in the last quarter of
the nineteenth century, grew dissatisfied with the romantic style and outlook,
and began to seek out new modes of poetic expression—one of the most
original was undoubtedly the Mexican Salvador Díaz Mirón. He was born in
Veracruz, in 1853, the same year as Martí. He studied in his native town
and in neighboring Xalapa (the most romantic of Mexican cities) and began
writing poems very early. His father was an important politician, and he felt
compelled to follow him into public life. By 1884, Porfirio Díaz was already
consolidating his grip on the country (he would remain in power until over-
thrown by the bloody 1910 revolution), and Díaz Mirón believed it his duty
to oppose his dictatorial rule. For many years, the writing of his intense,
elaborate poems, his fierce speeches in Congress, inflamed articles, and lethal
duels alternated in the most spectacular way. The very embodiment of *machismo*, Díaz Mirón killed several men in duels, the last of which forced
him, in 1892, to cease all political activity.

He did not collect his poems in book form until 1901, when he published *Lascas* (Stone Chips). By this time, however, his poems were already
widely known, and Darío had praised him in a Parnassian sonnet that exalted the
perfection of his verse and the spirit of freedom that inspired it. A fastidious
writer, always aiming at perfection, Díaz Mirón was also well versed in the
Spanish classics and, like Martí, knew how to blend old and new.

In the two poems reproduced here, one may recognize an echo of
Baudelaire's "Une Charogne." Yet they have a kind of "hardness" which is
perhaps even more reminiscent of Quevedo's somber sonnets.

Very close to Díaz Mirón in style and outlook, but working independently, Manuel Gutiérrez Nájera helped to promote the modernist revolution

with his brilliantly satirical poems and a literary journal, *Revista Azul* (1894), which became the most important periodical of the movement. He was born in 1859 and died at thirty-six, before he had time to collect his verse. But he was read by Martí, and probably helped to bring him closer to the new movement. With Díaz Mirón, Gutiérrez shares the glory of having introduced the new gospel to Mexican letters.

Two Poems

From Anthology of Mexican Poetry, *compiled by Octavio Paz and translated by Samuel Beckett (Bloomington: Indiana University Press, 1958), pp. 120–21.*

The Corpse

Like the bole of a fallen mountain tree.
A clear, majestic, pure, and lofty brow.
Black brows together drawn in the fine
and arching line that images the flight

of a bird lightly sketched against the sky.
Nostrils like a falcon's beak. Pallor
of ivory hair. Already verdureless
the pine fell and lies, part ringed with hoar.

The eyeball, stretching the ill-sutured lids,
emits a dark and glassy gleam of grief,
sheen of well water over its numbed depths.

With my handkerchief I fright and scatter
flies; and on the dead face a vague shadow
hovers, as of a condor, or of flight.

The Example

The corpse rotted from its exhibiting noose
like a horrible fruit from the bough,
witness to an unbelievable sentence,
swaying pendulous above the road.

The obscene nakedness, the protruding tongue,
and a high tuft of hair like a cockscomb,

lent it a comic look; at my horse's feet
a group of rapscallions sported and guffawed.

And the dismal remains, with lolling head,
scandalous and swollen on the green gibbet,
spread their gust of stench upon the breeze,

swinging with a censer's measured gravity.
And the sun rose in the immaculate blue,
and the land was like a poem of Tibullus.

3

JULIÁN DEL CASAL

Less famous than his countryman José Martí (selection 1), Julián del Casal is probably the most modernist of all Cuban poets. He hated nature and longed for the most exquisite artifacts of French culture. He modeled his life and verse on the decadents and wrote a series of ten sonnets describing with ecstatic delight Gustave Moreau's perverse paintings, which he had seen only in photographs. He also conducted a correspondence in French with the painter and writer Joris Karl Huysmans, the notorious author of *À Rebours* (Against Nature).

Poor, melancholy, and sickly, del Casal found in art and poetry a refuge against the overwhelming brightness of his native island. He could not stand the sun, and used to close doors and windows tightly against the glare of reality. He was born in 1863. He studied at a Jesuit college and later entered law school, but left before getting any degree. The death of his father forced him to obtain a modest position at the Department of Finance. A friend who had just returned from fabulous Paris brought him a trunk loaded with French books. In 1888 he managed to scrape some money together and went to Europe, but never traveled farther than Spain; left penniless after a few weeks, he had to return to Cuba without having seen Paris.

His first poems had been romantic, but already in 1892 he published *Nieve* (Snow), in which he would not only evoke the cold, exotic landscapes of Europe but also would reflect the influence of Baudelaire, Gautier, Verlaine, and some of the Spanish American modernists. But his principal master was Giacomo Leopardi, the Italian romantic; like him, del Casal was extremely unhappy, timid, and haunted by corruption and death. He also would die young, at thirty, of that most romantic of all diseases, tuberculosis, leaving a new volume of poetry (*Busts and Rhymes,* 1893) to be published posthumously. He was very likely homosexual, and so forced, by a society that expected its poets to be vigorously heterosexual, to express his feelings secretively and through a subtle use of metaphor. In a poem dedicated to Ludwig II of Bavaria and entitled "Flowers of Ether," del Casal left some hints as to his proclivities.

His poetry anticipated a whole line of the modernist movement. In the Colombian José Asunción Silva (1865–1896) one would find a similar refined sensitivity, a similar attraction toward the forbidden—in this case, a dead sister to whom Silva dedicated one of his most beautiful *Nocturnes*—and a similar early death. (Silva committed suicide when he was barely thirty.) Later, in the Uruguayan Julio Herrera y Reissig (selection 6), the same sort of love as del Casal's for the exotic and decadent, for the inaccessible luxuries of corrupted Paris, would function as a source for poetry. But it is in del Casal that the contrast between the overwhelming brightness of the island and the fabricated night of the poet's verse finds the most vivid, and perverse, expression.

Tropical Countryside

From "Paisaje del trópico," especially translated by Donald Walsh.

Dust and flies. Leaden atmosphere
where rumbles the clatter of the thunder
and, like swans in filthy slime,
white clouds in an ashen sky.

The sea stills its green slings,
and the lightning, above its bosom,
in the horizon's cloudless confine
traces its swift ruddy flash.

The drowsy tree nods,
a deep calm hovers for a long instant,
swift seagulls split the air,

the lightning bolt flashes in space,
and on the back of the steaming earth
the rain falls in crackling drops.

4

RUBÉN DARÍO

In less than two decades, Darío became the undisputed master of the new literature. In his lifetime he was recognized as the greatest Hispanic poet since the death of Quevedo. Although at the time of his death in 1916 a reaction against his poetry, and against modernism in general, was already visible, Darío's work has continued to this day to exert a profound influence in Spanish American letters. Any poem written in Spanish can be dated before or after him, as one of his best critics proclaimed.

Born in Nicaragua in 1867, he began by creating his own poetic persona: out of his rather common name, Félix Rubén García Sarmiento, he carved the shorter and more effective one, Rubén Darío, which carried associations with Darius, ancient King of Persia. He was an early and avid reader, and very soon began writing romantic poems. A brief trip to Paris when he was twelve served to confirm his admiration for Victor Hugo. Back home at the National Library, he had the chance to acquaint himself with the Spanish classics. In neighboring El Salvador he met Francisco Gavidia and began to take an interest in the poetry of the French Parnassians. He was also to read the Spanish Americans who were already exploring the possibilities of a new poetry.

But the most decisive journey he took was one south. For two years he lived in Chile (Santiago, Valparaiso), and there he discovered a group of young poets who were intimately familiar with the new French school, the symbolists. He also read two North American authors the French had adopted: Poe and Whitman. Darío rose splendidly to the occasion and in 1888 he produced *Azul* ... (Blue, as in the sky and in heraldry). It was a slim volume of prose and poetry, in which the young writer blended in a unique and curious harmony all the influences he had absorbed. He was romantic and Parnassian, classical and symbolist. But already his extraordinary mastery of meters, his uncanny ear, and his highly refined sense of irony were evident. The book caught the attention not only of all the young poets in Spanish America but also of the keenest Spanish critics. While deploring the excessive French influence, and what they called his "mental Gallicism," they acknowledged the emergence of a great poet.

After Chile, Darío went to Buenos Aires, already the largest Latin American city. There he completed his poetical campaign. Two books published simultaneously in 1896 were to consolidate his fame. One is a collection of critical essays, *Los raros* (The Strange Ones), in which he introduced to Spanish American readers creatures as exotic (then) as Martí and Lautréamont, Edgar Allan Poe and Verlaine, Walt Whitman and de Villiers de l'Isle-Adam, Ibsen and Max Nordau. They were *his* authors, or, at least, the kind of authors he liked to write about: unknown geniuses, controversial writers, ultradecadent poets.

The other book was *Prosas profanas* (literally, Profane Proses), a book of verses whose title played with the medieval meaning of prose—a Church hymn. The preface was a modernist manifesto. In it, Darío argued for a "useless" kind of poetry, refined, exotic, precious; a poetry of evasion from the crude realities of Latin American life and society; a poetry of his own. He hated (or pretended to hate) the times he was living in, and longed for the Versailles of Louis XIV, for classical Greece or ancient America. He was an aristocrat, proud of his elegant hands. Graciously he left democracy to Whitman. It was a text written to create scandal. It was meant to be insolent, and it achieved its purpose to perfection. The poems were splendid. Re-creating in Spanish the subtleties of French Parnassianism and the music of Verlaine, Darío transformed a rather austere and hard language into the most flexible and allusive of poetical instruments. A refined, tantalizing eroticism permeated all its pages. The parody of sophistication and luxury was so successful that to this day literal-minded readers are unable to detect it. But parody it was. Darío knew perfectly well he was living in Buenos Aires and not in Versailles and that he was writing in Spanish and not in Greek. It was this knowledge that allowed him to avail himself of a double vision. His writing ought to be read as a sincere imitation of certain sophisticated models, and as a nonetheless sincere effort to criticize those models through parody. In *Profane Proses* Darío produced a kind of summation of the work and achievements of the early modernists.

His next volume of verses, *Songs of Life and Hope* (1905), was published in Madrid. By that time, Darío had also been acknowledged in Spain as the master of the new poetry. A very important study of his poetry by the young Uruguayan critic, José Enrique Rodó (Three, 8), had been incorporated as a preface to the second edition of *Profane Proses* (Paris, 1901). Darío was at the zenith of his career. The new book was his best. The dazzling and deliberately superficial poetry of his younger years was still there, but a darker tone was already audible. The poet was getting old and beginning to discover the horrors of decay and certain death. His eroticism had become more agonized: the embrace no longer was simply a promise of ecstasy; it was also an unwilling rehearsal of death. (The French call orgasm "the little death.") Darío was a man of enormous appetites, and at thirty-eight he felt already like an old man. Too many drinks, too many women, even an excess of drugs, had destroyed his immense vitality. But he could not accept his own decline. He kept writing songs of hope while being permanently eroded by life. He was also beginning to realize that Latin America needed its own poets and that he could not leave everything to the many imitators of Whitman who were already proliferating in South America.

Although he was living in Europe as a diplomatic representative of his country at the time Teddy Roosevelt ordered the invasion of Panama (1903), Darío wrote a song that was a very outspoken political denunciation of Roosevelt's "Big Stick" policy. The pressures of his diplomatic position later impelled him to recant, in the poem "Salutation to the Eagle." But it is the song "To Roosevelt" that counted.

In the last years of his life, Darío continued to add some very important volumes to his canon: *The Errant Song* (1907), *Autumnal Poem* (1910), *Song to Argentina* (1910). The poet was still functioning splendidly—more mellowed and autumnal perhaps, and oppressed by irrational fears, a darkness of spirit—but the man was collapsing.

On the eve of the First World War he settled in Paris to edit a magazine, *Mundial* (Universal), that would become the rallying point for the new Latin American culture. Although it published some of the best writers in the Hispanic world, the magazine also became a showcase for the outlook of the new capitalistic, and scarcely democratic, regimes of the New World. His last years were a nightmare of drunkenness and physical decay. He died in 1916, completely destroyed, not yet fifty.

To represent Darío's work at all adequately, it would be necessary to select at least thirty poems. The eight presented here suffice merely to show some of his aspects: the elegant Parnassian poet of "Leda" and "Symphony in Gray Major" (which echoed a famous poem by Gautier); the nostalgic poet of "Far Away and Long Ago"; the anguished thinker of "Doom" and "Eheu!"; the bitter ironist of "To Roosevelt." But these are only some of his masks. They hardly represent a man who was (and is) Latin America's greatest poet.

Eight Poems

From Selected Poems of Rubén Darío, *translated by Lysander Kemp* *(Austin: University of Texas Press, 1965), pp. 69–70 and 82–83; and* An Anthology of Spanish Poetry from Garcilaso to García Lorca, *edited by Angel Flores and translated by Denise Levertov, Kate Flores, and Anita Volland (New York: Doubleday, 1961), pp. 215–16 and 225–27.*

Symphony in Gray Major

The sea, great mercury mirror,
reflects the zinc sheet of sky;
stain of faraway birds
on pale burnished gray.

Opaque round window, the sun
at a sick pace totters to the zenith;
a sea wind stretches
in shade, pillowed on its black
trumpet.

Under the pier the waves
groan, twitching leaden bellies.

A sailor sits on a coil of rope,
smoking, remembering
distant landfalls, a misty country.

This sea dog is old. Fiery rays
of Brazilian sun have scorched his face;
vicious Chinese typhoons have seen him
tilting his gin bottle.

Foam infused with saltpeter and iodine
has long been familiar with his red nose,
his crisp curls and athlete's biceps,
his canvas cap and drill shirt.

In the tobacco smoke he sees
that far-off misty land for which,
one golden, hot afternoon,
his brig set out in full sail.

Tropical siesta. The old man sleeps.
The scale of gray major envelops him.
It's as if an enormous
soft charcoal had been rubbed
over where the horizon used to curve.

Tropical siesta. An old cigala
tries out her obsolete, hoarse guitar;
a grasshopper begins
a monotone on his one-stringed fiddle.

                    Translated by Denise Levertov

Far Away and Long Ago

Ox of my childhood, steaming
under the flaring gold of Nicaraguan sun
on the fruitful farm, full of tropical harmony;
Pigeon of the
wind-sonorous, bird-musical, wild-
bull-roaring, ax-echoing forest:
I salute you both, for you are my life.

Heavy ox, you evoke the gentle
dawn that called the cows in to be milked,
when my life was all white and rose,
and you, cooing mountain dove,

stand for all there was of divine Spring
in my remote springtime.

Translated by Denise Levertov

Doom

Happy the tree, that scarcely feels,
And happier the hard stone not to feel at all,
For there is no pain greater than the pain of being alive,
Nor burden as heavy as conscious existence.

To be, and to know nothing, and to have no certain path,
And the fear of having been and a dread future . . .
And the hideous sureness of being dead tomorrow,
And suffering for life and for the dark and for

That which we do not know of and barely suspect,
And the flesh tempting with its cool grapes,
And the tomb that waits with its funeral wreaths,
And to know not whither we go,
Neither whence we come! . . .

Translated by Kate Flores

Eheu!

Here, beside the Latin sea,
I speak the truth:
I feel in rock and oil and wine
my own antiquity.

Oh how old I am, my God,
oh, how very old I am! . . .
From whence comes my singing?
And I, where am I bound?

The understanding of myself
has already cost me
many a moment of meditation
and the how and the when . . .

And this Latin splendor,
of what use was it to me
at the entrance of the dark mine
of the I and the not I? . . .

Contented wanderer of the clouds
I feel I can interpret
the secrets of the wind,
of the earth and of the sea . . .

Some few vague secrets
of being and not being
and fragments of consciences
of now and yesterday.

As in the midst of a desert
I started to cry out;
and looked up at the sun like a dead man
and then burst into tears.

Translated by Anita Volland

To Roosevelt

The voice that would reach you, Hunter, must speak
in Biblical tones, or in the poetry of Walt Whitman.
You are primitive and modern, simple and complex;
you are one part George Washington and one part Nimrod.
    You are the United States,
future invader of our naïve America
with its Indian blood, an America
that still prays to Christ and still speaks Spanish.

You are a strong, proud model of your race;
you are cultured and able; you oppose Tolstoy.
You are an Alexander-Nebuchadnezzar,
breaking horses and murdering tigers.
(You are a Professor of Energy,
as the current lunatics say.)

You think that life is a fire,
that progress is an irruption,
that the future is wherever
your bullet strikes.
            No.

The United States is grand and powerful.
Whenever it trembles, a profound shudder
runs down the enormous backbone of the Andes.
If it shouts, the sound is like the roar of a lion.
And Hugo said to Grant: "The stars are yours."

(The dawning sun of the Argentine barely shines;
the star of Chile is rising . . .) A wealthy country,
joining the cult of Mammon to the cult of Hercules;
while Liberty, lighting the path
to easy conquest, raises her torch in New York.

But our own America, which has had poets
since the ancient times of Nezahualcóyotl;
which preserved the footprints of great Bacchus,
and learned the Panic alphabet once,
and consulted the stars; which also knew Atlantis
(whose name comes ringing down to us in Plato)
and has lived, since the earliest moments of its life,
in light, in fire, in fragrance, and in love—
the America of Moctezuma and Atahualpa,
the aromatic America of Columbus,
Catholic America, Spanish America,
the America where noble Cuauhtémoc said:
"I am not on a bed of roses"—our America,
trembling with hurricanes, trembling with Love:
O men with Saxon eyes and barbarous souls,
our America lives. And dreams. And loves.
And it is the daughter of the Sun. Be careful.
Long live Spanish America!
A thousand cubs of the Spanish lion are roaming free.
Roosevelt, you must become, by God's own will,
the deadly Rifleman and the dreadful Hunter
before you can clutch us in your iron claws.

And though you have everything, you are lacking one thing:
   God!

Translated by Lysander Kemp

Philosophy

Come, spider, greet the sun and be of good will.
Come, toad, give thanks to God that you exist.
The shaggy crabs, like roses, all have thorns,
and the mollusks, reminiscences of women.

Learn to be what you are, embodied enigmas,
and leave the responsibility to the Norms,
who pass it on in turn to the All-Powerful—
(Come, cricket, sing in the moonlight; bear, come dance.)

Translated by Lysander Kemp

Leda

The swan in shadow seems to be of snow;
his beak is translucent amber in the daybreak;
gently that first and fleeting glow of crimson
tinges his gleaming wings with rosy light.

And then, on the azure waters of the lake,
when dawn has lost its colors, then the swan,
his wings outspread, his neck a noble arc,
is turned to burnished silver by the sun.

The bird from Olympus, wounded by love, swells out
his silken plumage, and clasping her in his wings
he ravages Leda there in the singing water,
his beak seeking the flower of her lips.

She struggles, naked and lovely, and is vanquished,
and while her cries turn sighs and die away,
the screen of teeming foliage parts and the wild
green eyes of Pan stare out, wide with surprise.

Translated by Lysander Kemp

Pity for Him Who One Day . . .

Pity for him who one day looks upon
his inward sphinx and questions it. He is lost.
And pity for him who pleads to joy or sorrow.
There are two gods, who are Ignorance and Forgetfulness.

We crystallize, in words and thoughts, what the tree
would like to say and what it says to the wind,
and what the animal manifests with its instincts.
But the only difference lies in the way of speaking.

Translated by Lysander Kemp

5

LEOPOLDO LUGONES

One of the first Argentine poets to come under Darío's influence was Leopoldo Lugones. He met the master in 1896, the year Darío had published *Profane Proses.* From that moment on, Lugones would develop his poetry in the context of modernism to achieve a total mastery of expression in verse, and become the most important Latin American poet of his generation.

He was born in Córdoba in 1874 and received a traditional Catholic education, but very early he discovered socialism and decided to move to cosmopolitan Buenos Aires, where Italian and Catalan immigrants had already introduced a slight ferment of anarchism. He began by writing exalted romantic verses, more or less imitating Victor Hugo. In his first volume, *The Golden Mountains* (1897), Hugo was mixed with Darío, whom Lugones had met only the year before. In his next book, *The Twilights of the Garden* (1905), he was already a complete modernist. He had discovered Alfred Samain and was writing dazzlingly sensuous verse whose influence on the younger Uruguayan poet Julio Herrera y Reissig (selection 6) would become the subject of long controversy.

In 1909 he published his most important volume of verses: *Lunario sentimental* (literally, Sentimental Moon Calendar). Following Jules Laforgue's ironic verses, which would also influence T. S. Eliot, Lugones created a totally artificial poetry, in which irony and humor did not detract from the most dazzling metaphors. In a sense, that book ended his modernist phase and inaugurated a new poetry, which Borges and other Argentine writers would attempt to rediscover some twelve years later (Part Four, 1).

Lugones was always the most fastidious of craftsmen and could not stand fixed in a single poetic mood, even if it were of his own invention. In 1910 he published *Secular Odes,* to celebrate Argentina's first centenary of independence. Later he would move to a new type of poetry, more traditional and with the rural subjects he had known so well in his childhood. The best of that poetry can be found perhaps in the posthumous *Ballads of Dry River* (1938).

Lugones was as fastidious in his prose as in his poetry. He wrote several books of essays, the best of which are those dedicated to the exaltation of *Martín Fierro* (Two, 7) and to Domingo Faustino Sarmiento (Two, 5). But he also excelled in the elaborate narratives of *The Gaucho War* (1906) and the collection of fantastic short stories called *The Strange Forces* (1906), both of which anticipated the fiction of Borges (Four, 1).

In the last two decades of his life, Lugones made a decision that was to alter radically the Argentine intelligentsia's attitude toward him: he abjured his socialist past and came more and more to the defense of army intervention in the political life of his country. When the army finally took over in 1930, Lugones was one of the few writers to support the coup. He became isolated and was attacked by many who had been his followers. This isolation, together with the sad outcome of a love affair with a young woman, was probably the reason for his taking his life in 1938. It was a paradoxical ending for a man who for at least thirty years had completely dominated Argentina's literary scene. The poem included here belongs to a volume called *The Faithful Book* (1912), in which the yet faithful Lugones sang his love for his wife. It shows his mastery and the uncanny flair for imagery and metaphor that several generations of poets would learn to envy.

White Solitude

From "La blanca soledad," especially translated by Donald Walsh.

Beneath the calm of sleep,
lunar calm of luminous silk,
night,
as if she were
the white body of silence,
lies down gently in the immensity.
And she lets
her hair down
in a prodigious foliage
of poplar groves.

Nothing lives but the eye
of the clock in the dark tower,
uselessly deepening the infinite
like an open hole in the sand.
The infinite,
rolled by the wheels
of the clocks,
like a cart that never arrives.

The moon digs a white abyss
of quietude, in whose hollow
things are corpses
and shadows live like ideas.
And one is amazed at how close
death is in that whiteness.
At how beautiful the world is

possessed by the antiquity of the full moon.
And the sad, sad yearning to be loved
trembles in the grieving heart.

There is a city in the air,
an almost invisible, suspended city
whose vague profiles
outline upon the clear night,
like watermarks upon a sheet of paper,
their many-sided crystallization.
A city so distant
that it gives anguish by its absurd presence.

Is it a city or a ship
in which we might gradually abandon the earth,
silent and happy,
and with such purity
that only our souls
would live in the full-moon whiteness? . . .

And suddenly a vague trembling
crosses through the serene light.
The lines vanish,
the immensity changes into white stone,
and all that remains in the fateful night
is the certainty of your absence.

6

JULIO HERRERA Y REISSIG

While Lugones's work covered a span of at least thirty years, the best
of the poetry produced by his contemporary, Herrera y Reissig, covered less than
ten. But his was some of the strangest and most original poetry of the whole
modernist movement. Herrera y Reissig was born in Montevideo in 1875, to one
of the principal Uruguayan families. One of his uncles, Julio Herrera y Obes, was
to become president in 1890; he was a ladies' man and left to posterity the legend
of his dandyism. (It has been said that the poet was his son.)

But if the family was illustrious, it was not wealthy. Julio (as he was always called) was partially brought up in the outskirts of Montevideo, in a small country place he was later to recall in very elaborate sonnets. At five he had the first of his attacks of rheumatic fever. Pampered from then on, he was to lead the life of a partial invalid, a dreamer, and a poet. His first verses were romantic, and the only book he published in his lifetime (actually a brochure) was a *Song to Lamartine,* in 1898. But very soon he would meet Roberto de las Carreras, a young poet two years his senior, who had recently returned from Paris. Julio immediately confiscated some of the books he brought with him, especially those of Alfred Samain.

In 1900, Julio suffered a serious heart attack and discovered he had tachycardia, a disease quite erratic and dramatic in its manifestations. His heart would beat very fast and, occasionally, even stop. To alleviate the pain and suspense, Julio began to take morphine. He probably never became an addict, but this practice became associated with him in the popular mind. By that time, the family had moved to a house in the old part of town, above one of the city's most notorious brothels. The house had a tower facing the River Plate, with an observation post for watching the boats that were coming to port. Julio took possession of the tower and immediately baptized it the Tower of Panoramas. Here he gathered his friends to drink and play the guitar in the intervals between very solemn poetry readings.

One day, Julio had the chance to listen to some very primitive recordings of Lugones's *The Twilights of the Garden* (see selection 5); before these poems were published in 1905, he had his own poems (entitled *The Abandoned Parks*) printed in some Uruguayan magazine. Some years later, a Venezuelan writer would accuse Lugones of plagiarizing Herrera y Reissig on the assumption that the latter poems had been written earlier. But Horacio Quiroga, who knew about the recordings, finally cleared the air with his testimony. The books Julio got from de las Carreras and Lugones's poems put him on the right track. With an urgency that probably was motivated by his unsteady heart, Julio moved at the turn of the century from the backwaters of romanticism to the forefront of modernism. In six years of frantic writing (1903–1909) he produced a completely new and unexpected poetry. Where Lugones had been erotic and sensual, Julio was perverse; where Lugones had been ironic and playful, Julio was grotesque. Everything the other did he did to excess, as if parody were his aim. In carrying Lugones's gift for metaphors to the extreme, Julio created some of the most extraordinary verse in the Spanish language. In the end, his poetry, especially the long poem called *The Tower of Sphinxes,* became so hermetic that to this day critics are trying to recapture the lost cipher, if any.

Although he married in 1907 and lived a quiet bourgeois life, he did not cease his poetic quest. The heart condition and the drugs probably heightened his perceptions. He also began to dabble in the occult, a subject that had similarly attracted Hugo and Darío. And he continued writing in spite of his bad heart. In the last years of his life he turned to the pastoral and evoked in a series of sonnets, *The Ecstasies of the Mountain,* the beautiful landscape of northern Spain he had never known. (There are no mountains in Uruguay, and besides,

Julio had traveled only as far as Buenos Aires.) But to that artificial genre he added his own knowledge of pastoral Uruguay. He was working on the proofs of his collected poems when he died of a heart attack in 1910. The book was published posthumously the same year with the title he had chosen: *The Pilgrims of Stone.*

If Julio was hardly known outside Uruguay during his lifetime, after his death he became very famous. His book had a second edition in Paris in 1913, and the young Latin American poets began to discover in his extraordinary poetry a way out of the modernist movement. In 1925 he was celebrated by the avant-gardists as the only Hispanic poet to be placed next to the futurists, the Dadaists, the cubists, and the expressionists they were reading so avidly.

The poems presented here show the quality of parody characteristic of his best poetry. Appearing rather late at the modernist banquet, he was still using the trappings of the grand style (mythological figures, bookish references to the past, eroticism, and luxury), but already he was underlining its exhaustion. It is a poetry that mocks its own values, to create a flamboyant display, almost a dress rehearsal of what many years later would be called camp.

Two Poems

From "Nirvana crepuscular" and "Fiesta popular de ultratumba," especially translated by Donald Walsh.

Twilight Nirvana

With her serpentine-colored garment
voluble Spring was laughing . . .
A trillion glow-worms of fine
emerald streaked the meadow.

Beneath a fleeting muslin air
all was idealized, as if it were
the vague panorama, the divine
materialization of a chimera . . .

In consubstantiation with that lovely
gray Nirvana of nature
you became inanimate . . . An unreal languor

flattered your face of provocative down,
and to the sound of my sighs your head
went to sleep like a bird upon my neck . . .

The People's Graveyard Festival

A great salon. A throne. Curtains. Grandstands.
(Adonis laughs with Eros over something that he has seen in
    Aspasia.)
The lunettes of the mirrors reveal their pallid days,
and on the ceiling and the carpet there are a thousand panoramas
    of Asia.

The lamps burn in yellow lecheries,
and the stoves flame into puberties of fire.
(Enter satyrs, gorgons, maenads, nymphs, and furies,
while the old Greek patriarch recites some verses.)

Some pages at the door wear golden uniforms;
ladies adorned with white veils cross the room.
(They announce: here are Goliath and a double-shaped lady
who is half fish, half Bluebeard and his two stilts.)

A good Terminus laughs at an ephebus who is bathing.
Everyone suddenly trembles. (Enter wiry Hercules.)
Petronius cries, "Salernum," Louis XI cries, "Champagne!"
A Pierrot cries, "Menelaus with horns and a shield!"

Everyone laughs; the only solemn ones are Juno and Mahomet,
Great Caesar and Pompey, Belisarius and other nobles
who were not very happy in love. Double dirges
are heard: it is Parca who appears . . .

Everyone trembles; the oldest pray, hide, mutter.
Sappho kisses her hand. Suddenly a great noise is heard,
it is Venus arriving; all undress, tremble, swear,
throw themselves to the ground, and there is heard only the
    immense roar

of a starving wild beast: the men rush forward to the goddess.
(By now no one is calm, all have lost their reason.)
They all kiss her, bite her, with frightful fury,
and Adonis weeps with rage . . . Amid that disorder

Pope Borgia is praying (while he pinches a girl);
just one bard protests: Lamartine, with angry voice;
to restore order, Marat was summoned. The quarrel
lasted a minute, and the scene came to nothing.

Enter Mercury with his wings on his heels; the messenger
encountered a deep silence. The great Voltaire winked,
as if to say, "How many pedants there are in the world
who think with their heels!" John looked at him askance,
and a journalist who was present became serious and very red.

Enter Aladdin and his lamp. Enter Cleopatra and Philip of
    Macedon.
Enter the Queen of Sheba. Enter Solomon and Croesus.
(With his eyes popping a rich bourgeois rushed forward,
a banker became speechless, and another became very stiff.)

"Mademoiselle Pompadour," announces a page. A thousand
    notes
suddenly vibrate; the men appear with wigs.
(A bald man applauds, and a decrepit old woman leaps with joy.)
The dancing begins: pavans, rounds, minuets, and gavottes.

Nimrod and Samson dance, Antaeus, Chiron, and Eurytus,
Juliet, Eloise, Saint Teresa, and Eulalia dance,
and the centaurs Caumantes, Grineo, Medon, and Clito.
(Not Hercules; jealous Omphale has forbidden him to dance.)

Enter Bacchus suddenly; everyone shouts "Wine! Wine!
(Burgundy, Italy and Oporto, Jerez, Cyprus, Cognac, Rum,
Gin, and even Brandy.) Long live the divine vine shoot,
long live Noah and Edgar Allan Poe, Byron, Verlaine, and
    Champagne!"

This said, they rush upon a cask. An obese friar
fell, his fall due no doubt (more than to the wine) to his own
    weight.
As they felt warm, Apuleius and Anacreon
bathed in a bucket. Enter Charon suddenly.

(All hasten to hide.) Of course there was some Spanish
moralist (one may presume) who called them drunkards;
the scandal took on an unheard-of magnitude,
until Satan arrived and, shouting frightfully,
said that he would gladly eat them all.

There were several incidents. Enter Attila and the floor sinks.
Aeolius puts out some candles. Danton speaks: a thunderclap is
    heard.
In the glass in which Galen
and Aesculapius drank, no one wished to drink.

A twenty-year-old stoic, afflicted by asthma,
was far away from everyone. "Give him this syrup at once,"
said Hippocrates, very serious. Byron muttered gravely,
"Apply to him a woman as a poultice."

A noisy laugh rang out in the hall. A gallant
dandy dressed in red shook hands with the poet
who had had such a bright idea (Great Byron, who was lame
as well as spoiled, did not abandon his stool
and gave Mephisto a most discreet bow.)

At this point there were discussions about which of the suicides
was most worthy of glory. Juliet said, "I have been
a queen of love; I would have given a thousand lives
to be joined with my Romeo." Werther said, "I did my duty,"
with a sublime gesture of personal arrogance.
Sappho and Petronius spoke, and even Judas the hanged one;
at last spoke up the cook of the famous King of France,
the brave Vatel: "I"—he said—"valorously killed myself
for more important things, because I couldn't find a fish!"

Everyone burst out laughing. (A page shouts, "Morpheus is
     here!")
All are silent, suddenly . . . all fall asleep.
Deep snores are heard.
(A madman named Delirium enters crouching.)

7

DELMIRA AGUSTINI

Women poets have existed since the origins of Latin American literature—the greatest Colonial poet was Sor Juana Inés de la Cruz (Part One, 11,
v)—but it was not until the advent of modernism that a distinctive feminine
poetry was created. Among the best writers of this particular group some were
born in the southern part of the Western Hemisphere: María Eugenia Vaz
Ferreira, Delmira Agustini, and Juana de Ibarbourou in Uruguay; Alfonsina
Storni in Argentina; Gabriela Mistral in Chile. The first two were modernists;
the others marked the transition toward a simpler, more direct, less elaborate

DELMIRA AGUSTINI

poetry. Juana de Ibarbourou and Gabriela Mistral were the only ones to achieve a really continental reputation, and Mistral (Three, 19, iv) was the first Latin American author to be awarded the Nobel Prize, in 1945.

But it was perhaps Delmira Agustini who better represented a certain concept of feminine poetry: a poetry of passion and sensuality, a poetry written to challenge social conventions and to exalt eroticism unabashedly. Born in the outskirts of Montevideo in 1887, Delmira (as she was always called even by the most conventional critics) was educated at home. A domineering, even tyrannical mother ruled her life to the last detail. She received the conventional education of girls of her bourgeois station in life: French, painting, piano lessons. Always under her mother's careful supervision, she developed a taste for poetry and began very early to compose poems that used the conventional poetic code to express her dreams of sensuality. When they began to be published, they astonished the critics. They could not understand how such a young and chaste girl knew so much. They were naturally wrong. She was not as young as she pretended (at the time it was normal to subtract a couple of years from any girl's age, especially if her mother wanted to appear young), and besides she did not know that much. Her eroticism was, like Leonardo's concept of painting, *una cosa mentale.* She borrowed her experience from poetry, not from real life. But she had one merit: to dare to write about such things in the Montevideo of the 1900s.

Roberto de las Carreras, who had helped Herrera y Reissig to discover the new French poets, helped her also. Years later, she would meet Darío briefly in 1912. He was fascinated by her beauty (she was fair and had the pink fleshiness men adored in those days) and liked her poetry very much. To promote her, he wrote a short prologue to one of her books, *The Empty Chalices* (1913), in which he declared that not since Saint Teresa had Hispanic literature produced verse of such intensity as Delmira's.

In that same year, real life intruded into her secluded princess's boudoir, when she married her fiancé, Enrique Job Reyes. The honeymoon was short. After a few days, she returned home, claiming, "I can't stand so much vulgarity." The prosaic character of everyday life was too much for her. She decided to start divorce proceedings but continued to see Enrique. In 1914, in one of their clandestine meetings in a cheap room, Enrique killed her and committed suicide. It was a gruesome end for the beautiful and sensual Delmira, and one that was amply exploited by the popular press of the day. No explanation, however, was given for the tragedy. Only quite recently it has been discovered that before her marriage she was in love with a notorious Don Juan, the Argentine writer Manuel Ugarte. But he had been in no hurry to initiate her and had preferred to wait until somebody else carried out this boring task. Did Enrique find out about Ugarte and decide to kill Delmira because he knew he would never truly possess her? Did she consent because she finally realized that erotic dreams had little to do with real sex? We shall never know. What we know is that all the eroticism she was capable of was (and is) in her poetry. There, like volcanic lava petrified forever, one would find a poetic imagination that dwelt in emptiness and fire, in thirst and anguish, in unrequited metaphorical passion.

My Loves

From "Mis amores," especially translated by Donald Walsh.

Today they have come back.
Along all the paths of night they have come
to weep at my bedside.
There were, there are so many of them!
I do not know which of them still live, which of them has died.
I shall mourn myself to mourn them all:
night drinks the tears like a black shawl.

There are heads made golden in the sun, as if ripened. . . .
There are heads touched by shadow and mystery,
heads crowned with an invisible thorn,
heads that the rose of illusion turns pink,
heads that bow to fathomless cushions,
heads that would like to rest in heaven,
some that do not get to smell of spring,
and many that have a fragrance of winter flowers.

All those heads grieve me like wounds. . . .
They grieve me like the dead. . . .
Ah! . . . and the eyes . . . the eyes grieve me most: they are
    double! . . .
Indefinite, green, gray, blue, black,
they burn if they shine;
they are caress, grief, constellation, Hell.
Upon all their light, upon all their flames,
my soul was illumined and my body tempered.
They gave me thirst from all those mouths. . . .
From all those mouths that flower my bed:
vessels red or pale with honey or bitterness,
with lilies of harmony or roses of silence
from all these vessels where I drank life,
from all these vessels where I drink death. . . .
The poisonous, intoxicating garden of their mouths
where it breathed their souls and their bodies
moistened with tears
has encircled my bed. . . .

And the hands, the hands heaped with secret
destinies and jeweled with rings of mystery . . .
There are hands that were born with caressing gloves,
hands that are heaped with the flower of desire,
hands in which one feels a never-seen dagger,
hands in which one sees an intangible scepter;
pale hands or dark, voluptuous or strong,
to all, all of them I managed to link a dream.

　　　With sadness of souls,
　　the bodies bow,
　　without veils, blessedly
　　dressed in desire.

　　Magnets of my arms, honeycombs of my heart,
as if at an unseen abyss they bow at my bed. . . .

　　Ah, among all the hands I have sought your hands!
Your mouth among the mouths, your body among the bodies,
of all the heads I want your head,
of all those eyes, I want only your eyes,
You are the saddest because you are the most beloved,
you arrived first because you came from farthest away . . .

　　Ah, the dark head that I have never touched
and the bright eyes that I gazed at so long!
The eye shadows that we deepened unconsciously the evening and
　　I,
the strange pallor that I doubled without knowing it,
　　　　come to me: mind to mind;
　　　　come to me: body to body.

　　You will tell me what you have made of my first sigh,
you will tell me what you have made of that kiss's dream. . . .
You will tell me if you wept when I left you alone. . . .
　　　　And you will tell me if you have died! . . .

　　If you have died,
my grief will slowly dress the room in mourning
and I shall clasp your shadow until my body dies away.
And in the sunken silence of the darkness,
and in the sunken darkness of the silence,
he will watch over us, weeping, dying,
our son: remembrance.

8

JOSÉ ENRIQUE RODÓ

In his lifetime, the Uruguayan essayist José Enrique Rodó was as famous as Darío (selection 4). He was then considered the best modernist writer in prose. His most popular book, *Ariel* (1900), made him the leader of the Latin American intelligentsia. Since his death in 1917, his reputation has suffered from endemic attacks. A radical shift in outlook brought about by World War I saw his elegant idealism, his aristocratic concept of democracy, his Parnassian style becoming more and more obsolete. New essayists, like the Peruvian Marxist Juan Carlos Mariátegui, or the Argentine sociopsychoanalyst Ezequiel Martínez Estrada, introduced new perspectives that made Rodó seem irrelevant. He had been the master of a doomed world, what the French called "La Belle Époque," and had very little to say to the new Latin American societies. But a purely political or sociological reading of Rodó misses the point of why his name and work meant so much at the time.

He was born in Montevideo in 1871, the last child of a Catalan father and an Uruguayan mother. When he was four, one of his eldest sisters taught him to read. He learned to revere the Spanish classics and the anti-Rosist writers (see Part Two, 4, 5, 6) his father had met when young. He never got a degree. He was a timid young man who preferred the silence of libraries to the noise of classrooms. All he learned, and he learned much, was in his father's library or in the library of the Atheneum.

He began to write and publish while he was still in school. In 1895 he founded with some friends of the same literary persuasion a magazine, solemnly called *The National Review of Literature and Social Sciences*. To it he contributed solid essays on Spanish American and Spanish letters, and a few more lyrical pieces. By the time the magazine ceased publication in 1897, he was a completely professional critic, the best in the River Plate area, and one of the best in the language. His second book, *Rubén Darío* (1899), confirmed his elevated status. Darío not only thanked him but used the essay as a preface to the second edition of his most famous book, *Profane Proses* (Paris, 1901).

It was, however, Rodó's third book, *Ariel*, that would achieve long-lasting fame. It assumed the guise of a long address by a teacher to his students on the last day of class. The students call him Prospero because of a statue of Ariel flying he has in his study. The gist of the new Prospero's advice can be summarized as follows: develop all your potentialities as men, do not let an early specialization constrict you; avoid a divorce between ethics and aesthetics—the good is better if beautiful; be always on the side of democracy, but preserve the aristocratic qualities of the mind; admire the greatness of the United States, but do not imitate its materialism. Published in 1900, the essay was written and read in the context of the Spanish-American War of 1898. It was a defense of Hispanic spiritualism (symbolized by Ariel) against United States materialistic power (Caliban). It became immediately popular: several pirate editions were printed in Spain and Spanish America. Rodó did not mind; he basked in the book's success.

Although the book attacked the United States, Rodó's stance was less political than the one taken by Martí and other modernists (see selections 1 and 4). He was more concerned with preventing blind imitation of the big northern neighbor, what he called "Nordomania," than with actual U.S. intervention in Latin American affairs. Years later, his views changed: after the invasion of Mexico and other, similar examples of the Big Stick policy, he denounced North American imperialism very strongly. At the time he wrote *Ariel*, however, he sought to keep the discussion at a more theoretical level.

The book was, in his mind, really a rehearsal of his next work, *The Motives of Proteus* (1909), in which he used the symbol of the elusive Greek god to analyze, in beautiful, almost poetic prose, the transformations of the personality by the forces of vocation, memory, and will. But while he created for his readers a world of idealism and beauty, he himself was a sad, isolated man. He had few friends, never received anybody in the somber old house he shared with his brothers and sisters (all single like him), and steadily drank himself to death.

In his public life, he was a professional optimist and a dedicated politician. Uruguay in those days was emerging very slowly from a long nightmare of revolutions and civil wars. As a member of the Chamber of Deputies (1902–1905, 1908–1914) and a political journalist, Rodó maintained until the last year of his life a strongly militant stance. Because he had opposed the government on some occasions, he was denied the recognition that was given to minor writers. But he was not dismayed and continued to participate in public life.

He longed for the pleasures of meditation, of reading and writing about permanent things; occasionally he could indulge in these pleasures. But it was not until 1916 that he managed to realize one of the dreams of his life: to visit Europe. He was sent as a literary correspondent of the Argentine magazine *Faces and Masks*. Very slowly he made his way through the South of France and Italy. But he was never to see Paris. He died in Palermo, in the same hotel where Wagner had written his *Parsifal*, completely alone and unattended.

Only a fraction of his rather voluminous life's work is devoted to pure criticism, to narrative and creative writing. But it is probably in these domains that his writings will be always relevant. If he failed to create in his *Ariel* a blueprint for the Latin America of the future, if, in his *Proteus*, he fell short of the kind of in-depth analysis Freud was already practicing, Rodó had achieved a different kind of creation. He had produced a prose that is still the most perfect of the modernist period; he had continued to develop the discussion of Latin American culture at the level set in the early nineteenth century by writers like Bello and Sarmiento (Two, 3, 5) and which would be continued later by essayists like Pedro Henríquez Ureña, Alfonso Reyes (Three, 19, v), and Jorge Luis Borges (Four, 1). From that point of view, Rodó is still relevant, one of the masters of Latin American literature.

The text presented here belongs to his most ambitious book, *The*

Motives of Proteus; it is a parable, written to illustrate the power of the will. But it is not the ethical value of the story that interests us today. It is the perfection of a narrative prose that aimed at sculptural beauty to create the illusion of reality.

The Granite Plain

From The Motives of Proteus, *translated by Angel Flores (London: George Allen & Unwin, 1929), pp. 351–53.*

It was a boundless, granite plain; its color, gray; not a wrinkle on its surface, sad and deserted, sad and cold, under an indifferent sky, under a sky of lead. And there was on the plain a gigantic old man, wrinkled, livid, beardless; there was a gigantic old man standing, straight as a bare tree. And the eyes of this man were cold like the plain and the sky, and his nose was sharp and hard like a sickle, and his muscles were rigid like that granite ground, and his lips no thicker than the blade of a sword. And near the old man there were three children, all stiff with cold, weak, wretched; three poor children, trembling before the haughty, indifferent old man.

The old man had a small seed in the palm of one hand. The extended forefinger of his other hand seemed to press against the emptiness of the air as against a thing of bronze. He grasped one of the children by his feeble neck and showed him the seed in the palm of his hand, and with a voice like the chilling whistle of a gale he said, "Dig a hole for this seed." And then he released the boy's trembling body, that sounded like a bag filled with pebbles as it fell upon the granite plain.

"Father," he sobbed, "how can I dig a hole in this hard, rocky land?"

"Gnaw one," he answered with a voice like the chilling whistle of a gale; and he raised one foot and placed it upon the boy's weak neck; and the teeth of the poor child scraping the rock sounded like a knife on a grindstone. Thus a long, long time passed; so long, in fact, that the boy had opened a hole in the rock as large as the hollow of a skull; but he kept on gnawing, gnawing always with a groan of agony; the poor boy gnawed under the foot of the old man as indifferent and immutable as the granite plain.

When the hole was large enough, the old man lifted his crushing foot; and if someone had been there he might have seen a still more pitiful sight: although the boy had white hair he was still a child. And the old man kicked him aside and lifted up the second boy, who had been watching and trembling all the time.

"Gather some soil for the seed," he said.

"Father," asked the unfortunate boy, "where is there any soil?"

"There is some in the wind," he answered, "gather it"; and with his thumb and forefinger he opened the wretched jaws of the child and made him face the wind. The floating dust of the air gathered on his panting tongue and jaws, and then the child vomited the dust in the form of slime; and a long, long time passed, and the indifferent, immutable old man on the granite plain showed neither impatience, nor eagerness, nor mercy.

When the cavity of rock was filled to the brim, the old man threw the seed into it and flung the boy aside like a piece of dry rind, and he did not see that grief had turned the young head white. Then he picked up the last small boy and, pointing to the buried seed, he said, "You must water that seed."

"Father, where is there any water?" asked the boy, trembling with anguish.

"Weep. There is water in your eyes," he answered; and he twisted the boy's weak hands and a flood of tears started from his eyes; the thirsty dust drank the tears. And this weeping lasted a long, long time, because the indifferent, immutable old man, standing on the granite plain, kept drawing tears from the weary eyes.

The tears kept dropping into the hole in the earth in a plaintive stream, and the seed appeared above the surface of the earth like a point. Then it sent out its first sprout, its first leaflets, and while the boy kept weeping, the new tree grew branches and leaves, and a long, long time passed until the tree had a strong trunk, a luxuriant foliage, leaves and flowers that perfumed the air. It rose high in the solitude, even higher than the indifferent, immutable old man on the granite plain.

The wind made the leaves of the tree rustle, the birds of the sky came to nest in the treetops, and its flowers matured into fruits, and then the old man freed the boy, who stopped weeping, but the child's hair was all white. The three children stretched out their greedy hands for the fruit of the tree; but the emaciated giant took them by the neck, like cubs, drew out another seed, and walked to a nearby rock. Raising his foot, he pressed the teeth of the first boy to the ground; and again the teeth gnawed the ground and grated under the foot of the old man, indifferent and immutable, erect, immense, and silent on the granite plain.

9

JAVIER DE VIANA

One of the most popular naturalists in Spanish American literature was the Uruguayan Javier de Viana. He introduced the techniques and attitudes of this school into the traditionally romantic domain of gauchesco literature. His gauchos were no longer the noble creatures Hernández or Acevedo Díaz had presented (see Part Two, 7, 8). Viana saw them as a degenerate race, not only obsolete but completely doomed, paralyzed by the forces of incest, superstition, and venereal disease. Zola's lumpen in *L'Assommoir* were Viana's model. To it he added some touches of Sacher-Masoch's perversions. Viana was born in 1868, in the outskirts of Montevideo, to a family that counted among its ancestors the forefathers of Uruguay. He spent his childhood on a ranch and got used to seeing rural life as the best possible type of existence. He learned the gaucho language and collected a treasure of stories and tales, which would become the basis of his narrative. He got his B.A. degree in Montevideo in 1887, one year exactly after his participation in one of the perennial revolutions organized against the government by the Blanco, or White, party. After graduation, he began to study medicine but quit in 1891 to devote himself to journalism and cattle raising.

In 1904 he again joined the revolutionary forces in a desperate, almost successful attempt to take power. After the defeat, he emigrated to Buenos Aires, where he would remain until 1918. He was already the author of two books of short stories (*Countryside*, 1896; *Gurí and Other Tales*, 1901) and a novel (*Gaucha*, 1899). But it was in the Argentine capital that he would become a professional man of letters, both as playwright and short-story writer. He was extremely successful in the latter capacity and published in the best magazines and literary sections of newspapers an endless stream of tales, some of which he would later collect in three volumes.

After his final return to Uruguay in 1918, he divided his attention between politics and journalism. He continued to write stories, with a facility that was dangerous for his reputation, and published eleven more volumes. He died in 1926. One more volume of stories was collected posthumously in 1934. All in all, seventeen volumes were published, and they do not exhaust his production in this genre. He wrote too fast, once boasting that he had completed four stories in one hour. Perhaps so. But such a rapid and massive output necessarily impaired the quality of his writing.

There are three clear stages in his work. The first contains his most ambitious, longer works, the ones published before 1904. The second represents a period of transition, in which Viana still aims at writing complex stories but is overwhelmed by the demands of the periodical press. In the last (the eleven-odd volumes after 1918) he writes with less care, more mechanically, although there are still some traces of his mastery left.

The excerpt presented here belongs to one of his longest stories, "Gurí." It tells the story of a young man who believes himself to be the victim of a spell. As a consequence he becomes impotent and is eventually destroyed by his fears. It is a somber, perverse tale, which Viana presents with meticulous detail. A few of the words he uses need some explanation because of the implicit symbolism. The nickname of the protagonist means "Boy," and it alludes to his naïveté in sexual matters; the "ombú" under which he discovers his impotence is a big tree that casts a wide, refreshing shadow but whose wood is useless for building a fire. The determinism of Gurí's fate was already embodied in his name and in the place where he met his destiny.

Gurí

From The Golden Land, *translated by Harriet de Onís, pp. 163–78.*

Six weeks went by, and Juan Francisco, Gurí, back on his own stamping grounds, completely taken up with the training of the race horse a rich rancher of Rincón de Ramírez had entrusted to his skill, dismissed from his mind all thought of Clara and the spells she might be trying to put on him. There in his familiar surroundings, leading an active life, his fears gradually faded away until they were no more than the memory of a bad nightmare.

His every thought was concentrated on the roan, a crossbreed of great promise that was to be matched against another crossbreed, a bay that belonged to a horse fancier of Yaguarón. The news of the race had spread far and wide, and excitement was running high. It was the topic of conversation around the fireplace in the ranch kitchens and at the roadside taverns. To the high stakes and the reputation of the two horses there was added the circumstance that one was from Uruguay and the other from Brazil, which gave the race something of an international character and piqued the pride of the spectators. And to further heighten interest, the two most skillful and best-known trainers were meeting too—Gurí, who was handling Núñez's roan, and the Indian Luis Pedro, who was handling Silveira Pintos's bay. Naturally neither of them spared any effort to have his horse in the best possible shape, spurred on by a rivalry of long standing, the desire to win, and the recompense that awaited the winner.

All these circumstances restored calm to Juan Francisco's spirit; and this calm in itself became his most effective cure, for it was clear that if a spell had been put on him, he would have felt the effects by this time. Having rid himself of his gloomy thoughts, he could take satisfaction in the fact that he had broken off his relations with Clara for good, a thought that raised him in his own estimation. Sometimes as he exercised the roan early in the morning, the oxygen-laden air from the hills produced in him a kind of gentle intoxication, an overflowing vitality, a great joy at being alive. When he remembered the terror he had felt at that hoot of an owl, which echoed for a moment and then was lost in space, he smiled, feeling that it had been a silly, childish thing to be so frightened by such a feeble portent. He still believed in ghosts, souls in torment, charms, spells, all manifestations of supernatural powers, divine and infernal; but he felt no fear, looking upon them as a remote danger, as one fears the lightning only when it storms. His peace of spirit made it possible for him to sort out his thoughts, put his mind in order. It gave him a chance to know Clara for what she was: depraved, overbearing, false, unreliable, incapable of loving anybody; but without enough determination or actual viciousness to commit a crime. In one of her frequent explosions of temper she might threaten to put a spell on him, but she would not have the purposefulness to carry it out. And that visit of Paula's and her story might very well have been a scheme, a lie invented by Clara to make him come back to her out of fear. To be sure, there was that question of the neckerchief that he could not get back from her; but was it not probable that it really was lost, or that she had given it away or thrown it out? He could not recall having seen her wear it for a long time, nor did he think she would have held out when he had her by the throat on the point of strangling her— The whole thing had been a farce, and he had been such a fool to swallow it and torment himself the way he had done. He had been seeing things, that was all; and although he was rather ashamed of his weakness, he smiled, forgot, and devoted all his attention and his time to the care of the roan that he was bringing into prime condition.

And the days slipped by, luminous, placid, like the blue firmament overhead, that incomparable autumn sky, beneath which nature, its laborious tasks at an end, takes on the calm, serene, almost august beauty of a proud matron.

This was Gurí's frame of mind that Sunday, the fifth of June, which had been set for the race. For a whole week people had been gathering: some from far off, those chronic vagabonds who can smell a good time miles away, like crows carrion; peddlers; owners of race horses; owners of bowling alleys, of knucklebones, of ninepins games; and, above all, the army of refreshment venders. Around Benito Cardoso's tavern a village seemed to have sprung up overnight; more than thirty tents had been pitched near the big stone buildings and in the big clumps of mataojo, without counting the nearby willow grove and the various ombús, all of which had been invaded by the crowd.

In the whole vicinity the only ones who had stayed home were the sick and the dogs: the first, because they could not go, the second, because by police ordinance no dogs were allowed. There were large crowds of strangers. The rich Brazilian ranchers of Yaguarón, of Cerro Largo, and Treinta y Tres came in a group, and were showing off their horses with their silver-trimmed saddle gear, their thick money belts full of gold. In their frank, gay, boisterous manner they rode about, laying heavy bets and taunting the backers of the roan: "It's got creeping paralysis and couldn't beat anything."

Along both sides of the track, a good track six hundred meters long, with a well-kept, roped-off grass border, eight or ten carriages and surreys were parked—which in the country is a huge collection of vehicles—and in each there were crowded eight, ten, a dozen stout women, squeezed into corsets and the silk dresses used only for special occasions, and girls decked out with all the ribbons they could find in their trunks. Each carriage was surrounded by a group of young men, relatives, acquaintances, suitors, or sweethearts.

At two in the afternoon the horses were brought out on the track and the interminable heats began. It was not until an hour and a half later that the starter's flag dropped. The bay took the lead, and the Brazilian visitors broke into howls of delight. But as the contest between the two rivals grew more intense, for a few seconds not a sound was heard. Then like a human avalanche the whole crowd rushed toward the goal. The race had been very close. The judges deliberated for a long time, and when order had finally been re-established, the chief of police pronounced the ritual phrase:

"Gentlemen! Attention! The roan is the winner by a nose."

Gurí, avoiding the congratulations of those who had bet on the roan, lost himself in the crowd and went into one of the tents where there were not so many people. It was run by an old woman and a young girl. It was poorly patronized, because the girl was known to be a flirt who led men on and then laughed at them, and her victims and those who knew her by reputation were giving her a severe letting alone. Vain, full of life, she was feeling the offense keenly. Her almond-shaped black eyes glittered hotly, and her sun-browned cheeks had a deep-red glow, like the fruit of the haw. Her Creole pride ran hot in her blood, and her young flesh was tormented by indomitable desires, and her mind, by voluptuous dreams. Her eighteen years imperiously demanded homage and caresses. Juan Francisco had approached her on more than one occasion, but she had laughed at his shyness and offended him with her disdain. But that afternoon she received him with great cordiality. The indifference of the others and the aureole of triumph that surrounded Gurí brought her down from her high horse, and she was affable and ingratiating. As she served him the coffee he had ordered, she asked him about the particulars of the race, smiling at him with a sweetness to which the boy was not accustomed.

"Have you seen the way the monkeys are buzzing around like a stirred-up hornets' nest? They came here as though they owned the place, and now that they've had to eat their brags and lost their money, they're as savage as a snake that's lost its poison."

And she laughed, happy over the local triumph and the defeat of the foreigners.

The entrance of some customers drew Rosa away. She went over to wait on them, friendly, chaffing, answering their teasing in kind, and looking over from time to time and winking at Juan Francisco, who sat quietly in the corner sipping his coffee.

The noise outside was deafening. Other races had been run, and people were arguing at the top of their lungs as to why this one had lost and the poor showing the other had made; there was an exchange of challenges and bets and jokes that were more like insults. There was the sound of singing, the strumming of a guitar, the wheezing of an accordion, the calls of boys selling pasties and fried cakes, drunken shouts, the laughter of women, the neighing of horses. And all this under a lowering sky, in an atmosphere heavy and foul with the sweat of so many people and horses, the reek of frying fat, of roasting meat, of simmering stews.

The tent was empty once more. Rosa selected from a tin platter the best custard-filled cake and handed it to Gurí.

"A poor person's gift," she said, "but each gives what he has."

Flattered at the attention, he took it, blushed, and stammered, "If you wanted to give all you have, it would be a rich person's gift—"

"Just listen to him!" she answered with an amused gesture as she turned her back.

It was getting dark. Juan Francisco got up to say goodbye. As he took Rosa's hand he drew her to him with the intention of giving her a kiss, but she ducked away.

"Not here, silly! They'll see us."

"Afterwards?"

"Maybe—"

"Honestly?"

"Get along with you," said the girl, giving him an affectionate shove. And when Juan Francisco looked back he met a look and a smile that were the equivalent of a formal promise. With his face on fire and his legs unsteady, he left the tent and went out into the crowd.

Night had fallen, dark and threatening rain. It was hard to see anything but the vague outline of people and horses, but in the tents the braziers and the kerosene lamps glowed, and the din continued. In the tavern there was gambling for heavy stakes at the green baize table surrounded by rich ranchers and presided over by the chief of police, a giant with an Indian cast of features who had committed a number of crimes himself, very fine in his cavalry lieutenant's uniform, and who was acting as croupier and playing at the same time.

About nine o'clock Gurí set out for Rosa's tent. Waiting for him at the entrance was the Indian Martiniano, an old Paraguayan with whom Gurí had an understanding.

"Where is she?" he asked in a low voice.

"Acoi hecomí," the old man answered in Guarani, to which Juan Francisco replied impatiently:

"Talk in Christian."

"She's there behind the tent."

Juan Francisco slipped away without another word, swore at a peg he stumbled over, and came upon Rosa, who, wrapped in a heavy poncho, was waiting for him.

The gaucho slipped his arm around the girl's waist under the blanket, at the same time pressing a long kiss on her cheek. Without moving, she said, "Be still; don't make any noise; the old woman hasn't gone to sleep yet, and she's as wary as a stray dog."

Gurí kept quiet, but his muscular arms tightened around the girl's plump waist, and his hot mouth, drunk with desire, kissed her feverishly on the mouth, the eyes, with all the ardor of his blood and his nature. She offered no resistance, yielding with delight, trembling from time to time in eager expectation.

About a quarter of an hour went by in this delightful dalliance. Then she freed herself.

"Wait a minute," she whispered, slipping noiselessly around the tent to the entrance. She came back quickly.

"The old woman is snoring," she said smiling, with a warm throb in her voice. "Where shall we go?"

Gurí stood perplexed. Where should they go? He hadn't even thought of that. But he settled it quickly in his primitive way.

"Right over there, under that big ombú behind the tavern."

She laughed. "What a pig! Like the dogs—"

"Just for tonight. Tomorrow I'll set you behind me on my horse and take you to a little house that's as warm as an oriole's nest."

"Easy, boy! Don't sell the hide before you've skinned the sheep. And after—"

He did not let her finish; he drew her toward him, held her tightly in his arms, and kissed her mouth. She said nothing and, clinging closely to him, followed him submissively to the enormous ombú whose spreading top rose majestically behind the white tavern.

The darkness was increasing, the noises were dying down. From inside the tents came faint flickers of light and muted snatches of sound.

Juan Francisco spread his poncho over the thick exposed roots of the ombú; then he drew her down beside him on the rough seat, and their mutual caresses fed the flames of their desire.

Suddenly a shiver ran down Gurí's spine. He recalled the threat, that terrible threat that he would lose his virility, that he would be a man only for Clara, and a cloud came over his spirit as when a flock of crows flies over a narrow valley. What if it was so? And with his spirit caught in this torturing doubt, he began to be afraid. His judgment became helpless, his will collapsed in the face of this mysterious spell to which distance was nothing and which was as irresistible and cruel as a malediction.

The first effect of a spell, the first harm from which all the others come, is the destruction of a man's sexual potency, of the supreme vital energy, and the end of his love life. This was solemnly vouched for by all familiar with witchcraft, and it must be true. Juan Francisco was gripped by fear, and the effects of his autosuggestion filled him with panic. For a time he had thought he was saved. Why? Had he had occasion to put it to the test? Why could the implacable enemy not have been lurking beside him, invisible, just waiting for the moment to deal him the mortal blow? When it begins to thunder is when one fears the lightning—

Rosa stirred impatiently, and he threw himself upon her in a frenzy, biting her as he kissed her, trying to forget and to forget himself, to cast away the black thought that was scratching at his mind with its spider's feet. But all his efforts were in vain. In the thick, cold blackness of the night he saw Clara's hovel, he saw the mulatto Gumersinda preparing her diabolical spells, he saw little Paula running away with eyes wide with fright, and he saw his former mistress smiling a devilish smile, her face set in a ferocious desire for revenge. A terrible struggle began in him between his will and the force of suggestion, a desperate combat of heroic charges and maddened retreats, of violent attacks and impotent onslaughts. It was like a man buried alive in a coffin of iron, wearing down his nails, bursting his muscles in his infinite desperation to save himself.

But every attempt met with defeat. His desperate efforts to cast out of his mind the memory of the fatal mischief were useless. And more frenzied, more enraged with every passing moment, unable to reason, moved only by animal impulses, his desire grew with his impotence. A jaguar held fast by two lassos could not have thrashed about more wildly or roared in madder despair than that unhappy lover.

Rosa, humiliated and exasperated, pushed him away with both hands and got to her feet. And with a voice trembling with hate and contempt, she threw these words at him, "You should have let me know you were gelded!"

Juan Francisco lay stretched face downward on his poncho, which was torn to shreds. He was motionless, like a steer that has been poleaxed. Around him everything was like thick, black crape against which winked glimmers of light, like the glow of fireflies in the canopied summer nights. Past, present, future, all lay motionless in his benumbed mind. This calm lasted for a long time, that profound calm which follows a great spiritual shock. Then the ideas began to move again, milling about, like a herd being sucked down by the waters of a heavy-running stream. Without anything to cling to, his mind went under. He tried to reconstruct what had happened, but he sank in a mire of disjointed memories. All he could grasp, all that was real, was his abasement, his moral death. His helpless soul floated on the torrent of his misfortune, as mute and somber as a mountain lion caught by flood waters on an island of wild hyacinths that the river drags along in its roaring tide.

A long time went by. A blazing streak of lightning made Gurí blink. A long, hoarse roll of thunder made his numb body shiver. With a great effort, he managed to pull himself into a sitting position on the roots of the ombú.

He opened his eyes wide and looked all around him, like a man rousing himself from a nightmare. It had grown colder and was raining hard. There was no longer any light in the tents, and no sound of voices. Inside the tavern the game was probably still going on around the green table, but the steady beat of the rain and the rumble of the thunder drowned out every other noise. In that dark loneliness only he kept vigil in the refuge of the giant ombú, impenetrable to water and to sun. And among that multitude which he sensed sleeping about him, unperturbed, dreaming of happiness, he alone was accursed, a being unworthy of living among other men, a miserable creature bowed down by the unbearable weight of a curse.

With another effort the gaucho got to his feet, weaving about as though drunk. He took two or three meaningless steps, and stopped to rub his eyes hard. He stood thus for a few moments, not knowing what to do. Then he tried to get his bearings, and, stumbling at each step, paying no attention to the rain or the mud, he managed to reach the place where he had tethered his horse. He slowly rolled up the tie rope, took his horse by the bridle, and returned to the ombú, where he had left his saddle. One by one, calmly and with his usual care, he arranged the different pieces. He cinched the girth tight, spread out the saddle pads evenly, taking care to put the oldest on top so the good ones would not get wet, unfastened his quirt from the saddle straps, slipped the bit in the horse's mouth, and mounted.

Where was he going? He did not know himself. He had become an automaton with no other guide than his instinct. When in danger the mountain lion makes a stand against a tree, the capybara plunges into the water, and the gaucho mounts his horse.

Gurí mounted, brought down the quirt, set spurs to the horse, and took off at a gallop, fleeing in terror from an enemy that was in his own soul and that he could not shake off, no matter how far he rode or where he tried to hide.

As he had forgotten to pick up his poncho, and the rain had turned into a downpour, in a little while he was soaked through. His baggy pants were sticking to his thighs, his boots were full of water; but none of this mattered to him, for he was not aware of it.

He had slackened the reins, and the horse was trotting uneasily, frightened by the thunder and the lightning. They were riding against a howling southwester, which tore at the horse's mane and buffeted the rider's face. The ground was oozing water, the brooks were overflowing, the fords were deep and slippery, but nothing could detain the wild, pathless flight of the young gaucho.

Neither the steady roll of the thunder aroused his mind, nor could the incessant flicker of the lightning bring light to his broken spirit. In his imagination he could see everything: the village, Clara, the hovel of their degrading love, the brutal scene of their breaking off. Then those tranquil months on the ranch when he affectionately and conscientiously trained the roan; the race, the pride of winning, the tent of the Paraguayans, the cup of coffee, the cake, and finally, Rosa, with her graceful body, her gay, young face, her hot eyes, and her caressing smile—the night, the ombú, his despairing impotence. Everything was present, clear, with a profusion of details, as vivid as a picture just seen. But this agglomeration of images did not produce any feeling; only his eyes saw them. As it was impossible for him to make any effort, he did nothing to drive them away, and besides they were not painful. The destruction of his personality had been complete, organically and emotionally; both feeling and will had disappeared, and all that remained was memory. His spirit was as insensible as his body; nothing, internal or external, left the slightest impress upon either. If he had come upon a lake in his path, he would have plunged into it, just as he would have advanced against a dagger held to his breast.

It was a long ride. For hours the young gaucho wandered aimlessly through the waterlogged fields. The next morning a gaucho who had spent the night gambling in Benito Cardoso's tavern was amazed, as he went to get his horse, to see a dun, saddled and grazing loose. He looked all round him for the rider and, not seeing him, went over to the horse and recognized it.

"Why, it's Gurí's! Wonder where the Indian is?"

As he observed it more closely, he noticed that the saddle was soaking wet, in spite of the fact that it was not raining any more; and this and the look of the horse, which told of a long trip, made him think its owner must have spent the night riding.

"Nobody but a man in love or a drunkard would have been riding around the country last night. And Gurí— But in any case that Indian would never turn a horse out saddled. Maybe he got into a fight."

He took the dun by the bridle and looked about in the grass, and it was not long before he saw an object that he quickly identified as Juan Francisco. At first the gaucho stood back, without venturing to touch him, thinking he might be wounded or dead, for the lad was stretched out full length in the mud, face down and motionless.

"Maybe he was hit by lightning," he muttered, and was about to cross himself when he looked up at the sky and, seeing that it was clear and serene, decided that the precaution was unnecessary. He drew closer and, bending over the boy, touched him on the shoulder.

"Friend Gurí," he shouted, "it's not such a good bed as to sleep in it all day."

As Gurí neither answered nor moved, the man drew back cautiously.

"Maybe he really is dead. But for my money—"

Prudence got the better of curiosity and, shrugging his shoulders, he observed philosophically, "Dead or soused, let the law handle it," and he headed for the tavern to report what he had found.

The first person he met was old Sosa, who, as soon as he heard the first words, rushed out toward the field. The gaucho followed close behind him.

"It's my opinion that he's pickled."

"That's impossible. I know Gurí like I know my own brand, and he never gets drunk. It must be something else. What if those—"

His guide understood what was in Sosa's mind and completed the phrase for him, "You think they might have beaten him up out of spite?"

They walked on until they found Juan Francisco lying in the same place and in the same position. The rancher bent over him, spoke to him without getting any answer, felt him, and, finding him alive, knelt down beside him and lifted his head. The lad was breathing slowly without opening his eyes or moving his lips. On his face, covered with mud, there was an expression of intense suffering. All Sosa's solicitous questions fell upon deaf ears. Finally he decided to carry him to the tavern with the help of the kindly gaucho.

They put him to bed on a cot in a little room in the back, where he lay all day completely immobile. It was impossible to get a word out of him or to make him take the different home remedies that were suggested. By evening Sosa, who was deeply worried by the lad's state, talked of sending for a doctor.

"A doctor! It's a long way from here to town, and before he got here the patient would have time to die or get well. Now if there was a good healer—"

Benito Cardoso felt it his duty to speak up. "If a healer is wanted there's one near here who knows as much medicine as any doctor and who has performed cures plenty of doctors would be proud of—"

"Who's that?"

"Don't you know who it is? It's the mulatto Luna. Take my word for it, the mulatto Luna knows more than all the doctors who've gone to school."

"The mulatto Luna," said Sosa thoughtfully. "I've heard of him. They say he knows his stuff. Does he live near here?"

"Oh, sure. Right over there, only six leagues away."

The mulatto Luna got there that evening and said after examining Gurí that his condition was serious. A high fever had set in, and the healer could not tell what was causing it. The day had been bad, and toward night he got much worse. The sick man was completely delirious, muttering words no one could make out and shuddering; at times his face would become contorted in a grimace of fear, as though he were seeing a legion of demons. He was seized by frequent convulsions that sent up his already high temperature. After great efforts he was finally made to swallow a brew the healer considered infallible; but it was two o'clock in the morning before the patient began to grow calmer and was able to sleep a little. The fever gradually dropped, the delirium calmed, and he seemed to be on the mend. But shortly after noon the fever came back following the same pattern.

Four days of anxious waiting went by like this, with momentary improvements followed by a complete relapse, to the despair of the healer and the deep sorrow of Gurí's kindly protector. In all this time it had been impossible to get a word out of the sick man which would throw any light on his state. In his delirium he would mutter strange words and phrases that made no sense; but when that disappeared he would sink into a brooding silence, against which all the attempts of the mulatto Luna and the affectionate efforts of the rancher to draw him out were useless. He spoke only once, and that was when the latter talked of sending to town for a doctor. No, it would be useless; he would not take any medicine. He only drank the healer's brews because they gave him momentary relief, but as for curing him, neither he nor anybody else could do that. He knew that he was going to die, and he was not afraid of death; he wanted to get it over with as soon as possible. Taking advantage of this opening, Sosa tried to get him to tell what he could about the cause of his ailment.

"Son," he said to him in a fatherly tone, "why won't you tell me what happened to you? Why don't you tell me, who has been like a father to you, who saw you come into the world, who raised you, and has always treated you like a son?"

Tears came into the black eyes of the kindly, venerable, gray-bearded rancher, noble and virile of countenance, as he pronounced these words.

Gurí, moved too by the suffering of the man for whom he felt the greatest affection and respect, murmured, closing his eyes as though to shut out a nagging vision, "I can't; don't ask me. Just let me die."

The rancher rebelled at the answer.

"That's not acting like a man," he said firmly.

Juan Francisco sat quickly up in the bed and, with eyes dilated, lips drawn back, and hands clenched, exclaimed in a hoarse, fierce voice, "I'm not a man any more!"

And as though the effort had finished him off, he fell back, as rigid and pale as a corpse.

"Gurí! Gurí! My son!" groaned the rancher, bending over the sick lad and shaking him to bring him back to consciousness. Unable to do so, he rushed out to find the healer, who was drinking maté in the kitchen. As the games were still going on and there were a number of people in the house, in a second the room was full of curious onlookers.

After long, anxious waiting the boy regained consciousness; but he did not say another word, and he seemed to be much worse.

Sosa and the healer grew more worried every day. Rosa had been indiscreet enough to make some remarks about what had happened under the ombú; remarks that spread through the neighborhood and changed with every telling, gathering many and fantastic details, arousing the curiosity of the country folk as they fell upon the fertile soil of their lush imagination, always prone to accept the supernatural.

By the eleventh day the fever had disappeared, but the illness was worse. Of that vigorous lad, overflowing with life, "with two cedar trunks for arms, and two *ñandubays* for legs," all that remained was a shadow, a pitiful creature consumed, crushed, devoured by a terrible moral malady. During the day he lay in a state of complete immobility, like a jacent statue; but as night came on, he began to writhe like one possessed. His hallucinations started with the twilight and lasted until dawn. Every twenty-four hours marked a steady decline; death was approaching rapidly.

While in the next room the chief of police and ten or twelve inveterate gamblers kept up their game night after night, in the little room where Gurí was guttering out, the rancher Sosa and the mulatto Luna kept solicitous watch, both at their wits' end.

"What is your opinion?" the rancher once asked.

And the old mulatto shook his head, where all his knowledge was in a muddle.

"I don't know, Don Sosa," he answered; "all I know is that poor Gurí is dying."

"But what is he dying of? You said the fever had left him, and if it isn't the fever any more, then what is killing him?"

The healer shook his head once more. "I don't know. I don't know anything. I do what I can and help all I can, but when I don't know, I don't know, and I come right out and say so, because I am not a doctor who can cure all kinds of sickness—or God, to undo witchcraft—"

Sosa looked at him steadily.

"Do you believe . . . ?" he asked.

"In what?"

"In witchcraft."

"Of course I do! I have seen more cases of it in my life than all the kisses my mother gave me."

"You think that Gurí . . . ?"

"I don't think anything. But if it isn't that a spell has been put on him . . . He's just exactly like others I have seen—and he's going the way they did."

"And don't you know anything for a spell?"

"I do—sometimes it works, sometimes it doesn't. In things having to do with the devil there are no rules, and it's nearly always useless. Besides, to do anything, you have to know where it comes from, who put it on him, how it happened . . . And the lad has a padlock on his mouth, like a barn door."

"And you can't try anything? Do we have to let him die, like a dog, like an animal with the plague?"

"That's the way it is, Don Sosa. Life is just lent to us, and we have to hand it over when the owner calls for it."

With this philosophical observation the old mulatto took up his bottle of rum, which he always had by him, and tilting it high, drank off a good share of the contents.

Juan Francisco kept getting worse; he saw his end approaching, and he awaited it calmly, with the proud, innate indifference of his race.

On the twenty-first day of his sickness, on an overcast, close afternoon that foretold a storm, his limbs began to grow numb and a sticky sweat beaded his brow. He no longer had strength to move. Those legs with muscles of steel that once clamped like a vise over the flanks of an unbroken colt were now only bone and skin; those arms that could check the rush of the wildest bull lay beside his body, inert, incapable of the slightest movement. Sosa, speaking to his companion and struggling to keep back the tears, summed it up in a beautiful figure of rustic rhetoric:

"He's like a tree that's been blasted by lightning."

The early hours of the night went by quietly. Sosa, crushed with sorrow, sat by the head of the cot smoking one cigarette of black tobacco after another, and drinking the matés the mulatto Luna handed him. A tallow candle stuck in a bottle stood on the floor at the foot of the bed. The charred wick was twisted around itself, and the feeble light barely picked out the dark face of the healer, leaving the room in a sad penumbra.

Juan Francisco continued in a state of sopor; his breathing grew slow and wheezy; his body and face were damp with a cold, viscous sweat. About midnight he awoke and with staring eyes in which the pupils glittered he cast a languid glance about the poor room.

Sosa drew near him and asked solicitously, "How are you, Gurí? How is it going?"

The lad smiled sadly with fleshless lips on which the smile was like a grimace of pain and whispered, "All right. This is it."

Then, still motionless, he fixed his glance on the ceiling, where he seemed to see reflected all the scenes of his life, all the images, all the recollections. His mind had acquired the lucidity that so often precedes death, and took satisfaction in passing a last review over the years lived, from which it was taking final leave. The certainty of his end had wiped out all his suffering, and he was savoring the pleasant state of well-being of his last moments. He recalled his childhood; he saw himself happy and strong along the banks of the Tacuari; he saw himself as a boy, enjoying the skill of his muscles in his hard, dangerous tasks; he saw himself free, master of his acts, in the land he loved; and then he saw his fatal meeting with Clara and the beginning of his undoing. With a kind of idle curiosity he wondered how the spell had been put on him. He remembered how it had been done in a case he had heard about: first, four daggers stuck to form a cross in the door of the house; then, an old woman—old Gumersinda—running a new needle threaded with red thread, which had to be new too, through the eyes of a green toad, and then sewing seven crosses with the thread in a neckerchief—his white neckerchief—which was then burned at midnight in a bonfire of green herbs having spellbinding powers. In this way the piece of clothing disappeared, and there was no way to undo the spell. That must have been the way it was put on him; he was sure as he recalled Paula's words. Old Gumersinda had asked, "To make him come back?" and Clara had answered, "No, to kill him!" And she was getting her wish; he was dying and in a miserable, miserable way after suffering the tortures of the damned. As though all the elements of his personality had come harmoniously together before his final passing, he recalled and evaluated everything. So much wretchedness in such a short time. That fateful night of the race was stamped on his mind: the old ombú with its wide-spreading branches seemed like a vicious monster; its thick, twisting surface roots, huge, cold snakes that had buried their venomous fangs in his body. When he left the place he was no longer a man. Rosa's stinging phrase still echoed in his ears and seared his soul as with quirt lashes. He had had that supreme insult thrown in his face and had not killed the person who dared to say it. He had not killed her because he had neither the courage nor the strength, because what she said was true: he was not a man any more. He, the last scion of an indomitable race, the last twig of the luxuriant tree that crowned the hills, he, the untamed gaucho, the gray fox, the fierce jaguar, lord of the open plains, had fled through the darkness, had spent the night cowering in the fields, seeking refuge like some cowardly varmint pursued by a pack of dogs. And with pistol and dagger in his belt, he had not thought of killing himself, he would not have been able to kill himself, because he was not a man any more. He, the pattern of the strong male, the breaker of mustangs, the herder who could cut out the wildest bull, the gaucho cast in the ancient mold, whose native intelligence disdained all teaching as an insult to his strength and bravery, was no longer a man. Degraded, humiliated, abased, he was dying shamefully in a bed, cut down by the curse of a vile woman, like an old dog wasting away in a corner, like a tree withering on the hillside. And leaving behind so many mustangs' backs, so many young bulls' horns! And above all, the country, the green, austere country, the unbounded open spaces and the pathless hills, the roaring rivers and the smiling sky, the diaphanous days and the nights of magnificent blackness; his country—land, nature, mother. Oh mother, in whose arms he would soon be at rest!

His face had taken on the waxy pallor of the dying; his nose grew sharper, his temples sank, his ears stood away from his head, and his lips hung pendulous.

Beside the bed the rancher, pale as a ghost at the approach of that doubly mysterious death, kept his eyes fixed on the candle that was almost burned down and cast barely a glimmer of light.

Outside the wind whistled and the heavy rain beat on the tin roof of the little room. There came a clap of thunder, so dry and sharp that it was like the explosion of a mine. Juan Francisco trembled. One last gleam came into his eyes, his lips parted, and in a horrible cry, voicing a superhuman despair, he roared:

"Clara! Clara! Clara!"

And that was all. There was the choking sound of the death rattle in his throat, and his lids fell halfway over his lightless eyes.

10

MARIANO AZUELA

If one had to choose a single novel to represent the Mexican Revolution of 1910, that novel would undoubtedly be Mariano Azuela's *The Underdogs*. In it Azuela portrayed the early days of an upheaval that aroused in Latin America at that time as much hope and enthusiasm as the Cuban Revolution in the early 1960s. Mexico was more than ready for change after the thirty-odd years of Porfirio Díaz's quasi-imperial regime. Francisco I. Madero, the man who led the anti-Díaz forces at the outbreak of the revolution, was a constitutionalist. He wanted Mexico to have a democratic regime that would restore elections and re-establish a free press. But the forces he unleashed were more radical, and fought for the agrarian reform that had been promised to the exploited peasants since the middle of the nineteenth century. The quick ouster of Díaz did not automatically bring about all these changes. After Madero's assassination by henchmen of General Huerta, the country was deeply divided among a number of warring factions. One of the most brilliant chieftains was Francisco (Pancho) Villa, and it was to his camp that Azuela was attracted.

Born in Jalisco in 1873, Azuela studied medicine in Guadalajara, and graduated in 1899. He began writing modernist prose, but one of his first important books was a realistic novel, *Andrés Pérez, Maderista* (1911), which depicted the hopes of the moderate party rallied around Madero. In 1914, Azuela joined the forces of Villa as a field doctor and obtained firsthand experience of guerrilla warfare. After Villa's defeat at Celaya, Azuela took refuge in El Paso, and it was there that he wrote *The Underdogs* (1916).

The novel covered more or less the same ground Azuela had covered with the Villistas. But instead of choosing as protagonist an educated man like himself, Azuela preferred to focus his narrative on a peasant, Demetrio Macías, who is pushed to the center of the revolutionary vortex without really having a clear idea of what he is fighting for. At the beginning of the novel, Macías is seen at the top of a ravine, with a group of his men, attacking the government forces; at the end of the book he will be at the bottom of the same ravine, being attacked by the same government forces. The Spanish title, *Los de abajo,* indicates more clearly than does the English translation the double meaning of "underdogs," because Macías and his men are literally *under*, at the bottom of the ravine, at the end of the story. The narrative thus has an essentially circular nature—for Azuela, a revolution was precisely that: something that revolves.

There are other perspectives in the novel. Apart from Macías's purely emotional attachment to revolution, the book presents the calculated, opportunistic attitude of Luis Cervantes, a cowardly intellectual concerned only with personal gain, and the more idealistic attitude of Solís, who despite his disillusionment fights on until he too is destroyed by the blind and violent social forces that have been unleashed.

In focusing the action on Macías's fate, Azuela underlined the fact that it was the destiny of the rebelling Indian peasants that really mattered. He viewed them very much as Hernández viewed his gauchos in *Martín Fierro* (see Part Two, 7): as cannon fodder for the ambitious schemes of politicians and landowners. Azuela's grim view of the first stage of the revolution did not detract from the power of his presentation of the epic struggle. His book is short and intense; it reads today as swiftly as it did sixty years ago. Despite its negative and pessimistic point of view, the book slowly came to be recognized as the most effective presentation of the Mexican Revolution. The first edition passed almost unnoticed, but in 1925 it was serialized in one of Mexico City's largest newspapers. In 1930, a major edition was published in Spain, making the book available all over the Hispanic world. Azuela was then recognized, with Gallegos, Rivera, and Güiraldes (selections 11, 12, 13), as one of the masters of the Latin American novel.

After *The Underdogs,* he wrote many books: some were biographies of famous Mexicans; some were experimental novels in the avant-garde style; some were satirical indictments of the new bourgeoisie that the final triumph of the revolution had produced. None of these books had the quality or the impact of his masterpiece. With *The Underdogs,* Azuela almost singlehandedly created a whole literary movement: the novel of the Mexican Revolution, which, through writers as diverse as Martín Luis Guzmán (Three, 14), Juan Rulfo (Five, 7), and Carlos Fuentes (Five, 13), has continued its development to this day.

In the chapters presented here, Azuela describes the early stages of Demetrio Macías's revolutionary career.

The Underdogs

From The Underdogs, *translated by E. Munguía Jr. (New York: The New American Library, 1962), pp. 14–38.*

I

"That's no animal, I tell you! Listen to the dog barking! It *must* be a human being."

The woman stared into the darkness of the sierra.

"What if they're soldiers?" said a man, who sat Indian-fashion, eating, a coarse earthenware plate in his right hand, three folded tortillas in the other.

The woman made no answer, all her senses directed outside the hut. The beat of horses' hoofs rang in the quarry nearby. The dog barked again, louder and more angrily.

"Well, Demetrio, I think you had better hide, all the same."

Stolidly, the man finished eating; next he reached for a *cántaro* and gulped down the water in it; then he stood up.

"Your rifle is under the mat," she whispered.

A tallow candle illumined the small room. In one corner stood a plow, a yoke, a goad, and other agricultural implements. Ropes hung from the roof, securing an old adobe mold, used as a bed; on it a child slept, covered with gray rags.

Demetrio buckled his cartridge belt about his waist and picked up his rifle. He was tall and well built, with a sanguine face and beardless chin; he wore shirt and trousers of white cloth, a broad Mexican hat and leather sandals.

With slow, measured step, he left the room, vanishing into the impenetrable darkness of the night.

The dog, excited to the point of madness, had jumped over the corral fence.

Suddenly a shot rang out. The dog moaned, then barked no more. Some men on horseback rode up, shouting and swearing; two of them dismounted, while the other hung back to watch the horses.

"Hey, there, woman: we want food! Give us eggs, milk, beans, anything you've got! We're starving!"

"Curse the sierra! It would take the Devil himself not to lose his way!"

"Guess again, Sergeant! Even the Devil would go astray if he were as drunk as you are."

The first speaker wore chevrons on his arm, the other red stripes on his shoulders.

"Whose place is this, old woman? Or is it an empty house? God's truth, which is it?"

"Of course it's not empty. How about the light and that child there? Look here, confound it, we want to eat, and damn quick too! Are you coming out or are we going to make you?"

"You swine! Both of you! You've gone and killed my dog, that's what you've done! What harm did he ever do you? What did you have against *him?*"

The woman re-entered the house, dragging the dog behind her, very white and fat, with lifeless eyes and flabby body.

"Look at those cheeks, Sergeant! Don't get riled, light of my life: I swear I'll turn your home into a dovecot, see?"

"By God!" he said, breaking off into song:

> "Don't look so haughty, dear,
> Banish all fears,
> Kiss me and melt to me,
> I'll drink up your tears!"

His alcoholic tenor trailed off into the night.

"Tell me what they call this ranch, woman," the sergeant asked.

"Limón," the woman replied curtly, carrying wood to the fire and fanning the coals.

"So we're in Limón, eh, the famous Demetrio Macías's country, eh? Do you hear that, Lieutenant? We're in Limón."

"Limón? What the hell do I care? If I'm bound for hell, Sergeant, I might as well go there now. I don't mind, now that I've found as good a remount as this! Look at the cheeks on the darling, look at them! There's a pair of ripe red apples for a fellow to bite into!"

"I'll wager you know Macías the bandit, lady? I was in the pen with him at Escobedo, once."

"Bring me a bottle of tequila, Sergeant: I've decided to spend the night with this charming lady. . . . What's that? The colonel? . . . Why in God's name talk about the colonel now? He can go straight to hell, for all I care. And if he doesn't like it, it's all right with me. Come on, Sergeant, tell the corporal outside to unsaddle the horses and feed them. I'll stay here all night. Here, my girl, you let the sergeant fry the eggs and warm up the tortillas; you come here to me. See this wallet full of nice new bills? They're all for you, darling. Sure, I want you to have them. Figure it out for yourself. I'm drunk, see: I've a bit of a load on and that's why I'm kind of hoarse, you might call it. I left half my gullet down Guadalajara way, and I've been spitting the other half out all the way up here. Oh well, who cares? But I want you to have that money, see, dearie? Hey, Sergeant, where's my bottle? Now, little girl, come here and pour yourself a drink. You won't, eh? Aw, come on! Afraid of your—er—husband . . . or whatever he is, huh? Well, if he's skulking in some hole, you tell him to come out. What the hell do I care? I'm not scared of rats, see!"

Suddenly a white shadow loomed on the threshold.

"Demetrio Macías!" the sergeant cried as he stepped back in terror.

The lieutenant stood up, silent, cold and motionless as a statue.

"Shoot them!" the woman croaked.

"Oh, come, you'll surely spare us! I didn't know you were there. I'll always stand up for a brave man."

Demetrio stood his ground, looking them up and down, an insolent and disdainful smile wrinkling his face.

"Yes, I not only respect brave men, but I like them. I'm proud and happy to call them friends. Here's my hand on it: friend to friend." Then, after a pause: "All right, Demetrio Macías, if you don't want to shake hands, all right! But it's because you don't know me, that's why, just because the first time you saw me I was doing this dog's job. But look here, I ask you, what in God's name can a man do when he's poor and has a wife to support and kids? . . . Right you are, Sergeant, let's go: I've nothing but respect for the home of what I call a brave man, a real, honest, genuine man!"

When they had gone, the woman drew close to Demetrio.

"Holy Virgin, what agony! I suffered as though it was you they'd shot."

"You go to father's house, quick!" Demetrio ordered. She wanted to hold him in her arms; she entreated, she wept. But he pushed away from her gently and, in a sullen voice, said, "I've an idea the whole lot of them are coming."

"Why didn't you kill 'em?"

"Their hour hasn't struck yet."

They went out together; she bore the child in her arms. At the door, they separated, moving off in different directions.

The moon peopled the mountain with vague shadows. As he advanced, at every turn of his way Demetrio could see the poignant, sharp silhouette of a woman pushing forward painfully, bearing a child in her arms.

When, after many hours of climbing, he gazed back, huge flames shot up from the depths of the canyon by the river. It was his house, blazing. . . .

II

Everything was still swathed in shadows as Demetrio Macías began his descent to the bottom of the ravine. Between rocks striped with huge eroded cracks, and a squarely cut wall, with the river flowing below, a narrow ledge along the steep incline served as a mountain trail.

"They'll surely find me now and track us down like dogs," he mused. "It's a good thing they know nothing about the trails and paths up here. . . . But if they got someone from Moyahua to guide them . . ." He left the sinister thought unfinished. "All the men from Limón or Santa Rosa or the other nearby ranches are on our side: they wouldn't try to trail us. That *cacique* who's chased and run me ragged over these hills is at Mohayua now; he'd give his eyeteeth to see me dangling from a telegraph pole with my tongue hanging out of my mouth, purple and swollen. . . ."

At dawn, he approached the pit of the canyon. Here, he lay on the rocks and fell asleep.

The river crept along, murmuring as the waters rose and fell in small cascades. Birds sang lyrically from their hiding places among the *pitaya* trees. The monotonous, eternal drone of insects filled the rocky solitude with mystery.

Demetrio awoke with a start. He waded the river, following its course which ran counter to the canyon; he climbed the crags laboriously as an ant, gripping root and rock with his hands, clutching every stone in the trail with his bare feet.

When he reached the summit, he glanced down to see the sun steeping the valley in a lake of gold. Near the canyon, enormous rocks loomed protrudent, like fantastic Negro skulls. The *pitaya* trees rose tenuous, tall, like the tapering, gnarled fingers of a giant; other trees of all sorts bowed their crests toward the pit of the abyss. Amid the stark rocks and dry branches, roses bloomed like a white offering to the sun as smoothly, suavely, it unraveled its golden threads, one by one, from rock to rock.

Demetrio stopped at the summit. Reaching backward, with his right arm he drew his horn which hung at his back, held it up to his thick lips, and, swelling his cheeks out, blew three loud blasts. From across the hill close by, three sharp whistles answered his signal.

In the distance, from a conical heap of reeds and dry straws, man after man emerged, one after the other, their legs and chests naked, lambent and dark as old bronze. They rushed forward to greet Demetrio, and stopped before him, askance.

"They've burnt my house," he said.

A murmur of oaths, imprecations, and threats rose among them.

Demetrio let their anger run its course. Then he drew a bottle from under his shirt and took a deep swig; then he wiped the neck of the bottle with the back of his hand and passed it around. It passed from mouth to mouth; not a drop was left. The men passed their tongues greedily over their lips to recapture the tang of the liquor.

"Glory be to God and by His Will," said Demetrio, "tonight or tomorrow at the latest we'll meet the Federals. What do you say, boys, shall we let them find their way about these trails?"

The ragged crew jumped to their feet, uttering shrill cries of joy; then their jubilation turned sinister and they gave vent to threats, oaths and imprecations.

"Of course, we can't tell how strong they are," said Demetrio as his glance traveled over their faces in scrutiny.

"Do you remember Medina? Out there at Hostotipaquillo, he only had a half a dozen men with knives that they sharpened on a grindstone. Well, he held back the soldiers and the police, didn't he? And he beat them, too."

"We're every bit as good as Medina's crowd!" said a tall, broad-shouldered man with a black beard and bushy eyebrows.

"By God, if I don't own a Mauser and a lot of cartridges, if I can't get a pair of trousers and shoes, then my name's not Anastasio Montáñez! Look here, Quail, you don't believe it, do you? You ask my partner Demetrio if I haven't half a dozen bullets in me already. Christ! Bullets are marbles to me! And I dare you to contradict me!"

"Viva Anastasio Montáñez," shouted Manteca.

"All right, all right!" said Montáñez. "Viva Demetrio Macías, our chief, and long life to God in His heaven and to the Virgin Mary."

"Viva Demetrio Macías," they all shouted.

They gathered dry brush and wood, built a fire and placed chunks of fresh meat upon the burning coals. As the blaze rose, they collected about the fire, sat down Indian-fashion and inhaled the odor of the meat as it twisted on the crackling fire. The rays of the sun, falling about them, cast a golden radiance over the bloody hide of a calf, lying on the ground nearby. The meat dangled from a rope fastened to a *huizache* tree, to dry in the sun and wind.

"Well, men," Demetrio said, "you know we've only twenty rifles, besides my thirty-thirty. If there are just a few of them, we'll shoot until there's not a live man left. If there's a lot of 'em, we can give 'em a good scare, anyhow."

He undid a rag belt about his waist, loosened a knot in it and offered the contents to his companions. Salt. A murmur of approbation rose among them as each took a few grains between the tips of his fingers.

They ate voraciously; then, glutted, lay down on the ground, facing the sky. They sang monotonous, sad songs, uttering a strident shout after each stanza.

III

In the brush and foliage of the sierra, Demetrio Macías and his threescore men slept until the halloo of the horn, blown by Pancracio from the crest of a peak, awakened them.

"Time, boys! Look around and see what's what!" Anastasio Montáñez said, examining his rifle springs. Yet he was previous; an hour or more elapsed with no sound or stir save the song of the locust in the brush or the frog stirring in his mudhole. At last, when the ultimate faint rays of the moon were spent in the rosy dimness of the dawn, the silhouette of a soldier loomed at the end of the trail. As they strained their eyes, they could distinguish others behind him, ten, twenty, a hundred. . . . Then, suddenly, darkness swallowed them up. Only when the sun rose, Demetrio's band realized that the canyon was alive with men, midgets seated on miniature horses.

"Look at 'em, will you?" said Pancracio. "Pretty, ain't they? Come on, boys, let's go and roll marbles with 'em."

Now the moving dwarf figures were lost in the dense chaparral, now they reappeared, stark and black against the ocher. The voices of officers, as they gave orders, and soldiers, marching at ease, were clearly audible.

Demetrio raised his hand; the locks of rifles clicked.

"Fire!" he cried tensely.

Twenty-one men shot as one; twenty-one soldiers fell off their horses.

Caught by surprise, the column halted, etched like bas-reliefs in stone against the rocks.

Another volley and a score of soldiers hurtled down from rock to rock.

"Come out, bandits. Come out, you starved dogs!"

"To hell with you, you corn rustlers!"

"Kill the cattle thieves! Kill 'em!"

The soldiers shouted defiance to their enemies; the latter, giving proof of a marksmanship which had already made them famous, were content to keep under cover, quiet, mute.

"Look, Pancracio," said Meco, completely black save for his eyes and teeth. "This is for that man who passes that tree. I'll get the son of a . . ."

"Take that! Right in the head. You saw it, didn't you, mate? Now, this is for the fellow on the roan horse. Down you come, you shave-headed bastard!"

"I'll give that lad on the trail's edge a shower of lead. If you don't hit the river, I'm a liar! Now: look at him!"

"Oh, come on, Anastasio, don't be cruel; lend me your rifle. Come along, one shot, just one!"

Manteca and Quail, unarmed, begged for a gun as a boon, imploring permission to fire at least a shot apiece.

"Come out of your holes if you've got any guts!"

"Show your faces, you lousy cowards!"

From peak to peak, the shouts rang as distinctly as though uttered across a street. Suddenly, Quail stood up, naked, holding his trousers to windward as though he were a bullfighter flaunting a red cape, and the soldiers below the bull. A shower of shots peppered upon Demetrio's men.

"God! That was like a hornet's nest buzzing overhead," said Anastasio Montáñez, lying flat on the ground without daring to wink an eye.

"Here, Quail, you son of a bitch, you stay where I told you," roared Demetrio.

They crawled to take new positions. The soldiers, congratulating themselves on their successes, ceased firing when another volley roused them.

"More coming!" they shouted.

Some, panic-stricken, turned their horses back; others, abandoning their mounts, began to climb up the mountain and seek shelter behind the rocks. The officers had to shoot at them to enforce discipline.

"Down there, down there!" said Demetrio as he leveled his rifle at the translucent thread of the river.

A soldier fell into the water; at each shot, invariably a soldier bit the dust. Only Demetrio was shooting in that direction; for every soldier killed, ten or twenty of them, intact, climbed afresh on the other side.

"Get those coming up from under! *Los de Abajo!* Get the underdogs!" he screamed.

Now his fellows were exchanging rifles, laughing and making wagers on their marksmanship.

"My leather belt if I miss that head there, on the black horse!"

"Lend me your rifle, Meco."

"Twenty Mauser cartridges and a half yard of sausage if you let me spill that lad riding the bay mare. All right! Watch me. . . . There! See him jump! Like a bloody deer."

"Don't run, you half-breeds. Come along with you! Come and meet Father Demetrio!"

Now it was Demetrio's men who screamed insults. Manteca, his smooth face swollen in exertion, yelled his lungs out. Pancracio roared, the veins and muscles in his neck dilated, his murderous eyes narrowed to two evil slits.

Demetrio fired shot after shot, constantly warning his men of impending danger, but they took no heed until they felt the bullets spattering them from one side.

"Goddamn their souls, they've branded me!" Demetrio cried, his teeth flashing.

Then, very swiftly, he slid down a gully and was lost. . . .

IV

Two men were missing, Serapio the candymaker, and Antonio, who played the cymbals in the Juchipila band.

"Maybe they'll join us further on," said Demetrio.

The return journey proved moody. Anastasio Montáñez alone preserved his equanimity, a kindly expression playing in his sleepy eyes and on his bearded face. Pancracio's harsh, gorillalike profile retained its repulsive immutability.

The soldiers had retreated; Demetrio began the search for the soldiers' horses which had been hidden in the sierra.

Suddenly Quail, who had been walking ahead, shrieked. He had caught sight of his companions swinging from the branches of a mesquite. There could be no doubt of their identity; Serapio and Antonio they certainly were. Anastasio Montáñez prayed brokenly.

"Our Father Who art in heaven, hallowed be Thy name. Thy kingdom come . . ."

"Amen," his men answered in low tones, their heads bowed, their hats upon their breasts. . . .

Then, hurriedly, they took the Juchipila canyon northward, without halting to rest until nightfall.

Quail kept walking close to Anastasio, unable to banish from his mind the two who were hanged, their dislocated limp necks, their dangling legs, their arms pendulous, and their bodies moving slowly in the wind.

On the morrow, Demetrio complained bitterly of his wound; he could no longer ride on horseback. They were forced to carry him the rest of the way on a makeshift stretcher of leaves and branches.

"He's bleeding frightfully," said Anastasio Montáñez, tearing off one of his shirt-sleeves and tying it tightly about Demetrio's thigh, a little above the wound.

"That's good," said Venancio. "It'll keep him from bleeding and stop the pain."

Venancio was a barber. In his native town, he pulled teeth and fulfilled the office of medicine man. He was accorded an unimpeachable authority because he had read *The Wandering Jew* and one or two other books. They called him "Doctor"; and since he was conceited about his knowledge, he employed very few words.

They took turns, carrying the stretcher in relays of four over the bare stony mesa and up the steep passes.

At high noon, when the reflection of the sun on the calcareous soil burned their shoulders and made the landscape dimly waver before their eyes, the monotonous, rhythmical moan of the wounded rose in unison with the ceaseless cry of the locusts. They stopped to rest at every small hut they found hidden between the steep, jagged rocks. ·

"Thank God, a kind soul and tortillas full of beans and chili are never lacking," Anastasio Montáñez said with a triumphant belch.

The mountaineers would shake calloused hands with the travelers, saying:

"God's blessing on you! He will find a way to help you all, never fear. We're going ourselves, starting tomorrow morning. We're dodging the draft, with those damned Government people who've declared war to the death on us, on all the poor. They come and steal our pigs, our chickens and corn, they burn our homes and carry our women off, and if they ever get hold of us they'll kill us like mad dogs, and we die right there on the spot and that's the end of the story!"

At sunset, amid the flames dyeing the sky with vivid, variegated colors, they described a group of houses up in the heart of the blue mountains. Demetrio ordered them to carry him there.

These proved to be a few wretched straw huts, dispersed all over the river slopes, between rows of young sprouting corn and beans. They lowered the stretcher and Demetrio, in a weak voice, asked for a glass of water.

Groups of squalid Indians sat in the dark pits of the huts, men with bony chests, disheveled, matted hair, and ruddy cheeks; behind them, eyes shone up from floors of fresh reeds.

A child with a large belly and glossy dark skin came close to the stretcher to inspect the wounded man. An old woman followed, and soon all of them drew about Demetrio in a circle.

A girl sympathizing with him in his plight brought a *jícara* of bluish water. With hands shaking, Demetrio took it up and drank greedily.

"Will you have some more?"

He raised his eyes and glanced at the girl, whose features were common but whose voice had a note of kindness in it. Wiping his sweating brow with the back of his palm and turning on one side, he gasped:

"May God reward you."

Then his whole body shook, making the leaves of the stretcher rustle. Fever possessed him; he fainted.

"It's a damp night and that's terrible for the fever," said Remigia, an old wrinkled barefooted woman, wearing a cloth rag for a blouse.

She invited them to move Demetrio into her hut.

Pancracio, Anastasio Montáñez, and Quail lay down beside the stretcher like faithful dogs, watchful of their master's wishes. The rest scattered about in search of food.

Remigia offered them all she had, chili and tortillas.

"Imagine! I had eggs, chickens, even a goat and her kid, but those damn soldiers wiped me out clean."

Then, making a trumpet of her hands, she drew near Anastasio and murmured in his ear:

"Imagine, they even carried away Señora Nieves' little girl!"

V

Suddenly awakening, Quail opened his eyes and stood up.

"Montáñez, did you hear? A shot, Montáñez! Hey, Montáñez, get up!"

He shook him vigorously until Montáñez ceased snoring and woke up.

"What in the name of . . . Now you're at it again, damn it. I tell you there aren't ghosts any more," Anastasio muttered out of a half-sleep.

"I heard a shot, Montáñez!"

"Go back to sleep, Quail, or I'll bust your nose."

"Hell, Anastasio, I tell you it's no nightmare. I've forgotten those fellows they hung, honest. It's a shot, I tell you. I heard it all right."

"A shot, you say? All right, then, hand me my gun."

Anastasio Montáñez rubbed his eyes, stretched out his arms and legs, and stood up lazily.

They left the hut. The sky was solid with stars; the moon rose like a sharp scythe. The confused rumor of women crying in fright resounded from the various huts; the men, who had been sleeping in the open, also woke up and the rattle of arms echoed over the mountain.

"You cursed fool, you've maimed me for life."

A voice rang clearly through the darkness.

"Who goes there?"

The shout echoed from rock to rock, through mound and over hollow, until it spent itself at the far, silent reaches of the night.

"Who goes there?" Anastasio repeated his challenge louder, pulling back the lock of his Mauser.

"One of Demetrio's men," came the answer.

"It's Pancracio," Quail cried joyfully. Relieved, he rested the butt of his rifle on the ground.

Pancracio appeared, holding a young man by the arms; the newcomer was covered with dust from his felt hat to his coarse shoes. A fresh bloodstain lay on his trousers close to the heel.

"Who's this tenderfoot?" Anastasio demanded.

"You know I'm on guard around here. Well, I hears a noise in the brush, see, and I shouts, 'Who goes there?' and then this lad answers, 'Carranza! Carranza!' I don't know anyone by that name, and so I says, 'Carranza, hell!' and I just pumps a bit of lead into his hoof."

Smiling, Pancracio turned his beardless head around as if soliciting applause.

Then the stranger spoke:

"Who's your commander?"

Proudly, Anastasio raised his head, went up to him and looked him in the face. The stranger lowered his tone considerably.

"Well, I'm a revolutionist, too, you know. The Government drafted me and I served as a private, but I managed to desert during the battle the day before yesterday, and I've been walking about in search of you all."

"So he's a Government soldier, eh?" A murmur of incredulity rose from the men, interrupting the stranger.

"So that's what you are, eh? One of those damn half-breeds," said Anastasio Montáñez. "Why the hell didn't you pump your lead in his brain, Pancracio?"

"What's he talking about, anyhow? I can't make head nor tail of it. He says he wants to see Demetrio and that he's got plenty to say to him. But that's all right: we've got plenty of time to do anything we damn well please so long as you're in no hurry, that's all," said Pancracio, loading his gun.

"What kind of beasts are you?" the prisoner cried. He could say no more: Anastasio's fist, crashing down upon his face, sent his head turning on his neck, covered with blood.

"Shoot the half-breed!"

"Hang him!"

"Burn him alive; he's a lousy Federal."

In great excitement, they yelled and shrieked and were about to fire at the prisoner.

"Sssh! Shut up! I think Demetrio's talking now," Anastasio said, striving to quiet them. Indeed, Demetrio, having ascertained the cause of the turmoil, ordered them to bring the prisoner before him.

"It's positively infamous, señor; look," Luis Cervantes said, pointing to the bloodstains on his trousers and to his bleeding face.

"All right, all right. But who in hell are you? That's what I want to know," Demetrio said.

"My name is Luis Cervantes, sir. I'm a medical student and a journalist. I wrote a piece in favor of the revolution, you see; as a result, they persecuted me, caught me, and finally landed me in the barracks."

His ensuing narrative was couched in terms of such detail and expressed in terms so melodramatic that it drew guffaws of mirth from Pancracio and Manteca.

"All I've tried to do is to make myself clear on this point. I want you to be convinced that I am truly one of your coreligionists. . . ."

"What's that? What did you say? Car . . . what?" Demetrio asked, bringing his ear close to Cervantes.

"Coreligionist, sir, that is to say, a person who possesses the same religion, who is inspired by the same ideals, who defends and fights for the same cause you are now fighting for."

Demetrio smiled:

"What *are* we fighting for? That's what I'd like to know."

In his disconcertment, Luis Cervantes could find no reply.

"Look at that mug, look at 'im! Why waste any time, Demetrio? Let's shoot him," Pancracio urged impatiently.

Demetrio laid a hand on his hair, which covered his ears, and stretching himself out for a long time, seemed to be lost in thought. Having found no solution, he said:

"Get out, all of you; it's aching again. Anastasio, put out the candle. Lock him up in the corral and let Pancracio and Manteca watch him. Tomorrow, we'll see. . . ."

VI

Through the shadows of the starry night, Luis Cervantes had not yet managed to detect the exact shape of the objects about him. Seeking the most suitable resting-place, he laid his weary bones down on a fresh pile of manure under the blurred mass of a *huizache* tree. He lay down, more exhausted than resigned, and closed his eyes, resolutely determined to sleep until his fierce keepers or the morning sun, burning his ears, awakened him. Something vaguely like warmth at his side, then a tired hoarse breath, made him shudder. He opened his eyes and feeling about him with his hands, he sensed the coarse hairs of a large pig which, resenting the presence of a neighbor, began to grunt.

All Luis' efforts to sleep proved quite useless, not only because the pain of his wound or the bruises on his flesh smarted, but because he suddenly realized the exact nature of his failure.

Yes, failure! For he had never learned to appreciate exactly the difference between fulminating sentences of death upon bandits in the columns of a small country newspaper and actually setting out in search of them, and tracking them to their lairs, gun in hand. During his first day's march as volunteer lieutenant, he had begun to suspect the error of his ways—a brutal sixty miles' journey it was, that left his hips and legs one mass of raw soreness and soldered all his bones together. A week later, after his first skirmish against the rebels, he understood every rule of the game. Luis Cervantes would have taken up a crucifix and solemnly sworn that as soon as the soldiers, gun in hand, stood ready to shoot, some profoundly eloquent voice had spoken behind them, saying, "Run for your lives." It was all crystal clear. Even his noble-spirited horse, accustomed to battle, sought to sweep back on its hind legs and gallop furiously away, to stop only at a safe distance from the sound of firing. The sun was setting, the mountain became peopled with vague and restless shadows, darkness scaled the ramparts of the mountain hastily. What could be more logical, then, than to seek refuge behind the rocks and attempt to sleep, granting mind and body a sorely needed rest?

But the soldier's logic is the logic of absurdity. On the morrow, for example, his colonel awakened him rudely out of his sleep, cuffing and belaboring him unmercifully, and, after having bashed in his face, deprived him of his place of vantage. The rest of the officers, moreover, burst into hilarious mirth and holding their sides with laughter begged the colonel to pardon the deserter. The colonel, therefore, instead of sentencing him to be shot, kicked his buttocks roundly for him and assigned him to kitchen police.

This signal insult was destined to bear poisonous fruit. Luis Cervantes determined to play turncoat; indeed, mentally, he had already changed sides. Did not the sufferings of the underdogs, of the disinherited masses, move him to the core? Henceforth he espoused the cause of Demos, of the subjugated, the beaten and baffled, who implore justice, and justice alone. He became intimate with the humblest private. More, even, he shed tears of compassion over a dead mule which fell, load and all, after a terribly long journey.

From then on, Luis Cervantes' prestige with the soldiers increased. Some actually dared to make confessions. One among them, conspicuous for his sobriety and silence, told him: "I'm a carpenter by trade, you know. I had a mother, an old woman nailed to her chair for ten years by rheumatism. In the middle of the night, they pulled me out of my house; three damn policemen; I woke up a soldier twenty-five miles away from my hometown. A month ago our company passed by there again. My mother was already under the sod! . . . So there's nothing left for me in this wide world; no one misses me now, you see. But, by God, I'm damned if I'll use these cartridges they make us carry, against the enemy. If a miracle happens (I pray for it every night, you know, and I guess our Lady of Guadalupe can do it all right), then I'll join Villa's men; and I swear by the holy soul of my old mother, that I'll make every one of these Government people pay, by God I will."

Another soldier, a bright young fellow, but a charlatan at heart, who drank habitually and smoked the narcotic marihuana weed, eyeing him with vague, glassy stare, whispered in his ear, "You know, partner . . . the men on the other side . . . you know, the other side . . . you understand . . . they ride the best horses up north there, and all over, see? And they harness their mounts with pure hammered silver. But us? Oh hell, we've got to ride plugs, that's all, and not one of them good enough to stagger round a water well. You see, don't you, partner? You see what I mean? You know, the men on the other side—they get shiny new silver coins while we get only lousy paper money printed in that murderer's factory, that's what we get, yes, that's ours, I tell you!"

The majority of the soldiers spoke in much the same tenor. Even a top sergeant candidly confessed, "Yes, I enlisted all right. I wanted to. But, by God, I missed the right side by a long shot. What you can't make in a lifetime, sweating like a mule and breaking your back in peacetime, damn it all, you can make in a few months just running around the sierra with a gun on your back, but not with this crowd, dearie, not with this lousy outfit. . . ."

Luis Cervantes, who already shared this hidden, implacably mortal hatred of the upper classes, of his officers, and of his superiors, felt that a veil had been removed from his eyes; clearly, now, he saw the final outcome of the struggle. And yet what had happened? The first moment he was able to join his coreligionists, instead of welcoming him with open arms, they threw him into a pigsty with swine for company.

Day broke. The roosters crowed in the huts. The chickens perched in the *huizache* began to stretch their wings, shake their feathers, and fly down to the ground.

Luis Cervantes saw his guards lying on top of a dung heap, snoring. In his imagination, he reviewed the features of last night's men. One, Pancracio, was pockmarked, blotchy, unshaven; his chin protruded, his forehead receded obliquely; his ears formed one solid piece with head and neck—a horrible man. The other, Manteca, was so much human refuse; his eyes were almost hidden, his look sullen; his wiry straight hair fell over his ears, forehead and neck; his scrofulous lips hung eternally agape. Once more, Luis Cervantes felt his flesh quiver.

VII

Still drowsy, Demetrio ran his hand through his ruffled hair, which hung over his moist forehead, pushed it back over his ears, and opened his eyes.

Distinctly he heard the woman's melodious voice which he had already sensed in his dream. He walked toward the door.

It was broad daylight; the rays of sunlight filtered through the thatch of the hut.

The girl who had offered him water the day before, the girl of whom he had dreamed all night long, now came forward, kindly and eager as ever. This time she carried a pitcher of milk brimming over with foam.

"It's goat's milk, but fine just the same. Come on now: taste it."

Demetrio smiled gratefully, straightened up, grasped the clay pitcher, and proceeded to drink the milk in little gulps, without removing his eyes from the girl.

She grew self-conscious, lowered her eyes.

"What's your name?" he asked.

"Camilla."

"Ah, there's a lovely name! And the girl that bears it, lovelier still!"

Camilla blushed. As he sought to seize her wrist, she grew frightened, and picking up the empty pitcher, flew out the door.

"No, Demetrio," Anastasio Montáñez commented gravely, "you've got to break them in first. Hmm! It's a hell of a lot of scars the women have left on my body. Yes, my friend, I've a heap of experience along that line."

"I feel all right now, Compadre." Demetrio pretended he had not heard him. "I had fever, and I sweated like a horse all night, but I feel quite fresh today. The thing that's irking me hellishly is that Goddamn wound. Call Venancio to look after me."

"What are we going to do with the tenderfoot we caught last night?" Pancracio asked.

"That's right: I was forgetting all about him."

As usual, Demetrio hesitated a while before he reached a decision.

"Here, Quail, come here. Listen: you go and find out where's the nearest church around here. I know there's one about six miles away. Go and steal a priest's robe and bring it back."

"What's the idea?" asked Pancracio in surprise.

"Well, I'll soon find out if this tenderfoot came here to murder me. I'll tell him he's to be shot, see, and Quail will put on the priest's robes, say that he's a priest and hear his confession. If he's got anything up his sleeve, he'll come out with it, and then I'll shoot him. Otherwise I'll let him go."

"God, there's a roundabout way to tackle the question. If I were you, I'd just shoot him and let it go at that," said Pancracio contemptuously.

That night Quail returned with the priest's robes; Demetrio ordered the prisoner to be led in. Luis Cervantes had not eaten or slept for two days, there were deep black circles under his eyes; his face was deathly pale, his lips dry and colorless. He spoke awkwardly, slowly: "You can do as you please with me. . . . I am convinced I was wrong to come looking for you."

There was a prolonged silence. Then:

"I thought that you would welcome a man who comes to offer his help, with open arms, even though his help was quite worthless. After all, you might perhaps have found some use for it. What, in heaven's name, do I stand to gain, whether the revolution wins or loses?"

Little by little he grew more animated; at times the languor in his eyes disappeared.

"The revolution benefits the poor, the ignorant, all those who have been slaves all their lives, all the unhappy people who do not even suspect they are poor because the rich who stand above them, the rich who rule them, change their sweat and blood and tears into gold. . . ."

"Well, what the hell is the gist of all this palaver? I'll be damned if I can stomach a sermon," Pancracio broke in.

"I wanted to fight for the sacred cause of the oppressed, but you don't understand . . . you cast me aside. . . . Very well, then, you can do as you please with me!"

"All I'm going to do now is to put this rope around your neck. Look what a pretty white neck you've got."

"Yes, I know what brought you here," Demetrio interrupted dryly, scratching his head. "I'm going to have you shot!"

Then, looking at Anastasio, he said:

"Take him away. And . . . if he wants to confess, bring the priest to him."

Impassive as ever, Anastasio took the prisoner gently by the arm.

"Come along this way, Tenderfoot."

They all laughed uproariously, when a few minutes later, Quail appeared in priestly robes.

"By God, this tenderfoot certainly talks his head off," Quail said. "You know, I've a notion he was having a bit of a laugh on me when I started asking him questions."

"But didn't he have anything to say?"

"Nothing, save what he said last night."

"I've a hunch he didn't come here to shoot you at all, Compadre," said Anastasio.

"Give him something to eat and guard him."

11

RÓMULO GALLEGOS

The publication of Rómulo Gallegos's *Doña Bárbara* in Madrid, in 1929, attracted the attention of the Hispanic reading public to the existence of a new school of Latin American narrative, and created a kind of mini-boom for it. The immediately ensuing publication there of books by Azuela, Rivera, and other, lesser novelists proved that the New World had already produced a group of writers that could rival the modernists in popularity (see selections 10, 12, 14).

Paradoxically, the novel in question was a rather conventional narrative that discovered in the Venezuelan plains the same type of conflict between civilization and barbarism that Sarmiento had presented in the Argentine Pampas (*Facundo*, 1845; see Part Two, 5) and Euclides da Cunha in the Brazilian Northeast (*Rebellion in the Backlands*, 1902; Two, 16).

Like them, Gallegos was also deeply concerned with his country's national destiny. He was born in Caracas in 1884. He began law school, but was too poor to complete it and became, like Sarmiento, a schoolteacher. In 1908 he was appointed director of a school in the provinces; later he headed more important institutes in Caracas. He began to write very early. He published a book of short stories and two novels in a realistic vein. At that time, Venezuela was still under the tyrannical rule of Juan Vicente Gómez.

For a while, Gallegos avoided politics and concentrated on writing his *Doña Bárbara* while living in Spain. The publication of the novel made him famous overnight. Even the dictator liked it, despite the fact that the book's theme was a denunciation of his rule and that the protagonist could be seen as a female counterpart of his own barbaric self. He admired Gallegos's mastery in presenting the landscape and characters of a region Gómez himself knew so well. He even offered the author a position in his government. But Gallegos refused to be honored, and left the country once again. He did not return until the dictator's death in 1935, after twenty-seven years of rule.

Gallegos was then appointed Minister of Education, and began a political career that eventually would lead him to the presidency, in 1947. He was ousted the following year by an army coup, but he managed to return in 1958, after the downfall of Pérez Jiménez, to be honored as his party's leading figure and Venezuela's national novelist. Although he was, like Sarmiento, a politician and an educator, it is as a novelist that he will be remembered.

After *Doña Bárbara* he wrote several other novels, two of which are perhaps even better: *Cantaclaro* (1934), about a popular folk singer, and *Canaima* (1935), about the vast Venezuelan jungles. But none of his other books ever matched the popularity of *Doña Bárbara*. The appeal of the book lies in the symbolic opposition between the two main characters: the beautiful and ruthless Doña Bárbara, absolute ruler of the plains, and the idealistic Dr. Santos Luzardo, a spokesman for law and civilization. Throughout, an epic confrontation between the two seems in prospect, but the prospect is never realized. Strictly speaking, the book is not so much a novel as a romance—that is, a work in which the symbolism of the setting and the characters are more important than the plot or action. Gallegos's eloquent descriptions of the landscape are all the more remarkable in that his personal knowledge of the plains was very limited. Up to the time of his writing *Doña Bárbara*, at least, it consisted of a single visit of a few days' duration. But those few days were enough. Like Sarmiento, who superbly described the pampas he had hardly seen, Gallegos created a literary prototype out of a very brief acquaintance with reality. The chapter here excerpted tells the story of Santos Luzardo's family and is devoted to an episode reminiscent of Prudencio Aguilar's killing in García Márquez's *One Hundred*

Years of Solitude (see Five, 14). It must be said, however, that the kind of dense, concentrated writing Gallegos offers here is not typical of the whole novel. Overall *Doña Bárbara* is lacking in stylistic precision or economy, though it compensates for this flaw through its strong symbolical appeal.

Doña Bárbara

From Doña Bárbara, *translated by Robert Malloy (New York: Pete Smith, 1948), pp. 18–23.*

In the wildest and most deserted part of the Arauca basin was situated the ranch of Altamira, originally some two hundred leagues of fertile savannas giving pasture to the immense herds which grazed in its fastnesses and containing one of the finest flocks of wild herons in the country.

It had been established years and years before by Don Evaristo Luzardo, one of those nomad cattlemen who used to—and still do—scour with their herds the vast prairies of the Cunaviche basin, passing from this to the basin of the Arauca, which was less remote from the centers of population. His descendants, real Plainsmen of "bare feet and side buttons" who never went beyond the boundaries of the ranch, improved and extended the property until they had converted it into one of the most important in the country; but when the family became rich and numerous, some of its members turned toward the cities, while the others remained under the palm-thatched roof of the ranch house; the peaceful patriarchal life of the earlier Luzardos was succeeded by separation, and this brought the discord which was to give them tragic fame.

The last owner of the original Altamira was Don José de los Santos, who, in order to save the property from the ruin of wholesale division, bought the interest of his fellow owners, an undertaking that cost him a long lifetime of toil and privation; but, upon his death, his children José and Panchita—the latter married to Sebastian Barquero—chose to divide, and the old establishment was succeeded by two, one the property of José, keeping its original name, the other taking the name of La Barquereña after its owner's surname.

Beginning at that time, because of an ambiguous phrase in the will which described the boundary line as "the palm grove of La Chusmita," discord arose between the brothers-in-law, for each declared that the phrase should be interpreted, to *his* advantage; and thus they commenced one of those endless litigations which make the fortunes of several generations of lawyers. It would have ended by ruining them, had not the same intransigency which was making them waste a fortune over an unproductive bit of land also made them determine, when a settlement was proposed, to have "all or nothing." And since both could not have all, they agreed that both should have nothing, and engaged to build a fence around the grove, which thus became enclosed and no part of either property.

But the matter did not end there. In the center of the grove was the bed of a channel which had dried up. In the winter this became a quagmire, a mudhole which was death to any man or beast attempting to cross it, and one day, when he spied in it a drowned steer belonging to the Barquero herd, José Luzardo protested to Sebastian Barquero, declaring that this was a violation of the neutral ground. The dispute became heated; Barquero swung his whip at the face of his brother-in-law, and the latter, whipping out his revolver, toppled Barquero from his horse with a bullet through his head. Then the reprisals commenced, and with the partisans killing each other off, the population, composed as it was of practically nothing but the various branches of the two families, was in the end nearly wiped out. And the seed of tragedy was born again in the breast of every single one.

When war broke out between Spain and the United States, José Luzardo, "true to his race," as he phrased it, sympathized with the mother country, while his eldest son Felix, a symbol of the new times, took the part of the "Yankees." The Caracas newspapers came to the ranch about once a month, and with the very first items of news, read by the son, for Don José was rapidly losing his sight, they became engaged in a fierce dispute which led to these bitter words from the old man:

"Anybody'd have to be mighty stupid to believe that those Chicago sausage-packers can beat us," to which Felix, livid and stammering with rage, replied, facing him defiantly:

"Maybe the Spaniards will win, but I won't stand for your insulting me for nothing."

Don José looked at him from head to foot, with an expression of scorn, and burst into a loud laugh. The son ended by losing his head, and drew his revolver from its holster; whereupon the father cut his guffaw short, and without any change of voice or position, but with a proud expression, said slowly:

"Shoot! But don't miss me, or I'll nail you to that wall with my lance-head."

This happened in the ranch house, shortly after supper, when the family was gathered around the lamp. Doña Asunción hastened to interpose, and Santos, who was about fourteen years old at that time, was stupefied with horror.

Whether overcome by the terrible calm of his father, or certain that the latter would carry out his threat if he shot and missed, or repenting of his violence—at any rate, Felix replaced the revolver in his holster and left the room. Shortly afterward, he saddled his horse, determined to leave his father's house, and it was in vain that Doña Asunción pleaded and wept. Meanwhile, as though nothing had happened, Don José had put on his glasses and read stoically the news items ending with the disaster at Cavite. But Felix was not content with leaving his home. He made common cause with the Barqueros against his own family in that war to the death, whose most pitiless advocate was his aunt Panchita, and which was winked at by the authorities, for it was the day of the caciques, and the Luzardos and Barqueros shared the lordship of the Arauca.

Nearly all the men of both families had fallen in personal encounters, when one night, when he knew there was to be a cockfight in the village and that his father would be there, Felix also went, under the joint influence of alcohol and his cousin Lorenzo Barquero, and burst in, shouting:

"Here's a Puerto Rican bantam. Not even a Yankee, but I want to see if there's any Spanish *cripple* to match him! I'll put him in with his spurs clipped to fight to the finish."

The unequal struggle had already ended with the victory of the "Yankees," and Felix had of course said that to provoke his father. Don José wanted to use a whip in correction of this insolence, but Felix flew to arms. So did the father, who returned home shortly afterward, dejected, grim, and suddenly grown old, to deliver this news to his wife:

"I've just killed Felix. They're bringing him in."

Going to the room where the first scene of the tragedy had occurred, he shut himself up in it, gave strict orders that he was not to be disturbed, removed the lance-head from his belt, and buried it in the wall where he had threatened to nail his son with it, that night of the tragic newspaper reading. For it was there, where he had threatened to kill his son, that he wished to have the murderous steel before his eyes until they should be closed forever, as a sign of expiation.

Shut up in that room, without so much as bread and water, without moving, almost without blinking his eyes; with the light from a single shutter, and eyes which would soon learn to do without light in the darkness, with his whole will bent on a horrible expiation for his deed—there he waited day after day for the death to which he had condemned himself, and there death found him, sitting up rigid in his chair, his gaze fixed on the blade stuck in the wall.

12

JOSÉ EUSTASIO RIVERA

Although *The Vortex* is read today especially for its brilliant description of the Amazonian jungle, which the novel presents almost as a fabulous living being, at the time it was published in 1924 it was mainly read for its terrifying indictment of the rubber industry. The Irishman Roger Casement had won a prize for his 1910–11 report on the horrors of the Putumayo River. Rivera came to know the basin ten years later, as a member of a commission sent to arbitrate a boundary dispute between Colombia and Venezuela. He then discovered the incredible beauty of the jungle but also learned about the brutal exploitation of the workers and could verify the truth of the sadistic tales of punishments and muti- lations. All this he described in an official report that later became the basis for the central part of his novel. When Rivera went back to Bogotá, he had a cause.

Rivera was born in Colombia in 1888, to a poor middle-class family. He graduated from law school in 1917 and tried to enter politics, but failed because he was considered too radical by the Conservative party his family supported. For two years (1918–1920) he lived on the Colombian plains, as legal adviser to a wealthy ranch owner. There he acquired a firsthand knowledge of one of the settings of his future novel.

Back in Bogotá, he became involved with a group of Parnassian poets and wrote sonnets with the perfection the school required. He collected them in a book, *The Promised Land* (1921). It was that same year that he visited the Amazon basin. When he came back, he ran for Congress and was elected. The publication of *The Vortex* in 1924 made him famous. The Uruguayan Horacio Quiroga was one of the first to recognize the book's outstanding qualities. He realized that his Colombian colleague had succeeded in doing on a larger scale what he himself had earlier achieved in his jungle tales: a new type of narrative in which social protest and imaginative writing were effectively blended. Quiroga's enthusiasm was such that he wrote Rivera, offering to write a preface for a forthcoming edition of the book. Although Rivera was moved ("Your words are gold to me," he wrote in a 1928 letter to Quiroga), it was too late: the edition was already out. Rivera died a few weeks afterward. The success of the book, however, had only begun. After a Madrid edition in 1930, the novel was con- stantly reprinted all over the Hispanic world.

Part of its success is due to the clever blending of fact and fiction. As a means of giving the novel some factual documentary basis, Rivera resorted to the well-known device of presenting himself as the editor of a journal kept by the protagonist, Arturo Cova. He has escaped Bogotá with Alicia, his two-months- pregnant mistress. After reaching the plains, they disappear into the Amazonian jungle. The journey lasts seven months—the term of Alicia's pregnancy. At the end, a sober note from the editor informs the reader that nothing is known about their fate: "The jungle devoured them" is the text's last line.

Like *Doña Bárbara*, the book is more a romance than a novel. Although there is some attempt to dissect Arturo's complex and rather perverse nature, the characters take second place to exalted descriptions of the natural setting. It is the jungle that is the book's true protagonist. With his lyrical style, Rivera evokes its primeval magic and terrifying power. The book also dwells extensively on the horrors of slavery and the display of human greed. In the chapter excerpted here, a group of rubber workers try to escape from their exploiters, only to fall into the path of an invasion of *tambochas,* the murderous ants that travel in armies; lost in the jungle labyrinths, they are destroyed by the physical or mental torture the jungle inflicts on them. The only survivor is Clemente, the guide, who has been searching for his son's grave and almost finds his own. With *The Vortex*, Rivera wrote the last great romantic tale of Latin American nature and opened the way for a certain type of novel that such later writers as Carpentier and Vargas Llosa (see Four, 3; Five, 17) would aim to perfect. It was no small achievement for a man for whom this book was the only attempt at novel writing.

The Vortex

From The Green Continent, *translated by K. James, pp. 32–43.*

One morning at sunrise came unexpected disaster. The sick workers who had remained in the main hut to doctor their livers suddenly heard shouts from the river. They hastily gathered on the rocky ledge. Floating down the middle of the stream, like enormous black ducks, were the balls of rubber; and behind them came a peon in a small dugout, pushing with his pole the spheres that tarried in the eddies and backwaters. As he herded his black flock into the inlet of the little bay, he raised a cry more frightful than any war cry:

"Tambochas! Tambochas! And the men are isolated!"

Tambochas! That meant suspending work, leaving shelter, throwing barriers of fire across the trail, and seeking refuge elsewhere. An invasion of carnivorous ants, born who knows where, emigrating to die as winter comes, sweeping the hills for leagues and leagues with the rustle and crackle of a distant forest fire. Wingless wasps, with red heads and lemon-colored bodies, scattering terror in their path because of their venomous bite and swarming multitudes. Every cave, every crevice, every hole—trees, shrubs, nests, beehives—everything suffered from the overpowering flow of that heavy and fetid wave that devours young birds, rodents, reptiles, and puts to flight whole villages of men and beasts.

The news spread consternation. The peons of the camp scurried around madly, gathering tools and equipment.

"On which side is the swarm coming?" asked Manuel Cardoso.

"On both banks, it seems. The tapirs and peccaries are plunging into the river from this side, but the bees are swarming on the other side."

"Who are the workers who are isolated?"

"Five in El Silencio swamp—they don't even have a boat."

"What can we do? They'll have to shift for themselves! We can't help. Who'd risk losing himself in these swamps?"

"I," replied old man Clemente Silva.

And a young Brazilian youth named Lauro Coutinho joined him.

"I'll go, too," he said. "My brother's there."

Gathering together what provisions they could, and supplied with arms and matches, the two set out along a trail that plunged into the jungle toward the Marie River.

They traveled hastily over oozing mud and through tangled under-brush, eyes and ears on the alert. Of a sudden, as the old man was clearing a path before him, forcing a trail toward El Silencio marsh, Lauro Coutinho stopped him.

"Now's the time to escape!"

The same thought had already crossed Don Clemente's mind, but he gave no sign of his pleasure at the suggestion.

"We should consult the others. . . ."

"I can assure you they'll agree—without hesitation."

And he was right. They found the five men on the following day, in a rude shelter, shooting craps on a handkerchief spread on the earth, drunk from the palmachonta wine they were imbibing from a gourd that went its ceaseless rounds.

"Ants? To hell with the ants! We laugh at tambochas! To escape, escape! With a guide like you—even from hell you could lead us!"

And there they go through the jungles with the illusion of freedom before them, laughing, full of plans, praising their guide, promising him their friendship, their remembrance, their gratitude! Lauro Coutinho has cut a palm leaf and carries it aloft like a banner. Souza Machado will not abandon his ball of crude rubber. It weighs ten pounds, but with its price he hopes to enjoy two nights of a woman's caresses, a white and fair woman, fragrant of roses and brandy. The Italian Peggi babbles of going to a city and getting a job as cook in a hotel where there is an abundance of leftovers and tips are generous. Coutinho the elder wants to marry a wench who boasts an income. The Indian Venancio wants to spend the rest of his days making dugouts. Pedro Fajardo aspires to buy a cottage that will shelter his blind old mother. Don Clemente dreams of finding the grave. It is a procession of unfortunates, a march from misery to death.

And which was the route they sought? The Curi-curiari River. From there they would go up the Río Negro, two hundred miles above Naranjal, passing to Umarituba to seek shelter. Señor Castanheira Fontes was a good man. He would help them. There a broad horizon would spread itself before them. In case of capture, the explanation was obvious; they were fleeing before the tambochas. Let them ask the foreman.

On the fourth day through the jungles the crisis began; food was scarce and the swamps interminable. They stopped to rest. They took off their shirts and tore them into strips to wrap around their legs, tortured by the leeches that lurked in the muddy waters. Souza Machado, made generous by fatigue, slashed his ball of rubber with a knife and shared it with his companions. Fajardo would not receive his portion. Souza took it. It was black gold and not to be despised.

A thoughtless one asked, "Where now?"

And all replied, reproachful, "Forward! of course."

But the guide was lost. He advanced doubtfully, feeling his way, yet without stopping or saying anything in order not to alarm the others. Three times within an hour he found himself back at the same swamp, but fortunately his companions did not recognize it. Concentrating all his being in his memory, he saw before him the map he had studied so often on the veranda at Naranjal. He saw the sinuous lines, spreading like a network of veins over a spot of palish green. Unforgettable names stood out: Teiya, Marie, Curi-curiari. But what a difference between this wilderness and the map, which shrinks in reproduction! Who would have thought that that piece of paper, scarcely large enough to be covered by his open hands, embraced such vast stretches, such dismal jungles, such deadly swamps! And he, experienced trail breaker, who so easily passed his finger from one line to another, spanning rivers and jungles, parallels and meridians—how could he ever have been fool enough to believe his feet would move as lightly as his fingers?

Inwardly he began to pray. If God would give him the sun but for a moment. . . . But nothing! Cold grayness—foliage sweating a blue vapor. Forward! The sun will not shine for the sad!

One of the men suddenly declared emphatically that he heard whistling. All stopped. Only a buzzing in his ears. Souza Machado wanted to be in the midst of the others. He swore the trees made uncanny gestures at him.

They grew nervous. Forebodings of misfortune pressed heavily upon them. A careless word and the repressed emotions might be released—in panic, rage, madness. Each struggled to resist. Forward!

Lauro Coutinho made a sorry effort to appear carefree. He bantered with Souza Machado, who had stopped to throw away the remains of his rubber ball. Machado attempted hilarity. They talked awhile. Then someone, I don't know who, asked Don Clemente some questions.

"Silence!" growled the Italian. "Remember that pilots and guides must not be spoken to!"

But old man Silva, stopping short, raised his arms as one who surrenders to captors and, facing his friends, sobbed, "We are lost!"

Instantly the unhappy group, with their eyes lifted to the lofty branches, howled like dogs, raising a chorus of blasphemy and prayer:

"Inhuman God! Save us, O God! We are lost!"

"We are lost!" Simple and common words—yet uttered in the jungles they strike terror in the heart. To the mind of the person who hears them comes the vision of a man-consuming hell, a gaping mouth swallowing men whom hunger and disappointment place in its jaws.

Neither vows, nor warnings, nor the tears of the guide, who promised to find his way again, could serve to calm the men's panic.

"This old fellow is to blame! He lost his way because he wanted to go to the Vaupes!"

"Wretch! Bandit! You were deceiving us. You were taking us to sell us, God knows where!"

"Yes, you criminal! But God blasted your schemes!"

Seeing that his crazed companions might kill him, old man Silva started to run, but the treacherous lianas of a tree caught his legs and tripped him. There they tied him up, while Peggi urged that they rip him to shreds. Then it was that Don Clemente spoke the words that saved him.

"You want to kill me?" he said. "How can you do anything without me? I'm your only hope!"

The men stopped mechanically.

"Yes, yes, it's necessary that he live in order to save us."

"But without letting him loose, or he'll escape!"

And although they would not unfasten him, they knelt before him to beg him to save them.

"Don't desert us!"

"Let's return to the hut!"

"If you abandon us, we'll starve!"

Don Clemente's explanations gradually made them amenable to reason. What had happened, he told them, was nothing unusual in the lives of guides and hunters. It was foolish to give up hope at the very first mishap, especially as there were so many ways of getting out of the difficulty. Why had they scared him? Why had they thought of the possibility of getting lost? Had he not told them again and again to resist all such thoughts, so easily aroused by the accursed jungles that seem eager to bewilder and confuse men? Had he not warned them not to look at the trees, because they beckon to one; not to listen to murmurings because they whisper things; not to speak, because the heavy foliage echoes back the voice? Far from following these instructions, they jested with the forest, and its witchery fell upon them, spreading from one to another as if by contagion; and he, too, although walking on ahead, had started feeling the influence of the evil spirits; the jungle began to move, the trees to dance before his eyes, the undergrowth to resist his efforts to blaze a trail; the branches hid from his knife, or sometimes sought to wrest it from him with a mighty grip. Who was to blame?

And now why the devil start yelling? And what good would shooting do? Who but the jaguar would run to find them? Would they like a visit from him? If so, they could wait until nightfall. He'd come then!

This terrified them and they were silent. Yet had they wished it, they could not have made their voices heard more than a couple of yards—their outcries had parched their throats. They spoke hoarsely, with the guttural pantings of geese.

Long before the sun was pluming with crimson those upper reaches they could not see, the smudge fire had to be lighted, for darkness falls upon the forest early. They cut branches on which to rest, scattering them on the mud, there to await the anguish of the inky shadows. Oh, the torture of a long night of hunger, of thoughts that terrify; yawning, always yawning, knowing that the next day the yawning will be worse! Oh, the depressing effect of the incessant sobbing in the shadows, of comforting words that are in vain, for they only hide death! Lost, lost! Sleeplessness brought its train of phantoms—and the agony of the helpless who feel unseen eyes spying on them from the darkness. The sounds came—the nocturnal voices, the creeping steps—silences as appalling as gaps in eternity.

Don Clemente, his head in his hands, searched his memory for some clarifying hint. Only the sky could help him. Let it only tell him where the light of dawn came. That would be enough to plan another route.

Through a clear space in the lofty ceiling of foliage, a skylight in the forest, he saw a fragment of blue, fractured by the riblike branches of a withered bough. He recalled his map again. To see the sun, to see the sun! That was the key. If those tall cones of green, which every day saw it pass over them, could only speak! Why should the silent trees refuse to tell a man what to do that he might not die? And, thinking again on God, he began to pray to the jungle, a prayer that begged forgiveness for the injury done the forests through bantering talk.

To climb one of those giants was next to impossible: the enormous trunks, the remote branches, dizziness lurking in the foliage to overtake the one who dared. If Lauro Coutinho, dozing nervously, were to try . . .

Silva was about to call him when a noise, as of rats gnawing on fine wood, scratched across the stillness. It was the teeth of his companions, chewing on the hard seeds of the vegetable ivory tree.

Don Clemente felt a surge of compassion. He would console them, even though by lying.

"What is it?" they whispered, bringing their shadowed faces near.

And anxious hands felt the knots of the cords that bound him.

"We are saved!"

Dulled with joy, they repeated the words: "Saved! Saved!" They knelt down and pressed the mud with their knees, for suffering had left them contrite. Without even asking what it was that offered them salvation, they gave vent to a hoarse prayer of thanks. It was enough that another promised it.

Don Clemente received embraces, entreaties of forgiveness, apologies to amend the wrong they had done him. Some took all the credit for the miracle:

"The prayers of my little mother!"

"The Masses that I offered!"

"The blessed amulet I carry!"

And meanwhile, in the shadows, death must have laughed!

Dawn broke.

The hope that sustained them accentuated the tragedy on their faces. Emaciated, feverish, with bloodshot eyes and fluttering pulses, they waited for the sun to rise. Their actions inspired fear. They had forgotten how to smile, or if they thought of smiling, only a frightful grimace moved their lips.

Vainly they searched for a place where they might see the sun. Then softly it began to rain. No one said a word. They understood. The sun was not to be theirs.

They decided to return, traveling over the trails traversed the previous day, skirting a swamp where footprints left tiny pools into which waters gurgled

—and wiped away the traces. Yet the guide stuck to the route. Silently they kept on until about nine in the morning, when they entered a heavy growth of coarse and matted bamboo. There they encountered flocks of rabbits and trogons, which, stupefied, ran between their legs seeking refuge. A few moments later and a sound as of swirling rapids was heard reverberating through the wilderness.

"Good God! The tambochas!"

Flight was the only thought then. Turning, they stumbled back and then plunged into the swamp until the stagnant waters swept over their shoulders. Better the leeches than the ants.

From there they watched the first swarm pass by. Like ashes thrown from a distant conflagration, clouds of fugitive roaches and coleoptera swept down to the waters, while the edges of the marsh grew dense with arachnids and reptiles, forcing the men to splash the foul waters so that the insects would not come toward them. A continual tremor agitated the ground, as if the vegetation of the jungles were boiling. From under trunks and roots came the tumultuous invaders; over the trees spread a dark stain, sheathing the trunks like a flowing shell that crept upward implacably to torture the branches, plunder the nests, swarm the apertures and cracks. A blind weasel, a tardy lizard, a newborn rat— these were coveted prey for the avaricious army which, grating shrilly, stripped the bones of flesh like some fast-dissolving acid.

How long did the martyrdom of those men last? Buried to the chin in the slimy liquid, with terror-stricken eyes, they watched the swarms of the enemy passing, passing, and again passing. Nerve-racking hours, during which they sipped and sipped the bitter depths of slow torture. When at length the last swarm was sweeping into the distance, they tried to emerge; but their limbs were numb, too weak to wrench themselves from the hungry mud that gripped them.

Yet they must not die there. They must struggle out. The Indian Venancio managed to grasp some plants and began to pull. Then he caught hold of a clump of reeds. Several stray tambochas gnawed the flesh of his hands, eating deeply. Little by little he felt the clammy mold that gripped him loosening its hold. His legs, as they tore from the bottom, cracked loudly. "Upa! Once more, and don't faint! Courage! Courage!"

He's out. The waters gurgled and bubbled in the hole he left.

Panting, on his back, he heard his despairing comrades calling on him for help. "Let me rest! Let me rest!"

An hour later, by means of branches and lianas, he had managed to get them all out.

This was the last time they suffered together. Which way had they been going? They felt their heads in flames, their bodies stiff. Pedro Fajardo began to cough convulsively. Of a sudden he fell, bathed in frothy blood that he vomited in an attack of hemoptysis.

But they could feel no pity for the dying man. Coutinho the elder advised them to lose no time. "Take his knife from his belt and leave him there. Why did he come if he was ill? He mustn't hamper us." So saying, he forced his brother to climb a copaiba to seek the sun.

The unfortunate youth bound his ankles with strips of shirt. Vainly he tried to grip the tree trunk. They raised him on their shoulders so that he might catch hold higher up. He continued his efforts, but the bark peeled off. He would slide down, to start anew. They held him up, propping him with long, forked branches and feeling their height tripled in their effort to help him. Finally he grasped the first branch. Stomach, arms, chest, and knees shed blood. "Do you see anything? Do you see anything?" they asked. And with his head he answered: "No!"

They no longer remembered to be silent in order not to provoke the jungle. An absurd violence filled them, and the fury of drowning people surged through them, the fury that knows neither friend nor relative, fighting off those who would clamber into a boat that can hold no more. With their hands they gesticulated heavenward as they called to Lauro Coutinho.

"You see nothing? Climb higher—and look well."

Lauro, on a branch, clutching the trunk, panted without replying. At such a height he seemed a wounded monkey, trying to squirm into frantic hiding from the hunter. "Coward! You must climb higher!" And those below, mad with rage, threatened him.

Suddenly, however, the youth started to descend. A roar of hate rose from the ground. Lauro, terrified, tried to explain. "More tambochas—coming —com—"

The last syllable died in his throat. The elder Coutinho, with a shot from his rifle, had pierced his chest. The youth fell like a plummet.

The fratricide stood still, his eyes on the crumpled, bleeding body.

"My God!" he broke out suddenly. "I've killed my brother—killed my brother!" Then, throwing away his gun, he fled. The others ran too, not knowing where. And they scattered never to meet again.

Many nights later Don Clemente heard them shouting, but he was afraid they would kill him. He, too, had lost all pity. The jungle possessed him. Then remorse set him weeping, although the need for saving his own life justified his act before his conscience. Eventually he went back to look for them. He found the skulls and a few femurs.

Without fire or gun, he wandered two months, reduced almost to imbecility, deprived of his senses, animalized by the jungle, despised even by death, chewing roots, husks, mushrooms like a herbivorous animal, with the sole difference that he had to watch what kind of fruit or berries the monkeys ate in order to avoid the poisonous ones.

But one morning he had a sudden revelation. He stopped before a cananguche palm, and to his mind came the tradition that tells how this species follows the sun, like a sunflower. Never had he given the matter any thought before. He spent anxious moments watching, and he thought he saw the lofty foliage slowly bending, with the rhythm of a head that took exactly twelve hours to move from the right shoulder over to the left. The secret voice filled his soul. Was it possible that this palm, planted in the wilderness like an index pointing to the blue, was showing him his route? True or false, he heard it speak. And he believed! That was all he needed—belief. And from the course the palm tree followed he plotted his own.

So it was that he reached the banks of the Tiquie. That river, narrow and curving, seemed more like a stagnant pond in the marshes than a stream. He began throwing leaves into the waters to see if they moved. The Albuquerque brothers found him thus occupied and, almost dragging him, took him to the shelter.

"Who's that scarecrow you've found?" the rubber-gatherers asked.

"A fugitive who can only say: 'Coutinho! . . . Peggi! . . . Souza Machado! . . .' "

Then after working there a year, he escaped in a dugout to the Vaupes.

Now he's sitting here in my company, waiting for dawn to break before going down to the shacks of Guaracu. Perhaps he's thinking of Yaguanari, of Yavarate, of his lost companions. "Don't go to Yaguanari!" he's always telling me. But I, remembering Alicia and my enemy, cry angrily:

"I'll go! I'll go, I'll go!"

13

RICARDO GÜIRALDES

Viana had presented the gaucho through naturalist eyes as a decadent race (see selection 9). It would be the task of the Argentine Ricardo Güiraldes to give the old prototype a new image. His *Don Segundo Sombra* would be a nostalgic hymn to the glory of a man and a world that had ceased to be. (The character's name means literally "shadow" in Spanish.) Its lyrical qualities and the facile character of its symbolism made the novel an instant success in both Latin America and Spain. Don Segundo was hailed as the epitome of the noble gaucho, and Güiraldes was acclaimed as Argentina's leading novelist.

He was born on a ranch in the province of Buenos Aires in 1886, to a wealthy family. His father had studied at Lausanne and Leipzig. When Ricardo was not yet two, the family moved to Paris and stayed there until 1890. By the time they came back, Ricardo spoke only French. But soon he discovered the real Argentina on his father's ranch. There he met Segundo Ramírez, the man he would eventually immortalize as Don Segundo Sombra. Ricardo learned from him everything about gaucho life and folklore. Don Segundo was a great story-teller, and the boy sat at his feet, absorbing the raw materials that many years later he would transform and refine in his masterpiece. Although he had to return to Buenos Aires each year for his schooling (French literature, German language, a smattering of architecture and law), it was the summers spent at the ranch that most truly molded Güiraldes.

In 1910 he went back to Paris to achieve his ambition of becoming a great writer. Anticipating Rudolph Valentino's role in *The Four Horsemen of the Apocalypse* (1920), he taught the wealthy patrons of the best nightclubs how to tango. He also took the first of his grand tours, to Italy, Greece, Germany, Russia, and India. Back home, he began to contribute stories about gaucho life to various popular literary journals, though with only limited success. Two books published in 1915—*The Crystal Cow Bell,* poems; and *Tales of Death and Blood*—went almost unnoticed. Güiraldes decided to return in leisurely fashion to France in 1916, via the Pacific and the Caribbean islands, where he absorbed the atmosphere of his next book, a novel, *Xaimaca* (1923). In Paris he met Valéry Larbaud, the ironical poet and storyteller of *Barnabooth,* and through him discovered the avant-garde writers.

He returned to Buenos Aires in 1920, a different man and a different artist. He sought contact with the younger ultraist poets (see Introduction to Part Four), edited with Borges an experimental magazine *Prow* (1924), and wrote *Don Segundo Sombra* (1926). The book was based on Güiraldes's own recollections of life on his father's ranch, but to make it more of a novel and closer to its models —Mark Twain's *Huck Finn,* Rudyard Kipling's *Kim*—he invented a melodramatic plot. The narrator is Fabio Cáceres, a bastard son who is protected by two old aunts and who finds a mentor in Don Segundo Sombra. The book is in form a *Bildungsroman,* and the action is presented through Fabio's reminiscences at three decisive moments of his life. In the first, he is fourteen years old and he evokes, on the banks of a stream, his childhood, his meeting with Don Segundo, and his slow apprenticeship in gaucho life. When he is nineteen, he recapitulates in his mind, as he stands on the banks of a river, the five glorious years spent working with Don Segundo. The last reminiscence comes when he is twenty-three and is found sitting on the banks of a pond. By this time, his real father has died, but not before acknowledging him in his will. Now Fabio is a man, and a wealthy ranch owner. He has had to sever his links with Don Segundo, who disappears into the horizon, as a shadow.

Even this brief summary makes apparent the overtly symbolic nature of the plot and characters. But what makes the novel so extremely attractive is its successful creation and sustaining of a mood of nostalgia. It is, in essence, an elegy. Don Segundo, moreover, is not merely a symbol, but exists as a fully rounded personality, with a notable capacity for a kind of subtle irony; and the stories he tells, and his counsel and reflections, are the best in gauchoesque literature since *Martín Fierro.* It is in that quality found so abundantly in writers like Hernández, Acevedo Díaz, and Viana—a strong narrative imagination, a resourcefulness in invention—that *Segundo Sombra* is most conspicuously deficient. And the elegance of style that was so warmly praised in its time no longer elicits the same admiration. Nonetheless, many individual episodes and chapters are of indisputable excellence. One of the best is the one excerpted here, in which the boy Fabio meets his hero for the first time. In it we discern the beginnings of a myth and a legend.

Don Segundo Sombra

From Don Segundo Sombra, *translated by Harriet de Onís (New York: The New American Library, 1966), pp. 13–20.*

Slowly, with my fishing rod over my shoulder and dangling my small victims heartlessly at my side, I made my way toward town. The street still was flooded by a recent thundershower, and I had to walk carefully to keep from sinking in the mud that clung to my sandals and almost sucked them off my feet. My mind was a blank as I took the narrow path that crept along the hedges of prickly pear, thorn, myrrh, following the rise of the ground, like hares seeking a level place to run.

The lane ahead of me stretched dark. The sky, still blue with twilight, lay in reflected shards in the puddles or in the deep wagon ruts, where it looked like strips of carefully trimmed steel.

I had reached the first houses, where the hour put the dogs on the alert. Fear twitched in my legs as I heard the growl of a dangerous mastiff not far off, but without a mistake I called all the brutes by name: Sentinel, Captain, Watcher. When some mutt set up a barking as swift as it was inoffensive, I disdainfully shied a clod at it.

I passed the graveyard and a familiar tremor ran down my spine, radiating its pallid chill to my calves and forearms. The dead, will-o'-the-wisps, ghosts, scared me far more than any encounter I might have with mortals in that neighborhood. What could the greediest robber hope for from me? I was on good terms with the slyest of them; and if one was so careless as to hold me up, he would be the loser by a cigarette.

The lane became a street, the outlying farms thickened into blocks of houses; and neither walls nor bead-tree hedges held any secrets for me. Here was a stand of alfalfa, there a patch of corn, a barn lot, or just brush. Now I could make out the first shanties, silent in their squalor and illumined only by the frail glow of a candle or stinking kerosene lamps. As I crossed a street I frightened a horse whose step had sounded farther off than it was; and as fear is catching, even from animal to man, I stood stock-still in the mud without daring to move. The rider, who seemed to me enormous in his light poncho, urged the horse on, whirling the whiplash past its left eye; but as soon as I tried to take a step the scared beast snorted like a mule and reared. A puddle cracked beneath his hoof with the sound of breaking glass. A high-pitched voice spoke calmly, "Steady, boy. Steady, boy."

Then trot and gallop splashed through the sleek mud.

I stood still and watched the silhouette of horse and rider disappear strangely magnified against the glowing sky. It was as if I had seen a vision, a shade, a something that passes and is more a thought than a living thing, a something that drew me as a pool swallows the current of a river into its depths.

Filled with my vision, I reached the first sidewalks, where I could make better time. Stronger than ever was the need I felt to get away, to leave this paltry town forever. I had glimpsed a new life, a life of motion and space.

In a whirl of dreams and doubts I kept on through the town and down the blackness of another alley to La Blanqueada. As I entered, the light made me pucker up my eyes. Behind the counter, as usual, stood the owner, and in front of him the half-breed Burgos was just finishing off a brandy.

"Good evening, gentlemen."

"Evening," mumbled Burgos.

"What you got?" asked the owner.

"There you are, Don Pedro." I showed him my string of catfish.

"All right. Want some rock candy?"

"No, Don Pedro."

"Couple packages of La Popular?"

"No, Don Pedro. Remember the last money you gave me?"

"Sure."

"It was round."

"And you made it roll?"

"You said it."

"All right. Here you are." He clinked several nickel coins down on the counter.

"Gonna set up the drinks?" grinned the half-breed.

"Sure—in the *Wouldn't You Like It* café."

"Anything new?" asked Don Pedro, for whom I was a kind of reporter.

"Yes, sir; a stranger."

"Where'd you see him?"

"At the crossing, as I was coming in from the river."

"And you don't know who he is?"

"I know he's not from here. There's no man as big as him in this town."

Don Pedro frowned, as if trying to concentrate on some half-forgotten memory. "Tell me, was he very dark?"

"I think so—yes, sir. And strong!"

As though talking of something extraordinary, the saloonkeeper muttered, "Who knows if it isn't Don Segundo Sombra!"

"It is!" I said, without knowing why, and I felt the same thrill as when at nightfall I had stood motionless before the portentous vision of that gaucho stamped black on the horizon.

"You know him?" Don Pedro asked the half-breed, paying no attention to my exclamation.

"Only what I've heard tell of him. The devil, I reckon, ain't as fierce as he's painted. How about serving me another drink?"

"Hm," went on Don Pedro. "I've seen him more than once. He used to come in here, afternoons. He's a man you want to watch your step with. He's from San Pedro. Had a run in, they say, with the police some time ago."

"I suppose he butchered somebody else's steer."

"Yes. But, if I remember rightly, the steer was a Christian."

Burgos kept his stolid eyes on the glass, and a frown wrinkled his narrow forehead of a pampas Indian half-breed. The fame of another man seemed to lessen his own as an expert with the knife.

We heard a gallop stop short at the door, then the soft hiss with which the country folk quiet a horse, and Don Segundo's silent figure stood framed in the doorway.

"Good evening," came the high-pitched voice, and it was easy to recognize. "How's Don Pedro?"

"Good. And you, Don Segundo?"

"I can't complain, thank God."

As they greeted each other with the customary courtesies, I looked the man over. He was not really so big. What made him seem so, as he appears to me even today, was the sense of power flowing from his body. His chest was enormous and his joints big-boned like those of a horse. His feet were short and high-arched; his hands thick and leathery like the scales of an armadillo. His skin was copper-hued and his eyes slanted slightly toward his temples. To talk more at ease he pushed his narrow-brimmed hat back from his forehead showing bangs cut like a horse's, level with his eyebrows. His attire was that of a poor gaucho. A plain pigskin belt girded his waist. The short blouse was caught up by the bone-handled knife from which swung a rough, plaited quirt, dark with use. His chiripá was long and coarse, and a plain black kerchief was knotted around his neck with the ends across his shoulders. He had split his *alpargatas* at the instep to make room for the fleshy foot.

When I had looked my fill at him, I listened to the talk. Don Segundo was looking for work, and Don Pedro was telling him where to find it; his constant business with the country people made him know everything that was going on at the ranches.

"At Galván's there are some mares they want broke. A few days ago Valerio was here and asked me if there was anyone I could recommend. I told him about Mosco Pereira, but if it suits you—"

"Seems to me it might."

"Good. I'll tell the boy they send to town every day. He generally drops in."

"I'd rather you said nothing. If I can, I'll go by the ranch myself."

"All right. Like a drink?"

"Well, I don't mind," said Don Segundo, sitting down at a nearby table. "Give me a glass of brandy, and thanks for the invitation."

Everything that had to be said was said. A calm silence filled the place. Burgos poured out his fourth glass. His eyes were bleary and his face expressionless. Suddenly, and for no apparent reason, he said to me, "If I was a fisher like you, I'd want to haul in a great big mud-bottom catfish." A sarcastic giggle underlined his words, and he kept looking at Don Segundo out of the corner of his eye. "They seem tough because they flop around and make such a fuss. But what can they do when they're nothing but niggers."

Don Pedro gave the half-breed a sharp look. Both of us knew what Burgos was like and that nothing could hold him when he turned ugly. The only one of the four of us who didn't understand the drift of things was Don Segundo, who went on sipping his liquor, his thoughts far away. The half-breed giggled again; he was proud of the comparison he had hit on. I longed to do something —something terrible if need be—to break the strain. Don Pedro was humming to himself. And the air was tense for us all, except for the stranger, who seemed to have neither understood nor felt the chill of our silence.

"A big mud-bottom catfish," repeated the drunk again. "But nothing but a catfish, for all it's got whiskers and walks on two legs like Christians. . . . I've heard there's a lot of 'em in San Pedro. That's why they say:

'Anyone from San Pedro
Is either a chink or a mulatto.' "

Twice he repeated the rhyme in a voice that grew thicker and more insolent.

Don Segundo looked up and, as if just realizing that the half-breed's words were meant for him, said calmly, "Come, friend, I'll soon begin to think you're trying to start something."

So unexpected were the words, so amusing the expression of surprise on his face, that we had to smile despite the ugly turn the talk was taking. The drunk himself was nonplussed, but only for a moment.

"Yeah? I was beginning to think everybody around here was deaf."

"How could a catfish be deaf, with the big ears they got? But me? I'm a busy man and I can't take care of you now. When you want to fight with me, let me know at least three days in advance."

We burst out laughing, in spite of the amazement this calm that verged on foolhardiness aroused in us. Again he began to grow in my imagination. He was the "masked man," the "mystery man," the man of silence, who inspires a wondering admiration in the pampas.

The half-breed Burgos paid for his drinks, muttering threats. I followed him to the door and saw him hide in the shadow. Don Segundo got up and took his leave of Don Pedro, who was pale with fear. The drunk was going to kill this man to whom my heart went out! As if speaking to Don Pedro, I warned Don Segundo, "Watch out!"

And then I sat down on the doorsill, my heart in my mouth, waiting for the fight that was sure to come.

Don Segundo stood on the threshold, looking from side to side. I understood that he was getting his eyes used to the dark, so as not to be taken by surprise. Then, keeping to the wall, he started toward his horse.

The half-breed stepped from the shadow feeling sure of his man and let loose his knife aimed straight at the heart. I saw the blade cut the night like the flash of a gun. With incredible swiftness Don Segundo dodged, and the knife shattered against the brick wall with the clang of a bell. Burgos stepped back two paces and waited for what must be his death. The triangular blade of a small knife glittered in Don Segundo's fist. But the attack did not come. Don Segundo bent calmly over, picked the broken steel from the ground, and said in his ironic voice, "Here you are, friend. Better get it fixed. This way, it's no good even to skin a sheep."

The attacker kept his distance. Don Segundo put away his own little knife and again held out the fragments of the blade.

"Take it, friend."

The bully came forward, his head low, moved by a force stronger than his fear. His clumsy fist took the hilt of the knife, now harmless as a broken cross. Don Segundo shrugged and walked toward his horse. And Burgos followed him. Don Segundo mounted and made ready to move into the night. The drunk came close, seeming to have recovered the gift of speech.

"Listen, friend," he said and raised his sullen face, in which only the eyes were alive. "I'm gonna have this knife fixed for whenever you need me." The dull bully's mind could think of only one act of thanks: to offer his life to the other. "Now, shake."

"Sure thing," agreed Don Segundo, as calm as ever. "Put it there, brother."

And without further ado he went down the narrow street, while the half-breed stood seeming to struggle with a thought too great and radiant for him.

I went striding along beside Don Segundo, who kept his horse at a walk.

"You know that fellow?" he asked, muffling himself in his voluminous poncho with a leisurely gesture.

"Yes, sir. I know him well."

"Seems sort of foolish, don't he?"

14

MARTÍN LUIS GUZMÁN

If Azuela (selection 10) presented the Mexican Revolution from the viewpoint of the common man, Martín Luis Guzmán was more interested in showing, at close quarters, the intricate political machinations and struggles to which the Revolution gave rise, the ways in which power was achieved and used. Guzmán was fifteen years younger than Azuela, and that disparity was alone enough to create a difference, in both perspective and tone, between their respective works. With Guzmán, a cooler, more precisely documented assessment of the Revolution began to emerge.

Born in Mexico in 1887, Guzmán belonged to a distinguished family and had a sound education. He was barely twenty-three when Madero overthrew Porfirio Díaz's long-entrenched and corrupt regime. As a journalist he covered Carranza's revolt against Huerta, the assassin of Madero. Guzmán came to meet Pancho Villa personally and for a while accompanied his troops, observing everything and taking notes.

Out of his experiences he wrote *The Eagle and the Serpent*, which presented in brilliant narrative form the historical events he had witnessed at firsthand. The book, published in 1928, became one of the most successful literary accounts of the Revolution. A Spanish edition in two volumes helped promote its diffusion in Latin America.

With Sarmiento's *Facundo* and Da Cunha's *Rebellion in the Backlands* (Two, 5, 16), the book has generally been numbered among the best Latin American works on a historical theme—a judgment substantiated by the dual nature of its achievement, as both historical chronicle and fascinating narrative. A significant contributing factor was Guzmán's particular approach to the treatment of historical events. As he said once, he did not disdain to add a "touch of poetic fancy" here and there to bring out more clearly the "essence" of historical facts.

In his later works, Guzmán used much the same formula: The novel *The Shadow of the Leader* (1930) was based on an actual 1927 episode of the power struggle between the rival chiefs Obregón and Calles. *Memoirs of Pancho Villa* (1940) pretended to be its hero's autobiography; its style reflected the characteristic flavor and tone of his manner of speech, and it sounded very much like him. *Historical Deaths* (1959), brief, minutely detailed reconstructions of the last moments of two revolutionary leaders, represented a subtle blend of fact and fiction. But it is *The Eagle and the Serpent*, with its extraordinary drive and power, that makes Guzmán a major figure. The title alludes to the Mexican national coat of arms, which shows an eagle engaged in deadly battle with a serpent. For Guzmán, the symbols of a remote Aztec past are alive in revolutionary Mexico. The chapter excerpted here presents one of Villa's lieutenants, Rodolfo Fierro, executing captured prisoners in a very exhibitionistic fashion. With its precise descriptions of Fierro's skill, it stands as a portrayal of an extreme and hyperbolic machismo. Even the name "Fierro" ("iron," in Spanish) has symbolic connotations. The chapter conveys admirably the climate of violence and moral corruption that made the Mexican Revolution almost too unbearable to record. With this work, Guzmán was one of the first to attempt to do it thoroughly.

The Eagle and the Serpent

From The Golden Land, translated by Harriet de Onís, pp. 325-34.

My interest in Villa and his activities often made me ask myself, while I was in Juárez, which exploits would best paint the Division of the North: those supposed to be strictly historical or those rated as legendary; those which were related exactly as they had been seen, or those in which a touch of poetic fancy brought out their essence more clearly. These second always seemed to me truer, more worthy of being considered history.

For instance, where could one find a better painting of Rodolfo Fierro —and Fierro and Villa's movements were two facing mirrors that reflected each other endlessly—than in the account of how he carried out the terrible orders of his chief after one of the battles, revealing an imagination as cruel as it was fertile in death devices. This vision of him left in the soul the sensation of a reality so overwhelming that the memory of it lives forever.

That battle, which was successful in every way, had left not less than five hundred prisoners in Villa's hands. Villa ordered them to be divided into two groups: the Orozco volunteers, whom he called "Reds," and the Federals. And as he felt himself strong enough to take extreme measures, he decided to make an example of the prisoners in the first group and to act more generously with the second. The Reds were to be executed before dark; the Federals were to be given their choice of joining the revolutionary troops or returning home, after promising not to take up arms again against the Constitutionalist cause.

Fierro, as might have been expected, was put in charge of the execution, and he displayed in it that efficiency which was already winning him great favor with Villa, his "chief," as he called him.

It was growing late in the afternoon. The revolutionary forces, off duty, were slowly gathering in the little village that had been the objective of their offensive. The cold, penetrating wind of the Chihuahua plains was beginning to blow up, and the groups of cavalry and infantry sought protection against the groups of buildings. But Fierro—whom nothing and nobody ever held back—was not to be put out by a cool breeze that at most meant frost that night. He cantered along on his horse, whose dark coat was still covered with the dust of battle. The wind was blowing in his face, but he neither buried his chin in his breast nor raised the folds of his blanket around his face. He carried his head high, his chest thrown out, his feet firm in the stirrups, and his legs gracefully flexed under the campaign equipment that hung from the saddle straps. The barren plain and an occasional soldier that passed at a distance were his only spectators.

But he, perhaps without even thinking about it, reined his horse to make it show its gaits as though he were on parade. Fierro was happy; the satisfaction of victory filled his being; and to him victory was complete only when it meant the utter rout of the enemy; and in this frame of mind even the buffeting of the wind, and riding after fifteen hours in the saddle, were agreeable. The rays of the pale setting sun seemed to caress him as they fell.

He reached the stable yard where the condemned Red prisoners were shut up like a herd of cattle, and he reined in a moment to look at them over the fence rails. They were well-built men of the type common in Chihuahua, tall, compact, with strong necks and well set up shoulders on vigorous, flexible backs. As Fierro looked over the little captive army and sized up its military value and prowess, a strange pulsation ran through him, a twitching that went from his heart or from his forehead out to the index finger of his right hand. Involuntarily the palm of this hand reached for the butt of his pistol.

"Here's a battle for you," he thought.

The cavalrymen, bored with their task of guarding the prisoners, paid no attention to him. The only thing that mattered to them was the annoyance of mounting this tiresome guard, all the worse after the excitement of the battle. They had to have their rifles ready on their knees, and when an occasional soldier left the group, they aimed at him with an air that left no room for doubt as to their intentions, and, if necessary, fired. A wave would run over the formless surface of the mass of the prisoners, who huddled together to avoid the shot. The bullet either went wide or shot one of them down.

Fierro rode up to the gate of the stable yard. He called to a soldier, who let down the bars, and went in. Without taking off his serape, he dismounted. His legs were numb with cold and weariness, and he stretched them. He settled his two pistols in their holsters. Next he began to look slowly over the pens, observing their layout and how they were divided up. He took several steps over to one of the fences, where he tied his horse to a fence board. He slipped something out of one of the pockets of his saddle into his coat pocket and crossed the yard, at a short distance from the prisoners.

There were three pens that opened into one another, with gates and a narrow passageway between. From the one where the prisoners were held, Fierro went into the middle enclosure, slipping through the bars of the gate. He went straight over to the next one. There he stopped. His tall, handsome figure seemed to give off a strange radiance, something superior, awe-inspiring, and yet not out of keeping with the desolation of the barnyard. His serape had slipped down until it barely hung from his shoulders; the tassels of the corners dragged on the ground. His gray, broad-brimmed hat turned rose-colored where the slanting rays of the setting sun fell on it. Through the fences the prisoners could see him, his back turned toward them. His legs formed a pair of herculean, glistening compasses: it was the gleam of his leather puttees in the light of the afternoon.

About a hundred yards away, outside the pens, was the officer of the squad in charge of the prisoners. Fierro made signs to him to come closer, and the officer rode over to the fence beside Fierro. The two began to talk. In the course of the conversation Fierro pointed out different spots in the enclosure in which he was standing and in the one next to it. Then he described with gestures of his hand a series of operations, which the officer repeated, as though to understand them better. Fierro repeated two or three times what seemed to be a very important operation, and the officer, now sure about his orders, galloped off toward the prisoners.

Fierro turned back toward the center of the stable yard, studying once more the layout of the fence, and the other details. That pen was the largest of the three, and the first in order, the nearest to the town. On two sides gates opened into the fields; the bars of these, though more worn-out than those of the farther pens, were of better wood. In the other side there was a gate that opened into the adjoining pen, and on the far side the fence was not of boards, but was an adobe wall, not less than six feet high. The wall was about a hundred and thirty feet long, and about forty feet of it formed the back of a shed or stalls, the roof of which sloped down from the wall and on the one side rested on the end posts of the lateral fence, which had been left longer, and on the other on a wall, also of adobes, which came out perpendicular from the wall and extended some twenty-five feet into the barnyard. In this way, between the shed and the fence of the adjoining lot, there was a space closed on two sides by solid walls. In that corner the wind that afternoon was piling up rubbish and clanging an iron bucket against the wellhead with an arbitrary rhythm. From the wellhead there rose up two rough forked posts, crossed by a third, from which a pulley and chain hung, which also rattled in the wind. On the tiptop of one of the forks sat a large whitish bird, hardly distinguishable from the twisted points of the dry pole.

Fierro was standing about fifty steps from the well. He rested his eye for a moment on the motionless bird, and as though its presence fitted in perfectly with his thoughts, without a change of attitude or expression, he slowly pulled out his pistol. The long polished barrel of the gun turned into a glowing finger in the light of the sun. Slowly it rose until it pointed in the direction of the bird. A shot rang out—dry and diminutive in the immensity of the afternoon—and the bird dropped to the ground. Fierro returned his pistol to its holster.

At that moment a soldier jumped over the fence into the yard. It was Fierro's orderly. It had been such a high jump that it took him several seconds to get to his feet. When he did, he walked over to where his master was standing.

Without turning his head Fierro asked, "What about them? If they don't come soon, we aren't going to have time."

"I think they're coming."

"Then you hurry up and get over there. Let's see, what pistol have you got?"

"The one you gave me, chief. The Smith & Wesson."

"Hand it over here and take these boxes of bullets. How many bullets have you got?"

"I gathered up about fifteen dozen today, chief. Some of the others found lots of them, but I didn't."

"Fifteen dozen? I told you the other day that if you kept on selling ammunition to buy booze, I'd put a bullet through you."

"No, chief."

"What do you mean: 'No, chief'?"

"I do get drunk, chief, but I don't sell the ammunition."

"Well, you watch out, for you know me. And now you move lively so this stunt will be a success. I fire and you load the pistols. And mind what I tell you: if on your account a single one of the Reds gets away, I'll put you to sleep with them."

"Oh, chief!"

"You heard what I said."

The orderly spread his blanket out on the ground and emptied onto it the boxes of cartridges that Fierro had just given him. Then he began to take out one by one the bullets in his cartridge belt. He was in such a hurry that it took him longer than it should have. He was so nervous that his fingers seemed all thumbs.

"What a chief!" he kept thinking to himself.

In the meantime behind the fence of the adjoining barn lot soldiers of the guard began to appear. They were on horseback, and their shoulders showed above the top fence rail. There were many others along the other two fences.

Fierro and his orderly were the only ones inside the barnyard; Fierro stood with a pistol in his hand, his serape fallen at his feet. His orderly squatted beside him lining up the bullets in rows on his blanket.

The commander of the troop rode up through the gate that opened into the next lot, and said, "I've got the first ten ready. Shall I let them out for you?"

"Yes," answered Fierro, "but first explain things to them. As soon as they come through the gate, I'll begin to shoot. Those that reach the wall and get over it are free. If any of them doesn't want to come through, you put a bullet into him."

The officer went back the same way, and Fierro, pistol in hand, stood attentive, his eyes riveted on the narrow space through which the soldiers had to come out. He stood close enough to the dividing fence so that, as he fired, the bullets would not hit the Reds that were still on the other side. He wanted to keep his promise faithfully. But he was not so close that the prisoners could not see, the minute they came through the gate, the pistol that was leveled at them twenty paces off. Behind Fierro the setting sun turned the sky into a fiery ball. The wind kept blowing.

In the barnyard where the prisoners were herded, the voices grew louder, but the howling of the wind made the shouts sound like herders rounding up cattle. It was a hard task to make the three hundred condemned men pass from the last to the middle lot. At the thought of the torture waiting for them, the whole group writhed with the convulsions of a person in the grip of hysteria. The soldiers of the guard shouted, and every minute the reports of the rifles seemed to emphasize the screams as with a whipcrack.

Out of the first prisoners that reached the middle yard, a group of soldiers separated ten. There were at least twenty-five soldiers. They spurred their horses on to the prisoners to make them move; they rested the muzzles of their rifles against their bodies.

"Traitors! Dirty bastards! Let's see you run and jump. Get a move on, you traitor!"

And in this way they made them advance to the gate where Fierro and his orderly were waiting. Here the resistance of the Reds grew stronger; but the horses' hoofs and the gun barrels persuaded them to choose the other danger, the danger of Fierro, which was not an inch away, but twenty paces.

As soon as they appeared within his range of vision, Fierro greeted them with a strange phrase, at once cruel and affectionate, half ironical and half encouraging. "Come on, boys; I'm only going to shoot, and I'm a bad shot."

The prisoners jumped like goats. The first one tried to throw himself on Fierro, but he had not made three bounds before he fell, riddled by bullets from the soldiers stationed along the fence. The others ran as fast as they could toward the wall—a mad race that must have seemed to them like a dream. One tried to take refuge behind the wellhead: he was the target for Fierro's first bullet. The others fell as they ran, one by one; in less than ten seconds Fierro had fired eight times, and the last of the group dropped just as his fingers were touching the adobes that by the strange whim of the moment separated the zone of life from the zone of death. Some of the bodies showed signs of life; the soldiers finished them off from their horses.

And then came another group of ten, and then another, and another, and another. The three pistols of Fierro—his two and that of his orderly—alternated with precise rhythm in the homicidal hand. There were six shots from each one, six shots fired without stopping to take aim and without pause, and then the gun dropped on to the orderly's blanket, where he removed the exploded caps, and reloaded it. Then, without changing his position, he held out the pistol to Fierro, who took it as he let the other fall. Through the orderly's fingers passed the bullets that seconds later would leave the prisoners stretched lifeless, but he did not raise his eyes to see those that fell. His whole soul seemed concentrated on the pistol in his hand, and on the bullets, with their silver and burnished reflections, spread out on the ground before him. Just two sensations filled his whole being: the cold weight of the bullets that he was putting into the openings of the barrel, and the warm smoothness of the gun. Over his head one after another rang out the shots of his "chief," entertaining himself with his sharp-shooting.

The panic-stricken flight of the prisoners toward the wall of salvation —a fugue of death in which the two themes of the passion to kill and the infinite desire to live were blended—lasted almost two hours.

Not for one minute did Fierro lose his precision or aim or his poise. He was firing at moving human targets, targets that jumped and slipped in pools of blood and amidst corpses stretched out in unbelievable positions, but he fired with no concern other than that of hitting or missing. He calculated the deflection caused by the wind, and corrected it with each shot.

Some of the prisoners, crazed by terror, fell to their knees as they came through the gate. There the bullet laid them low. Others danced about grotesquely behind the shelter of the wellhead until the bullet cured them of their frenzy or they dropped wounded into the well. But nearly all rushed toward the adobe wall and tried to climb it over the warm, damp, steaming heaps of piled-up bodies. Some managed to dig their nails into the earth coping, but their hands, so avid of life, soon fell lifeless.

There came a moment in which the mass execution became a noisy tumult, punctuated by the dry snap of the pistol shots, muted by the voice of the wind. On one side of the fence the shouts of those who fled from death only to die; on the other, those who resisted the pressure of the horsemen and tried to break through the wall that pushed them on toward that terrible gate. And to the shouts of one group and the other were added the voices of the soldiers stationed along the fences. The noise of the shooting, the marksmanship of Fierro, and the cries and frantic gestures of the condemned men had worked them up to a pitch of great excitement. The somersaults of the bodies as they fell in the death agony elicited loud exclamations of amusement from them, and they shouted, gesticulated, and gave peals of laughter as they fired into the mounds of bodies in which they saw the slightest evidence of life.

In the last squad of victims there were twelve instead of ten. The twelve piled out of the death pen, falling over one another, each trying to protect himself with the others, in his anxiety to win in the horrible race. To go forward they had to jump over the piled-up corpses, but not for this reason did the bullet err in its aim. With sinister precision it hit them one by one and left them on the way to the wall, arms and legs outstretched, embracing the mass of their motionless companions. But one of them, the only one left alive, managed to reach the coping and swing himself over. The firing stopped and the troop of soldiers crowded into the corner of the adjoining barn lot to see the fugitive.

It was beginning to get dark. It took the soldiers a little while to focus their vision in the twilight. At first they could see nothing. Finally, far off, in the vastness of the darkling plain they managed to make out a moving spot. As it ran, the body bent so far over that it almost seemed to crawl along on the ground.

A soldier took aim. "It's hard to see," he said as he fired.

The report died away in the evening wind. The moving spot fled on.

Fierro had not moved from his place. His arm was exhausted, and he let it hang limp against his side for a long time. Then he became aware of a pain in his forefinger and raised his hand to his face; he could see that the finger was somewhat swollen. He rubbed it gently between the fingers and the palm of his hand and for a good space of time kept up this gentle massage. Finally he stooped over and picked up his serape, which he had taken off at the beginning of the executions. He threw it over his shoulders and walked over to the shelter of the stalls. But after a few steps he turned to his orderly, "When you're finished, bring up the horses."

And he went on his way.

The orderly was gathering up the exploded caps. In the next pen the soldiers of the guard had dismounted and were talking or singing softly. The orderly heard them in silence and without raising his head. Finally he got slowly to his feet. He gathered up the blanket by the four corners and threw it over his shoulder. The empty caps rattled in it with a dull tintinnabulation.

It was dark. A few stars glimmered, and on the other side of the fence the cigarettes shone red. The orderly walked heavily and slowly and, half feeling his way, went to the last of the pens and in a little while returned leading his own and his master's horses by the bridle; across one of his shoulders swung the haversack.

He made his way over to the stalls. Fierro was sitting on a rock, smoking. The wind whistled through the cracks in the boards.

"Unsaddle the horse and make up my bed," ordered Fierro. "I'm so tired I can't stand up."

"Here in this pen, chief? Here . . . ?"

"Sure. Why not?"

The orderly did as he was bidden. He unsaddled the horse and spread the blankets on the straw, making a kind of pillow out of the haversack and the saddle. Fierro stretched out and in a few minutes was asleep.

The orderly lighted his lantern and bedded the horses for the night. Then he blew out the light, wrapped himself in his blanket, and lay down at the feet of his master. But in a minute he was up again and knelt down and crossed himself. Then he stretched out on the straw again.

Six or seven hours went by. The wind had died down. The silence of the night was bathed in moonlight. Occasionally a horse snuffled. The radiance of the moon gleamed on the dented surface of the bucket that hung by the well and made clear shadows of all the objects in the yard except the mounds of corpses. These rose up, enormous in the stillness of the night, like fantastic hills, strange and blurred in outline.

The blue silver of the night descended on the corpses in rays of purest light. But little by little that light turned into a voice, a voice that had the unreality of the night. It grew distinct; it was a voice that was barely audible, faint and tortured, but clear like the shadows cast by the moon. From the center of one of the mounds of corpses the voice seemed to whisper:

"Oh! Oh!"

The heaped-up bodies, stiff and cold for hours, lay motionless in the barnyard. The moonlight sank into them as into an inert mass. But the voice sounded again:

"Oh . . . Oh . . . Oh . . ."

And this last groan reached to the spot where Fierro's orderly lay sleeping and brought him out of sleep to the consciousness of hearing. The first thing that came to his mind was the memory of the execution of the three hundred prisoners; the mere thought of it kept him motionless in the straw, his eyes half open and his whole soul fixed on the lamentation of that voice:

"Oh . . . please . . ."

Fierro tossed on his bed.

"Please . . . water . . ."

Fierro awoke and listened attentively.

"Please . . . water . . ."

Fierro stretched out his foot until he touched his orderly.

"Hey, you. Don't you hear? One of those dead men is asking for water."

"Yes, chief."

"You get up and put a bullet through the sniveling son-of-a-bitch. Let's see if he'll let me get some sleep then."

"A bullet through who, chief?"

"The one that's asking for water, you fool. Don't you understand?"

"Water, please," the voice kept on.

The orderly took his pistol from under the saddle and started out of the shed in search of the voice. He shivered with fear and cold. He felt sick to his soul.

He looked around in the light of the moon. Every body he touched was stiff. He hesitated without knowing what to do. Finally he fired in the direction from which the voice came. The voice kept on. The orderly fired again. The voice died away.

The moon floated through the limitless space of its blue light. Under the shelter of the shed Fierro slept.

15

LIMA BARRETO

While Machado de Assis (Part Two, 14) never wrote as a mulatto, one of his followers, Lima Barreto, never wrote as a white man. He had been influenced by the Russian novel, and he himself was a character out of Dostoevsky, one of "the insulted and injured." He was born in Rio de Janeiro in 1881, and could say, as does one of his characters, "I was born poor, I was born a mulatto." Despite his humble origins, he attempted to get a degree in engineering; but he had to leave the polytechnic school after the second year. He turned to journalism and, to supplement his modest income, became a clerk at the Ministry of War. There was a streak of madness in his family (his father died insane), and he himself was an alcoholic.

His literary output was irregular: five completed novels and six volumes of miscellaneous prose, plus an intimate *Journal.* All these works were written somewhat carelessly, in some twenty years of frantic activity, interrupted by long periods lost to drunkenness.

His earliest novel, *Clara dos Anjos,* begun in 1904, was not completed until the last years of his life and was only published posthumously (1923–24, in serial form; 1948, as a book). In it the chief obsession of Barreto's life is already discernible. The protagonist is a mulatto woman, seduced by a young white man. His second novel, *Life and Death of M. J. Gonzaga de Sá,* begun in 1906–7 and published in 1919, was the story of a bureaucrat. The third novel, *Memories of Isáias Caminha, Notary Public,* was the first to be published by him, in 1909. The Dostoevskyan influence is obvious in this story of a mulatto who tries to get a degree in Rio but succeeds only as a journalist. A bitter satire of the corrupt Brazilian journalism Baretto knew so well, it anticipated his masterpiece, *The Sad End of Policarpo Quaresma* (1911, in serial form; 1915, as a book). The protagonist is a kind of mediocre Don Quixote, a bureaucrat at the army arsenal who has an obsessive concern with punctuality, and whose only weakness is to conceive impractical projects (one of these, among many: to establish the indigenous tongue Tupí-Guaraní as Brazil's official language). At the outbreak of the 1893 naval revolt against the dictatorial president Floriano Peixoto (the Iron Marshal), Quaresma comes to the defense of the government. Although he has never previously held army rank, he is appointed commander of a battalion. His adventures bring him eventually to a sad end, as the title indicates, but there is nothing sad in Barreto's lively satirical presentation of the Brazilian army, as shown in the chapter excerpted here. The author was obviously profiting from the years spent at the Ministry of War in close observation of people and mores.

His last novel published in his lifetime, *Numa and the Nymph* (1915), was a political satire. After having lampooned journalism, bureaucracy, and the army, Barreto chose another sacred institution and applied to his bitter task the same enthusiasm. This time the protagonist is a congressman whose political speeches are written by his wife's lover.

In the last years of his life, Barreto became a socialist. The triumph of the Russian Revolution convinced him that the day of social justice had come. He was working on his last novel, *The Cemetery of the Living,* about his experiences in a hospital for madmen and drunkards, when he died in 1922. Fragments of the book were published in 1953. In all his works, Barreto used satire very effectively to shatter the carefully preserved surface of Brazilian society, a surface that both Alencar and Machado (Part Two, 12 and 14) had already corroded with their irony. But Barreto went further than these predecessors, and opened the way for the successful social novelists of the 1930s and 1940s.

The Sad End of Policarpo Quaresma

From O triste fim de Policarpo Quaresma, *especially translated by Gregory Rabassa.*

Eight o'clock in the morning. The haze still envelops everything. On the land side the lower portions of the nearby buildings can scarcely be distinguished; on the sea side at this hour sight is powerless against those whitened, fluctuating shadows, against that wall of opaque fuzz that condenses here and there in apparitions, in the likeness of things. The sea is calm: there are long intervals between weak wave laps. A small, dirty stretch of beach can be seen, covered with algae, and the marshy smell seems stronger in the mist. To the left and to the right is the unknown, the Mystery. But that thick paste of diffuse clarity is peopled with sounds. The whine of nearby saws, the whistles of factories and locomotives, the squeak of hoists on ships fill that undecipherable and taciturn morning; and one can even hear the rhythmic noise of oars cutting the sea. In that setting one would think that it is Charon bringing his boat to one of the shores of the Styx.

Heads up! They all scrutinize the curtain of pasty mist. The faces are disturbed; it seems that demons are about to rise up out of the bosom of the fog.

The sound is no longer heard: the long boat has withdrawn. The faces breathe with relief.

It's not night, it's not day; it's not sunrise, it's not sunset; it's the hour of anguish, it's the light of uncertainty. At sea, there are neither stars nor sun to steer by; on land, birds die from colliding with the white walls of the houses. Our misery is more complete and the lack of those mute frames for our activity gives a greater sense of our isolation in the bosom of great nature.

The sounds continue, and because nothing can be seen, they seem to come from the depths of the earth or to be auditory hallucinations. Reality only comes to us from the stretch of sea that can be seen, waves lapping at long intervals, weakly, tenuously, fearfully, meeting the sand of the beach, which is dirty with seaweed, algae, and sargasso.

After the sound of oars the soldiers have lain down in groups on the grass behind the beach. Some are already dozing; others search with their eyes for the sky through the mist that wets their faces.

Corporal Ricardo Coração dos Outros, a bayonet on his belt and a cap on his head, sits on a rock off to one side, all alone, and gazes out at that distressing morning.

It's the first time he's seen the fog close to the sea like that, where all the strength of its despair can be felt. Usually he has eyes only for clear and purple sunrises, soft and fragrant; this misty, ugly dawn is something new for him.

Under his corporal's uniform the minstrel is not weary. That free life outside the barracks is good for his soul; the guitar is inside there, and on off-duty hours he practices, humming in a low voice. He can't let his fingers get rusty. . . . He is a little annoyed at not being able to open up his chest from time to time.

The commandant of the detachment is Quaresma, who maybe would let him . . .

The major is inside the house that serves as headquarters, reading. His favorite study is artillery now. He has bought manuals; but because his education is deficient, from artillery he goes to ballistics, from ballistics to mechanics, from mechanics to the calculus and analytic geometry; he goes on down the steps; he goes to trigonometry, to geometry, to algebra, and to arithmetic. He passes along that chain of related sciences with the faith of an inventor. He learns a most elementary notion after a rosary of research, from textbook to textbook; and in that way he spends his days of military idleness involved in mathematics, in disagreeable mathematics, so hostile to brains that are no longer young.

The detachment has a Krupp cannon, but he has nothing to do with the death-dealing apparatus; nevertheless, he studies artillery. In charge of the cannon is Lieutenant Fontes, who shows no obedience whatsoever to the patriot major. Quaresma is not upset by that; he goes along, slowly learning to serve as touchhole and submit to the subordinate's arrogance.

The commandant of the Cruzeiro do Sul post, Bustamante with his Mosaic beard, is still at headquarters, overseeing the battalion's affairs. The unit has few officers and very few enlisted men; but the state pays on the basis of four hundred. There's a lack of captains, the number of second lieutenants is just right, that of first lieutenants almost, but there is already one major, who is Quaresma, and the commandant, Bustamante, who out of modesty only makes himself a lieutenant colonel.

There are forty soldiers in the detachment under the command of Quaresma, three second lieutenants, two first lieutenants; but the officers don't appear very often. They're either sick or on leave, and only he, the ex-farmer from Sossêgo and a second lieutenant, Polidoro, the latter only at night, are on duty.

A soldier entered: "Commandant, sir, can I go eat?"

"Yes. Send me Corporal Ricardo."

The soldier went out, limping in his high shoes; the poor man wore those protective articles as a punishment. As soon as he found himself in the woods on the way home, he took them off and felt the breath of freedom on his face.

The commandant went to the window. The fog was breaking up. One could already see the sun, which was shining like a disk of ruddy gold.

Ricardo Coração dos Outros appeared. He looked comical in his corporal's uniform. His blouse was extremely short, hitched up; his cuffs were fully exposed; and his pants were too long and dragged on the ground.

"How are you, Ricardo?"

"Fine. How are you, major?"

"All right."

Quaresma cast that sharp, slow look of his on his underling and friend: "You're upset about something, right?"

The troubador felt happy with the commandant's interest: "No . . . What I mean to say, major, yes . . . If it went on like this to the end it wouldn't be bad. . . . The devil of it is when there's shooting. . . . One thing, major. Couldn't I, maybe, those times when there's nothing to do, go into the mango trees and do a little singing?"

The major scratched his head, stroked his goatee, and said, "I, I don't know. . . . It's . . ."

"You know that singing low is like rowing on a dry run. . . . They say that in Paraguay . . ."

"All right. Go sing there, but don't holler, all right?"

They were silent for a while. Ricardo was about to leave when the major told him, "Have them bring me my lunch."

Quaresma ate dinner and lunch right there. It was not unusual for him to sleep there too. The meals were furnished him by a nearby lunch stand, and he slept in a room in that imperial edifice. For the house where the detachment was billeted had been the emperor's bathhouse on the former estate of Ponta do Caju. Also there was the Rio Douro railroad station and a large, noisy sawmill. Quaresma went to the door, looked at the dirty beach, and was surprised that the emperor would have wanted to swim there. The fog was breaking up completely.

The shape of things was emerging from the bosom of that mass of heavy mist; satisfied, as if the nightmare had passed. First the low parts rose up, slowly; and finally, almost suddenly, the high parts.

On the right were Saúde, Gamboa, the merchant ships: three-masted galleys, steam freighters, haughty sailing ships—which were coming out of the mist—and at moments it all had the look of a Dutch landscape; on the left were Rapôsa Cove, Retiro Saudoso, horrendous Sapucaia, and the Ilha do Governador, the blue range of the Órgãos, tall enough to touch the sky; across the way the Ilha dos Ferreiros with its coal deposits; and stretching one's sight out across the calm sea, Niterói, whose mountains had just emerged outlined against the blue sky by the light of that tardy morning.

The mist disappeared and a rooster crowed. It was as if joy were returning to the earth; it was a hallelujah. The creaking, the whistles, the hoists had a festive accent of contentment.

Lunch arrived and the sergeant came to tell Quaresma that there were two desertions.

"Two more?" The major seemed surprised.

"Yes, sir. One-twenty-five and three-twenty didn't answer roll call today."

"Take care of it."

Quaresma was having lunch. Lieutenant Fontes, the cannon man, came in. He almost never slept there. He spent the night at home, and during the day he would come to see how things were going.

Early one morning he wasn't there. The darkness was still deep. The soldier on watch saw out in the distance a shape moving in the shadows, sliding along the surface of the sea. It had no light: only the movement of that dark spot and the slight glow of the water revealed a boat. The soldier gave the alarm; the small detachment took up its positions, and Quaresma appeared.

"The cannon! Quick! Let's go!" the commandant ordered. And immediately he added nervously, "Wait a minute."

He ran to the house and went to consult his manuals and tables. He delayed, and the launch was getting closer. The soldiers were thunderstruck, and one of them took the initiative: he loaded the piece and fired.

Quaresma reappeared on the run, startled, and said, his words shortened by his panting, "Take good aim . . . distance . . . height . . . angle . . . You always have to keep the effect of the shot in sight."

Fontes arrived, and when he heard about the episode the next day, he laughed a great deal. "Come, major, you think you're practicing on the firing range. Just fire straight ahead!"

And that was how it went. Almost every afternoon there was a bombardment of the forts from the sea and from the forts at the sea; and both ships and forts emerged unharmed from such terrible experiences.

There was one occasion, however, when they hit the mark, and then the newspapers told the story: "Yesterday Fort Acadêmico got off a wonderful shot. Its cannon placed a shell on the *Guanabara.*" On the following day, at the request of the battery on the Pharoux docks, which was the one that made the shot that hit its mark, the same newspaper corrected its story. Days passed, and the incident was already forgotten when a letter appeared from Niterói claiming the honors of the shot for the fortress at Santa Cruz.

Lieutenant Fontes arrived and was examining the cannon with the air of an expert. There was a trench made of alfalfa bales, and the mouth of the piece stuck out through the strands of straw like the snout of some wild animal hiding in the grass.

He looked at the horizon after a careful examination of the cannon, and he was examining the Ilha das Cobras when he heard the moan of a guitar and a voice singing:

"I promise by the Most Holy Sacrament"

He went to the place where the sounds were coming from and came across this beautiful picture: in the shade of a large tree the soldiers were lying or sitting in a circle around Ricardo Coração dos Outros, who was singing his wounded dirges.

The soldiers had finished eating lunch and drinking their cane liquor and were so enraptured with Ricardo's song that they didn't notice the arrival of the young officer.

"What's going on?" he asked sternly.

The soldiers all got up saluting; and Ricardo, his right hand profiled at his cap and his left clutching the guitar, which rested on the ground, made his excuses: "Lieutenant, sir, it was the major who gave his permission. You know, sir, that if we didn't have permission we wouldn't be playing around."

"All right. But I don't want any more of this," the officer said.

"But," Ricardo objected, "Major Quaresma . . ."

"Major Quaresma's not here. I won't have it, I said!"

The soldiers broke up and Lieutenant Fontes went into the old imperial house to look for the major of the Cruzeiro do Sul post. Quaresma was still at his studies, a rock of Sisyphus, but a voluntary one for the glory of the nation. Fontes went in and said, "What's all this, Mr. Quaresma? Do you permit songfests in the detachment?"

The major had forgotten about the matter and was startled at the young man's severe, gruff air. Fontes repeated, "Do you allow enlisted men to sing tunes and play the guitar on duty?"

"But what harm is there in it? I heard that during the war . . ."

"What about discipline? And respect?"

"All right, I'll stop it," Quaresma said.

"You don't have to. I already did."

Quaresma didn't become annoyed, he saw no reason for annoyance, and he said softly, "You did the right thing."

He immediately asked the officer for the method of finding the square root of a decimal fraction; the young man showed him and they were chatting cordially about everyday things. Fontes was engaged to Lalá, the third daughter of General Albernaz, and he was waiting for the uprising to end so they could get married. For an hour the conversation between the two dealt with that little family matter which was linked to that thunder, those shots, that solemn dispute between two ambitions. Suddenly the bugle cut the air with its metallic voice. Fontes cocked his ear. The major asked, "What call is that?"

"Battle stations."

The two of them went out, Fontes in perfect uniform and the major tightening his sword belt, having difficulty, tripping over the venerable sword, which insisted on getting between his short legs. The soldiers were already in the trenches, clutching their weapons. The cannon alongside had the ammunition it needed. A launch was approaching slowly, its high prow aimed at the position. Suddenly a gush of thick smoke came from on board: "A shot!" a voice shouted. They all got down, the ball passed over, humming, singing, harmless. The launch continued advancing boldly. Besides the soldiers there were onlookers, young boys, watching the shooting, and it had been one of them who had shouted, "A shot!"

And that was how it always went. Sometimes they would come quite close to the troops, interfering with their duties; at other times one of the civilians would approach the officer and very delicately ask, "Would you let me try a shot?" The officer gave his permission, the crew loaded the piece, the man aimed, and a shot took off.

With time the revolt had become a festival, fun for the city. When a bombardment was announced, the terrace of the Passeio Público filled up in seconds. It was as if it were a moonlit night during the times when it had been fashionable to enjoy it in the old garden of Dom Luís de Vasconcelos, watching the solitary star turn the water silver and fill the sky.

Binoculars were for rent, and old men and young women, young men and old women followed the bombardment like a theatrical production: "Santa Cruz fired! Now it's Aquidabã! There it goes." And in that way the revolt was becoming something familiar, getting into the habits and customs of the city.

On the Pharoux docks the small boys, newsboys, shoeshine boys, vegetable vendors stayed behind the entrance ways, urinals, trees, watching, waiting for bullets to fall; and when one happened to fall, they all ran in a group to grab it as if it were a coin or piece of candy.

Bullets became fashionable. There were tie clasps, watch fobs, mechanical pencils all made from small rifle bullets; collections were also made of the middle-sized ones, and their metal casings, scoured, polished, filed down, decorated the consoles and glass cabinets of middle-class homes; the large ones, the "melons and squashes," as they were called, decorated gardens as flowerpots or sculpture.

The launch kept on shooting; Fontes fired. The cannon vomited out its projectile, drew back a little, and then was placed back in position. The boat answered and the boy shouted, "A shot!"

There were always boys who announced the enemy's shots. As soon as they saw the quick shooting and the smoke there in the distance on the ship, the slow, heavy gush, they would shout, "A shot!"

There was one in Niterói who had his quarter hour of fame. They called him "Thirty-Réis," and the newspapers of the time got involved and took up a collection for him. A hero! The revolt passed and he was forgotten, the same as the *Luci*, a beautiful launch that was becoming an entity in the imagination of the *urbs*, interesting it, creating enemies and admirers.

The boat stopped provoking the fury of the Caju position, and Fontes gave instructions to his chief gunner and went off.

Quaresma retired to his room and went on with his military studies. Most of the days that passed on that edge of the city were no different from that one. The events were the same, and the war fell into the banality of a repetition of the same episodes.

16

GRACILIANO RAMOS

Unlike Lima Barreto, a marginal, almost isolated writer, Graciliano Ramos was placed exactly in the center of an important movement of renovation in Brazilian letters. With José Lins do Rêgo and Jorge Amado (selections 17, 18), he was chiefly responsible for the success of the Northeast circle of novelists which dominated Brazilian fiction of the 1930s and '40s. This group came into existence after the First Congress of Northeast Regionalists, which met in Recife in 1926. Under the inspiration of Gilberto Freyre, the well-known sociologist and author of the masterpiece *Masters and Slaves* (1933), the group tried to define a new vision of Brazilian culture and emphasized the need for a more accurate presentation of the part of Brazil that Euclides da Cunha had described so apocalyptically in his 1902 *Rebellion in the Backlands* (Part Two, 16).

At the time, the group was reacting against what it felt to be the excessive cosmopolitanism of an earlier school, centered in São Paulo, which had defined its task as the liberation of Brazilian letters and language from the old-fashioned Portuguese rhetoric and poetic diction. This latter movement was called modernism because it took form during the celebration of a Week of Modern Art in 1922. (This group must not be confused with the Spanish American modernists of the late 1880s and '90s—see introduction to Darío, selection 4.) The Brazilian modernists were initially inspired by the Italian futurists and corresponded to the avant-garde. Opposing them, the Northeast group urged a return to local subjects and problems, a larger concern with social and political issues, and a renewed concept of regionalism.

Today, the differences between the modernists and the Northeast writers seem less important than their common assumptions. Both groups believed in a need for drastic change in artistic vision and linguistic expression; both were deeply concerned with the creation of a totally independent Brazilian literature; both achieved their goals in the work of their best writers.

Graciliano Ramos deserves a place among the best. Born in a small town in Alagoas state in 1892, he did not learn to read until he was nine. Later he went to school in Maceió, the state capital, but never received a degree. After working in his father's business, he went to Rio to work for a newspaper. In 1915 he returned home to a modest bureaucratic position. He eventually attained high public office, becoming director of the Alagoas State Press and director of Public Education. In 1936, however, his career came to a halt: he was imprisoned on charges of being a Communist. This was at a time when Getulio Vargas's Fascist Estado Novo (New State) was at its height. Ramos had to spend several years in different prisons in Pernambuco and Rio. Out of his experience he wrote a somber, intense, long book, *Memoirs of Prison Life,* which was published the year he died (1953).

His literary work overall is relatively limited in extent: four novels, one book of childhood memoirs (1945), one of short stories, and one of travels in Eastern Europe. An introvert, shy to the point of total silence, Ramos was reticent to publish his first book. He was already forty-one when *Caetés* appeared in 1933. During his early years he had been influenced by Gorky and by certain masters of Portuguese and Brazilian fiction: Eça de Queiroz among the former; Machado de Assis and Raul Pompéia (Two, 14, 15) among the latter.

His first three novels used the well-known Machadoan device of narrator-protagonists. Through their eyes, Ramos explored the sad, useless lives of men fighting to survive in a land of greed and hunger, torn by feelings of impotence or obsessive ambition, degraded by adultery or crimes of passion. But in his most famous work, *Barren Lives* (1938), he dropped this approach to describe directly and in the sparest style the plight of a poor family in its fight against the Northeast's endemic droughts. Each chapter is autonomous—in fact, they were originally published as separate stories—and the whole structure of the novel reveals a great concern with form and style. In many respects, it is a book closer in spirit and tone to the Mexican Juan Rulfo's *Pedro Páramo* (Five, 7) than to the more exuberant works of his own Brazilian colleagues, Lins do Rêgo and Jorge Amado.

Although Ramos avoided explicit psychological analysis in *Barren Lives* (he had indulged in it to excess in his previous novel, *Anguish,* 1936), he managed to reveal, more by implication than by direct statement, the inner life of his destitute characters through their relationship with the pitiless milieu and with their fellow animals. The sun, a dog (as in the chapter excerpted here), and a shadow were as legitimate characters in this tale as the human beings. Ramos's masterpiece proved that regionalism need not be shallow and that concentration on very small incidents and simple people did not necessarily detract from a novel's scope and depth. In his work he succeeded in accomplishing not only the aims of the Northeast group but those of the avant-garde modernists as well. It was no small achievement.

The Dog

From Barren Lives, *translated by Ralph Edward Dimmick (Austin:* University of Texas Press, 1965), pp. 86–92.

The dog was dying. She had grown thin and her hair had fallen out in several spots. Her ribs showed through the pink skin and flies covered dark blotches that suppurated and bled. Sores on her mouth and swollen lips made it hard for her to eat and drink.

Fabiano, thinking she was coming down with rabies, tied a rosary of burnt corncob about her neck. The dog, however, only went from bad to worse. She rubbed against the posts of the corral or plunged impatiently into the brush, trying to shake off the gnats by flapping her dangling ears and swishing her short, hairy tail, thick at the base and coiled like a rattlesnake's.

So Fabiano decided to put an end to her. He went to look for his flintlock, polished it, cleaned it out with a bit of wadding, and went about loading it with care so the dog wouldn't suffer unduly.

Vitória shut herself up in the bedroom, dragging the children with her. They were frightened and, sensing misfortune, kept asking, "Is the dog going to be hurt?"

They had seen the lead shot and the powder horn, and Fabiano's gestures worried them, causing them to suspect that the dog was in danger.

She was like a member of the family. There was hardly any difference to speak of between her and the boys. The three of them played together, rolling in the sand of the riverbed or in the loose manure, which, as it piled up, threatened to cover the goat pen.

The boys tried to push the latch and open the door, but Vitória dragged them over to the bed of tree branches, where she did her best to stop their ears, holding the head of the older between her thighs and putting her hands over the ears of the younger. Angry at the resistance they offered, she tried to hold them down by force, grumbling fiercely the while.

She too had a heavy heart, but she was resigned. Obviously Fabiano's decision was necessary and just. The poor dog!

Listening, she heard the noise of the shot being poured down the barrel of the gun, and the dull taps of the ramrod on the wadding. She sighed. The poor dog!

The boys began to yell and kick. Vitória had relaxed her muscles, and the bigger one was able to escape. She swore.

"Limb of Satan!"

In the struggle to get hold of the rebel again she really lost her temper. The little devil! She gave him a crack on the head, which he had plunged under the bedcovers and her flowered skirt.

Gradually her wrath diminished and, rocking the children, she began grumbling about the sick dog, muttering harsh names and expressions of contempt. The sight of the slobbering animal was enough to turn your stomach. It wasn't right for a mad dog to go running loose in the house. But then she realized she was being too severe. She thought it unlikely that the dog had gone mad and wished her husband had waited one more day to see whether it was really necessary to put the animal out of the way.

At that moment Fabiano was walking in the shed, snapping his fingers. Vitória drew in her neck and tried to cover her ears with her shoulders. As this was impossible, she raised her arms and, without letting go of her son, managed to cover a part of her head.

Fabiano walked through the lean-to, staring off toward the brauna trees and the gates, setting an invisible dog on invisible cattle.

"Sic 'em, sic 'em!"

Crossing the sitting room and the corridor, he came to the low kitchen window, from which, on examining the yard, he saw the dog scratching herself, rubbing the bare spots of her hide against the Jerusalem thorn. Fabiano raised the musket to his cheek. The dog eyed her master distrustfully and slipped sulkily around to the other side of the tree trunk, where she crouched with only her black eyes showing. Bothered by this maneuver on her part, Fabiano leaped out the window and stole along the corral fence to the corner post, where he again raised the arm to his cheek. As the animal was turned toward him and did not offer a very good target, he took a few more steps. On reaching the catingueira trees, he adjusted his aim and pulled the trigger. The load hit the dog in the hindquarters, putting one leg out of action. The dog began to yelp desperately.

Hearing the shot and the yelps, Vitória called upon the Virgin Mary, while the boys rolled on the bed, weeping aloud. Fabiano withdrew.

The dog fled in haste. She rounded the clay pit, went through the little garden to the left, passed close by the pinks and the pots of wormwood, slipped through a hole in the fence, and reached the yard, running on three legs. She had taken the direction of the shed but, fearing to meet Fabiano, she withdrew toward the goat pen. There she stopped for a moment, not knowing where to go, and then set off again, hopping along aimlessly.

In front of the oxcart her other back leg failed her, but, though bleeding profusely, she continued on her two front legs, dragging her hindquarters along as best she could. She wanted to retreat under the cart, but she was afraid of the wheel. She directed her course toward the jujube trees. There under one of the roots was a deep hole full of soft dirt in which she liked to wallow, covering herself with dust against the flies and gnats. When she would arise, with dry leaves and twigs sticking to her sores, she was a very different-looking animal.

She fell before reaching this distant refuge. She tried to get up, raising her head and stretching out her forelegs, but her body remained on its flank. In this twisted position she could scarcely move, though she scraped with her paws, digging her nails into the ground, pulling at the small pebbles. Finally she drooped and lay quiet beside the heap of stones where the boys threw dead snakes.

A horrible thirst burned her throat. She tried to look at her legs but couldn't make them out, for a mist veiled her sight. A desire came over her to bite Fabiano. She set up a yelp, but it was not really a yelp, just a faint howl that grew weaker and weaker until it was almost imperceptible.

Finding the sun dazzling, she managed to inch into a sliver of shade at the side of the stones.

She looked at herself again, worried. What was happening to her? The mist seemed ever thicker and closer.

A good smell of cavies drifted down to her from the hill, but it was faint and mingled with that of other creatures. The hill seemed to have grown far, far away. She wrinkled her muzzle, breathing the air slowly, desirous of climbing the slope and giving chase to the cavies, as they jumped and ran about in freedom.

She began to pant with difficulty, feigning a bark. She ran her tongue over her parched lips, but felt no relief. The smell was ever fainter: the cavies must certainly have fled.

She forgot them and once more had the desire to bite Fabiano, who appeared before her half-glazed eyes with a strange object in his hand. She didn't recognize it, but she began to tremble, sure that it held a disagreeable surprise for her. She made an effort to avoid it, pulling in her tail. Deciding it was out of harm's way, she closed her leaden eyes. She couldn't bite Fabiano; she had been born near him, in a bedroom, under a bed of tree branches, and her whole life had been spent in submission to him, barking to round up the cattle when the herdsman clapped his hands.

The unknown object continued to threaten her. She held her breath, covered her teeth, and peered out at her enemy from under her drooping eyelids. Thus she remained for some time, and then grew quiet. Fabiano and the dangerous thing had gone away.

With difficulty she opened her eyes. Now there was a great darkness. The sun must certainly have disappeared.

The bells of the goats tinkled down by the riverside; the strong smell of the goat pen spread over the surroundings.

The dog gave a start. What were those animals doing out at night? It was her duty to get up and lead them to the water hole. She dilated her nostrils, trying to make out the smell of the children. She was surprised by their absence.

She had forgotten Fabiano. A tragedy had occurred, but the dog did not see in it the cause of her present helplessness nor did she perceive that she was free of responsibilities. Anguish gripped at her small heart. She must mount guard over the goats. At that hour there should be a smell of jaguars along the riverbanks and in the distant tree clumps. Fortunately the boys were sleeping on the straw mat under the corner shelf, where Vitória kept her pipe.

A cold, misty, winter night enveloped the little creature. There was no sound or sign of life in the surroundings. The old rooster did not crow on his perch, nor did Fabiano snore in the bed of tree branches. These sounds were not in themselves of interest to the dog, but when the rooster flapped his wings and Fabiano turned over, familiar emanations let her know of their presence. Now it seemed as if the ranch had been abandoned.

The dog took quick breaths, her mouth open, her jaw sagging, her tongue dangling, void of feeling. She didn't know what had happened. The explosion, the pain in her haunch, her difficult trip from the clay pit to the back of the yard faded out of her mind.

She was probably in the kitchen, in among the stones on which the cooking was done. Before going to bed, Vitória raked out the coals and ashes, swept the burnt area of the earthen floor with a broom, and left a fine place for a dog to take its rest. The heat kept fleas away and made the ground soft. And when she finally dozed off, a throng of cavies invaded the kitchen, running and leaping.

A shiver ran up the dog's body, from her belly to her chest. From her chest down, all was insensibility and forgetfulness, but the rest of her body quivered, and cactus spines penetrated the flesh that had been half eaten away by sickness.

The dog leaned her weary head on a stone. The stone was cold; Vitória must have let the fire go out very early.

The dog wanted to sleep. She would wake up happy, in a world full of cavies, and would lick the hands of Fabiano—a Fabiano grown to enormous proportions. The boys would roll on the ground with her in an enormous yard, would wallow with her in an enormous goat pen. The world would be full of cavies, fat and huge.

17

JOSÉ LINS DO RÊGO

Graciliano Ramos's masterpiece presented only one side of the fabulous Northeast: the fate of peasants destroyed by endemic droughts. It was José Lins do Rêgo's task to encompass in eight of his novels that whole complex world.

He was born in Paraíba in 1901, into a wealthy family that owned a sugar mill. From childhood, he came to know very well the land and the people of a region that in some aspects was similar to the South of the United States: the economy of the Northeast was also based on a single crop (sugar in this case) and dependent on cheap slave labor, and it developed a paternalistic, almost feudal society which came to crisis when slavery was abolished and the old sugar mills were replaced by factories. Although Lins do Rêgo went to Recife to study law and even got a degree, he was more interested in studying his own roots than in establishing a practice. While in Recife he had met Gilberto Freyre, the sociologist most responsible for a new understanding of the Northeast. Later in Alagoas, he would meet Graciliano Ramos and Rachel de Queiróz, who in 1930 wrote a pioneering novel on the devastating drought of 1915. Those meetings were decisive. Between 1932 and 1943, Lins do Rêgo published six related novels, which came to be known as the "sugar-cane cycle." Using the Balzacian device of connecting the novels by interlinked appearances of members of the same cast of characters, Lins do Rêgo devoted the first three of the series to the development of Carlos de Melo, a boy brought up (like the author) in a sugar mill. (These three novels have been published in English under the collective title *Plantation Boy*.) The fourth and fifth novels of the cycle follow the adventures of Ricardo, a black urchin who was one of Carlos's companions at the sugar mill; but this time he is seen as a young man in Recife, getting involved in political strikes.

The last novel of the cycle was published almost ten years later. It is Lins do Rêgo's masterpiece. Vast in scope, *Dead Fires* presents the decadent Northeast society from all possible points of view. Instead of a linear narrative that generally followed the experience of one central protagonist, as in the previous five novels, *Dead Fires* intertwined the lives and adventures of several main characters. Decadent landowners of old-style mills, aggressive new industrialists, bandits and fools, and blacks of all shades occupy the vast canvas. Among them, Vitorino Carneiro da Cunha, called Vitorino Papa-Rabo (Asshole Eater) by the black urchins, is a major creation. A sort of pitiful, grotesque Don Quixote, endlessly fighting imaginary or irreverent enemies, Vitorino brings to Lins do Rêgo's world a new dimension. In the chapter excerpted here he can be seen in full.

Two other novels, written before and after *Dead Fires*, respectively, completed Lins do Rêgo's great enterprise. In *Beautiful Stone* (1938), he reconstructed the crushing of a group of religious fanatics who practiced human sacrifice; the story was like a page torn from da Cunha's *Rebellion in the Backlands* (Part Two, 16). *Cangaceiros* (1953) covered similar ground and even used some of the characters of the previous book, but it focused on the bandits who terrorized the countryside and were generally at the service of the wealthy landowners.

Lins do Rêgo wrote three more novels in a more romantic or sentimental vein; he even attempted an urban novel, *Eurydice* (1947), with psychoanalytical undertones. But his strength lay in the evocation, vivid and nostalgic, of a world he had known in his childhood. In many respects, his outlook, if not his style, was similar to that of Ricardo Güiraldes (selection 13). Like Güiraldes, he was haunted by the past and believed men were greater, more heroic, then.

The following is a glossary of Portuguese terms that appear in this selection:

AROEIRA   (Braz., bot.) pepper tree

BOGARI   (Braz., bot.) Arabian jasmine

CABREIRA   hedge-like bush in semiarid lands

CAJÁ   hog-plum

CAJÀZEIRA   hog-plum tree

CARDEIRO   silk-cotton tree

COMADRE   godmother in relation to the godchild's parents; child's mother in relation to the godparents

COMPADRE   godfather in relation to the godchild's parents; father in his relationship with his child's godfather

JASMIM-DO-CÉU   plant of the plumbaginaceous family (*Plumbago capensis*) originally from southern Africa

MASSAPÊ   (Braz.) black, clayey soil suitable for sugar-cane growing

MOLEQUE   Negro urchin

PITOMBEIRA   (Braz., bot.) variety of soapberry (tree)

QUICÊ, QUICÉ   (N. Braz.) useless old knife, especially one without a point or handle

SERTÃO   hinterland, backland, the interior

TANAJURA   (Braz., entom.) female sauba ant (tropical leaf-cutting ant)

Dead Fires

From Fogo Morto, *especially translated by Susan Hertelendy.*

Pedro Boleeiro, the coachman, arrived at Master José Amaro's door with a message from Colonel Lula for the craftsman to go to the plantation and fix the cart's harness. The master listened to the message, let the Negro talk freely, and then, because it upset him, he opened up with the other man.

"Everybody thinks that Master José Amaro is a servant. I'm a professional, Seu Pedro, a professional who values himself. When Colonel Lula passes by, he takes his hat off as if doing me a favor. He never stops to ask how I'm doing. He has his pride; I have mine. I live on his land; I don't pay rent because my father lived here in the days of his father-in-law. I was a child in these surroundings. What's all this pride for? It wouldn't cost him a thing to step over and ask about my health. My father used to tell me that the Baron of Goiana was not such a high-hat. He was well mannered with little people. And the Baron of Goiana—he had something to brag about; he owned a lot of sugar-cane plantations; a man with plenty of cash stacked away. I'm poor, Seu Pedro, but I'm a man who never lowers himself to anyone."

"Master Zé, this isn't my fault. The man told me to call you; all I'm doing is giving you the message."

"I know, I'm not saying anything out of the ordinary. What I'm telling you, I'd tell anyone. What I can't deal with is poor people like this good-for-nothing Vitorino fawning on the big ones like a dog without a master. Colonel Lula wants me to fix the harness of his cart. So I'll go."

"It's all rotten, Master Zé. I can't put pressure on it, or it'll fall apart completely. That thing has been around for ages."

"That's because you people aren't careful with other people's things. You break everything."

"That's not so, Master Zé. It's really shot."

"Colonel Lula is pigheaded; he's a haughty man. I never saw such a squeamish plantation owner. I've never seen that man on foot overseeing his plantations. Just watch Colonel José Paulino. He's never off a horse's back. And he's really rich. Not Colonel Lula—forever seated in his buggy like a king."

"It depends on how you look at it. Now take old Costa de Mata de Vara; he doesn't ride horses so as not to wear out the animal's hoofs."

"I'm talking about *people*, Seu Pedro. Don't come to me with that beast. That's a beast. And a very common one too. He came over one time to order a saddle from me. He nearly talked my head off. He talked and talked and offered me peanuts in the end. I didn't hold back from saying, 'Captain Costa, that's my daily bread. I can't afford to give presents to rich people.' Hell, I gave it to him straight!"

"And Colonel Lula doesn't hang back either, Master Zé. That's a hell of a stingy man if ever there was one."

"That's in his blood, Seu Pedro, that's in his blood. They say his old man was the same sort. He was ousted because of the '48 revolution. They say he died in the woods. My father used to speak about that '48 war. They killed a cousin of the Baron of Goiana, a certain Nunes Machado. Colonel Lula's father hung around with those people. They finished him off. His wife became kind of crazy and the son is—well, you know what."

"True, Master Zé, that man is kind of batty. I don't want to say anything, but just between the two of us, I'm even scared to live with those people."

"Nonsense, Seu Pedro. That's because you're young. I knew their former coachman there, old Macário. I never saw a man as loyal as he was to the Colonel. He died of old age. They say that Macário originally came from Pernambuco to work for the Colonel because of his father. He had been the old Holanda's gunman in the war of '48. And he was a true macho. In the Colonel's quarrel with Quinca Napoleão, old Macário one day went up to that bastard Quinca and said, 'Look, major sir, my life is worth nothing, but yours is worth a lot. The Colonel can't be insulted.' I like a man like that Macário."

"But Master Zé, don't you pay rent?"

"My father never paid it. We're on this land since the Colonel's father-in-law was alive. Here I stay. Colonel Lula never mentioned it to me. And I tell you: he isn't a bad man. What I can't get used to is his pride. What's all that snootiness for, why so stuck-up? The earth really eats us up in the end. So tell the Colonel I'll take care of his job tomorrow."

When Pedro the coachman left, Master Zé's mind was on Colonel

Lula. He had known many owners of sugar-cane plantations, had worked for all kinds of people, but to tell the truth the Colonel was like no one else. What was Santa Fé compared to the neighborhood plantations? First-class *massapê* lowlands, some highlands with woods; a good parcel of land, small, but large enough for a man to live on very well with his family. Captain Tomás, father of Dona Amélia and father-in-law of Colonel Lula, had lived there.

He had known him as a boy, but his father spoke of the man as upright, hard-working, and resolute. He was even an important politico in the liberal party and the owner of a good stock of slaves. Then came Colonel Lula de Holanda. He had lived with the Colonel for over thirty years and had not changed since the death of Captain Tomás. He had come in that carriage, in real style, and that way he lived. Master José Amaro couldn't explain, he couldn't understand the life of this plantation owner to whom he owed his house and the land on which he stood.

Outside it was a beautiful May day. Everything was green and the warm sun dried the puddle-filled road. The *cajá* trees or *cajàzeiras* offered shade, and along the stakes the flowers of creepers decorated with blue and purple the little corral where old Sinhá bred her pigs. The animals screeched in the clear morning. Master José Amaro's thoughts left Colonel Lula and were taken over again by the woman who crossed before him with a bundle of twigs on her back. He wanted to speak to her, but he stopped in the middle of the word that was about to come out of his mouth and, in order to discipline himself, hammered more violently at the sole he was working on. It was Sinhá his wife, and he couldn't hide his hate for her. Now he saw his daughter leave the house and walk toward the pigsty with a pot on her head. She really was his daughter, but something in her was against him. Master José saw her open-legged, dragging walk and wanted to speak to her, to say something that would hurt her. He hammered harder at the sole and felt his leg hurt. He struck the hammer with more violence and hate. This was his family. A single daughter, with no marriage in sight, no fiancé, no life resembling that of normal people.

"Good morning, Master Zé."

It was Laurentino the painter returning from Santa Rosa.

"I finished the jobs yesterday afternoon. It was hard work. The Colonel is giving a tremendous party. They say even the governor will be there. He is marrying his youngest daughter off too."

"Did they paint the entire house?"

"The whole thing is a beauty. Master Rodolfo is there installing plumbing for running water in the bathroom. When Colonel José Paulino spends, he really spends."

"I've seen a lot happen. Two weeks ago when you passed by here, I was telling you that the old man of Santa Rosa doesn't count on me for anything. And I don't take it back now. You come by to tell me about the grandness of his house. You're quite mistaken, it doesn't make my mouth water."

"Nonsense, Master Zé, you're suspicious of everything. I know you can't stand the Colonel, but that's going too far."

"That's enough, Seu Laurentino; I'm a poor man, a professional with no belongings. And I'm content; I'm not complaining. You can spread the news: 'Master José Amaro doesn't envy anybody.' Whoever has his money can stick it up his ass."

"Master, I didn't come to argue."

"I'm not arguing, man of God. This is no argument. Can't I even tell the truth?"

"All right, Master Zé, all right. Forgive me."

"I've got nothing to forgive. If I wanted to, I'd be in Goiana and very rich on my own. No one's wealth makes me suffer."

There was a short silence. On the waterspout the canary sang in trills. And Master José Amaro's *quicé* knife hissed on the sole.

"Seu Laurentino," he went on, "a man's worth is measured by what he is, not by what he has. You've been eating at Colonel José Paulino's table and came to my house to make me envious."

"You're wrong, Master Zé. I'm not that kind of a man. It's not the first time that I eat at a rich man's table."

"No, I'm not wrong. I can tell."

A horse could be heard trotting by in the muddy road. The two looked up and, in the light fog old José Paulino, with his whip at hand and wearing a Panama hat, passed by.

"Good morning," he said from a distance.

Laurentino the painter rose to lift his hat. Master José Amaro grumbled an angry good morning through his clenched teeth. Their conversation ended. The morning shone everywhere. From the kitchen came the sizzling sound of bacon in the clay frying pan.

"Well, Master Zé, I'm on my way."

"That's how it is, Seu Laurentino, these hands here will cut no sole for that man."

"O.K., Master, I'll see you."

What a devil of an old man, thought Laurentino the painter. What a poisonous nature. Sticking his nose into other people's lives. He has something to say about everything.

He was walking along the road to Pilar when a fellow on horseback came trotting toward him. He thought it might be Father José João, who enjoyed riding as if he were in no hurry to get anywhere, but it was Vitorino Papa-Rabo, or Asshole-Eater, on his spotted mare. He wanted to sneak by through the short cut, but Vitorino yelled after him, "What are you afraid of?"

"Nothing, Captain Vitorino."

"You all think I'm a beast. I'm a man to be respected."

"I'm not saying the contrary."

"You can call me captain. I'm a captain, like Lula de Holanda is a colonel. You do me no favor."

Standing at the roadside, Laurentino the painter listened to the old man's nagging. The spotted mare stood there with her bones showing, in her old, worn saddle, her tattered blanket, and her frazzled rope bit.

"I'm a man to be respected. I was coming down the road and some bastard kids ran out to insult me. That's insolence. I'm a white man like José Paulino. He's my cousin. And these scoundrels don't leave me alone. Do you hear me, Seu Laurentino? Lula de Holanda travels in a carriage to see if he can get some idiot to marry his daughter. Don't think I'm anybody's fool, Seu Laurentino."

One of the mare's eyes watered and the broken rein buried itself deep in her mouth. The painter wanted to take his leave, but Vitorino had more to say. The old man's badly shaved large face and his white hair showing under the dirty cloth hat gave him the air of a forlorn clown.

"Have a good trip, Captain Vitorino. I must be home soon."

"Tell those dogs that they can call on Captain Vitorino Carneiro da Cunha any time they want to see a real man."

And in his fury he dug his spurs into the mare. The animal jumped sideways, almost throwing her rider to the ground. Vitorino straightened up and yelled, "Pack of dogs!"

A Negro urchin hidden behind a *cabreira* bush suddenly jumped in front of the animal to scare her: "Papa-Rabo, Papa-Rabo!"

Vitorino cracked his whip in the air with all his might.

"Papa-Rabo is your mother, you son-of-a-bitch."

And the urchin kept hounding the infuriated old man with his taunts. Vitorino wished the mare were strong enough to run down the impertinent *moleque*. He rammed the spurs in, but nothing happened; the same lazy pace, that dragging of old bones. Farther ahead another *moleque* yelled, "The crupper fell."

Vitorino displayed violent indignation, a terrible despair. "Pack of dogs. I am Vitorino Carneiro da Cunha, a respectable white man."

He talked to himself and gestured as if carrying on a dialogue with an enemy. He cracked the whip with a madman's fury. "This damned beast won't move!"

And he mercilessly punished the mare. Along the silent road the soft steps of the saddle horse scared the lizards away. Captain Vitorino Carneiro da Cunha crossed the Santa Fé plantation belonging to Colonel Lula de Holanda. The great pepper tree there was haunted. He did not believe it. He feared no thing living or dead. A woman in a red skirt passed by.

"Good morning, Seu Vitorino."

"Hold your tongue, I'm not of your kind. 'Captain Vitorino.' I paid a patent for that."

"Forgive me, Seu Vitorino."

"Get lost. Go after your machos."

"Shut up, you old lecher."

Vitorino started to raise his whip against her. The woman ran up the bank yelling insults. "You cheap old bastard. You're known all over the place, you old dog."

"Papa-Rabo," they screamed farther ahead.

"It's your mother."

The woman left the road and Captain Vitorino continued his trip. A little more and he would reach Master José Amaro's house. Yes, it was José Amaro da Silva, enfranchised citizen, his compadre José Amaro. Had it been his choice, his son Luís's godfather would have been his cousin José Paulino. But his wife had picked the saddler. Stubborn, willful, pigheaded woman. He would have liked to call out, fill his mouth with the good sound of "my compadre José Paulino." That damned woman had to pick the other one.

His son Luís was in the navy. He would be a man of position. The birds sang in the trees that shaded Captain Vitorino as he returned home. Everyone who saw him mocked him. He was no man to take jeers. He was Captain Vitorino Carneiro da Cunha, of a good family from Várzea do Paraíba. A baron cousin of his had been in the state government. Before going home he would stop for a chat with his compadre José Amaro. The craftsman's family was not like his own, but the man was white; his father was the son of a sailor from Goiana.

And thus Vitorino, father of Luís, who had been baptized at the missions of Friar Epifânio in Pilar, approached the door of the master saddler, his compadre.

"Good morning, Compadre," the rider cried out at the door.

"Good morning, Compadre. Won't you get down?"

Vitorino got off the mare, tied the halter to the fence, and moved toward the shop. Master José Amaro stared at him scornfully. He always felt ill at ease in the company of this poor man, who was not worthy of respect. That aimless life, that wandering back and forth without really doing anything or taking care of anything, was undignified. He was the godfather of Vitorino's son, and he had felt glad when he learned that the boy had joined the navy. At least he wouldn't grow to be like his father, an idiot wandering around aimlessly.

Old Vitorino stared at his compadre as he would at an inferior. He was a saddler, a manual worker, and therefore shouldn't be taken into account by a white person like himself.

"Working hard, Compadre José Amaro?"

"As usual, Compadre Vitorino, as usual."

"I've also been pushing myself so hard I don't even have time for a rest. This lousy election doesn't give me a break. And, by the way, Compadre, I've been meaning to tell you: I need your vote. Major Ambrósio put me on a ticket for councilman. I'm counting on your vote. They know what Captain Vitorino Carneiro da Cunha is worth. I'm going to be a big shot, my compadre. This time José Paulino will see what his cousin Vitorino is worth."

The saddler's wife appeared at the window.

"Good afternoon, Compadre Vitorino; how is Comadre Adriana?"

"Good afternoon, Comadre Sinhá. The old woman isn't too well. She's got a hell of a case of jealousy. As if I were some kind of a stud. Damn that woman, Comadre, she's been setting spies on me everywhere."

"But Compadre, you don't straighten out either."

"If I did any more, Comadre, I'd be a monk." And he broke out in a roaring laughter. Master José Amaro, sour-faced, acted as if he hadn't heard a word of the old man's chatter.

"Compadre, I wish you had seen what a hit I was at Maravalha's dance. And don't forget there was a bunch of young studs around with their horns just showing. And I, in my old age, was surrounded by more girls than I could handle. They wouldn't lay off of me. True, I'm not young any more, but those young tomcats can't scare me off."

"Well, then, Compadre, don't you think that Comadre Adriana has reasons to keep an eye on you?"

"What do I care about an old woman's worries? An old horse needs new grass, Comadre Sinhá."

José Amaro's sour face showed clear disapproval of their chatter. His wife noticed it and took her leave. "So, Compadre, tell Comadre Adriana to show up. I have some roosters ready for castration. Only she knows how to do those things."

After his wife withdrew, José Amaro stared firmly at the animal tied to the fence. "It's down to the bones, Compadre."

"It's not due to lack of care. She has enough hay, I give her corn, I do everything possible. It's old age. The bitch doesn't even whinny at studhorses any more. And when an animal doesn't do that any more, it's nearing its end. But, Compadre, I cut our conversation short. I was speaking about the election, right? I count on your vote. Let's put José Paulino out of politics once and for all. Ambrósio knows about my prestige. He knows I'm man enough to carry two hundred votes to the ballot box. Those relatives of mine from Várzea are mistaken. Captain Vitorino Carneiro da Cunha has friends. Can I count on your vote?"

A *moleque* on horseback passed by along the road and, seeing old Vitorino, stopped and hollered for the whole world to hear: "Papa-Rabo, Papa-Rabo."

Vitorino raised his flabby body, picked up a stone, and ran after the boy. "Papa-Rabo is your mother."

And he ran with such impetus that he stumbled over the roots of the *pitombeira* and fell flat on his face like a ripe tomato. Master José Amaro rose so as to hold him up. The old man had almost lost his speech. He was white as chalk and his body was weak. He recovered after drinking a glass of water and then, still panting, said, "It's just as you see, Compadre. That's how they chase me."

People from the house came to cheer him up.

"I fell. Thank you. I'll take care of these hoodlums. These are doings of Juca from Santa Rosa. These runts will pay for it. I'll cut the bastard's face with a horsewhip."

Master Amaro spoke softly to his compadre: "Compadre Vitorino, I don't want to say anything, but this is all your fault."

"What's my fault? Can't you see that this is political harassment? They're afraid of my electorate. Damned ruffians. I'll show everybody who this old Vitorino Carneiro da Cunha is. I don't refuse a fight. If they want a brawl, let's have it."

Master José Amaro kept silent while Captain Vitorino, now recovered from the shock, chattered away: "I'll beat José Paulino to the ground. Colonel Rêgo Barros is on his way. He's a military man who gives justice where it's due. He'll be governor. With him around, no thief will stay out of jail. Dantas Barreto is in Pernambuco. Franco Rabelo in Ceará. Lula de Holanda should be head of the party here in Pilar. His father was a man of authority in Pernambuco. I heard he was in the war of '48. That's why I like the people from the *sertão*. My father owned land in Cariri; he had thirty gunmen. Over there they pull the trigger, Compadre. That's what I like."

It was getting dark, and a dog's desperate barking came from the direction of the river. Then a dry shot was heard in the silence.

"It's Manuel de Úrsula, hunting cavies," Captain Vitorino said. "That scoundrel is one of those who have no respect for me. You can be sure, Compadre, that I'll bring some kind of misery to Várzea. I'll have someone's tripes out on the floor. Well, I'm off." And he yelled in the direction of the house, "Comadre, I'll be seeing you."

"May God accompany you, Compadre."

"And so, Compadre, can I count on your vote?"

Master José Amaro almost left the question without an answer.

"Can I count on it?"

"The elections are far away, Compadre."

And Vitorino mounted the poor mare stepping in the iron stirrups. "I'm at your service."

And the horse took off at its tired pace. Vitorino's shadow grew in the disappearing afternoon. He looked like a giant in the remaining light of the sun as it covered the *cajàzeiras*. The mare jumped to one side as if it would fall apart. The captain thrust his spurs into the animal's sides and disappeared behind the big *cabreira* bush. Master José Amaro still saw him before the road's curve. He rode away gesticulating, shaking his liana riding whip in the air as if he were striking enemies. Right then, in the distance, the high voice of a boy was heard screaming, "Papa-Rabo, Papa-Rabo."

And the yelping of dogs covered the hoarse shout of the captain: "It's your mother."

The muffled echo answered from the other side. Master José Amaro busied himself carrying his things into the house. He saw his daughter arriving with a water pitcher on her head. His wife prodded the hens onto the perch. In the yard, a guinea hen's shrieking sounded human. Old Sinhá's voice filled everything: "Shhh, shhh."

Master Amaro walked a little way toward the edge of the road. A swarm of *tanajura* ants flew low and fell to the ground, too weak to pick themselves up again. They were too fat. The Negro Manuel de Úrsula passed by with a shotgun on his shoulder and two dogs tied with a long rope.

"Good afternoon, master. Are you taking in the afternoon's air?"

"Just watching the time roll by."

"The *moleques* up there managed to get old Vitorino down on the ground. They tied a rope on the road, the old man's horse stumbled and threw the poor creature. They're devilish rascals. I put Seu Vitorino back on his horse. He took off insulting every creature on this earth. He even told me he had had a fight with Laurentino the painter and that he beat the man up. This Seu Vitorino still needs straightening out."

The dead cavies' blood poured through the Negro's feed bag. Master José Amaro remained silent.

"If you wish, master, here's a little cavy for you. It's so fat, it's just like chicken."

And he took out a cavy and left it on the grass. "It's heavy food. For those who are wounded, it's just like poison."

Master José Amaro thanked the man for his gift. And the Negro left with the growling dogs. It was almost night. No voice was heard from the house. The hens on the perch quieted down for sleep.

"Hey, girl, take this inside."

The grass became sticky with blood. That dark blood made the saddler sick. He felt nauseated; he couldn't stand to see an animal's blood. He took some mud and covered the stains. Sinhá had already put all the livestock to sleep. The pigs in the pen nuzzled the earth, grunting. The billy goat lay in the shed. That blood had made the saddler sick. He didn't have the nerve to throw the animal away. Sinhá would make a stew, and next day he wouldn't even think about that dirty blood any more. A kerosene lamp filled the room with dimming light. The new sole leather, just in from Itabaiana, gave off a strong smell. At that moment, the saddler felt like talking with his family, opening up to them, receiving a caress from his daughter. He rarely felt that way. It was much too hard; it was like having a thorny *cardeiro* inside him. Just then Colonel Lula's buggy passed along the road. Its shining lamps and tinkling bells filled the empty night with life.

"It's Dona Amélia going to the May celebrations," his wife said.

"That's the life they want," the saddler answered.

As if coming from the end of the world, the bells were still heard.

"That's why they don't get ahead."

"Shut up, you heretic."

"I don't believe in a man who's always hanging around priests."

The house returned to its silence.

"Poor Compadre Vitorino and poor Comadre Adriana in that constant suffering. You can't imagine what she has to take, Zeca."

"It's that poor woman's fate. She was born like that and will die like that."

A pleasant breeze came into the saddler's house from the night. The flowers of the *bogari* and of the *cajàzeiras* gave off a sweet perfume, and the *jasmim-do-céu* opened up to the moon that had just stuck her head out.

"Is it full moon today?"

"Yes. Didn't you see how Compadre Vitorino acted?"

The two walked to the house door. They saw the starry night and the peace of the world, of that large silent world. A dog started barking in torment and finally howled as if in deep pain.

"That's for the moon."

"It's for the moon. The dog is suffering very much."

A cloud covered the sky and everything became dark. Suddenly the world cleared again in a white light.

"Zeca, watch out for the dampness. It'll make you cough."

The master closed the window.

"There are too many mosquitoes coming in. I'm going to take a short walk." And he left.

"Watch out for the dampness, Zeca."

The saddler was overcome by peace, by tender sadness; he was going to watch the moon as it bathed Colonel Lula de Holanda's lowlands with milk from above the *cajàzeiras*. He walked along the road; he wanted to be alone, to live alone, to feel everything alone. The night invited him to take a walk, which was something he never did. He was always nailed to that stool like a Negro in a cangue. And he kept walking. As he approached Lucindo Carreiro's house, he stopped for a while. A white specter came in his direction. He waited for the figure to pass by. It was a messenger from Santa Rosa, the Negro José Guedes.

"Good evening, Master Zé, looking for something?"

"Just walking, stretching my legs."

The Negro left. By the pond the frogs filled the world with an endless croaking. And the fireflies crawled on the ground in fear of the moon. Everything was so beautiful, so different from his house. He wanted to go on farther. And what if he left the road? He took the shortcut that led to the river. There he found the Negress Margarida, who was going to fish.

"What are you doing around here, Master José Amaro?"

He gave some excuse and returned in the other direction. He smelled the whole earth. It was a smell of open flowers, of ripe fruits. Master José Amaro was returning home as if he had discovered a new world. When he arrived, his wife was already afraid. "What were you doing out this late, Zeca? Leave it to those who are moon-struck!"

He kept silent, closed the entrance door, and went to the hammock with the heart of a new man. He didn't sleep. He heard everything that came from outside. He heard his daughter's snoring. What was the matter with her? Then he remembered the cavy's blood soiling the green grass. The smell of new sole leather filled the house. Master José Amaro saw a very white moon entering through the tiles of the roof. And he slept with the rays that spread dots throughout his room. Sinhá snored like the pigs in the pen.

Next day the story that Master José Amaro was turning into a werewolf had spread everywhere. He had been found in the woods awaiting the hour of the devil; human blood had been seen at the door of his house.

18

JORGE AMADO

It has been argued that Jorge Amado does not belong to the Northeast school. His novels have their venue farther south, in Bahía and its hinterland; he is twenty years younger than Graciliano Ramos, eleven years younger than Lins do Rêgo. Nevertheless, he began to publish his novels in the early 1930s, at the same time his two elders were publishing their own earliest works of fiction; he shared with both of them a concern for the land and the people of Brazil's northern regions, and for a long time he practiced a kind of critical regionalism that was very much in their line.

He was born in Pirangí in 1912, the son of a cacao planter. He was sent to Rio to study law and got a degree, but was more attracted to journalism and politics. He became a follower of Luis Carlos Prestes, the Communist leader whose biography he wrote (*The Knight of Hope*, 1945). For a time, while the fascist regime of Getulio Vargas was still in power in Brazil, he had to live in Argentina. Later, he became disillusioned with the Soviet Union and returned permanently to his native land.

His fictional output is large: at least fourteen novels and two books of long tales. The first novels were published as a response to Lins do Rêgo's sugar-cane cycle. In Amado's case, however, cacao was the main crop, and the perspective was also different. While Lins do Rêgo's vision was basically nostalgic, Amado's was more critical, even satirical. His political ideology impelled him to present a grotesque world, symmetrically divided between Good (the poor exploited workers) and Evil (the hideous capitalists). The same Manichean outlook found expression in the cycle of urban novels that explored the lower life of Bahía's port district and attempted to document (especially in *Jubiabá*, 1935) the awakening of a social conscience in a member of what Marx called the lumpenproletariat. (Orthodox Marxists, of course, could argue that the possibility of a lumpen's conversion into a useful comrade was at least debatable.) But despite the simplistic nature of Amado's ideological stand, the novels were written in a brilliant oral style and displayed the author's gift for storytelling. If he failed as a sociopolitical analyst, he was at his best when describing simple people. This is evident in the chapter of *Sea of the Dead* (1936) excerpted here. On the basis of a popular song by the Bahian troubadour Dorival Caymmi on the theme of the sweetness of death at sea, Amado built up a supple, poetical structure of recurrent motifs and images which admirably conveyed the fatalism of sailors.

Since his break with Communism, Amado has written several very successful novels in a different vein, devoid of any political bias. They are saturated in Bahía's colorful and sensual folklore and have larger-than-life characters. The most famous is *Gabriela, Clove and Cinnamon* (1958). Although Amado does not attain Ramos's stature or Lins do Rêgo's larger range, his fictional world is still worth knowing.

Sea of the Dead

Especially translated by Donald Walsh.

I
The Storm

Night had closed in early. No one was expecting it, when it fell, heavy with clouds, upon the city. The lights on the wharf were still dark, and in the Lighthouse of the Stars there was as yet no glow of little lamps brightening the glasses of rum. And many boats were still furrowing the waters of the sea when the wind brought the black-clouded night.

The men looked at one another in wonder. They gazed out over the blue ocean, as if asking where that night came from, unexpectedly, so much before its time. Yet it did come, heavy with clouds preceded by the cold wind of dusk, like a fearful miracle darkening the sun.

Night arrived that evening with no music to greet it. The clear voice of the Vesper bells did not echo through the city. On the wharf, no Negro had appeared with his guitar. No accordion greeted night from the prow of a boat. Not even the monotonous baticum of the candomblés and the macumbas had rolled down from the hills. Why, then, did night arrive, without waiting for its customary musical welcome, or the summons of the bells, or the cadence of guitars and accordions, or the mysterious playing of religious instruments? Why did it come thus, before its hour, outside its time?

That night was strange and anguished. The men were uneasy and the sailor drinking alone in the Lighthouse of the Stars ran toward his boat as if to save it from irretrievable disaster. And the woman on the tiny Market Wharf, waiting for the boat of her loved one, began to tremble, not with the icy wind or the frozen rain, but with a chill that came from her anxious heart, filled with the evil omen of the sudden night.

Because both the sailor and the dark woman were almost consubstantial with the sea, they knew well that if the night advanced the hour of its coming, many men were to die among its salty waves, ships would not complete their voyage, and widows would wet with tears their children's heads. They knew this. That night that came so suddenly was not the true night, the night of moonlight and stars, of music and love. The true night came at its own hour, when the bells rang and on the wharf a Negro was singing to his guitar a song of homesickness. The night that had arrived, heavy with clouds, brought by the wind, was the squall that sank ships and tossed men into the air. The storm is the false night.

The rain beat down furiously, washed the wharf clean, pounded the sand, lashed the ships lying offshore, stirred up the depths, and drove away all those who were waiting for the liner to dock.

A man in the hold had told his mate that a storm was blowing.

Like an extravagant monster, a crane moved through the wind and the rain, loaded with bales. The waters beat like pitiless ashes upon the Negroes on the hold. The wind rushed swiftly, whistling, knocking things down, terrifying the women. The black shadow of the rain blinded the men. Only the black cranes were moving. A boat listed heavily and two men fell into the sea. One of them was young and strong. Perhaps he murmured a name in that last moment. It was surely not an oath, because it sounded gently through the storm.

The wind tore the sail from the boat and dragged it to the wharf like a tragic omen. The belly of the waters swelled, the waves dashed against the dike. The dories moved jerkily by the lumber wharf, and the boatmen decided not to return that night to the little villages of the Reconcavo. The sail of the foundered sloop blew against the breakwater, and the lights went out abruptly on all the boats. The women began to chant the prayer for the dead, and the eyes of the men searched the sea.

Opposite his glass of rum, the Negro Rufino no longer smiled. In that storm Esmeralda would not come.

The lights came on. But they were weak and flickering. The men who were waiting for the liner could distinguish nothing. They had entered the sheds and they could scarcely make out the shape of the crane and that of the loaders who slouched through the rain. But they could not see the hoped-for ship aboard which were friends, parents, brothers and sisters, lovers, perhaps. Nor the man who was weeping down there in third class. On the face of the man who was crossing the paths of the sea, in the third class of a ship that docked at twenty different ports, the rain mingled with the tears, and the memory of the lampposts of his village merged with the foggy lights of the stormy city.

Captain Manuel, the sailor who knew most about those waters, decided not to go out with his boat that night. Love is a pleasant thing on stormy nights, and the flesh of Maria Clara smells of the sea.

The lights of the old fort were dark. Also the lanterns on the boats. And then, of a sudden, the city too was dark. Even the cranes stopped, and the stevedores took refuge in the sheds.

Guma, seeing that darkness from his boat, the *Valiant*, grew fearful. His hand grasped the rudder and the boat veered to one side.

The wharf was deserted.

Only Livia, thin, with drenched hair that clung to her face, stayed facing the boat dock, looking at the angry waves. She heard the amorous groans of Maria Clara. But her thoughts and her eyes were on the sea. The wind shook her like a reed and the rain lashed her face, her legs, and her hands. But she stood still, her body thrust forward, peering into the darkness, hoping to discover the red lantern of the *Valiant* crossing through the storm, lighting up the starless night, announcing the arrival of Guma.

II
Song Book of the Wharf

Abruptly, and as rapidly as it came, the storm went off to other waters, sinking other ships.

Livia could hear now the groans of Maria Clara. But they were no longer sharp cries of pleasure and of pain, cries of a wounded animal, piercing the storm with an air of challenge. Now that through the city, through the wharf, through the sea, true night was spreading, the night of love and music, the night of stars and moonlight, love on the boat of Captain Manuel was sweet and tranquil. The groans of Maria Clara were like sobs of stifled joy, almost a song. Livia turned her gaze for a moment from the tranquil sea and heard those heavings. Soon Guma would come; the *Valiant* would cross the bay and she would hold him in her dark arms, and they too would be groaning with love.

Now the storm had ended and she was no longer afraid. Before long the glimmer of the boat's red lantern would shine faintly on the dark sea.

Little waves slapped against the stones of the dike and the boats rocked gently. In the distance, the lights shone on the wet pavements of the city. Groups of men, no longer in a hurry or afraid, moved toward the great elevator.

Livia looked again out over the water. She had not seen Guma for a week. She had remained in the old cabin on the wharf. This time she did not go with him on the ever fresh adventure of his trip across the bay and up the calm river. It would have been better had she been with him when the storm broke. For surely Guma would have feared for the life of his companion; and yet Livia would have had no fear at all, because she would know that she was close to him, who knew all the paths of the sea, whose eyes were brighter than lanterns, and whose hands were firm on the rudder.

Soon Guma would be coming. He would arrive drenched, strong and smiling, telling stories, with Livia's name, and beneath it an arrow like a flourish, tattooed on his arm. Livia smiled. She turned her dark, shapely body, facing the place filled with the groans of Maria Clara.

The wharf was dark; here and there a ship's lantern was shining, but she could see clearly only Captain Manuel's boat filled with the noise of groaning. There it was, moored to the wharf, rocking on the waves. On it, a man and woman were making love, and the sound of their groans came to Livia. Later, in only a little while, it would be she who on the prow of a boat would press Guma's strong body to hers, she who would kiss his dark hair, who would smell the salt savor of his body, the savor of death that would still be on his eyes, so recently escaped from the storm. And her sighs of love would be sweeter than those of Maria Clara, for they would be filled with the long wait and the anguish that had pierced her. Maria Clara would stop her loving to listen to the music of sobs and laughter that would burst from her lips when Guma pressed her, held her in his arms wet from the sea.

A boat passes and its captain says good evening to Livia. Farther off, a group examines the sail of the foundered sloop. The sail, very white and torn, is near the wharf. Some of the men run to their dories to go in search of the bodies. But Livia thinks of Guma, who is still to arrive, and of the love that is waiting for her. She will be happier than Maria Clara, who did not wait and who was not afraid.

"Do you know who was drowned, Livia?"

Livia shuddered. But that sail is not the *Valiant*'s sail. The sail of his boat is bigger and would not tear that way. She turned and asked Rufino: "Who?"

"Raimundo and his son. They were drowned near the city. It was a wild storm."

That night, thought Livia, Judith will have no love in her cabin, nor on her husband's boat. Jacques, Raimundo's son, is dead. She will go over there afterward, after Guma comes, after they have killed the saudade, after they have loved.

Rufino looks at the rising moon. "They have gone out to search for the bodies. . . ."

"Does Judith know?"

"I'm going now to tell her. . . ."

Livia looked at the Negro. He was gigantic and smelled of rum. He had certainly been drinking in the Lighthouse of the Stars. Why must he look at the full moon that rides skyward on the sea and brightens everything with a silver radiance?

Maria Clara still sobs with love. Livia too will love when Guma arrives, drenched by the storm, smelling of the sea. How beautiful the sea is, all whitened by the moon!

Rufino still does not move. From the old fort comes music. An accordion plays and they sing:

"The night is for love. . . ."

A heavy, Negro voice. Rufino looks at the moon. Perhaps he too thinks that Judith will have no love that night. Nor ever any more. . . . Her man has died in the sea.

"Come and love on the waters that shine beneath the moon. . . ."

Livia asks Rufino: "Does Judith still live with her mother?"

"No. The old woman sailed off toward Cachoeira," he says, fretfully, looking at the moon.

A Negro sings in the old fort, but his song will not console Judith. With a gesture, Rufino says, "Well, I'm going over there. . . ."

"I'll be there shortly. . . ."

Rufino took a few steps, and then stopped.

"It's very sad. . . . Hard to say . . . to say that he died. . . ."

And he scratched his head. Livia became sad. Judith will never love again. Never again will she love on the sea at the hour when the moon shines. For her, night will not be for love, but for tears.

Rufino stretched out his hand. "Why don't you come with me, Livia? You know how to say . . ."

But love is waiting for Livia. Guma will be coming soon on the *Valiant;* soon the red lantern will shine; soon the hour will come when their two bodies meet; soon he will sail across the mantle of light that the moon has spread upon the sea. Love is waiting for her. Livia cannot go. That day, after her fear, after the vision that filled her with anguish, of Guma drowning, Livia wants only love, she wants joy, she wants groans of possession. No. She cannot go to weep with Judith, who will never love again.

"I am watching to see if Guma comes, Rufino."

Will the Negro think badly of her? But Guma can't be much longer. And she added, "I'll come afterward."

Rufino waved his hand. "Good night, then."

"Good night."

Rufino took a few listless steps. He looked at the moon and began to listen to the man who was singing.

"Come and love on the waters that shine beneath the moon. . . ."

Then he turned toward Livia. "Do you know that she is pregnant?"

"Judith?"

"Yes, she is."

And he began to walk, staring at the moon. From the old fort they are singing:

"The night is for love. . . ."

Maria Clara groans and laughs in the arms of her man. Livia starts out almost running, calling to Rufino, outlined faintly in the distance.

"I'm going with you. . . ."

They walk along. Livia goes on watching the sea for a long time. Who can tell whether that lantern shining far off is not the *Valiant*'s lantern? . . .

*   *   *

Judith is a mulatto and her belly is big now under her misshapen percale dress. Everyone is silent. The Negro Rufino waves his hands, finding no place to put them, and looks at the others with frightened eyes. Livia is a gesture of pure consolation, her hands sheltering Judith's head. Other people have come now to bring their sympathy, and they stand around the room, waiting for the bodies that the men went to search for in the sea. From where Judith lies come broken sobs, and Livia's hands move with fond gestures. Then Captain Manuel comes, and Maria Clara, with swollen eyes.

There is nothing left now to recall the storm. Maria Clara no longer groans with love. Why, then, does Judith weep? Judith is a widow now, and the men are waiting for two bodies.

Gladly would the Negro Rufino flee to the joy of Esmeralda's arms. He is oppressed by the sadness of the house, by Judith's grief; he doesn't know what to do with his hands, and he knows that he will suffer even more when the body arrives and Judith has her last meeting with the man who loved her, who gave her a child, who possessed her body.

Livia is the one who is brave. And she is even more beautiful thus. Who wouldn't like to marry her, to be wept for by her when he died in the sea? Livia is at that moment a sister to Judith. Surely she too would like to flee and go to wait for Guma at the edge of the wharf and spend a night beneath the stars.

Judith's suffering distresses them all, and Maria Clara thinks that some day Manuel may be left in the sea, on a stormy night, and that Livia may give up waiting for Guma to bring her the news. She clutches the arm of Manuel, who asks, "What's the matter with you?"

But she is weeping and Manuel is silent. They have brought a bottle of rum. Livia leads Judith to the bedroom. Maria Clara goes with them, taking Livia's place, and weeps with the widow, weeps for herself.

Livia returns to the other room. The men are talking now in low voices. They are discussing the storm, the fate of the father and son who died that night.

"The old fellow was a real man!" said one Negro. "He had courage enough for three."

Another began to tell a story:

"Do you remember that storm in June? Well, Raimundo . . ."

Someone uncorked the bottle of rum. Livia crossed through the group and looked out the door. She listened to the murmur of the calm sea, its unchanging, everyday murmur. Guma must arrive soon and will surely come to look for her at Judith's house. Even across the blackness of the wharf she can make out the sails of the boats. Suddenly the same fear strikes her that struck Maria Clara. What if they should come one night to bring her the news that Guma was at the bottom of the sea, and that the *Valiant* was wandering without course, without rudder, without guide? Then she knew how completely she was Judith's sister, the sister of Maria Clara too, the sister of all the women of the sea, women with a common destiny: to wait on a stormy night for news of their husbands' death.

From the bedroom comes the sound of Judith's sobbing. She was left with a child in her belly. Perhaps one day she will have to weep too for the death of that son in the sea.

In a group in the outer room, a man says, "He saved five men. . . . It was a terrible night. Many saw that night the mother of waters. Raimundo . . ."

Judith goes on sobbing in the bedroom. It is the destiny of all of them. The men of the wharf have only one path in their lives: the path of the sea. They set out upon it because that is their destiny. The sea is the master of them all. From the sea come all their joys and all their sorrows, because the sea is a mystery that not even the most weather-beaten sailors understand; not even those ancient skippers who no longer put to sea, who only mend sails and tell stories. Who has deciphered the mystery of the sea? From the sea come music, love, and death. Is it not, perhaps, upon the sea that the moon seems most beautiful? The sea is ever-changing. Like it, too, is life for men on the boats. Who among them ever spent his last years like landsmen who fondle grandchildren and unite the family for Sunday dinner? None of them walks with that firm tread of the landsmen. Each of them has someone in the depths of the sea: a son, a brother, an arm, a sunken boat, a sail torn to shreds by the storm.

But also, who among them cannot sing those songs of love in the nights by the wharf? Who among them cannot love violently and gently? Because each time that they sing and that they love may well be for the last time. When they say goodbye to their wives they do not give quick kisses like landsmen starting out to work. They give long farewells; hands that wave as if they beckoned. . . .

Livia looks at the men who are climbing the slope. They are in two groups. The lanterns give a phantasmagoric quality to this funeral procession. As if she felt their arrival, Judith redoubles her sobbing. It is enough to see the men with bared heads to know that they are bringing the bodies.

Father and son died in the storm. There is no question that one of them tried to save the other, and both perished in the sea. Away in the background, coming from the fort, coming from the wharf, coming from the boats, coming from some distant and indefinable place, an inspiriting music accompanies the bodies.

"Sweet is death in the sea. . . ."

Livia sobs. She shelters Judith in her bosom, but she sobs too; she sobs with the certainty that her day will come, and Maria Clara's, and the day for all of them.

The music comes to them across the wharf.

"Sweet is death in the sea. . . ."

But at that moment not even the presence of Guma, who walks in the cortege and who found the bodies, can console the heart of Livia.

A distant music, from the old fort, perhaps, singing "Sweet is death in the sea," bespeaks the fate of Judith's husband.

The bodies are now stretched out in the room; Judith weeping, kneeling next to her husband. The men around her. Maria Clara with the fear that one day her Manuel too may drown.

But why think of this, why think of death, of sadness, when love is waiting for her? Because now they are on the prow of the *Valiant*, Livia stretched out on the deck, under the furled sail, looking at her man quietly smoking his pipe. Why think of death, of men who struggle against the waves, when her man is there, saved from the storm, smoking a pipe which is the fairest star on that sea? And yet Livia is thinking. She is sad because he does not hold her close in his tattooed arms. And she is waiting for him with her hands beneath her head, her breasts showing under the blouse that the night breeze, now gentle, lifts and stirs. The boat also stirs gently.

Livia waits and the waiting makes her beautiful: she is the loveliest woman on the wharf or on any of the boats. No captain has a wife like Guma's. Everyone says so, and they smile at her when they see her pass. They would like to hold her in their storm-toughened arms. But she belongs only to Guma. She married him in the church of Montserrat, where fishermen, boatmen, and masters of ships are married. Even the sailors that voyage distant seas, in enormous ships, come to get married in the church of Montserrat, their church, that clings to the hill and looks out to sea. She married Guma there and, since then, in the nights on the wharf, on their boat, in the rooms of the Lighthouse of the Stars, on the sand of the wharf, they have loved and linked their bodies upon the sea and beneath the moon.

And today, after she had waited for him so long in the midst of the storm, today when she desires him so much because she was so much afraid, Guma smokes without thinking of her. That is why she remembers Judith, who will never again be loved; for whom night will be always the hour of weeping. She remembers her kneeling next to her man, looking at his face, that face that no longer moved, no longer smiled; a face that had slipped now beneath the waves, eyes that were now seeing Yemanjá, the mother of waters.

Livia thinks angrily of Yemanjá. She is the mother of waters, the mistress of the sea, and therefore men who live upon the waves fear her and love her. Yemanjá punishes. She never shows herself to men except when they die in the sea. Those who die in the storm are her favorites. And those who die to save others, those go with her, into the sea, like a ship, sailing to all the ports, crossing all the seas. No one finds the bodies of these men, because they go with Yemanjá. To see the mother of waters, there are many who have thrown themselves smiling into the sea, and have appeared no more. Can she be asleep with them all in the depths?

Livia thinks of her resentfully. At this hour she will be with the father and son who died in the storm, and they will be fighting over her, they who were so close together all their lives. Perhaps the father died trying to save the son. When Guma found the bodies, the old man's hand was grasping the shirt of the son. They died friends, and now—who knows?—perhaps because of Yemanjá, the mistress of the sea, the woman that only the dead can look upon, they are fighting: Raimundo drawing his knife, which the men did not find in his belt and which he must have taken with him. They are struggling perhaps in the depths of the ocean to learn which of them is to sail with her to the cities on the other side of the earth.

Judith who weeps, Judith who carries a child in her belly, Judith who will end her days in cruel toil, Judith who will never love a man again, must have been forgotten by now, because the mother of waters is blond and has long hair and is nude beneath the waves, scarcely covered by her long tresses which gleam faintly when the moon passes over the sea.

The landsmen—what do they know?—say that they are moonbeams on the sea. But the sailors, the masters of ships, the boatmen laugh at the ignorant landsmen. *They* know that it is the hair of the mother of waters who peers up to see the full moon. It is Yemanjá who comes to watch the moon. That is why men stand gazing at the silvered sea on moonlit nights. They know that the mother of waters is there.

The Negroes play guitars, accordions, dance the batuque, and sing. It is the tribute that they pay to the mistress of the sea. Others smoke their pipes to light up the paths, so that Yemanjá can see her way. All love her and even forget their wives when the hair of the mother of waters is spread upon the sea.

And so Guma stands, looking at the silver curves of the water and hearing the music of the Negro who invites them to die, singing, "Sweet is death in the sea," for the drowned will go to meet the mother of waters, the loveliest woman in the world. Guma stares at her hair, forgetting Livia, with her body stretched out, offering her breasts; Livia who waited so long for the hour of love; Livia who saw the storm destroying everything, sinking boats, killing men; Livia who was so much afraid. . . . How she would like to hold him in her arms, to kiss his mouth and discover on it whether he was afraid when the lights darkened; to clasp him to her body and know if the sea had drenched him!

Nevertheless, he stands there, Livia forgotten, thinking only of Yemanjá, the mistress of the sea. Perhaps even envying the father and son who died in the storm and who now are seeing worlds that only sailors on great steamships know. Livia is filled with hatred, with a desire to weep, to leave the sea, to go far away.

A boat passes. Livia raises her head and turns to see it better.

They call to Guma, "Good evening, Guma!"

Guma waves his hand. "A good trip to you!"

Livia looks at him. Now that a cloud has hidden the moon and that Yemanjá has gone, Guma puts out his pipe and smiles. She crouches, joyful, feeling herself already in his arms.

"Where can that Negro be singing?" says Guma.

"I don't know. Maybe in the fort."

"Lovely music!"

"Poor Judith!"

Guma looks back at the sea.

"You're right. . . . Life is going to be hard for her! And with a child in her belly! . . ."

His face darkens, and he looks at Livia. She is lovely, lying there, offering herself. Her hands are not made for drudgery. If he should be left in the sea, she would have to belong to another man to go on living. Her hands are not made for drudgery. This thought fills him with deep anger. Livia's breasts are showing under her blouse. All the men on the wharf desire her. All would like to possess her because she is the loveliest. And when it came his turn to go with Yemanjá? He would like to kill her as she lay there, so that she would never belong to another.

"And what if one day my boat should founder and I should be food for fishes?"

Her laughter was forced.

And once again the voice of the Negro pierces the night.

"Sweet is death in the sea. . . ."

"Would you work to earn your living too? Or would you go off with another man?"

She began to cry with fear. She also fears that day when her man will be left at the bottom of the sea, never to return, that day when he will go with Yemanjá, the mistress of the sea, the mother of waters, to roam the oceans and the land. She straightens up and her arms clasp Guma's neck.

"Today I was afraid. . . . I waited for you at the edge of the wharf. It seemed to me that you would never come. . . ."

But Guma came. Yes, he knew how anxiously Livia waited; how much she feared. He came to her arms, to her love.

A voice sings in the distance:

"Sweet, oh sweet, is death in the sea. . . ."

And now the hair of Yemanjá, mistress of the sea, no longer shines beneath the moon. What stopped the Negro's music were the love groans of Livia, the woman on the wharf that all men desire, and who now, on the prow of the *Valiant,* is loving her man, because she feared so much for him and is still so much afraid.

The winds of the storm are far away now. The waters from the clouds of the false night are falling on other ports. Yemanjá will roam with other bodies through other lands. Now the sea is calm and pleasant. The sea is the friend of the masters of ships. Is the sea not their road, their street, their home? Is it not on the sea, on the prow of its boats, that they love and beget their sons?

Yes, Guma loves the sea and Livia loves it too. The sea is beautiful thus, in the blue night, endless blue, mirror of the stars, filled with the lanterns of boats, filled with the lanterns of embers in pipes, filled with murmurs of love. The sea is the friend, the pleasant friend, of all those who live on it.

And Livia smells the savor of the sea on Guma's flesh.

The *Valiant* sways like a hammock.

FIVE SPANISH AMERICAN
POSTMODERNIST POETS

By the time of Rubén Darío's death in 1916, Spanish American modernism had substantially run its course (see selection 4). Even before Darío died, some of the late modernists, such as Julio Herrera y Reissig (6), were already pointing the way toward the avant-garde movements to come. And as early as 1917, Vicente Huidobro was participating in Paris in the poetic experiments of Apollinaire and Pierre Reverdy. Despite these signs of the advent of a new era, a few Spanish American poets of the period 1910 to 1930 continued to work in accordance with modernist principles, or modified them so subtly that they seemed to be concerned not to break openly with the movement. They were original and even highly idiosyncratic writers, but they did not make their originality into a matter for scandal, as the avant-garde poets did. Working separately, and almost unnoticed at first, they helped to ease the transition between modernism and the avant-garde.

Of the five selected here to represent this trend, only one (the Chilean Gabriela Mistral) achieved continental fame, and even received, in 1945, the first Nobel Prize to be awarded a Latin American writer. A second (the Mexican Alfonso Reyes) had won a wide and appreciative audience in Spanish America, but exclusively as a prose stylist. The other three were less popular. One (the Argentine Macedonio Fernández) went almost unnoticed until the early forties. Nevertheless, they were all as instrumental as their better-known colleagues in making possible the extraordinary flowering of Latin American poetry in this century.

I / JOSÉ JUAN TABLADA

A singular poet who blended the most *outré* effects of Nerval, Baudelaire, and Gautier with the experiments of Apollinaire and Max Jacob, the Mexican José Juan Tablada was born in 1871 and died in 1945, after a thirty-year exile in New York. His controlled, sparse verse owed much to a form developed in Japan in the seventeenth to nineteenth centuries: the haiku. The extreme economy of this type of poem—three lines with a total of seventeen syllables—attracted Tablada's attention after a trip to Japan in 1900. It had also attracted the interest of French poets. (In 1924 the distinguished journal *Nouvelle Revue Française* received a thousand entries for a haiku competition.) Some of the most important Anglo-Saxon poets, such as Ezra Pound and Wallace Stevens, adopted the form, and even tampered with it. For Tablada, the haiku became the best means of conveying his precise, minute observations of the world—an instrument that served in his hands to transfigure reality like a magnifying glass.

Poems

From Anthology of Mexican Poetry, *compiled by Octavio Paz and translated by Samuel Beckett (Bloomington: Indiana University Press, 1958), pp. 150–52, 155–58; and* New Poetry of Mexico, *edited by Octavio Paz, José Emilio Pacheco, and Homero Aridjis (New York: E. P. Dutton, 1970), pp. 213–17.*

Haiku of a Day

I

Tender willow,
almost gold, almost amber,
almost light. . . .

II

The geese on their
clay trumpets sound
false alarms.

III

Royal peacock, slowly fulgurant,
through the democratic barnyard
you pass like a procession. . . .

IV

Although he never stirs from home
the tortoise, like a load of furniture,
jolts down the path.

V

The garden is thick with dry
     leaves:
on the trees I never saw
so many green, in spring. . . .

VI

Lumps of mud, the toads
along the shady path
hop. . . .

VII

The bat, in the night,
essays the swallow's flight
so as to fly by day. . . .

VIII

Restore to the bare bough,
nocturnal butterfly,
the dry leaves of your
     wings!

IX

The nightingale beneath
the awe of heaven raves
its psalm to the sole
     star.

X

The brilliant moon
working through its web
keeps the spider awake.

Haiku of the Flowerpot

I

The multicolored mushroom seems
a Japanese toad's
parasol.

II

The dragonfly strives patiently
to fasten its transparent cross
to the bare and trembling bough.

The Idol in the Porch

On the morning
sky a stone of sun
shows its broad basalt
face on high
at the edge of a pool of obsidian,
and the mouth seems to pour
dribble of human blood
and helianthi of death. . . .

It is the great grindstone
of the solar corn
that makes the bread of days
in the mills of eternity.

Stone of chronologies,
synthesis of years and days,
breathing in silent song
the unconquerable dread
of old mythologies. . . .
On it the flowered and divining months
string pallid alabaster moons
like hollow skulls on the *zompantli*
in the temple.

XI

Sea the black night,
the cloud a shell,
the moon a pearl.

III

Ants on inert cricket crawling.
Memory
of Gulliver in Lilliput.

IV

Mingled, in the quiet evening,
chimes of Angelus and bats
and swallows fly.

About this Table of the Law
the months assemble, mystic,
        sworded,
in warlike song, murmur of prayer,
as about a King. . . .

And at the close of the belated
        days
the Nemontani. . . . Five, in masks,
with thistly aloe leaves!

Days in whose nights the moon
dissolves like turbid chalchuite,
days when shadow-stained the sun
        gold shines
like tiger skin, like sunflower. . . .

Like the Tropic other days
are rich and sonorous, and when the
        jaguar roars
and clouds of parakeets arise
it is as though the forest took to
        wing.

And the flash of the macaws
sears the sky—clamor and oriflamme
and gleam and echo seem
flung by the legion of the God of
    Battles.

And in broad day the quetzals' tails
soar and whirl like Catherine wheels,
like showering stars, flying flowers,
fountains of emerald, gushing, falling
in sprays of willow. . . .

The great anaconda writhes
like sinuous water,
and the thicket quivers
its vast bulk, cold and chill,
inlaid with flowers, encrusted with
    stars,
in strict geometry.

Other evenings the wild herds of
    bison
pour across the plain,
their humps rolling like hills
or stormy sea asurge with billows.

In the tall bamboo the macaws
    screech;
with dreadful crunching,

trailing havoc,
an earthquake plunges through the
    brake:
the Tapir.

The iguana has changed the
    sunflower of its iris
and the armadillo fled
to hiding in its carapace.
Huddled in its shell, wound in a ball,
it rolled through the mountain all
    night and day
and safe to the valley came.

From the azure where it hovered
the pursuing eagle
deemed it dead. . . .
And soon the armadillo, like a holy
desert hermit, rose into the sun.

It escaped the eagle's claw,
but in the end changed into a guitar
beneath a southern
Zapatist's hand
full of patriot love
of the Promised Land,
the armadillo at the foot
of the Idol of the Porch
sings the song.

The Parrot

Parrot identical with that
of grandmother, grotesque voice
of kitchen, corridor and terrace.

With the first rays of the sun
the parrot breaks into his cry
and into his bitter song,
to the sparrow's consternation
who only sings El Josefito. . . .

Choleric and gutteral
he makes little of the cook,

apostrophizing as he goes
the pot of hotch.

When the parrot, treading on
my feet, traverses the brick
    floor,
the black cat, curled up in a
    ball,
fixes him with amber eye,
glowering diabolic sulphur
at this green and yellow demon,
nightmare of its somnolence.

Flying Fish

Struck by the sun's gold
the pane of the sea bursts into splinters.   *Translated by W. S. Merwin*

Alternating Nocturne

New York night gold
  Cold walls of Moorish lime
Rector's foxtrot champagne
  Mute houses and strong gates
And gazing back
  Over the silent roofs
The petrified soul
  The white cats of the moon
Like the wife of Lot

And nevertheless
  it is always
    the same
     in New York
      or Bogotá

     Moon . . . !

Translated by Eliot Weinberger

Southern Cross

Those women with sea-coral
  movements
have orchid-red hair and lips.
The monkeys at the Pole are albino
amber and snow they dance up and
  down
dressed in the aurora borealis

There's an Oleomargarine
ad in the sky
Here we have the quinine tree
and Our Lady of Sorrows

the Zodiac wheels around in the
  night
of yellow fever
rain keeps all the tropics
in a glass cage

It's time to streak across the dusk
like a zebra toward the Island of
  Lastyear
where the murdered women break
  sleep
    Translated by Hardie St. Martin

II / MACEDONIO FERNÁNDEZ

The Argentine Macedonio Fernández (1874–1952) was already fifty-four when his first book came out. It was a complex, almost unreadable essay on metaphysics entitled, literally, *Not All Vigil Is the One of the Open Eyes* (meaning: we may be more truly awake and aware when sleeping). Two years later, he edited a collection of miscellaneous prose pieces under the title *Papers of a Newcomer*, some of which were masterpieces of nonsensical humor. Both books had been published at the insistence of a group of devoted disciples, among whom Jorge Luis Borges (Part Four, 1) was prominent. Fernández's reluctance was understandable: he was less a writer than a talker, and when he did condescend to write, he never bothered to correct or even to organize his papers.

Two more books were published during his lifetime, but even these were deliberately left unfinished: *A Novel That Begins* (1941), and *Continuation of Nothing* (1945). After his death his faithful family managed to assemble two additional books out of his papers: *Poems* (1953) and a sort-of-novel, *Museum of the Novel of the Eternal She* (1967), which consists of twenty narrative chapters, preceded by fifty-six prologues and completed by three epilogues. Fernández had taken all this trouble to prove once and for all that he was not a writer.

Compared to his prose works, his poetry was more conventional. He wrote little, but he produced some very fine individual poems. The best are those dedicated to his dead wife, the Eternal She of his writings. Eliot Weinberger's translation captures the mood and the rhythm of this moving tribute.

Elena Beauty Death

From "Elena Bellamuerte," especially translated by Eliot Weinberger.

It is not you, Death, who could
through mystery turn my mind
as pallid as you,
for I have seen at rest within you
the stainless gaze of a child,
of she who summoned you when she left,
and, leaving without you, left me, with you,
and did not fear for me.
She, whom the eagerness of love had made deceitful,
wanted to say:
"Watch well this summoning, this leaving;
of her work I carry none,
nor did I ever vex her;
her reign over me has not been exercised;
I have not followed her way;
nor do I wear her pallor,
nor her seedy clothes,
but rather the light of my first day,
and the proud garments that mother
measured in spring,

and in summer now are cut short;
nor do I carry pain gripped to me,
but look! before you is the joy of a child
who, under the tenderness and security
of her mother's gaze, plays
(and bold with love I do play to extremes—
see how I act with you,
how I tell it to your tears—)
hidden from her eyes.
Sure of her terror
to cure with a quick slap."
For I have seen how you began
the descent of your flight so coldly
to rest in the heart of the loving,
and how quickly you raised
such courteous sweetness,
because love reigned,
because love defended itself
from death there.

Oh Elena, oh child,
to magnify our love
we delayed our first encounter,
for most of all love loves
those who play before loving
and who, before the hour of loving,
look at each other, children
—and this you knew, this grave knowledge
your burning soul guarded;
the grave thought of love that everyone knows—
so in great tenderness, in passion,
I invent that you wanted this parting,
for in such deep hour
my dull male mind would see you a child.
It was your parting so smooth, triumphant,
as a wave calms returning
from shore to the vast gulf,
as if your cold loved face were a depth of sea.
On your face a wave's end
sleeps through caresses as though
in a fantasy of being your friend
and of showing you that there
absence or dream but no death exists;
that your pillow does not seek
a dying in another death, rather

a dream in dreams:
child sleeping in its mother.

And you slept in innocent victory.
You slept? Words cannot say it.
It was only a sweet wanting to sleep,
only a sweet wanting to leave,
and a burning wanting to cling,
a burning wanting to cling to me.
Where do I seek you, anxious soul,
soul longing, searching soul?
Where my journey takes me
—soul, weariless follower—
may my word reach you.
That which was understood,
understood at its parting,
in a burning hopeful scheme.

And if it isn't so—don't interrupt me!
And if it isn't so, it's because it's much more.

Creature of the obstinance of love
who unwove time,
who called her to her first day,
was obedient to her obstinance,
and involved her face,
and drenched her head,
and clutched at her hair,
the light of her first sacred day,
docile to the sacred fancy
of a woman's last hour
in that worldly toil.

And she told me,
smiling so at that hour:
"Let me play, smile. It is an instant
when your being trembles.
I take with me your understanding.
I leave knowing torpid male love
will not be yours."

Child and teacher of death,
false in saintly games
of a single, burning destiny.
Maddening sham

who with a word had
tears flowing.

That which turns serious, beating heavily,
breast of the maiden confused
by love's closeness,
and gives itself courage and resolution
for the hardest tests, that which
was left only for whom it was intended,
hidden, and to show itself again,
Loving.

I knew death but not that parting.
Death is beauty and it left me taught
of a child's game
which put forth to smiling death
a head of fantasies
battered by love's tangles.

And what a child's game you wanted!
Child of false death
with more tears than the most ardent show.
What fierce struggle your weary head made
when you dropped it to sleep
your "death" on the pillow
called Awake Tomorrow.
Eyes and soul such masters of tomorrow
that without turning bitter in tears
they induced so much weeping.
So much certainty in the being of a child;
her eyes were dry: all in turn cried.
Oh child of this Awake Tomorrow
who, in the light of her first day became hidden,
submitting to Light, Time and Death
in the loving diligence
of serving the sacred deceit
of the deepest fancy in the lightest game
of the ultimate human desire of she
who today is no longer human.

Death is Beauty.
But enthusiastic death
to part deathless in the light of a first day
is Divinity.

Grave and graceful artifice
of smiling death.
Oh what a child's game you managed,
Elena, victorious child,
to the heights of God the deceiver
in the last hour of a woman.

My being lost in the courtesies
of such elegance,
of a soul to all love raised.
When it will be that to all, love,
its life served, has raised
to its battered, broken lips the last cup,
it may try one more time,
the eternal Time of the soul, the gaze
of which today has only the being of Hope,
as only from Hope have I being.

III / RAMÓN LÓPEZ VELARDE

Although the Mexican poet Ramón López Velarde (1880–1921) moved to Mexico City when he was twenty-eight, in spirit he never left the small town where his poetic sensibility had taken shape. He was, in the best sense of the word, a provincial poet: a poet of love and pain in the melancholic afternoon, of loneliness and death, of sudden flashes of sensuality, of deep religious feelings. In his youth he had admired Leopoldo Lugones's poetry very much (see selection 5), or at least that part of Lugones's poetry which was ironic, sentimental, and intimate. He had also admired Herrera y Reissig (6) but had refrained from following him in his most "decadent" experiments. After receiving a law degree in San Luis Potosí, his career was interrupted by the Mexican Revolution. He was a Maderist and became involved in the political life of his province. The publication of his first volume of verses was delayed until 1916. But it was the second volume, *Worries* (1919), which made him famous. After his death, a third book came out, *The Heart's Beat* (1932), which confirmed his exceptional qualities. Today he is considered, with José Juan Tablada, a prime innovator of the new Mexican poetry.

Poems

From Anthology of Mexican Poetry, *translated by Samuel Beckett, pp. 178–81; and* New Poetry of Mexico, *translated by Douglas Eichhorn and Donald Justice, pp. 191–93, 201–3.*

Wet Earth

Wet earth of liquid evenings when the rain
whispers and girls soften
under the redoubled pelting of the drops
on the roof terrace.

Wet earth of odoriferous evenings when
misanthropy toils up to the lascivious
solitudes of air and on them lights
with the last dove of Noah;
while the thunder crackles tirelessly
along the miry clouds.

Wet evenings of steaming earth when I
acknowledge I am made
of clay, for in its summer tears, beneath
the auspice of the light that is half gone,
the soul turns to water on the nails
of its cross.

Evenings when the telephone invites
naiads known for their knowingness,
who leave their bath for love,
to strew their fatuous tresses on the bed
and to lisp, with perfidy and profit,
damp and panting monosyllables
as the fine rain harries the windowpanes. . . .

Evenings like an alcove under the sea,
its bed its bath;
evenings when a maiden
grows old in front of her extinguished hearth,
waiting for a swain to bring her a live coal;

evenings when on earth
angels descend to plow unerring furrows
on edifying fallows;
evenings of supplication and Pascal candle;
evenings when the squall
incites me to inflame
each frigid maiden with the opportune coal;

evenings when, my soul
oxidized, I feel
an acolyte of camphor,
slightly swordfish, slightly
Saint Isidore Labrador. . . .

The Malefic Return

Better not to go back to the village,
to the ruined Eden lying silent
in the devastation of the shrapnel.

Even to the mutilated ash trees,
dignitaries of the swelling dome,
the lamentations must be borne of
the tower riddled in the slinging winds.
And on the chalk of all
the ghostly hamlet's walls
the fusillade engraved
black and baneful maps,
whereon the prodigal son might trace,
returning to his threshold,
in a malefic nightfall,
by a wick's petrol light,
his hopes destroyed.

When the clumsy mildewed key
turns the creaking lock,
in the ancient
cloistered porch
the two chaste gyps
medallions will unseal narcotic lids,
look at each other and say, "Who is that?"

And I shall enter on intruding feet,
reach the fatidic court
where a well curb broods

with a skin pail dripping
its categoric drop
like a sad refrain.

If the tonic, gay, inexorable sun
makes the catechumen fountains boil
in which my chronic dream was wont to bathe;
if the ants toil;
if on the roof the crawy call resounds
and grows aweary of the turtledoves
and in the cobwebs murmurs on and on;
my thirst to love will then be like a ring
imbedded in the slabstone of a tomb.

The new swallows, renewing
with their new potter beaks
the early nests;
beneath the signal opal
of monachal eventides
the cry of calves newly calved
for the forbidden exuberant udder
of the cud-chewing Pharaonic cow
who awes her young;
belfry of new-aspiring peal;
renovated altars;
loving love
of well-paired pairs;
betrothals of young
humble girls, like humble kales;
some young lady
singing on some piano
some old song;
the policeman's whistle . . .
and a profound reactionary sorrow.

The Dream of the Black Gloves

I dreamed the city lay within
the very deadest of dead seas.
It was an early winter morning
and drops of silence drizzled down.

No sign of life but for the echoes
of mass bells tolling for some rite
in an oceanic chapel, far away.

Suddenly you come out to meet me,
brought back to life and wearing your black gloves.

That I might fly to you, the Holy Ghost
lent to my skeleton His wings.

Holding me fast with your black gloves,
you lured me to the ocean of your breast,
and our four hands were reunited
midway between your bosom and my own,
as if they were the four foundations
supporting the framework of the galaxies.

Your flesh, was it preserved upon each bone?
The dark question of love was guarded by
the total prudence of your black gloves.

Oh, prisoner of the Valley of Mexico!
My flesh . . .* of your perfection
will remain now bone of my bone;
and the dress, that dress, in which your body
was laid to rest in the Valley of Mexico;
and that mannequin, made of some dark stuff
you picked up on a pleasure trip. . . .

But in the early morning of my dream,
our hands, on an eternal circuit,
lived the apocalyptic life.

A strong . . . as though in a dream,
free as a comet, and on its flight
the ashes and . . . of the cemetery
seemed pleasing to me as a rose. . . .

Translated by Donald Justice

The Chandelier

to Alejandro Quijano

In the radiant spire
that my personal essence
illuminates and perfects,
and where a hand from heaven

---

*The ellipses indicate illegible passages in the text.

and another from earth
set the crown upon my temple;
in the orgy of morning
where drowning in blue
I am like emery
and central and essential as the rosebush;
in the glory where, mellifluous,
I am diligently chaste
because the alive and the lifeless
are joyfully offered me as nourishment;
in this mystic gluttony
where my Christian name
is an incandescent cabal
enlarging and annihilating all;
I have discovered my symbol
in the chandelier formed like a ship
dangling its shrewd crystal and earnest prayer
from creole domes.

O chandelier, o ship, before the altar
we, a secret pair, fulfill
a single commandment: worship!

Vessel, you who give light
to divine basins:
in your clear presence
my humanity swells and oranges,
for in mute eminence
the flight of my gulls
and the sobbing smoke from my fleets
are anchored to you.

O chandelier, o ship: God sees your pulsing
and knows you are humbled—
not for being old nor tarnished—
in the sacred domes!

You brighten your high prayer
with the spirit of these regions.

You do not know the terror
of islands of lepers,
the polar home
of Don Juanish bears,
the magnetic bay

of sexual swoons,
the equatorial cranes
like scruples in flight,
and so before the Lord
you paralyze what you know
like the odor given off by your best flower.

Like your chimera,
I crystallize without deception
the hot coals of my igneous spring,
hoist my joy and sickness on high
and hang my wounds like prisms.

Chandelier, you who like me
are sick of the absolute,
and point your expert prow
toward a golden archipelago without grief;
chandelier, magical skiff:
my recalcitrant dreams
grow hushed as a zero
on your seaworthy crystal,
still lofty, and reverent.

Translated by Douglas Eichhorn

IV / GABRIELA MISTRAL

With the exception of her compatriot Pablo Neruda (see Part Four, 12), no other Latin American poet has had such a following as Gabriela Mistral. Born in an impoverished region of Chile in 1889, she was self-educated and fought hard to become, at fifteen, a schoolteacher. In 1914, she won a prize with her "Sonnets to Death," in which she sang both of a lost love and the suicide of a man she had loved. In 1922, some friends published in New York a first collection of her verses, *Desolation.* By then she was the most widely read and recited of all Spanish American poets. Mothers sang her lullabies to their children; schoolteachers taught her songs to their pupils; poets of both sexes imitated her. She wrote not only about lost love but also about loneliness, about a frustrated maternal urge, about God and pain. She had been influenced early by the Chilean modernists and the Mexican Amado Nervo. She found in Delmira Agustini (Three, 7) a kindred desperate soul, but her love was untainted by sensuality. She was more in debt to the Bible and Saint Teresa, although her religion was never mystical. Her poetry was sometimes harsh and prosaic; her verses had an obsessive beat. But in her best volumes (*The Felling of Trees,* 1938;

Wine Press, 1954) she achieved a sort of stark and uncompromising beauty that came very close to justifying the 1945 Nobel Prize she received at a time when Reyes, Neruda, and Borges were all still very active.

Poems

From An Anthology of Spanish Poetry from Garcilaso to García Lorca, *edited by Angel Flores and translated by Muriel Kittel and Kate Flores (New York: Anchor, 1961), pp. 292–93, 298;* Latin American Writing Today, *translated by Doris Dana, pp. 15–17;* Anthology of Contemporary Latin American Poetry, *edited by Dudley Fitts and translated by Donald Walsh (New York: New Directions, 1942), pp. 39–43.*

The Liana

In the secret of night
my prayer climbs like the liana,
gropes like a blind man,
sees more than the owl.

Up the stalk of night
that you loved, that I love,
creeps my torn prayer,
rent and mended, uncertain and
    sure.

Here the path breaks it,
here breezes lift it,
wind flurries toss it,
and something I don't know
hurls it to earth again.

Now it creeps like the liana,
now geysers up, at every thrust
received and returned.

My prayer is, and I am not.
It grows, and I perish.
I have only my hard breath,
my reason and my madness.
I cling to the vine of my prayer.

I tend it at the root
of the stalk of night.

Always the same glory
of life, the same death,
you who hear me and I who see you.
The vine tenses, snaps, recoils,
lacerates my flesh.

Grasp the weakening tip
when my prayer reaches you
so that I may know you have it,
sustain it the long night.

Of an instant night hardens,
hard as ipecac, as eucalyptus:
becomes black stretch of road
and frozen hush of river.
My liana climbs and climbs
till tendrils touch your side.

When the vine breaks, you raise it,
and by your touch I know you.
Then my breath catches,
my ardor rekindles, my message
    flames.

I grow still. I name you. One by one
I tell you all your names.
The liana caresses your throat,
binds you fast, entwines you, and
    rests.

My poor breath quickens
and words become flood.
My prayer, moored, at last
grows quiet, at last is still.

Then I know the dark vine
of my blood is anchored,
the broken skein of my body

unraveled in prayer;
and I learn that the patient
cry, broken, mends;
climbs again and climbing,
the more it suffers, the more attains.

Gather up my prayer tonight.
Take it and hold it.
Sleep, my love, let my sleep
fall to me in prayer,
and as we were on earth,
so do we remain.

Translated by Doris Dana

The Prayer

Thou knowest, Lord, with what flaming boldness
my word invokes Thy help for strangers.
I come now to plead for one who was mine,
my cup of freshness, honeycomb of my mouth,

lime of my bones, sweet reason of life's journey,
bird trill to my ears, girdle of my garment.
Even those who are no part of me are in my care.
Harden not Thine eyes if I plead with Thee for this one!

He was a good man, I say he was a man
whose heart was entirely open; a man
gentle in temper, frank as the light of day,
as filled with miracles as the spring of the year.

Thou answerest harshly that he is unworthy of entreaty
who did not anoint with prayer his fevered lips,
who went away that evening without waiting for Thy sign,
his temples shattered like fragile goblets.

But I, my Lord, protest that I have touched—
just like the spikenard of his brow—
his whole gentle and tormented heart:
and it was silky as a nascent bud!

Thou sayest that he was cruel? Thou forgettest, Lord, that
    I loved him,

and that he knew my wounded heart was wholly his.
He troubled forever the waters of my gladness?
It does not matter! Thou knowest: I loved him, I loved him!

And to love (Thou knowest it well) is a bitter exercise;
a pressing of eyelids wet with tears,
a kissing-alive of hairshirt tresses,
keeping, below them, the ecstatic eyes.

The piercing iron has a welcome chill,
when it opens, like sheaves of grain, the loving flesh.
And the cross (Thou rememberest, O King of the Jews!)
is softly borne, like a spray of roses.

Here I rest, Lord, my face bowed down
to the dust, talking with Thee through the twilight,
through all the twilights that may stretch through life,
if Thou art long in telling me the word I await.

I shall weary Thine ears with prayers and sobs;
a timid greyhound, I shall lick Thy mantle's hem,
Thy loving eyes cannot escape me,
Thy foot avoid the hot rain of my tears.

Speak at last the word of pardon! It will scatter
in the wind the perfume of a hundred fragrant vials
as it empties; all waters will be dazzling;
the wilderness will blossom, the cobblestones will sparkle.

The dark eyes of wild beasts will moisten,
and the conscious mountain that Thou didst forge from stone
will weep through the white eyelids of its snowdrifts;
Thy whole earth will know that Thou hast forgiven!

Translated by Donald Walsh

Ballad

    He went by with another;
I have seen him go.
Ever fair was the wind
and the path full of peace.
My eyes, my poor eyes
have seen him go!

He is falling in love with another
upon the flowering earth.
The thorn bush is blooming;
a song goes floating by.
And he is falling in love with another
upon the flowering earth!

He has kissed the other
on the shores of the sea;
the orange blossom moon
was gliding over the waters.
And my blood did not anoint
the sea's expanse!

He will go away with the other
for all eternity.
There will be fair skies
(God wishes to keep still.)
And he will go with the other
for all eternity!

Translated by Muriel Kittel

Absence

My body leaves you drop by drop.
My face leaves in a deaf anointment;
My hands are leaving in loosed mercury;
My feet leave in two tides of dust.

Everything leaves you, everything leaves us!

My voice is leaving, that made you a bell
Closed to all except ourselves.
My gestures leave, that before your eyes
Round on spindles wound themselves,
And the gaze is leaving that fixed on you
Gave forth juniper and elm.

With your very breathing I am leaving you:
I am exuded like your body's mist.
Asleep and waking I am leaving you,
And in your most faithful recollection I am already blurred,
And in your memory faded with those
Born in neither field nor wood.

Would I were blood, and leaving in the palms
Of your labor, and in your mouth of attar of grape.
In your sinews I should leave, and be burned
In your motions I could never hear again,
And in your passion pounding in the night
Like the dementia of lonely seas!

Everything leaves us, everything leaves us!

Translated by Kate Flores

V / ALFONSO REYES

A true humanist and a man of prodigious energy, the Mexican Alfonso
Reyes (1889–1959) wrote poetry and fiction, tragedies and comedies, memoirs,
essays, and criticism, all with the same apparent ease and skill. His *Complete
Works* now encompass eighteen volumes and there still remains to augment
them a seemingly inexhaustible archive of manuscripts and papers, among which
are several volumes of a precise *Journal* and thousands of letters. The bulk of his
work is such as to make him, paradoxically, unreadable. But he deserves to be
rescued from the excesses of his creativity and his own obsessive tendency to
collect everything he ever wrote.

Alfonso Reyes, the son of a Mexican general who died in the Revolution (Martín Luis Guzmán chronicled his tragic death—see selection 14),
was educated in France and Spain and spent many years as a diplomat in
Paris, Buenos Aires, and Rio de Janeiro. Back in Mexico in 1939, he devoted
the last twenty years of his life to completing a formidable list of writings.
When he died, he was the most respected literary figure in Latin America.
Borges once said about him that he was the best prose stylist in Spanish. Perhaps he was, but he was also a very distinguished poet—intimate, subtle, impeccably elegant, as the selection presented here demonstrates. He was also
one of the first Spanish Americans to be influenced by English poetry to the
point of blending its deliberate prosaism with the more traditional Spanish
popular vein. As a translator, he excelled in his versions of Homer, Sterne,
and Chesterton.

Poems

From Anthology of Mexican Poetry, *compiled by Octavio Paz and translated by Samuel Beckett (Bloomington: Indiana University Press, 1958), pp. 188–90, 194–96.*

Tarahumara Herbs

The Tarahumara Indians have come down,
sign of a bad year
and a poor harvest in the mountains.

Naked and tanned,
hard in their daubed lustrous skins,
blackened with wind and sun, they enliven
the streets of Chihuahua,
slow and suspicious,
all the springs of fear coiled,
like meek panthers.

Naked and tanned,
wild denizens of the snow,
they—for they thee and thou—
always answer thus the inevitable question:
"And is thy face not cold?"

A bad year in the mountains
when the heavy thaw of the peaks
drains down to the villages the drove
of human beasts, their bundles on their backs.

The people, seeing them, experience
that so magnanimous antipathy
for beauty unlike that to which they are used.

Into Catholics
by the New Spain missionaries they were turned
—these lionhearted lambs.
And, without bread or wine,

they celebrate the Christian ceremony
with their *chicha* beer and their pinole,
which is a powder of universal flavor.

They drink spirits of maize and peyotl,
herb of portents,
symphony of positive aesthetics
whereby into colors forms are changed;
and ample metaphysical ebriety
consoles them for their having to tread the earth,
which is, all said and done,
the common affliction of all humankind.
The finest Marathon runners in the world,
nourished on the bitter flesh of deer,
they will be first with the triumphant news
the day we leap the wall
of the five senses.

Sometimes they bring gold from their hidden mines
and all the livelong day they break the lumps,
squatting in the street,
exposed to the urbane envy of the whites.
Today they bring only herbs in their bundles,
herbs of healing they trade for a few nickels:
mint and cuscus and birthroot
that relieve unruly innards,
not to mention mouse-ear
for the evil known as "bile";
sumac and chuchupaste and hellebore
that restore the blood;
pinesap for contusions
and the herb that counters marsh fevers,
and viper's grass that is a cure for colds;
canna seeds strung in necklaces,
so efficacious in the case of spells;
and dragon's blood that tightens the gums
and binds fast the roots of loose teeth.

(Our Francisco Hernandez
—the Mexican Pliny of the Cinquecento—
acquired no fewer than one thousand two hundred
magic plants of the Indian pharmacopoeia.
Don Philip the Second,
though not a great botanist,

contrived to spend twenty thousand ducats
in order that this unique herbarium
might disappear beneath neglect and dust!
For we possess the Reverend Father Moxo's
assurance that this was not due to the fire
that in the seventeenth century occurred
in the Palace of the Escurial.)

With the silent patience of the ant
the Indians go gathering their herbs
in heaps upon the ground—
perfect in their natural natural science.

Scarcely . . .

Sometimes an effluence rises,
made of nothing, from the ground.
Suddenly, hiddenly,
a cedar sighs its scent.

We who are a secret's
tenuous dissolution,
our soul no sooner yields
than dream wells over.

What a poor thing the wandering
reason, when in the still,
sunlight seems to fall
upon me from your memory!

Monterrey Sun

No doubt: the sun
dogged me when a child.
It followed at my heels
like a Pekinese;
   disheveled and soft,
   luminous and gold:
   the sun that sleepy dogs
   the footsteps of the child.

It frisked from court to court,
in my bedroom weltered.
I even think they sometimes

shooed it with a broom.
And next morning there
it was with me again,
   dishevely and soft,
   luminous and gold,
   the sun that sleepy dogs
   the footsteps of the child.

   (I was dubbed a knight
by the fire of May:
I was the Child-Errant
   and the sun my squire.)

Indigo all the sky,
all the house of gold.
How it poured into me,
the sun, through my eyes!
A sea inside my skull,
go where I may,
and though the clouds be drawn,
oh what weight of sun
upon me, oh what hurt
within me of that cistern
of sun that journeys with me!

No shadow in my childhood
but was red with sun.
Every window was sun,
windows every room.
The corridors bent bows
of sun through the house.
On the trees the coals
of the oranges burned redhot,
and in the burning light
the orchard turned to gold.
The royal peacocks were

kinsmen of the sun.
The heron at every step
it took went aflame.

And me the sun stripped bare
the fiercer to cleave to me,
    dishevely and soft,
    luminous and gold,
    the sun that sleepy dogs
    the footsteps of the child.

When I with my stick
and bundle went from home,
to my heart I said:
Now bear the sun awhile!
It is a hoard—unending,
unending—that I squander.
I bear within me so
much sun that so much sun
already wearies me.

No shadow in my childhood
but was red with sun.